More Praise for *Uncommon Ground*

"An intellectually pathbreaking book. *Uncommon Ground* is loaded with fresh and provocative essays that probe our conceptions of nature, historicizing the divorce of the 'natural' from the human that plagues contemporary environmentalism. It succeeds brilliantly in showing that 'nature' is a human construction—romanticized in parks and wilderness preserves, commercialized in ecoshops and resort attractions. It argues convincingly that what we have constructed we can reconstruct—by ending the divorce and attending to the myriad roles that nature plays in our metropolitan lives."
—Daniel J. Kevles, Koepfli Professor of the Humanities, California Institute of Technology

"This is a groundbreaking, deeply felt, and deeply thoughtful book. *Uncommon Ground* goes a long way toward reinventing our understanding of humanity's impact on nature—and how nature has meanwhile been reinventing us."
—Tony Hiss, author of *The Experience of Place*

"A major intellectual watershed. Whether discussing the rainforest or the shopping mall, *Uncommon Ground* is a luxuriant garden of new and challenging ideas about the social construction of nature. Most importantly, as an uncompromising critique of an increasingly reactionary Wilderness metaphysics it frames a vision of a more inclusive, and populist, environmental politics."
—Mike Davis, author of *City of Quartz*

"An extraordinary feat from some of the foremost environmental thinkers of our time."
—Yi-Fu Tuan, J. K. Wright and Vilas Professor, University of Wisconsin

W.W. Norton & Company / New York / London

UNCOMMON GROUND

*Rethinking
the Human Place
in Nature*

William Cronon, editor

The seminar and conferences from which this book emerges were sponsored by the University of California's Humanities Research Institute with the support of a grant from the Nathan Cummings Foundation.

The publisher and authors gratefully acknowledge permission to reprint "The Albino Gorilla" from *Mr. Palomar,* by Italo Calvino, copyright © 1983 by Giulio Einaudi editore s.p.a., Torino, English copyright © 1985 Harcourt Brace & Company, reprinted by permission of Harcourt Brace & Company and Reed Consumer Books, on pp. 81–83.

Library of Congress Cataloging-in-Publication Data
Uncommon ground : toward reinventing nature / William Cronon, editor.
p.   cm.
Includes bibliographical references and index.

ISBN 0-393-03872-6
ISBN 0-393-31511-8 pbk.

1. Environmentalism—Congresses.   2. Environmental policy—United
States—Congresses.   I. Cronon, William.
GE195.U53 1995
363.7—dc20   95-2147

W. W. Norton & Company, Inc., 500 Fifth Avenue, New York, N. Y. 10110
W. W. Norton & Company Ltd., 10 Coptic Street, London WC1A 1PU

5 6 7 8 9 0

Contents

BEGINNINGS

PARADISE LOST AND FOUND

List of Illustrations

The Albums

Scattered through this book are albums of "found objects": texts, images, photographs, advertisements, and so on, each of which seems to us to raise provocative questions about the different meanings of nature in the modern world. Aside from a paragraph at the start of each album, we have generally chosen to let these found objects speak for themselves, with little or no editorial commentary. We encourage you to peruse them at your leisure, lingering long enough to consider their intended and unintended meanings, their juxtapositions with adjacent images, and their relation to the arguments we offer in our essays.

Acknowledgments

THIS BOOK HAD ITS ORIGINS IN AN INTERDISCIPLINARY SEMINAR ON THE
theme "Reinventing Nature" held at the University of California's Humanities Research Institute (HRI) in Irvine during the spring of 1994. The seminar received generous financial support not only from HRI itself but also
from the Nathan Cummings Foundation, whose president, Charles Halpern, played a crucial role in instigating and promoting our work. We owe a
great debt to the University of California, to the Nathan Cummings Foundation, and to Charles Halpern for making this book possible, and the campus of the University of California at Irvine proved to be an ideal place for
us to live and work together.

At Irvine seminar participants enjoyed the wonderful generosity and
intellectual support of one of the finest humanities institutes in the country.
In particular, we would like to thank Mark Rose, former director of HRI,
for the energy, grace, and insight he brought to all phases of our work
together. Without Mark the seminar would never have come into being, nor
would its efforts have been nearly so productive and exciting for all who
participated. We were fortunate indeed to have found ourselves in his care.
We feel no less grateful to the rest of the institute's staff as well. Debra
Massey, HRI's assistant director, responded to even our most unusual
requests with unfailing enthusiasm and good humor, always making sure
that we had what we needed to move forward productively with our work.
Chris Aschan, who served as the research assistant for our group (ably aided
by Peter Catapano), tracked down obscure documents, assembled packets

13

of photocopies, and in general facilitated our discussions and writings in every conceivable way. Mia Larson played an especially crucial role in the formative phases of the group, attending to all manner of details involved in planning our activities together. Sauni Hawes saw to our travel and conference needs, while Linda Arias made sure that our finances and lodgings were in good order. And Suzanne Reed kept the lines of communication open for all of us.

Other individuals made important contributions to one or another phase of our work. Although they were unable to contribute to this book, Ann Bermingham and Victor M. Sher participated in many of our conversations and played powerful roles in shaping our ideas. Daniel Botkin had to drop out of the seminar for personal reasons, but we benefited from his presence at our initial planning meeting.

Our group took several field trips that were important in shaping our understanding of the ways in which the abstract questions we were discussing express themselves in real, concrete landscapes and environments. The staff of Sea World in San Diego gave us an unusual behind-the-scenes tour, for which we are grateful—even though Sea World later refused to give us permission to publish images of their theme park in this book, thereby illustrating in quite a different way one of the themes we discuss here! We gained a much better understanding of California fire ecology from visiting the site of the Laguna Canyon fire after talking with Scott E. Franklin, Michael Lindsey, Gary A. Medeiros, and Timothy S. Neely. We very much appreciate the hospitality we were shown by Michael Hamilton, resident director of the University of California's field station near Idyllwild, who helped educate us about California mountain and desert ecosystems. (The rest of the group would like also to thank seminar member Michael Barbour, field trip impresario extraordinaire, for organizing our two ecological field trips.) Giovanna Di Chiro and Una Halloran (with guidance from Norma Alarcon) organized a daylong discussion of the environmental justice movement in California, at which we had the opportunity to talk with key activists in the Los Angeles area: Kathleen Allen, Robert Gottlieb, Penny Newman, and Laura Pulido. Finally, Mike Davis took us on a field trip through Los Angeles as only he can, providing what was unquestionably one of the highlights of our stay at Irvine.

Steve Forman, our editor at W. W. Norton and Company, did a superb job of shepherding this rather unusual and complicated book through publication; we're grateful for his enthusiasm and his tolerance of the special production challenges it posed. We appreciate the work Otto Sonntag did as copyeditor, and JoAnne Metsch's work on book design. Gregory Summers and H. Sarah Nyala did yeoman work as research assistants in gathering the copyright permissions for the illustrations and found objects.

Being part of the Reinventing Nature seminar at the Humanities Research Institute was a rare intellectual and personal experience for every member of our group, and we are deeply grateful to everyone who made it possible.

Contributors

Michael G. Barbour is professor of plant biology at the University of California at Davis. His research interests are in the ecology of wildland vegetation, including desert scrub, salt marsh, coastal dune plants, and montane conifer forests in North America, Argentina, Australia, and Israel. He is the coauthor or coeditor of standard textbooks on plant biology (*A Brief Introduction to Plant Biology*, 2nd ed., 1984), plant ecology (*Terrestrial Plant Ecology*, 2nd ed., 1987), California vegetation (*California's Changing Landscapes*, 1993), and North American vegetation generally (*North American Terrestrial Vegetation*, 1988, 2nd ed. to be published in 1996), as well as the author or coauthor of nearly one hundred journal articles.

William Cronon is the Frederick Jackson Turner Professor of History, Geography, and Environmental Studies at the University of Wisconsin at Madison. He is an American historian specializing in environmental history, frontier history, and western history. His books include *Changes in the Land: Indians, Colonists, and the Ecology of New England* (1983) and *Nature's Metropolis: Chicago and the Great West* (1991). He is a past president of the American Society for Environmental History.

Susan G. Davis is associate professor of communication at the University of California at San Diego, where she teaches courses on the history of culture and communication. Her first book, *Parades and Power: Street Theatre in Nineteenth Century Philadelphia* (1988), explored popular uses of public

15

space. Her *Spectacular Nature*, a study of the Sea World marine theme park in San Diego, will be published by the University of California Press in 1996.

Giovanna Di Chiro is a lecturer in environmental studies and women's studies at the University of California at Santa Cruz and a doctoral candidate in the History of Consciousness Program. The author of "Defining Environmental Justice: Women's Voices and Grassroots Politics," *Socialist Review* 22, no. 4 (1993): 93–130, she is writing a dissertation on environmental and social justice in the United States and India.

Jeffrey C. Ellis is a doctoral candidate in American history at the University of California at Davis. His dissertation is entitled "When Green Was Pink: Environmental Dissent in Cold War America."

Donna J. Haraway is a professor in the History of Consciousness Board at the University of California at Santa Cruz, where she teaches feminist theory, cultural and historical studies of science and technology, and women's studies. She is the author of *Crystals, Fabrics, and Fields: Metaphors of Organicism in Twentieth-Century Developmental Biology* (1976), *Primate Visions: Gender, Race, and Nature in the World of Modern Science* (1989), and *Simians, Cyborgs, and Women: The Reinvention of Nature* (1991). Her next book, *Modest_Witness@Second_Millenium.FemaleMan © Meets OncoMouse™*, a series of essays on feminism and technoscience, is forthcoming in 1995.

Robert Harrison is associate professor of French and Italian literature at Stanford University. His published books include *The Body of Beatrice* (1989), *Forests: The Shadow of Civilization* (1992), and, most recently, (in French) *Rome, la pluie: A quoi bon la littérature?* (1994).

N. Katherine Hayles, professor of English at the University of California at Los Angeles, writes and teaches on literature and science in the twentieth century. Her books include *Chaos Bound: Orderly Disorder in Contemporary Literature and Science* (1990). She is currently completing *Virtual Bodies: Evolving Materiality in Cybernetics, Literature, and Information* (forthcoming).

Carolyn Merchant is professor of environmental history, philosophy, and ethics in the College of Natural Resources at the University of California at Berkeley. She is the author of *The Death of Nature: Women, Ecology, and the Scientific Revolution* (1980), *Ecological Revolutions: Nature, Gender, and Science in New England* (1989), and *Radical Ecology: The Search for a Livable World* (1992), as well as numerous articles on the history of science, environmental history, and women and the environment. She is the editor of *Major Problems in American Environmental History* (1993) and *Key Concepts in Critical Theory: Ecology* (1994). A new book, *Earthcare: Women and the Environment,* will be published in 1995.

Kenneth R. Olwig is a senior research fellow at the Humanities Research Center, Menneske & Natur, at Odense University, Denmark. He is working on an international project concerning the evolution of the concepts of nature, landscape, and environment, as exemplified by changing attitudes toward water use. He is an associate professor in geography and is the author of *Nature's Ideological Landscape* (1984).

Jennifer Price is completing her Ph.D. in history at Yale University. She has published an essay in William H. Shore, ed., *The Nature of Nature: New Essays from America's Finest Writers on Nature* (1994), and is working on a book entitled *Flight Maps: Encounters with Birds in Modern American Culture.* She lives in Boulder, Colorado.

James Proctor is assistant professor of geography and environmental studies at the University of California at Santa Barbara. His Ph.D. dissertation, "The Owl, the Forest, and the Trees: Eco-Ideological Conflict in the Pacific Northwest" (1992), explored the ethical and ideological underpinnings of the heated conflict surrounding spotted owl protection in the Pacific Northwest.

Candace Slater is professor of Spanish and Portuguese at the University of California at Berkeley. Her most recent book, *Dance of the Dolphin: Transformation and Disenchantment in the Amazonian Imagination* (1994), looks at the theme of change in folk stories told throughout much of present-day Amazonia. She is at work on a book-length study of perceptions in nature in Amazonia.

Anne Whiston Spirn is professor of landscape architecture and regional planning at the University of Pennsylvania. Her book, *The Granite Garden: Urban Nature and Human Design* (1984), won the President's Award of Excellence from the American Society of Landscape Architects, and she edited a special issue of *Landscape Journal* (Fall 1988) on the theme "Nature, Form, and Meaning." Since 1984 she has worked in inner-city neighborhoods on the design of community open space and urban landscape plans.

Richard White is a professor of history at the University of Washington. His writings on environmental history, western history, and Native American history include *The Roots of Dependency: Subsistence, Environment, and Social Change among the Choctaws, Pawnees, and Navajos* (1983), *The Middle Ground: Indians, Empires, and Republics in the Great Lakes Region, 1650–1815* (1991), *It's Your Misfortune and None of My Own: A New History of the American West* (1991), and *The Organic Machine* (1995).

Foreword to the Paperback Edition

WHEN *UNCOMMON GROUND* WAS FIRST PUBLISHED, WE WERE DISMAYED BUT NOT entirely surprised by how controversial the book proved to be for some of its readers. These essays were written just before a powerful conservative resurgence produced a Republican-dominated Congress that quickly distinguished itself as the most hostile toward environmental protection in all of U.S. history. Americans who cared about the natural environment suddenly found themselves confronting what looked to be a political juggernaut committed to dismantling a quarter century's worth of hard-won environmental legislation. *Uncommon Ground* showed up in bookstores when the anti-environmental assault still looked like it might prove horribly successful. Because the book is sometimes critical of certain widely shared modern beliefs about the human place in nature—beliefs that more than a few environmentalists embrace without always considering their full implications—some readers saw it as participating in the general backlash and so reacted angrily to its arguments.

Now, thankfully, as this paperback edition goes to press, we have clear evidence that the would-be counter-revolution has met much greater resistance than its supporters had hoped. There has been widespread public revulsion at efforts to gut the laws protecting air, water, endangered species, and the public lands. Legislators who at first thought they could make political hay by leading the anti-environmental charge have gone scurrying for green fig leaves to obscure their true intentions. Although the struggle to defend and extend our existing environmental protections is by no means over, the threat no longer seems as irresistible as it did when the book came out.

Given this new, more optimistic context, we hope we can be forgiven for asking our readers to resist any impulse they may have to react to *Uncommon Ground* as a hostile attack on the environmental movement. These essays were meant to be quite the opposite. The criticisms we offer—whether of environmentalism in particular or of American ideas of nature in general—are intended to encourage greater reflection about the complicated and contradictory ways in which modern human beings conceive of their place in nature. Some of us come to these criticisms after long involvement with environmentalism and its political struggles, and the last thing we want is to undermine the movement or its long-term agendas. We believe that criticism is ultimately about building up rather than tearing down. Our goal is greater understanding and self-knowledge, qualities which, far from weakening environmentalism, should only strengthen and deepen the insights it has to offer.

These essays take as their starting point one key insight. It is simply that "nature" is a human idea, with a long and complicated cultural history which has led different human beings to conceive of the natural world in very different ways. Far from inhabiting a realm that stands completely apart from humanity, the objects and creatures and landscapes we label as "natural" are in fact deeply entangled with the words and images and ideas we use to describe them. Even when we travel through a beautiful mountain landscape in the Sierra Nevada or a remote rainforest in the Amazon—places that on their surface may seem as uncontaminated by humanity as anywhere on earth—we cannot help experiencing them not just as natural environments but as cultural icons. We turn them into human symbols, using them as repositories for values and meanings which can range from the savage to the sacred. At one moment they can stand for nature red in tooth and claw; at another, they can seem to be the purest earthly embodiment of sacred nature. What we find in these places cannot help being profoundly influenced by the ideas we bring to them.

Stated so simply, this hardly seems a radical proposition; it is in some ways so obvious that one might almost regard it as a truism. So why do some readers find it so threatening and objectionable? Three possible reasons suggest themselves. One is that environmentalism has often asserted its moral authority by invoking nature as an uncontested and transcendent category whose appeal is so compelling that no right-thinking person could resist it. As soon as we label something as "natural," we attach to it the powerful implication that any change from its current state would degrade and damage the way it is "supposed" to be. But in fact we are rather selective about the parts of nature we choose to view in this way. It is in some sense "natural" that very large numbers of human beings should die from epidemic disease each year, and yet this does not prevent the vast majority of people—to say nothing of the entire infrastructure of modern medicine—from trying to resist that fate. Manipulating landscapes and growing seasons to produce agricultural crops is of course a profoundly unnatural enterprise, and yet almost all of the human race depends for its survival on doing just that. Indeed, civilization itself could hardly be less "natural"—even though it is civilization which has spawned modern environmentalism and taught us to value nature in the highly civilized ways we now do.

So one problem with asserting that "nature" is as much a human idea as a non-human thing is to undermine the uncontested nature of nature. If what we mean by "nature" reflects our own assumptions about the world around as, we must offer much subtler arguments to defend our beliefs about what we should and should not do with that world. It is not nearly enough to assert that something is "natural" and assume that this will end all discussion of what is to be done. Just as importantly, once we recognize that not all human groups and cultures view nature in the same way, it becomes at least more complicated to assert that one group's ideas of nature should take precedence over another's. At a minimum, we need to enter into a dialogue with other people about why they think as they do, and this can seem to make the work of protecting nature more difficult. But much as we might long for a world in which our own ideas were self-evident truths and those of our adversaries were false or downright evil, the world we actually inhabit almost never works this way. The essays in *Uncommon Ground* assert that we should be willing to question some of our own moral certainty in an effort to understand why we ourselves think of nature as we do, and why others do not always agree with us. Recognizing that "nature" may not be quite as natural as we think can be an important step in this direction, even if it threatens some of our dearest beliefs.

This leads to a second possible reason why *Uncommon Ground* has proven so controversial. Asserting that "nature" is an idea is far from saying that it is only an idea, that there is no concrete referent out there in the world for the many human meanings we attach to the word "nature." And yet this is precisely the way some readers choose to interpret the message of this book. It is almost as if they believe that we must make a choice: *either* the world is made of pure matter, inhabited by objectively real plants and animals in objectively real landscapes that are completely unaffected by the ideas we may have of them, or it is made of pure idea, a fantasy we invent and carry around in our heads that has nothing whatsoever to do with anything other than ourselves.

The latter proposition is so ludicrous that it is hard to see how any sane person could hold it—and in fact none of the authors of these essays do. But at least for humanity, a world of pure matter is no less absurd, for ideas do exist and have real consequences in the world. Yosemite is a real place in nature—but its venerated status as a sacred landscape and national symbol is very much a human invention. The objects one can buy in stores like The Nature Company certainly exist in nature—but that does not begin to explain how they came to inhabit some of the most upscale malls in modern America. The bomb that exploded over Hiroshima could hardly have been more material, expressing as it did some of the most fundamental laws of matter—and yet it also could not possibly have existed without the human ideas that described those laws and applied them to this very particular piece of technology, to say nothing of the use to which that technology was put.

Some readers apparently fear that the critical perspectives offered in *Uncommon Ground* point toward a world in which anything goes, in which everything becomes relative to our own ideas and there is no stable ground on which we can hope to make a stand in defending the natural world. If one person's ideas are as good as any other's, how can we defend some uses (and non-uses) of nature over others? How can we protect the environment if everything is up for grabs? The answer, of course, is that not everything is up for grabs, and not all ideas or uses of nature are equally defensible. There are very real material constraints on our ideas and actions, and if we fail to take these into account, we are doomed to frustration if not outright failure. The material nature we inhabit and the ideal nature we carry in our heads exist always in complex relationship with each other, and we will misunderstand both ourselves and the world if we fail to explore that relationship in all its rich and contradictory complexity. The essays in this book try to suggest some of the things we can learn if we reflect as much on nature as an idea as we do on nature as material reality. They suggest that environmentalism is as much a cultural prospect as a "natural" one.

There is perhaps one final reason why this book has provoked some readers into regarding it as an anti-environmental tract. We live in a time when political discussion favors extreme positions and sound bites. In the struggle to attract attention and support for one's own views, the temptation is very great to caricature those of one's adversaries. The result is a rhetorical landscape of polarities, in which stark oppositions arise and cartoons become our most common way of conducting what passes for reasoned debate. In such a world, you're either for the environment or against it, and any inquiry that points toward more challenging or difficult ways of framing the discussion can seem threatening. The crucial task of self-criticism is all too easily avoided because it can seem to lend aid and comfort to the enemy.

Such aversion to criticism is understandable, but ultimately disastrous. There is no question that our purpose in writing *Uncommon Ground* was to ask hard questions that would encourage environmentalists and others to rethink some of their own most basic assumptions about nature and its meanings. Confronting such questions is never easy, and we do not claim to have answered them adequately in the pages of this book. We nonetheless regard this kind of self-criticism as crucial to the future of environmentalism, and to the human project of living on the earth in a responsible way. The struggle to live rightly in the world is finally not just about right actions, but about the ideas that lie behind those actions. At a time when threats to the environment have never been greater, it may be tempting to believe that people need to be mounting the barricades rather than asking abstract questions about the human place in nature. Yet without confronting such questions, it will be hard to know which barricades to mount, and harder still to persuade large numbers of people to mount them with us. To protect the nature that is all around us, we must think long and hard about the nature we carry inside our heads.

William Cronon

Madison, Wisconsin
June 1996

BEGINNINGS

Introduction:
In Search of Nature

William Cronon

IT WAS HARD NOT TO BE PREOCCUPIED BY THE FIRES. NIGHT HAD ALREADY fallen by the time the jet started its approach into Orange County. As the lights of Los Angeles began to glow on the far horizon, I found myself gazing toward them with unaccustomed watchfulness and anxiety, searching for places that might be brighter, less orderly, more *flickering* than the rest. For several days we had been reading about the wildfires that were ravaging the hillsides of southern California, and we had even considered canceling our gathering when it looked for a time as if the campus of the University of California at Irvine might lie in their path. The news of the past twenty-four hours had been good, however, so I and more than a dozen colleagues were now flying into the city with reasonable assurance that we would not get swept up in the holocaust. I nonetheless scanned the hillsides, and will never forget the lone mountaintop that still blazed on the city's margins. From afar it looked like nothing so much as a volcano, the flames massed into a single enormous blaze, which made it seem that an entire forest was burning at once. Seen from the comfortable seat of a Boeing 727, it looked otherworldly, as if a wayward band of giants had made camp for the night and were still heaping fuel on their fire. The orange light filled the valley below as our plane continued its descent, and I craned my neck backward for as long as I could to watch the flames leaping toward heaven. It is not often that one looks down from the sky to see a city or a mountain burning in the night.

I did not know it at the time, but we had come to California to ponder the meaning of those flames. It was October 1993, and the ostensible purpose of our meeting was the prosaic one of planning an academic seminar. Two years earlier I had been approached by Mark Rose, then director of the University of California's Humanities Research Institute in Irvine, about organizing a residential seminar that would explore contemporary environmental problems from a broadly humanistic interdisciplinary perspective. The offer he dangled before me proved irresistible: I could focus the seminar on any questions that seemed worthy of our attention, and I could collect whichever scholars seemed best suited to grapple with those questions. The institute would raise the funds to cover our expenses, and we would live together on the campus of the University of California at Irvine for the spring semester of 1994 to conduct our research. We would have only two primary responsibilities: we were to hold daylong weekly meetings at which we would struggle to advance our understanding of the questions we posed, and we were to produce a book at the end of our time together that would share with the rest of the world what we learned from each other. It was an extraordinary opportunity, one that would almost surely never come our way again, which is why I and virtually every scholar I approached leapt at the chance to participate.[1]

Most of us had never met each other as we gathered in the smoke-filled air and the furnace-like heat of the Santa Ana winds for that first October meeting. True to our interdisciplinary mandate, we were an eclectic bunch, representing academic fields ranging from history to geography, from ecology to literary criticism, from landscape architecture to environmental studies, from critical theory to law. We had come together under the rubric "Reinventing Nature," and the task we had set ourselves was nothing less than to rethink the meaning of nature in the modern world. Lest this seem too grandiose, we took as our point of departure two key insights that have emerged from the work of scholars and scientists over the past quarter century. Let me discuss them in turn.

First, recent scholarship has clearly demonstrated that the natural world is far more dynamic, far more changeable, and far more entangled with human history than popular beliefs about "the balance of nature" have typically acknowledged. Many popular ideas about the environment are premised on the conviction that nature is a stable, holistic, homeostatic community capable of preserving its natural balance more or less indefinitely if only humans can avoid "disturbing" it. This is in fact a deeply problematic assumption. The first generation of American ecologists, led at the start of the twentieth century by the Nebraska scientist Frederic Clements, believed that every ecosystem tended to develop toward a natural climax community much as an infant matures into an adult. This climax, according to Clements and his followers, was capable of perpetuating itself forever unless something interfered with its natural balance.

Popular ideas of the natural world still reflect a fairly naive version of this belief, even though professional ecologists began to abandon Clementsian ideas almost half a century ago. By the 1950s, as Michael Barbour explains in his essay for this volume, scientists were realizing that natural systems are not nearly so balanced or predictable as the Clementsian climax would have us believe and that Clements's habit of talking about ecosystems as if they were organisms—holistic, organically integrated, with a life cycle much like that of a living animal or plant—was far more metaphorical than real.[2] Furthermore, the work of environmental historians has demonstrated that human beings have been manipulating ecosystems for as long as we have records of their passage. All of this calls into question the familiar modern habit of appealing to nonhuman nature as the objective measure against which human uses of nature should be judged. Recognizing the dynamism of the natural world, in short, challenges one of the most important foundations of popular environmental thought. Part of our job in Irvine was to consider the ways in which such thinking might have to change to accommodate this first, key insight.

The second of our two starting insights was perhaps even more challenging to popular conceptions of nature, and it soon emerged as the central dilemma to which our research group kept returning. The work of literary scholars, anthropologists, cultural historians, and critical theorists over the past several decades has yielded abundant evidence that "nature" is not nearly so natural as it seems. Instead, it is a profoundly human construction. This is not to say that the nonhuman world is somehow unreal or a mere figment of our imaginations—far from it. But the way we describe and understand that world is so entangled with our own values and assumptions that the two can never be fully separated. What we mean when we use the word "nature" says as much about ourselves as about the things we label with that word.[3] As the British literary critic Raymond Williams once famously remarked, "The idea of nature contains, though often unnoticed, an extraordinary amount of human history."[4]

What happens to environmental politics, environmental ethics, and environmentalism in general once we acknowledge the deeply troubling truth that we can never know at first hand the world "out there"—the "nature" we seek to understand and protect—but instead must always encounter that world through the lens of our own ideas and imaginings? By "environmentalism" in this book we generally mean the broad cultural movement in the decades since World War II that has expressed growing concern about protecting nature and the environment against harms caused by human actions. Our emphasis throughout is primarily on environmental ideas in American popular culture rather than on the more systematic thinking of those who have devoted their professional lives to understanding the environment (people whose ideas have in fact profoundly shaped our own thinking in writing this book). Popular concern about the environment often implicitly appeals to a kind of naive realism for its intellectual foundation, more or less assuming that we can pretty easily recognize nature when we see it and thereby make uncomplicated choices between natural things, which are good, and unnatural things, which are bad. Much of the moral authority that has made environmentalism so compelling as a popular movement flows from its appeal to nature as a stable external source of nonhuman values against which human actions can be judged without much ambiguity. If it now turns out that the nature to which we appeal as the source of our own values has in fact been contaminated or even invented by those values, this would seem to have serious implications for the moral and political authority people ascribe to their own environmental concerns.

Here, then, were the chief questions our seminar sought to tackle: How should popular conceptions of nature and the environment change in the face of these insights? What would a more historically and culturally minded way of understanding nature look like, which would take seriously not just the natural world but the human cultures that lend meaning and moral imperatives to that world? Can our concern for the environment survive our realization that its authority flows as much from human values as from anything in nature that might ground those values? And if the answer to this last question is yes—as surely it must be—then how can a more self-critical understanding of what we mean by nature enhance our efforts to protect the environment in ways that are both sustainable and humane?

Our own conviction in writing this book is that however threatening such questions might seem, they cannot be evaded. We know that by asking them, our essays may be perceived by some as hostile to environmentalism, part of a general backlash against the movement. And yet nothing could be further from the truth. Indeed, it is precisely because we sympathize so strongly with the environmentalist agenda—with the task of rethinking and reconstructing human relationships with the natural world to make them more just and accountable—that we believe these questions *must* be confronted. To ignore them is to proceed on intellectual foundations that may ultimately prove unsustainable. We believe that any movement that merits the most passionate support of its followers—as environmentalism surely does—also deserves their most thoughtful and soul-searching criticism. Troubling as such criticism can sometimes seem, its goal in the end must be to deepen and enrich our understanding of the problems we struggle to solve, by helping us see the unexamined, sometimes contradictory, assumptions at the core of our own beliefs—assumptions that can distract and defeat us if we embrace or act on them unthinkingly. Our goal in writing this book is to contribute to an ongoing dialogue among all who care about the environment. The outcome of that dialogue, we hope, will be a renewed environmentalism that will enter the twenty-first century more aware of its own history and cultural assumptions, and thereby renewed in its mission of protecting the natural world by helping people live more responsibly in it.

Stated so broadly, our central questions may strike the reader as being all too abstract and academic, the kind of impressive-sounding but ultimately irrelevant ivory-tower trivialities with which professors so often distract themselves while more practical folk get on with the real work of the world.

From the beginning, the members of our group were conscious that our project might be viewed in this way, and we worked hard not to fall into disembodied academic abstraction. In fact, one of our secondary agendas in this book has been to try to demonstrate the practical relevance for practical problem solving of humanistic disciplines that are rarely even consulted by policymakers and activists who devote themselves to environmental protection. People often appeal to the natural and social sciences in trying to understand environmental problems; we hope that after reading this book they will appeal to the humanities as well.

The challenge we faced was how to make this case as persuasively as possible. At that first October meeting, I repeatedly reminded my colleagues that we would be writing a book together and that it should speak not just to us or to our academic peers but to the much broader public—people who care about the environment and wish to understand why they relate to it as they do. As we cast about for ways to show such readers that the real-world problems of everyday life raise fascinating questions about the human place in nature and how people think of it, Donna Haraway proposed that we begin by discussing what she called "found objects": texts, photographs, advertisements, paintings, anything that would exemplify as concretely and vividly as possible the ideas of nature we wished to explore. Each of us, she suggested, should bring in an image or a text that would force the group to think about nature in new and unexpected ways. The resulting gallery of "found objects" would give us a rich and wonderfully playful tool for launching our discussions and getting to know one another's different perspectives at the same time.

Like so many of Donna's contributions to the group, it was a brilliant proposal. When we regathered in Irvine three months later, we arrived with an odd collection of found objects that would shape our discussions for the rest of our time together. Some were as quirky as a box of Heritage O's breakfast cereal—manufactured by a Canadian company called Nature's Path Foods, Inc.—or an advertisement for the computer game SimCity 2000, "the ultimate city simulator." Others were as serious as a discussion of ecological sustainability in a scientific journal or a *New York Times* article on the problems faced by native peoples in the Amazon rain forest. Each provoked lively discussion, and a few became so central to our thinking that we kept returning to them throughout the semester.

Probably the group's favorite found object was a collection of newspaper articles and tourist brochures that Richard White distributed on the Rocky Mountain Arsenal, in Denver, Colorado. Built during World War II and once a major Department of Defense manufacturing facility, the 17,000-acre site was used for nearly forty years to produce a long list of extraordinarily toxic substances: aldrin, dieldrin, atrazine, chlordane, mustard gas, phosgene, methyl parathion, napalm, and many others. Along the way, hundreds of millions of gallons of highly poisonous chemicals were deposited in landfills and waste basins on the site. As a result, the Rocky Mountain

Arsenal is now among the worst toxic waste dumps in the United States. But that is not all it is. Partly because the site is so toxic that most people have avoided it for decades, it has emerged as one of the West's most remarkable wildlife refuges. Its wildlife populations are more diverse and abundant than those anywhere else in the central Rockies, so the arsenal staff now devotes considerable energy not just to cleaning up toxic waste but to promoting environmental education at the site. More and more visitors come to the arsenal to enjoy its "natural" wonders, leading some to dub it the "Nation's Most Ironic Nature Park."[5]

The paradoxes of such a place are endlessly fascinating. Here we have one of the nation's most polluted landscapes, which is also among its richest wildlife preserves. In trying to figure out what to do with it, we face the dilemma of deciding whether to clean up its waste dumps even if doing so might endanger the creatures that now make their homes there. How do we choose between the animals that seem to be thriving at the arsenal and the people who fear that it threatens the value of their homes and the health of families? There is nothing natural, surely, about the arsenal's toxicity—and yet that toxicity is itself one of the most important things supporting the wild nature for which the place is now celebrated. The familiar categories of environmentalist thinking don't seem to work here, since we have no clear indication of what would be "natural" or "unnatural" to do in such a case. Instead, it leaves us with an all too familiar riddle: How can we act in an uncertain world where our familiar compass bearings don't work as well as we once thought they did, and how must we change the way we think in order to reorient ourselves and act responsibly?

The ability to blur the boundaries between "natural" and "unnatural" is precisely what makes the Rocky Mountain Arsenal and other found objects so useful for encouraging us to question our assumptions about what nature means and how we should relate to it. In the pages that follow, we have gathered a number of our most provocative found objects into what we call "albums," located at the end of each major part of the book. Our original found objects about the Rocky Mountain Arsenal, for instance, appear in an album following this introduction, so you can read for yourself about the site and think about the dilemmas and paradoxes it poses. Although the found objects in most of these albums are only rarely addressed in our individual essays, our hope is that you will soon perceive their direct relevance to the themes we discuss throughout the book. Indeed, once you have become accustomed to the quirky eclecticism of these texts and images, we hope you will begin to collect others for yourself, for you will find, as we did, that they are all around us. Virtually every newspaper, magazine, and television newscast offers equally vivid examples, as do the landscapes and environments in which we make our homes. All can serve as grist for daily reflection about the many meanings of nature in our ordinary lives.

That was certainly what happened to us in Irvine. It is not too much to say that for many of us, southern California became the most vivid found object of all, continually echoing and reflecting the ideas we discussed in our weekly meetings. Just before we arrived, a 6.8 magnitude earthquake shook the area around Northridge, severely damaging many neighborhoods in the northern reaches of the Los Angeles Basin. Although its effects on Irvine were slight—the occasional aftershock adding just a smidgeon of excitement to our otherwise calm existence—together with the October fires it became a symbol of the tenuously ambivalent relationship between nature and humanity in this vast California metropolis. Add to these "natural" problems the longstanding economic recession that California's defense-dependent economy has suffered from the end of the Cold War, as well as the disaster that has overtaken the University of California system as a result of property tax reform and the ensuing fiscal crisis, and you get a recipe for deep malaise in a state whose residents often in the past seemed unaccustomed to that emotion. Those of us who came to the seminar from outside Los Angeles arrived to find a lot of soul-searching about whether the California dream might finally be over or might even have been an illusion in the first place.

My favorite symbol of this malaise was the handwritten cardboard sign my family and I saw on the back of a U-Haul trailer in Carlsbad, New Mexico, during our drive from Wisconsin to Irvine. It showed a crude map of California inside a circle with a diagonal line slashed across it. Beneath this image were written these words:

THE CALIFORNIA DREAM:
EARTHQUAKES
FIRES
FLOODS
MUDSLIDES
RIOTS
RECESSION
CROWDING
TRAFFIC JAMS
SMOG
WE'RE GOING HOME TO TEXAS!

Since we too were pulling a U-Haul, we introduced ourselves to the family responsible for this sign and asked what part of California they were leaving. Their answer: Irvine.

This is a good story and an amusing found object, but it's worth reading the sign once again to consider its evidence that the California dream is over. Its most noteworthy feature is the way it unhesitatingly mingles problems that seem completely natural with problems that seem completely human. Earthquakes, surely, can't be blamed on anything but the natural movements of the San Andreas and its associated faults, while one would hardly be inclined to blame anyone but people for riots or traffic jams (though we might argue for quite a while about *which* people to hold responsible for such things). Often when we label a problem as "natural," we imply that there's not much we can do about it. It's just the way things are, and we'd better get used to it. Although the engineers of southern California have devoted immense energy to designing structures capable of withstanding large earth movements, and although Californians for the most part seem inclined to trust the engineers' assurances that these structures are safe, many people make their peace with the shaking earth by fatalistically accepting its inevitability. All one can do in the end is hope that when the Big One comes, the house that collapses won't be one's own. Earthquakes are natural and can be tolerated as such, at least until an experience at the upper end of the Richter scale shakes one's faith in fatalism.

But interesting problems lurk beneath the surface here. It is not at all clear, for instance, that even earthquakes are as natural as the previous paragraph would suggest. The Northridge quake affected different neighborhoods and structures in very different ways. Sometimes this was because of underlying strata and fault systems that concentrated the shaking motion in unexpected places like Santa Monica. But neither the underlying geology nor anything else in nature explains why some of the most severely damaged buildings were apartment complexes with unreinforced garages on their first floors. Such architecture is the product of economy and culture, not nature. Likewise, no feature of the natural environment can explain why some neighborhoods—Balboa Boulevard in Granada Hills, for instance—were able to rebuild so quickly following the quake, while others—Hollywood Boulevard near Western Avenue, for instance—became virtual ghost towns. These differences in the way the earthquake affected the built environment reflect differences in the social environment, not the natural one.[6] Most suggestive of all, perhaps, is the reminder that some of the worst effects of the quake occurred in places where people had consciously chosen to ignore key features of the local landscape. In the San Francisco quakes of 1906 and 1989, some of the most severe damage happened where people had built houses and highways on landfills in old wetlands. In the Northridge quake of 1994, no single effect was more disruptive to the lives of more people than the closing of the heavily trafficked Santa Monica Freeway. And yet the only place where that highway collapsed was a stretch of ground that bears the place-name La Cienaga—"swamp" in Spanish.[7] Although it may be perfectly natural in an earthquake for wetlands to shake more violently than drier ground, there is nothing natural—common though it may be—about building highways or houses in such places.

The cardboard sign on that U-Haul trailer did not specifically blame nature for its authors' flight from California. Instead, it mocked what it called the California Dream with a litany of disasters that for more than just this one family had turned the dream into a nightmare. The sign made no distinction between natural and unnatural hazards, and this surely says something important about the way people often think about the environment in general. Problems like smog, which represent the mingled effects of complex natural and human causes, are so diffuse in their origins and so normal a feature of life in the Los Angeles Basin that they might as well be natural. After a while they become second nature to us, and we do our best to ignore them. For someone who fears being trapped inside it, even a traffic jam or a riot can seem like a force of nature—vast and inescapable, something we can accept or flee but not change. Treating such things as normal and inevitable in effect naturalizes them, placing them beyond our control and excusing us from having to take responsibility for them, making it easier to pretend that they have little or nothing to do with our own actions.

Here one is reminded of another California nightmare listed on that sign: wildfires like the ones still burning as we gathered in Irvine for our first meeting that October. When we walked over to look at the apartments in which most of us would live, we tried not to think about the blackened, smoldering hillsides we couldn't help seeing on a horizon that was far too close for comfort. Several months later our resident ecologist, Michael Barbour, would take us on an extraordinary field trip to the site of the Laguna Canyon fire, which had burned nearly 14,000 acres and devastated dozens of homes before dying out less than a mile from the Irvine campus. Such fires are, of course, a natural feature of California's coastal chaparral ecosystems, which contain some of the most flammable vegetation on earth. Standing amid the ruins of once beautiful houses, surrounded by plants that were already sending up vigorous green shoots from the ashes, we could see all too easily why the buildings had gone up in smoke. Indeed, we were able to pinpoint the area where the next chaparral fire is almost certain to occur, given the age of the vegetation and the accumulated fuel load. It too will destroy many homes. If the rains cooperate in just the wrong way, such a fire will be followed by devastating mudslides like the ones we saw at Malibu, producing landscapes without so much as a blade of grass. At Malibu, the mud flowed down in knee-deep rivers through the posh beachhouses that blocked its path to the sea. California Dream indeed!

The irony is that the people who build in exposed locations like these— the locations most susceptible to the fire and mud—are often those with the greatest ability *not* to do so. Hillside real estate with ocean vistas commands prices in Los Angeles that only the wealthiest homeowners can afford. The engineering and architectural feats that permit houses to stand with elaborate props on slopes that would make even a mountain goat think twice before ascending are nothing less than astonishing for anyone accustomed to living on flatter ground. To spend millions of dollars to live suspended in midair above fire-prone vegetation on soil with only the most tenuous commitment to remaining in place, all within a few dozen miles of the San Andreas Fault, would seem to make no sense at all. And yet even while standing in the ashes with scenes of devastation in all directions, one can easily see why people build here anyway. The views from these places are breathtaking. The sight of such a landscape each time you step out your

Foundations of burned houses overlooking Laguna Canyon fire area. *(Photograph by William Cronon)*

front door is a reminder of what it means to be alive—even if that reminder ultimately kills you. Since World War II, roughly 75,000 upper-income homes have been built on hillside lots by people seeking a room with a view.[8] They presumably have at least some inkling of the attendant dangers, though it is surprisingly easy to forget the quakes and the fires and the mud while gazing out on the intoxicating blue of the Pacific. Why do they do it? They put themselves and their families at risk for the simple reason that they want to be close to nature.

This is the chief paradox of southern California, the feature of its environment that makes it such a perfect place for meditating on the complex and contradictory ideas of nature so typical of modernity. Many of the vices for which the region is most infamous—indeed, virtually every item on that U-Haul sign—are simply the mirror opposites of the virtues for which it once was, or still is, famous. Without the faults and the quakes, the landscape would never have acquired its astonishing physical relief, the mountains that climb so abruptly out of that stunning ocean. The slopes that offer such breathtaking views also tilt the shattered bedrock and unconsolidated soil well past their angle of repose, tempting them to head downslope at the least invitation. The vegetation keeps the sight lines open, without cluttering the horizon with trees, and is often the only thing holding the soil in place— but it is also very fond of burning. The glorious climate, with its endless sunny days, rarely provides the rainfall that might clear the air of smog, or

GIVE THE CANYONS A BREAK!

WILDERNESS AT WORK

WHAT WILL HAPPEN NEXT

Despite the lifeless appearance of the blackened hillsides, natural recovery is already underway. The remaining ash contains nutrients that will aid in the regeneration of the affected plant communities. Outlined below is the anticipated evolution of the landscape.

1. The heat of the fire activates the germination of many native seeds. Other plants regenerate by root sprouting.

2. Some of the first plants to reappear on the blackened landscape will be colorful wildflowers, including poppies and lupines.

3. Over the next few years, the native shrubs (Toyon, California Sagebrush, Lemonadeberry, Buckwheat) will begin to reappear.

4. As various plant communities regenerate to pre-fire levels of diversity, associated wildlife (California Gnatcatcher, Coastal Cactus Wren, Mule Deer, Bobcat) will return.

Mature Chaparral | Fire | 1 Year After Fire | 5 Years After Fire | 10 Years After Fire | 25 Years After Fire

WHAT YOU CAN DO TO HELP!

Respect the wilderness. Please stay out of burned areas!

The fire has left the wilderness in a fragile state. Premature access could damage plants that are trying to come back after the fire, as well as further traumatize displaced animals.

Be patient! All land managers are working together to reopen the canyons to public access as soon as possible.

Explore one of Orange County's other wilderness areas while the canyons heal.

ALISO & WOOD CANYONS REGIONAL PARK	714 / 831-2790
CASPERS WILDERNESS PARK	714 / 728-0235
CLEVELAND NATIONAL FOREST	909 / 736-1811
O'NEILL REGIONAL PARK	714 / 868-0965
WHITING RANCH WILDERNESS PARK	714 / 589-4729

Contact land managers for future access and volunteer information.

CRYSTAL COVE STATE PARK	714 / 494-3539
LAGUNA COAST WILDERNESS PARK	714 / 854-7108
IRVINE COMPANY OPEN SPACE RESERVE	714 / 832-7478

"Give the Canyons a Break! Wilderness at Work." *(County of Orange, EMA/Parks & Recreation)*

the water this metropolis needs to quench its insatiable thirst. The automobiles that produce the smog and jam the highways are also the means for fulfilling the ultimate suburban dream, enabling their owners to put a great distance between workplace and home, and permitting them on weekends to head out to the beach or the freedom of the hills. The crowding is but an ironic measure of the city's success, for the people who come in pursuit of the dream are all too often seduced into thinking they can leave behind the very problems they bring with them. As for the riots, they are a grim reminder, like so many other features of this favored landscape, that the troubles we ignore always come back to haunt us. Not even going home to Texas—that land of droughts and floods and hurricanes and tornadoes, to say nothing of urban sprawl and racial strife and the boom-and-bust economy—will save us in the end.

What better place than southern California, in short, to explore the contradictory meanings of nature in the modern world—not because southern California is unique but because it perfectly exemplifies so many tendencies of modern American culture. As our group proceeded with its work, we soon discovered that certain themes and motifs kept recurring in our discussions, each attached to some significant way of thinking about nature, and each also having important physical analogues in the landscapes around us. The individual essays in this book address these themes and motifs in far greater detail than this introduction can, but perhaps it would be useful here to offer a quick guided tour of the several versions of nature that most concerned us. The list I offer is anything but comprehensive, but it certainly identifies some of the most important ways that contemporary Americans think about nature. Perhaps the most important lesson to remember while reading this list, as I noted at the beginning, is that none of these natures is natural: all are cultural constructions that reflect human judgments, human values, human choices. We *could* choose to think about nature differently, and it is surely worth pondering what would happen if we did.

To make this provocative claim is, of course, to fly in the face of what people commonly mean when they speak of "nature," because one of the most important implications of that word is that the thing it describes is *not* of our own making. This is the view of nature the essays in this book most explicitly seek to critique. We might call it *nature as naive reality*. It is in fact one of the oldest meanings that the word "nature" carries in the English language: the sense that when we speak of the *nature* of something, we are describing its fundamental essence, what it really and truly *is*.[9] Indispensable as the usage may be, it is dangerous for what it tempts us to assume: the very thing it seeks to label is too often obscured beneath the presumption of naturalness. When we refer to "the nature of *x*," we usually imply that there is no further need to analyze or worry about that nature. We need not ask where it came from or on what contingencies it depends, for it is simply the way *x* is. Its meaning is transparent and uncomplicated, so we can take it for granted as a given: that is its nature.

A central tenet of modern humanistic scholarship is that everything we humans do—our speech, our work, our play, our social life, our ideas of ourselves and the natural world—exists in a context that is historically, geographically, and culturally particular, and cannot be understood apart from that context. If we wish really to make sense of a document like the Declaration of Independence, for instance, we dare not assume that the people who wrote it used words or conceived of the world precisely as we do. Unless we are willing to make the imaginative leap backward to immerse ourselves in the cultural universe of their time and place, we will make grievous errors in understanding what they meant. Moreover, we cannot assume that the people who subsequently read that document understood it as its authors did: the Declaration of Independence no doubt meant something very different to Jefferson Davis and Abraham Lincoln in 1861 from what it meant to Thomas Jefferson in 1776 or to Martin Luther King, Jr., in 1963. And so we take on the immensely challenging burden of trying to understand the *changing* meanings and *different* cultural contexts that have characterized human life and thought in all their infinite particularity.

This is why humanists are often so suspicious of arguments that appeal to something called "human nature." That term compresses such diverse and complex phenomena into such a flat, colorless cartoon that it erases most of the things scholars wish to understand. It assumes as an uncontested fact that humanity can be captured in a single, monolithic description, when the burden of proof for actually demonstrating such a claim would for all but the crudest assertions be so immense as to be practically impossible. The same can be said for the concept of nature itself. Our ways of thinking about the natural world are powerfully shaped by our time, our place, and our culture. When people use the word "nature" to refer to the whole of creation, they are echoing a long semantic history that tracks backward to the medieval church and even to classical antiquity, implying without much reflection that nature is One Thing with One Name, a monolith that can be described holistically in much the same way as God. Nature in Western culture is the product of a monotheistic religious tradition; it is often unrecognizable for people whose cultures have not taught them to worship a lone deity.[10]

This is not the place to offer a comprehensive history of nature in Western thought. For the purposes of this book, I simply wish to argue that the burden of proof should be with those who assert the universal nature of nature, for the evidence against such a view is enormous. Ideas of nature never exist outside a cultural context, and the meanings we assign to nature cannot help reflecting that context. The main reason this gets us into trouble is that nature as essence, nature as naive reality, wants us to see nature as if it *had* no cultural context, as if it were everywhere and always the same. And so the very word we use to label this phenomenon encourages us to ignore the context that defines it. If we wish to understand why we think of nature as we do—for instance, even so basic a matter as why the object of this sentence is expressed as a singular noun—then we cannot afford to fall into the trap that this word has laid for us. If we wish to understand the values and motivations that shape our own actions toward the natural world, if we hope for an environmentalism capable of explaining why people use and abuse the earth as they do, then the nature we study must become less natural and more cultural.

The appeal to nature as naive reality is often linked to a second major cluster of ideas that surround this word: *nature as moral imperative.* One need not travel a very great distance in speaking of "the nature of *x*" to get from "this is the way *x* really *is*" to "this is way *x ought* to be." The great attraction of nature for those who wish to ground their moral vision in external reality is precisely its capacity to take disputed values and make them seem innate, essential, eternal, nonnegotiable. When we speak of "the natural way of doing things," we implicitly suggest that there can be no other way, and that all alternatives, being unnatural, should have no claim on our sympathies. Nature in such arguments becomes a kind of trump card against which there can be no defense, at least not as long as our opponents share our values—and how could they not, if those values are as natural as we claim? Only a fool or an incorrigible sinner could fail to respond to so compelling a moral imperative. This habit of appealing to nature for moral authority is in large measure a product of the European Enlightenment. By no means all people in history have sought to ground their beliefs in this particular way. Indeed, it would have been far more common in the past for people in Western traditions to cite God as the authority for their beliefs. The fact that so many now cite Nature instead (implicitly capitalizing it as they once might have capitalized God) suggests the extent to which Nature has become a secular deity in this post-romantic age.

Because the values that people attach to nature as moral imperative are so dependent on cultural context, it makes little sense to discuss this phenomenon in the abstract. Nature as moral imperative always implies a very particular vision of what ideal nature is supposed to be. For some modern Americans, ideal nature is clearly a pristine wilderness, as I argue elsewhere in this book. For others, as Kenneth Olwig notes in his essay, ideal nature is the pastoral countryside or the small town, while others still would celebrate the suburb or even the city as the natural home of humankind. It hardly needs saying that nothing in physical nature can help us adjudicate among these different visions, for in all cases nature merely serves as the mirror onto which societies project the ideal reflections they wish to see.

The Judeo-Christian tradition nonetheless has one core myth that is so deeply embedded in Western thought that it crops up almost anytime people speak of nature. It is so widespread in modern environmental thinking that it deserves to be labeled as a separate cluster of ideas in its own right: *nature as Eden.* Candace Slater, Carolyn Merchant, and Kenneth Olwig were responsible for introducing this concept to our seminar in Irvine, and their essays explore it in detail. It quickly became one of the most fertile topics we discussed. Candace in particular argued that a great many environmental controversies revolve around what she calls "Edenic narratives," in which an original pristine nature is lost through some culpable human act that results in environmental degradation and moral jeopardy. The tale may be one of paradise lost or paradise regained, but the role of the narrative is always to project onto actual physical nature one of the most powerful and value-laden fables in the Western intellectual tradition. The myth of Eden describes a perfect landscape, a place so benign and beautiful and good that the imperative to preserve or restore it could be questioned only by those who ally themselves with evil.

Nature as Eden encourages us to celebrate a particular landscape as the ultimate garden of the world. In her essay, Candace Slater demonstrates that the Amazon rain forest now plays this role for a great many people in the United States and Europe who have never actually seen that forest for themselves. Kenneth Olwig points to the ways in which Yosemite offered nineteenth-century Americans an ideal combination of pristine wilderness and pastoral garden, turning it into a nationalist symbol of paradise. And for many of us in the Reinventing Nature group, it also seemed that Eden, albeit a problematic Eden, existed right on our doorsteps, in Irvine and southern California generally. The awe-inspiring views of the Pacific that tempt wealthy homeowners into the path of the fires are only one manifestation of the love affair with nature that is so near the core of southern California culture. Los Angeles has fewer public parks per capita than most other American cities, but it possesses nearly eighty miles of beachfront unequaled by any other city in the world.[11] Marketed even in the late nineteenth century as the ultimate garden suburb, a city with no downtown but with houses in grassy yards everywhere, Los Angeles and its neighbors have long participated in the Edenic myth. As Reyner Banham has written, "Whatever man has done subsequently to the climate and environment of Southern California, it remains one of the ecological wonders of the habitable world. Given water to pour on its light and otherwise almost desert soil, it can be made to produce a reasonable facsimile of Eden."[12]

The city's developers make their living by selling Eden, and they know their business well. The real estate section of the *Los Angeles Times* is unquestionably the largest and most colorful I have ever seen. Each Sunday brought a sheaf of promotional literature for the subdivisions whose explosive growth we could monitor every time we took a drive. The advertisements promised not only the social attractions of living in a planned community—the reassuring safety of gated entrances staffed round the clock by security guards, the convenience of nearby schools and shopping malls, the recreational opportunities of adjacent country clubs and golf courses— but also the *natural* attractions of a community whose planners really care, they tell us, about protecting the environment. Irvine bills itself as the largest planned community in the nation and has served as the prototype for many of its neighbors. Dove Canyon, on the eastern outskirts of Irvine, offers would-be buyers "the more perfect world you've promised yourself, and it's time you made it your home."[13] The developers of Rancho Santa Margarita—"where the west begins. Again"—explain, "It all started years ago with a vast rancho rich in history and natural beauty. And then came a dream. To develop the land into a master-planned community while carefully protecting all that makes the land so wonderful and beautiful." Even though this "may look like a vacation destination, it isn't. It's a hometown."[14] Just so are we able to regain paradise if only we can afford the down payment.

Like the original garden, these new Edens are not without their problems. Conflicts often erupt over the particular vision of nature—God's or Satan's—they are meant to express. While we were living in Irvine, an Edenic controversy swirled around a small bird called the gnatcatcher. It had been proposed as an endangered species so that environmentalists could avail themselves of the federal courts to prevent further development of the bird's coastal sage scrub habitat—the very habitat most at risk to be turned into spanking new versions of Eden by the developers. In May 1994 a federal judge overturned the bird's listing under the Endangered Species Act, thereby throwing open the remaining chaparral to development. For the environmentalists this was tantamount to casting it into Satan's hands; for the developers it assured that the subdivided paradises of Orange County could continue to expand. As one environmentalist declared, "This is absolutely a step in the wrong direction, one that could have a devastating impact on the habitat protection program" of the entire Orange County landscape. Developers, on the other hand, celebrated the court's rejection of what they saw as environmentalist efforts "to illegitimately twist the Endangered Species Act into a tool for stopping development in general."[15] The point here is not the particular merits of either argument but the fact that a single small animal has for peculiar legal and cultural reasons been made to bear the entire burden of defending or delimiting Eden. In the gnatcatcher case, both sides appealed to a common moral tradition—both employed Edenic language to defend their case—even though the natures they sought to protect on the coastal hills could hardly have been more different.

This is not unusual. Consider the case of the homeowners association in Laguna Niguel that decided after a closed meeting to resolve a long-standing dispute among its members by cutting down two hundred of the town's eucalyptus trees, most of them located in the middle of people's yards. What problem justified such drastic intervention? Residents living high up on the community's slopes were having their views of the ocean blocked by the fast-growing trees. They naturally felt that their quality of life and the value of their houses were being jeopardized, since the premium prices they had paid for their properties had been predicated on the open view. Homeowners farther down the slope, on the other hand, not having the same views or property values to protect, just as naturally prized the trees for the cool shade they offered on the hot hillsides. Feelings ran so high that the tree cutters were at one point threatened with a shotgun, and several homeowners wept openly as their trees came down. One woman who had lost fourteen eucalyptuses on her property said that before their removal, "it was like living in a park setting. I hope this is illegal what they have done, because if not, it's definitely immoral."[16]

Here again there is no clear right or wrong: both sides were merely defending their corner of Eden, trying to protect the nature they valued so highly. The violence of their disagreement testifies to how important our views of nature can be in defining who we think we are and the kinds of lives we wish to lead. In the United States, and especially in southern California, Eden is never far beneath the surface in shaping what we imagine to be the perfect home in the perfect natural setting. Ever since the Puritans arrived in Boston to build their fabled city on a hill to serve as a beacon for all the world, Americans have hankered after the Protestant mission of reforming an old world and a faded dream by starting over again. In this land of new beginnings, the place to which people most wish to return is inevitably some version or another of the original garden, the paradise that would have been ours if only we hadn't lost our way.

Nowhere in the United States are these impulses more powerfully expressed than in California. Continent's end has long been the final resting stop on the great frontier migration, the last best place for starting over. It would be hard to buy property in Orange County without being influenced by the real estate literature that promises paradise for the price of a mortgage. And there is nothing necessarily wrong with this. Most of us, I suspect, have some notion of where we would most like to live if we could have the home of our heart's desire. Trouble surfaces only when, as so often happens, one person's Eden comes into conflict with another's, much as God's plans for paradise collided with Satan's. Then the Edenic myth becomes the vehicle for casting our adversaries into the heart of darkness, demonizing them as allies of the dark angel who so long ago seduced us into this, our present exile in a fallen world. Even those who do not subscribe to the Judeo-Christian imagery can fall victim to its moral dualism, because that is how Eden tempts us. It is a place of absolute good and absolute evil, of actions that are unambiguously right and wrong. When we project its polarized, black-and-white myth onto the ambiguous world of gray on gray that we actually inhabit, the power of its imagery sparks our passions but darkens our vision. It buys clarity at the expense of understanding by tempting us to reenact its most ancient of stories rather than listen for whether there might be some other tale to tell.

I initially introduced Eden as a special case of nature as moral imperative, but these disputes and the work of the real estate developers suggest that Eden can point in another direction as well: *nature as artifice, nature as self-conscious cultural construction.* What is so striking about the southern California landscape is the extent to which it has been transformed into a vision of nature utterly different from the ecosystems that once characterized the region. In this, it represents a more extreme example of the careful manipulation of natural systems that Anne Whiston Spirn describes Frederick Law Olmsted performing as he helped found the profession of landscape architecture. Olmsted sought to design *with* nature, and the paradox of his success is that many of his most important creations are no longer even recognized as such: people look at them now and see nature, not Olmsted. In less sensitive hands than Olmsted's, artifice can triumph even more completely. Once we believe we know what nature *ought* to look like—once our vision of its ideal form becomes a moral or cultural imperative—we can remake it so completely that we become altogether indifferent or even hostile toward its prior condition. Taken far enough, the result can be a landscape in which nature and artifice, despite their apparent symbolic opposition, become indistinguishable because they finally merge into one another.

One might go so far as to say that the replacement of nature by self-conscious artifice is a key defining quality of the modern landscape. If so, Irvine is a near-perfect example of the genre. Like many planned communities in southern California, it takes its inspiration in part from that amazing planned environment in Anaheim a few miles to the north: Disneyland. There, Disney's imagineers succeeded in replicating on a very small plot of land a jungle, a Louisana bayou, a desert, a coral reef, a miniaturized English countryside, even the most famous mountain in the Alps. The landscaping of Disneyland is rarely less than brilliant, with each different habitat and playground screened from its neighbors with carefully controlled sight lines, plantings, and sound baffles. The animals in these landscapes always perform perfectly on cue as the tourists pass by, because most are machines that reproduce the appearances of nature without its bothersome misbehaviors. The streets are constantly swept by uniformed attendants so that no litter ever lingers for long, and are also steam-cleaned each night to make sure they are ever immaculate. Social problems are carefully excluded from the theme park, along with the people who might inflict those problems on this land where fantasy and commercial profit reign supreme. It is in all ways an extraordinary place, a triumph of artifice over nature.

The same might be said of Orange County itself. Here's how the California Office of Tourism sells the place to visitors:

It's a theme p .rk—a seven-hundred-and-eighty-six square mile theme park—and the theme is "you can have anything you want."

It's the most California-looking of the Californias: the most like the movies, the most like the stories, the most like the dream.

Orange County is Tomorrowland and Frontierland, merged and inseparable. 18th century mission. 1930s art colony. 1980s corporate headquarters. . . .

The temperature today will be in the low 80's. There's a slight offshore breeze. Another just-like-yesterday day in paradise.

Come to Orange County. It's no place like home.[17]

Ansel Adams, Campus Park, the Commons, and Library Administration Buildir. University of California at Irvine, shortly after construction. *(Sweeney/Rubin Ansel Adams Fiat Lux Collection, California Museum of Photography, University of California at Riverside)*

Like Disneyland, Orange County is a place where planners, designers, and real estate developers have remade nature to make it conform to their own ideal. One has only to look at Ansel Adams's photographs of the first buildings at the University of California at Irvine to see how completely the landscape has been transformed. As recently as the late 1960s, the university sat virtually alone in a vast empty grassland, the dryness and openness of the vegetation visible in all directions. Today one has to walk to the edge of the campus to see any remnants of this grassland, which have been set aside as a nature preserve—a preserve that incidentally could easily serve as the corridor for bringing wildfire to this community if the Santa Ana winds should ever blow in the wrong direction on a day when the hills are burning. Elsewhere the original vegetation has given way to the succulent ice plant, the spicy-smelling eucalyptus, and all the other non-native plantings that have turned this semiarid land into a subtropical paradise. As Banham says, water is all it takes to build Eden in this place.

What most struck many of us after living in Irvine for a time was not just the transformation of the local ecosystem but the way its idealized nature reflects underlying assumptions about order and community. It is a city where everything has been given its proper place so that nothing need ever interfere with anything else. Everything is well under control. The major city streets are carefully designed so that each block has only a single point of access, with the result that cars can travel at fifty-five miles per hour on streets that in any other city would be posted at least fifteen to twenty miles per hour lower. Traffic flow is almost as brilliantly managed here as in Disneyland: the bumper-to-bumper cars so characteristic of Los Angeles often disappear when freeways reach the margins of Irvine. The highway engineers have finally made their peace with U-turns, so much so that they become the chief device permitting high-speed movement on limited-access streets. Bike lanes are everywhere, often completely separated from cars on roads designed solely for two-wheeled vehicles. Parks wind their way along the major drainage channels, so those who wish to bike or stroll beside the cement-lined creeks can easily do so to take in the view.

The only problem is that all this meticulously arranged openness somehow never quite becomes *public:* private space rarely seems to become public place. One experiences the parkland of Irvine, like the freeways, privately, as an individual, without any real sense that one is doing so as the member of a community. The same is true of the ubiquitous shopping malls, the parks, even the UC-Irvine campus. Many of us in the seminar had the feeling months after our arrival that we were still trying to find Irvine: even now, I couldn't tell you where to locate the downtown—it was designed not to have one—nor could I give you directions for finding any but a small handful of places. For all the care lavished on this planned community— maybe even because of that care—it is an extraordinarily difficult place to navigate. I once asked a woman at the checkout counter in my local supermarket how to get to another store less than a mile away. Even though she had lived in the city for several years, she just shook her head and said she wasn't sure. "I used to drive a cab," she remarked, "and I always tried to say no when they wanted me to pick up someone in Orange County. Nothing makes sense here. I'm still always getting lost." The curving streets are undoubtedly part of the problem, but so is the planner's impulse to keep everything neatly segregated from everything else. The local geography seems designed to reveal itself on a strictly need-to-know basis. One can search in vain to find an address on any of the major streets, a problem one typically solves by getting directions in advance, always starting from the nearest shopping mall. Like the walls and gates behind which so many people live here, this is perhaps just another way of protecting privacy. It certainly prevents one from having any clear sense of relationship to a larger community.

For me the most powerful symbol of this impressively planned, well-controlled, elegantly designed landscape was right in our own yard. I have never lived in a house with a more immaculate garden. There was no grass anywhere in sight, and nothing we needed to mow. Instead, the garden was filled with palms and ferns and mosses whose succulent leaves and deep green hues bespoke an unfailing supply of water. Each night, at odd intervals we could never predict in advance, a computer in our garage turned on the sprinklers and gave our lovely plants the drink they so needed after their long hot day in the California sun. The water that quenched their thirst (and our own) probably traveled hundreds of miles from the Owens Valley or the Colorado River to make our private backyard Eden possible—though it is a token of this strange land that I will never know for sure which distant river was sacrificed to make our green space possible (and to be fair, the garden was maintained with gray water recycled from other uses). Despite the luxuriance and richness of the garden, we never raised a finger to take care of it. That work was done by Mexican American gardeners who arrived at discreetly chosen times when their activities would not disturb the calm of our pastoral retreat.

It was all so peaceful, so Edenic and natural, that one would surely have thought it would be easy to get used to. And yet somehow I never did. I admired the beauty and the ingenious contraptions that made it possible, and I was grateful for the hard work I did not have to do. But I never quite felt at home. For some perverse reason the garden memory that remains most vivid in my mind is of the snails that slithered across our walkway each night after the sprinklers had done their work. We could never see them as we made our way home in the evening, so almost every night we winced as their shells crunched loudly beneath our feet, forcing us to clean mashed snail slime from our shoes before going inside. (Worse still were the mornings, when I occasionally stepped on them barefoot while groping for the morning paper in the dark.) The snails were the one element of this garden that had somehow escaped automation and control, the one example of nature doing its own thing instead of what the planners had prescribed. Never mind that the snails could hardly have been native to the place and depended just as much as our succulent plants on the artificial rain that our computer delivered each night. Because they didn't fit the plan, they somehow seemed more natural.

I will return to those snails in a moment. Orange County is a place so constructed that it verges on becoming still another form of nature: *nature as virtual reality.* This was a theme that Katherine Hayles and Donna Haraway introduced to our discussions in Irvine, and I think we were all surprised by how influential the idea became for the rest of us. We live in a time when the proliferation of networked computers, the power of morphing and fractal geometry, the ever more persuasive illusions of Industrial Light and Magic, the anarchic world of the Internet, and so many other features of the electronic universe make it increasingly possible to inhabit a cultural space

Snails on garden walkway, University Hills, Irvine, California. *(Photograph by William Cronon)*

whose analogues in nature seem ever more tenuous. Katherine shared with our group numerous examples of computer simulations and graphics that came close to constructing an alternative reality. We speculated together about the possibility that computer viruses might serve as the models for new silicon-based life forms that would live out their lives in electronic space. Some computer scientists now believe that the most effective way to create artificial intelligence will be to devise small self-replicating programs capable of mutating and undergoing evolution inside our machines, the idea being that they will eventually develop the complexity, self-referentiality, and autonomy needed to produce a consciousness akin to our own. At first glance the idea seemed bizarre to all of us, but the more we considered it, the more plausible it became.

The fascinating thing about virtual reality is that although it initially appears to be the least natural of human creations, the most disembodied and abstracted expression of modernity's alienation from nature, it can in fact serve as a powerful and rather troubling test of whether we really know what we're talking about when we speak of nature. One would think that the virtual would stand in pure opposition to the real, but when you put them next to each other this is not nearly so obvious. Yes, a person using computerized sensory apparatus to move through virtual space could hardly be more isolated from the surrounding environment. And yet the better the simulation, the more difficulty we begin to have in distinguishing it from the real. The more engaged we become with experiencing it, the more plausible it begins to seem as an alternative to the world we know—indeed, an alternative with real advantages. Even more than the planned landscape of Orange County, virtual reality seems to hold out the seductive promise of total control, an environment we can manipulate to our heart's content because it apparently offers no resistance to our fantasies. Some go so far as to imagine that it will ultimately enable us to escape the confines of our own bodies, so that the information in our neurons and synapses can be downloaded into a computer where our mind, our consciousness, our very being can shed its husk of flesh and finally enable us to fulfill the age-old dream of becoming, like the gods, immortal. This is not just science fiction; it is a plausible description of a future in which virtuality will become as real and natural to us as nature is today.

Many of us no doubt recoil from such a vision, but as the members of our group learned in Irvine, it is easier to recoil than to explain why we do so. Unnatural though they may seem, virtual consciousness and virtual reality emulate many more features of the "natural" world than one might at first assume. Katherine Hayles takes up some of these issues in her essay for this book, and I will not try to reproduce the intricacies of her argument here. Instead, I will offer just two observations. First, the dream of complete control is no more assured in a virtual world than in this supposedly more natural one. Among the many surprising features of virtuality is the fact that the closer it comes to emulating real life, the more chaotic and unpredictable it seems to become. Programs designed to do one thing often turn out to do another, evolving in ways their original authors could not have anticipated. The more complex the systems become, the more they emulate the kinds of behaviors we so often see in nature. As in the real world, these often prove much harder to control, much more capable of taking us by surprise, than we could ever have imagined.

Just as strikingly, the real world we now inhabit already contains many elements in which the natural and the virtual mingle in such subtle ways that it can be surprisingly difficult to distinguish between them. This is among the lessons of Disneyland, in which plastic trees and mechanical animals mimic quite amazingly their counterparts in nature. Susan Davis took our group on a field trip to Sea World, where we watched Shamu™, the killer whale, perform its tricks—or rather its "behaviors," as the Sea World staff insists on calling them—in a great tank of water with an enormous television screen standing behind to magnify the performance for the delighted audience. The images on the screen, backed by the resonant narration of James Earl Jones, were as important to the performance as the live animal and its trainers. Susan's essay in this book discusses the complex ways in which this corporate theme park manipulates visitors' experience of its creatures, raising the question of what is natural and what is virtual in such a place.

Sea World implicitly exemplifies one of the most powerful cultural constructions that shapes modern American attitudes toward nature: *nature as commodity,* a thing capable of being bought and sold in the marketplace quite apart from any autonomous values that may inhere in it. Market exchange and commodified relations with nature have been transforming the landscape of America, indeed, of the entire planet, for centuries. Few cultural conceptions have had greater ecological impact. Whether one looks at the destruction of the great herds of bison or flocks of passenger pigeons in the nineteenth century, the extirpation from North America of whole ecosystems like the tallgrass prairie, or the increasing assaults on biodiversity worldwide, the immense power of a political economy based on culturally commodified nature is everywhere apparent, producing an alienation from the natural world—and from the effects human actions have thereon—that is all too characteristic of modernity. Looking at the environment in this way comes so easily to members of modern Western cultures that it is virtually second nature. It is present in the trading pits of the Chicago Board of Trade, where all manner of natural resources become commodities, and it is no less present in places like Sea World, where nature itself—or rather, a particular *idea* of nature—is bought and sold as a consumable experience. The peculiar tendency of many cultures in the modern capitalist world to view nature in this way is yet another kind of virtual reality, a construction so comfortable that it seems utterly commonsensical, universal, and *natural* to those who inhabit it—no matter how problematic its consequences may be.

Jennifer Price gives another example of commodified nature in her essay on The Nature Company, which many members of our group visited in Orange County's famous South Coast Plaza shopping mall. Surrounded by some of the most upscale stores in America, the Nature Company manages the neat trick of standing in apparent opposition to its glitzy surroundings by offering a calm woodsy space where shoppers can enjoy the pleasures of our national pastime—shopping—while still affirming their green values by purchasing recycled greeting cards, rustic bird feeders, ecologically educational toys, ambient environmental sound CDs, and hand-made crafts from the indigenous peoples of the rain forest. What the Nature Company sells is not so much nature as authenticity—or what passes for authenticity in a consumer culture. It reassures its customers that they can participate in consumerism with their values intact, go to the mall and still get back to nature. Standing in the midst of such a store, surrounded by its many beautiful objects and basking in the image of nature it wants to sell us, we can legitimately ask whether this might not be yet another kind of simulation, another form of virtual space.

But theme parks and shopping malls are by no means the only ways in which the virtual and the natural are converging in our time. It is well worth remembering that some of the most dramatic environmental problems we appear to be facing as we enter the twenty-first century exist mainly as simulated representations in complex computer models of natural systems. Our awareness of the ozone hole over the Antarctic, for instance, depends very much on the ability of machines to process large amounts of data to produce maps of atmospheric phenomena that we ourselves could never witness at first hand. No one has ever seen the ozone hole. However real the problem may be, our knowledge of it cannot help being virtual.

The same is even more true of the phenomenon called global warming, which many people now take to be an absolute fact of nature. Like the ozone hole, it too is probably real, but our knowledge of it could hardly be more simulated. The computer models on which we base our predictions of what will happen as concentrations of greenhouse gases rise are in fact still so unsophisticated that they cannot even do an accurate job of predicting *past* climatic change, let alone change in the future. Load into them the data for 1900, and the weather they will predict for our present time bears little resemblance to what we are now experiencing. Given this rather awkward weakness in their software, the modelers have had to resort to a less troublesome forecasting technique. They run their programs forward in time, once using the data for today's mixture of atmospheric gases, and once with doubled levels of carbon dioxide. After the computer has done its job, they compare the two runs and describe what will happen when we double the carbon dioxide. The only trouble is that this description is of the simulated doubling of a modeled gas in a virtual atmosphere, all of which bears only the most hypothetical relationship to the future world, for which we of course have no empirical data whatsoever. The model's ability to predict the future is no more assured than its proven inability to predict the past.[18] But

because the phenomenon being predicted is so complex, because its consequences could be so catastrophic, and because we have no better way to
investigate it, we have no choice but to rely on these flawed tools. In a very
real sense, global warming is the ultimate example of a virtual crisis in virtual
nature—which is far from saying that it is unreal. Instead, it is proof that
the virtual and the natural can converge in surprising ways.

None of this is very reassuring for environmentalists and others who look
to nature as the ultimate foundation for their moral vision. In the face of
culturally constructed landscapes and increasingly virtual experiences of the
world, many of us would not be at all unhappy if nature would reassert its
own authority over all this human unreality. This may be one reason why
environmentalists so often seem drawn to prophecies of ecological doom
that offer elaborate descriptions of the disasters that will soon occur because
of our misdeeds against the earth. The genre is familiar enough to constitute
yet another nature for our list. It is the nightmare inversion of Eden to
which that eloquent U-Haul sign bore witness: *nature as demonic other,
nature as avenging angel, nature as the return of the repressed.* It can range
from something as trivial as those uncooperative snails in our Irvine garden,
to natural disasters like earthquakes or floods, to the hypothetical horrors
of global warming. At whatever scale we experience them, these things represent a nonhuman world that despite our best efforts we never quite succeed in fully controlling. Often we come close enough that we congratulate
ourselves prematurely for our own triumph—and then are surprised when
the long-silent fault or the hundred-year flood suddenly reveals our hubris.
As one man wrote to *Time* magazine following the Northridge quake, "If
Mother Nature has proved one thing, it is that she can be a real bitch."[19]

Even beyond the earthquake and the fires, California offered numerous
examples of nature in apparent rebellion during our stay. Early in the year
reports surfaced of a high school in nearby Westminster where 292 students
had been infected with tuberculosis by a single classmate, twelve of them
with drug-resistant forms that would respond slowly to treatment if they
responded at all. A little later the newspapers announced that the first killer
bees had finally made it to California, and offered dire predictions of what
this would mean for people who would now have to worry about being
stung by them.[20] More dramatically, in April a young woman jogging near
her home in the Sierra Nevada foothills was stalked and pulled from the trail
by a female mountain lion and then quickly mauled to death. The lioness
was hunted down and shot, lest she kill again. The woman left behind two
small children; the lion, a seven-week-old cub. It undoubtedly says something about people's ideas of nature, perhaps even their ideas of human
nature, that public appeals on behalf of these young orphans soon yielded
$9,000 for the two children . . . and $21,000 for the cub.[21]

What is interesting about such events is not that they occur. After all,
what could be more natural than a mountain lion killing its prey or a great
fault relieving its pent-up strain? What is really intriguing is the meaning we

ENTERING
MOUNTAIN
LION
COUNTRY

A RISK

You are entering a wilderness park.

Mountain Lions are present and unpredictable. Be cautious. They are generally elusive, but have been known to attack without warning.

Your safety cannot be guaranteed. You are advised to stay alert for potential dangers. CHILDREN MUST BE ATTENDED BY AN ADULT.

Please respect the wilderness and its wildlife.

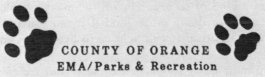

COUNTY OF ORANGE
EMA/Parks & Recreation

"Entering Mountain Lion Country: A Risk." *(County of Orange, EMA/Parks & Recreation)*

assign to them, for we have an inveterate habit of turning them into moral fables. The snails in my Irvine garden become small gruesome symbols of the limits to human control. The earthquakes exemplify nature's terrifying randomness—and also people's hubris in pretending that rare, irregular events can safely be ignored simply because they cannot be predicted. The mountain lion can serve as a token of nature's savagery—or as the innocent victim of human beings who in their efforts to live closer to nature unthinkingly invade the lion's home. Every environmental disaster, all the way up to global warming, stands as a potential indictment of the ignorant or culpable human actions that contributed to it.

The human inclination is to transform all such events into stories that carry a moral lesson. Nature as demonic other is Job's whirlwind, the horror of random suffering that is all the more terrifying because it offers no discernible justification for the pain it inflicts on the innocent and the guilty alike. Nature as the avenging angel is the dark side of the Eden story, the punishment that follows in the wake of our having listened to Satan's seductive advice. It is this story that makes us shake our heads so knowingly even as we sympathize with the families that lost their homes in the Laguna Canyon fire. *It's too bad,* we say, *but they brought it on themselves by building there. What did they expect? After all, the fires are only natural.* We do this even though we ourselves have almost surely made similar bargains with nature, whether we live in the fault zone or the floodplain or the path of great storms. When we become victims, these things are never our fault, though it is easy enough for us to see how others have foolishly placed themselves in harm's way.

People are drawn to nature as avenging angel for much the same reason that they are drawn to nature as Eden. It should by now be clear that the two are in fact opposite sides of the same moral coin. The one represents our vision of paradise: the good that is so utterly compelling that we feel no hesitation in claiming nature as our authority for embracing it. The other is our vision of hell: the place where those who transgress against nature will finally endure the pain and retribution they so justly deserve. There is a wonderfully attractive clarity in this way of thinking about nature, for it turns the nonhuman world into a moral universe whose parables and teachings are strikingly similar to those of a religion. We need such teachings, for they give meaning and value to our lives. To the extent that environmentalism serves as a kind of secular religion for many people in the modern world, it is capable of doing great good if it can teach us the stories, as religions often try to do, that will help us to live better, more responsible lives.

And yet: we must never forget that these stories are *ours*, not nature's. The natural world does not organize itself into parables. Only people do that, because this is our peculiarly human method for making the world make sense. And because people differ in their beliefs, because their visions of the true, the good, and the beautiful are not always the same, they inevitably differ as well in their understanding of what nature means and how it should be used—because nature is so often the place where we go searching for the fulfillment of our desires. This points to one final vision of nature that recurs everywhere in this book: *nature as contested terrain.*

Over and over again in these essays, we encounter the central paradox of this complex cultural construct. On the one hand, people in Western cultures use the word "nature" to describe a universal reality, thereby implying that it is and must be common to all people. On the other hand, they also pour into that word all their most personal and culturally specific values: the essence of who they think they are, how and where they should live, what they believe to be good and beautiful, why people should act in certain ways. All these things are described as *natural,* even though everything we know about human history and culture flies in the face of that description. The result is a human world in which these many human visions of nature are always jostling against each other, each claiming to be universal and each soon making the unhappy discovery that even its nearest neighbors refuse to acknowledge that claim.

The history of environmentalism is fraught with this paradox. In his essay Jeffrey Ellis explores the long-standing search by leading environmental intellectuals for what he calls "the root cause," which will trace all environmental problems back to a single source: overpopulation, capitalism, what have you. Their vehement disagreements have ironically stemmed from their shared wish to discover a universal explanation for what are almost surely multicausal phenomena. James Proctor analyzes recent debates about the future of old-growth forests in the Pacific Northwest and discovers adversaries whose different ethical systems lead them to very different visions of what the nature of the region should be. Giovanna Di Chiro describes the history of the environmental justice movement, detailing the many ways in which its struggles to achieve safer and healthier environments for women, workers, and people of color have been systematically ignored by most mainstream environmental organizations—precisely because these groups do not agree on what counts as a nature worth protecting. Richard White comes at the same problem from a very different angle by arguing that many twentieth-century Americans, including most who call themselves environmentalists, have forgotten what it means to know nature through work. As a result, they defend an ideal of nature that almost inevitably brings them into conflict with those who earn their living by working on the land.

In each of these instances, as in all the others I have discussed in this introduction, we see the many ways in which people disagree deeply about the meaning of nature. Perhaps the most important message of this book is that such disagreement is inevitable—one might even be tempted to say natural—given the universalizing tendencies that lie at the very core of this human construct called nature. The question "Whose nature?" again emerges as central. As soon as we project our values onto the world and begin to assert their primacy by calling them natural, we declare our unwillingness to consider alternative values that in all likelihood are no less compelling for the people who hold them dear. Nature becomes our dogma, the wall we build around our own vision to protect it from competing views. And like all dogmas, it is the death of dialogue and self-criticism. This is its seductive power. This is the trap it has set for us.

As we try to make sense of these many natures all claiming to be one, we would do well to stop hoping that any single one of them can ever finally triumph. Nature will *always* be contested terrain. We will never stop arguing about its meanings, because it is the very ground on which our debates must occur. This is *not* to say that all visions of nature are equally good, or that we can never persuade others that one of them is better, truer, fairer, more beautiful than another. It is simply to state that such persuasion will never occur if all we do is assert the naturalness of our own views. Tempting as it may be to play nature as a trump card in this way, it quickly becomes a self-defeating strategy: adversaries simply refuse to recognize each other's trump and then go off to play by themselves. This can often feel quite satisfying, since it reinforces our dogma and makes it that much easier to berate our enemies and celebrate our own moral superiority. But it is surely not a very promising path for trying to understand our differences. Without such understanding, the prospect for solving environmental problems, to say nothing of working toward a juster world for all the peoples and creatures of the earth, would seem very grim indeed.

And where is nature in all this? Does the world consist of nothing more than people disagreeing with each other about the meanings of words and values? Surely not. As Robert Harrison eloquently argues in the final essay of this book, it is the radical *otherness* of nature with which we have constantly to contend. The fact that it lies forever beyond the borders of our linguistic universe—that it does not talk back to us in a language we can easily understand—permits us to pretend that we know what it really is and to imagine we can capture its meaning with this very problematic word "nature." And yet it is never so. Just when we think we have gotten our picture right, just when we think that Eden is once again ours, the alien other reasserts itself. The snails appear in the garden, the fires return to the chaparral, the ground quakes beneath our feet. The reality of nature is undeniable. The difficulty of capturing it with words—not even with the word "nature" itself—is in fact one of the most compelling proofs of its autonomy.

One last found object can perhaps speak for nature as a way of bringing this introduction to a close. The campus of the University of California at Irvine is built around a great circular green space called Aldrich Park. Like so many other features of Irvine, it is a carefully planned and constructed place. Its symbolic role on the campus is to offer a representation of nature—pastoral, parklike, Edenic—at the heart of the university. The planners' self-conscious goal, as the university now describes it, was for the campus landscape "to be both educational and aesthetic," so Aldrich Park has been planted as a kind of arboretum with dozens of different tree species representing natives from California as well as exotics from all over the world.[22] If you like, you can pick up a map with every single tree marked and labeled to aid your botanizing. By examining where all these trees come from, and by thinking of the vast amount of human labor that has gone into rearranging this landscape, you will begin to understand just how artificial this natural green space really is.

The paths in the park have been carefully laid out to prevent people from traveling straight across it. They do so quite cleverly, inviting the walker in by means of a well-crafted optical illusion that makes it look as if they do go straight across; only after one is already committed to one's route is one permitted to see that the lines that at first seemed straight are in fact curved and broken. This forces anyone who needs to get to the other side of campus to proceed via a series of curvilinear walkways that frustrate every attempt to get to one's destination by the most efficient route. No doubt this is intended to remind visitors that mere efficiency is not the point of life. The

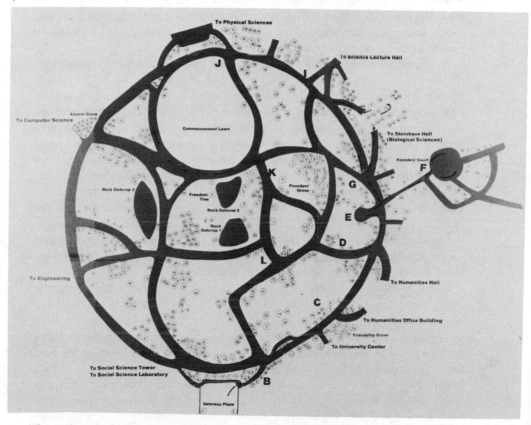

The park at the heart of the campus: an Irvine tree tour. *("UCI Tree Tour: A Natural History Walk in Aldrich Park," University of California at Irvine, 1990)*

planners who designed this landscape are encouraging us—nay, forcing us for our own good—to slow down, become more meditative, and enjoy a brief respite in nature's greenery before getting back to work. I have to confess that I found these deceptive pathways rather irritating. Perhaps this irritation betokens my inability to shed my linear consciousness and appreciate nature in a more organic way, but I could not help seeing these paths as just one more example of the planners' ubiquitous efforts to control and manipulate my experience of their world, forcing me to conform to their sense of the proper way to appreciate this natural area they had constructed on my behalf. As a result, I usually ignored the designated walkways and tramped straight across the lawn.

Ironically, this obstinacy on my part meant that I did not get to the center of the park, where those curving paths were trying to lead me, until the very end of my time in Irvine. One morning, feeling frustrated by a problem I couldn't seem to solve in my essay for this book, I headed out across the park with no particular destination in mind, wandering the paths more or less at random as I brooded about my question. Even this was probably not what the planners had intended, since I was so lost in thought that I did not much notice the landscape through which I was passing until I suddenly realized I had come to a place I had never been before.

At the center of Aldrich Park are two rock outcrops, helpfully designated on the campus map as "Rock Outcrop 1" and "Rock Outcrop 2." Strikingly set off from the rest of the lawn by their stony appearance and the exotic pines that are planted around them, they form a kind of sacred grove where the designers clearly intended us to linger. Some of the rocks have been arranged to form a circular sitting area, and a wind chime hangs from one of the trees. Make no mistake about it: like everything else in Irvine, this is a carefully designed simulacrum of the nature we are meant to appreciate here. As the university's brochure explains, "Although the rock outcrops are natural features of the area, they were not always as prominent a part of the landscape. Initially they were partially buried, lichen-covered outcroppings. Additional area was exposed using fire hoses and high pressure jets of water to allow a larger area for planting succulents."[23] African irises and various aloes have been the beneficiaries of this artifice.

But as I stopped before the outcrops and realized that I had somehow never seen them before, it didn't matter to me that the succulents had been imported from afar and that, for all I knew, the rocks had been moved here by a bulldozer. The stone itself was strikingly beautiful, and it gave me the seat I needed to meditate on. So I sat down on Rock Outcrop 1 and stayed there for half an hour. The air was cool and the sky hazy, and as a bird called quietly from one of the pines, I found my mind moving back and forth between the thoughts in my own head and the landscape around me. Because the problem I was trying to solve had something to do with wildness, I ran my hand over the outcrop and meditated, as the planners no doubt intended I should do, about the meaning of the stone and my relationship to it. No epiphany occurred, and I certainly did not experience any mystical flash of enlightenment. Still, it was a beautiful moment in a lovely place, and I left with a much clearer sense of where I was going and what I wanted to say.

Rock Outcrop 1 could hardly be more cultural a construction. Exposed to view by powerful jets of water, planted with exotic species, cast in the form of a shrine, surrounded by a pastoral park, and embedded in a community whose every feature has been planned down to the smallest detail—what could be less natural? Furthermore, the meditative moment I experienced in the quiet of that glade was itself a culturally constructed act I had learned from a long line of romantic and pastoral poets: Henry David Thoreau and William Wordsworth had helped teach me what I was supposed to do and feel on that rock. After everything I have said here, I will not be so foolish as to assert that my feelings there were either natural or universal. My thoughts that morning were surely different from those of many other people I can imagine visiting the place. I'm sure, for instance, that the landscape architects who made it the centerpiece of their creation experience it very differently from me, no doubt feeling a professional pride of authorship when they sit amid these trees and having a much more comprehensive sense of how the outcrop fits into their overall design for the campus: like so many other planners, they command the bird's-eye view. I suspect that the construction workers who labored to make this land seem natural feel a different kind of authorship in relation to it, especially since many of them probably do not regard this as the sort of place to which they themselves would make regular pilgrimages. The Mexican American gardeners who tend the aloes on these rocks surely have a far more physical relationship to this soil than I do, and probably have rather ambivalent feelings about privileged walkers like myself who can choose at any time we wish to enjoy a few moments of idle leisure amid their handiwork. Even the university people who regularly come here no doubt have very different ways of seeing it: I'm sure that members of the geology department, for instance, experience it in ways quite unlike the ways in which members of the English department experience it. It is easy enough to see that for students this secluded spot tends to serve as an evening rendezvous for lovers, whose admiration for the nature they find here is no doubt earthier than my own. What each of us finds here, in other words, is not One Universal Nature but the many different natures that our cultures and histories have taught us to look for and find.

And yet the rock remains, as do the trees and the birds, the wind and the sky. They are first and foremost themselves, despite the many meanings we discover in them. We may move them around and impose our designs upon them. We may do our best to make them bend to our wills. But in the end they remain inscrutable, artifacts of a world we did not make whose meaning for themselves we can never finally know. Acknowledging their autonomy and otherness does not spare us the task of trying to make human sense of what they seem to tell us. It does not prevent us from making false assumptions about them, nor does it make any clearer what obligations we owe them. We will argue about such things forever, and the arguments will not vanish just because we appeal to nature to defend our case. But if we listen closely, we human beings can learn a great deal from the tales we tell of such a place. This silent rock, this nature about which we argue so much, is also among the most important things we have in common. That is why we care so much about it. It is, paradoxically, the uncommon ground we cannot help but share.

UNNATURAL NATURE

Our favorite found object, the one to which our conversations kept returning and from which we learned the most, was the Rocky Mountain Arsenal in Denver, Colorado. Constructed during World War II for the manufacture of chemical weapons, it served that purpose for nearly forty years before being abandoned. It soon emerged as one of the most toxic waste sites in the nation—and one of the richest wildlife refuges in the West. It has been called "The Nation's Most Ironic Nature Park," and its paradoxical juxtapositions of toxicity and wilderness raise all sorts of interesting questions about what people mean when they use words like "natural" and "unnatural" to apply to such a place. The texts that follow consist of excerpts from the 1991 scenic wall calendar that the arsenal distributed to members of the public, as well as clippings from the *Denver Post*.

THE NATION'S MOST IRONIC NATURE PARK...

Flourishing wildlife,
toxic waste and an epic history
make Denver's Rocky Mountain
Arsenal the nation's most
ironic nature park. Legislation
now pending before Congress
could make it official. RMA's
17,000 acres — containing the
former Army chemical weapons
facility and Shell pesticides plant —
are proposed as the nation's first
wildlife refuge on a Superfund
site. The prospect of millions
of visitors at RMA calls for new
thinking about "environmental
education." RMA could help
us learn about our history,
the survival of nature in an
urban/industrial environment,
the realities of hazardous waste
and our hopes for the future.

"The Nation's Most Ironic Nature Park." (*Courtesy Urban Design Forum, Denver, Colorado*)

The Rocky Mountain Arsenal was the last chemical weapon manufacturing facility built by the United States during the World War II era. Thousands of Army and civilian workers labored long hours in the Arsenal's plants. Production of chemical weapons by the United States deterred the enemy from initiating chemical warfare in World War II and the Korean conflict. Fortunately, the chemical weapons manufactured at the Arsenal were never used and subsequently the site served as a primary location for destruction of such weapons.

Following the war, private industry was encouraged to use military facilities to foster economic growth. Several companies used the Arsenal site to produce pesticides and synthetic resins. Currently, the sole operational mission at the Arsenal is clean-up of environmental contamination resulting from past operations. No weapons are produced or stored at the site, and the only chemicals present are used in or produced by the clean-up effort.

The Arsenal's site on the Colorado prairie has endured many changes. Dinosaurs once wandered here. Buffalo herds, native American settlements, domestic livestock and the farmer's plow all made their marks on the land. Then came weapons and chemical plants. Despite its wartime legacy, the Arsenal's future holds the promise for new uses that will benefit people and the environment. Through all of time's tests, life has persisted here. This calendar offers a view of the wildlife that endures and thrives at the Arsenal in the shadow of urban and agricultural development.

Texts from a scenic calendar: Introduction. (Rocky Mountain Arsenal 1991 Calendar: Denver's Urban Wildlife Refuge

APRIL

A HISTORY

Long ago the area that is now the Rocky Mountain Arsenal was part of a vast inland sea. After millions of years a rolling prairie, dominated by native grasses and bison, succeeded the ancient sea. Nomadic groups of Arapaho and Cheyenne Indians were among the early peoples known to live in the area.

7

In the mid-nineteenth century southwestern Adams County, where the Arsenal is located, was part of Kansas Territory and reserved for the Indians. When early pioneers realized the value of this land, they quickly staked their claims as they arrived by oxcart and covered wagon. Alfalfa, wheat and other crops replaced wild buffalo grass and blue grama. Where skin tepees had stood a commercial community sprang up with towns like Derby, Commerce Town and Adams City forming the hub for various industries.

14
● New Moon

With the outbreak of World War II, the United States Armed Forces were faced with the need to manufacture chemical and incendiary weapons. Construction of a weapons plant on the site of the Rocky Mountain Arsenal began on Saturday June 13, 1942 and by December of that year it was in operation. Mustard, lewisite and chlorine gases were made in quantity. The Arsenal munitions plant went on standby in May 1947 and was started up again in 1950 when the United States entered the Korean conflict. The production of GB nerve agent began in 1956.

21

After the war, an Arsenal facility was leased by private industry for the production of insecticides and synthetic resins.

28
Full Moon

Chemical weapons production stopped in the late 1960's and in 1982 Shell closed its factory at the Arsenal. Today, the principal mission at the Arsenal is contamination clean-up.

S   M   T   M

TOUR INFORMATION: 303-289-0232

Texts from a scenic calendar: April, A History. (Rocky Mountain Arsenal 1991 Calendar: Denver's Urban Wildlife Refuge)

JUNE

SUNDAY

EDUCATION

"Look! A deer! . . . Two Deer!" "Where?" "Over there!" "At three o'clock are three mule deer bucks. Two are lying down and if you look closely you can see their antlers sticking up above the grass. Good eyes!" The double decker bus shifts to the right as everyone jumps up to see the animals. The enthusiasm and excitement on the bus grow and all eyes search for more wildlife.

This is a classic beginning to a tour at the Rocky Mountain Arsenal. The Arsenal provides an urban community with the unique opportunity to view a diversity of prairie wildlife and learn more about the Arsenal's unique past.

The combination of abandoned weapon plants, thriving wildlife and an active environmental clean-up effort exemplifies how our society's values and needs have changed over time. The Arsenal is an incredible learning laboratory. Visitors can learn about ecological principles, wildlife conservation and management, the history of chemical weapon and pesticide production and the resulting contamination.

The U. S. Fish and Wildlife Service, the U. S. Army and Shell Oil Company are working together to develop educational programs for all age groups and many diverse interests regarding the Arsenal. Bus tours and outreach programs are available through the U. S. Fish and Wildlife Service and the U. S. Army. Teacher curriculums are being created for use in the schools. Through an active public involvement program the future of the Arsenal is in good hands and entrusted to informed minds.

THINGS TO SEE IN JUNE:

Mule and white-tailed deer fawns, northern orioles, goslings, prairie dogs, white pelicans, burrowing owls, cottontails and jackrabbits, lark buntings, coyotes.

PLANTS - groundsel, sand verbena, fleabane, prickly poppy, tumble mustard.

TOUR INFORMATION: 303-289-0232

2

9

16
Father's Day

23

30

Texts from a scenic calendar: June, Education. (Rocky Mountain Arsenal 1991 Calendar: Denver's Urban Wildlife Refuge)

AUGUST

RECREATION

"How's fishing?" The small boy grinned and answered, "It's fun! I especially like it when we throw the fish back." "Really, why?" asked the biologist. "Cause I like to see it swim off to its friends."

The lakes of the Rocky Mountain Arsenal offer anglers one of the premier warm water fishing opportunities in the Colorado Front Range. Northern pike weigh up to 20 pounds, large mouth bass up to 10 pounds. Channel catfish and bluegills put up a good fight for the Arsenal's catch and release angler. Fishing Lake Ladora and Lake Mary is not for everyone, particularly those who like to take their fish home to eat. Although the water is not contaminated the lake bottom sediments have traces of chemicals, because these lakes were used for industrial cooling in the chemical manufacturing process. Therefore, fishing is a catch and release program and the fish grow very large.

The primary recreation at the Arsenal is watching wildlife. Guided wildlife bus tours and visits to the Eagle Watch (a viewing blind overlooking a bald eagle winter roost) are popular. Recreational users and potential users must remember that the primary mission of the site is contamination clean-up. Access is carefully controlled to ensure the safety of visitors.

THINGS TO SEE IN AUGUST:

White-tailed and mule deer fawns, prairie dogs, cottontails and jackrabbits, burrowing owl families, herons, Swainson's hawks, kingbirds, coyotes, migrating turkey vultures, osprey.

PLANTS - bush morning glory, sunflower, cow-pen daisy, broom butterweed, wild buckwheat.

TOUR INFORMATION: 303-289-0232

4

11

18

25
Full Moon

S	M	T
	1	2
7	8	9
14	15	16
21	22	23
28	29	30

Texts from a scenic calendar: August, Recreation. (Rocky Mountain Arsenal 1991 Calendar. Denver's Urban Wildlife Refuge)

DECEMBER

LESSONS LEARNED

1

Whenever United States Armed Forces have been called to duty - during World War II, the Korean conflict, and the Vietnam War - the Rocky Mountain Arsenal has also served by producing special munitions as a deterrent to opposing forces. In these times of crisis millions of bombs, shells, and rockets were quickly assembled by Army and civilian workers.

8

In times of war, the urgency of the situation often overshadowed concerns for the environment. The Army and private companies used state-of-the-art disposal practices, but little was known of the effects on the environment. We learned the hard way that the environment is fragile. The once standard and acceptable disposal practices are now known to have caused serious ecological consequences in many instances.

15

The primary mission of the United States Army at the Rocky Mountain Arsenal is clean-up of contamination, resulting from four decades of industrial and military operations. An important part of this project, however, is the study of technical causes and effects of environmental damage so that in the future, even in times of national crisis, service to our country is also service to our natural world.

22

THINGS TO SEE IN DECEMBER:

Bald eagles, mule deer and white-tailed deer, prairie dogs, cottontails and jackrabbits, coyotes, ferruginous hawks, rough-legged hawks, golden eagles.

29

Eagle Watch

TOUR INFORMATION: 303-289-0232

NOV

S	M	T
3	4	5
10	11	12
17	18	19
24	25	26

Texts from a scenic calendar: December, Lessons Learned. (Rocky Mountain Arsenal 1991 Calendar: Denver's Urban Wildlife Refuge)

Arsenal billions away from being picnic site

By Mark Obmascik
Denver Post Environment Writer

No expert would dispute this depressing fact about the Rocky Mountain Arsenal: If all of the facility's polluted soil were dumped into a ditch 3 feet wide and 3 feet deep, it would stretch from Denver to China.

The billion dollar arguments begin when someone suggests that someone else actually should clean all that earth.

The U.S. Army and Shell Oil Co., which poisoned the arsenal with thousands of tons of toxic wastes from chemical weapon and pesticide production, are willing to clean up the land to a certain point. But state officials want the property to be a suitable site for Sunday picnics.

For about the same price, the government could build Denver's $1.8 billion replacement for Stapleton Airport.

With such giant stakes, it's no surprise that five years of wrangling by dozens of lawyers has failed to answer one short question: How clean should the Rocky Mountain Arsenal be?

"I'd like to get this case to come to a head before I die or commit some bad behavior for which I would be impeached," lamented U.S. District Court Judge Jim Carrigan, who has been trying to persuade the three parties to strike some kind of compromise.

At the center of the dispute is the future of 27 square miles owned by federal taxpayers in the middle of the metropolitan area. Army and Shell officials say it's just unrealistic to ever make the arsenal safe for drinking water wells, home building, vegetable gardens or lakes with edible fish.

Gov. Roy Romer has said he wants to make the arsenal a "Central Park of the West." And the Adams County Commission in 1975 approved a resolution asking federal officials to convert the arsenal, described by the Army as the most polluted place in America, into a national park.

The problem is, the state must rely on the Army and Shell to pay for virtually everything it wants.

The massive legal struggle, one of the biggest and most complex in the history of American jurisprudence, began on Oct. 5, 1983, when Shell filed a lawsuit demanding that 250 of its insurance companies pay its share of the arsenal cleanup.

Two months later, on Dec. 9, 1983, the U.S. Army sued Shell for $1.8 billion as compensation for the environmental devastation the oil giant left behind at the arsenal. The state sued the Army and Shell later that same day in a multi-million dollar environmental damage claim.

Three years later, on Nov. 14, 1986, the state sued the Army, demanding that the federal government obey state laws during the draining of Basin F, a 93 acre dumping pond that once contained 240 million gallons of toxic wastes.

Shell alone has spent more than $40 million to defend itself against the Army lawsuit. Neither Shell nor the insurance companies will say how many tens of millions of dollars they have spent on the more than 50 full-time lawyers litigating that case, which is expected to end in closing arguments next week.

But the state litigation against the Army and Shell could drone on for years, despite an agreement last year that divided cleanup costs between the two polluters. That proposal calls for Shell to spend $320 million of the first $700 million, and 20 percent of the balance. Taxpayers would pay the remainder. Assuming a bill of $2 billion, the taxpayers would pay more than two-thirds of the total.

The Army and Shell say costs can be held down only by establishing early cleanup exemptions that will forever leave some pollution at the arsenal. State officials say that's tantamount to creating a permanent toxic waste dump just northeast of Denver.

"This is really our one shot to clean up a big site in metropolitan Denver," said Michael Hope of the state Attorney General's office. "What if the state wants to use the arsenal for something else 50 years from now? What the Army and Shell are talking about doing now is only a partial cleanup."

To convert the arsenal into a park, it would have to be clean enough for "kids to eat dirt," Hope said.

The state wields considerable leverage for now over the arsenal cleanup. The Army wants to tout the Rocky Mountain Arsenal as a leading example of how it intends to accomplish complicated cleanups of many other military installations across America. And Shell wants a quick settlement to reduce bad publicity.

No matter how the legal dispute is resolved, the federal government will end up owning the land and be responsible for decisions on future land use. In practical terms, the arsenal will remain off-limits to the public until it is clean enough for someone to issue liability insurance.

This often has been a daunting requirement at relatively clean recreational facilities such as Standley Lake. No one has set a price tag on the insurance it would take to open a former nerve gas and pesticide production facility to the public.

Mark Obmascik, "Arsenal Billions Away from Being Picnic Site." (Courtesy Denver Post, February 14, 1987)

20 bald eagles dare to roost at Arsenal

By Lou Chapman
Denver Post Environmental Writer

The Rocky Mountain Arsenal contains what's called the "most polluted square mile in America," but now it's also a home to America's endangered national symbol, the bald eagle.

Twenty eagles have taken up residence at the Arsenal, once used to make chemical weapons and pesticides and now a federal Superfund cleanup site.

The eagles, an endangered species in Colorado, began building a communal roost in a grove of trees along First Creek in the Arsenal's southeastern corner last November, Army officials said Friday.

Researchers don't know whether the eagles will stay at the Arsenal permanently or will move to higher elevations as the weather warms.

If the birds are just wintering at the Arsenal, they probably will return for subsequent winters, experts said.

Whatever the birds' travel plans are, the decision is completely theirs. As members of an endangered species, the eagles are protected from any activities that would disturb them or disrupt their roost.

The eagles' protected status could have an impact on how the Army goes about cleaning up the contaminated soil and groundwater at the Arsenal. The presence of the roost may even be a good enough reason for the Federal Aviation Administration to reconsider the environmental impact of expanding Stapleton International Airport, which lies immediately to the south.

Certainly, the eagles will be considered in any plans for a new airport east of the Arsenal, officials said.

"But right now I can't see there's any conflict with air navigation," said Walt Barbo, manager of the regional office of the FAA.

Right now officials don't know enough about the eagles and the new home to predict if it will affect either ongoing Stapleton expansion or construction of the new airport.

The four adult and 16 immature eagles are being watched carefully by the consulting firm that is helping the Army investigate the extent of contamination at the Arsenal.

The U.S. Fish and Wildlife Service also is very interested in the birds, in part because the agency's regional office is studying the effect of contamination on eagles in Colorado and Utah.

"All of a sudden, we have a large concentration of bald eagles at the Arsenal that we can study," said Jeff Opdycke of the agency's field office in Grand Junction.

Opdycke and his staff also noticed an unusually large population of ferruginous hawks at the Arsenal recently. That species is being considered for inclusion on the endangered species list.

"I guess we didn't fully appreciate the value of the Arsenal as a wildlife habitat until this year."

Some might say that is putting it mildly.

Beginning in 1942, the Arsenal produced tons upon tons of military supplies that included nerve gas, mustard gas, hydrazine rocket fuel and white phosphorous grenades. Shell Oil Co. and smaller companies made pesticides and herbicides at the Arsenal until 1982.

Seepage from the Arsenal has polluted nearby groundwater sources, and one 93-acre pond of liquid hazardous waste and its surrounding land have been dubbed "the most polluted square mile in the United States" by the U.S. Environmental Protection Agency.

Lou Chapman, "20 Bald Eagles Dare to Roost at Arsenal." *(Courtesy* Denver Post*)*

PARADISE
LOST
AND
FOUND

The Trouble with Wilderness;

or,

Getting Back to the Wrong Nature

William Cronon

THE TIME HAS COME TO RETHINK WILDERNESS.

This will seem a heretical claim to many environmentalists, since the idea of wilderness has for decades been a fundamental tenet—indeed, a passion—of the environmental movement, especially in the United States. For many Americans wilderness stands as the last remaining place where civilization, that all too human disease, has not fully infected the earth. It is an island in the polluted sea of urban-industrial modernity, the one place we can turn for escape from our own too-muchness. Seen in this way, wilderness presents itself as the best antidote to our human selves, a refuge we must somehow recover if we hope to save the planet. As Henry David Thoreau once famously declared, "In Wildness is the preservation of the World."[1]

But is it? The more one knows of its peculiar history, the more one realizes that wilderness is not quite what it seems. Far from being the one place on earth that stands apart from humanity, it is quite profoundly a human creation—indeed, the creation of very particular human cultures at very particular moments in human history. It is not a pristine sanctuary where the last remnant of an untouched, endangered, but still transcendent nature can for at least a little while longer be encountered without the contaminating taint of civilization. Instead, it is a product of that civilization, and could hardly be contaminated by the very stuff of which it is made. Wilderness hides its unnaturalness behind a mask that is all the more beguiling because it seems so natural. As we gaze into the mirror it holds up for us, we too easily imagine that what we behold is Nature when in fact we see the reflection of our own unexamined longings and desires. For this reason, we mistake ourselves when we suppose that wilderness can be the solution to our culture's problematic relationships with the nonhuman world, for wilderness is itself no small part of the problem.

To assert the unnaturalness of so natural a place will no doubt seem absurd or even perverse to many readers, so let me hasten to add that the nonhuman world we encounter in wilderness is far from being merely our own invention. I celebrate with others who love wilderness the beauty and power of the things it contains. Each of us who has spent time there can conjure images and sensations that all the more hauntingly real for having engraved themselves so indelibly on our memories. Such memories may be uniquely our own, but they are also familiar enough to be instantly recognizable to others. Remember this? The torrents of mist shoot out from the base of a great waterfall in the depths of a Sierra canyon, the tiny droplets cooling your face as you listen to the roar of the water and gaze up toward the sky through a rainbow that hovers just out of reach. Remember this too: looking out across a desert canyon in the evening air, the only sound a lone raven calling in the distance, the rock walls dropping away into a chasm so deep that its bottom all but vanishes as you squint into the amber light of the setting sun. And this: the moment beside the trail as you sit on a sandstone ledge, your boots damp with the morning dew while you take in the rich smell of the pines, and the small red fox—or maybe for you it was a raccoon or a coyote or a deer—that suddenly ambles across your path, stopping for a long moment to gaze in your direction with cautious indifference before continuing on its way. Remember the feelings of such moments, and you will know as well as I do that you were in the presence of something irreducibly nonhuman, something profoundly Other than yourself. Wilderness is made of that too.

And yet: what brought each of us to the places where such memories became possible is entirely a cultural invention. Go back 250 years in American and European history, and you do not find nearly so many people wandering around remote corners of the planet looking for what today we would call "the wilderness experience." As late as the eighteenth century, the most common usage of the word "wilderness" in the English language referred to landscapes that generally carried adjectives far different from the ones they attract today. To be a wilderness then was to be "deserted," "savage," "desolate," "barren"—in short, a "waste," the word's nearest synonym. Its connotations were anything but positive, and the emotion one was most likely to feel in its presence was "bewilderment"—or terror.[2]

Many of the word's strongest associations then were biblical, for it is used over and over again in the King James Version to refer to places on the margins of civilization where it is all too easy to lose oneself in moral confusion and despair. The wilderness was where Moses had wandered with his people for forty years, and where they had nearly abandoned their God to worship a golden idol.[3] "For Pharoah will say of the Children of Israel," we read in Exodus, "They are entangled in the land, the wilderness hath shut them in."[4] The wilderness was where Christ had struggled with the devil and endured his temptations: "And immediately the Spirit driveth him into the wilderness. And he was there in the wilderness for forty days tempted of Satan; and was with the wild beasts; and the angels ministered unto him."[5] The "delicious Paradise" of John Milton's Eden was surrounded by "a steep wilderness, whose hairy sides / Access denied" to all who sought entry.[6] When Adam and Eve were driven from that garden, the world they entered was a wilderness that only their labor and pain could redeem. Wilderness, in short, was a place to which one came only against one's will, and always in fear and trembling. Whatever value it might have arose solely from the possibility that it might be "reclaimed" and turned toward human ends—planted as a garden, say, or a city upon a hill.[7] In its raw state, it had little or nothing to offer civilized men and women.

But by the end of the nineteenth century, all this had changed. The wastelands that had once seemed worthless had for some people come to seem almost beyond price. That Thoreau in 1862 could declare wildness to be the preservation of the world suggests the sea change that was going on. Wilderness had once been the antithesis of all that was orderly and good—it had

Thomas Cole, *Expulsion from the Garden of Eden,* 1827–28. *(Gift of Mrs. Maxim Karolik for the M. and M. Karolik Collection of American Paintings, 1815–1865, courtesy Museum of Fine Arts, Boston)*

been the darkness, one might say, on the far side of the garden wall—and yet now it was frequently likened to Eden itself. When John Muir arrived in the Sierra Nevada in 1869, he would declare, "No description of Heaven that I have ever heard or read of seems half so fine."[8] He was hardly alone in expressing such emotions. One by one, various corners of the American map came to be designated as sites whose wild beauty was so spectacular that a growing number of citizens had to visit and see them for themselves. Niagara Falls was the first to undergo this transformation, but it was soon followed by the Catskills, the Adirondacks, Yosemite, Yellowstone, and others. Yosemite was deeded by the U.S. government to the state of California in 1864 as the nation's first wildland park, and Yellowstone became the first true national park in 1872.[9]

By the first decade of the twentieth century, in the single most famous episode in American conservation history, a national debate had exploded over whether the city of San Francisco should be permitted to augment its water supply by damming the Tuolumne River in Hetch Hetchy valley, well within the boundaries of Yosemite National Park. The dam was eventually built, but what today seems no less significant is that so many people fought to prevent its completion. Even as the fight was being lost, Hetch Hetchy became the battle cry of an emerging movement to preserve wilderness. Fifty years earlier, such opposition would have been unthinkable. Few would have questioned the merits of "reclaiming" a wasteland like this in order to put it to human use. Now the defenders of Hetch Hetchy attracted widespread national attention by portraying such an act not as improvement or progress but as desecration and vandalism. Lest one doubt that the old biblical metaphors had been turned completely on their heads, listen to John Muir attack the dam's defenders. "Their arguments," he wrote, "are curiously like those of the devil, devised for the destruction of the first garden—so much of the very best Eden fruit going to waste; so much of the best Tuolumne water and Tuolumne scenery going to waste."[10] For Muir and the growing number of Americans who shared his views, Satan's home had become God's own temple.

The sources of this rather astonishing transformation were many, but for the purposes of this essay they can be gathered under two broad headings: the sublime and the frontier. Of the two, the sublime is the older and more pervasive cultural construct, being one of the most important expressions of that broad transatlantic movement we today label as romanticism; the frontier is more peculiarly American, though it too had its European antecedents and parallels. The two converged to remake wilderness in their own image, freighting it with moral values and cultural symbols that it carries to this day. Indeed, it is not too much to say that the modern environmental movement is itself a grandchild of romanticism and post-frontier ideology, which is why it is no accident that so much environmentalist discourse takes its bearings from the wilderness these intellectual movements helped create.

Although wilderness may today seem to be just one environmental concern among many, it in fact serves as the foundation for a long list of other such concerns that on their face seem quite remote from it. That is why its influence is so pervasive and, potentially, so insidious.

To gain such remarkable influence, the concept of wilderness had to become loaded with some of the deepest core values of the culture that created and idealized it: it had to become sacred. This possibility had been present in wilderness even in the days when it had been a place of spiritual danger and moral temptation. If Satan was there, then so was Christ, who had found angels as well as wild beasts during His sojourn in the desert. In the wilderness the boundaries between human and nonhuman, between natural and supernatural, had always seemed less certain than elsewhere. This was why the early Christian saints and mystics had often emulated Christ's desert retreat as they sought to experience for themselves the visions and spiritual testing He had endured. One might meet devils and run the risk of losing one's soul in such a place, but one might also meet God. For some that possibility was worth almost any price.

By the eighteenth century this sense of the wilderness as a landscape where the supernatural lay just beneath the surface was expressed in the doctrine of the *sublime,* a word whose modern usage has been so watered down by commercial hype and tourist advertising that it retains only a dim echo of its former power.[11] In the theories of Edmund Burke, Immanuel Kant, William Gilpin, and others, sublime landscapes were those rare places on earth where one had more chance than elsewhere to glimpse the face of God.[12] Romantics had a clear notion of where one could be most sure of having this experience. Although God might, of course, choose to show Himself anywhere, He would most often be found in those vast, powerful landscapes where one could not help feeling insignificant and being reminded of one's own mortality. Where were these sublime places? The eighteenth-century catalog of their locations feels very familiar, for we still see and value landscapes as it taught us to do. God was on the mountaintop, in the chasm, in the waterfall, in the thundercloud, in the rainbow, in the sunset. One has only to think of the sites that Americans chose for their first national parks—Yellowstone, Yosemite, Grand Canyon, Rainier, Zion—to realize that virtually all of them fit one or more of these categories. Less sublime landscapes simply did not appear worthy of such protection; not until the 1940s, for instance, would the first swamp be honored, in Everglades National Park, and to this day there is no national park in the grasslands.[13]

Among the best proofs that one had entered a sublime landscape was the emotion it evoked. For the early romantic writers and artists who first began to celebrate it, the sublime was far from being a pleasurable experience. The classic description is that of William Wordsworth as he recounted climbing the Alps and crossing the Simplon Pass in his autobiographical poem *The*

Prelude. There, surrounded by crags and waterfalls, the poet felt himself literally to be in the presence of the divine—and experienced an emotion remarkably close to terror:

> The immeasurable height
> Of woods decaying, never to be decayed,
> The stationary blasts of waterfalls,
> And in the narrow rent at every turn
> Winds thwarting winds, bewildered and forlorn,
> The torrents shooting from the clear blue sky,
> The rocks that muttered close upon our ears,
> Black drizzling crags that spake by the way-side
> As if a voice were in them, the sick sight
> And giddy prospect of the raving stream,
> The unfettered clouds and region of the Heavens,
> Tumult and peace, the darkness and the light—
> Were all like workings of one mind, the features
> Of the same face, blossoms upon one tree;
> Characters of the great Apocalypse,
> The types and symbols of Eternity,
> Of first, and last, and midst, and without end.[14]

This was no casual stroll in the mountains, no simple sojourn in the gentle lap of nonhuman nature. What Wordsworth described was nothing less than a religious experience, akin to that of the Old Testament prophets as they conversed with their wrathful God. The symbols he detected in this wilderness landscape were more supernatural than natural, and they inspired more awe and dismay than joy or pleasure. No mere mortal was meant to linger long in such a place, so it was with considerable relief that Wordsworth and his companion made their way back down from the peaks to the sheltering valleys.

Lest you suspect that this view of the sublime was limited to timid Europeans who lacked the American know-how for feeling at home in the wilderness, remember Henry David Thoreau's 1846 climb of Mount Katahdin, in Maine. Although Thoreau is regarded by many today as one of the great American celebrators of wilderness, his emotions about Katahdin were no less ambivalent than Wordsworth's about the Alps.

> It was vast, Titanic, and such as man never inhabits. Some part of the beholder, even some vital part, seems to escape through the loose grating of his ribs as he ascends. He is more lone than you can imagine. . . . Vast, Titanic, inhuman Nature has got him at disadvantage, caught him alone, and pilfers him of some of his divine faculty. She does not smile on him as in the plains. She seems to say sternly, why came ye here before your time? This ground is not prepared for you. Is it not enough that I smile in the valleys? I have never made this soil for thy feet, this air for thy breathing, these rocks for thy neighbors. I cannot pity nor fondle thee here, but forever relentlessly

drive thee hence to where I *am* kind. Why seek me where I have not called thee, and then complain because you find me but a stepmother?[15]

This is surely not the way a modern backpacker or nature lover would describe Maine's most famous mountain, but that is because Thoreau's description owes as much to Wordsworth and other romantic contemporaries as to the rocks and clouds of Katahdin itself. His words took the physical mountain on which he stood and transmuted it into an icon of the sublime: a symbol of God's presence on earth. The power and the glory of that icon were such that only a prophet might gaze on it for long. In effect, romantics like Thoreau joined Moses and the children of Israel in Exodus when "they looked toward the wilderness, and behold, the glory of the Lord appeared in the cloud."[16]

But even as it came to embody the awesome power of the sublime, wilderness was also being tamed—not just by those who were building settlements in its midst but also by those who most celebrated its inhuman beauty. By the second half of the nineteenth century, the terrible awe that Wordsworth and Thoreau regarded as the appropriately pious stance to adopt in the presence of their mountaintop God was giving way to a much more comfortable, almost sentimental demeanor. As more and more tourists sought out the wilderness as a spectacle to be looked at and enjoyed for its great beauty, the sublime in effect became domesticated. The wilderness was still sacred, but the religious sentiments it evoked were more those of a pleasant parish church than those of a grand cathedral or a harsh desert retreat. The writer who best captures this late romantic sense of a domesticated sublime is undoubtedly John Muir, whose descriptions of Yosemite and the Sierra Nevada reflect none of the anxiety or terror one finds in earlier writers. Here he is, for instance, sketching on North Dome in Yosemite Valley:

> No pain here, no dull empty hours, no fear of the past, no fear of the future. These blessed mountains are so compactly filled with God's beauty, no petty personal hope or experience has room to be. Drinking this champagne water is pure pleasure, so is breathing the living air, and every movement of limbs is pleasure, while the body seems to feel beauty when exposed to it as it feels the campfire or sunshine, entering not by the eyes alone, but equally through all one's flesh like radiant heat, making a passionate ecstatic pleasure glow not explainable.

The emotions Muir describes in Yosemite could hardly be more different from Thoreau's on Katahdin or Wordsworth's on the Simplon Pass. Yet all three men are participating in the same cultural tradition and contributing to the same myth: the mountain as cathedral. The three may differ in the way they choose to express their piety—Wordsworth favoring an awe-filled bewilderment, Thoreau a stern loneliness, Muir a welcome ecstasy—but they agree completely about the church in which they prefer to worship.

Muir's closing words on North Dome diverge from his older contemporaries only in mood, not in their ultimate content:

> Perched like a fly on this Yosemite dome, I gaze and sketch and bask, oftentimes settling down into dumb admiration without definite hope of ever learning much, yet with the longing, unresting effort that lies at the door of hope, humbly prostrate before the vast display of God's power, and eager to offer self-denial and renunciation with eternal toil to learn any lesson in the divine manuscript.[17]

Muir's "divine manuscript" and Wordsworth's "Characters of the great Apocalypse" were in fact pages from the same holy book. The sublime wilderness had ceased to be a place of satanic temptation and become instead a sacred temple, much as it continues to be for those who love it today.

But the romantic sublime was not the only cultural movement that helped transform wilderness into a sacred American icon during the nineteenth century. No less important was the powerful romantic attraction of primitivism, dating back at least to Rousseau—the belief that the best antidote to the ills of an overly refined and civilized modern world was a return to simpler, more primitive living. In the United States, this was embodied most strikingly in the national myth of the frontier. The historian Frederick Jackson Turner wrote in 1893 the classic academic statement of this myth, but it had been part of American cultural traditions for well over a century. As Turner described the process, easterners and European immigrants, in moving to the wild unsettled lands of the frontier, shed the trappings of civilization, rediscovered their primitive racial energies, reinvented direct democratic institutions, and thereby reinfused themselves with a vigor, an independence, and a creativity that were the source of American democracy and national character. Seen in this way, wild country became a place not just of religious redemption but of national renewal, the quintessential location for experiencing what it meant to be an American.

One of Turner's most provocative claims was that by the 1890s the frontier was passing away. Never again would "such gifts of free land offer themselves" to the American people. "The frontier has gone," he declared, "and with its going has closed the first period of American history."[18] Built into the frontier myth from its very beginning was the notion that this crucible of American identity was temporary and would pass away. Those who have celebrated the frontier have almost always looked backward as they did so, mourning an older, simpler, truer world that is about to disappear forever. That world and all of its attractions, Turner said, depended on free land—on wilderness. Thus, in the myth of the vanishing frontier lay the seeds of wilderness preservation in the United States, for if wild land had been so crucial in the making of the nation, then surely one must save its last remnants as monuments to the American past—and as an insurance policy to protect its future. It is no accident that the movement to set aside national parks and wilderness areas began to gain real momentum at precisely the time that laments about the passing frontier reached their peak. To protect wilderness was in a very real sense to protect the nation's most sacred myth of origin.

Among the core elements of the frontier myth was the powerful sense among certain groups of Americans that wilderness was the last bastion of rugged individualism. Turner tended to stress communitarian themes when writing frontier history, asserting that Americans in primitive conditions had been forced to band together with their neighbors to form communities and democratic institutions. For other writers, however, frontier democracy for communities was less compelling than frontier freedom for individuals.[19] By fleeing to the outer margins of settled land and society—so the story ran—an individual could escape the confining strictures of civilized life. The mood among writers who celebrated frontier individualism was almost always nostalgic; they lamented not just a lost way of life but the passing of the heroic men who had embodied that life. Thus Owen Wister in the introduction to his classic 1902 novel *The Virginian* could write of "a vanished world" in which "the horseman, the cow-puncher, the last romantic figure upon our soil" rode only "in his historic yesterday" and would "never come again." For Wister, the cowboy was a man who gave his word and kept it ("Wall Street would have found him behind the times"), who did not talk lewdly to women ("Newport would have thought him old-fashioned"), who worked and played hard, and whose "ungoverned hours did not unman him."[20] Theodore Roosevelt wrote with much the same nostalgic fervor about the "fine, manly qualities" of the "wild rough-rider of the plains." No one could be more heroically masculine, thought Roosevelt, or more at home in the western wilderness:

> There he passes his days, there he does his life-work, there, when he meets death, he faces it as he has faced many other evils, with quiet, uncomplaining fortitude. Brave, hospitable, hardy, and adventurous, he is the grim pioneer of our race; he prepares the way for the civilization from before whose face he must himself disappear. Hard and dangerous though his existence is, it has yet a wild attraction that strongly draws to it his bold, free spirit.[21]

This nostalgia for a passing frontier way of life inevitably implied ambivalence, if not downright hostility, toward modernity and all that it represented. If one saw the wild lands of the frontier as freer, truer, and more natural than other, more modern places, then one was also inclined to see the cities and factories of urban-industrial civilization as confining, false, and artificial. Owen Wister looked at the post-frontier "transition" that had followed "the horseman of the plains," and did not like what he saw: "a shapeless state, a condition of men and manners as unlovely as is that moment in the year when winter is gone and spring not come, and the face of Nature is ugly."[22] In the eyes of writers who shared Wister's distaste for modernity, civilization contaminated its inhabitants and absorbed them into the faceless, collective, contemptible life of the crowd. For all of its troubles and dangers, and despite the fact that it must pass away, the frontier had been a better place. If civilization was to be redeemed, it would be by men like the Virginian who could retain their frontier virtues even as they made the transition to post-frontier life.

The mythic frontier individualist was almost always masculine in gender: here, in the wilderness, a man could be a real man, the rugged individual he was meant to be before civilization sapped his energy and threatened his masculinity. Wister's contemptuous remarks about Wall Street and Newport suggest what he and many others of his generation believed—that the comforts and seductions of civilized life were especially insidious for men, who all too easily became emasculated by the femininizing tendencies of civilization. More often than not, men who felt this way came, like Wister and Roosevelt, from elite class backgrounds. The curious result was that frontier nostalgia became an important vehicle for expressing a peculiarly bourgeois form of antimodernism. The very men who most benefited from urban-industrial capitalism were among those who believed they must escape its debilitating effects. If the frontier was passing, then men who had the means to do so should preserve for themselves some remnant of its wild landscape so that they might enjoy the regeneration and renewal that came from sleeping under the stars, participating in blood sports, and living off the land. The frontier might be gone, but the frontier experience could still be had if only wilderness were preserved.

Thus the decades following the Civil War saw more and more of the nation's wealthiest citizens seeking out wilderness for themselves. The elite passion for wild land took many forms: enormous estates in the Adirondacks and elsewhere (disingenuously called "camps" despite their many servants and amenities), cattle ranches for would-be rough riders on the Great Plains, guided big-game hunting trips in the Rockies, and luxurious resort hotels wherever railroads pushed their way into sublime landscapes. Wilderness suddenly emerged as the landscape of choice for elite tourists, who brought with them strikingly urban ideas of the countryside through which they traveled. For them, wild land was not a site for productive labor and not a permanent home; rather, it was a place of recreation. One went to the wilderness not as a producer but as a consumer, hiring guides and other backcountry residents who could serve as romantic surrogates for the rough riders and hunters of the frontier if one was willing to overlook their new status as employees and servants of the rich.

In just this way, wilderness came to embody the national frontier myth, standing for the wild freedom of America's past and seeming to represent a highly attractive natural alternative to the ugly artificiality of modern civilization. The irony, of course, was that in the process wilderness came to reflect the very civilization its devotees sought to escape. Ever since the nineteenth century, celebrating wilderness has been an activity mainly for well-to-do city folks. Country people generally know far too much about working the land to regard *un*worked land as their ideal. In contrast, elite urban tourists and wealthy sportsmen projected their leisure-time frontier fantasies onto the American landscape and so created wilderness in their own image.

There were other ironies as well. The movement to set aside national parks and wilderness areas followed hard on the heels of the final Indian wars, in which the prior human inhabitants of these areas were rounded up and moved onto reservations. The myth of the wilderness as "virgin," uninhabited land had always been especially cruel when seen from the perspective of the Indians who had once called that land home. Now they were forced to move elsewhere, with the result that tourists could safely enjoy the illusion that they were seeing their nation in its pristine, original state, in the new morning of God's own creation.[23] Among the things that most marked the new national parks as reflecting a post-frontier consciousness was the relative absence of human violence within their boundaries. The actual frontier had often been a place of conflict, in which invaders and invaded fought for control of land and resources. Once set aside within the fixed and carefully policed boundaries of the modern bureaucratic state, the wilderness lost its savage image and became safe: a place more of reverie than of revulsion or fear. Meanwhile, its original inhabitants were kept out by dint of force, their earlier uses of the land redefined as inappropriate or even illegal. To this day, for instance, the Blackfeet continue to be accused of "poaching" on the lands of Glacier National Park that originally belonged to them and that were ceded by treaty only with the proviso that they be permitted to hunt there.[24]

The removal of Indians to create an "uninhabited wilderness"—uninhabited as never before in the human history of the place—reminds us just how invented, just how constructed, the American wilderness really is. To return to my opening argument: there is nothing natural about the concept of wilderness. It is entirely a creation of the culture that holds it dear, a product of the very history it seeks to deny. Indeed, one of the most striking proofs of the cultural invention of wilderness is its thoroughgoing erasure of the history from which it sprang. In virtually all of its manifestations, wilderness represents a flight from history. Seen as the original garden, it is a place outside of time, from which human beings had to be ejected before the fallen world of history could properly begin. Seen as the frontier, it is a savage world at the dawn of civilization, whose transformation represents the very beginning of the national historical epic. Seen as the bold landscape of frontier heroism, it is the place of youth and childhood, into which men escape by abandoning their pasts and entering a world of freedom where the constraints of civilization fade into memory. Seen as the sacred sublime, it is the home of a God who transcends history by standing as the One who remains untouched and unchanged by time's arrow. No matter what the angle from which we regard it, wilderness offers us the illusion that we can escape the cares and troubles of the world in which our past has ensnared us.[25]

This escape from history is one reason why the language we use to talk about wilderness is often permeated with spiritual and religious values that reflect human ideals far more than the material world of physical nature. Wilderness fulfills the old romantic project of secularizing Judeo-Christian values so as to make a new cathedral not in some petty human building but in God's own creation, Nature itself. Many environmentalists who reject traditional notions of the Godhead and who regard themselves as agnostics or even atheists nonetheless express feelings tantamount to religious awe when in the presence of wilderness—a fact that testifies to the success of the romantic project. Those who have no difficulty seeing God as the expression of our human dreams and desires nonetheless have trouble recognizing that in a secular age Nature can offer precisely the same sort of mirror.

Thus it is that wilderness serves as the unexamined foundation on which so many of the quasi-religious values of modern environmentalism rest. The critique of modernity that is one of environmentalism's most important contributions to the moral and political discourse of our time more often than not appeals, explicitly or implicitly, to wilderness as the standard against which to measure the failings of our human world. Wilderness is the natural, unfallen antithesis of an unnatural civilization that has lost its soul. It is a place of freedom in which we can recover the true selves we have lost to the corrupting influences of our artificial lives. Most of all, it is the ultimate landscape of authenticity. Combining the sacred grandeur of the sublime with the primitive simplicity of the frontier, it is the place where we can see the world as it really is, and so know ourselves as we really are—or ought to be.

But the trouble with wilderness is that it quietly expresses and reproduces the very values its devotees seek to reject. The flight from history that is very nearly the core of wilderness represents the false hope of an escape from responsibility, the illusion that we can somehow wipe clean the slate of our past and return to the tabula rasa that supposedly existed before we began to leave our marks on the world. The dream of an unworked natural landscape is very much the fantasy of people who have never themselves had to work the land to make a living—urban folk for whom food comes from a supermarket or a restaurant instead of a field, and for whom the wooden houses in which they live and work apparently have no meaningful connection to the forests in which trees grow and die. Only people whose relation to the land was already alienated could hold up wilderness as a model for human life in nature, for the romantic ideology of wilderness leaves precisely nowhere for human beings actually to make their living from the land.

This, then, is the central paradox: wilderness embodies a dualistic vision in which the human is entirely outside the natural. If we allow ourselves to believe that nature, to be true, must also be wild, then our very presence in nature represents its fall. The place where we are is the place where nature is not. If this is so—if by definition wilderness leaves no place for human beings, save perhaps as contemplative sojourners enjoying their leisurely reverie in God's natural cathedral—then also by definition it can offer no solution to the environmental and other problems that confront us. To the extent that we celebrate wilderness as the measure with which we judge civilization, we reproduce the dualism that sets humanity and nature at opposite poles. We thereby leave ourselves little hope of discovering what an ethical, sustainable, *honorable* human place in nature might actually look like.

Worse: to the extent that we live in an urban-industrial civilization but at the same time pretend to ourselves that our *real* home is in the wilderness, to just that extent we give ourselves permission to evade responsibility for the lives we actually lead. We inhabit civilization while holding some part of ourselves—what we imagine to be the most precious part—aloof from its entanglements. We work our nine-to-five jobs in its institutions, we eat its food, we drive its cars (not least to reach the wilderness), we benefit from the intricate and all too invisible networks with which it shelters us, all the while pretending that these things are not an essential part of who we are. By imagining that our true home is in the wilderness, we forgive ourselves the homes we actually inhabit. In its flight from history, in its siren song of escape, in its reproduction of the dangerous dualism that sets human beings outside of nature—in all of these ways, wilderness poses a serious threat to responsible environmentalism at the end of the twentieth century.

By now I hope it is clear that my criticism in this essay is not directed at wild nature per se, or even at efforts to set aside large tracts of wild land, but rather at the specific habits of thinking that flow from this complex cultural construction called wilderness. It is not the things we label as wilderness that are the problem—for nonhuman nature and large tracts of the natural world *do* deserve protection—but rather what we ourselves mean when we use that label. Lest one doubt how pervasive these habits of thought actually are in contemporary environmentalism, let me list some of the places where wilderness serves as the ideological underpinning for environmental concerns that might otherwise seem quite remote from it. Defenders of biological diversity, for instance, although sometimes appealing to more utilitarian concerns, often point to "untouched" ecosystems as the best and richest repositories of the undiscovered species we must certainly try to protect. Although at first blush an apparently more "scientific" concept than wilderness, biological diversity in fact invokes many of the same sacred values, which is why organizations like the Nature Conservancy have been so quick to employ it as an alternative to the seemingly fuzzier and more problematic concept of wilderness. There is a paradox here, of course. To the extent that biological diversity (indeed, even wilderness itself) is likely to survive in the future only by the most vigilant and self-conscious management of the ecosystems that sustain it, the ideology of wilderness is potentially in direct conflict with the very thing it encourages us to protect.[26]

The most striking instances of this have revolved around "endangered species," which serve as vulnerable symbols of biological diversity while at the same time standing as surrogates for wilderness itself. The terms of the Endangered Species Act in the United States have often meant that those hoping to defend pristine wilderness have had to rely on a single endangered species like the spotted owl to gain legal standing for their case—thereby making the full power of sacred land inhere in a single numinous organism whose habitat then becomes the object of intense debate about appropriate management and use.[27] The ease with which anti-environmental forces like the wise-use movement have attacked such single-species preservation efforts suggests the vulnerability of strategies like these.

Perhaps partly because our own conflicts over such places and organisms have become so messy, the convergence of wilderness values with concerns about biological diversity and endangered species has helped produce a deep fascination for remote ecosystems, where it is easier to imagine that nature might somehow be "left alone" to flourish by its own pristine devices. The classic example is the tropical rain forest, which since the 1970s has become the most powerful modern icon of unfallen, sacred land—a veritable Garden of Eden—for many Americans and Europeans. And yet protecting the rain forest in the eyes of First World environmentalists all too often means protecting it from the people who live there. Those who seek to preserve such "wilderness" from the activities of native peoples run the risk of reproducing the same tragedy—being forceably removed from an ancient home—that befell American Indians. Third World countries face massive environmental problems and deep social conflicts, but these are not likely to be solved by a cultural myth that encourages us to "preserve" peopleless landscapes that have not existed in such places for millennia. At its worst, as environmentalists are beginning to realize, exporting American notions of wilderness in this way can become an unthinking and self-defeating form of cultural imperialism.[28]

Perhaps the most suggestive example of the way that wilderness thinking can underpin other environmental concerns has emerged in the recent debate about "global change." In 1989 the journalist Bill McKibben published a book entitled *The End of Nature,* in which he argued that the prospect of global climate change as a result of unintentional human manipulation of the atmosphere means that nature as we once knew it no longer exists.[29] Whereas earlier generations inhabited a natural world that remained more or less unaffected by their actions, our own generation is uniquely different. We and our children will henceforth live in a biosphere completely altered by our own activity, a planet in which the human and the natural can no longer be distinguished, because the one has overwhelmed the other. In McKibben's view, nature has died, and we are responsible for killing it. "The planet," he declares, "is utterly different now."[30]

But such a perspective is possible only if we accept the wilderness premise that nature, to be natural, must also be pristine—remote from humanity and untouched by our common past. In fact, everything we know about environmental history suggests that people have been manipulating the natural world on various scales for as long as we have a record of their passing. Moreover, we have unassailable evidence that many of the environmental changes we now face also occurred quite apart from human intervention at one time or another in the earth's past.[31] The point is not that our current problems are trivial, or that our devastating effects on the earth's ecosystems should be accepted as inevitable or "natural." It is rather that we seem unlikely to make much progress in solving these problems if we hold up to ourselves as the mirror of nature a wilderness we ourselves cannot inhabit.

To do so is merely to take to a logical extreme the paradox that was built into wilderness from the beginning: if nature dies because we enter it, then the only way to save nature is to kill ourselves. The absurdity of this proposition flows from the underlying dualism it expresses. Not only does it ascribe greater power to humanity than we in fact possess—physical and biological nature will surely survive in some form or another long after we ourselves have gone the way of all flesh—but in the end it offers us little more than a self-defeating counsel of despair. The tautology gives us no way out: if wild nature is the only thing worth saving, and if our mere presence destroys it, then the sole solution to our own unnaturalness, the only way to protect sacred wilderness from profane humanity, would seem to be suicide. It is not a proposition that seems likely to produce very positive or practical results.

And yet radical environmentalists and deep ecologists all too frequently come close to accepting this premise as a first principle. When they express, for instance, the popular notion that our environmental problems began with the invention of agriculture, they push the human fall from natural grace so far back into the past that all of civilized history becomes a tale of ecological declension. Earth First! founder Dave Foreman captures the familiar parable succinctly when he writes,

> Before agriculture was midwifed in the Middle East, humans were in the wilderness. We had no concept of "wilderness" because everything was wilderness and *we were a part of it*. But with irrigation ditches, crop surpluses, and permanent villages, we became *apart from* the natural world. . . . Between the wilderness that created us and the civilization created by us grew an ever-widening rift.[32]

In this view the farm becomes the first and most important battlefield in the long war against wild nature, and all else follows in its wake. From such a starting place, it is hard not to reach the conclusion that the only way human beings can hope to live naturally on earth is to follow the hunter-gatherers back into a wilderness Eden and abandon virtually everything that civilization has given us. It may indeed turn out that civilization will end in ecological collapse or nuclear disaster, whereupon one might expect to find any human survivors returning to a way of life closer to that celebrated by Foreman and his followers. For most of us, though, such a debacle would be cause for regret, a sign that humanity had failed to fulfill its own promise and failed to honor its own highest values—including those of the deep ecologists.

In offering wilderness as the ultimate hunter-gatherer alternative to civilization, Foreman reproduces an extreme but still easily recognizable version of the myth of frontier primitivism. When he writes of his fellow Earth Firsters that "we believe we must return to being animal, to glorying in our sweat, hormones, tears, and blood" and that "we struggle against the modern compulsion to become dull, passionless androids," he is following in the footsteps of Owen Wister.[33] Although his arguments give primacy to defending biodiversity and the autonomy of wild nature, his prose becomes most passionate when he speaks of preserving "the wilderness experience." His own ideal "Big Outside" bears an uncanny resemblance to that of the frontier myth: wide open spaces and virgin land with no trails, no signs, no facilities, no maps, no guides, no rescues, no modern equipment. Tellingly, it is a land where hardy travelers can support themselves by hunting with "primitive weapons (bow and arrow, atlatl, knife, sharp rock)."[34] Foreman claims that "the primary value of wilderness is not as a proving ground for young Huck Finns and Annie Oakleys," but his heart is with Huck and Annie all the same. He admits that "preserving a quality wilderness experience for the human visitor, letting her or him flex Paleolithic muscles or seek visions, remains a tremendously important secondary purpose."[35] Just so does Teddy Roosevelt's rough rider live on in the greener garb of a new age.

However much one may be attracted to such a vision, it entails problematic consequences. For one, it makes wilderness the locus for an epic struggle between malign civilization and benign nature, compared with which all other social, political, and moral concerns seem trivial. Foreman writes, "The preservation of wildness and native diversity is *the* most important issue. Issues directly affecting only humans pale in comparison."[36] Presumably so do any environmental problems whose victims are mainly people, for such problems usually surface in landscapes that have already "fallen" and are no longer wild. This would seem to exclude from the radical environmentalist agenda problems of occupational health and safety in industrial settings, problems of toxic waste exposure on "unnatural" urban and agricultural sites, problems of poor children poisoned by lead exposure in the inner city, problems of famine and poverty and human suffering in the "overpopulated" places of the earth—problems, in short, of environmental justice. If we set too high a stock on wilderness, too many other corners of the earth become less than natural and too many other people become less than human, thereby giving us permission not to care much about their suffering or their fate.

It is no accident that these supposedly inconsequential environmental problems affect mainly poor people, for the long affiliation between wilderness and wealth means that the only poor people who count when wilderness is *the* issue are hunter-gatherers, who presumably do not consider themselves to be poor in the first place. The dualism at the heart of wilderness encourages its advocates to conceive of its protection as a crude conflict between the "human" and the "nonhuman"—or, more often, between those who value the nonhuman and those who do not. This in turn tempts one to ignore crucial differences *among* humans and the complex cultural and historical reasons why different peoples may feel very differently about the meaning of wilderness.

Why, for instance, is the "wilderness experience" so often conceived as a form of recreation best enjoyed by those whose class privileges give them the time and resources to leave their jobs behind and "get away from it all"? Why does the protection of wilderness so often seem to pit urban recreationists against rural people who actually earn their living from the land (excepting those who sell goods and services to the tourists themselves)? Why in the debates about pristine natural areas are "primitive" peoples idealized, even sentimentalized, until the moment they do something unprimitive, modern, and unnatural, and thereby fall from environmental grace? What are the consequences of a wilderness ideology that devalues productive labor and the very concrete knowledge that comes from working the land with one's own hands?[37] All of these questions imply conflicts among different groups of people, conflicts that are obscured behind the deceptive clarity of "human" vs. "nonhuman." If in answering these knotty questions we resort to so simplistic an opposition, we are almost certain to ignore the very subtleties and complexities we need to understand.

But the most troubling cultural baggage that accompanies the celebration of wilderness has less to do with remote rain forests and peoples than with the ways we think about ourselves—we American environmentalists who quite rightly worry about the future of the earth and the threats we pose to the natural world. Idealizing a distant wilderness too often means not idealizing the environment in which we actually live, the landscape that for better or worse we call home. Most of our most serious environmental problems start right here, at home, and if we are to solve those problems, we need an environmental ethic that will tell us as much about *using* nature as about *not* using it. The wilderness dualism tends to cast any use as *ab*-use, and thereby denies us a middle ground in which responsible use and non-use might attain some kind of balanced, sustainable relationship. My own belief is that only by exploring this middle ground will we learn ways of imagining a better world for all of us: humans and nonhumans, rich people and poor, women and men, First Worlders and Third Worlders, white folks and people of color, consumers and producers—a world better for humanity in all of its diversity and for all the rest of nature too. The middle ground is where we actually live. It is where we—all of us, in our different places and ways—make our homes.

That is why, when I think of the times I myself have come closest to experiencing what I might call the sacred in nature, I often find myself remembering wild places much closer to home. I think, for instance, of a small pond near my house where water bubbles up from limestone springs to feed a series of pools that rarely freeze in winter and so play home to waterfowl that stay here for the protective warmth even on the coldest of winter days, gliding silently through steaming mists as the snow falls from gray February skies. I think of a November evening long ago when I found myself on a Wisconsin hilltop in rain and dense fog, only to have the setting sun break through the clouds to cast an otherwordly golden light on the misty farms and woodlands below, a scene so unexpected and joyous that I lingered past dusk so as not to miss any part of the gift that had come my way. And I think perhaps most especially of the blown-out, bankrupt farm in the sand country of central Wisconsin where Aldo Leopold and his family tried one of the first American experiments in ecological restoration, turning ravaged and infertile soil into carefully tended ground where the human and the nonhuman could exist side by side in relative harmony. What I celebrate about such places is not *just* their wildness, though that certainly is among their most important qualities; what I celebrate even more is that they remind us of the wildness in our own backyards, of the nature that is all around us if only we have eyes to see it.

Indeed, my principal objection to wilderness is that it may teach us to be dismissive or even contemptuous of such humble places and experiences. Without our quite realizing it, wilderness tends to privilege some parts of nature at the expense of others. Most of us, I suspect, still follow the conventions of the romantic sublime in finding the mountaintop more glorious than the plains, the ancient forest nobler than the grasslands, the mighty canyon more inspiring than the humble marsh. Even John Muir, in arguing against those who sought to dam his beloved Hetch Hetchy valley in the Sierra Nevada, argued for alternative dam sites in the gentler valleys of the foothills—a preference that had nothing to do with nature and everything with the cultural traditions of the sublime.[38] Just as problematically, our frontier traditions have encouraged Americans to define "true" wilderness as requiring very large tracts of roadless land—what Dave Foreman calls "The Big Outside." Leaving aside the legitimate empirical question in conservation biology of how large a tract of land must be before a given species can reproduce on it, the emphasis on big wilderness reflects a romantic frontier belief that one hasn't really gotten away from civilization unless one can go for days at a time without encountering another human being. By teaching us to fetishize sublime places and wide open country, these peculiarly American ways of thinking about wilderness encourage us to adopt too high a standard for what counts as "natural." If it isn't hundreds of square miles big, if it doesn't give us God's-eye views or grand vistas, if it doesn't permit us the illusion that we are alone on the planet, then it really isn't natural. It's too small, too plain, or too crowded to be *authentically* wild.

In critiquing wilderness as I have done in this essay, I'm forced to confront my own deep ambivalence about its meaning for modern environmentalism. On the one hand, one of my own most important environmental ethics is that people should always to be conscious that they are part of the natural world, inextricably tied to the ecological systems that sustain their lives. Any way of looking at nature that encourages us to believe we are separate from nature—as wilderness tends to do—is likely to reinforce environmentally irresponsible behavior. On the other hand, I also think it no less crucial for us to recognize and honor nonhuman nature as a world we did not create, a world with its own independent, nonhuman reasons for being as it is. The autonomy of nonhuman nature seems to me an indispensable corrective to human arrogance. Any way of looking at nature that helps us remember—as wilderness also tends to do—that the interests of people are not necessarily identical to those of every other creature or of the earth itself is likely to foster *responsible* behavior. To the extent that wilderness has served as an important vehicle for articulating deep moral values regarding our obligations and responsibilities to the nonhuman world, I would not want to jettison the contributions it has made to our culture's ways of thinking about nature.

If the core problem of wilderness is that it distances us too much from the very things it teaches us to value, then the question we must ask is what it can tell us about *home*, the place where we actually live. How can we take the positive values we associate with wilderness and bring them closer to home? I think the answer to this question will come by broadening our sense of the otherness that wilderness seeks to define and protect. In reminding us of the world we did not make, wilderness can teach profound feelings of humility and respect as we confront our fellow beings and the earth itself. Feelings like these argue for the importance of self-awareness and self-criticism as we exercise our own ability to transform the world around us, helping us set responsible limits to human mastery—which without such limits too easily becomes human hubris. Wilderness is the place where, symbolically at least, we try to withhold our power to dominate.

Wallace Stegner once wrote of

the special human mark, the special record of human passage, that distinguishes man from all other species. It is rare enough among men, impossible to any other form of life. *It is simply the deliberate and chosen refusal to make any marks at all.* . . . We are the most dangerous species of life on the planet, and every other species, even the earth itself, has cause to fear our power to exterminate. But we are also the only species which, when it chooses to do so, will go to great effort to save what it might destroy.[39]

The myth of wilderness, which Stegner knowingly reproduces in these remarks, is that we can somehow leave nature untouched by our passage. By now it should be clear that this for the most part is an illusion. But Stegner's deeper message then becomes all the more compelling. If living in history means that we cannot help leaving marks on a fallen world, then the dilemma we face is to decide what kinds of marks we wish to leave. It is just here that our cultural traditions of wilderness remain so important. In the broadest sense, wilderness teaches us to ask whether the Other must always bend to our will, and, if not, under what circumstances it should be allowed to flourish without our intervention. This is surely a question worth asking about everything we do, and not just about the natural world.

When we visit a wilderness area, we find ourselves surrounded by plants and animals and physical landscapes whose otherness compels our attention. In forcing us to acknowledge that they are not of our making, that they have little or no need of our continued existence, they recall for us a creation far greater than our own. In the wilderness, we need no reminder that a tree has its own reasons for being, quite apart from us. The same is less true in the gardens we plant and tend ourselves: there it is far easier to forget the otherness of the tree.[40] Indeed, one could almost measure wilderness by the extent to which our recognition of its otherness requires a conscious, willed act on our part. The romantic legacy means that wilderness is more a state of mind than a fact of nature, and the state of mind that today most defines wilderness is *wonder*. The striking power of the wild is that wonder in the face of it requires no act of will, but forces itself upon us—as an expression of the nonhuman world experienced through the lens of our cultural history—as proof that ours is not the only presence in the universe.

Wilderness gets us into trouble only if we imagine that this experience of wonder and otherness is limited to the remote corners of the planet, or that it somehow depends on pristine landscapes we ourselves do not inhabit. Nothing could be more misleading. The tree in the garden is in reality no less other, no less worthy of our wonder and respect, than the tree in an ancient forest that has never known an ax or a saw—even though the tree in the forest reflects a more intricate web of ecological relationships. The tree in the garden could easily have sprung from the same seed as the tree in the forest, and we can claim only its location and perhaps its form as our own. Both trees stand apart from us; both share our common world. The special power of the tree in the wilderness is to remind us of this fact. It can teach us to recognize the wildness we did not see in the tree we planted in our own backyard. By seeing the otherness in that which is most unfamiliar, we can learn to see it too in that which at first seemed merely ordinary. If wilderness can do this—if it can help us perceive and respect a nature we had forgotten to recognize as natural—then it will become part of the solution to our environmental dilemmas rather than part of the problem.

This will only happen, however, if we abandon the dualism that sees the tree in the garden as artificial—completely fallen and unnatural—and the tree in the wilderness as natural—completely pristine and wild. Both trees in some ultimate sense are wild; both in a practical sense now depend on our management and care. We are responsible for both, even though we can claim credit for neither. Our challenge is to stop thinking of such things according to a set of bipolar moral scales in which the human and the non-human, the unnatural and the natural, the fallen and the unfallen, serve as our conceptual map for understanding and valuing the world. Instead, we need to embrace the full continuum of a natural landscape that is also cultural, in which the city, the suburb, the pastoral, and the wild each has its proper place, which we permit ourselves to celebrate without needlessly denigrating the others. We need to honor the Other within and the Other next door as much as we do the exotic Other that lives far away—a lesson that applies as much to people as it does to (other) natural things. In particular, we need to discover a common middle ground in which all of these things, from the city to the wilderness, can somehow be encompassed in the word "home." Home, after all, is the place where finally we make our living. It is the place for which we take responsibility, the place we try to sustain so we can pass on what is best in it (and in ourselves) to our children.[41]

The task of making a home in nature is what Wendell Berry has called "the forever unfinished lifework of our species." "The only thing we have to preserve nature with," he writes, "is culture; the only thing we have to preserve wildness with is domesticity."[42] Calling a place home inevitably means that we will *use* the nature we find in it, for there can be no escape from manipulating and working and even killing some parts of nature to make our home. But if we acknowledge the autonomy and otherness of the things and creatures around us—an autonomy our culture has taught us to label with the word "wild"—then we will at least think carefully about the uses to which we put them, and even ask if we should use them at all. Just so can we still join Thoreau in declaring that "in Wildness is the preservation of the World," for *wildness* (as opposed to wilderness) can be found anywhere: in the seemingly tame fields and woodlots of Massachusetts, in the cracks of a Manhattan sidewalk, even in the cells of our own bodies. As Gary Snyder has wisely said, "A person with a clear heart and open mind can experience the wilderness anywhere on earth. It is a quality of one's own consciousness. The planet is a wild place and always will be."[43] To think ourselves capable of causing "the end of nature" is an act of great hubris, for it means forgetting the wildness that dwells everywhere within and around us.

Learning to honor the wild—learning to remember and acknowledge the autonomy of the other—means striving for critical self-consciousness in all of our actions. It means that deep reflection and respect must accompany each act of use, and means too that we must always consider the possibility of non-use. It means looking at the part of nature we intend to turn toward our own ends and asking whether we can use it again and again and again—

sustainably—without its being diminished in the process. It means never imagining that we can flee into a mythical wilderness to escape history and the obligation to take responsibility for our own actions that history inescapably entails. Most of all, it means practicing remembrance and gratitude, for thanksgiving is the simplest and most basic of ways for us to recollect the nature, the culture, and the history that have come together to make the world as we know it. If wildness can stop being (just) out there and start being (also) in here, if it can start being as humane as it is natural, then perhaps we can get on with the unending task of struggling to live rightly in the world—not just in the garden, not just in the wilderness, but in the home that encompasses them both.

Constructing Nature: The Legacy of Frederick Law Olmsted

Anne Whiston Spirn

FREDERICK LAW OLMSTED (1822–1903) LEFT A LEGACY OF WONDERFUL places, from Central Park to Boston's "Emerald Necklace," from Niagara Falls to Yosemite. Few people now recognize these as built landscapes. Most are startled to learn that New York's Central Park was constructed, that even the Ramble is an "artful wilderness," and that Boston's Fens and Riverway were molded out of polluted mudflats, planted to grow into tidal marsh and floodplain forest. Even those few who recognize Central Park and the Fens as constructions are surprised at how extensively the experiences of Niagara Falls and Yosemite are shaped by design, for these have come to stand as monuments of nature untouched by human artifice.[1]

Olmsted's contemporaries certainly recognized that landscapes like Central Park and the Fens were designed and built. After all, they were familiar with the previous appearances of those sites and the lengthy and ambitious process of transformation. However, this popular realization soon faded. Olmsted was so skillful at concealing the artifice that both the projects he had so brilliantly constructed and the profession he had worked so hard to establish became largely invisible. Today the works of the profession of landscape architecture are often not "seen," not understood as having been designed and deliberately constructed, even when the landscape has been radically reshaped. Many landmarks of landscape architecture are assumed to be works of nature or felicitous, serendipitous products of culture. This blindness prevents their appreciation as artful answers to knotty questions of conflicting environmental values and competing purposes.

91

Olmsted is justly recognized and remembered for his built works, but his legacy consists of far more than *places*. He was a pragmatic visionary who, through a fusion of theory and practice, shaped the American landscape from city to wilderness. He was a pivotal figure in the formative years of the conservation movement and struggled with issues that still face American society. In his report on Yosemite he urged that such extraordinary places be made accessible to all and not remain the property of an elite. At Niagara he worked with the "processes of nature" to form a frame for the falls. At Biltmore he constructed a forest "out of whole cloth" and planned its management for pleasure and utility. In Boston's Fens and Riverway he employed the lessons of a lifetime to transform urban landscapes polluted by waste into habitats that enhanced human health, safety, and welfare, while they reintroduced a sense of the wild into the heart of the city.

Much of Olmsted's work, written and built, is remarkably fresh a century after his retirement, but its potential has not been fully explored and realized. Projects that should have been widely replicated were forgotten, then occasionally reinvented, or they were misunderstood, then poorly imitated. Lately, admirers have praised the pastoral scenery of Olmsted's urban parks, while critics have attacked his ideas that exposure to such scenery would improve the morals of working-class people.[2] Admirers and critics alike have focused upon the specifics of his expression, whether formal or verbal, and have neglected the larger significance of his vision and methods. Olmsted's legacy needs reclaiming.

Yosemite

YOSEMITE WAS THE FIRST TRACT OF WILD LAND SET ASIDE BY AN ACT OF Congress, in 1864, "for public use, resort, and recreation."[3] There was no precedent in the United States for such an action, and Olmsted was asked to chair a commission to recommend what should be done with Yosemite. In 1865 he outlined the case for preserving Yosemite and the strategies for managing it. His view was frankly anthropocentric: Yosemite should be preserved because it had value for humans; to be in a place surrounded by "natural scenery" promoted human health and welfare. Such scenery, he felt, should never be private property, but should be held in trust for public purposes, for its importance to the nation was comparable to strategic, defensive points along national boundaries. Without government action to assure "free enjoyment" for all citizens, Olmsted predicted, places like Yosemite would become "rich men's parks" and the public would be barred from the beneficial effects of its scenery. He cited the example of Great Britain, where "the enjoyment of the choicest natural scenes in the country" was the "monopoly . . . of a very few, very rich people."[4]

In 1865, the year of Olmsted's report, several hundred people visited Yosemite. Visitors had to hire a guide and horses and travel three to four days, for forty miles along a "very poor trail." Olmsted's proposals for Yosemite were deceptively simple: provide free access for all visitors in a manner that preserved the valley's scenic qualities. He proposed that a public road be constructed to connect Yosemite with the nearest road and that five cabins be built in the valley, convenient to camping places and each providing at least one free room for public use. He proposed paths and prospects to shape visitors' experience of Yosemite by directing their movement and gaze. To enhance an individual's experience of this scenery without the distracting intrusion of "artificial construction," he recommended building a narrow, one-way trail in a circuit around the valley, concealed by trees so that it would be invisible to viewers gazing from one side to another.[5]

Olmsted read his report to the other commissioners and a handful of journalists and friends in August 1865. He returned to New York soon after this meeting, and the report was never submitted to the California legislature. There is evidence that it was suppressed by several commissioners who felt that it conflicted with their own political and financial interests (one held the sole charter to build a toll road from the nearest railroad to Yosemite and to run a stagecoach line along it).[6] One of the journalists present at the reading, Samuel Bowles, was publisher of the *Springfield Republican*. He reported Olmsted's ideas and urged that New York preserve such places as Niagara Falls for popular use.[7]

To Olmsted the significance of Yosemite lay in the quality of its scenery— "the union of the deepest sublimity with the deepest beauty of nature"—not in any one scene or series of views, but in the whole.[8] Although he noted the economic significance of such scenery, its benefit to public health and welfare concerned him most intensely. Olmsted was convinced that the "contemplation of natural scenes of an impressive character" had lasting beneficial physical, mental, and moral effects, particularly if it occurred "in connection with relief from ordinary cares, change of air and change of habits." Furthermore, he believed that such contemplation increased the subsequent capacity for happiness and that the lack of such opportunity could lead to depression and mental illness.[9] What was it about natural scenery that accounted for such an effect? In its contemplation, he said, the mind was "occupied without purpose," producing an enjoyment of the moment, an escape from stresses of the present and worries about the future; it exercised and refreshed both mind and body. In his extended description of the values of natural scenery, Olmsted was describing the effect he believed it had upon himself. He frequently suffered nervous ailments of one sort or another, from which he found relief in "natural scenery," as opposed to "artificial pleasures" such as "theatres, parades, and promenades."[10]

Olmsted predicted that within a century millions of visitors would come to Yosemite each year and advised that precautions be taken to manage the landscape so that these visitors would cause the least damage, for "the slight harm which the few hundred visitors of this year might do, if no care were taken to prevent it, would not be slight if it should be repeated by mil-lions."[11] Today Yosemite is one of the most popular national parks, with about 2.5 million visitors per year. It is also an urban park, serving the surrounding metropolitan regions of California and Nevada. Bumper-to-bumper traffic often clogs the road through the valley, and trucks haul out more than twenty tons of garbage per day.[12] The air is polluted by car exhaust. Earth and plants along the main trails are pummeled and trampled by those who make the pilgrimage to Yosemite. Such are the conditions in other national parks, in Yellowstone, in Acadia, in landscapes like Niagara that have come to embody a cultural ideal of nature.

The question Olmsted posed in 1865 remains unresolved: how to admit all the visitors who wish to come without their destroying the very thing they value? The moment people come to a place, even as reverent observers, they alter what they came to experience. Preventing the destructive effects of human visitation requires management of water and soil, plants and ani-mals, and people (and this is now routine at national parks and forests). Yet management is something most people don't associate with wilderness; even the *idea* of management is anathema to some. This is because they see wil-derness as something separate from humanity—as untouched by human labor and culture, on the one hand, and as a place where one's behavior is free and unconstrained, on the other. Both ideas are problematic; both

Traffic congestion at Yosemite, 1980. *(Courtesy Carl Steinitz, Department of Landscape Architecture, Graduate School of Design, Harvard University)*

result, ultimately, in the destruction of what they value.[13] Ironically, Olmsted's concealment of the artifice of his intervention (a tradition continued today in the national parks) permits the misconception that places like Yosemite are not designed and managed.

Olmsted's work at Central Park and at Yosemite was informed by similar ideas about the value of natural scenery, the importance of free public access, and the necessity for managing the landscape (albeit concealed) to realize the value of both the scenery and the access. He advocated both the preservation of remote wild lands and the restoration of urban landscapes that had been ravaged by human use, and he continued to work across this spectrum of environments for the rest of his career.

Niagara Falls

NIAGARA FALLS IS MORE THAN A BIG WATERFALL. FOR AMERICANS IT IS *the* waterfall. Niagara has long been, for many, the epitome of the sublime, offering the experience of a powerful natural feature of superhuman scale that inspires awe and fear. To others it has been a spectacle, a source of cheap power, a historic landmark, a livelihood. Niagara has never meant the same thing to everyone, and its meanings have changed over time, reflections of cultural context. The falls and their frame have been repeatedly reconstructed, literally and figuratively, their form and meaning revisited by generation after generation. (See illustrations on pp. 163–67.)

Niagara Falls was a popular tourist destination throughout the early nineteenth century. By the 1860s, however, it had become a natural wonder that failed to astonish. Water flow over the falls was diminished by diversions for power and industry, and visitors had to pick their way along muddy paths bordered by dilapidated factories. On his return from California and Yosemite, Olmsted joined the campaign to establish Niagara Falls as a public reservation and restore its scenic qualities.[14] Here was sublime scenery that was freely accessible to urban populations. Niagara provided Olmsted with the opportunity to apply the ideas he had outlined in his report on Yosemite. In 1879 he was appointed a consultant to the state survey that studied the falls and recommended that the state of New York repurchase property along the Niagara River and the American Falls (the state had sold the land bordering the Niagara River and Falls in 1806). The state survey also proposed that the landscape around Niagara be designed as a frame within which the falls could be experienced in diverse ways.[15]

In 1886, after Olmsted had lobbied for the preservation of Niagara for over twenty years, he and his partner Calvert Vaux were hired to prepare a plan for Niagara Reservation.[16] Their report of 1887 analyzed the disappointment of first-time visitors to Niagara and identified two types of response: the failure of the falls to meet expectations and the distraction posed by the "objectionable artificial character" of the context.[17] They concluded that no improvement could "increase the astonishing qualities of Niagara"[18] and therefore focused on enclosing river and falls within a frame of "natural scenery." This required the removal of all "artificial" structures: mills, other industrial buldings, and the "illuminating apparatus" used to project red, white, and blue lights on the falls at night.[19] In some areas they proposed merely to remove walls along the riverbank and allow the river "to take its course."[20] In others they planned to "hasten the process already begun" by nature,[21] thereby achieving more than the "unassisted processes of nature."[22] For example, they recommended that stone retaining walls along the mainland shore be removed, the shoreline reshaped, and the old stone reused to form low walls with pockets of soil and planted with "willows, rushes, ferns, irises, . . . and other water side plants of the region" so that they looked just like the "natural, low, rocky shores of the neighboring islands."[23] Though Olmsted and Vaux were "far from thinking that all that is required to accomplish the designed end is to 'let Nature alone,' " this was the very impression they sought to create by their "unobtrusive" interventions.[24]

Olmsted and Vaux designed paths and prospects—carriageways with views, shoreline footpaths, and overlooks with railings to prevent crowds from tumbling into the chasm. The plan choreographed the experience of the visitors to accommodate their large numbers (as many as ten thousand per day) and their diverse expectations and to prevent destruction of the scenic qualities they came to see.[25] Most visitors arrived by train in large numbers; to disperse these crowds, picnic areas and other attractions were provided near the train station, with paths leading off toward the river and the falls. Olmsted recognized that most visitors would be satisfied with a short walk to the falls and a brief view of the spectacle. For those who preferred to contemplate the sublime scenery in solitude, there were footpaths along the river to more remote areas.

Olmsted's plan of 1887 successfully accommodated tourists with diverse values and expectations, but failed to address the fundamental conflict at Niagara Falls in coming decades—the tension between scenic landmark and source of power. By 1909 the view enclosed by the frame of natural scenery so carefully designed by Olmsted and Vaux was of "American Falls Running Dry."[26] (See the photograph on p. 164, showing only a trickle of water flowing over the falls.) The conflict between sublime scenery and material resources was not limited to Niagara.[27] The split in the conservation movement—between those who would preserve sublime scenery and those who supported managed use of the material resources it represented—grew wider and progressively more bitter through the twentieth century. Future reconstructions of Niagara occurred against this changing cultural backdrop.

The conflict between the consumption of the falls as symbolic scenery and as a source of power has been addressed by one international board after another and been the subject of multiple treaties between Canada and the United States. The specific proposals of each successive board reveal the changing cultural context within which Niagara was seen. The recommendations of the international boards set up in 1926 and in 1967 provide striking similarities to and telling differences with the report by Olmsted and Vaux in 1887.

The 1926 board was appointed to determine how the "vanished beauty" of Niagara Falls might be restored.[28] The board investigated commercial, hydrological, and aesthetic issues (water use, tourism, patterns of water flow and erosion, and the relationship between water depth and the greenish-blue color of the Horseshoe Falls) and employed this data "to plan the betterment of the spectacle by using water to greater scenic advantage."[29] To this end, they proposed the use of concealed weirs to divert more water over the American Falls, to raise the water level in the rapids, and to "throw more water against the head of Goat Island."[30] Since tourists visited mainly in the summer, they suggested that power companies be permitted to divert water (10,000 cubic feet per second on each side) from October 1 to April 1.[31]

The 1967 board was set up to investigate "measures necessary to preserve or enhance the beauty of the American Falls," with specific concern for the prevention of erosion and accumulation of fallen rock that was transforming the falls from a waterfall into a cascade.[32] As they had been in 1887 and 1926, the concerns were aesthetic and symbolic, for the falls were deemed "one of the most spectacular natural phenomena in the world" and "a symbol of international amity and cooperation."[33] In an elaborate series of studies spanning seven years, the board probed, sampled, tested, modeled, and evaluated the American Falls. A temporary dam was built to drain the falls for five and a half months, so that the dry river bottom and rock face could be inspected, photographed, and mapped and so that instruments could be installed in fissures to measure water pressure and ground movement.[34] All this information was used to construct a model of the American Falls one-fiftieth its actual size, with turbulence, mist, illumination, and volume of water all carefully simulated. The model was built so that rocks at the base (talus) could be removed, and a committee of landscape architects charged with the task of "choosing a permanent arrangement of talus that would have the most dramatic effect."[35] Finally, the flow of water over the "real" Niagara Falls was reduced and then increased from 8,000 to 15,000 cubic feet per second and the visual effects recorded and evaluated. (See illustrations on pp. 165–67.)

After all this manipulation of the falls, both actual and virtual, the International Joint Commission concluded that "man should not interfere with the natural process," for the falls are a "reminder of man's relationship with his environment. Indeed, this is the very essence of their attractiveness."[36] Let the talus accumulate, and do not stabilize the rock mass, because to alter the falls would be "to create, on a grand scale, an artificial waterfall in a formal park. It would interfere with the geologic process and would be contrary to the recent emphasis on environmental values."[37] The commission also recommended that guidelines be set to prevent the "intrusion of . . . towers . . . and commercial features whose appearance on the skyline will result in an artificial encirclement that will overshadow and stifle the magnificence of the Falls."[38] By the 1970s it was not just Niagara Falls but Olmsted's plan that seemed worthy of preservation.[39]

In some ways, the three sets of recommendations are remarkably similar. All emphasize the falls' visual appearance, referring to Niagara as a "spectacle," and all advocate a frame of "natural" scenery. In his report Olmsted carefully explained his ideas about the value of natural scenery and its benefits to health, but the later reports take this value as self-evident, leaving their own assumptions unexamined. Why is the "natural" frame preferred to the urban in 1929 and the 1970s? Note the perjorative implications of the words "artificial" and "formal," as opposed to "natural" scenery in the 1975 report. Why must the city be screened from view? Frank Lloyd Wright's Fallingwater, one of the most powerful architectural images of the twentieth century, gains its appeal from the juxtaposition of building and waterfall. Why not Niagara? There is evident in 1974 a fear that this would diminish the falls, "overshadow" and "stifle" their "magnificence."

The three groups differ in whether they propose to manipulate the falls as opposed to the frame. Olmsted dismissed the idea that the falls themselves could be altered; the 1920s board felt that the water flow above the falls could and should be shaped to magnify the spectacle; the 1970s commission acknowledged that the falls could be manipulated (and its board's had done so), but recoiled from the act. Olmsted was working during a time when sublime landscapes like those of Niagara and Yosemite were seen as creations of God or nature; they could be framed but not constructed. The board of 1926 was working when projects such as the Grand Coulee Dam were being conceived as a progressive union of nature and culture, an organic machine, a manufactured sublime. By the 1960s people had the failed promise of Grand Coulee and all those other dams in the backs of their minds, along with the connections they represented to the development of the atomic bomb and the excesses of industrial agriculture described in Rachel Carson's *Silent Spring*.[40] There was a sense of guilt over what humans had wrought, as well as a notion that nature (not just the scenery) was fragile and required human protection, that human actions could "emasculate" the falls.[41] Still, it is curious that in 1974 the commission deemed it all right to construct the frame, but not the falls; to alter the amount of water flowing over the falls, but not move the rocks.

Niagara Falls is shaped by water flowing, rocks falling, and trees growing, by artists and tourists, by journalists and landscape architects, by engineers and workers who divert the water. Niagara is constructed through processes of nonhuman nature, through water use and treaties, through paintings and postcards, memory and myth. Even the most awesome landscapes are products of both nature and culture, and they change in predictable and unpredictable ways in response to both. Olmsted employed the shaping capacity of water flow and of plant growth and reproduction to design over time. Through writing and lobbying, he influenced public perception of Niagara in his own time, but he could not anticipate the future social and political events that would continue to shape Niagara.

Biltmore

BILTMORE, ONCE THE HOME OF GEORGE VANDERBILT, IS NOW PART OF THE Pisgah National Forest. Driving up the entrance road through a lush, mature forest, one finds it difficult to imagine that this landscape was constructed—made, as Olmsted put it, "out of the whole cloth."[42] Vanderbilt assembled his huge estate near Asheville, North Carolina, through the purchase of many small farms and woodlots. He retained Olmsted in 1888 to advise him on the improvement of his newly acquired property. The site was unpromising, Olmsted reported, the soil was "extremely poor and intractable,"[43] the woods were "miserable, all the good trees having again and again been culled out and only runts left."[44] Vanderbilt had thought to plant a pastoral landscape of groves and grass, but Olmsted warned that he would "get very poor results at great cost."[45] Instead, he persuaded Vanderbilt to underwrite America's first large-scale experiment in forestry. Olmsted's plan for the estate included a park and garden near the house,

Biltmore Forest prior to improvement. *(Gifford Pinchot,* Biltmore Forest: An Account of Its Treatment, and the Results of the First Year's Work *[Chicago: Lakeside Press, 1893], courtesy Francis Loeb Library, Graduate School of Design, Harvard University)*

farmlands "on the river bottom chiefly to keep and fatten live stock with a view to manure," and the remainder as forest.[46] Thousands of acres of scrubby, second-growth woodland and old fields were ultimately planted as forest and managed for economic return and aesthetic enjoyment.[47]

By January 1891 work was well under way, with white pines planted on three hundred acres of old fields, nursery stock readied for the forest, and gangs of workmen assembled to take out "the poor and dilapidated trees of the existing woods."[48] A large nursery was established at Biltmore to supply forest trees and shrubs in the quantity required and variety desired.[49] In 1891 the recently established nursery included about 100,000 trees and bushes "of merchantable size" and about 500,000 seedlings and cuttings that had been propagated there.[50]

Olmsted saw in Biltmore an opportunity to demonstrate the promise of forestry techniques for the management of land used for recreation.[51] Working with a private client, he hoped to avoid the frustrations and misunderstandings he had met in public projects, such as Central Park, where public protest thwarted his plans for landscape management. In Central Park, Olmsted had planted trees thickly, with the intention of culling the weaker trees later, and had introduced "nurse" trees to shelter more tender species intended ultimately to predominate. Years later, when workers cut the trees as planned, park visitors sometimes stood in front of the trees and tried "to wrest the axe from the hand of the woodsman."[52] Olmsted and J. B. Harrison wrote "Observations on the Treatment of Public Plantations, More Especially Related to the Use of the Axe" in 1889 to persuade the public that landscape management includes the creative use of the ax as well as the generative act of planting seeds. The chance to work with a single client must have seemed a welcome relief and an opportunity to gain a powerful patron for forestry. Olmsted encouraged Vanderbilt to become involved in the management of his forest as a suitable, long-term, and "most interesting rural occupation."[53]

At Biltmore, Olmsted nurtured the future development of American forestry in more ways than one. Gifford Pinchot, later the first director of the U.S. Forest Service, visited Biltmore upon his return from studying forestry in Europe and was soon employed to work on a management plan. Pinchot later recalled his excitement: "Here was my chance. Biltmore could be made to prove what America did not yet understand, that trees could be cut and the forest preserved at one and the same time."[54] Working under Olmsted at Biltmore was Pinchot's first job, which included an apprenticeship in public relations, as well as in forestry. Among his first assignments was the preparation of an exhibit and pamphlet on the project for the Chicago world's fair of 1893, which was sent to thousands of newspapers and prompted much commentary.[55] Pinchot continued to work at Biltmore after Olmsted's retirement in 1893, but also took on other jobs as a consulting forester. His successor at Biltmore as resident forester, Alvin Schenck, established the Biltmore Forest School in 1897, the first such school in America.[56] By the

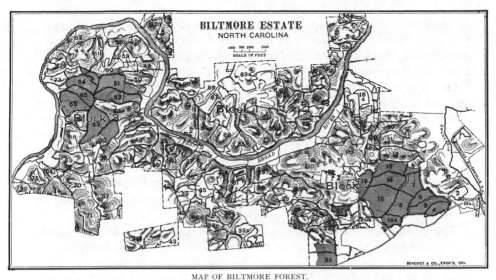

MAP OF BILTMORE FOREST.

BLOCKS BOUNDED BY RED LINES; COMPARTMENTS NUMBERED FROM 1 TO 92; FOREST LANDS, GREEN; IMPROVEMENT CUTTINGS, DARK GREEN.

Biltmore Forest, 1893. *(Gifford Pinchot,* Biltmore Forest: An Account of Its Treatment, *and the Results of the First Year's Work [Chicago: Lakeside Press, 1893], courtesy Francis Loeb Library, Graduate School of Design, Harvard University)*

early 1900s, however, it became clear that the forest was a financial fiasco in the short term and would yield no economic return for many years. If one of the richest men in America couldn't afford an experiment in forest management, then who could? Pinchot's experience at Biltmore convinced him that the long time frame required by forest management demanded that forest reserves be managed by public agencies.

Pinchot's notion that "trees could be cut and the forest preserved at one and the same time" lies at the core of some of the most bitter disputes of the environmental movement during the last century. They split the ideals of the Forest Service from those of the National Park Service, the goals of the Sierra Club from those of Resources for the Future. They lie at the heart of the debate over the fate of forests, from the wilds of Oregon to the streets of Dayton.

Trees cannot be cut and "the forest" preserved unless there is agreement on what a forest is and whom it is it for. Is it everyday habitat or sacred symbol, mental image or material resource? Is it for plants, animals, or people? And which ones—for native oaks or Norway maples; for spotted owls or English sparrows; for hikers or hunters, naturalists or lumbermen; for local residents or distant populations? There are many kinds of forests, and the answers depend upon the context of a particular place.[57] Since an old-growth forest and an urban forest of trees in city parks and streets are not the same, different priorities should inform their management.

For Olmsted it was appropriate to apply the same methods of forest management to trees in urban parks and to those in rural woodlands. He published his pamphlet on forestry as applied to Central Park in 1889 as he was commencing work at Biltmore. Nearly a century later, the city forester of Dayton, Ohio, found himself embroiled in a controversy much like the one Olmsted encountered at Central Park, when he proposed a sustained management program for Dayton's urban forest. The forester planned to harvest diseased and dying street and park trees while they were still marketable, using the proceeds to pay for the cost of removing and planting new trees. The local Sierra Club and Audubon Society chapters opposed the program, citing loss of wildlife habitat in rotten trunks and fallen trees and the desire to "let nature take her course." They sued the city and won, forcing the abandonment of the program.[58] Preservation versus conservation—this, in a nutshell, is the core dilemma of environmentalism.

The powerful lesson of Biltmore is what human impulse can accomplish given sufficient time, with an eye to restoration and beauty, as well as to utility. One hundred years ago there was no forest at Biltmore, just cut-over woods and infertile fields. Now there is forest. Olmsted had the designer's faith that he could make something better, not worse. Key to his belief in himself was the ability to envision the future shape of the landscape, to guide it over time, and to imagine human intervention as potentially beneficial, not inevitably detrimental. He aimed to demonstrate how human intervention could make a forest more beautiful *and* more productive, provided one pursued long-term goals and a gradual return on investment, rather than short-term gain and maximum profit.

Olmsted took a long-term view of landscape construction and development. Unlike a building, a landscape is never "finished" after construction; it grows and changes, season by season, year by year. The form of a landscape can be fundamentally changed through the way it is managed. As design through time, landscape architecture often entails a succession of designs, sometimes requiring the alteration or even the deliberate destruction of early phases through growth, succession, or thinning, for example. At Central Park, Olmsted had envisioned a design that had to be implemented over several decades after the initial construction. And the forest at Biltmore would mature well beyond his own lifetime; at the age of eighty-eight he could say, "The entire undertaking looks to results that can be fully realized only after many years, and, except to a botanist, its value lies in its promises and experiments rather than its actualities."[59]

The Fens and the Riverway

IN OCTOBER 1893 OLMSTED WROTE TO HIS PARTNERS FROM BILTMORE, warning them to turn down any business that would distract them from the Boston work, especially the Riverway, and to follow that work carefully, day by day: "The aims are novel, the conditions are novel. You cannot trust

Biltmore entrance drive under construction, ca. 1890s. *(Courtesy National Park Service, Frederick Law Olmsted National Historic Site)*

Biltmore entrance drive. *(Courtesy National Park Service, Frederick Law Olmsted National Historic Site)*

to usage." The Boston works, he said, would be "points to date from in the history of American landscape architecture, as much as Central Park. They will be the openings of new chapters of the art."[60]

Boston's Fens and Riverway were built over nearly two decades (1880s–1890s) as an urban "wilderness," the first attempt anywhere, so far as I know, to *construct* a wetland. These projects, built on the site of tidal flats and floodplains fouled by sewage and industrial effluent, were designed to purify water and protect adjacent land from flooding. They also incorporated an interceptor sewer, a parkway, and Boston's first streetcar line; together, they formed a landscape *system* designed to accommodate the movement of people, the flow of water, and the removal of wastes. This skeleton of park, road, sewer, and public transit structured the growing city and its suburbs. The latter features were not part of the original park plan; Olmsted persuaded the city engineer to approve the construction of a tidal marsh instead of a concrete flood basin. He got the city to adopt a radical expansion of the project's scope and concept.

Olmsted's contemporaries knew full well that these parks were constructed, for they had seen and smelled the filthy, stinking, muddy mess the Fens replaced; the recognition of the transformation was part of their social meaning and aesthetic power. Today these works are admired, but are widely assumed to be preserved bits of "nature" in the city, rather than places that were designed and built, daring experiments of engineering, ecology, landscape design, and city planning.

The Fens and the Riverway yielded new knowledge and techniques, but not without trial and error. While Olmsted based his design upon a general understanding of natural processes of water movement—tides, currents, and flooding—and plant growth and succession, gained from experience with

The Fens and Boston, ca. 1925. *(Courtesy National Park Service, Frederick Law Olmsted National Historic Site)*

The Fens and Boston, 1983. *(Courtesy Alex S. MacLean/Landslides)*

Constructing the Riverway, 1892. *(Courtesy National Park Service, Frederick Law Olmsted National Historic Site)*

The Riverway, 1920. *(Courtesy National Park Service, Frederick Law Olmsted National Historic Site)*

projects such as that at Niagara, he had no existing models to guide him. Yet he undertook this risky experiment on a project that was in the public spotlight. In collaboration with the city's engineer, he worked out a plan for the basin to receive rising floodwaters and a design for the tidal gate that would enhance water circulation and regulate water exchange between the Fens and the river.[61] Olmsted engaged Charles Sprague Sargent, director of the Arnold Arboretum, to advise him on plant selection and methods for establishing the marsh. In the first phase, in 1883, more than 100,000 plants—grasses, flowers, shrubs, and vines—were planted in a space of two and a half acres.[62] These included many species, both native and exotic, so that if some died, others would survive. Some plants were also intended as "nurses" to shelter more tender plants from sun and wind until they took hold. Securing the plants and finding a contractor capable of this novel construction proved difficult. Almost all the plants died before the end of the first year and had to be replaced. Furious and mortified, Olmsted wrote the contractor, "The mere loss of so many plants is the smallest part of the disaster. The whole plan is a wreck."[63] The Fens were replanted, and within ten years the marshy landscape looked as if it had always been there.

Not only the function but also the appearance of the Fens and Riverway were revolutionary; up to this time, urban parks had been designed mainly in the formal or pastoral styles.[64] Olmsted introduced this "wild" appearance to bring the advantages of "natural scenery" found in places like Yosemite to "those who cannot travel":

> Cities are now grown so great that hours are consumed in gaining the "country," and, when the fields are reached, entrance is forbidden. Accordingly, it becomes necessary to acquire, for the free use and enjoyment of all, such neighboring fields, woods, pond-sides, river-banks, valleys, or hills as may present, *or may be made to present,* fine scenery of one type or another.[65]

The idea of constructing parks that imitated the appearance of the regional landscape of forest, prairie, and floodplain was pursued later in the early-twentieth-century work of Jens Jensen and the Prairie school. Superficially, Jensen's "Prairie River" in Chicago looked very similar to the Fens, but the aims of the two projects, and the two men, were very different. Olmsted imitated "natural scenery" because he believed that contact with such scenery would improve human health. Jensen used native plants and imitated the scenery of the region for political reasons. Jensen's "Prairie River" and other projects were ideological works with a chauvinistic agenda where "native" plants and the local landscape were seen as superior to "foreign" plants and places.[66] In this they reflected contemporary ecological theories of plant "communities" as embodying similarities to human communities and, by extension, as justifying certain human activities as "natural."[67] It was the understanding of landscape *processes* applied to landscape restoration and human health, safety, and welfare that made the Fens and the Riverway so significant. Olmsted imitated the local landscape in the service of these goals, and he often included hardy, exotic plants, along with native species.[68] Jensen emphasized visual appearance and the use of native plants; there was no underlying function of reclamation, flood control, and health. The fact that Jensen's work and Olmsted's resemble each other in visual appearance has led many later designers to confuse and conflate the intentions of these two quite dissimilar men.[69]

The Fens and the Riverway anticipated by nearly a century the introduction of "ecological" planning and design in landscape architecture in the 1960s, the recent appreciation of urban "wilds," and the "new" field of landscape restoration. In the 1970s eight thousand acres of freshwater marsh in Boston's Charles River watershed were purchased by the U.S. government to serve as "natural storage areas" for floodwaters. Heralding the project as revolutionary, the authors of the plan were unaware of the more radical precedent of the Fens, where wetlands were built, not preserved. Also in the 1970s the Woodlands, a new community for 150,000 people near Houston, was planned around a "natural drainage system" of preserved and constructed streams and swales. In the 1960s landscaped drainage channels and detention basins were built in Denver as parkland designed to prevent floods.[70]

Why were Olmsted's landmark achievements in the Fens and the Riverway—projects that should have been widely replicated models—first forgotten and then repeatedly reinvented? The answer lies mainly in the cultural conception of nature and of city: on the one hand, their "natural" appearance concealed their construction; on the other, the persistent mental opposition of nature and city gradually eroded the memory of Olmsted's contribution. For several decades after Olmsted's death, his successors continued to propose this type of project. Landscape architects like Frederick Law Olmsted, Jr., and John Nolen were important figures in the development of city planning as a "new" profession in the early 1900s. They served as the first presidents of the American City Planning Institute, offered the first course in city planning, and founded the first departments of city planning in American universities.[71] By the 1950s, however, city planning was emphasizing social and economic concerns over aesthetic and environmental issues and was moving increasingly away from "physical" planning, to a focus on the formulation of policies.[72]

Disasters might have been avoided in other sections of Boston if projects similar to the Fens and the Riverway had been implemented. In Roxbury and Dorchester, for example, streams were buried in sewers and houses built on low-lying land in the 1880s and 1890s. Most of these houses have long since been abandoned and demolished, after leaky sewers saturated the soil and owners failed to maintain the buildings. In some areas 90 percent of the original floodplain is now vacant, open land once again. How paradoxical that people perceive these vacant lots on the floodplain as "unnatural" and the landscapes of the Fens and the Riverway as "natural"! Olmsted's

Vacant land on floodplain in inner-city neighborhood, Boston, 1985. *(Anne Whiston Spirn, personal collection)*

example has guided my own work on the reconstruction of these and other inner-city landscapes in Boston and Philadelphia.[73] Boston's combined sewers overflow after rainstorms, making Olmsted's concept as appropriate as ever. Restored landscapes on low-lying vacant lands could be designed to serve as both parks and storm-water storage areas, as the Fens and Riverway once did and the parks in Denver now do, to prevent flooding and promote good water quality.

And the fate of the Fens itself? The Fens functioned as planned for only a short time. In 1910, just fifteen years after construction, the Charles River Dam was built, diminishing the importance of the Fens for flood control. Since the dam converted the Charles from a brackish into a freshwater river, many of the plants died, and then the site was used as a convenient dumping ground for dirt and debris from subway excavations.[74] The Fens of today bears little resemblance to that of Olmsted. In the 1980s the Massachusetts Department of Environmental Management engaged consultants to prepare a plan for the "preservation" of the Fens because of its importance as a historic landscape. A team of historians, preservationists, and landscape architects proposed that the Fens be restored to their original appearance, thus treating them like an ornamental object, used solely for strolling, looking, and thinking. The plan to preserve the Fens is a pale imitation that mocks the meaning and misses the significance of the original. Its intended function could have been restored: a place where floodwaters, flowing off roofs and streets, course and pool, filling the basin, dropping their silty load before entering the river, a place linked to the system of sewers that sustains the health and safety of Boston's citizens. The restoration could have amended a sewer system that now pollutes the water it is meant to protect; this would have been a restoration effort in the spirit of the original.

How could the planners miss such an obvious idea in this "age of ecology"? What was the value the planners thought they were restoring—that of the scenery? Their proposal demonstrates a fundamental misunderstanding of the project's significance: the comprehensive scope of its functions, the dialogue between cultural and natural processes, the relevance for present urban problems. Their failure to perceive this relevance is both amazing and sobering. Our short individual and collective memories present a major human conundrum. How can human communities manage landscape change that takes place over a hundred years or more, when people's perceptions and priorities change from generation to generation, or even from election to election? What one generation starts, another may overturn or fail to finish. Humans may not have the right "attention span" to manage environmental change, and this may be the species's fatal flaw.[75] Perhaps this is the value of history—as an attempt to extend the time frame of our memory beyond the human lifetime. The only problem is that history represents selective memory.

Reclaiming Olmsted, Reconstructing Nature

> In reclaiming and reoccupying lands laid waste by human improvidence or malice . . . the task is to become a co-worker with nature in the reconstruction of the damaged fabric.
> —George Perkins Marsh, *Man and Nature* (1864)

OLMSTED'S PROJECTS EMBODY THIS PRINCIPLE. THE MARSHES, MEADOWS, and forests he conceived in Boston, Biltmore, and Niagara were built of materials that were both given and worked: earth, rock, water, and plants of the place; dredged mud, quarried stone, channeled water, and bred plants. His landscapes were constructed by human imagination, human labor, and processes of nonhuman nature. Olmsted's drawn plans and on-site adjustments guided the labor of others—dredging, grading, planting, pruning, tending. He envisioned how the trees, shrubs, grasses, and flowers that he caused to be planted would grow, beget and nurture other plants, live, and die, and how water, flowing through the channels he molded, would modify further the shorelines he shaped. Olmsted shaped sites like Yosemite more indirectly through the influence of his writings on policy and through the application, after his death, of lessons learned from his work at Niagara. Olmsted's values and ideas inspired the landscapes he conceived; but these were shaped in turn by the culture of his time, class, and gender.

In employing natural and cultural processes as "co-workers," Olmsted foresaw some results and failed to anticipate others. He successfully matched the form of the landscapes he designed to the rhythms of nonhuman processes and the spatial structure they created, and he planned within a frame of time and space appropriate to the processes involved. He sought common solutions to social and environmental problems by defining every project as comprehensively as possible, expanding its scope when necessary. But Olmsted was generally more skilled at taking account of physical and biological processes than at accounting for social and political processes. Time and again, his projects were destroyed or fundamentally altered because he failed to take such processes into account.[76]

Olmsted invented methods of practice, advanced the discipline of landscape architecture, and set a standard for professional conduct. He undertook risky innovation to advance the field, avoided short-term expedience in favor of long-term interests, and put public service before personal gain. But he also believed that professionals were a privileged elite whose expert opinions should not be questioned, and he failed to appreciate the power of popular culture to affect people's attitudes toward his projects.

Olmsted's legacy was double-edged; his ideas and the work that stemmed from them contained the seeds of both success and failure. Even as he established and expanded the influence of his profession, landscape architecture, in his own time, he planted the seeds of its invisibility. On the one hand, he understood physical and biological processes and applied that knowledge inventively. On the other, he disguised the artifice, so that ultimately the built landscapes were not recognized and valued as human constructs. He planted trees to look like "natural scenery" and then felt frustrated when people, accepting the scenery as "natural," objected to cutting the trees he had planned to cull. His concealment of the art was so successful that it backfired. His notion of the social utility of natural scenery was lost; ultimately, it was viewed as decorative, not functional. Ironically, it was the "natural" appearance of his work that prevented people from appreciating how it fulfilled a broad range of functions.[77]

Landscapes blur the boundaries between the human and the nonhuman. Most people cannot distinguish between the parts of Biltmore Forest that merely grew and those that were planted, between the shores of Niagara that were shaped solely by river's flow and plants' growth and those planted to resemble them. Calling some landscapes "natural" and others "artificial" or "cultural" ignores the fact that landscapes are never wholly one or the other. Such thinking promotes the persistent, common conception of the city as a degraded environment and wilderness as a pristine place untainted by human presence. Seeing humans, ourselves, as solely or mainly a contaminating influence prevents us from appreciating the potential beneficial effects we might have and limits what we can imagine as possible.

Olmsted offers an example to emulate, not imitate. In reclaiming his legacy, we should do so selectively, learning from both his successes and his failures, retaining those ideas that are still relevant and discarding others as relics. We may apply some of the principles upon which his work is based but not imitate the work itself; employ and celebrate the physical and biological *processes* that connect human and nonhuman nature but not always copy the outward *appearance* of natural features, not always try to conceal the design. We may embrace his notion of environmental benefits for all without adopting his belief that exposure to natural scenery will improve morals. And we may embrace his high standards for professional conduct while rejecting his notion of professional privilege.

Olmsted represented a middle ground—which eroded in the twentieth century—between John Muir's idea of nature as "temple" and Gifford Pinchot's idea of nature as "workshop." To Muir a wilderness like Yosemite was sacred ground: "our holy Yosemite," as he put it.[78] Grazing the meadows and cutting the trees was sacrilege—plundering paradise. To Pinchot, Yosemite's water and timber were material resources to be conserved and used. Olmsted could reconcile reverence and use, and he did this through art. He could speak of the sacred qualities of Yosemite, the "reverent mood" it evoked, yet still condone cutting and planting trees and shaping the scene, because he could envision future groves and glades still sublime. Like Olmsted, most designers believe that their work will make the world a better place, or at least improve some small part of it.

Failure to recognize the Fens and the Riverway as *designed*, as an artful, deliberate reconstruction of landscapes laid waste by human occupation, blinds us to the possibility of such transformations elsewhere. Recognition demands that renewal accompany use, that we not just abandon those places whose original appeal or value has been destroyed through human use but also take responsibility for creating life-sustaining habitats. Failure to acknowledge the constructedness of Niagara Falls and Yosemite conceals their connection to landscapes where the human is more dominant. Acknowledging the role of human ideas and purposes in constructing these landscapes forces us to clearly confront the *human* values we inevitably project upon such places. Demystifying the construction of these extraordinary places celebrates the human ability to shape them and promotes the possibility of fostering similar qualities in ordinary landscapes.

To deny the dynamic reality of the nonhuman world is also misleading and potentially destructive. Rain, rivers, mountains, trees, and birds are not just figments of human imagination; they *exist*. We perceive them only through our own human senses, refer to them by names we have given them, and employ them to tell our own stories, but they also have an existence outside that which *we* grant them. Failure to appreciate the dynamic, autonomous role of nonhuman features and phenomena promotes the illusion that humans can construct and control everything. Recognition prompts an understanding of human limitations, admits the possibility of unforeseen consequences, and recommends caution for undertakings so large in scale that unanticipated consequences might spell disaster.

All landscapes are constructed. Garden, forest, city, and wilderness are shaped by rivers and rain, plants and animals, human hands and minds. They are phenomena of nature *and* products of culture. There is always a tension in landscape between the reality and autonomy of the nonhuman and its cultural construction, between the human impulse to wonder at the wild and the compulsion to use, manage, and control. Landscapes of city and wilderness represent poles of a continuum in the history and intensity of human intervention. Seen thus, they bracket a range of environments, some destructive of life and some life-sustaining, some structured largely by human habitation, some a reminder that the human is only one possibility among many. For the world is not infinitely malleable; nature may be constructed, but it is not *only* a construction.

Amazonia as Edenic Narrative

Candace Slater

FEW PLACES IN THIS WORLD CONJURE UP SUCH POWERFUL IMAGES AS DOES Amazonia—great snakes, immense rivers, Indians with feather halos, and, above them all, a glittering canopy of green. I can remember, as a child, poring over a book of Donald Duck's adventures in a wondrous tangle of trees, vines, and butterfly-like flowers labeled "The Amazon Jungle." And yet, while Americans today are far more apt to speak of the biodiverse "rain forest" than to refer to Donald's teeming jungle, the idea of an enchanted Amazon remains very strong. Outsiders who rely primarily on the mass media for images of the region are almost always surprised, if not disappointed, to learn that over half of its residents now live in cities, that Indians make up less than 2 percent of the population, and that the rainbow-colored forest is itself composed of vegetation that often seems monotonous to the untutored eye. Accustomed to noble, if beleaguered, natives and thoroughly villainous miners, they are startled to discover tribes whose members have turned to mining or who do a brisk business with mineral and logging companies.

In the following pages, I argue that the tendency to see the Amazon—or Amazonian nature—as a kind of Eden fosters a skewed and largely static approach toward a multilayered and decidedly fluid reality. The problem is not just that this vision is often false or exaggerated but that it obscures the people and places that actually exist there.

Although native peoples and the rain forest are essential elements of Amazonia, an insistence on seeing the one as an idealized embodiment of the other conceals the multiplicity of worlds that lie within the region's borders. To the extent that an abstract Edenic landscape crowds out the teenage rubber tapper in a faded World Cup T-shirt, the stinging smoke of factories in a treeless city ringed by forest, or the lone plant sprouting in the cracks of a sunbaked roof, it impoverishes our vision of Amazonia, as well as of a larger natural world that demands not just to be respected but, first of all, to be rethought.

Because the Edenic Rain Forest (as opposed to the specific and non-interchangeable rain forests that exist in Amazonia and elsewhere) results in policy decisions that wreak havoc on the lives of both trees and people, it not just invites but demands attention. The persistent idea, for instance, of the Amazon as exuberantly fertile has continued to propel large-scale colonization schemes.[1] The actual fragility of Amazonian soils, however, has resulted in the burning of vast tracts of land for pasture, which then goes barren after a few years.

Biological reserves provide another excellent example of how Edenic schemes can backfire. Intended to shore up nature's bounty from would-be intruders, some of these projects actually threaten a long-standing equilibrium between the human and the nonhuman worlds. The vast state and federal reserves on the Trombetas River in Brazilian Amazonia, for instance, have created hunger in communities founded two centuries ago by runaway slaves. Actively supported by powerful multinational mining interests eager to seize title to lands that the Brazilian constitution recognizes as communal property, the reserves withhold an array of natural resources from the fishermen, subsistence farmers, and extractivists who have long cultivated and preserved these riches.[2] At the same time, the mining companies, which ostentatiously defend endangered animals such as caimans and mountain lions, continue to turn whole lakes and rivers red with bauxite wastes.

"Edenic narratives," as I would call them, are presentations of a natural or seemingly natural landscape in terms that consciously—or, more often, unconsciously—evoke the biblical account of Eden. These narratives underlie and color much of what we accept as fact about particular people and places. Because of Amazonia's spectacular topography and immense biological variety, it is especially likely to generate these sorts of Edenic accounts.[3] And yet, while my focus here is on a very specific corner of the globe, the dynamic I describe in the following pages is by no means limited to an Amazonia that is both geographic entity and province of the imagination.

There are two major types of Edenic stories. The first sort is directly linked to the account of Adam and Eve that appears in Genesis. This story presupposes an initial state of harmony and perfection in which human beings live as one with other divine creations. Next, it posits the notion of human separability from, and potential mastery over, nature. These ideas are implicit in God's initially giving humankind dominion over "the fish of the sea, and over the fowl of the air, and over the cattle, and over all the earth, and over every creeping thing that creepeth upon the earth." Finally, "strict" accounts of Eden include an obligatory Fall from grace following Adam and Eve's refusal to obey the divine mandate not to eat of the Tree of Knowledge. They conclude with the exile from the garden that imposes upon human beings the necessity of labor and thus challenges their original mastery over nature.

The second sort of narrative offers a less ordered and less orthodox reworking of elements contained in the biblical story of the garden. While these "new Edenic" or "quasi-Edenic" stories recall aspects of the account in Genesis, they do not share its carefully prescribed beginning, middle, and end. Many of these tales are actually "after-Eden" stories that highlight nostalgia for a perfect past or deep fears about continuing loss. Such stories may imply hopes for the rediscovery of paradise (the recovery, for instance, of an original state of innocence and plenty through a return to nature). They also may focus on the construction of a new Eden through the alliance of nature with technology or the radical replacement of the first by the second.

Although this second category is far more inclusive than the first, not all stories of Amazonia, or of nature, are Edenic even in this considerably looser sense. The region's biodiversity, for instance, may foster a quasi-Edenic vision of a new garden to which the entire human race lays claim. But this same biological wealth also may inspire a variety of cyber-fables in which humans extract from a recalcitrant nature the elements through which they can construct their own new, unabashedly "unnatural" world. Biodiversity also may serve as the focus of an ecocentric story in which human beings find themselves forced to play an ambiguous or unaccustomed supporting role.

And yet, while it is possible to imagine various sorts of non-Edenic stories, a very high proportion of existing accounts of Amazonia are definitely Edenic or, more commonly, quasi-Edenic narratives. Landscapes with an unmistakable moral and aesthetic component appear in many cultures, and ideas of a sublime garden or a Land Without Evil are not inherently Judeo-Christian. The central paradox of the biblical story, however, which sees humans at once as integral parts of the natural world they seek to dominate and as forever alien from the rest of nature (which appears to turn upon them in the garden), is played out in extremely powerful ways in contemporary Western societies, including the United States.

Although Edenic stories are always cosmic dramas with panhuman implications, the presence of a universalizing impulse that implies the underlying presence of a single, master narrative about human beings and nature does not keep the elements from forming different constellations in different times and places. Moreover, different sorts of natural spaces may be Edenic (or non-Edenic) in different ways. Thus, while the two terms most frequently associated with Amazonia for much of its postconquest history—"wilderness" and "jungle"—both suggest Edenic underpinnings, they are by no means synonyms. Even though meanings change over time, the wilderness is apt to conjure up visions of a primeval landscape reminiscent of a world before the Fall. The jungle, in contrast, is in many ways a counterpoint to the garden that God fashioned as a home for human beings. Although it, like the wilderness, is an arena for adventure (Donald Duck's green labyrinth was, above all else, exciting), one does not embark on a safari in order to commune with nature and a more "natural" past.

In the minds of most present-day Americans, the wilderness's most salient characteristic is its lack of direct utility. Originally a place of wild beasts (from the Old English *wilddēoren*), it is "a tract or region uncultivated and uninhabited by human beings" or, as the U.S. Wilderness Act proclaims, "a place where man remains a visitor." As such, it necessarily lies on the fringes of civilization. Both the savage, desolate plain and the pristine, majestic Yosemite of an Ansel Adams photograph are foils to, and potential respites from, an agitated world of routines and obligations. Although wild spaces may be good for inspiration and re-creation, they steadfastly eschew more direct sorts of intervention. Even minor human alterations make a wild place something else.

As early as the beginning of the twentieth century, the word "wilderness" had come to signal not just an invitation to adventure but also an incipient nostalgia for unspoiled origins. In the account of his voyage of discovery through Amazonia, entitled *Through the Brazilian Wilderness,* Theodore Roosevelt dwells on the challenges that "blood-crazy fish" and "brutish" caimans pose for the "true wilderness wanderer."[4] At the same time, however, he expresses definite twinges of nostalgia for an older past he finds embodied in the Nambikwara tribe. The nakedness of these Amazonian Indians (who would fascinate the French anthropologist Claude Lévi-Strauss in his own later quest for origins) causes Roosevelt to compare them to "Adam and Eve before the Fall."[5] "It was an interesting sight," he remarks, "to see these utterly *wild, friendly savages,* circling in their slow dance, and chanting their *immemorial melodies,* in the brilliant tropical moonlight, with the river rushing by in the background, through the lonely heart of the wilderness."[6]

In contrast to a supposedly empty wilderness that sets Roosevelt to musing on an "immeasurably remote" past, the jungle evokes a still-savage present. The Sanskrit root *jangala,* meaning "dry" or "desert," recalls the original sense of wilderness as a barren wasteland. And yet, while the jungle, like the wilderness, may be "the dwelling-place of wild beasts," the term has acquired connotations of excess that contrast with the wilderness's spare, essential quality. Similar in sound to both "jumble" and "jangle" (one older spelling is actually "jangal"), "jungle" suggests a tortuous complexity. Although travelers may lose their way in either a wilderness or a jungle, the latter is distinguished less by the vast solitude that makes it a fitting stage for either contemplation or heroic action than by its disordered and disorienting growth.

Both the wilderness and the jungle possess strong moral connotations.

The wilderness, for its part, has retained vestiges of the desolation and peril that formerly made a wilderness condition "one of straits, wants, deep distresses, and most deadly dangers."[7] Even the most enthusiastic participants in the present-day encounter groups and academic conferences devoted to "Recovering the Wild" would probably steer clear of a moral wilderness.

To the extent that it suggests an unsullied, original state, the wilderness possesses a decidedly Edenic aura. The multitudes of tourists who set off for Yellowstone or the Grand Canyon to commune with nature are seeking a sense of freedom and of temporary isolation, a carefully bounded space in which to feel unbounded. ("Oh for a lodge in some vast wilderness," exclaimed one English poet well over two centuries ago.)[8]

If wilderness has become increasingly attractive to Americans of various social classes, the jungle has retained, and even intensified, its negative connotations. While some jungles hold out the promise of discovery and forbidden pleasures (and in this sense it is possible to imagine a "jungle getaway" and a "jungle haven"), many others are off-putting. In its guise as Green Hell—a frequent epithet for Amazonia during the first part of this century— the jungle is an emphatically nonparadisal space. A figurative as well as literal maze (of housing laws, for instance), it is also a place of ruthless struggle for survival ("Man, it's a real jungle out there," one may say with a grimace). Rife with disease ("jungle fever") and decay ("jungle rot"), it is home to beasts and unsavory characters such as hoboes or tramps. Whereas the human inhabitants of a wilderness tend to embody its positive aspects (they are "natural," though always uncommon, people), jungle dwellers are more apt to incarnate its off-putting traits. The dark-skinned, when not black-hearted, native inhabitants of Joseph Conrad's *Heart of Darkness* are thus not only physically other but morally ambiguous.[9]

The far-reaching implications of the terms "jungle" and "wilderness" are evident in news items and TV documentaries with names such as "Wilderness Sojourn," "Jungle Yields to Civilization," and "Bigtime Industry Invades Emerald Wilds." To illustrate some of these divergences as they relate to Amazonia, I have chosen to take a close look at two short newspaper articles about Amazonian Indians. Islands of type in a sea of ads for luxury services and items, these pieces on the Kayapó and Yanomami emphasize the larger context of international capitalism in which U.S. discussions of the Amazon occur. Written in the early 1990s, they were among half a dozen news items I first selected as "found objects" on the basis of their physical appearance. On further reflection, however, I came to view these reports as particularly striking illustrations of superficially contradictory, yet fundamentally similar, approaches to native peoples.[10] The narrative analysis that follows emphasizes the presence of Edenic elements that reappear in countless discussions of the Amazon as well as of various other, apparently unrelated environmental and nature issues.

The first piece, "Brazil Creates Reserve for Imperiled Amazon Tribe," describes the Brazilian government's establishment of a reserve for the

Yanomami Indians. Its author, James Brooke, regularly writes about the Amazon for the *New York Times*. The second, "Battle over Rich Brazilian Lands," by Jack Epstein of the *San Francisco Chronicle*, focuses on the Kayapó Indians' commercial dealings. Although both reporters also refer to Amazonia as a rain forest—a term to which I later return—the first identifies the land as "wilderness," while the other alludes to one group of Amazonian Indians as "jungle maharajahs." Whereas the "Stone Age Yanomami" conjure up a primordial past, the Kayapó have eaten from the Tree of Capitalism occupying the jungle's verdant heart.

The Brooke article chronicles the creation of an Indian reserve in the extreme north of Amazonia. By substituting the term "imperiled Amazon tribe" for the more specific "Yanomami" in his title, the author emphasizes the broader outlines of the conflict and the largely generic quality of the people whom it involves. At the same time, his repeated references to the land as wilderness signals its primal character and foregrounds the issue of its use. How, one wonders, can the Yanomami lay claim to an area that is implicitly unsettled? They can do so, suggests the author, because their nomadic interactions with the landscape do not alter it in a lasting way. On

Brazil Creates Reserve for Imperiled Amazon Tribe

By JAMES BROOKE
Special to The New York Times

SAO PAULO, Nov. 17 — Overriding mining interests and military protests, President Fernando Collor de Mello has moved to reserve a stretch of Amazon rain forest as a homeland for the Yanomami Indians, a tribe virtually untouched by modern civilization whose ways date from the Stone Age.

The new reserve, coupled with a slightly smaller park across the border, in Venezuela, will allow the Yanomami, South America's last major untouched tribe, to roam freely over 68,331 square miles of Amazon wilderness, an area the size of Missouri.

"We struggled for 20 years for what has just happened," said Claudia Andujar, coordinator of the Commission for the Creation of a Yanomami Park, a private group based here.

With the fate of South America's 23,000 Yanomami an international cause, Napoleon A. Chagnon, an American anthropologist, echoed widespread American and European euphoria when he said today in a telephone interview, "This will go a long way to making cultural survival of the Yanomami a real possibility."

Military Resists Move

But not everyone was clapping in Brasilia on Friday when Mr. Collor signed a decree reserving 1 percent of Brazil's land mass for the nation's estimated 9,000 Yanomami. At the signing ceremony, Gen. Carlos Tinoco, the Army Minister, pointedly abstained from joining the applause.

Charging that foreign interests secretly seek to create an independent Yanomami nation, influential elements of Brazil's military have argued that Brazil should clear a 12-mile-wide border strip to separate Brazil's Yanomami from Venezuela's Yanomami.

Searching for a mission after the collapse of international Communism, Brazil's conservative generals are increasingly taking nationalist stands on the Amazon.

"The innocence and purity of some idealists is exploited in order to keep dormant the potential of the Brazilian Amazon," warned a recent study by the Superior War College, Brazil's elite military institute.

Describing Indian and other reserves as "liberated zones" under international control, the military document predicted, "It would take a great Brazilian effort for their elimination, probably resorting to war."

But the army's political standing has been weakened in recent days by newspaper reports of fixed bidding practices for equipment procurements.

Rebuffing the army's national security arguments, Mr. Collor's announcement came on the national holiday marking the military's abolition of Brazil's monarchy in 1889.

Brazilian "sovereignty continues intact, and even reinforced," Mr. Collor said of the park. Two weeks ago, he approved 71 other Indian reserves, covering 42,471 square miles.

Mr. Collor ignored economic objections raised by governors of two states where the park will be located, Amazonas and Roraima.

Rich in gold, tin, diamonds and zinc, the park area is virtually papered with 698 requests by mining companies for exploration rights. Once an area becomes an Indian reserve, mining contracts are subject to approval by Indian communities and mediation by Brazil's Indian protection agency, Funai.

The New York Times
Reserves in Brazil and Venezuela have been set aside for the tribe.

Single-Handedly

Invented by Breguet, the "Jump Hour" automatic watch with hour display and minute hand. Crafted in platinum with a porcelain dial, from a limited series numbered by the maker, $46,000. Enlarged to show detail.

TIFFANY & CO.

NEW YORK · FIFTH AVENUE AND 57TH STREET · 800-526-0649 · ©T & CO. 1991

James Brooke, "Brazil Creates Reserve for Imperiled Amazon Tribe," with accompanying Tiffany & Co. advertisement. (*New York Times, November 19, 1991, © 1991 by the New York times Company and Tiffany & Co., reprinted by permission*) some level, then, not only is the land Yanomami but the Yanomami *are* the land, which resists history and change itself.

The very first sentence of the article identifies the Yanomami as "a tribe virtually untouched by modern civilization." In the Edenic divide between nature and culture, they thus weigh in on the side of nature. This identification is particularly interesting, given the Yanomami's former media image as a particularly fierce and savage people.[11] Although Brooke does not go so far as to call these Indians *un*civilized, "South America's last major untouched tribe" remains emphatically separate from the surrounding world.

Not unlike the deer and buffalo that meander through that classic celebration of the U.S. frontier—"Home on the Range"—the Yanomami want nothing more than "to roam freely." But if the tribe cheerfully ignores the gold, tin, and diamonds glittering beneath the surface of its ancestral homeland, a host of mining companies metaphorically litter its surface with petitions for exploration rights.

Misplaced fears about national security prompt similar opposition from Brazilian military leaders. Their demand for a twelve-mile-wide border would not only divide a people who long have inhabited a region spanning part of present-day Brazil and Venezuela but also transform a preserve of nature into a military enclave and geopolitical entity. President Fernando Collor's refusal to accede to pressure exerted by the formerly all-powerful armed forces elates Brazilian environmental groups while creating "widespread American and European euphoria."

From the standpoint of its analysis as an Edenic (or quasi-Edenic) narrative, this article reveals two particularly interesting facets. The first is the absence of the Yanomami from the persons the reporter quotes or paraphrases. The second is the framing of a debate about a people's destiny exclusively in terms of land.

The Yanomami are conspicuously silent in an article that purports to describe their plight. Although Brooke cites many different individuals, not one belongs to the tribe. Moreover, despite the American anthropologist Napoleon A. Chagnon's assertion that the creation of a reserve "will go a long way to making *cultural* survival [my italics] of the Yanomami a real possibility," the article says almost nothing about culture. Instead, the terms in which both their advocates and their opponents evoke the Yanomami are strongly reminiscent of U.S. debates about endangered species. Because U.S. conservation laws protect not habitats but species, much debate over land usage hinges on threats to the survival of particular life forms.

The Yanomami in this article come across very much like another particularly noteworthy biological entity whose survival happens to require the protection of a very large amount of land. Just as endangered species do not argue on their own behalf, so the tribe's non-Indian supporters speak for them in this article. "Untouched by modern civilization," the Indians cannot be expected to join a thoroughly present-day debate. But the 23,000

Yanomami also remain silent because, in the end, the real focus of the article is less on their destiny as a people than on the fate of that vast habitat whose future is interwined with theirs. The tribe's "imperiled" status demands and reaffirms the continuing identity of that part of Amazonia as wilderness on the map that serves as the article's lone illustration.

To the extent that the Yanomami's survival guarantees the continued preservation of the rain forest as wilderness, the tribe's position is not unlike that of the songbird called the California gnatcatcher. As the presence of the gnatcatcher on the endangered species list blocks its nesting ground from real estate development, and as its loss of privileged status opens these same lands to large-scale human exploitation, a great deal rests upon a pair of tiny wings. "All that space for a mere bird?" demand pro-development interests. "What about the thousands of people who would benefit from projects on that same land?" "The gnatcatcher's very existence is threatened by the assault upon its fragile habitat," reply conservationists. "How can we, who share this planet, knowingly participate in its extinction?"

I do not mean to imply that Brooke or any other of the individuals in this article would equate the Yanomami with gnatcatchers or other animal species. Nonetheless, a sense of the ways in which the role of the Yanomami is structurally not unlike that of the gnatcatcher helps explain their silence here. Likewise, an awareness of the power of other, simultaneous debates over wilderness and endangered species outside the confines of Amazonia aids in understanding how the Brazilian government could perceive the creation of an Indian reserve as strengthening national sovereignty. Clearly, the park implies the loss of immediate revenues. But through the ostentatious subordination of national interests and short-term economic gain to more global, international concerns, Brazil stands to reap potentially greater profits in terms of future investments by foreign agencies anxious to appear sensitive to indigenous populations and environmental issues.

The newspaper article "Battle over Rich Brazilian Lands" appears to tell a very different story. If the central problem associated with the wilderness is use, the major difficulty posed by jungles is the riotous abundance that impedes clear passage or clear view. Accordingly, the subtitle "Indians Accused of Being 'Jungle Maharajahs'" conjures up a tangled snarl of economic interests very different from the Yanomami's pristine, if endangered, space. In contrast to their "primitive" and "dirt-poor" cousins, the money-hungry Kayapó find themselves enmeshed in a seemingly impenetrable thicket of opposing economic, demographic, and environmental interests.

The separate narrative structures of the two articles underscore differences in the authors' presentations of the two tribes. Whereas Brooke presents the Brazilian chief executive as a voice of reason in the triumphant creation of a Yanomami reserve, Epstein offers a range of opinions that appear more or less equally weighted. While, for instance, some environmentalists denounce the Kayapó's activities as "absurd, illegal, immoral and wrong," one senior scientist for the Environmental Defense Fund calls attention to

A8 San Francisco Chronicle ★★★★★   WORLD   WEDNESDAY, DECEMBER 29, 1993

Battle Over Rich Brazilian Lands

Indians accused of being 'jungle maharajahs'

By Jack Epstein
Chronicle Foreign Service
A-Ukre, Brazil

Environmentalists say they are heretics. Brazilian officials accuse them of breaking the law. Others call them politically incorrect Indians.

But the chiefs in this remote Kayapo Indian village in the southern Amazon basin say they just want to make a buck. And they do not mind selling the trees and gold around them to do so.

By keeping 15 percent of the gold that miners find on the tribe's 42,000-square-mile reserve and charging loggers $50 per cubic foot of mahogany, the 14 Kayapo Indians will earn an estimated $15 million a year.

The Brazilian constitution bans commercial use of natural resources by outsiders on Indian reserves unless those uses are approved by Congress.

The illegal extraction operations on their constitutionally protected reserve have allowed the 6,000-member tribe to become the richest among Brazil's 250,000 Indians — and have put the Kayapo at the center of a national debate about indigenous rights.

The Kayapo have managed to displease environmentalists who expect them to be natural conservationists and Brazilian politicians who believe that Indians have been given control over too much of the vast Amazon region.

Kayapo leaders defend their actions by pointing out that the government is broke and that its agency for Indian affairs, FUNAI, halted most aid and programs in the early 1980s.

In such a situation, asked longtime tribal spokesman Paulinho Paiakan, "Isn't what we are doing better than asking for a handout?"

The debate over the use of Indi-

an lands comes at a tense time for this country's estimated 180 tribes.

Human rights groups say that 84 percent of Indian reserves have been invaded by small farmers, prospectors and loggers. In August, 16 members of the Yanomami tribe — a primitive group that has had little contact with the outside world — were killed by Brazilian gold miners across the northern border in Venezuela.

And a current congressional review of the 1988 constitution, due to conclude in March, may eventually strip away millions of acres set aside as Indian reserves.

The Kayapo say the criticism against them are a ploy by non-Indians to wrest control of their lucrative enterprises.

"Why is this question of use now?" asked Stephen Schwartzman, senior scientist for the Environmental Defense Fund in Washington. The local elite wants their land and the mahogany. There are many economic interests at play."

Backed by major landowners and mining and logging firms, Amazon politicians are leading the movement to revise the constitutional statute that gives Brazil's indigenous peoples — who account for 0.3 percent of the population — 198 million acres, or 10 percent of the nation's land surface.

"There's too much land for too few Indians," Gilberto Mestrinho, governor of Amazonas state, recently told a Pan-American conference on rain forest development. "Show me another country that does that."

Mestrinho's message has caught on in Congress. A recent poll of 436 congressmen by the Folha de São Paulo newspaper found 47 percent in favor of reducing the size of Indian lands and only 29 percent supporting the current allocation.

Indian defenders, however, say that shrinking the existing boundaries would be unjust.

"They used to own all of it," declared Francisco de Oliveira, the

FUNAI director in Redenção, a market center at the edge of the Amazon, 190 miles from A-Ukre. "I would ask those who would change the law: Who's got the other 90 percent?"

A survey by the Indianist Missionary Council shows that less than 1 percent of Brazil's landowners control almost 49 percent of these, 151 individuals own properties with more than 247,000 acres, according to the nation's leading news magazine, Veja.

In the state of Acre, for example, a businessman named Pedro Aparecido Dotto owns a ranch the size of El Salvador.

But critics say the Kayapo are allowing the rain forest to be destroyed for money.

Brazilian journalists have dubbed the tribe "Kayapo Inc." and its leaders "jungle maharajahs." Articles tell of chiefs who frequent brothels in Redenção and buy airplanes, city apartments and cars.

Ecologists embarrassed by the

Kayapos' commercial stratagems are pressuring the government to overturn the tribe's contracts with outsiders. They recently won several lawsuits in which loggers have been heavily fined for doing business with Indians.

"What the Kayapo are doing is absurd, illegal, immoral and wrong," said Congressman Fabio Feldman, a leading environmentalist.

A visit to A-Ukre, or "the place where the river bottom is noisy" in the Kayapo language, will never bring to mind the image of Fortune 500 corporate headquarters.

The village is accessible only by small plane from Redenção, and its 200 residents live crowded together in about 30 large thatched-roof huts arranged in a circle. The only trace of modern consumerism is a large TV set hooked up to a satellite dish near the village center.

When village chiefs recently allowed two American reporters to

visit, they echoed the self-empowerment arguments made by American Indians who have built casinos and bingo parlors on their reservations.

They conceded that some chiefs had enriched themselves, but they claimed that most proceeds are spent on such necessities as food, medicine and schools.

The chiefs also say their business acumen has kept them from the same fate as the dirt-poor Yanomami.

"You never hear of a Kayapo being killed by gold miners or loggers," said Divino Ferreira, owner of a Redenção lumber company. "Everyone accepts their contracts."

The reluctance of outsiders to use force against the Kayapo is explained largely by the tribe's high media profile. Visitors to the tribal reserve have included camera crews from Britain's Granada TV and pop star Sting.

Kayapo men sat under the canopy near the village center of A-Ukre weaving bamboo strips to decorate their wooden spears; in a nod to modern life, the tribe purchased a satellite dish

BY JACK EPSTEIN/SPECIAL TO THE CHRONICLE

Jack Epstein, "Battle over Rich Brazilian Lands," with accompanying Jewelry Exchange advertisement. (*San Francisco Chronicle, December 29, 1993, reprinted with permission of San Francisco Chronicle, Jack Epstein, and the Jewelry Exchange*)

the local economic interests at play behind the outcry. In response to conservative politicians' complaints that there is "too much land for too few Indians," the tribe's supporters point out that one percent of Brazilian landowners control almost half of the country's surface.

At first glance, the Kayapó—who do indeed speak out here—appear to embrace modernity. Clever naïfs of a sort more apt to appear on travel pages than in international news items, they appropriate Western technology in a manner meant to be disjunctive and, on some level, amusing to the newspaper reader. "Isn't what we are doing better than asking for a handout?" they demand with an indignation worthy of any poor-but-proud American scrambling to stay off the county welfare roles.

And yet, at the same time that the Kayapó consort with rock stars and foreign television reporters, these eager converts to modern civilization remain staunch traditionalists. Despite repeated forays into the prickly undergrowth of venture capitalism, tribe members continue to speak in unison, inhabit remote places with exotic names that underscore their distance from mainstream society, and, for all their wealth, embrace "primitive," communal ways.

Significantly, even though the Kayapó speak out in a manner that sets them apart from the Yanomami, they always do so as a collectivity. While the great majority of voices in the article are those of individuals ("Gilberto Mestrinho, governor of Amazonas state," "Congressman Fábio Feldmann, a leading environmentalist"), the only Kayapó identified by name is a "long-time tribal spokesman." The reporter's claim that anonymous village chiefs echo the self-empowerment arguments of U.S. Indians further suggests the existence of a single, tribal voice.

The Kayapó's continuing residence in exotic-sounding locations adds a note of appealing local color. The obviously non-European roots of the name A-Ukre ("the place where the river bottom is noisy") stresses the continuing separation of "this remote Kayapó Indian village" from mainstream Brazilian society. The accompanying photograph of two non-European-looking men in native dress weaving bamboo strips to decorate their wooden spears reemphasizes the Kayapó's cultural and physical distance from the outside world, which appears in the background in the form of a satellite dish. The reporter goes on to explain that even though A-Ukre's two hundred residents have become rich by most standards, they still choose to live "crowded together" in large thatched-roof huts arranged in a circle. By implication, money—and the new technologies symbolized by the TV dish—have not significantly altered the tribe's deep, and deeply Edenic, association with the land.

Epstein at no point mentions the fierce, long-standing debates between the spokesman Paiakan and tribal members with different viewpoints. Limiting his focus to one of a string of Kayapó villages, not all of which have such poetic names, he stresses A-Ukre's distance from the city of Redenção rather than its often troubling proximity to various smaller population centers. As a glance at the photograph of these "traditional" people reveals rubber sandals on the feet of the two men in the foreground, a coffee thermos among the bamboo, and a third Indian in shirt, pants, and shoes, the satellite dish is clearly neither "the only trace of modern consumerism" nor a mere "nod to modern life."

The systematic exclusion of a series of non-Edenic and potentially contradictory elements from his account of the Kayapó suggests that the reporter's focus is ultimately less on this particular group of people than on the "Rich Brazilian Lands" they control. Thus, while the second item says considerably more about the Kayapó than the first does about the Yanomami, both are less about indigenous communities than about apparently irreconcilable economic and environmental claims.

Despite a number of obvious differences between the two accounts of Indian territories, both set up a conflict in which the U.S. reader ultimately is not forced to take sides. Although military officers and miners want one thing in the first piece and the Yanomami's supporters another, "Brazilian sovereignty continues intact, and even reinforced" in reference to the park. In like manner, while different parties express opposing viewpoints about the Kayapó, the fact remains that Brazilian Indians legally cannot sell the resources on lands officially designated tribal property. The law-abiding, ecologically minded outsider therefore need not choose between the Kayapó's right to remain upon the lands to which they have been given formal title and the state's obligation to prohibit commercial activities that endanger natural riches.

In the end, the Kayapó need protection from unscrupulous outsiders who would lure them into a treacherous thicket of illegal ventures. As a result, environmentalists serving as self-appointed stewards of both forest and forest dwellers "have won several lawsuits" against logging interests. To the degree that members of the tribe come across as vulnerable newcomers to a jungle rife with human predators, the article recalls similar accounts of abuses perpetrated against U.S. Indian groups.

A report entitled "Managers of Indian Casino Are Indicted," which appears alongside an account of the gnatcatcher controversy in Orange County on the front page of a recent issue of the *Los Angeles Times*, provides a good point of comparison. As the title indicates, its subject is the fraudulent actions of a group of non-Indian managers who set up an intermediary firm to lease "illegal gambling devices" to the Palm Springs Morongo tribe. Exploiting the series of court decisions that give native groups control over their own lands (and thus the right to establish and operate its own casinos), nefarious outsiders quickly turn what was "merely a card room and bingo hall" into a morass of fast-paced electronic wagering machines.[12] In the process, they cheat the unsuspecting tribe out of millions of dollars.

Although the article says nothing whatsoever about nature or environmental issues, it recalls the Kayapó piece not only in its presentation of native peoples as easy targets for unscrupulous, wilier others but also in its description of the competing legal, economic, and social interests for which they serve as pawns. No one argues that the Morongo have jurisdiction over their own land, but the desire to channel gambling proceeds into state coffers makes California officials hostile to the idea of independent Indian casinos. Just as international environmental groups committed to protecting biologically rich lands may express their true interests through a focus on the land's inhabitants, so these officials present their desire to control gambling—and their unsolicited removal of the slot machines associated with the crooked managers—as a concern for supposedly vulnerable Indians. In this manner, both the Morongo and the Kayapó are drawn into much larger legal tangles, in which the real issue is the exact uses of the lands that are theirs by law.

On the surface, the Yanomami fulfill Edenic expectations by providing a handy bridge to a past free of polluted oceans, cancer clusters, and toxic dumps. The Kayapó, in contrast, challenge outsiders' expectations by cheerfully peddling the mahogany and gold they "should," by virtue of their identity as Indians, conserve. In the last analysis, however, the authors share a vision of the Amazon as a threatened paradise that demands protection, whether from greedy outsiders or from its own traditional guardians, caught up in the invasive thorns and nettles of economic change.

In their presentation of Indians as embodiments of the landscape and unfailing champions of nature, our two examples resemble countless other news reports on Amazonia. Still, while their authors are in no way alone in their presentations of Amazonia as a wilderness or jungle, the dominant image of the region today is unquestionably the rain forest. For this reason it is worth considering some of the associations that make the rain forest different from a wilderness or a jungle (either of which it may also, technically, be). Although it has absorbed and transformed a number of older meanings associated with these other terms, the rain forest has at the same time acquired a life of its own.

At first glance, "rain forest" (*floresta pluvial,* in Spanish and Portuguese) is about as straightforward and noncontroversial a term as one could hope to find. And yet, this "woodland with an annual rainfall of one hundred inches, marked by lofty, broad-leaved evergreen trees forming a continuous canopy" has acquired, over the last two decades, ever stronger Edenic overtones.[13] While Amazonians themselves tend to employ the decidedly unsensational *mata* ("woods"), outsiders' growing use of "rain forest" as a synonym for Amazonia marks important changes in the way that many persons see the region. This shift also underscores yet deeper transformations in prevailing ideas of what nature is, or ought to be.

Unlike "wilderness" and "jungle," whose ancient histories generate multipage dictionary citations, "rain forest" is a relatively modern term. Entries in the *OED* span less than a century and occupy a comparatively scant space on the page. Although the first example cited, a translation from the German *Regenwald,* bears a date of 1898, and although botanists and plant biologists have used the word for the last century, "rain forest" did not makes its way into a number of dictionaries before the late seventies and early eighties.[14] Its increasing popular usage coincides with the emergence of environmentalism as a powerful political and social movement, as well as with a giant spurt in state-sponsored economic development throughout many rain forest regions, including, above all, the Amazon.

The single most important difference between a rain forest and a wilderness resides in the former's greater openness to use. A rain forest may sustain different sorts of settlement and cultivation without any threat to its identity. Although trees are essential to a forest, an unspecified number can disappear without the forest's requiring a new name. Thus, while some rain forests may be wildernesses and others jungles, the term permits a far greater manipulation of nature.

The rain forest's potential for varying degrees of exploitation suggests the presence of new economic, as well as environmental, interests in Amazonia. The compression of two words into a single noun is, in many ways, a marketing phenomenon. Not by coincidence, the composite form "rainforest" has increasingly come to double as an adjective. Cost Plus importers, for instance, carry an entire line of Brazilian Rainforest gels, lotions, shampoos, and, improbably, "sea salts." The Rainforest Products wagon (purveyor of rattles, whistles, seed and feather ornaments, and potpourri in rainbow-colored packets) does a brisk business in southern California shopping malls, while Rainforest Crunch has found a niche in numerous specialty shops and upscale supermarkets. Various tourist agencies now offer "rainforest ecotours." Lavishly illustrated books with titles such as *Tropical Rainforest* and *Rainforests: A Celebration* are available in nature boutiques and bookstores. And the Environmental Affairs division of the McDonald's fast-food chain began handing out fliers entitled "Our rainforest policy" in 1990.[15]

Not just its commercial applications but also the seeming scientific rigor that puts "rain forest" in the same class as "environment" and "biome" makes it attractive to a non-Amazonian public reared on high technology. What, after all, could be less subjective than calibrated moisture? The rain forest's aura of neutrality distinguishes it from the jungle as well as from the wilderness, both of which, as we have seen, have strong, and sometimes quite negative, moral connotations.

Its freedom from heavily weighted, often pejorative associations allows users of the term "rain forest" to signal a different sort of relationship to nature. Over the past few decades the rain forest has acquired a conspicuously more positive, as well as more resolutely tropical, air.[16] As a result, while both jungle and rain forest have come to be defined as specifically tropical woodlands, one is an emerald haven or "living cathedral," in which countless scores of living things take refuge, whereas the other is a tangled hell.[17] In contrast to a jungle, which normally throws up a series of barriers to humans, rain forests oppose impenetrable growth with exuberant abundance.

Beautiful in the extreme, the rain forest is also intensely vulnerable. Because its stability depends on a complex equilibrium, a single false step can destroy the fragile fulcrum on which its majesty is poised. Most jungles are collections of haphazard growth that can protect themselves all too well against trespassers. Wildernesses need above all to be left to their own devices (thus, the need to establish reserves such as the Yanomami park). The rain forest, however, demands considerably more of humans. The call "Save the Rainforest!"—emblazoned on countless T-shirts, shopping bags, and rain forest confections—underscores a perceived need for active intervention.

This rain forest, which has become increasingly ensconced in the popular imagination, is also distinguished by its radiance. Free of the suffocating darkness that engulfs the jungle explorer, its glistening greenery exudes a perpetual mist suggesting breath and life. The iridescent birds perched above gleaming waterfalls distinguish it from the deep and tangled jungle, whose shadowy depths strike fear into intruders. The redemptive light at the end of a dark tunnel of environmental destruction, the rain forest holds out the hope that all has not been lost and that even catastrophic damage may somehow be erased. Its luminous distance encourages the outsider to imagine a struggle between obvious victims (the "virgin land") and equally obvious villains (miners, loggers, ranchers) in which he or she is in no way complicit.

The flier that describes the McDonald's Corporation's rain forest policy offers striking proof of the force of this radiant image. Widely distributed in hamburger restaurants throughout the United States as well as various foreign countries between 1990 and 1993, and still available in many locations, this flier portrays a shimmering woodland on its front side.[18] An explanation of the company's commitment to environmental principles appears upon the back. The light that fans out beneath the caption "Our rainforest policy" reveals a jewel-toned bower, which promises delectation and refreshment. Bright as the golden arches that proclaim McDonald's presence on the landscape, this appealing scene awakens both concern and admiration.

The problem with this picture—and with the Edenic notions implicit in it—is its dubious relationship to anything resembling a readily recognizable rain forest. Because the heavy canopy of a rain forest normally blocks out the sort of light that floods the leafy floor here, permitting very little surface vegetation of the type that abounds here, this picture appears to be of some other sort of woodland. The lack of epiphytes ("air plants" that grow on other plants or objects on which they depend for support), which are standard in most rain forests, confirms this impression.[19]

The trees in question are actually temperate conifers completely alien to the tropics for which the flip side of the flier expresses such deep concern.[20]

Our rainforest policy. 5

Tropical rainforests play an important role in the Earth's ecology. And their destruction threatens the delicate environmental balance of our planet.

For the record: NOWHERE IN THE WORLD DOES McDONALD'S® PURCHASE BEEF RAISED ON RAINFOREST (OR RECENTLY DEFORESTED RAINFOREST) LAND.

In fact, McDonald's has a strict corporate policy against using rainforest beef.

"...it is McDonald's policy to use only locally produced and processed beef in every country where we have restaurants. In those isolated areas where domestic beef is not available, it is imported from approved McDonald's suppliers from other countries. In all cases, however, McDonald's does not, has not, and will not permit the destruction of tropical rainforests for our beef supply... This policy is strictly enforced and closely monitored. Any McDonald's supplier who is found to deviate from this policy or cannot prove compliance with it will be immediately discontinued."

In the U.S., we use only 100% pure U.S. domestic beef. In Canada, we use only 100% pure Canadian beef. And in Europe, we use only European Economic Community grown and approved beef.

McDonald's will continue to monitor its beef suppliers and adopt policies and practices aimed at protecting the global environment on which we all depend.

FOR MORE INFORMATION WRITE:
McDonald's Environmental Affairs,
McDonald's Corporation, Oak Brook, Illinois 60521.

© 1990 McDonald's Corporation

"Our rainforest policy." *(Courtesy McDonald's Corporation, © 1989)*

Compounding the irony, the abundance of new growth belies some sort of relatively recent disturbance. Although this disturbance may have had natural causes, non-natural causes—above all, logging—remain a distinct possibility. The image chosen to illustrate the call to preserve "the delicate environmental balance of our planet" is therefore, more accurately, a portrait of destruction.

The drawback of Edenic imagery is definitely not a lack of power to move viewers. Like the newspaper reports about the Kayapó and the Yanomami, McDonald's sunstruck forest encourages concern for rain forests in general, if not for Amazonia in particular. To the degree that both the flier and these articles trigger interest in an area of the world that otherwise might seem hopelessly remote, Edenic images are positive and useful.

The real difficulty with Edenic representations is not even that they are partially untrue, if not downright false. Romanticizations of a particular place and people, they dehumanize through idealization. But, as I suggested at the outset of this discussion, they are yet more destructive in their tendency to supplant something that actually exists.

The very notion of Amazonia as "the rain forest"—or "the wilderness" or "the jungle"—greatly oversimplifies the region's complex patchwork of forest, scrublands, floodplains, and savannas. Each of these terms' stress upon the landscape tends to underplay or deny the role of the human beings who have transformed it over many centuries. The widely different cities that are now home to over half the Amazonian population have no place in the worlds any of the three suggests, except as demonic counterpoints to an idyllic countryside. Furthermore, those human beings who do appear in this narrow scheme are usually forced into too-simple, Manichean roles. Instead of complex groups and individuals with varying needs and desires, they become endangered species or unfaithful guardians.

My purpose in this brief analysis is not to single out for criticism examples chosen precisely for their resemblance to countless others. The ubiquity and real appeal of images such as the ones that appear here lead one to wonder what escape there may be from Edenic thinking.

The most obvious answer is that no total escape is possible. Eden may be so entrenched in Western ways of thinking about nature that it is impossible wholly to elude it. Although one can be more or less aware of the power of Edenic logic—and this awareness makes a great difference in how we portray and understand ourselves as well as others—the idea that we could invent another language is dubious at best.[21] Even if we were to ban the words "wilderness," "jungle," and "rain forest" from all writing on the Amazon in favor of a wholly different vocabulary, it is quite likely that our new words would soon carry the old meanings.

Moreover, it is not certain that wholesale dismissal of Edenic metaphors in regard to Amazonia would be advisable, even if it were possible. They are too tightly bound up with the history of the Amazon and our own conceptions of the relationship between human beings and nature to be dismissed so simply. In addition, Edenic schemes may be appropriated for a wide variety of ends. Indians and rubber tappers, in particular, have shown themselves to be admirably fluent in Greenspeak and Edenese. If newspaper reporters and TV cameramen want them to act as extensions of the natural landscape, they obligingly don parrot feather halos in dramatic appearances before the Brazilian Congress or quickly invent "time-honored rituals" such as hanging rubber trees with long black ribbons that force outsiders to decry the death of Chico Mendes.[22]

The fact that the Yanomami appear silent in some outsiders' presentations of them does not stop them from exploiting their imposed role as embodiments of the land. Likewise, the epithet "jungle maharajahs" does not keep the Kayapó from publicly chiding government officials for their anti-environmental policies. Outsiders' tendency to see Indians much as they see whales or dolphins may distress or amuse native peoples, who nonetheless remain ready and willing to use others' perceptions of them to further their own ends.

What is important, then, is an awareness not only of the power and depth of Edenic thinking but of our susceptibility to paradisal images that speak to our own needs and desires. It is well worth asking not just *how* we can save the rain forest but *why* we want to do so. Whom do we wish to benefit? And why focus our efforts on Amazonia instead of Africa, Antarctica, or northern California? Before we try to answer these essential questions, however, we must ask what we mean by "the rain forest." What exactly do we think we want to safeguard? It will be hard enough to reverse the acrid course of recent history in Amazonia. But it is impossible to rescue something that does not exist.

My conclusion takes the form of a personal confession. When I first started doing research in the Amazon some seven years ago, I had very little intrinsic interest in environmental issues or even in nature. For me, Amazonia was a skinny child selling chewing gum and forest herbs on a city sidewalk and the heartbeat of a boat's motor in the almost cool of night. The Amazon was also a lone fisherman casting his net upon a mercury-curdled river and international mining interests that continued to further their own economic programs through strategic references to ecology. It troubled me that many of my students, friends, and neighbors did not seem aware of anything beyond The Rain Forest or particularly interested in how environmental questions impinged not just on trees and animals but on countless human lives.

Over time I have come to appreciate the degree to which today's common images of Amazonia build on very fundamental conceptions of nature. In the process, I have become increasingly interested in far larger definitions and debates about the natural world and the multiple natures of that thing we are quick to call nature. It is my hope that if an interest in Amazonia can prompt a growing concern for, and engagement in, a whole range of environmental problems, the opposite also can occur. The individual who begins to recognize Edenic narratives in many different places will necessarily see Amazonia with new eyes. And, in place of paradise, there will be—among many other things—the child, the boat, the river.

Reinventing Eden: Western Culture as a Recovery Narrative

*Carolyn Merchant**

A PENOBSCOT INDIAN STORY FROM NORTHERN NEW ENGLAND EXPLAINS the origin of maize. A great famine had deprived people of food and water. A beautiful Indian maiden appeared and married one of the young men of the tribe, but soon succumbed to another lover, a snake. On discovery she promised to alleviate her husband's sorrow if he would plant a blade of green grass clinging to her ankle. First he must kill her with his ax, then drag her body through the forest clearing until all her flesh had been stripped, and finally bury her bones in the center of the clearing. She then appeared to him in a dream and taught him how to tend, harvest, and cook corn and smoke tobacco.[1]

This agricultural origin story taught the Indians not only how to plant their corn in forest clearings but also that the earth would continue to regenerate the human body through the corn plant. It features a woman, the corn maiden, and a male lover as central actors. It begins with the state of nature as drought and famine. Nature is a desert, a poor place for human existence. The plot features a woman as savior. Through a willing sacrifice in which her body brings forth new life, she introduces agriculture to her husband and to the women who subsequently plant the corn, beans, and squash that sustain the life of the tribe. The result is an ecological system based on the planting of interdependent polycultures in forest gardens. The story type is ascensionist and progressive. Women transform nature from a desert into a garden. From a tragic situation of despair and death, a comic, happy, and optimistic situation of continued life results. In this story the valence of

132

women as corn mothers is good; they bring bountiful gifts. The valence of nature ends as a good. The earth is an agent of regeneration. Death is transformed into life through a reunification of the corn mother's body with the earth. Even death therefore results in a higher good.[2]

Into this bountiful world of corn mothers, enter the Puritan fathers bringing their own agricultural origin story of Adam and Eve. The biblical myth begins where the Indian story ends, with an ecological system of polycultures in the Garden of Eden. A woman, Eve, shows "the man," Adam, how to pick fruit from the Tree of the Knowledge of Good and Evil and to harvest the fruits of the garden. Instead of attaining a resultant good, the couple is cast out of the garden into a desert. Instead of moving from desert to garden, as in the Indian story, the biblical story moves from garden to desert. The Fall from paradise is caused by a woman. Men must labor in the earth by the sweat of their brow to produce food. Here a woman is also the central actress and, like the Indian story, the biblical story contains violence toward women. But the plot is declensionist and tragic, not progressive and comic as in the Indian story. The end result is a poorer state of nature than in the beginning. The valence of woman is bad. The end valence of nature is bad. Here men become the agents of transformation. They become saviors, who through their own agricultural labor have the capacity to re-create the lost garden on earth.[3]

According to Benjamin Franklin, Indians quickly perceived the difference between the two accounts. Franklin satirically writes that when the Indians were apprised of the "historical facts on which our [own] religion is founded, such as the fall of our first parents by eating an apple, . . . an Indian orator stood up" to thank the Europeans for their information. "What you have told us . . . is all very good. It is, indeed, bad to eat apples. It is much better to make them all into cider. We are much obliged by your kindness in coming so far to tell us these things which you have heard from your mothers; in return I will tell you some of those which we have heard from ours."[4]

Historical events reversed the plots of the European and the Indian origin stories. The Indians' comic happy ending changed to a story of decline and conquest, while Euramericans were largely successful in creating a New World garden. Indeed, the story of Western civilization since the seventeenth century and its advent on the American continent can be conceptualized as a grand narrative of fall and recovery. The concept of recovery, as it emerged in the seventeenth century, not only meant a recovery from the Fall but also entailed restoration of health, reclamation of land, and recovery of property.[5] The recovery plot is the long, slow process of returning humans to the Garden of Eden through labor in the earth. Three subplots organize its argument: Christian religion, modern science, and capitalism. The Genesis story of the Fall provides the beginning; science and capitalism, the middle; recovery of the garden, the end. The initial lapsarian moment (i.e., the lapse from innocence) is the decline from garden to desert as the first couple is cast from the light of an ordered paradise into a dark, disorderly wasteland.

The Bible, however, offered two versions of the origin story that led to the Fall. In the Genesis 1 version, God created the land, sea, grass, herbs, and fruit; the stars, sun, and moon; and the birds, whales, cattle, and beasts—after which he made "man in his own image . . . ; male and female created he them." Adam and Eve were instructed, "Be fruitful, and multiply, and replenish the earth, and subdue it," and were given "dominion over the fish of the sea, and over the fowl of the air, and over every living thing that moveth upon the earth." In the Genesis 2 version, thought to have derived from a different tradition, God first created the plants and herbs, next "man" from dust, and then the garden of Eden with its trees for food (including the Tree of Life and the Tree of the Knowledge of Good and Evil in the center) and four rivers flowing out of it. He then put "the man" in the garden "to dress and keep it," formed the beasts and fowls from dust, and brought them to Adam to name. Only then did he create Eve from Adam's rib. Genesis 3 narrates the Fall from the garden, beginning with Eve's temptation by the serpent, the consumption of the fruit from the Tree of the Knowledge of Good and Evil (which in the Renaissance becomes an apple), the expulsion of Adam and Eve from the garden "to till the ground from which he was taken," and finally God's placement of the cherubims and flaming sword at the entrance of the garden to guard the Tree of Life.[6]

During the Renaissance, artists illustrated the Garden of Eden story through woodcuts and paintings, one of the most famous of which is Lucas Cranach's 1526 painting of Eve offering the apple to Adam, after having been enticed by the snake coiled around the tree of the Knowledge of Good and Evil. Writers from Dante to Milton depicted the Fall and subsequent quest for paradise, while explorers searched for the garden first in the Old World and then in the New. Although settlers endowed new lands and peoples with Eden-like qualities, a major effort to re-create the Garden of Eden on earth ultimately ensued. Seventeenth-century botanical gardens and zoos marked early efforts to reassemble the parts of the garden dispersed throughout the world after the Fall and the Flood.[7]

But beginning in the seventeenth century and proceeding to the present, New World colonists have undertaken a massive effort to reinvent the whole earth in the image of the Garden of Eden. Aided by the Christian doctrine of redemption and the inventions of science, technology, and capitalism ("arte and industrie"), the long-term goal of the recovery project has been to turn the earth itself into a vast cultivated garden. The strong interventionist version in Genesis 1 legitimates recovery through domination, while the softer Genesis 2 version advocates dressing and keeping the garden through human management (stewardship). Human labor would redeem the souls of men and women, while cultivation and domestication would redeem the earthly wilderness. The End Drama envisions a reunification of the earth with God (the Parousia), in which the redeemed earthly garden merges into

Lucas Cranach, *Adam and Eve*, 1526. *(Courtesy Courtauld Institute Galleries)*

a higher heavenly paradise. The Second Coming of Christ was to occur either at the outset of the thousand-year period of his reign on earth (the millennium) or at the Last Judgment, when the faithful were reunited with God at the resurrection.[8]

Greek philosophy offered the intellectual framework for the modern version of the recovery project. Parmenidean oneness represents the unchanging natural law that has lapsed into the appearances of the Platonic world. This fallen phenomenal world is incomplete, corrupt, and inconstant. Only by recollection of the pure, unchanging forms can the fallen partake of the original unity. Recovered and Christianized in the Renaissance, Platonism provided paradigmatic ideals (such as that of the Garden of Eden) through which to interpret the earthly signs and signatures leading to the recovery.[9]

Modern Europeans added two components to the Christian recovery project—mechanistic science and laissez-faire capitalism—to create a grand master narrative of Enlightenment. Mechanistic science supplies the instrumental knowledge for reinventing the garden on earth. The Baconian-Cartesian-Newtonian project is premised on the power of technology to subdue and dominate nature, on the certainty of mathematical law, and on the unification of natural laws into a single framework of explanation. Just as the alchemists had tried to speed up nature's labor through human intervention in the transformation of base metals into gold, so science and technology hastened the recovery project by inventing the tools and knowledge that could be used to dominate nature. Francis Bacon saw science and technology as the way to control nature and hence recover the right to the garden given to the first parents. "Man by the fall, fell at the same time from his state of innocency and from his dominion over creation. Both of these losses can in this life be in some part repaired; the former by religion and faith; the latter by arts and science." Humans, he asserted, could "recover that right over nature which belongs to it by divine bequest," and should endeavor "to establish and extend the power and dominion of the human race itself over the [entire] universe."[10]

The origin story of capitalism is a movement from desert back to garden through the transformation of undeveloped nature into a state of civility and order.[11] Natural resources—"the ore in the mine, the stone unquarried [and] the timber unfelled"—are converted by human labor into commodities to be exchanged on the market. The good state makes capitalist production possible by imposing order on the fallen worlds of nature and human nature. Thomas Hobbes's nation-state was the end result of a social contract created for the purpose of controlling people in the violent and unruly state of nature. John Locke's political theory rested on the improvement of undeveloped nature by mixing human labor with the soil and subduing the earth through human domination. Simultaneously, Protestantism helped to speed the recovery by sanctioning increased human labor just as science and technology accelerated nature's labor.[12]

Crucial to the structure of the recovery narrative is the role of gender encoded into the story. In the Judeo-Christian tradition the original oneness is male and the Fall is caused by a female, Eve, with Adam, the innocent bystander, being forced to pay the consequences as his sons are pushed into developing both pastoralism and farming.[13] While fallen Adam becomes the inventor of the tools and technologies that will restore the garden, fallen Eve becomes the nature that must be tamed into submission. In the Western tradition it is fallen nature in opposition to which male science and technology are directed. The good state that keeps unruly nature in check is invented, engineered, and operated by men. The good economy that organizes the labor needed to restore the garden is likewise a male-directed project.

Nature, in the Edenic recovery story, appears in three forms. As original Eve, nature is virgin, pure, and light—land that is pristine or barren, but that has the potential for development. As fallen Eve, nature is disorderly and chaotic; a wilderness, wasteland, or desert requiring improvement; dark and witchlike, the victim and mouthpiece of Satan as serpent. As mother Eve, nature is an improved garden, a nurturing earth bearing fruit, a ripened ovary, maturity. Original Adam is the image of God as creator, initial agent, activity. Fallen Adam appears as the agent of earthly transformation, the hero who redeems the fallen land. Father Adam is the image of God as patriarch, law, and rule, the model for the kingdom and state. These meanings of nature as female and agency as male are encoded as symbols and myths into American lands as having the potential for development, but needing the male hero, Adam. Such symbols are not essences, because they do not represent characteristics necessary or essential to being female or male. Rather, they are historically constructed meanings deriving from the origin stories of European settlers and European cultural and economic practices transported to and developed in the American New World. That they may appear to be essences is a result of their historical construction in Western history, not their immutable characteristics.

The Enlightenment idea of progress is rooted in the recovery of the garden lost in the Fall—the bringing of light to the dark world of inchoate nature. The lapsarian origin story is thus reversed by the grand narrative of Enlightenment that lies at the very heart of modernism. The controlling image of Enlightenment is the transformation from desert wilderness to cultivated garden. This complex of Christian, Greco-Roman, and Enlightenment components touched and reinforced each other at critical nodal points. As a powerful narrative, the idea of recovery functioned as ideology and legitimation for settlement of the New World, while capitalism, science, and technology provided the means of transforming the material world.

Greco-Roman Roots of the
Recovery Narrative

IN CREATING A RECOVERY NARRATIVE THAT REVERSED THE LAPSARIAN moment of the Fall, Europeans reinforced the Christian image of the precipitous Fall from the Garden of Eden with pagan images of a gradual decline from the golden age. Hesiod (eighth century B.C.E.[?]) told of the time of immortal men who lived on Olympus, where all was "of gold" and "the grain-giving soil bore its fruits of its own accord in unstinted plenty, while they at their leisure harvested their fields in contentment amid abundance."[14] Ovid, in the *Metamorphoses* (A.D. 7), pictured the golden age as a time when a bountiful (unplowed) mother earth brought forth grains, fruits, honey, and nectar and people were peaceful, "unaggressive, and unanxious." Only in the decline of the subsequent silver, bronze, and iron ages did strife, violence, swindling, and war set in.[15]

Whereas Hesiod and Ovid offered elements that reinforced the Fall, Virgil and Lucretius introduced components of a recovery story that moved from "savagery" to "civilization." Nature was a principle of development, deriving from the Latin word *nascere*, "to be born." Each stage of development was inherent in the preceding stage, an actualization of a prior potential. The word "nation" derived from the same word; hence the state was born from the state of nature.[16] Virgil (70–19 B.C.E.) depicted a narrative of development from nature to nation that moved through four stages mimicking the human life cycle: (1) death and chaos, a world filled with presocial "wild" peoples (winter), to (2) birth and the pastoral, in which people grazed sheep on pastured lands (spring), to (3) youth or farming by plowing and planting gardens (summer); to (4) maturity, or the city (Rome) in the garden (fall). For Virgil these four stages were followed by a return to death and chaos, whereas in the Christian myth the recovery was followed by redemption and a return to the original garden. Yet within each of Virgil's stages lies the potential to lapse prematurely into the earlier chaotic, or "savage," state. The second, or pastoral, stage is like the Christian Garden of Eden—its loss is mourned and its innocence yearned for—but in the Roman story, it passes "naturally" to the third, or agricultural, stage.

Virgil's *Georgics* narrates the agricultural period in which humans actively labor in the earth to cultivate it and themselves. Both society's potential and the earth's potential are actualized and perfected. When farmers till the ground and tend their crops, nature's bounty brings forth fruits: "Father Air with fruitful rains" descended on the "bosom of his smiling bride" to feed her "teeming womb."[17] The *Aeneid* reveals the fourth stage—the emergence of Rome as a city of culture and civilization within the pastoral and agricultural landscapes—*urbs in horto*—the city in the garden. The four developmental phases of nature and nation exist both temporally as stages and spatially as zones. The city is an actualization of movement from a chaotic "wild" periphery to a pastoral outer zone, a cultivated inner zone, and a "civilized" central place. Because nature is viewed as a cyclical development, the decline and fall of Rome is preordained in the final return to winter and chaos. Yet out of chaos comes a second golden age as "the great line of the ages is born anew." The "virgin" (Justice) returns, and a "newborn boy" appears "at whose coming the iron race shall first cease and a golden race will spring up in the whole world." At this point the Roman and Christian versions of a second return converge, offering Europeans and Americans the possibility of the recovery an Edenic golden age.[18]

Lucretius provides the elements for Thomas Hobbes's origin story of capitalism and the good state as an emergence from the "state of nature." Lucretius' *De Rerum Naturum* (Of the nature of things) closely prefigures Hobbes's *Leviathan*. For both Lucretius and Hobbes the early state of human nature is disorderly, lawless, and chaotic. According to Lucretius, before the discovery of plow agriculture, wild beasts consumed humans and starvation was rampant.[19] But early civilization, nurtured by the taming of fire and the cooking of food, foundered on the discovery of gold, as violent wars were spawned by human greed. Just as Hobbes saw individual men in the state of nature as unruly and warlike, so Lucretius lamented that "things down to the vilest lees of brawling mobs succumbed, whilst each man sought unto himself dominion and supremacy." Just as Hobbes argued that people voluntarily gave up their ability to kill each other in the state of nature and entered into a civil contract enforced by the state, so Lucretius held that people out of their own free will submitted to laws and codes. The creation of civil law thus imposes order on disorderly humans, offering the possibility of recovery from the state of nature.[20]

Yet Lucretius' poem, as it came down to the Renaissance, ended not in recovery but in death, as plague and pestilence overcame Athens. The poem breaks off on a note of extreme pessimism and utter terror as piles of dead bodies burn on funeral pyres and all hope is forsaken. Like Lucretius, Hobbes (who was also deemed an atheist) offered a profoundly pessimistic view of nature, human nature, and divinity. Humans who are basically competitive and warlike contest with each other on the commons and in the marketplace in the creation of a capitalist economy.[21]

Like civilization, nature for Lucretius ends in death and a return to the chaos of winter. As did humans, the earth, whose name was mother, went through stages of life and death. She brought forth birds, beasts, and humans. The fields were like wombs, and the earth's pores gave forth milk like a mother's breasts. Yet when the earth had aged, she was like a worn-out old woman.[22]

In the seventeenth century the Greek cyclical stories of nature and human society that ended in death and destruction were converted to the Christian redemption story during the battle between ancients and moderns. The declensionist narrative depicting a slide downward from golden age to iron age, from original wisdom to ignorance, from human giants to midgets was transformed by hope of recovery. Both nature and human nature were capable of redemption. Science and technology offered the means of transforming nature; labor in the earth, the means of saving human souls. The earth could be plowed, cultivated, and improved as human beings mixed their labor with the soil. (For Locke, as opposed to Hobbes, the state of nature is good.) Thus both the cultivated earth and cultivated humans would be prepared for the final moment of redemption, or Parousia, when earth would merge with heaven, re-creating the original oneness. With the discovery of the New World, a new earth could be reconstructed with the image of the original garden as paradigm.

The American Heroic Recovery Narrative

IN AMERICA THE RECOVERY NARRATIVE PROPELLED SETTLEMENT AND "improvement" of the American continent by Europeans. Euramerican men acted to reverse the decline initiated by Eve by turning it into an ascent back to the garden. Using science, technology, and biblical imagery, they changed first the eastern wilderness and then the western deserts into cultivated gardens. Sanctioned by the Genesis origin story, they subdued the "wilderness," replenished the earth, and appropriated Indian homelands as free lands for settlement. Mercantile capitalism cast America as the site of natural resources, Africa as the source of enslaved human resources, and Europe as the locale of resource management. Timber, barrel staves, animal hides, herbal medicines, tobacco, sugar, and cotton were extracted from nature in the great project of "improving" the land. Men, as fallen Adam, became the heroic agents who transformed and redeemed fallen nature.[23]

In New England, European settlers converted a "hideous and desolate wilderness" into "a second England for fertileness" in the space of a few decades. The Pilgrim migration, as recorded in the text of William Bradford, conforms to the six elements of the mythic heroic narrative identified by the Russian folklorist Vladimir Propp: (1) the hero's initial absence, (2) his transference from one place to another, (3) the combat between hero and villain, (4) the hero's receipt of a gift, (5) the victory, and (6) the final repair of the hero's initial absence.[24] In this case the hero, Bradford, leads his people through trials and tests in the struggle to re-create the garden in the New World.

In the preparatory, or first, phase of the New England recovery story, the land is absent of the hero. Indian lands are vacant, corn fields have been abandoned, and the Indians themselves have succumbed to disease. As John Cotton later explained it, "When the Lord chooses to transplant his people, he first makes a country . . . void in that place where they reside."[25] In the second, or transference, phase, the hero, William Bradford, is transported from Old England to New England by ship. A spatial translocation takes place between two kingdoms, that of the Antichrist (the fleshpots of Old England) and the New Canaan, or promised land of New England. In the third, or combative, phase, the hero is tested through struggle with the villain—the devil acting through nature. The mythic struggle between hero and villain is played out as a struggle between Bradford and the wilderness—the tempestuous ocean and the desolate forest, a land filled with "wild beasts and wild men." Bradford's faith in God and his leadership of his people are continually called on, as storms wreak havoc with the small ship, the *Mayflower,* and the little band of settlers struggles to survive the grim winter on the shores of an unforgiving land. In the fourth phase, the hero receives a gift from a helper, in this case, "a special instrument sent [from] God," through the Indian Squanto, who not only speaks the Pilgrims' own language but shows them how to "set their corn, where to take fish, and to procure other commodities." The fifth phase is the victory of the hero, as the corn is harvested, cabins and stockade are built, and the struggling band survives its first year. Nature, as wilderness, has been defeated. In the sixth and climactic phase, the hero's initial absence has been repaired, the misfortunes are liquidated, and the Pilgrims are reborn. They celebrate their triumph over wilderness by their first harvest, achieved through the miracle of the re-created garden. By filling and replenishing the land, the recovery of the garden in the New World has been launched and the American recovery myth created.[26]

Pilgrim victory was followed by Puritan victory when the Massachusetts Bay Colony added thousands of additional settlers to the new land, repeating the heroic journey across the Atlantic to advance the Edenic recovery. As the *Arabella* left England for the New World in 1629, Puritan refugees listened to John Winthrop quoting Genesis 1:28, "Be fruitful and multiply, and replenish the earth and subdue it." The Boston pastor Charles Morton followed both the Genesis origin story and the Baconian ideal when he wrote in 1728 that because of the sin of the first parents, agriculture and husbandry must be used to combat weeds and soil sterility through fencing, tilling, manuring, and draining the land. The almanac maker Nathaniel Ames in 1754 helped to justify the mechanistic science of the body in Edenic terms when he informed his readers that the divine artificer initially had made the body of man "a machine capable of endless duration," but that after Eve's ingestion of the forbidden apple the living principle within had fallen into disharmony with the body, disrupting the smooth functioning of its parts.[27]

In the Chesapeake region, by the early eighteenth century, tobacco planters had converted an "unjustly neglected" and "abused" Virginia into a ravishing garden of pleasure. Robert Beverley predicated Virginia's potential as a "Garden of the World," akin to Canaan, Syria, and Persia, on his countrymen's ability to overcome an "unpardonable laziness."[28] Tobacco cultivation became the means of participating in the European market, while simultaneously improving the land through labor. But the recovery was ever in danger from new lapsarian moments if people allowed themselves to indulge too much in laziness, narcotics, or alcohol. During the eighteenth and nineteenth centuries, migrants from the original colonies and immigrants from Europe explored, settled, and "improved" the uplands west of the Atlantic coast, the intervales of the Appalachian Mountains, and the lowlands of the Mississippi valley.

In the late 1820s and 1830s Thomas Cole of the Hudson River school of painters depicted the American recovery narrative and the dangers of both the original and the subsequent lapsarian moments. His *Expulsion from the Garden of Eden* (1827–28) contrasts the tranquil, original garden on the right with the bleak, chaotic desert on the left, while in the center God expels Adam and Eve through a gate. (See p. 71.) The garden features a meandering stream and luxuriant vegetation, while the desert comprises barren rock, hot winds, a wild cataract, an erupting volcano, and a wolf attacking a deer. *The Oxbow* (1836) portrays the possibility of recovery through re-creating the garden on earth. The painting moves from dark wilderness on the left to an enlightened, tranquil, cultivated landscape on the right, bordering the curve of the peaceful Connecticut River. In the background, cutover scars in the forest on the hill apparently spell the Hebrew letters "Noah," which when viewed upside down from a God's-eye view form the word *shaddai,* meaning "the Almighty." God's presence in the landscape recognizes God's covenant with Noah and anticipates the final reunion of God and the earth at the Parousia. Humans can therefore redeem the land itself as garden, even as they redeem themselves through laboring in the earth.[29]

In a series of paintings from the 1830s, Cole depicted the movement from "savagery" to "civilization" and the problem of lapsing back into the darkness of wilderness. Of an 1831 painting, *A Wild Scene,* he wrote, "The first picture must be a savage wilderness . . . the figures must be savage—clothed in skins & occupied in the Chase— . . . as though nature was just waking from chaos."[30] A subsequent series, *The Course of Empire,* followed Virgil's stages of emergence from "savagery": The Savage State, the Pastoral State, Consummation of Empire, Destruction of Empire, and Desolation, to warn of lapsarian dangers that thwart progress and end in the ruin of civilization.

Ralph Waldo Emerson eulogized the recovered garden achieved through human dominion over nature in glowing rhetoric: "This great savage country should be furrowed by the plough, and combed by the harrow; these rough Alleganies should know their master; these foaming torrents should be bestridden by proud arches of stone; these wild prairies should be loaded with wheat; the swamps with rice; the hill-tops should pasture innumerable sheep and cattle. . . . How much better when the whole land is a garden, and the people have grown up in the bowers of a paradise."[31] Only after intensive development of the eastern seaboard did a small number of nineteenth-century urban artists, writers, scientists, and explorers begin to deplore the effects of the "machine in the garden."[32]

Similarly, Euramericans acted out the recovery narrative in transforming the western deserts during the second half of the nineteenth century. The elements of the story again conform to the elements of Propp's heroic narrative. The land is absent of the heroes—the migrants themselves. They are transferred across inhospitable desert lands; engage in combat with hostile Indians, diseases, and starvation; receive gifts from God in the form of gold and free land; emerge victorious over nature and Indian; and liquidate the initial absence of the hero by filling and replenishing the land. In filling the land through settlement, the migrants heeded John Quincy Adams's 1846 call for expansion into Oregon: "to make the wilderness blossom as the rose, to establish laws, to increase, multiply, and subdue the earth, which we are commanded to do by the first behest of the God Almighty." They likewise heard Thomas Hart Benton's call to manifest destiny that the white race had "alone received the divine command to subdue and replenish the earth: for it is the only race that . . . hunts out new and distant lands, and even a New World, to subdue and replenish."[33]

With the Reverend Dwinell, they commemorated the 1869 joining of the Central Pacific and Union Pacific railroads, using the Bible to sanction human alteration of the landscape. "Prepare ye the way of the Lord, make straight in the desert a highway before our God. Every valley shall be exalted, and every mountain and hill shall be made low and the crooked shall be made straight and the rough places plain." And in settling, ranching, and plowing the Great Plains, they reversed the biblical Fall from Eden by turning the "Great American Desert" into yet another "Garden of the World." The reclamation of arid lands west of the hundredth meridian through the technologies of irrigation fulfilled the biblical mandate to make the desert blossom as the rose, while making the land productive for capitalist agriculture.[34]

At the end of the nineteenth century, Frederick Jackson Turner's essay on the closing of the frontier in American history epitomized the heroic recovery narrative. The six phases of the heroic victory are again present in Turner's narrative, although it warns of impending declension as the frontier closes. (1) The frontier is defined by the absence of settlement and civilization. "Up to and including 1880, the country had a frontier of settlement, but at present the unsettled area has been . . . broken." (2) Europeans are transferred across space as the succession of frontier lines moves west, and they "adapt . . . to changes involved in crossing the continent." Stand at Cumberland Gap and watch the procession—the buffalo following the trail to the salt lick, the trapper, the miner, the rancher, and the farmer follow each other in succession; stand at South Pass a century later and watch the same succession again. (3) The individual hero is in combat with the villain—again the wilderness, Indians, and wild beasts. "The wilderness masters the colonist." The encounter with wilderness "strips off the garments" of European civilization and "puts him in the log cabin of the Cherokee and Iroquois." (4) The heroes receive the gift of free land. But "never again," Turner warns, "will such gifts of free land offer themselves." (5) The encounter with the frontier transforms hero into victor. "Little by little he transforms the wilderness, but the outcome is not the old Europe. . . . Here is a new product that is American." (6) Democracy and American civilization "in a perennial rebirth" fill the land, liquidating the initial absence. "Democracy is born of free land."[35] With frontier expansion, temporal recovery through science and capitalism merges with spatial recovery through acquisition of private property.

Indians in the Recovery Narrative

THE HEROIC RECOVERY NARRATIVE THAT GUIDED SETTLEMENT IS NOTABLE for its treatment of Indians. Wilderness is the absence of civilization. Although most Euramericans seemed to have perceived Indians as the functional equivalent of wild animals, they nevertheless believed the Indian survivors had the potential to be "civilized" and hence to participate in the recovery as settled farmers. American officials changed the Indians' own origin stories to make them descendants of Adam and Eve; hence they were not indigenous to America. Thomas L. McHenry, who formulated Indian policy in the 1840s, said that the whole "family of man" came from "one original and common stock," of which the Indian was one branch. "Man . . . was put by his creator in the garden, which was eastward in Eden, whence flowed the river which parted, and became into four heads; and that from his fruitfulness his [the Indian] species were propagated." The commissioner of Indian affairs in 1868 deemed them "capable of civilization and christianization." A successor in 1892 argued that since Indian children were "made in the image of God, being the likeness of their Creator," they had the "same possibilites of growth and development" as other children. An Indian baby could become "a cultivated refined Christian gentleman or lovely woman."[36]

Euramericans attempted to transform Indians from hunters into settled farmers first by removing them to lands west of the Mississippi, then to reservations, and later by allotting them 160-acre plots of private property. Thomas Jefferson saw them as capable of participating in the recovery narrative when he told a delegation in 1802 that he would be pleased to see them "cultivate the earth, to raise herds of useful animals and to spin and weave."[37] With Indians largely vanquished and moved to reservations by the 1890s, twentieth-century conservationists turned "recovered" Indian homelands into parks, set aside wilderness areas as people-free reserves where "man himself is a vistor who does not remain," and managed forests for maximum yield and efficiency. With the taming of wilderness, desert, and "wild men," the recovery story reached an apparently happy ending.[38]

But Indians, for the most part, rejected the new narrative. With some exceptions, they resisted the roles into which they were cast and the lines they were forced to speak. They objected to characterizations of their lands as wilderness or desert, calling them simply home. As Chief Luther Standing Bear put it, "We did not think of the great open plains, the beautiful rolling hills, and winding streams with tangled growth, as 'wild.' Only to the white man was nature a wilderness and only to him was the land 'infested' with 'wild' animals and 'savage' people. To us it was tame. Earth was bountiful. . . ."[39]

While adopting the Christian religion, Indians often emphasized those aspects compatible with traditional beliefs and participated in the ceremonial and celebratory aspects with greater enthusiasm than in the more austere, otherworldly practices.[40] Although taught to read and cipher, they often rejected white society's science and technology as useless for living. As Franklin satirized the colonists' effort, the Indians, when offered the opportunity to attend the College of William and Mary in Virginia, politely considered the matter before refusing:

> Several of our young people were formerly brought up at the colleges of the northern provinces; they were instructed in all your sciences; but when they came back to us they were bad runners; ignorant of every means of living in the woods; unable to bear either cold or hunger; knew neither how to build a cabin, take a deer, or kill an enemy; spoke our language imperfectly, and were therefore neither fit for hunters, warriors, or counsellors; they were totally good for nothing. We are however, none the less obliged by your kind offer, tho' we decline accepting it; and to show our grateful sense of it, if the gentlemen of Virginia will send us a dozen of their sons, we will take great care of their education, instruct them in all we know, and make men of them.[41]

Female Nature in the Recovery Narrative

An account of the history of American settlement as a lapsarian and recovery narrative must also consider the crucial role of nature conceptualized as female in the very structure of the plot. The rhetoric of American settlement is filled with language that casts nature as female object to be transformed and men as the agents of change. Allusions to Eve as virgin land to be subdued, as fallen nature to be redeemed through reclamation, and as fruitful garden to be harvested and enjoyed are central to the particular ways in which American lands were developed. The extraction of resources from "nature's bosom," the penetration of "her womb" by science and technology, and the "seduction" of female land by male agriculture reinforced capitalist expansion.[42]

Images of nature as female are deeply encoded into the texts of American history, art, and literature and function as ideologies for settlement. Thus Thomas Morton in praising New England as a new Canaan likened its potential for development by "art and industry" to a "faire virgin longing to be sped and meete her lover in a Nuptiall bed." Now, however, "her fruitfull wombe, not being enjoyed is like a glorious tombe."[43] Male agriculturalists saw in plow technology a way to compel female nature to produce. Calling Bacon "the grand master of philosophy" in 1833, the Massachusetts agricultural improver Henry Colman promoted Bacon's approach to recovering the garden through agriculture. "The effort to extend the dominion of man over nature, he wrote, "is the most healthy and most noble of all ambitions." He characterized the earth as a female whose productivity could help to advance the progress of the human race. "Here man exercises dominion over nature; . . . commands the earth on which he treads to waken her mysterious energies . . . compels the inanimate earth to teem with life; and to impart sustenance and power, health and happiness to the countless multitudes who hang on her breast and are dependent on her bounty."[44]

A graphic example of female nature succumbing to the male plow is provided by Frank Norris in his 1901 novel *The Octopus*, a story of the transformation of California by the railroad. Here the earth is female, sexual, and alive. Norris writes,

> The great brown earth turned a huge flank to [the sky], exhaling the moisture of the early dew. . . . One could not take a dozen steps upon the ranches without the brusque sensation that underfoot the land was alive, . . . palpitating with the desire of reproduction. Deep down there in the recesses of the soil, the great heart throbbed once more, thrilling with passion, vibrating with desire, offering itself to the caress of the plough, insistent, eager, imperious. Dimly one felt the deep-seated trouble of the earth, the uneasy agitation of its members, the hidden tumult of its womb, demanding to be made fruitful, to reproduce, to disengage the eternal renascent germ of Life that stirred and struggled in its loins. . . .[45]

In Norris's novel the seduction of the female earth was carried out on a massive scale by thousands of men operating their plows in unison on a given day in the spring. "Everywhere throughout the great San Joaquin," he wrote, "unseen and unheard, a thousand ploughs up-stirred the land, tens of thousands of shears clutched deep into the warm, moist soil."[46] And Norris leaves no doubt that the men's technology, the plow, is also male and that the seduction becomes violent rape:

> It was the long stroking caress, vigorous, male, powerful, for which the Earth seemed panting. The heroic embrace of a multitude of iron hands, gripping deep into the brown, warm flesh of the land that quivered responsive and passionate under this rude advance, so robust as to be almost an assault, so violent as to be veritably brutal. There, under the sun and under the speckless sheen of the sky, the wooing of the Titan began, the vast primal passion, the two world-forces, the elemental Male and Female, locked in a colossal embrace, at grapples in the throes of an infinite desire, at once terrible and divine, knowing no law, untamed, savage, natural, sublime.[47]

The narrative of frontier expansion is a story of male energy subduing female nature, taming the wild, plowing the land, re-creating the garden lost by Eve. American males lived the frontier myth in their everyday lives, making the land safe for capitalism and commodity production. Once tamed by men, the land was safe for women. To civilize was to bring the land out of a state of savagery and barbarism into a state of refinement and enlightenment. This state of domestication, of civility, is symbolized by woman and "womanlike" man. "The man of training, the civilizee," reported *Scribner's Monthly* in November 1880, "is less manly than the rough, the pioneer."[48]

But the taming of external nature was intimately linked to the taming of internal nature, the exploitation of nonhuman nature to the exploitation of human nature. The civilizing process not only removed wild beasts from the pastoral lands of the garden; it suppressed the wild animal in men. Crèvecoeur in 1782 noted that on the frontier "men appear to be no better than carnivorous animals . . . living on the flesh of wild animals." Those who farmed the middle settlements, on the other hand, were "like plants," purified by the "simple cultivation of the earth," becoming civilized through reading and political discourse.[49] Or as Richard Burton put it in 1861, "The civilizee shudders at the idea of eating wolf."[50] Just as the earth is female to the farmer who subdues it with the plow, so wilderness is female to the male explorer, frontiersman, and pioneer who tame it with the brute strength of the ax, the trap, and the gun. Its valence, however, varies from the negative satanic forest of William Bradford and the untamed wilderness of the pioneer (fallen Eve) to the positive pristine Eden and mother earth of John Muir (original and Mother Eve) and the parks of Frederick Law Olmsted. As wilderness vanishes before advancing civilization, its remnants must be preserved as test zones for men (epitomized by Theodore Roosevelt) to hone male strength and skills.[51]

Civilization is the final end, the telos, toward which "wild" nature is destined. The progressive narrative undoes the declension of the Fall. The "end of nature" is civilization. Civilization is thus nature natured, *Natura naturata*—the natural order, or nature ordered and tamed. It is no longer nature naturing, *Natura naturans*—nature as creative force. Nature passes from inchoate matter endowed with a formative power to a reflection of the civilized natural order designed by God. The unruly energy of wild female nature is suppressed and pacified. The final, happy state of nature natured is female and civilized—the restored garden of the world.[52]

John Gast depicts this ascensionist narrative in his 1872 painting *American Progress*.[53] On the left, toward the west is *Natura naturans*, nature active, alive, wild, dark, and savage, filled, as William Bradford would have put it, with "wild beasts and wild men." Buffalo, wolves, and elk flee in dark disorder accompanied by Indians with horses and travois. On the right, coming from the east, advancing to the west, is *Natura naturata*— nature ordered, civilized, and tamed. No longer to be feared or sexually assaulted, she floats angelically through the air in flowing white robes, emblazoned with the star of empire. She carries telegraph wires in her left hand, symbols of the highest level of communication—language borne through the air, the word or logos from above. The domination of logic or

John Gast, *American Progress. (Courtesy Gene Autry Museum, Los Angeles, California)*

pure form is repeated in the book grasped in her right hand touching the coiled telegraph wires. She represents the city, the civil, the civic order of government—the highest order of nature. She is pure Platonic form impressed on female matter, transforming and ordering all beneath her.[54]

Most important, however, it is American men who have prepared her way. They have dispelled the darkness, fought the Indian, killed the bear and buffalo. Covered wagons bearing westward pioneers, gold rush prospectors, and the pony express precede her. Farmers plowing the soil next to their fenced fields and rude cabins have settled and tamed the land. Stage coaches and trains follow, bringing waves of additional settlers. At the far right is the Atlantic civilization, where ships bearing the arts of the Old World arrive in the New World. The painting itself is a lived progressive narrative. Its east-to-west movement is a story of ascent and conquest.

A similar image was captured by Emanuel Leutze in his famous mural in the U.S. Capitol, *Westward the Course of Empire Takes Its Way,* painted in 1861, illustrating a line from a poem by George Berkeley. At the center of the mural on a rock outcrop pointing west toward barren "virgin" land is a madonna-like grouping of a pioneer with his wife and child. Below pass men with guns mounted on horses followed by covered wagons bearing women representing civilization. Their way is prepared by men cutting the forest with axes and uprooting trees that lie in the party's way. Below, in the mural's frame, is a view of San Francisco's golden gate flanked by portraits of explorers William Clark and Daniel Boone. Like Gast's *American*

Emanuel Leutze, *Westward the Course of Empire Takes its Way. (Courtesy National Museum of American Art, Smithsonian Institution, Washington, D.C. Bequest of Sara Carr Upton.)*

Progress, the scene is a dynamic moment in the transformation of "virgin" nature into female civilized form through the agency of men.

A third example is the 1875 painting *Progress of America,* by Domenico Tojetti. A female liberty figure personifying progress drives a chariot with a mounted American eagle pulled by two white horses. On the left, American Indians and buffalo flee into darkness and disorder in the advance of civilization, while on the right behind the liberty icon, female figures representing agriculture, medicine, mechanics, and the arts accompany her advance. Women bearing a tablet symbolizing literacy follow in front of a train bringing commerce and light to a barren "virgin" landscape.

A fourth representation is that of *Civilization,* painted by George Willoughby Maynard in 1893. A white female figure dressed in white robes is seated on a throne decorated with cornucopias. She holds the book of knowledge on her lap and points to its written words as the epitome of enlightenment and education. The book represents the logos, the light or word from above. The figure's Anglo-Saxon whiteness excludes the blackness of matter, darkness, and dark-skinned peoples.

All four images portray movement from dark, barren, virgin, undeveloped nature, or *Natura naturans,* to final Platonic, civilized, ideal form, *Natura naturata.* In the first two images, male agents effect the transformation from the undeveloped disorder of the desert to the ordered, idealized

Domenico Tojetti, *Progress of America*. (*Courtesy Collection of the Oakland Museum of California, Gift of the Kahn Foundation*)

landscape. The final two paintings reveal the outcome, an enlightened world made safe for educated Euramerican men and women.

The City in the Garden

THE CITY REPRESENTS THE NEXT STAGE OF THE RECOVERY NARRATIVE—THE creation of the city in the garden (Virgil's *urbs in horto*) by means of the capitalist market. The city epitomizes the transformation of female nature into female civilization through the mutually reinforcing powers of male energy and interest-earning capital. Frank Norris in his second novel, *The Pit* (1903), reveals the connections.[55] In writing of Chicago and the wheat pit at the Board of Trade (a story brilliantly told in William Cronon's *Nature's Metropolis,* inspired in part by Norris's book),[56] Norris depicts the city as female. The city is the locus of power that operates in the natural world, sweeping everything towards its center. It is the bridge between civilized female form and the raw matter of the surrounding hinterlands, drawing that matter towards it, as natural resources are transformed into capitalist commodities. Chicago, writes Norris,

the Great Grey City, brooking no rival, imposed its dominion upon a reach of country larger than many a kingdom of the Old World. For thousands of miles beyond its confines was its influence felt. Out, far out, far away in the snow and shadow of Northern Wisconsin forests, axes and saws bit the bark

George Willoughby Maynard, *Civilization. (Courtesy National Academy of Design)*

of century-old trees, stimulated by this city's energy. Just as far to the south-ward pick and drill leaped to the assault of veins of anthracite, moved by her central power. Her force turned the wheels of harvester and seeder a thousand miles distant in Iowa and Kansas. Her force spun the screws and propellers of innumerable squadrons of lake steamers crowding the Sault Sainte Marie. For her and because of her all the Central States, all the Great Northwest roared with traffic and industry; sawmills screamed; factories, their smoke blackening the sky, clashed and flamed; wheels turned, pistons leaped in their cylinders; cog gripped cog; beltings clasped the drums of mammoth wheels; and convert-ers of forges belched into the clouded air their tempest breath of molten steel.[57]

The city transforms the matter of nature in the very act of pulling it inward. Like Plato's female soul of the world, turning herself within herself, the city provides the source of motion that permeates and energizes the world around it, the bridge between raw changing matter and final civilized form. In Norris's novel, men at first seem subordinate to the city's higher force, acting merely as agents in the preordained purpose of transforming nature into civilization. They facilitate the change from *Natura naturans* into *Natura naturata,* from natural resource into fabricated product. Operating the steam engines, sawmills, factories, lumber barges, grain ele-vators, trains, and switches that make Chicago an industrial city, workers shout and signal as trains daily debouch businessmen bringing with them trade from country to city. This process of "civilization in the making," says Norris, is like a "great tidal wave," an "elemental," "primordial" force, "the first verses of Genesis." It "subdu[es] the wilderness in a single genera-tion," through the "resistless subjugation of . . . the lakes and prairies."[58]

Yet behind the scenes, other men, the capitalist speculators of the Chicago Board of Trade, attempt to manipulate the very forces of nature, pushing the transformation faster and faster. Capitalism mystifies by converting liv-ing nature into dead matter and by changing inert metals into living money.[59] To the capitalist puppeteers, nature is a doll-like puppet con-trolled by the strings of the wheat trade that changes money into interest-earning capital. Male minds calculate the motions that control the inert mat-ter below.

To Norris's capitalist, Curtis Jadwin, nature is dead. Only money is alive, growing and swelling through the daily trade of the wheat pit. With the bulls and bears of the marketplace the only apparent living things he encounters, Jadwin fails utterly to account for the earth and the wheat as alive. Yet as Jadwin, the bull trader, corners the market to obtain complete control over the bears, driving the price higher and higher, the living wheat planted by hundreds of farmers throughout the heartland rises from the soil as a gigantic irrepressible force. The capitalist's manipulation of apparently dead nature has immense environmental consequences. Jadwin, Norris writes, had "laid his puny human grasp upon Creation and the very earth herself." The "great mother . . . had stirred at last in her sleep and sent her omnipotence moving through the grooves of the world, to find and crush the disturber of her appointed courses."[60]

But in the late nineteenth century, as the frontier closes, forests disappear, and the land is made safe for civilization, American men begin to lament the loss of wild nature. There is an apparent need to retain wilderness as a place for men to test maleness, strength, and virility and an apparent association of men with nature.[61] Similarly, women are symbolized as the moral model that suppresses internal sexual libido. But nature as wilderness does not *become* male, nor does civilization *become* female in a reversal of the so-called universal association of female to nature and male to culture identified by Sherry Ortner.[62] There is no real reversal of male/female valences in the closing chapters of the story of frontier expansion. In the story of American progress, males continue to be the transforming agents between active female nature and civilized female form, making the land safe for women and men alike, suppressing both unpredictable external nature and unruly internal nature.

Nor are nature and culture, women and men, binary opposites with universal or essential meanings. Nature, wilderness, and civilization are socially constructed concepts that change over time and serve as stage settings in the progressive narrative. So too are the concepts of male and female and the roles that men and women play on the stage of history. The authors of such powerful narratives as laissez-faire capitalism, mechanistic science, manifest destiny, and the frontier story are usually privileged elites with access to power and patronage. Their words are read by persons of power who add the new stories to the older biblical story. As such the books become the library of Western culture. The library, in turn, functions as ideology when ordinary people read, listen to, internalize, and act out the stories told by their elders—the ministers, entrepreneurs, newspaper editors, and professors who teach and socialize the young.

The most recent chapter of the book of the recovery narrative is the transformation of nature through biotechnology. From genetically engineered apples to Flavr-Savr tomatoes, the fruits of the original (evolved) garden are being redesigned so that the salinated irrigated desert can continue to blossom as the rose. In the recovered Garden of Eden, fruits will ripen faster, have fewer seeds, need less water, require fewer pesticides, contain less saturated fat, and have longer shelf lives. The human temptation to engineer nature is reaching too close to the powers of God, warn the Jeremiahs who depict the snake coiled around the Tree of the Knowledge of Good and Evil as the DNA spiral. But the progressive engineers who design the technologies that allow the recovery to accelerate see only hope in the new fabrications.

The twentieth-century Garden of Eden is the enclosed shopping mall decorated with trees, flowers, and fountains in which people can shop for nature at the Nature Company, purchase "natural" clothing at Esprit, sample organic foods and Rainforest Crunch in kitchen gardens, buy twenty-first-century products at Sharper Image, and play virtual reality games in which SimEve is reinvented in Cyberspace. This garden in the city re-creates the pleasures and temptations of the original garden and the golden age where people can peacefully harvest the fruits of earth with gold grown by the market. The mall, enclosed by the desert of the parking lots surrounding it, is covered by glass domes reaching to heaven, accessed by spiral staircases and escalators affording a vista over the whole garden of shops. The "river that went out of Eden to water the garden" is reclaimed in meandering streams lined with palm trees and filled with bright orange carp. Today's malls feature stone grottoes, trellises decorated with flowers, life-sized trees, statues, birds, animals, and even indoor beaches that simulate paradigmatic nature as a cultivated, benign garden. With their engineered spaces and commodity fetishes, they epitomize consumer capitalism's vision of the recovery from the Fall.[63]

Critiques of the Recovery Narrative

THE MODERN VERSION OF THE RECOVERY NARRATIVE, HOWEVER, HAS BEEN subjected to scathing criticism. Postmodern thinkers contest its Enlightenment assumptions, while cultural feminists and environmentalists reverse its plot, depicting a slow decline from a prior golden age, not a progressive ascent to a new garden on earth. The critics' plot does not move from the tragedy of the Fall to the comedy of an earthly paradise but descends from an original state of oneness with nature to the tragedy of nature's destruction. Nevertheless, they too hope for a recovery, one rapid enough to save the earth and society by the mid-twenty-first century. The metanarrative of recovery does not change, but the declensionist plot, into which they have cast prior history, must be radically reversed. The postmodern critique of modernism is both a deconstruction of Enlightenment thought and a set of reconstructive proposals for the creation of a better world.

The identification of modernism as a problem rather than as progress was sharply formulated by Max Horkheimer and Theodor Adorno in the opening sentences of their 1944 *Dialectic of Enlightenment*: "The fully enlightened earth radiates disaster triumphant. The program of the enlightenment was the disenchantment of the world; the dissolution of myths and the substitution of knowledge for fancy." They criticized both Francis Bacon's concept of the domination of nature and Karl Marx and Friedrich Engels's optimism that the control of nature would lead to advancement. They faulted the reduction of nature to mere number by mechanistic science and capitalism: "Number becomes the canon of the Enlightenment. The same equations dominate bourgeois justice and commodity exchange. . . . Myth turns into enlightenment and nature into mere objectivity."[64]

Among the critics of modernism are many feminists and environmentalists who propose a reversal that will initiate a new millennium in the twenty-first century. Cultural feminists and ecofeminists see the original oneness as female, the *terra mater* of the neolithic era, from which emerged the consciousness of differences between humans and animals, male and female, people and nature, leading to dominance and submission. The advent of patriarchy initiates a long decline in the status of women and nature. Men's plow agriculture took over women's gathering and horticultural activities, horse-mounted warriors injected violence into a largely peaceful Old European culture, and male gods replaced female earth deities in origin stories. In the proposed recovery, Eve is revisioned as the first scientist, Sophia as ultimate wisdom, and the goddess as symbol of female power and creativity. Feminist religious history redirects inquiry into the gendered nature of the original oneness as both male and female. The recovery would therefore be a feminist or an egalitarian world.[65]

Feminist science sees the original mind as having no sex, and hence accessible to male and female minds alike. It has been men, many feminists would argue, who have invented the science and technology and organized the market economies that have made nature victim in the ascent of "man." For such feminists the new narrative would entail reclaiming women's roles in the history of science and asserting female power in contemporary science and technology. Hence both sexes can participate in the recovery.[66]

Environmentalism, like feminism, reverses the plot of the recovery narrative, seeing history as a slow decline, not a progressive movement that has made the desert blossom as the rose. The recovery story is false; an original garden has become a degraded desert. Pristine nature, not innocent man, has fallen. The decline from Eden was slow, rather than a precipitous lapsarian moment as in the Adam and Eve origin story. Over the millennia from the paleolithic to the present, nature has been the victim of both human hubris and social changes that overcome "the necessities of nature" through domestication, cultivation, and commodification of every aspect of an original, evolved, prehuman garden. So-called advances in science, technology, and economy actually accelerate the decline.[67]

As the twentieth century draws to a close and the second great millennium since the birth of Christ reaches its end, the environmental decline approaches a crisis. The greenhouse effect, the population explosion, the destruction of the ozone layer, the extinction of species, and the end of wilderness are all subplots in a grand narrative of environmental endism. Predictions of crisis, such as those of Paul Ehrlich in "Eco-Catastrophe" (1969), the Club of Rome in *Limits to Growth* (1972) and Bill McKibben in *The End of Nature* (1989), abound, as first (evolved, prehuman) nature is totally subsumed by humans and the human artifacts of second (commodified) nature.[68]

Like feminists, environmentalists want to rewrite the modern progressive story. Having seen the plot as declensionist rather than progressive, they nevertheless opt for a recovery that must be put in place by the mid-twenty-first century. "Sustainability" is a new vision of the recovered garden, one in which humanity will live in a relationship of balance and harmony with the natural world. Environmentalists who press for sustainable development see the recovery as achievable through the spread of nondegrading forms of agriculture and industry. Preservationists and deep ecologists strive to save pristine nature as wilderness before it can be destroyed by development. Restoration ecologists wish to marshal human labor to restore an already degraded nature to an earlier, pristine state. Social ecologists and green parties devise new economic and political structures that overcome the domination of human beings and nonhuman nature. Women and nature, minorities and nature, other animals and nature will be fully included in the recovery. The regeneration of nature and people will be achieved through social and environmental justice. The End Drama envisions a postpatriarchal, socially just ecotopia for the postmillennial world of the twenty-first century.[69]

Chaos Theory and Partnership Ethics

SEEING WESTERN HISTORY AS A RECOVERY NARRATIVE, WITH FEMINISM AND environmentalism as reversals of the plot, brings up the question of the character of the plot itself. The declensionist and progressive plots that underlie the meta-narrative of recovery both gain power from their linearity. Linearity is not only conceptually easy to grasp; it is also a property of modernity itself. Mechanistic science, progress, and capitalism all draw power from the linear functions of mathematical equations—the upward and downward slopes of straight lines and curves. To the extent that these linear slopes intersect with a real material world, they refer to a limited domain only. Chaos theory and complexity theory suggest that only the unusual domain of mechanistic science can be described by linear differential equations. The usual—that is, the domain of everyday occurrences, such as the weather, turbulence, the shapes of coastlines, and the arrhythmic fibrillations of the human heart—cannot be so easily described. The world is more complex than we know or indeed can ever know. The comfortable predictability of the linear slips away into the uncertainty of the indeterminate—into discordant harmonies and disorderly order.

The appearance of chaos as an actor in science and history in the late twentieth century not only is symptomatic of the breakdown of modernism, mechanism, and, potentially, capitalism but suggests the possibility of a new birth, a new world, a new millennium—the order-out-of-chaos narrative of Ilya Prigogine and Isabelle Stengers. But chaos theory also fundamentally destabilizes the very concept of nature as a standard or referent. It disrupts the idea of the "balance of nature," of nature as resilient actor or mother who will repair the errors of human actors and continue as fecund garden (Eve as mother). It questions the possibility that humans as agents can control and master nature through science and technology, undermining the myth of nature as virgin female to be developed (Eve as virgin). Chaos is the reemergence of nature as power over humans, nature as active, dark, wild, turbulent, and uncontrollable (fallen Eve). Ecologists characterize "mother nature" as a "strange attractor," while turbulence is seen to be encoded with gendered images of masculine channels and feminine flows.[70] Moreover, in the chaotic narrative, humans lose the hubris of fallen Adam that the garden can be re-created on earth. The world is not created by a patriarchal God ex nihilo, but emerges out of chaos. Thus the very possibility of the recovery of a stable original garden—the plot of the recovery meta-narrative—is itself challenged.

Recognition of history as a meta-narrative raises the further question of the relativity of the histories through which we are educated and of our own lives as participants in the plots they tell. Like our nineteenth-century counterparts, we live our lives as characters in the grand narrative into which we have been socialized as children and conform as adults. That narrative is the story told to itself by the dominant society of which we are a part. We internalize narrative as ideology. Ideology is a story told by people in power. Once we identify ideology as a story—powerful and compelling, but still only a story—we realize that by rewriting the story, we can begin to challenge the structures of power. We recognize that all stories can and should be challenged.

But can we actually step outside the story into which we have been cast as characters and enter into a story with a different plot? More important, can we change the plot of the grand master narrative of modernism? Where do I as author of this text stand in relationship to it? As a product of modernism, mechanism, and capitalism, I have internalized the values of the recovery narrative I have sought to identify. I participate in the progressive recovery narrative in my daily work, my wages for intellectual labor, my aspirations for a better material life, and my enjoyment of the profits my individual achievements have wrought. Yet I also believe, despite the relativism of environmental endism, that the environmental crisis is real—that the vanishing frogs, fish, and songbirds are telling us a truth. I am also a product of linear thinking and have set up this recovery narrative to reflect the very linearity of progressive history. This is history seen from a particular point of view, the view I have identified as the dominant ideology of modernism. I also believe my recovery narrative reflects a fundamental insight into how nature has been historically constructed as a gendered object.

Yet both history and nature are extremely complex, complicated, and nonlinear. What would a chaotic, nonlinear, nongendered history with a different plot look like? Would it be as compelling as the linear version, even if that linear version were extremely nuanced and complicated? A postmodern history might posit characteristics other than those identified with modernism, such as a multiplicity of real actors; acausal, nonsequential events; nonessentialized symbols and meanings; many authorial voices, rather than one; dialectical action and process, rather than the imposed logos of form; situated and contextualized, rather than universal, knowledge. It would be a story (or multiplicity of stories) that perhaps can only be acted and lived, not written at all.

I too yearn for a recovery from environmental declension—for my own vision of a postpatriarchal, socially just ecotopia for the third millennium. My vision entails a partnership ethic between humans (whether male or female), and between humans and nonhuman nature. For most of human history, nonhuman nature has had power over humans. People accepted fate while propitiating nature with gifts, sacrifices, and prayer (often within hierarchical human relationships). Since the seventeenth century, however, some groups of people have increasingly gained great power over nature and other human groups through the interlinked forces of science, technology, capitalism (and state socialism), politics, and religion.

A partnership ethic would bring humans and nonhuman nature into a dynamically balanced, more nearly equal relationship. Humans, as the bearers of ethics, would acknowledge nonhuman nature as an autonomous actor that cannot be predicted or controlled except in very limited domains. We would also acknowledge that we have the potential to destroy life as we currently know it through nuclear power, pesticides, toxic chemicals, and unrestrained economic development, and exercise specific restraints on that ability. We would cease to create profit for the few at the expense of the many. We would instead organize our economic and political forces to fulfill peoples' basic needs for food, clothing, shelter, and energy, and to provide security for health, jobs, education, children, and old age. Such forms of security would rapidly reduce population growth rates, since a major means of providing security would not depend on having large numbers of children, especially boys. A partnership ethic would be a relationship between a human community and a nonhuman community in a particular place, a place that recognizes its connections to the larger world through economic and ecological exchanges. It would be an ethic in which humans act to fulfill both human needs and nature's needs by restraining human hubris. Guided by a partnership ethic, people would select technologies that sustained the natural environment by becoming co-workers and partners with nonhuman nature, not dominators over it.

A partnership ethic implies a remythicizing of the Edenic recovery narrative or the writing of a new narrative altogether. The new myth would not accept the patriarchal sequence of creation, or even the milder phrase "male and female, created he them," but might instead emphasize simultaneous creation, cooperative male / female evolution, or even an emergence out of chaos or the earth. It would not accept the idea of subduing the earth, or even dressing and keeping the garden, since both entail total domestication and control by human beings. Instead, each earthly place would be a home, or community, to be shared with other living and nonliving things. The needs of humans and nonhumans would be dynamically balanced. If such a story can be rewritten or experienced, it would be the product of many new voices and would have a complex plot and a different ending. As in the corn mother origin story, women and the earth, along with men, would be active agents. The new ending, however, will not come about if we simply read and reread the story into which we were born. The new story can be rewritten only through action.

A L B U M

SUBLIME
NATURE

No site was more important to nineteenth-century Americans as a symbol of sublime, wild nature than Niagara Falls. In the eyes of those who saw it, it was one of the wonders not just of the natural world but of the American nation, a powerful cultural symbol of the pristine, unfallen nature that had vanished from Europe but that could still be found in the United States. In the decades following the Civil War, however, the falls became an object of growing concern. Were tourism and industrial development conspiring to destroy Niagara's beauty? What could be done to make sure that the falls would not "fail to astonish" visitors? In the twentieth century planners went so far as to construct elaborate models of the falls, and even manipulated the flow of water over Niagara itself, in an effort to reconstruct their natural beauty. Rarely has so much time, energy, and money been spent trying to determine the ideal form a natural wonder should take.

Herman Moll, "The Falls of Niagara," 1732. *(From* A New and Exact Map of the Dominion of the King of Great Britain on the Continent of North America, *courtesy of the Library of Congress)*

Arthur Lumley, "Niagara Seen with Different Eyes," 1873. *(*Harper's Weekly, *August 9, 1873, courtesy of the Iconographic Collection, Neg. WHi(x3)49508 State Historical Society of Wisconsin)*

American Falls running dry, February 16, 1909. *(Anne Whiston Spirn, personal collection)*

American Falls "Dewatered." *(From International Joint Commission,* Preservation and Enhancement of the American Falls at Niagara: An IJC Report to the Governments of Canada
and the United States, *1975, plate 5, courtesy of the Francis Loeb Library, Graduate School of
Design, Harvard University)*

Virtual Niagara under construction. *(Hydro-Electric Power Commission of Ontario, American Falls International Board,* Preservation and Enhancement of the American Falls at Niagara: Interim Report to the International Joint Commission, Appendix B: Aesthetics, *December 1971, courtesy of the Francis Loeb Library, Graduate School of Design, Harvard University)*

Virtual Niagara: present state of American Falls *(Hydro-Electric Power Commission of Ontario, American Falls International Board, Preservation and Enhancement of the American Falls at Niagara: Interim Report to the International Joint Commission, Appendix B: Aesthetics, December 1971, courtesy of the Francis Loeb Library, Graduate School of Design, Harvard University)*

Virtual Niagara: proposed reconstruction of American Falls *(Hydro-Electric Power Commission of Ontario, American Falls International Board, Preservation and Enhancement of the American Falls at Niagara: Interim Report to the International Joint Commission, Appendix B: Aesthetics, December 1971, courtesy of the Francis Loeb Library, Graduate School of Design, Harvard University)*

AT
WORK
AND
PLAY

"Are You an Environmentalist or Do You Work for a Living?": Work and Nature

Richard White

IN FORKS, WASHINGTON, A LOGGING TOWN BADLY CRIPPLED BY BOTH OVER-cutting and the spotted owl controversy, you can buy a bumper sticker that reads "Are You an Environmentalist or Do You Work for a Living?"[1] It is an interesting insult, and one that poses some equally interesting questions. How is it that environmentalism seems opposed to work? And how is it that work has come to play such a small role in American environmentalism?

Modern environmentalists often take one of two equally problematic positions toward work. Most equate productive work in nature with destruction. They ignore the ways that work itself is a means of knowing nature while celebrating the virtues of play and recreation in nature. A smaller group takes a second position: certain kinds of archaic work, most typically the farming of peasants, provides a way of knowing nature. Whereas mainstream environmentalism creates a popular imagery that often harshly condemns all work in nature, this second group is apt to sentimentalize certain kinds of farming and argue that work on the land creates a connection to place that will protect nature itself. Arguments that physical labor on the land establishes an attachment that protects the earth from harm have, however, a great deal of history against them.

There are, of course, numerous thoughtful environmentalists who recognize fruitful connections between modern work and nature, but they operate within a larger culture that encourages a divorce between the two. Too often the environmental movement mobilizes words and images that widen the gulf. We need to reexamine the connections between work and nature.

171

They form perhaps the most critical elements in our current environmental crisis. The attitudes of most Americans toward work indicate fundamental problems with how we conceive of the natural world and our place in it. By failing to examine and claim work within nature, environmentalists have ceded to the so-called wise-use movement valuable cultural terrain. The loss of natural terrain can only follow. The wise-use movement confuses real work with invented property rights. It perverts the legitimate concerns of rural people with maintaining ways of life and getting decent returns on their labor into the special "right" of large property holders and corporations to hold the natural world and the public good hostage to their economic gain. As long as environmentalism refuses to engage questions of modern work and labor, wise use will prosper and our children, in the end, will suffer.

There is no avoiding questions of work and nature. Most people spend their lives in work, and long centuries of human labor have left indelible marks on the natural world. From pole to pole, herders, farmers, hunters, and industrial workers have deeply influenced the natural world, so virtually no place is without evidence of its alteration by human labor. Work that has changed nature has simultaneously produced much of our knowledge of nature. Humans have known nature by digging in the earth, planting seeds, and harvesting plants. They have known nature by feeling heat and cold, sweating as they went up hills, sinking into mud. They have known nature by shaping wood and stone, by living with animals, nurturing them, and killing them. Humans have matched their energy against the energy of flowing water and wind. They have known distance as more than an abstraction because of the physical energy they expended moving through space. They have tugged, pulled, carried, and walked, or they have harnessed the energy of animals, water, and wind to do these things for them. They have achieved a bodily knowledge of the natural world.

Modern environmentalism lacks an adequate consideration of this work. Most environmentalists disdain and distrust those who most obviously work in nature. Environmentalists have come to associate work—particularly heavy bodily labor, blue-collar work—with environmental degradation. This is true whether the work is in the woods, on the sea, in a refinery, in a chemical plant, in a pulp mill, or in a farmer's field or a rancher's pasture. Environmentalists usually imagine that when people who make things finish their day's work, nature is the poorer for it. Nature seems safest when shielded from human labor.

This distrust of work, particularly of hard physical labor, contributes to a larger tendency to define humans as being outside of nature and to frame environmental issues so that the choice seems to be between humans and nature. "World War III," Andy Kerr of the Oregon Natural Resources Council likes to say, "is the war against the environment. The bad news is, the humans are winning."[2] The human weapon in Kerr's war is work. It is logging, ranching, and fishing; it is mining and industry. Environmentalists, of course, also work, but they usually do not do hard physical labor, and they often fail to think very deeply about their own work and its relation to nature.

Like Kerr, most Americans celebrate nature as the world of original things. And nature may indeed be the world we have not made—the world of plants, animals, trees, and mountains—but the boundaries between this world of nature and the world of artifice, the world of things we have made, are no longer very clear. Are the cows and crops we breed, the fields we cultivate, the genes we splice natural or unnatural? Are they nature or artifice? We seek the purity of our absence, but everywhere we find our own fingerprints. It is ultimately our own bodies and our labor that blur the boundaries between the artificial and the natural. Even now we tamper with the genetic stuff of our own and other creatures' bodies, altering the design of species. We cannot come to terms with nature without coming to terms with our own work, our own bodies, our own bodily labor.

But in current formulations of human relations with nature there is little room for such a reconciliation. Nature has become an arena for human play and leisure. Saving an old-growth forest or creating a wilderness area is certainly a victory for some of the creatures that live in these places, but it is just as certainly a victory for backpackers and a defeat for loggers. It is a victory for leisure and a defeat for work.

Work and play are linked, but the differences matter. Both our work and our play, as Elaine Scarry has written, involve an extension of our sentient bodies out into the external world. Our tools, the products of our work, become extensions of ourselves. Our clothes extend our skins; our hammers extend our hands. Extending our bodies into the world in this manner changes the world, but the changes are far more obvious in our work than in our play. A logger's tools extend his body into trees so that he knows how the texture of their wood and bark differs and varies, how they smell and fall. The price of his knowledge is the death of a tree.[3]

Environmentalists so often seem self-righteous, privileged, and arrogant because they so readily consent to identifying nature with play and making it by definition a place where leisured humans come only to visit and not to work, stay, or live. Thus environmentalists have much to say about nature and play and little to say about humans and work. And if the world were actually so cleanly divided between the domains of work and play, humans and nature, there would be no problem. Then environmentalists could patrol the borders and keep the categories clear. But the dualisms fail to hold; the boundaries are not so clear. And so environmentalists can seem an ecological Immigration and Naturalization Service, border agents in a socially dubious, morally ambiguous, and ultimately hopeless cause.

I have phrased this issue so harshly not because I oppose environmentalism (indeed, I consider myself an environmentalist) but precisely because I think environmentalism must be a basic element in any coherent attempt to address the social, economic, and political problems that confront Americans at the end of the century. Environmentalists must come to terms with work because its effects are so widespread and because work itself offers both a fundamental way of knowing nature and perhaps our deepest connection with the natural world. If the issue of work is left to the enemies of environmentalism, to movements such as wise use, with its single-minded devotion to propertied interests, then work will simply be reified into property and property rights. If environmentalists segregate work from nature, if they create a set of dualisms where work can only mean the absence of nature and nature can only mean human leisure, then both humans and nonhumans will ultimately be the poorer. For without an ability to recognize the connections between work and nature, environmentalists will eventually reach a point where they seem trivial and extraneous and their issues politically expendable.

Given the tendency of environmentalists to exaggerate boundaries, to make humans and nature opposing sides in a bitter struggle, any attempt to stress the importance of work needs to begin by blurring the boundaries and stressing human connections with nature. Work once bore the burden of connecting us with nature. In shifting much of this burden onto the various forms of play that take us back into nature, Americans have shifted the burden to leisure. And play cannot bear the weight. Work entails an embodiment, an interaction with the world, that is far more intense than play. We work to live. We cannot stop. But play, which can be as sensuous as work, does not so fully submerge us in the world. At play we can stop and start.[4] A game unfinished ultimately means nothing. There is nothing essential lost when recreation is broken off or forgone. Work left unfinished has consequences.

It is no accident, then, that the play we feel brings us closest to nature is play that mimics work. Our play in nature is often itself a masked form of bodily labor. Environmentalists like myself are most aware of nature when we backpack, climb, and ski. Then we are acutely aware of our bodies. The labor of our bodies tells us the texture of snow and rock and dirt. We feel the grade of the incline. We know and care about weather. We are acutely conscious of our surroundings; we need to read the landscape to find water and shelter. We know where the ground is soft or hard. We (some of us better than others) know the habits of fish because we seek to kill and eat them. The most intense moments of our play in nature come when it seems to matter as much as work: when the handhold in the rock matters; when we are four days from the trailhead and short on food; when whitewater could wreck a craft. It is no wonder that the risks we take in nature become more extreme. We try to make play matter as if it were work, as if our lives depended on it. We try to know through play what workers in the woods, fields, and waters know through work.

This confusion of work and play, the segregation of nature from real work, and the denigration of modern labor are complicated phenomena. Among the sources of confusion are two widespread convictions shared by many Americans. The first is that the original human relation with nature was one of leisure and that the first white men in North America glimpsed and briefly shared that relation. The second (not wholly reconcilable with the first) is that the snake in the garden was the machine. It tempted humans away from whatever benign possibilities work in nature once held. These two assumptions need critical examination.

We supposedly still get a hint of an earlier and proper relation between humans and nature embedded in the first conviction, which connects nature and leisure during our own excursions into the backcountry. In buttressing this belief in a connection with nature through play, we tend to mask the ways humans have known the natural world through work.

To make the case for an original relation with nature in North America that predates work, modern environmental writers—and, I suspect, many environmentalists—tell stories that make it seem as if play provided a primal and pristine contact with nature that work ruined. In effect, popular environmental writing tells an old Judeo-Christian story. Work is a fall from grace. In the beginning no one labored. In the beginning there was harmony and no human mark on the landscape. This is also the story told in the backcountry. This, we say, is how it must have appeared to the first white man: the mythical first white man whose arrival marks not just specific changes but the beginning of change itself. We identify our acts in the backcountry with the acts of historic figures emblematically connected with nature, and we make their work seem the equivalent of our play.

The first white man is, I think, a critical figure in our confusion about work and nature. We are pious toward Indian peoples, but we don't take them seriously; we don't credit them with the capacity to make changes. Whites readily grant certain nonwhites a "spiritual" or "traditional" knowledge that is timeless. It is not something gained through work or labor; it is not contingent knowledge in a contingent world. In North America, whites are the bearers of environmental original sin, because whites alone are recognized as laboring. But whites are thus also, by the same token, the only real bearers of history. This is why our flattery (for it is usually intended to be such) of "simpler" peoples is an act of such immense condescension. For in a modern world defined by change, whites are portrayed as the only beings who make a difference.

In telling stories about the first white man, environmentalist writers aren't just narrating a history. These accounts pretend to be history, but they are really just-so-stories about the paradise before labor. Over the last two decades academic historians have produced a respectable body of work on humans and the environment in North America that concentrates on how Indian peoples shaped the natural world they lived in.[5] But, by and large, this literature either has not penetrated popular treatments of nature or has been dismissed. The first white man always enters an untouched paradise. The first white man must also always be a *white man*. French métis trappers and traders penetrated and lived in the West long before more-famous first white men came along, but they tend to drop from the accounts. Working people of mixed race entering a region of modified nature can't carry the story line of the wonder of a world before work.

The most popular first white men remain Lewis and Clark and Daniel Boone. Daniel Boone is Wendell Berry's first white man.[6] Bill McKibben uses Lewis and Clark, and so does Philip Shabecoff, a good and intelligent environmental journalist. In *A Fierce Green Fire*, his recent history of the environmental movement, Shabecoff follows his first white men through lands "unchanged by humans."[7] The last of the first white men was Bob Marshall, who, consciously imitating Lewis and Clark, often gets credit for walking through the last areas in North America unseen by human beings. But the Central Brooks Range of Alaska, where Marshall hiked, had been inhabited by the Nunamiut in the nineteenth century, and they had returned in the 1940s. It is very unlikely that the areas Marshall traveled had been unvisited.[8]

These first white men are fascinating and sympathetic historical figures in their own right, but my concern with them is as cultural figures constructed by environmentalism. They are made into viewers of a natural world "as," according to McKibben, "it existed outside human history."[9] But it is not nature that exists outside human history; it is the first white men who do so. For environmentalist writers depict not how these travelers actually saw the natural world but instead how we would have seen it in their place. In this construction the first white men travel through nature untouched by human labor and are awed by it. Shabecoff's brief account in *A Fierce Green Fire* is typical. He quotes a journal entry by William Clark praising the scenery "in a country far removed from the civilized world." Shabecoff admits some "slight impact" on the environment from European introductions such as horses and guns, but he stresses how much of the continent was "unchanged by humans." Lewis and Clark serve both to reveal the untouched continent and to set its destruction in motion.[10]

This is not, however, the most likely or persuasive reading of what Lewis and Clark saw and did. They were, first of all, quite aware that they were moving through landscapes where human work had altered nature. Lewis and Clark described Indians farming, hunting, fishing, and grazing their animals. Their journey west was punctuated by fires set by Indians to shape the landscape, influence the movement of animals, or signal each other.[11] They described a landscape that we know, partly through their accounts, was already in the midst of wrenching change as a result of human labor.[12]

Nor did Lewis and Clark spend much time being staggered by the beauty and the sublimity of what they saw. They are not blind to the beauty of the world, but they are matter-of-fact: "the country still continues level fertile and beautifull," Lewis noted in a typical entry.[13] Even when touched, as in the Missouri Breaks, by "Seens of Visionary enchantment," what engages far more of Lewis's and Clark's attention is the laborious work of moving upstream.[14] Their labor gives them their most intimate knowledge of the country. In describing work, their writing becomes expansive and detailed. They are not just seeing the country. They are feeling it; they are literally enmeshed in it. Here are Clark and Lewis describing their struggle to pass through the Missouri Breaks. First Clark: "we Set out, and proceeded on with great labour . . . . & the banks were So muddey & Slippery that the men could Scercely walk. . . ." The land near the river, the land they struggle through, is "much hard rock; & rich earth, the Small portion of rain which has fallen causes the rich earth as deep as is wet to Slip into the river or bottoms." Now Lewis:

> the men are compelled to be ⟨much⟩ in the water even to their armpits, and the water is yet very could, and so frequent are those point that they are one fourth of their time in the water, added to this the banks and bluffs along which they are obliged to pass are so slippery and the mud so tenacious that they are unable to wear their mockersons, and in that situation draging the heavy burthen of a canoe and walking ocasionally for several hundred yards over the sharp fragments of rocks which tumble from the clifts and garnish the borders of the river; in short their labour is incredibly painfull. . . .[15]

What most deeply engaged these first white men with nature, what they wrote about most vividly, was work: backbreaking, enervating, heavy work. The labor of the body revealed that nature was cold, muddy, sharp, tenacious, slippery. Many more of their adjectives also described immediate, tangible contact between the body and the nonhuman world. Environmental writers have edited this out; they have replaced it with a story of first white men at strenuous play or in respectful observation.

We have masked the work of first white men. We have equated their work with our play. We have implicitly presumed that the journey of first white men must have been one long backpack across the West. But they did not gain knowledge of nature through play; they knew and connected with the world through work. And we unwittingly admit as much when we make our own play mimic their work.

This masking of knowledge gained through work is typical of one environmentalist approach to labor, but the actual role of labor is easily unmasked. Examples of human knowledge of nature gained through labor are readily apparent if we look. For millennia humans have known animals largely through work. Work gave the people who trained and worked with animals a particular knowledge of them. "There is something about a horse that isn't an engine you know," Albert Drinkwater, a British Columbia horse logger, explained, "a horse won't work for everybody the same. He'll work for one man and he'll pretend to pull for the other one." "The horses themselves became . . . part of the man that drove them."[16] Today the animals we know most intimately are pets; they share our leisure, not our work. We find working partnerships only in a few odd places. One of them is the circus. There the joint labor of humans and animals survives as entertainment.

Circuses where humans and animals connect for a common task are today often marked as unnatural or even cruel. Animals that work are pitied and presumed abused. But such pity is misplaced in the circus world that Diana Cooper describes in her recent book *Night after Night*. To work intimately with a trained animal is, she says, to know something nonhuman, vividly and deeply. She writes of trainers as being "deep in their work, focused on the animals and their human partners and what they are all creating together."[17] It is the trainer "who, through *knowing* Toto, has taught him what he needs to know."[18] And what trainers learn about elephants and horses is not only something about elephants and horses in general but also a deeply particular knowledge of individual elephants and horses. This is a knowledge we possess because we have bodies with which to work. Embodied, we encounter not ideas of the world but other bodies. We confront the intransigent materiality of the world itself. To know an elephant or a horse through work is to know that for all the general knowledge of horses or elephants you may have, what also matters is a knowledge of this particular elephant at this particular time.

It is precisely this recognition of how work provides a knowledge of, and a connection to, nature that separates a minority of environmentalists, particularly those sympathetic to Wendell Berry, from the dominant environmentalist denigration of work. But this second, minority position limits such good work to labor done without modern machines. They rely, to varying degrees, on the second conviction of modern environmentalism regarding the work in nature under examination here. In doing such work, people supposedly once had a truer, more benign relation with the natural world, one that technology has severed. It is supposedly modern work, not work itself, that has made us into dangerous monsters. Consequently, both our salvation and the land's can be found by harking back to a time before modern technology, to a time, in Shabecoff's telling, before the "new machines" degraded the landscape.[19]

The demonization of modern machines and the sentimentalization of archaic forms of labor allows a bifurcation of work into the relatively benign and even instructive, and the modern and destructive. Nowhere does this bifurcation show up more than in agriculture. Some, but again hardly all, environmentalists romanticize peasants, non-Western farmers, and even some premodern American farmers granting them an earth knowledge derived from their work. But in an age of vast, mechanized agribusinesses, in a land where farmers have given way to growers and where the very category "farmer" has now disappeared from the census, environmentalists grant no such knowledge to most modern farmers.

John Berger doesn't write from such motives, but his essays on peasants and peasantry, *Pig Earth*, can stand as examples of peasant knowledge.[20] In these communities "working is a way of preserving knowledge."[21] There are no peasants in the United States, but there are farmers who embody some of the peasants' working knowledge of the land. Farmers in the mountains of New Mexico, for example, once shared the life Berger describes.

Jacobo Romero was a New Mexican farmer in the Sangre de Cristo Mountains of New Mexico. Along with the Rio de las Trampas, a small river that is really little more than stream, he is the central figure in William deBuys and Alex Harris's haunting *River of Traps*. Romero knew nature through work. Like Berger's peasants, "inexhaustibly committed to wresting life from the earth," he was so wedded to a particular place that to move him would have been to change who and what he was. He worked his land along the river, and his work yielded knowledge that could be passed on. Working—how one works, how one wields a spade, how one handles a horse—imparts a bodily knowledge and a social knowledge, part of what Pierre Bourdieu calls habitus. Such knowledge is connected with physical experience, but it is not derived solely or often even directly from physical experience. Working communicates a history of past work; this history is turned into a bodily practice until it seems but second nature. This habitus, this bodily knowledge, is unconsciously observed, imitated, adopted, and passed on in a given community. Our work in nature both reinforces and modifies it.[22]

Luckily, in *River of Traps* Bill deBuys and Alex Harris were outsiders, too old and slow to learn in the usual way. Jacobo Romero had to articulate and explain what would otherwise be second nature at their age. His first and most telling injunction was "never to give holiday to the water," but instead "to put every drop to work."[23] To deBuys and Harris, watching Romero fulfill this injunction is to watch his shovel become a "tool of art." He tuned the water, "watching and listening to it like a technician attending his instruments, amplifying the flow here, muting it there, adjusting, repairing and rearranging."[24] He knew his ditches and fields intimately and precisely; he knew them because he worked them. He knew how to work water, because, from years of working with water he knew that "you got to let the water show you. You take your time, and sooner or later the water will show you."[25]

Wendell Berry is the environmental writer who has most thoughtfully tried to come to terms with labor like that of Romero or Berger's peasants. He is not only one of the few environmental writers who takes work seriously; he also has the impressive consistency of actually laboring in his own fields. But Berry quite purposefully and pointedly makes his own labor archaic and unusual; he relies on animal power and urges others to do this same. It is advice best taken by literary farmers. It is only Wendell Berry's writing, after all, that enables him to farm with horses. Such work resembles gardening, a favored model these days for a reconciliation with nature.[26] It is admirable; it yields lessons and insights, but it does not yield a living. It is not really our work in the world. Environmentalists still withhold from modern workers—those who work with machines that depend on more than muscle or wind for their power, those who gain their livelihood from work—the possibility of connections to and knowledge of nature.

The inroads that Wendell Berry, or Jacobo Romero, or Berger's peasants make into the general environmentalist disdain for work in nature are ultimately dead ends. For such work is always either vanishing or unable to yield a living. Wendell Berry and Jacobo Romero serve only as additional critiques of modern farming, logging, fishing, ranching, and industry. They don't change the basic message that modern work is the enemy of nature.

How modern work came to be alienated from nature has become the subject of another just-so-story. This story, ironically, is often told by workers themselves. It is not racialized, like the story of the first white men, but it is just as gendered: it treats work and machines as if they were male or female. Once, this story says, there was real manly work that took skill and strength and was rooted in the natural world. This was the work of Berger's peasants or Jacobo Romero. But this good work has now been contaminated by machines.

This story, like the story of the first white man, uses history without being a history. There certainly is a very real sense in which machinery did both deskill workers and alienate them from nature. As work became less physically demanding, as it required less bodily knowledge, workers who once possessed the skills now made irrelevant by machines felt robbed of something valuable. Old loggers in Coos Bay, Oregon, for example, denigrate modern logging. Their own work among the big trees demanded judgment, strength, and hours of strenuous labor on a single tree, all of which might be lost if the tree fell wrong and broke. But modern loggers harvest "pecker poles." The old loggers knew big timber, but loggers are cutting "dog hair these days."[27] This is, of course, hardly the view of modern loggers, although they, too, prefer the harvest of old growth.[28]

In the nineteenth and early twentieth centuries, blue-collar workers regarded physical work as a mark of manhood. They often saw the machines that broke their connection with nature as emasculating them; they associated these machines with women. Charley Russell was a working cowboy before he became a cowboy artist. When he lamented the end of the West, he mourned a world where work in nature defined manhood. Machines that didn't need real men, which could be run by women, had broken the tie between labor and nature.

Invention has made it easy for man kind, but it has made him no better. Machinery has no branes. A lady with manicured fingers can drive an automobile with out maring her polished nails. But sit behind six range bred horses with both hands full of ribbons these are God made animals and have branes. To drive these over a mountain rode takes both hands feet and head and its no ladys job.[29]

A man did real work with "God made animals"; a woman could handle machines "with out maring her polished nails." Machines associated with women broke a male connection with female nature, thus creating an almost domestic drama. Clearly for Russell, machines broke the old connections forged by manly labor.

But this division between good work close to nature and bad work, the work of machines that alienated men from nature, doesn't hold up to historical scrutiny. First of all, archaic labor and peasant labor, for all the knowledge they yielded, were not necessarily kind to the land. Bill deBuys, who works for the Nature Conservancy, deeply admired Jacobo Romero and his work. He was his neighbor and worked beside him. But he has no illusions that such knowledge protected the land from harm. DeBuys has shown how the agriculture of Jacobo and his neighbors took a toll on the land even as his work created knowledge of natural world and forged a deep connection with it.[30]

A connection with the land through work creates knowledge, but it does not necessarily grant protection to the land itself. There is a modern romanticism of place that says that those who live and depend on a place will not harm it. Its conservative version is wise use. Its environmentalist version appears in bioregionalism or in the work of Wendell Berry. Berry regards his own writing as depending on "work of the body and of the ground."[31] He regards himself as being very much of a place. In part his connection is from deep familiarity, but it also comes from the pleasure he takes in the work of restoring that place by hand. Yet he restores land that others, who were just as fully of this place, destroyed through their work. Berry writes as if working in nature, of being of a place, brought a moral superiority of sorts. Such rootedness supposedly offers a solution to our problematic relationship with the nonhuman world. I do not think this is necessarily true.[32] The choices are neither so simple nor so stark. Both destructive work and constructive work bring a knowledge of nature, and sometimes work is destructive and restorative at the same time, as when we cut or burn a meadow to prevent the encroachment of forest.

The intellectual, social, and political costs of limiting our choice to these two attitudes toward work and nature are immense. Condemning all work in nature marks environmentalists, as the Forks bumper sticker declares, as a privileged leisure class. Approving of archaic work while condemning modern work marks environmentalists as quaint reactionaries; they seem oblivious to the realities of the modern world. Environmentalists appeal to history to maintain these positions, but they turn history into just-so-stories.

We need to do better. The choice between condemning all work in nature and sentimentalizing vanishing forms of work is simply not an adequate choice. I am not interested in replacing a romanticism of inviolate nature with a romanticism of local work. Nor am I interested in demonizing machines. Environmentalists need to come to terms with modern work. The problem *is not* that modern work has been defiled by machines. Women who did much of the backbreaking labor on American farms before electricity have never, to the best of my knowledge, grown nostalgic for the work of pumping and carrying water or cleaning clothes on zinc washboards or any of what Senator George Norris of Nebraska called "the unending punishing tasks" of rural life.[33] Anyone in doubt about the hopes for liberation through machines and the kind of labor in nature that prompted those hopes should read the literature surrounding rural electrification; it described the tedium and social cost of this work in graphic detail.[34]

Coming to terms with modern work and machines involves both more complicated histories and an examination of how *all* work, and not just the work of loggers, farmers, fishers, and ranchers, intersects with nature. Technology, an artifact of our work, serves to mask these connections. There are clearly better and worse technologies, but there are no technologies that remove us from nature. We cannot reject the demonization of technology as an independent source of harm only to accept a subset of technologies as rescuing us from the necessity of laboring in, and thus harming, nature. We have already been down this road in the twentieth century.

In the twentieth century technology has often become a container for our hopes or our demons. Much of the technology we now condemn once carried human hopes for a closer and more intimate tie to nature. Over time the very same technology has moved from one category to another. Technology that we, with good reason, currently distrust as environmentally harmful—hydroelectric dams, for example—once carried utopian environmental hopes. To Lewis Mumford, for instance, dams and electricity promised an integration of humans and nature. Mumford saw technology as blurring the boundaries between humans and nature. Humans were "formed by nature and [were] inescapably . . . part of the system of nature." He envisioned a Neotechnic world of organic machines and "ecological balance."[35]

In an ironic and revealing shift, Mumford's solution—his liberating technology, his union of humans and nature—has become redefined as a problem. It is not just that dams, for example, kill salmon; they symbolize the presence of our labor in the middle of nature. In much current environmental writing such blurred boundaries are the mark of our fall. Nature, many environmentalists think, should ideally be beyond the reach of our labor. But in taking such a position, environmentalists ignore the way some technologies mask the connections between our work and the natural world.

The idea that pure nature, separate from our work, might no longer exist can prompt near hysteria. Bill McKibben fashioned a best-seller, *The End of Nature*, from that possibility. For McKibben global warming proved the final blow. "We have changed the atmosphere and thus we are changing the weather. By changing the weather, we make every spot on earth man-made and artificial."[36] "We have deprived nature of its independence, and that is fatal to its meaning. Nature's independence *is* its meaning; without it there is nothing but us."[37]

Now, nature as I have used it in this essay is only an idea. When we use the word "nature," we assert a unity, a set of relations, and a common identity that involves all the things humans have not made. Nature is, in this sense, purely cultural. Different cultures produce different versions of nature. Although nature is only an idea, it is unlike most other ideas in that we claim to see, feel, and touch it. For in everyday speech we use the word not only to describe a unity of all the things we have not made but also to name a common quality—the natural—possessed by seemingly disparate things: for example, sockeye salmon, Douglas fir, and cockroaches. When we see rocks, animals, or rivers in certain settings, we say we are seeing nature.

McKibben admits that his nature is only an idea, but that only raises the question of why he is so upset over the end of an idea. The answer is, I think, that McKibben, like the rest of us, doesn't really carry the distinction between nature as an idea and nature as the living, breathing world around us over into daily life or practice.[38] It is hard to read his *The End of Nature* without thinking that he considers our modern, Western construction of nature to be largely congruent with a real world that is also ending. Most human beings can, after all, easily accommodate a change in the meaning of a word. We all change our minds. We don't often pine for old definitions and ideas. What we miss more are people, animals, landscapes that have vanished. And if all McKibben is lamenting is the loss of an idea, then he is a man who lives far more deeply in his head than in the natural world he writes about. It is as if, all the while insisting on the distinction between mothers and motherhood, he mourned the death of his mother, not, so he claimed, for her own sake, but because *the idea* of motherhood has for him died with her.

To the extent to which McKibben is upset and not merely being histrionic, it is hard not to suspect that it is the end of what he regards as the natural world itself that upsets him. Thunderstorms, mountain ranges, and bears persist, but without the ability to draw a clear line between weather, mountains, animals, and plants and the consequences of our labor, they have ceased for McKibben to be natural, and we have become unable to "imagine that we are part of something larger than ourselves."[39]

If McKibben's angst is widely shared, then the issue of our contamination of nature is a serious one indeed. For while it is in part the deleterious effects of our labor that McKibben objects to, it is ultimately the ability of our labor to touch all aspects of the natural world, even the climate, that dismays him. The popularity of McKibben's book indicates that for many of us the meaning of the world depends on clear boundaries, pure categories, and the separation of nature out there from us, our bodies, and our work in here. This is, I think, a common American reaction to the modern world, and it is worth some notice. This fixation on purity and this distrust of our own labor—along with our casual, everyday ahistoricism that robs us of any sense of how our current dilemmas developed—explain at least some of our own inability to deal with mounting environmental problems, bitter social divisions, and increasing despair about our relations with the rest of the planet.

When McKibben writes about his work, he comments that his office and the mountain he views from it are separate parts of his life. They are unconnected. In the office he is in control; outside he is not. Beyond his office window is nature, separate and independent. This is a clean division. Work and nature stand segregated and clearly distinguished.

I, like McKibben, type at a keyboard. On this clear June day I can see the Olympic Mountains in the distance. Like McKibben, I do modern work. I sort, compile, analyze, and organize. My bodily movement becomes electrical signals where my fingers intersect with a machine. Lights flicker on a screen. I expend little energy; I don't sweat, or ache, or grow physically tired. I produce at the end of this day no tangible product; there are only stored memories encoded when my fingers touched keys. There is no dirt or death or even consciousness of bodily labor when I am done. Trees still grow, animals still graze, fish still swim.

But, unlike McKibben, I cannot see my labor as separate from the mountains, and I know that my labor is not truly disembodied. If I sat and typed here day after day, as clerical workers type, without frequent breaks to wander and to look at the mountains, I would become achingly aware of my body. I might develop carpal tunnel syndrome. My body, the nature in me, would rebel. The lights on this screen need electricity, and this particular electricity comes from dams on the Skagit or Columbia. These dams kill fish; they alter the rivers that come from the Rockies, Cascades, and Olympics. The electricity they produce depends on the great seasonal cycles of the planet: on falling snow, melting waters, flowing rivers. In the end, these electrical impulses will take tangible form on paper from trees. Nature, altered and changed, is in this room. But this is masked. I type. I kill nothing. I touch no living thing. I seem to alter nothing but the screen. If I don't think about it, I can seem benign, the mountains separate and safe from me as the Adirondacks seem safe from McKibben as he writes his essays for the *New Yorker*. But, of course, the natural world has changed and continues to change to allow me to sit here, just as it changes to allow McKibben to write. My separation is an illusion. What is disguised is that I—unlike loggers, farmers, fishers, or herders—do not have to face what I alter, and so I learn nothing from it. The connection my labor makes flows in only one direction.

My work, I suspect, is similar to that of most environmentalists. Because it seems so distant from nature, it escapes the condemnation that the work that takes place out there, in "nature," attracts. I regularly read the *High Country News,* and its articles just as regularly denounce mining, ranching, and logging for the very real harm they do. And since the paper's editors have some sympathy for rural people trying to live on the land, letters from readers denounce the paper for not condemning these activities enough. The intention of those who defend old growth or denounce overgrazing is not to denounce hard physical work, but that is, in effect, what the articles do. There are few articles or letters denouncing university professors or computer programmers or accountants or lawyers for sullying the environment, although it is my guess that a single lawyer or accountant could, on a good day, put the efforts of Paul Bunyan to shame.[40]

Most humans must work, and our work—all our work—inevitably embeds us in nature, including what we consider wild and pristine places. Environmentalists have invited the kind of attack contained in the Forks bumper sticker by identifying nature with leisure, by masking the environmental consequences of their own work. To escape it, and perhaps even to find allies among people unnecessarily made into enemies, there has to be some attempt to come to terms with work. Work does not prevent harm to the natural world—Forks itself is evidence of that—but if work is not perverted into a means of turning place into property, it can teach us how deeply our work and nature's work are intertwined.

And if we do not come to terms with work, if we fail to pursue the implications of our labor and our bodies in the natural world, then we will return to patrolling the borders. We will turn public lands into a public playground; we will equate wild lands with rugged play; we will imagine nature as an escape, a place where we are born again. It will be a paradise where we leave work behind. Nature may turn out to look a lot like an organic Disneyland, except it will be harder to park.

There is, too, an inescapable corollary to this particular piece of self-deception. We will condemn ourselves to spending most of our lives outside of nature, for there can be no permanent place for us inside. Having demonized those whose very lives recognize the tangled complexity of a planet in which we kill, destroy and alter as a condition of living and working, we can claim an innocence that in the end is merely irresponsibility.

If, on the other hand, environmentalism could focus on our work rather than on our leisure, then a whole series of fruitful new angles on the world might be possible. It links us to each other, and it links us to nature. It unites issues as diverse as workplace safety and grazing on public lands; it unites toxic sites and wilderness areas. In taking responsibility for our own lives and work, in unmasking the connections of our labor and nature's labor, in giving up our hopeless fixation on purity, we may ultimately find a way to break the borders that imprison nature as much as ourselves. Work, then, is where we should begin.

Looking for Nature at the Mall:
A Field Guide to
the Nature Company

Jennifer Price

Entry

PERHAPS, LIKE MOST PEOPLE, YOU FIRST ENCOUNTERED THE NATURE COMpany by chance. Say it was a Saturday afternoon at South Coast Plaza, the upscale mega-mall in southern California, and while searching for an exit after three hours of shopping, you stopped in your tracks. "Customers often exclaim, 'Wow!' when entering" the store, begins the Nature Company's press release.[1] I don't recall the exact mall where I had my own first run-in—around 1989, in the St. Louis Union Station, or perhaps the Bridgewater Commons in central New Jersey—but that approximately describes my reaction. Since then I've sought out Nature Company stores in a variety of malls, invariably on expedition from the Banana Republic, and every new encounter makes roughly the same impact.

The Nature Company's marketing director recently told *Time* that people "come in and say, 'Ahhh!' "[2] "Wow," however, better expresses my own assortment of feelings. "Wow" is subtler, more ambivalent. I marvel at the wondrous array of bird feeders, kites, telescopes, jewelry, and geodes, and at the trademark bins of wind-up dinosaurs, rubber animal noses, and cow-moo noise boxes. As a birder and hiker, I linger by the shelves of natural history books, binoculars, and wildlife videos. But I marvel equally at the apparent brazenness of it all. The Nature *Company*? The very name provokes my deepest suspicions. In South Coast Plaza? Nature itself, after all, comes unpackaged. While nature is by definition down-to-earth, not to mention outdoors, the Nature Company is so forthrightly upscale, commercial, and slick. It inhabits a forty-acre indoor shopping mall. "I bought a beautiful pair of gardening shears there," a friend mused to me, "but I felt somehow manipulated. It feels inauthentic"—but her brother gives her husband terrific Nature Company wildlife ties for Christmas. "It feels fake," another friend complained, having just bought a spectacular geode. If the Nature Company feels vaguely troubling to some of its patrons, it beckons irresistibly.

Nature stores are multiplying. The late 1980s saw the rise of two types of environmental store—the eco-store, which sells nature-friendly products like efficient light bulbs, and the more successful nature store, which markets "nature-oriented" items like animal sculptures, bug T-shirts, and glow-in-the-dark stars.[3] The Nature Company, the nature store prototype, has spawned a profusion of clones—the Natural Selection, the Ecology House, Nature's Own Imagination, and the company's most serious competitor, Natural Wonders. The Nature Company itself was founded in Berkeley in 1973, by a young couple, Tom and Priscilla Wrubel, who had served together in the Peace Corps. When they opened a small store "devoted to the observation, understanding and appreciation of the natural world," they hoped it might fill a useful niche for a "population taking to the wilderness in record numbers," and for a generation of new parents, like themselves, who wished to inaugurate children into the joys of nature.[4] Within ten years the Wrubels had opened four stores in the Bay Area. In 1983, seeking expansion capital, they sold the outfit to the CML Group in Acton, Massachusetts, a parent group that now also owns NordicTrack and Smith & Hawken—according to *Business Week*, "a package of yuppie goodies unlike anybody else's."[5] The Nature Company now runs 124 stores in the United States, 3 in Canada, 12 in Japan, and 7 in Australia.[6] Among its competitors, it remains the major success story. Under CML's guidance, the company has ridden the rising tides of baby-boomer income, upscale mega-mall construction, and environmental concern. Clearly, the urbanites who took to the wilderness in the 1970s have now taken to the malls as well. And who among us frequents the wilderness more often than the mall? If you want to explore the particular reinventions of nature in the 1990s, you must at some point make a trip to South Coast Plaza, or to the mall and nature store nearest you.

This essay, then, is a brief meditation on the Nature Company that raises, and tries to answer, a set of questions about these encounters. What is the Nature Company selling us, exactly? Why has the Nature Company sited most of its stores in upscale malls, within bowling distance of shops like Emporio Armani and the Banana Republic? Why do people say "wow"? Why do I harbor such deep suspicions, yet make the Nature Company my first stop for holiday shopping? Why is the Nature Company easier to run into than to find? But most of all, why have many of us been looking for nature at the mall? And can we find it there?

Natural Selection

WHAT DOES THE NATURE COMPANY SELL, EXACTLY? IMAGES OF NATURE, pieces of nature, and tools for going out into nature. The company markets over twelve thousand products.[7] It sells bird feeders, paperweights, wind chimes, field guides, note cards, music, and videos. Herb teas, bat shelters, rain gauges, field hats, Swiss army knives, Rainforest Crunch, plastic periscopes, and amethyst geodes. Stuffed tigers, Zuni fetishes, petrified wood, rock polishers, dinosaur everything, star charts, and galaxy boxer shorts.[8] At first glance, it seems that anything that has to do with nature must be here. But the Nature Company isn't a continent, a forest, or biome. It's 2,900 square feet of retail space—a very small space for all of nature—and what lives here must sell.[9] The company must define "nature-oriented" quite carefully. There's a principle of natural selection at work here. If we've been looking for nature at the mall, what nature have we been looking for?

It is easiest to begin with what the company does *not* sell. As nature stores draw boundaries around nature, what do they turn away at the doors? The Nature Company will not sell any "trophy" items that require the killing of animals—no butterflies, seashells, furs, or mounted heads.[10] They avoid products that anthropomorphize animals. The popular children's book *Goodnight Moon*, therefore, is non grata here because the bunny wears pajamas and sleeps in a bed.[11] Anthropomorphizers, as a species, are relatively non grata as well: you will discover almost no human images on the posters, and not too many human voices on the CDs (and no Enya, though often requested). Domestic animals are in short supply. The company's bias clearly runs toward wilder, nonhuman forms of nature.

Nature Company personnel themselves tend to describe their enterprise with the terms "authenticity," "quality," "uniqueness," and "whimsy."[12] So the toy animals here will not smile or wag their tails. The dolphins and cicadas on the keychains are accurate replicas.[13] The bat puppets look like real bats, the piggy banks like real pigs, and the angelfish bathtub toys like real angelfish.[14] The wind-up dinosaurs in the "ning-ning" bins (the Wrubels' children coined the term) come in bright colors "in line with new scientific thought," and the inflatable emperor penguins are anatomically correct.[15] Nature Company products apparently can be humorous, but not maudlin, kitschy, or cliché. They can be inexpensive, but not cheap. The company markets real rocks and plastic grasshoppers, but not real grasshoppers or plastic rocks. Dolphin keychains and stone bird sculptures, but no I-♥-dolphins bumper stickers or plastic pink flamingos.

Of all Nature Company products, perhaps the items that limn the stores' boundaries most visibly are the ones that don't, if you think about it, look like nature, or send you out into it. For example, the company sells handmade paper lamps, and Amish oak-hickory rockers. And why Zuni fetishes? The company enjoys a brisk business in Native American crafts and in indigenous and ethnic music. "Each product," according to the company's literature, ". . . introduces customers to an aspect of the natural world," so how do the lamps connect you to nature?[16] They don't—at least not directly. The Zulu baskets satisfy the entrance criteria not because they are nature but because they, like the brightly colored wind-up dinosaurs, are "authentic" or "unique." The Nature Company draws boundaries around not so much what nature *is* as what nature *means* to us. Items like *Viento de los Andes,* a CD of Andean folk music, get in by association, since nature and indigenous cultures have both come to connote a simpler and more authentic reality. The piggy bank must look like a real pig; but more important, it comes with "layers and layers of associations," including "French farmyards," "childhood dreams," and "the good old days."[17] The Nature Company bills itself as your direct connection to the natural world, but I'll argue it's more accurately a direct line to the meanings we've invested in nature.

And if the Nature Company sells over twelve thousand products, it's hawking a small handful of large ideas. What does nature mean? Few of us would do a double take on the Polish folk-art candles, or doubt that Papua New Guinean drumming creates the proper shopping atmosphere. (And why *do* so many people ask for Enya in a nature store?) The meanings that Americans have traditionally invested in "nature" are keystones of modern middle-class culture. We are well versed. To begin with, think of the Nature Company as a market bazaar for the meanings that many of the essays in this book explore.[18] Here you can buy pocket *Waldens* and John Muir field hats to enjoy nature as "wilderness"—an untamed natural realm, a solitary refuge from the city, that's ideally as unpeopled (and as devoid of cows and cats) as the Nature Company's poster collection. Here nature is also a destination for "adventure," brought to life by the subgenre of books that the company's head book buyer calls "tales of personal adventure in a wild land."[19] The displays of Zuni fetishes and Zulu baskets associate nature nearly interchangeably with indigenous peoples. The whale and eagle calls on the *Glacier Bay* CD "create moods and emotions within us"—so "nature" here, much like the "nature" that Susan Davis finds at Sea World, is also an exterior world that fosters an interior world of emotions and feelings.[20] To appreciate this brand of "nature," Davis argues—to be caring and sensitive, in short the right sort of person—has become a peculiarly middle-class obsession. *What* meanings of nature does the Nature Company market? But we also have to ask *whose* nature is on sale here.[21] The company's emphasis on children certainly plugs into longtime, distinctly middle-class traditions of using nature to educate children's emotional lives. And the entire inventory stands as a monument to the middle-class, white-collar vision of "nature" as something we enjoy in our leisure time.

Whether for critique, respite, or balance, middle-class Americans have co-opted nature as counterpoint to modern everyday life, and what seem to be its often troubling hallmarks. "Nature" has long been drafted into service as a palliative for urbanism, anonymity, commercialism, white-collar work, artifice, alienation, and the power of technology. On the first page of *Walden,* Thoreau contrasted nature to "civilized life"—and many since have agreed.[22] In modern America harvesting nature for a psychic yield has become a defining middle-class pastime. We graft meanings onto nature to make sense out of modern middle-class life, and then define ourselves by what we think nature means. Authenticity, simplicity, reality, uniqueness, purity, health, beauty, the primitive, the autochthonous, adventure, the exotic, innocence, solitude, freedom, leisure, peace. No one item at the Nature Company means everything, but nearly every single product draws from this pool of meanings. To shop at the Nature Company is to experience familiar ideas tumbling from the shelves.

Each generation and demographic slice of middle-class Americans has customized this pool of meanings to fit its own experience of modernity. And in the 1990s, according to *Forbes,* CML's target consumer group is the "affluent middle-aged." *Business Week* calls them the "yuppie leisure market."[23] The Nature Company targets the Wrubels' and my own generation, those born between about 1948 and 1962, and while few of us gracefully accept the term "yuppie," nature here is defined in ways that have become especially meaningful to us. For children of the 1950s and 1960s, "nature" assuages middle-class post–World War II anxieties about conformity, artifice, and anonymity. The Nature Company also strives to make its customers "feel good about themselves," and CML's parallel mission— quoted on the cover of its annual report, with a breathtaking photograph of Mount Rainier from the Nature Company—is to "enhance people's health, understanding of the natural world, and sense of well-being." In the slightly different words of an investment analysis firm, CML markets "products for stress relief."[24] In the 1980s and 1990s, "nature" has become a key therapeutic resource for the baby boomers' virtual obsessions with stress relief, self-improvement, and emotional healing. If you choose to site the Nature Company birdbath fountain indoors, "the sound of running water has a calming, beautiful effect." And the video *Tranquility,* a "moodtape" of sunrises, clouds, and "peaceful ocean waves," "designed to create a soothing and harmonious atmosphere," is an especially good bet to sell well.[25]

Perhaps the Nature Company's most innovative touch is its vaunted emphasis on humor, for a consumer generation with a notorious forever-young outlook. On a recent visit to South Coast Plaza, I found the kids book *Everyone Poops* scattered liberally around the store. Laughter in the mainstream American nature tradition has been notably scarce. Not too many jokes in Emerson—"nature" must not be trivialized—so the Nature Company walks a fine line here. But as an earthly source of "whimsy," "nature" encourages the children of baby boomers to be children. Kites, bubble kits, and paint-a-snakes encourage the parents to remain playful and young, and to stay trustworthy over thirty.

The store sounds like fun, and it is. So why do I feel ambivalent? I finger everything in the ning-ning bins, but maintain a cool reserve. Why does the store "feel fake" to some of its patrons? Well, to begin with, the Nature Company is not nature. And among the set of meanings we've attached to the natural world, perhaps the most overarching and powerful is that nature is *not* a shifting set of human meanings. It's tangible, secure, rocklike, stable, self-evident, definable, real. In a word, it's natural. Not that we don't know or acknowledge that nature means definable things to us, like "solitude" or "relaxation." But the meanings seem universal, indelible, indigenous to the rocks and trees themselves. And nature, we tend to assume, is for everyone, or should be. "Nature" is not constructed, like a movie, to tell a story that appeals to a definable audience in a certain time and place.

Ordinarily, if you buy your pruning shears at the hardware store, or your bird guide at a bookstore, these convictions don't face any serious threat. In fact, my friend testified that a trip to Ace Hardware for gardening tools would not feel like an "inauthentic" experience, nor would she feel "manipulated." In the garden, too, where you're surrounded by what is undeniably real and tangible about nature, nature feels securely natural. But here, where the Nature Company has brought together thousands of nature-oriented products, the boundaries we've drawn around "nature" begin to look visible. If you compile the complete pool of meanings, and stack and shelve them all together in one room in a mall, they begin to look like meanings. And in this upscale venue, practically neighbors with Emporio Armani, *whose* meanings these are becomes an almost palpable question. Few of us will respond with, "Aha, so the meaning of nature is not so self-evident or universal after all." The response, I think, is closer to "um, wow." The store invites us in, but plants the vague suspicion that nature is a very human, historically shifting idea—not precisely what most of us are shopping for.

The Nature Company is engaged in a highly tricky pursuit. It's marketing a product—middle-class meanings of nature—to target consumers who tend to question the product's existence. The company also markets "authenticity," "uniqueness," and "simplicity" in the extravagant maw of South Coast Plaza. It's a lucrative business if you can do it, but the very meanings that the "Nature" in "the Nature Company" immediately call to mind—the antimodern associations that are the company's real commodity—provoke many nature lovers to doubt the most basic features of the enterprise. The Nature Company, tapping flawlessly into the market for anatomically correct inflatable penguins, and a perfect place to go to encounter what nature means to America's "affluent middle-aged" in the late twentieth century, inevitably breeds some mistrust among its clientele.

Habitat

YET THE COMPANY AND ITS COMPETITORS HAVE CHOSEN TO SITE MOST OF their stores in shopping malls, of all places. Why sell "nature" at the mall, a place many of us think of as "unnatural"? Why hawk "authenticity" at the mall, a place whose reputation for generic-ness is so notorious that we call it "the mall"? And why the biggest, most expensive malls? The Nature Company, which pioneered the mall as home for nature stores, now leases space in many dozens of upscale malls and most of the country's mega-malls. It is not difficult to predict where to find one. In Denver, the Cherry Creek Mall. In St. Louis, the Galleria and Union Station. In Los Angeles, the Century City Shopping Center, and the Beverly Center in Beverly Hills. In Orange County, South Coast Plaza. The Mall of America has one. "Mall" and "nature" may sound like opposites, but Nature Company stores posted net sales of $162 million in 1993.[26] In the course of our efforts to mitigate the materialism and artifice of life in the 1990s, why has it become somehow logical to make regular trips to these symbolic hotbeds of conspicuous consumption?

Shopping malls—they've been called "worlds of artifice," "gardens of delight," and "palaces of consumption." And since the 1950s, when they began to dot the suburban landscape, they've been targets for derision, or at least ambivalence. In the 1970s Joan Didion described them as "toy garden cities in which no one lives but everyone consumes."[27] They've been accused of being identityless, devoid of character, with television a major culprit in the postwar homogenization of American culture. With interstate highways, they've homogenized the American landscape. Lost along the corridors of chain-outlet shoe stores, you could be anywhere. The mall, as they say, is every place and no place.[28]

In the 1980s mall developers set out to inject more individuality into their installations, outfitting the new mega-malls with more character, and giving face-lifts to most of the larger upscale malls built in the 1960s and 1970s— exactly the malls the Nature Company has moved into.[29] Some malls now look like European villages, or Mexican haciendas. Tropical settings have been especially popular (in no trivial part because plants like figs and rhodo-dendrons grow well in indoor climate-controlled spaces). The Mall of America, Minneapolis's mall of all malls, contains within its ninety-six acres an "East Broadway" avenue, a mock European railway station, a seven-acre theme park with a Minnesota woodland motif, and the Rainforest Café, with live animals, waterfalls, fog, and a " 'star-filled' sky."[30] The new malls, in other words, *simulate* place.[31] Drawing from the world over, mall developers have converted real places into décor and motif, mixing and matching as if the earth were a giant Lego set or salad bar. (The Los Angeles malls tend to simulate Los Angeles, a city notorious as both a simulation of place and an outsize shopping mall.) Like the Foot Locker and Benetton stores, the Greek agora and Italian piazza are cookie-cutter pieces of the world that mall architects tuck ready-made into any mall in any city. They are places out of place.

The Nature Company markets rocks, geodes, gold slivers, wildflower seeds, petrified wood. It is a kind of one-store global assemblage itself. And most of the nature here is simulated—the plastic whales and sculpted giraffes, the inflatable penguins, the spiders on the T-shirts, the posters and postcards and videos of Alaska and New Zealand and Tanzania. We are globe-coasters all, and the natural world has remained near center stage during the late-twentieth-century postmodern collapse of space. The Nature Company invites us to touch every part of the globe. And you can browse the earth's wild things close to home, because the company has installed similar assemblages in malls in thirty-four states and two Canadian provinces, in Australia, and in the giant malls in Japan's underground railway stations. The stores at South Coast Plaza (store no. 7), the St. Louis Galleria (no. 60), and the Century City Shopping Center (no. 21) all stock the same giraffe ties, *Virtual Nature* videos, and inflatable globes.[32] At the Century City center, a breezy outdoor mall on LA's west side, the Nature Company faces Rand-McNally, a "map and travel store." Next door at the Market food court, you can eat at Bueno Bueno, Gulen's Mediterranean Cuisine, DeMartino's Pizzeria, Raja, La Crepe, or Kisho An. When I shopped at the center last June, El Portal Luggage, also next to the Nature Company, was featuring World Cup posters in its windows, two doors down from Toys International and within sight (a tree and a bush across from the globes and atlases in the Rand-McNally window) of United Colors of Benetton. In the Nature Company itself, the "now playing" CD combined Western instrumental forms with Baka Pygmy music from the border of Congo and Cameroon. I sifted through the zebra and panda footprint stamps, but decided to buy the polar bear.

If one harbors theoretical doubts about the mall as a fitting habitat for a nature store, the Nature Company feels instinctively well sited, because encounters with nature in the 1990s have become as simulated and as disconnected from place as "the mall" itself. Even we city dwellers who hike and camp, and who make seasonal vacation pilgrimages to wild places, encounter nature far more often in everyday urban haunts—on our living-room walls, on television (on PBS and on car commercials), and in shops. We've filled our homes and offices with images of nature from everywhere. So many of our daily encounters with nature transpire quite separately—separated by miles, or by feats of simulation, or both—from real pieces of nature rooted in specific places. *Where* do we look for nature most often in the 1990s? Not in the "where" where we generally think of nature as being. It's not surprising that one of the more successful Nature Company stores not in a mall is in the Pittsburgh airport.

Nature itself still seems to many of us to be nothing if not rooted in place. Along with "natural" and "authentic," "place" is among the most powerful in the pool of meanings we've attached to nature. "Nature" counters the pervasive, often troubling placelessness of modern life that the mall so definitively represents. In this fast-paced, ever-changing world, we count on nature not only to stay constant in meaning but to stay put. A poster of the Antarctic or the Amazon rain forest inspires, among other things, a spirit of place. Just as collecting all our meanings for "nature" into one store plants the suspicion that "nature" is a middle-class grab bag of ideas, does bringing all the world's places together imply the rootlessness of modern encounters with nature? If the posters connect me to nature and place, they can also instill a sneaking sensation of detachment.

The Nature Company's stated mission is to connect us to nature, not disconnect us. So which does it do? Well, postmodern globe coasting works both ways. We know more about the entire natural world than people have at any time before, but may also know less about any one piece of it. The toy plastic whale in the "Ocean Authentics Collection" can teach its owner about the blue whale and the circumpolar oceans the species inhabits. What it most basically does, on the other hand, is bring a miniature, reasonably accurate image of a whale into one's life. What you do with it is up to you. To a child in suburban Chicago, the palm-size whale might look like an endangered blue whale, and possibly like the largest animal that ever lived. And it might look like Jonah, Shamu, Monstro, or Willy in *Free Willy*. It might look like a to-be-named companion for a Mighty Morphin Power Ranger. The distance from the Pacific makes the whale unusually open to interpretation.[33]

Of course, if Nature Company products actually connect us less to nature itself than to what nature means, then a bit of distance might work wonders. Far from the ocean, the plastic whale reduces easily to a motif, a feeling, an association—like "freedom" or "beauty," or perhaps "solitude." *Glacier Bay*, one of the company's best-selling CDs, comes with a booklet that reads, "ALASKA— . . . a superlative for natural beauty and unbounded wilderness."[34] It's "for relaxation," a store manager told me—so I bought one. The music has a New Age dreamlike quality. It's a quiet, flowing mélange of flute, cello, whales, eagles, and waves, which sounds not unlike the flute, cello, frogs, wrens, and flowing water on the Costa Rican *Cloud Forest* CD. It's self-identified mood music, in which the humpback whale makes a cameo appearance. From a boat in the bay itself, would coastal Alaska be relaxing? Isn't the far North notorious as mosquito country? And why, I've always wondered, does the music composed to evoke the natural world always sound like flute? In suburban somewhere, however, after a stressful day at work (even if you read the booklet notes on natural history), Glacier Bay reduces to a handful of abstractions, like "beauty," "wilderness," and "relaxation." The call of the humpback whale promotes human peace of mind. The arctic landscape and its animals become shadowy realities, subordinate to these meanings. And what better place to sell these abstractions than in the placeless vacuum of the mall?

Ironically, and mindful of its audience, the Nature Company designs its stores specifically to assuage modern anxieties about malls and the meltdown of place. The dark slate exterior, and the stream flowing through the open window display, can immobilize you on your stroll through the mall, as if you'd stumbled onto a landmark in a maze. The store looks like a distinctive place. Inside, in contrast to the bright open interiors of its neigh-

The Nature Company store front at Cherry Creek Mall, Denver, Colorado. *(Philip J. Deloria)*

bors, the Nature Company looks more like sun and shadows, and not cluttered though intricately niched. The Nature Company likens the design to a "dappled forest."[35] And browsing here feels a bit akin to taking a nature walk in that forest. The company sets products low on the shelves, often out of their boxes, inviting you to touch, experience. Videos attract customers to stop and watch. Open the mineral drawers, turn the posters, put a quarter in the Rainforest Meter, read a book on the couch in the book nook, all to the accompaniment of music inspired by nature. The store promotes a mall version of a Thoreauvian encounter.

The mall architects use some natural touches themselves. The recent spate of upscale-mall renovations rely liberally on the addition of skylights, greenery, and fountains—like the St. Louis Galleria's "garden court," with topiary bird mobiles and a fountain about eight stores long. In fact, I'll argue that such face-lifts have been undertaken precisely to attract the baby boomers—now the chief commanders of disposable income—who object to the generic, placeless aura of the malls they grew up on. Build a fountain, they will come: developers install nature like a sign to affluent middle-class shoppers, saying this place is a real place, and it's for you. The Nature Company has simply maximized this design strategy. In the artifice of the mall, the store feels like a sylvan refuge. It's a green hole among the bright lights and echoes. To anyone at all anxious about malls, it's a relief. "I suppose I should state," a *New York Times* columnist reported on his enjoyable first run-in with the Nature Company, on a Sunday trip to the Bridgewater Commons, "that shopping bores me and malls make me yearn for the relative tranquillity of a dentist's chair."[36] The Nature Company attracts nature lovers precisely by inhabiting a notoriously placeless site.

In sum, while the mall makes perfect, intuitive sense as a place to look for nature in these placeless times, it's also a smart sales tactic. The *Glacier Bay* CD perhaps makes best cognitive sense in a mall, but it also sells rapidly. I'm not questioning the sincerity with which the Nature Company pursues its mission to connect us to nature. The company simply speaks two languages—the language of "authenticity" and "uniqueness," and the language of profits. It has to—the mall has sales-per-square-foot requirements for its tenants. Also, as Tom Wrubel has said, "there's nothing we sell here that they really need."[37] The *Tranquility* moodtape may be meaningful, but it's an optional item in most people's lives. Selling the Nature Company's products demands a fair bit of strategy.

Fortunately, the mall itself specializes in the strategic marketing of things people don't really need. It can be hard to find something you *do* need. Why, for example, in the entire acreage of the mall, can't you find a bar of Dial soap? The motives behind mall design lie in the answers to the questions so many of us have asked. Why are there so few entrances, and only one map? Why is it so hard to find the rest rooms? Why can't I ever remember which floor the Gap is on? And why can't we find the car?[38] Nearly every square inch of the mall, from the tenant locations to the curves in the hallways, hews to a science that the shopping-center industry has been refining since the 1950s, in which "Discourage direct navigation" might be the supreme law.[39] It's been statistically proven that the longer we stay, the more we buy.[40] Hence, no Dial. No drugstores, Safeway, or dry cleaners. Necessities encourage beeline, goal-oriented, quick-exit shopping. "It's a hard place to run into for a pair of stockings," a companion of Joan Didion's remarked.[41] The upscale mall pulls in shoppers (or "invitees," as the shopping-mall literature refers to us) through a few well-spaced entrances, and keeps us rambling around inside (the current average mall visit lasts three hours) to stimulate the impulse purchase.[42] After one's first run-in with the Nature Company, like any other store it can be difficult to relocate. In the mall, looking for nature can become a quite literal search.

For a company that markets items like moodtapes and plastic polar bears—things one's core consumers might not intentionally set out to find—the mall is therefore the optimal site. The architecture of the mall will careen more than a few "invitees" through one's doors. Inside the Nature Company store itself, if you careen into the compasses while you're searching for the Rainforest Crunch, you may be tempted to buy one. Have patience, though. You'll find the candy eventually, next to a telescope, though en route you may decide to buy a wind-up dinosaur. The company deploys mall savvy, maneuvering its customers to stay and browse. Even the catalog has no index, and is organized as much by color as by item. But the company's real genius has been to design its private retail store to feel un-retail, for a consumer profile that harbors above-average angst about malls and shopping. If the store itself feels like a refuge, the search for items feels like an outdoor adventure. Friends tell me they play with the toys and watch the videos, but don't buy much—well, except for fish magnets and wind chimes. The design is so successfully antimall that sometimes patrons don't even quite notice when they've purchased something unnecessary.

In sum, if my friend "felt manipulated"—upon emerging from a trip to the Nature Company with her new pair of gardening shears—she's absolutely justified. But do the Nature Company's strategic maneuvers necessarily constitute grounds for complaint? Many of us enjoy browsing there. The "dappled forest" design pulls me into a private retail enterprise, but also adds a little sunshine to my trip to the mall. And does the company manipulate me more objectionably than the Gap or the Banana Republic does? "Nature," of course, triggers my suspicions here. "Nature," many of us like to think, is antonym and antidote to modern materialism. The Nature Company *feels* more manipulative, because it sells "nature," not jeans. Just as the very meanings the company markets make some customers uneasy about what nature the company sells, and where, we're a little suspicious that they sell it at all.

The main reason, after all, that we've been looking for nature in the mall is that the mall is the place where you buy things. And it's the buying and selling, I'm convinced, that engenders the greatest uneasiness. Why are we looking for nature with our credit cards? "If nature is so important to us," asked the *New York Times* columnist who'd rather enjoyed his run-in with the Nature Company ("we bought something we didn't need and didn't mind a bit"), "then why, on earth, weren't the people in the store outside experiencing it instead of indoors buying it?" And while searching for his car in the parking lot, he felt increasingly troubled, but not mostly because he'd forgotten the computer paper he'd come to the mall to buy. Rather, he voiced a deep anxiety that many of us share—"Is it possible that people in our culture have become so estranged from nature that their only avenue to it is consumerism?"[43]

Ecology

AMERICANS SPEND A TREMENDOUS AMOUNT OF TIME BUYING THINGS. SHOPping ranks second only to TV watching as a leisure-time pursuit—except that not everyone watches TV.[44] Even those of us who consume comparatively little consume quite a lot, making regular shopping trips to the mall and to the store, filling our homes, offices, and cars with necessities, luxuries, gadgets, equipment, art, décor, and knickknacks. We have filled our lives with an abundance of *things*. Consumerism, since the turn of the century the nation's economic foundation, has increasingly evolved into a way of moving through the world. In these globe-connected, high-tech times, we obviously make only some tiny percentage of the items we personally use. And in an urban society of comparative anonymity *and* an abundance of commodities, we use the things we buy to define ourselves. The clothes, the sound system, the books, the computers, the kind of car and the bumper stickers: these have become key tools not only for keeping busy but for creating distinctive self-identities.[45] Gifts, too—and one could argue that an upscale mall is a giant gift arcade—have become abundant fuel for modern social relationships. We give gifts to mark important events, to reward and motivate, and to tell stories about the places we've traveled. And shopping itself can often be as much a social outing as a quest for goods.[46] Buying something is at once an economic act, a social act, and an act of creativity and imagination. And it's been shown that many Americans prefer shopping to sex.[47]

Hence we approach the natural world, just like everything else, instinctively as consumers. It's perfectly logical (I think inevitable) to articulate a vision of nature, to learn about nature, to share one's enthusiasms through the common arts of shopping for things, buying them, using and displaying them, and giving them to others. The bird feeder imports nature into one's life. The Yosemite calendar becomes a daily utterance about what nature means ("majesty"? "solitude"?). The ready-to-install waterfall marks the garden's owner as the kind of person who knows and values what nature means. A Saturday-afternoon browse through geodes, bat puppets, and rain forest posters at the Nature Company can be a value-forming experience, and fun too—and with a friend or partner, an affirmation of shared values. The nature store is an excellent, logical place to reiterate, enjoy, and share one's commitments to nature. On a birthday an inflatable emperor penguin—the company's best-selling inflatable—binds an adult gift giver to a child, fosters shared meanings, purveys values about people and animals and places from one person to another.[48]

If a run-in with the Nature Company sets one's consumer instincts into motion, the store can also trigger a nature lover's anticonsumer instincts. After all, for many of us "nature" *counters* consumption—"simple," "primitive," and "natural," it's a palliative for modern materialism—and the whole store flashes NATURE like a neon warning sign. If I define myself with the things I buy, I define myself also by what I think "nature" means. At the Nature Company, I am an anticonsumer consumer. The company itself, meanwhile, not surprisingly designs its stores to encourage its patrons with anticonsumer fears to relax. You can put a quarter in the Rainforest Meter and send your money off to a good cause. You can buy a book about tropical deforestation. The company makes serious, extensive efforts to be a place where one can consume responsibly and well.

The Nature Company is nothing if not ironic. It's a plexus of contradictions. And no ironies get more complicated here than those swirling around consumption. So on the one hand, many of us flatly assume, like the *Times* columnist, that nature should be experienced, not consumed—that shopping, in contrast to a day's hike up a mountain, is a less "real" or "authentic" encounter with nature. On the other hand, at the Nature Company you can buy "authentic," "quality" things—a lifelike bronze frog for $995, for example, that *connotes* "authenticity." The company also sells recycling kits. A percentage of profits goes to the Nature Conservancy. At the Nature Company you consume to preserve nature. Nevertheless, in South Coast Plaza, a monument to overconsumption, it's tempting to think about shopping as a quantity more than a quality experience. Perhaps the Nature Company, like its neighbors, sells too many quality things, and too much nature—if there are five hundred ways to shop for a better world, perhaps we shop too much.[49] At the same time, some products here are made from recycled materials. The company makes a concerted effort to locate their recycled items, like the luminaria, "waste not" stationery, and flying animals wrapping paper.

Most of the company's products, however, have not been recycled—and this, I think, points to the most stubborn irony about consumption here, and the most deeply buried. Every "nature-oriented" item, whether recycled or not, is literally manufactured from nature. When I "consume" an inflatable penguin, I'm literally consuming natural resources like oil, wood, minerals, and energy. Who thinks about that? Who thinks of the *Glacier Bay* whale calls as "petroleum" more than "freedom"? Looking for what nature means, we can lose track of nature itself—but doubly ironic, if the real arctic landscape recedes as we graft abstract meanings onto it, its oil might be right in our laps. While pondering whether consumerism is a proper way to connect to nature, we miss the most literal, direct connections. Does the Nature Company connect people to nature? Absolutely— perhaps too much. Can we find nature at the mall? It would be impossible not to. Nature provides the raw materials the mall is made from.

The mall is generally designed to downplay or disguise all these connections, natural and economic, to the world outside (as Marx might have pointed out long ago). Mall developers deliberately sequester all traces of producing, sending, and receiving—for example, by relegating business offices to the basement, and by trucking in goods in the early morning hours before the invitees arrive to shop.[50] Retail stores, too, are designed to be like slices of magic, bearing few traces of where products came from (other than "made in China"), of how they got to suburban Chicago, or where your money will go after you trade it for a shirt. Shopping malls—"gardens of delight," "palaces of consumption." The Nature Company calls its store a "magical space."[51] But while the Nature Company may be Oz, like the mall it's also a flowchart.

The Nature Company actually parts its curtain wider than most companies do. It emphasizes its recycled items. It identifies the selected products for which a percentage of profits go to the Nature Conservancy, Cultural Survival, and other groups. But the flowchart looks more complex. Begin with the company's self-description, in an informational sheet for the sales staff—"Although the public would hardly be aware of it, there is, in fact, an order to the magic in the form of eight professionally managed buying departments."[52] The Nature Company sources products in Brazil, China, Zaire, Portugal, Chile, and the Philippines, among other countries.[53] It has its thousands of products shipped to a distribution center in Kentucky, which reships them to the 146 stores in four countries.[54] Profits from these products go to far too many places to map, but among other places, the eight buying departments; 850 sales employees; a vice president of real estate development; a director of public relations, image, and special events; a company naturalist; mall managers and leasing agents; advertising agencies; the CEO and the president of CML, who earned $1.38 million and $1.37 million, respectively, in fiscal year 1993; and among CML's stockholders, Reader's Digest, the Ford Foundation, my phone company US West, the Bank of Tokyo, IBM, and GE.[55]

"Commodity consumption," the historian Jean-Christophe Agnew has written, has not "enhanced our appreciation of the remote consequences of our acts or . . . clarified our responsibilities for them."[56] I spent $180.18 at the Nature Company while researching this essay—mostly on gifts. Items like the polar bear footprint stamp (made in China) and the *Glacier Bay* CD (recorded in San Francisco, with notes printed in Canada) connect me to the lives and working conditions of people worldwide who mine, plant, assemble, and transport the company's materials and products. The hummingbird feeder on my porch connects me to the CML chairman's hefty campaign contributions, which in the 1980s flowed to his friend President Bush.[57] These items also connect me to *nature*—to the pieces of nature worldwide that the Nature Company's operations touch upon and that stockholder companies mine with the profits. In sum, to shop at the Nature Company is to plug into the flows of energy and resources, economic power and influence that define the modern American capitalist economy. And one of the touchstones of this economy has been its ravenous global consumption of natural resources. Like any successful company, the Nature Company has been expanding as rapidly as possible. Perhaps the perfect metaphor for the Nature Company is a famous outdoor sculpture by Isamu Noguchi at South Coast Plaza, called *California Scenario,* a strikingly serene landscape of rock and cactus and water. If you turn around, you see its perfect reflection in the thirty-story glass walls of the Great Western Bank.[58]

And who controls the bulk of this economic activity? The shoppers the company draws—whose "nature" the Nature Company markets—are exactly the generation and class who own and invest substantial capital, who reap the material benefits. CML's target consumers, whom *Business Week* labels the "yuppie leisure market," are "folks [with] lots of money to spend and a seemingly irrepressible urge to spend it." They control, according to *Forbes,* "a great deal of the economy's discretionary income."[59] If we are globe coasters all, the globe now belongs to the higher-income baby boomers not only figuratively but literally. The *Glacier Bay* CD channels serenity into my leisure hours, and channels profits from Alaskan oil mining into my portfolio. As Susan Davis writes, the kind of person who "appreciates" nature is likely to be the kind of person who consumes a lot of it. Here, I think, is the irony that lies at the very heart of the new nature stores. It's an "ur"-irony, if you will, near the core of middle-class encounters with nature in the 1990s. The Nature Company markets twelve thousand products that, on the one hand, sustain American middle-class ideas of nature that mitigate the materialism and artifice of modern capitalist society and, on the other hand, sustain, through the creation of artifice, the capitalist overconsumption of resources that underpins American middle-class life.

Exit

I HAVE A MOUNTAIN FOR A BACKYARD, A LOVELY PINE-CLAD SLICE OF THE foothills of the Rockies at the edge of Boulder, Colorado, where I hike often, and where these ironies tend not to chase me into the woods. At the Nature Company, however, the ironies always threaten to surface—which returns me squarely to "wow," because at the heart of my ambivalence lies not the company but myself. I'm uneasy about what "nature" the company is hawking, and where, but mostly I'm resisting my vague suspicion that this is, after all, a very logical place for me to be. The Nature Company all but spells out the contradiction between the meanings I look for in the natural world, which chafe against modernity, and the very modern whats, whos, wheres, and hows of my everyday encounters. I cherish nature as a universal source of meaning, and as a counterpoint to modern placelessness, artifice, and materialism. But I use "nature" like a vessel for all my middle-class generational angst about urban life in the nineties. I encounter nature most often out of place, in the city, through artifice and simulation. And I am a consumer.

It's 1995, and I doubt that my brushes with nature are going to become simpler or more direct, less mediated, or any less tangled in a consumer economy. They're not likely to detach themselves from this historical place and time. So it's time to consider that my engagements with nature may be as ineluctably modern as the rest of my life—to acknowledge that these encounters, as much as the mountain hikes, are *real* encounters, and to take responsibility for them. Begin with what "nature" means to me. As human beings, we inevitably invest nature with meanings that define both the natural world and our place within it. But if "nature" means a host of antonyms for modern life, then it's difficult (as many authors in this book argue) to envision an urban habitat, a modern everyday life, that uses nature at all, much less wisely or sustainably.[60] Nature is my mountain at the edge of town, but it's also, as Giovanna Di Chiro argues, the place where people live and work. "Nature" has to mean something that people can convert to human artifice, make into livable cities, and consume—a host of meanings that might infuse modern cities with more of what I like about my hikes in the pines (and better preserve the mountain). What "nature" should I look for at a nature store? Rugged remote mountains, savannas, and deserts, and plastic polar bears and wind-up dinosaurs. Also cityscapes, rooftops, and neighborhoods, some human images on the posters, and a few inflatable cows and cats.

We have access to the entire globe in these postmodern high-tech times, and it's a wondrous diverse place, which we'll inevitably simulate in plastic. We'll buy miniature polar bears and blue whales, and ponder our connections to them. But globe coasters so easily become casual tourists, collecting pieces of nature more than connecting to them, investing distant places and species with meanings that satisfy our desires but say little about the actual places themselves. It's easy to lose track of the real ocean and the real blue whale. But if we're going to cruise the earth's natural places by means of replicas and photos, should we keep better track of nature itself?

It's easy, too, to forget that brightening our lives with plastic animals requires the aggressive *use* of distant pieces of nature. I'm going to consume nature as meaning, but equally inevitably as raw materials. Keeping track of the nature I import into my life—this desk, this computer, in sum my large material world of stuff—seems to me an especially daunting, intractably modern charge. The Nature Company itself has recently installed "field stations" in some of its stores, to encourage patrons to keep track of nature close to home. The Cherry Creek Mall station in Denver, for example, stocks maps and guides for the natural areas in the surrounding Rockies and plains—the places I personally love and spend my weekends. But a "field station" might also chart nature through the cities of Denver and Boulder— mapping, for example, where our water comes from and where the garbage goes. It should, I think, attempt to keep track not only of the nature we preserve but of what we consume. And inside the Nature Company itself, is it possible to consume responsibly and well? The nature store might not be the most congenial site for posing the most challenging questions to an American nature lover—*Who* consumes exactly what nature, and how much?

There are, in sum, some difficult decisions to make. Is the Nature Company "a gracious balance between commerce and environmental consciousness"?[61] Should we be using the sounds of Glacier Bay to relax? And should I buy the inflatable penguin for my nephew on his birthday? Those turn out to be extraordinarily spacious, complicated questions.

Putting on a price tag. *(Drawing by Roger Roth,* New York Times, *May 7, 1989, Illustration © 1989 Roger Roth. Reprinted by permission of the illustrator.)*

"Touch the Magic"[1]

Susan G. Davis

THE TELEVISION COMMERCIAL OPENS ON A LITTLE BOY, HIS FACE PRESSED TO glass, "in absolute amazement," as a gigantic black-and-white killer whale swims past. The scene dissolves to a seal jumping, and then to an old man hugging a small girl. On the audio track a male singer asks, "Do you remember . . . the feeling of wonder? . . . Bring back the smile to the child inside of you. . . ."[2]

The scene dissolves back to the tank of the black-and-white whale, where an athletic, wet-suited man is thrust into the air on the whale's nose. As the stadium crowd cries out at the sight, the singer intones, "Touch the magic. . . . Touch the world that you once knew."

Now the visual and aural pace of the commercial turns quiet and gentle. A little girl dips her hand into a tide pool, grasps a starfish, and turns it over. Another little girl and her grandfather lean over a wall to pet a dolphin as the chorus fades away, singing, "From the heart, Sea World touches you. . . ."

The images on the television screen alternate between shots of human groups and shots of animals. Waddling penguins dissolve into shots of a little girl waddling in imitation. A flock of flamingos is intercut with a woman in a wheelchair and a little boy watching dolphins at a glass wall. A mother duck swims by with her brood, and a small boy swings on a playground rope. The male singer returns to tell us that we will have good friends forever in this place.

The chorus swells in song as a pair of killer whales performs a synchronized jump: "A world apart. . . . That brings our world together. . . ." People in the stadium crowd throw back their heads and laugh. A father takes a picture of his wife and children, a mother tends her baby, a courting man and woman snuggle.

At the commercial's conclusion, the camera returns to the little boy and girl at the edge of the killer-whale tank. They approach the clear wall, and the camera lingers a few seconds in close-up as, with faces pressed close to the glass, they try to touch the black-and-white whale. The whale's head is close to the children; it appears to gaze back. Stringed instruments surge, and the chorus sings, "From the heart . . . Sea World touches you." Then silence for a few reverent seconds, as the television screen displays a blue, white, and black logo and the words "Sea World: Make Contact." And, at the very bottom of the screen, "An Anheuser-Busch Theme Park."

"Touch the Magic," as the television commercial is titled, is the center-piece of a recent advertising campaign for the Busch Entertainment Company's four Sea World theme parks.[3] From the spring of 1993 through the spring of 1994, Busch Entertainment urged millions of prime-time viewers to "make contact."[4] At the simplest level the powerful "Touch the Magic" images sum up the product. A visit to a Sea World park, the commercial argues, is not just a day out of the house; it's a "magical," "touching" experience that "brings our world together."

In this essay I want to explore Sea World's nature magic as it appears in this commercial and as it is constructed and delivered at the theme parks. "Touch the Magic" is a rich text, presenting many ideas about the meaning of nature in contemporary American culture. It summarizes, as the Sea World parks elaborate, twentieth-century mass culture's dominant arguments about human relations to nature. Carefully thought-out and expensively produced, this piece of publicity is a tiny but typical portion of a much larger field of images and arguments emanating from the corporate media. As such, it is part of a media world that helps shape how Americans understand nature and the environment. "Touch the Magic" has much to tell us about how Anheuser-Busch in particular and large businesses in general represent nature to vast audiences.

A look at Anheuser-Busch and its theme parks will help contextualize "Touch the Magic." Anheuser-Busch is the planet's largest brewer. The company controls 43 percent of the U.S. beer market and in 1993 saw about $11.6 billion in sales worldwide.[5] While Busch Entertainment does not report theme park attendance figures to the public, this subsidiary is very successful. With the second-largest total attendance of the five U.S. theme park chains, Busch Entertainment is expanding abroad. (Attendance at the Disney parks far outranks that of all other contenders.) At a conservative guess, the four Sea Worlds together entertain about 11.35 million paying visitors annually, most of them North Americans. These visits alone evidence a wide exposure to and interest in Anheuser-Busch's powerful and colorful representations of nature.[6]

Nature exhibits and marine animals are the central themes of the Sea Worlds. Superficially, the ways the parks present nature seem varied. At the San Diego park, for example, some settings mimic the new environmental zoo. The ARCO Penguin Encounter is a sort of living diorama that simulates parts of the Antarctic environment. At Orlando and San Diego the shark exhibits carry customers on a moving walkway and through a Plexiglas tube, to encounter the "Terrors of the Deep." "Rocky Point Preserve" re-creates a bit of the Northwest coast in San Diego and houses dolphins and sea otters, albeit in separate tanks.

Despite all the variety within individual parks, however, Sea World's nature is not only highly artificial but also standardized. Busch Entertainment has overarching supervision of the parks, so each new exhibit or entertainment is carefully vetted in St. Louis. Successful displays from one park are exported to the others, as are the animal shows. And the killer whale in "Touch the Magic" is more than just a striking creature; it is a registered trademark. "Shamu" appears at all four Sea Worlds, in shows that emphasize similar themes of loving, caring, and closeness between whales and people. Among the most popular attractions at all the parks are the pools holding dolphins, sea stars, rays, and skates that visitors can handle and feed. The themes of "touch" and "contact" in the television commercial connect directly to one of the most appealing facets of a visit to any Sea World— the opportunity to encounter and pet wild animals.

Sea World's reconstructed nature is, in the 1990s, a highly commercial production. Like all theme parks, each Sea World draws customers and keeps them spending as long as possible by offering a diverse, even clashing, array of activities and diversions. Ice skating extravaganzas, power boat shows, game arcades, and sky rides coexist with aquariums and tide pools. Lush landscaping and gardens provide a backdrop for country music concerts, company picnics, and disco dancing. The animal shows, though, are the major draw. But compared with an old-fashioned zoo, a publicly supported museum, or a free park, Sea World is very expensive. In 1994 a child's admission to Orlando's Sea World was $29.95, the highest in the theme park industry.[7] Just as important as admissions for each park's profits are the almost endless concession stands, boutiques, and gift shops offering refreshments and souvenirs of many sorts. As a student in one of my undergraduate classes aptly put it, "Sea World is like a mall with fish."[8]

Anheuser-Busch is not the only company profiting from theme park nature. The Sea Worlds subsidize some of their displays with corporate sponsorships. Although "Touch the Magic" ignores this by presenting Sea World's environment as if it were noncommercial, a good number of the displays inside the parks have outside funding. In San Diego, ARCO helps present the Penguin Encounter, Home Federal Bank sponsors Rocky Point Preserve, and am-pm mini-markets support the shark reef. But many other businesses and manufacturers, from Kodak film to Pepsi-Cola and Southwest Airlines, take part in joint promotional and advertising ventures inside and outside the parks.[9] Perhaps more important, the parks provide a kind of advertising *and* public relations for the parent company. For example, besides selling Anheuser-Busch's Budweiser beers and Eagle snack foods, the Sea Worlds' "hospitality centers" feature "micro-breweries" and free beer tasting. The theme parks house and display the company's trademark Clydesdale horses, converting the registered trademark of one corporate division into an attraction at a wholly owned subsidiary. And, of course, associating Anheuser-Busch and its products with animals, nature, education, and families positions the world's largest brewer as environmentally and socially concerned.[10] At the Sea World theme parks, advertising, marketing, and public relations are so thoroughly collapsed into entertainment and recreation that it is very hard to tell what is publicity and what is "just fun." Inside the park the advertising–promotional–public relations mix is an intricate maze.

Given this commercial and promotional environment, it is striking that the nature theme park styles itself a public facility.[11] To do this the Sea Worlds draw on today's concern with environmental issues and animals, and they emphasize education. Busch Entertainment and Anheuser-Busch make much of their involvement with research on whales and dolphins, their efforts at fostering the reproduction of species (including a few endangered species), and their part in marine animal rescue and rehabilitation efforts.[12] Sea World's rescue and research activities are also heralded in educational programs offered to public school systems, courses taught at the parks, and credentialing programs for teachers. Anheuser-Busch estimates that 650,000 children annually participate in education programs inside the Sea World parks. Direct satellite broadcasts now reach an estimated 16 million viewers via schools throughout the United States.[13]

This push by a private entertainment corporation into the public school classroom is not unique. "Channel One" of Whittle Communications is only the most famous recent example. On the environmental education front, the Walt Disney Company is at work on a curriculum for use in the California public schools. Procter & Gamble, one of the world's largest consumer goods producers and the world's biggest advertiser, has recently developed and distributed a free packet of "Decision Earth" materials for elementary school use.[14] However, Busch's expansion into public education suggests that the Sea World theme park is a new kind of institution. Unlike the older amusement park, the nature theme park combines the search for private profits through entertainment with an attempt to occupy the cultural space and functions of the nonprofit, publicly funded zoo, natural history museum, or aquarium. Courses are taught, whales are bred, and the nesting patterns of the least tern are studied at the theme park. But these activities are inseparable from Sea World's marketing and Anheuser-Busch's public relations. Education, corporate image, and luxuriant profits go hand in hand.

"Touch the Magic" is just one small segment of the mass of pictures and print that Busch Entertainment commissions from ad agencies to support not just its theme parks but all its marine-themed products. Like all theme parks, the Sea Worlds are integral to a media culture that extends far beyond their physical boundaries.[15] For example, the Sea Worlds create whale- and dolphin-based entertainment specials. These network television shows, like the satellite broadcasts mentioned above, serve to advertise and promote the park as a tourist destination, while the theme park helps build an audience for the television programs.[16] Aggressive public relations departments make sure that the parks' animal-saving activities are regularly featured and highlighted in network entertainment and news programming. At present, Anheuser-Busch lacks only a syndicated television show to deliver to the widest possible audience filmed and animated media products based on its performing celebrity animals.[17] Many other Sea World–themed commodities result from licensing agreements: stuffed animals, postcards, T-shirts, story books, nature study books, and video tapes only begin the list of commodities marketed through the parks.[18] Again, the products support the parks, while these support the goods far outside the theme park gate. In creating and distributing its own imagery so extensively, Sea World has gone far beyond the traditional educational functions of the zoo or natural history museum, even while it claims to be providing those services.

This sprawling commercial operation is the context for "Touch the Magic." Let's return to the world of the nature theme park as proposed by the ad. In a very real sense, the expansive corporation is as much the author of the television commercial as any copywriter or video producer. What stories does Anheuser-Busch use "Touch the Magic" to tell? How do the commercial and the company ask the audience to think about relationships between humans and the natural world? What happens if we touch the magic?

"Touch the Magic" presents a condensed, more perfect world. The advertisement does a good job of delivering Sea World's visual richness. As other scholars have stressed, theme parks and television are intimately connected media. Not only does the advertisement aim to reproduce the qualities of the park, but the park in many ways tries to be "televisual." The advertisement compresses a richness of experience into the visual mode, and so does the park, which pays careful attention to color, detail, landscape, and sight lines. Sea World's leafy foliage and expensive plantings, its brightly colored birds and massing fish, the contrast of sun and shade, wet and dry, and the variety of its surfaces are all emphasized in the ad. Here is a wealth of things to see and touch.

Sea World defines nature as an overwhelmingly visual experience, but its way of seeing extends beyond kaleidoscopic abundance. In the commercial and the theme park, we see animals, greenery, and performers with an easy immediacy. As in other heavily photographic media, such as *National Geographic* or the television program "Nature," our approach to nature is simple and unobstructed. Our sight is unimpeded—we see nature in a way that we rarely could out in the "real world," where brush and trees block a view or murky water hides the fish. Like television, the parks are full of tricks of visual purification. The many carefully realistic aquariums, for example, are designed to make the unseen visible. Sea World assures us that its way of seeing nature will be natural.[19]

At the same time that we are tempted by perfect seeing, great distances are collapsed and we are promised adventure. As "Touch the Magic" offers to take viewers to spectacularly inaccessible, invisible, or little-known places, so Sea World designs a mass version of nature tourism implicitly built on an older tradition of exploration. A trip to the park is a condensed voyage that circles and surveys the world, without requiring us to go very far from home. Again, this is similar to the experience offered by other mass media, most famously *National Geographic* magazine.[20] Sea World is full of exhibits structured like a journey: the customer consults a map of the "World," navigates a place in line, and finally, slowly draws near. The supposedly strange sight is nevertheless thoroughly familiar from popular culture and the literature of travel and tourism: a penguin-packed Antarctic ice floe, a Polynesian atoll seething with sharks, a "forbidden reef" infested with moray eels, the rugged stretch of the Pacific Northwest coast, a ghostly sea bottom in the "Bermuda Triangle." On the one hand, this selective tour of the globe defines nature as exotic and remote. On the other, without ever calling up a precise history, the theme park offers its customers a chance to stand in the shoes of the European discoverers as they mapped the non-European world.

While Sea World locates this highly visual nature in an implied historical narrative of exploration, it paradoxically decontextualizes nature. Indeed, what customers don't see is as significant as what they do. At Sea World crowds of people watch a natural world seemingly uncrowded, unpeopled. Any human cultures or histories of the environments shown in the dioramas linger only as background information. At the "Shark Encounter" we see no Pacific Islanders, but the mysterious sound of drums enhances the carefully painted and sculpted set. Ersatz totem poles frame the park's centerpiece show, "Shamu New Visions," which is introduced with a (genuine?) Northwest Coast Indian story about a boy and a whale.[21] Otherwise, long human connections to animals and environments vanish. In Sea World's presentation nature and animals have been discovered and are being protected in a pristine state by white North Americans. This pristine state is physically produced within the context of intense consumerism.

The most extreme examples of decontextualization are also the most popular: the trained animal performances. The theme park exhibits rebuild nature and bring the faraway close. But in the whale stadium nature is isolated and held up to the collective gaze. The surprise, awe, and wonder of crowds focus on individual animals. In these shows performers seem to push the possibilities of animal bodies and animal-human interactions to their limits, Shamu's launching the trainer off its snout being only the most famous example.

There is one exception to the decontextualization of nature: Sea World's technicians and scientists are ever present in the theme park frame. In its stories of exploration, Sea World always identifies itself with pioneering experts. Again, the trained killer whales are the famous and telling examples. Long a part of Northwest Coast Native American knowledge and mythology, orcas were first kept in captivity and developed as an entertainment resource by Sea World's founders in the mid-1960s. Anheuser-Busch makes much of this "pioneering" role, casting Sea World's success in inducing killer whales to reproduce successfully in captivity as an important scientific accomplishment.[22] In the Sea World version of natural history, the theme park itself brings exciting unknown things to public awareness, and the audience travels vicariously with the experts. Similarly, the Sea World Penguin Encounter in San Diego claims the capacity to support the penguin reproductive cycle. While visitors to a natural history museum's dioramas might view a scene that looks like part of Antarctica, at the ARCO-sponsored exhibit they are treated to something new in mass culture—the proliferating Antarctic. It appears that the skill of the theme park enterprise itself has made life multiply.[23]

Besides creating a larger-than-life, decontextualized nature, as the ad argues, Sea World has another magical effect. Having decontextualized nature, Sea World makes it a powerful carrier of human emotions. In "Touch the Magic" intense emotion is signaled by physical contact (the hugs and kisses in the crowd), power and speed (the trainer rocketing off the nose of the killer whale), and sound (the sentimental music track). Visuals and music underscore the ad's verbal references to happy feelings: "Bring back the smile to the child inside of you."

Here nature is not only about seeing, exploring, and collecting; it is about relationships, feelings, and families. "Touch the Magic" shows people close to each other, in groups and couples. Similarly, animals appear in flocks or pairs. We see two whales, two dolphins, and a mother duck leading her brood. Animal groupings parallel human groupings of families and potential families (boy- and girlfriends).

As the ad's theme underscores, relationships at Sea World are intimate, expressed through touch. Grandparents hug children, parents watch their kids cavort and clown, a young woman cuddles her boyfriend. Even that ambivalent image of human community—the crowd—seems not to consist of strangers. Laughing, close together, the people enjoy themselves. The advertisement's argument is that the theme park as a cultural space can help bring people closer together—across boundaries of gender, races, handicaps, and generations, and perhaps even across the barriers of anonymity that separate people in crowds and audiences. As the song has it, Sea World is "another world . . . that brings our world together."[24]

But "Touch the Magic" contains a tension it sets up, resolves temporarily, and then calls up again. Gentle physical contact takes place not just among people but also between people and animals. The ad's opening and closing shots feature one of Sea World's most famous advertising images: the children and Shamu pressed nose to nose, reaching out to one another. But their intimacy is incomplete: the transparent barrier of Plexiglas allows humans and whales to come close while keeping them separated. Since the nose-to-nose shot precedes and follows so many images of direct contact between people, and between people and animals, it seems to express a fantastic wish for a total merging with wild nature.

The stark print text "Make contact with another world" accompanying the nose-to-nose image emphasizes Sea World's claim to create a kind of communication that is otherwise impossible. Making contact with "another world" may mean several things. Certainly the video shot of children and whale separated but trying to touch each other implies that nature and wild animals constitute a world distinct from humans, one that humans should wish to approach more closely. The notion of far-away worlds trying to contact us might be here, too—in a reference to spirits and unseen forces or, perhaps, as in science fiction, to other planets and parallel universes.[25] Given the surrounding emphasis on relationships, however, it seems more likely that the other world of nature is also an interior world, one of emotions and feelings. We've already been exhorted to remember feelings, to "bring back the smile to the child inside of you." "Touch the Magic" suggests that the theme park offers customers access not only to nature and exotic animals but to themselves. Asking us to "remember the feeling of wonder" and "bring back the smile" suggests that we need to return to authentic feelings.

In short, communication and contact with nature promise to remake people. This is familiar: most contemporary advertising presents the product as magically transforming the consumer herself from an alienated and isolated state to a meaningful, whole identity.[26] Consumer products also promise to alter social identities, and perhaps a visit to Sea World is no different. To make contact with nature is to have real feelings and to become someone different and more desirable. But how does this transformation work?

First, as other authors in this volume are at pains to show, nature is a vast complex of ideas as well as a biological world. This is part of what makes the idea of a more intimate contact with it so evocative, powerful, and magical. Sea World offers its customers transformation through contact with a long historical tradition of nature's social meanings, a tradition the theme park version of nature, with its emphasis on visual realism and scientific expertise, paradoxically obscures.[27]

For at least the last two hundred years, Europeans and Euro-Americans have made nature a visual, touchable, "out there" object. Making nature literally "another world," Euro-Americans endowed it with cultural and spiritual properties. At the same time, art and literature emphasizing labor and the complex interactions between humans and the biological world have been marginalized in the Euro-American aesthetic tradition.[28] Appreciation of this aestheticized, separate version of nature has been used to distinguish people from each other and to normalize the differences between them. For example, in the eighteenth century, as Raymond Williams argues, the gentry justified its expanding property rights and dominance over the rural poor through aesthetic practices. Sculpting nature into country estates, celebrating it in pastoral poetry, manipulating it in the form of lovingly landscaped gardens, the gentry literally naturalized its vast social and economic power.[29] In the nineteenth century appreciating nature by viewing it, painting it, or hiking through it helped factory owners and businessmen define themselves as rational and sensitive men, especially in comparison with rural and urban workers.[30] Toward the end of this period, zoos and museums did more than popularize the global scientific world view and integrate nature into a Euro-centered colonial map. Their boards of directors also hoped museums would teach respect for law and "natural order" to the urban, immigrant working classes, whom they saw as having anarchic, un-American ideas.[31]

For at least two centuries the propertied have used nature as a material and a symbolic resource and as a favored tool of improvement aimed down the social scale at class and racial others. And while nature education in classrooms and summer camps has surely had many democratic and socially progressive uses, it has also been closely tied to efforts to model a hierarchical social order. The right sort of person, as advocated by nature educators, was an English-speaking, self-controlled, property-respecting, refined middle-class citizen. Sea World's nature magic partakes of this uplifting tradition. As "Touch the Magic" argues, contact with nature creates or affirms a customer's identity as a caring, sensitive person. A visit to Sea World offers nature as a source of rational pleasure—albeit in a context of irrational prices and endless throw-away souvenirs. There are no gut-wrenching, mind-blowing roller coasters here. Perhaps a visit to Sea World also helps customers distance themselves, however little they think about it, from people defined as uneducated, insensitive, and irrational.

In "Touch the Magic" Sea World's visitors dress casually but well. They are mostly white adults with children, respectfully excited by the sights they behold. The ad reflects Sea World's marketers' understanding of their audience as defined by age, income, ethnicity, and education. Although Sea World's managers, like most white Americans, are reluctant to speak in terms of social class or to acknowledge a racial pattern among their customers, market research for the San Diego park reveals that their audience is heavily southern Californian and white, with a very high level of income and education.[32] The San Diego park describes its customers as consisting heavily of "parents" who are "usually college educated and . . . interested in learning about ocean life."[33] It is not that the people who run Sea World do anything active to keep ethnic minorities out of the park.[34] Indeed, the education programs recruit minority children via public school field trips.

But considering the multiethnic demographics of the five southern California counties, the whiteness of Sea World's paying audience seems to be an example of extreme self-selection.[35] Perhaps the high admission prices alone tend to keep poor people away; however, other expensive theme parks in southern California, most notably Disneyland and Six Flags–Magic Mountain, have strong followings among people of color. Is it possible that the version of nature marketed by Sea World appeals positively to white people as part of being appropriately middle-class? Conversely, does Sea World's discrete, aestheticized nature seem unfriendly or irrelevant to working-class people and nonwhites? Whatever the answer, Sea World's marketers clearly craft their nature product for the affluent.

The children in the ad give another clue that Sea World's nature magic is in part about social class. In white middle-class culture, the positive association between children and animals, children and nature, reaches far back.[36] Children are supposed to have special things to gain from contact with nature, but perhaps these special things are related as much to social ideals as to children's practical growth.[37] According to long-standing theories of education, nature and the outdoors teach the child about the inner self.[38] And, at a more mundane level, contact with nature is thought to lay the groundwork for the child's future success in biology or some other important science. It is not that any of these ideas are entirely false. But in this ideal of childhood, nature, social mobility, and the sense of self all run together. The nature-children-class connection is expressed in the century-old middle-class emphasis on suburban yards, summer homes, summer camps, and nature study in the classroom.[39] That "Touch the Magic" and all Sea World's advertisements and publicity feature children learning points to the theme park's claim that it helps produce the right sort of person. That children are shown learning in the context of the family implies that the park also helps reproduce social position.

So perhaps "Touch the Magic" and Sea World itself show us that mass-mediated nature is constructed to appeal to its consumers as much in terms of who they want to be, as individuals and members of families and communities, as in terms of the aesthetics of clarity and purity. In any case, when Sea World claims to create feelings of awe, wonder, and joy, we might understand this as an argument that awe, wonder, and joy—as opposed to fear, boredom, hostility, or exhaustion—are feelings the "right sort" of person should have in the presence of nature.

While the desires and identities of Sea World's customers have a long past, something new is happening in the theme park, too. Touching the magic of nature is a way of making contact with a world of possibilities as well as a way of finding one's feelings and confirming a social identity. All of Sea World's and Anheuser-Busch's important publicity materials appeal strongly to the environmental interests of the American public, carefully positioning the corporation as at once a good environmental citizen and a responsible producer of goods. It is in the context of wishes and worries about the future, I think, that Anheuser-Busch and Sea World try to redirect popular environmental concerns. In the process of presenting nature as something for people to contact and care about, the company is arguing for nature's reinvention.

Once again, the shot of the children pressed nose to nose with Shamu is suggestive. This image sums up all Sea World's urgings about "making contact," but specifically making contact with another form of higher life, not just scenery and science. The promise of mutuality between whale and people is what is different. Traditional zoos and aquariums, the aesthetic theorist John Berger writes, reveal people's distance from the world of nature by bringing them close to animals. Because animals are turned into spectacle, and because their boredom and passivity is inescapable, zoos underline the extreme marginalization of nature from human life in industrial society.[40] The new zoo and the nature theme park actively try to override this disappointing perception by showing animals in more natural-looking environments, where they seem to have privacy, autonomy, and the ability to avoid the human gaze.[41] The aesthetic of the new zoo does not reverse the long separation of humans and nature, but it makes nature seem less dominated, less captive.

"Touch the Magic," however, makes a different argument for Sea World. If we look closely at the way the killer whales are represented in Sea World's commercials, we see that the whale appears to be meeting the children's gaze. It is looking back, and this is exactly what Berger argues zoo animals can never do. Why should the whale seem to be trying to make contact? Certainly the audience is being asked to have feelings with and about whales, but is it possible that by seeming to reach out, the whales ask people to join with them? Sea World constructs itself as "another world," a parallel world in a watery realm, and the parks surely argue that orcas parallel humanity, or at least that segment of humanity defined as Sea World customers. The largest, most popular mammals on display, the orcas are always discussed in terms of social organization, intelligence, and especially reproduction. Much of the pleasure of watching their performances comes from seeing them humanized. Orcas are made to seem so like us—caring for their babies, working hard for their rewards, and getting the better of their foolish trainers—that a subtle identification takes place. Perhaps without intending it, Sea World asks its audience to form a relationship with nature —under the theme park's auspices. But which relationship? What prospect for humanity's relationship to nature is being promised to the audience as it makes contact?

The relationship Sea World proposes between humans and nature emerges more clearly when we recall that all the park's publicity contains claims for the social and scientific responsibility of the company and Anheuser-Busch. The nature images and animal performances flowing through the overlapping channels of entertainment, advertising, and promotion all tell the same story: Sea World and Anheuser-Busch conserve, protect, study, and foster nature. In this context, contact between whale and children invokes the beginning of a journey into the future, in which the protected, biologically reproducing animal and the learning, socially reproducing children travel together under the same, benign auspices. The right sort of person not only expresses interest in animals and science; she trusts and knows that companies like Anheuser-Busch are taking good care of nature. This caretaking goes beyond paying taxes, making donations to appropriate philanthrophic organizations, or establishing foundations. Corporate America is taking care of nature right down to the structure of DNA, and in the process, as Donna Haraway argues, it is transforming definitions of humanity, community, and nature. At the theme park customers collaborate in this corporate assumption of responsibility as audiences and consumers. As a neighbor of mine said to me, "Even the high admission fees are worth it, because they do such good things for the oceans there." And as a line from one of Sea World's shows has it, "Just by being here, you're showing that you care."

For all its seductive imagery, "Touch the Magic" is just one commercial, a tiny piece of media culture. But it is a good example of how much corporate culture hopes its audiences will understand nature and environmental issues. It is not that Sea World and Anheuser-Busch made up the idea of nature as pure, separate from humans, and under the benign care of experts and multinational capital. Rather, Anheuser-Busch, its parks division, and the collaborating sponsors have very intelligently recast and reworked some much older ways of seeing nature, in part for purposes of direct commercial appeal and profit, in part as a more general strategy for creating a positive public view of a very large corporation. In the process "Touch the Magic," Sea World, and many similar mass media products advance a vision of nature's future that is consonant with the interests of corporate America. The green public relations version of nature not only obscures a long history of relationships between humans and nature; it makes democratic pressures for environmental preservation, safety, and health invisible. Although parks like Sea World and ads like "Touch the Magic" appeal to popular environmental concern, neither the problems of pollution and resource exhaustion nor solutions from outside the corporate sphere have a place in the Sea World scenario. Rather, nature theme parks show corporations like Anheuser-Busch rising to the conservation occasion with spontaneous good will.

Anheuser-Busch holds no monopoly on this corporate-friendly version of nature. The same story is told, with variations, in many streams of the mass media. The arguments of Sea World's nature magic resemble those conjured in corporate-image campaigns such as Chevron's "People Do" ads or the Du Pont "Ode to Joy" commercials.[42] The nature magic is also familiar from other kinds of television, film, and print. Environmentalists, students of environmental history, and communication scholars would do well to take mass-media representations of nature and environmental issues seriously. Environmental public relations, "green advertising," and nature programming occupy a significant proportion of network and cable television broadcast hours.[43] Nature magic is summoned in much, though certainly not all, of what one can see on the corporately sponsored Public Broadcasting System or the commercial Discovery Channel.[44] Its core ideas radiate into the larger culture from many different sources. But arguably the "walk-through TV" environment of the theme park—the synthesis of entertainment and advertisement that reaches into the day-care center, school, library, bookstore, and home—is more thoroughgoing than any earlier medium. Because it is at work on so many levels, Sea World's privately produced version of nature takes up a huge amount of space. This space is physical and cultural, imaginative and psychic. As Candace Slater argues in this volume, such a spectacular but limited way of seeing nature necessarily displaces or hides other kinds of connections and contacts that need to be made. In the late twentieth century what are the alternatives to theme park nature? Where can missing connections be picked up?

In asking these questions about nature theme parks, we must recognize that most Americans—scholars included—live in the vast environment of mass-mediated culture, as surely as we drive cars and eat cheeseburgers. And we must confront the fact that many older forms of popular contact with nature and science that once enjoyed public support in the form of tax-based funding have been extensively reorganized. Zoos and natural history museums always had an elite bias; they often communicated the social vision of their philanthropic funders and directors. The establishment of national parks may have expressed, in part, an elitist wilderness aesthetic. But these institutions were not, in theory or practice, private property. Operating with some governmental funding and oversight, they were open to pressure for popular use and had to respond to often conflicting concerns.[45] As basically nonprofit institutions, zoos and museums were spared the pressure of having to turn every square foot of exhibit space into profits. But today aquariums, museums, zoos, and state and national parks are increasingly tied into the same tourist economies that shape theme parks; at the same time, declining tax support means that they are forced to rely heavily on corporate funding. The new funds come with new strings attached—for example, the need to show that the zoo or museum has the appropriate audience demographics. All these institutions rely more and more on blockbuster exhibitions or special events that can be promoted to garner paying audiences.[46] Because funds are tighter, and corporate support unreliable, at many museums admission is no longer free or even modestly priced. The gift shop has become crucial to the institution's budget. As zoos and museums compete with theme parks, shopping malls, and television, they resemble these commercial forms ever more closely.

Nevertheless, what remains of the public educational sphere deserves the support of environmental activists just as much as the corporate version of nature demands critical analysis. San Diego's small and underfunded Museum of Natural History offers a good example. Competing directly with Sea World of California for visitor dollars, and often drawing on Sea

World staff for resources, the museum has been forced to promote itself as an attraction for regional tourists, even while it struggles to provide a local educational resource. Despite its reliance on local corporate sponsorship, the museum has been able to mount some small but sophisticated exhibitions on serious environmental issues. These have covered topics ranging from the relationship between development, land use, and habitat destruction in San Diego County to the *Exxon Valdez* oil spill and to scientific controversies over global warming. If they are small and limited, spaces such as this one have great potential for enlivening informed debate about what nature is and how we might struggle to rethink its problems. Try to imagine a theme park mounting a thoughtful exhibit on ocean pollution—a problem of grievous immediacy in southern California.[47] While we criticize commercial culture's nature, we also need to create and support sites for less magical images and information. Defending older quasi-public spaces from the tyranny of the bottom line is one way to do this. To argue for public spaces for environmental discourse is not to argue for doing away with entertainment. Neither do I disdain people who enjoy the remarkable qualities of animals. But not all entertainment should be commercial, and education should not be collapsed into public relations and a ruthless drive for corporate profits.

Definitions of nature and the solutions to its problems are now massively authored by the private sphere of conglomerate, corporate culture, at the same time that corporations claim to further the public good. Sea World's theme park nature is only one example, but it is striking that it asks America's most affluent, educated, and influential citizens to trust nature's future, and their own, to the corporate matrix. Finding a new environmental ground depends on contentious debate, not on easy consensus that corporations and citizens are each doing their part. To conduct this debate, it is vitally important that all Americans have a wide range of ideas, information, and images to draw on.

SYMBOLIC NATURE

The impulse to use elements of the natural world to serve as cultural symbols is as old as human language itself. But the uses to which nature can be put are always specific to particular cultures at particular moments in their histories. What we see in nature and what we say about it reveal as much about who we think we are as about what we think nature is. The found objects here form a highly eclectic mix, revealing the malleability of symbolic nature. What does an eagle mean? Compare its role in commemorating the apotheosis of a Roman emperor with its presence on the American dollar bill, its role in selling gasoline for CITGO with its work for the U.S. Postal Service and the Central Intelligence Agency. But don't stop there. Consider the role of nature in marketing the state of Arizona as paradise or in selling breakfast cereal as an icon of our ancient natural heritage. Nature is everywhere around us, a sea of symbolic meanings, no matter how natural or unnatural it may seem to us.

Emperor Nero's apotheosis. *(Courtesy Bibliothèque Municipale, ville de Nancy)*

Nazi eagle. *(Das Deutsche Hausbuch*, Berlin, 1943. *Courtesy University of Wisconsin–Madison Libraries.)*

Great Seal of
the United States,
one-dollar bill.

Seal, Central Intelligence Agency. *(Courtesy U.S. Central Intelligence Agency)*

U.S. Express Mail eagle. *(Permission to reproduce granted by United States Postal Service)*

"CITGO: You Can Feel the Pride." *(Courtesy CITGO Petroleum Corporation)*

New spin on ecological power

Once again, environmentalists are learning the hard way that every up side has a down side.

Outside magazine reports in its April issue that environmentalists are enthralled with Altamont Pass near San Francisco, where dozens of windmills generate electrical power without emitting an ounce of hydrocarbons. Less thrilled is the U.S. Fish and Wildlife Service, whose agents find about two dozen birds a month that have been julienned by the whirling blades.

Worse yet, these are not just chopped chickadees and butterflied bluejays: Most are birds of prey like red-tailed hawks, American kestrels and the endangered golden eagle, of which only about 1,500 remain in California. The state energy commission estimated about 40 golden eagles get turned into eagle cutlets every year by the Ronco Raptor-matics in the sky.

The Fish and Wildlife Service is pledging to fight expansion of the wind-power industry if the problem of hacked-up hawks and cut-up kestrels can't be solved. But the state Sierra Club chapter has temporarily joined forces with the industry, pending a study of protective measures that might keep the birds out of the blades.

The conundrum is reminiscent of those studies proving that washing cotton diapers was no more environmentally friendly than tossing the disposable ones. Such trade-offs will become more and more visible as our environmental sophistication increases.

Ronco Raptor Matic. *("New Spin on Ecological Power," editorial, courtesy* Wisconsin State Journal, *March 16, 1994)*

"The Little House at the Bottom of the Sea." *(Courtesy Chevron Corporation)*

"Other Worlds Do Exist."
(Courtesy Arizona Office of Tourism and Moses Anshell)

The natural cereal box: Heritage O's. *(Courtesy Nature's Path Foods, Inc.)*

CONTESTED TERRAINS

Ecological Fragmentation
in the Fifties

Michael G. Barbour

Introduction

SOMETHING PROFOUNDLY IMPORTANT HAPPENED AMONG AMERICAN ECOLO-
gists during the decade of the 1950s. What took place and why it occurred
at just that time are the subjects of this essay.

One ironic legacy of that period is that the language and perceptions of
many of today's nature conservationists are considered to be "unnatural" by
most ecologists. For example, the preservation of endangered species and
ecosystems is currently argued on the basis of a nature described as tightly
organized, interdependent, and highly coevolved. "Everything is connected
to everything else" was the way Barry Commoner expressed it in his first
law of ecology.[1] The loss of an endangered species to extinction, according
to this view of nature, will have repercussions that ripple out through the
surrounding ecosystem of which it was once a part. The ecologists of the
1950s disputed—disproved, many insisted—that nature was so interdependent. Prior to the 1950s nature was simplistic and deterministic; after the
1950s nature became complex, fuzzy edged, and probabilistic.

The ecologists of the 1950s were actors in the long-running story of
holism yielding to reductionism, a theme in the history of science. Holism,
according to the *Random House Dictionary of the English Language*, is a
theory that wholes are more than "the mere sum of their parts." The word
was invented by the South African philosopher and politician Jan Christiaan
Smuts less than eighty years ago, but the concept of holism has long been at
the base of human thought about the surrounding world. Animism,
vitalism, and religions are all examples of holistic world views. They seek to

explain behavior by adding an element beyond the mere atoms, organs, or parts of which an individual—or the earth—is composed. Each layer of complexity has emergent properties that make it unique beyond the parts of which it is composed. In contrast, reductionists argue that a sufficient explanation for the behavior of any object or any ecosystem comes from a dissection and study of the object's component parts. The behavior, then, of a single human being can be understood and predicted once we know all the biochemical and cellular details that make up that person.

The holistic-reductionist debate played out in the 1950s was formulated by two vegetation ecologists, Frederic Clements and Henry Gleason. Clements argued that groups of species living together in a given habitat were highly organized into natural, integrated units called communities. Gleason countered that such communities were only constructs of human thought and that in reality the distribution and behavior of every species were unbounded by imagined holistic bonds to all the surrounding species. By 1960 the majority of ecologists had shifted their opinion of the community from Clements's view to Gleason's, and in so doing they overturned a half century of scientific rhetoric. It was a revolution.

Clements and Gleason, Holism and Reductionism

SELF-CONSCIOUS PLANT ECOLOGY IN AMERICA BEFORE 1950 WAS DOMI-nated by the holistic thoughts of Frederic Edward Clements. Clements was born in the grasslands of Nebraska in 1874. He was voraciously curious about the natural world, making collections of flowering plants, algae, fungi, and lichens. "Any botanical article, without reference to the language, was read, and every plant, whether desmid or tree, was interesting," his student Homer Shantz later wrote about his adviser's university years.[2] Clements received his Ph.D. in botany two years before the turn of the century, in a heady and expanding time for the young science of ecology. His research goal became nothing less than the explanation of vegetation patterns over the world's surface, especially in relation to regional climate. By the time he died, in 1945, his great energy and aggressive intellect had made his theory of vegetation so dominant that even one of his critics admitted he was "by far the greatest individual creator of the modern science of vegetation."[3]

Clements had argued that natural vegetation tended over time to become organized into discrete units separated by narrow or broad ecotones. These units, which he named formations or associations (and which others have come to call communities), are uniform over large areas. Each area has its own characteristic climate. That is, every climatic region will over time (other factors not interfering) develop its own association vegetation type, and that association is in balance with the climate. Factors that interfere include unique geologic substrates and drainages and episodic disturbances.

Associations are as natural as species or atoms; they are fundamental units in the hierarchy of life and not mere human constructs. The floristic composition within any community is homogeneous throughout its range, he wrote, because the component species are tightly interdependent upon each other. Moreover, if an assocation is disturbed by fire, logging, grazing, cultivation, or flood, it recovers its original species composition and appearance over time (once the disturbance ceases) in a process he called succession. The path of succession leads faithfully back to the regional association because only this community is in balance with the climate. Clements called this final phase of succession a climax. A single climatic region, Clements wrote, has only a single possible climax. Thus all successions should ultimately, with sufficient time, lead to the same end point, whether time zero starts on bare rock, on the lee slope of a hill, or at the edge of a pond. This is the "monoclimax" corollary to Clements's basic hypothesis about vegetation.

Because each unit is so constant, its boundaries so discrete, its location with respect to regional climate so predictable, and the path of succession so reminiscent of the ontogeny of an individual from conception to maturity, Clements equated these units with organisms. "As an organism, the formation arises, grows, matures and dies. . . . The climax formation is the adult organism of which all the initial and medial stages are but stages of development. . . . The concept of holism is as nearly as possible a replica of nature's observed process." Clements's ideas about vegetation have been variously labeled as the holistic, organismic, or association-unit theory.[4]

If we look at a landscape through Clements's eyes, we see a simple, harmonious patchwork pattern. For example, the foothills of California that face the Great Central Valley show juxtaposed patches of grassland, chaparral scrub, woodland, and forest. Each patch corresponds to a different association unit. Each patch contains its own set of component species, and each patch narrowly abuts the next. Moreover, each patch can be quickly recognized by the presence of certain large overstory species, which are said to dominate the rest. Thus, by looking for oak trees in the landscape, we can know that all the tens of other vascular plant species that are part of oak woodland are sure to be present; or by looking for the presence of chamise shrubs, we can similarly know that all the tens of other species that are part of chaparral scrub are surely present as well. The entire foothill landscape, covering more than ten million acres, contains only a handful of natural units. We can map these units easily and with confidence use each unit as an indicator or predictor of many subtle differences in the soil and climate. The Clementsian landscape is a balance of nature, a steady-state condition maintained so long as every species remains in place. Everything is cooperatively and interdependently linked; if one element is disturbed, the whole will be changed. When the landscape is stressed or disturbed, and then released from stress, we can predict the route and rate of recovery (the process of succession) back to the pre-disturbance landscape. The process of quantitatively describing a Clementsian landscape is made easy by the discreteness of each patch. Clements recommended placing several samples, which he called quadrats, well within each type of patch and noting the abundance of plant species in each sample. Patch edges and the transitions were not to be sampled. In other words, he recommended subjective, intensive sampling rather than random, extensive sampling.

The historian Ronald Tobey called the association-unit theory a (micro-) paradigm in the sense of Thomas Kuhn.[5] A paradigm represents a world view that is shared and maintained by many persons (ecologists in this case) at one time. A paradigm is maintained until enough contrary information accumulates to prompt a few scientists to substitute a different world view. Their example quickly leads to a wholesale shift in opinion by other scientists. A paradigm shift, or revolution, can often be speeded up by the death or retirement of its founders.

The central tenet of the association-unit paradigm is that plant communities are objective reality. That is, plant species are organized into natural, recognizable units of vegetation called formations, associations, or communities, and these entities are steady-state balance points in nature that exhibit stability and constancy over time.

Clementsian orthodoxy adds several more tenets to this paradigm: (1) the member species of an association are interdependent and function together as a single organism; (2) associations develop in an irreversible, predictable direction—albeit at variable rates—along a structured sequence over time in a process called succession; and (3) the end (climax) state of succession is the single matrix of plant and animal life most suited to a given climatic region (the monoclimax corollary).

Another view of vegetation, antithetical to the association-unit theory, was also in the literature of the mid-twentieth century. Called the individualistic or continuum concept, it was simultaneously and independently proposed by several ecologists in Europe and America. The American proponent was Henry Allen Gleason, born into a rural Illinois setting in 1882.[6] Like Clements, he was a schoolboy collector of wild plants. While an undergraduate at the University of Illinois, he took a biology course from two pioneering ecologists—Charles Adams and Stephen Forbes—later to become presidents of the Ecological Society of America. His subsequent doctoral research at Columbia University was entirely taxonomic, but his career interests and publications included both plant taxonomy and vegetation ecology. Mathematics also attracted him, and Gleason made some of the earliest attempts to quantify biotic diversity.

Gleason had an unusual eye for detail.

When I first began field work, the association was an organism. It had to be: Clements said so. But as time went on and I became better acquainted with more kinds of vegetation, it became ever clearer that an association and an organism had essentially nothing in common. Next it became evident that two separate patches of the same association were never exactly alike . . . and that the degree of likeness was roughly inversely proportional to their distance apart. . . . Every variation of the environment, whether in space or in time . . . produces a corresponding variation in the structure of the vegetation.[7]

In 1917 and again in 1926 and 1939, Gleason published his theory of vegetation, which he called the "individualistic concept."[8] According to this theory, formations and associations are not real, natural units; they are merely artifacts and human constructs or abstractions. Groups of species do not appear and rise and fall in abundance synchronously across the landscape; entire collections of co-occurring species are not interdependent. Rather, each species spreads out as an independent entity, individualistically distributed according to its own genetic, physiological, and life-cycle characteristics and according to its way of relating both to the physical environment and to other species.

The foothill landscape that Clements saw so cleanly, Gleason saw as indescribably complex. One now sees the dizzying distribution of all species, not just oak trees or chamise shrubs. The landscape at this level of detail is a continuum of change. Many grassland species are not limited to the patches of grassland, but also occur beneath oak trees in the woodland; the range of many chaparral shrubs extends into woodland, where they are simply more scattered than in the chaparral; occasional isolated oak trees grow in the center of grassland patches. Where, then, does woodland end and grassland or chaparral begin? The landscape is no longer a simple patchwork quilt of just a few sharp-edged repeating pieces, and vegetation units can no longer be mapped objectively with confidence. Every patch of grassland, for example, is different. In fact, every square foot of grassland in a single patch is different. Gleason argued that if one samples this landscape randomly and extensively—instead of subjectively and intensively, as Clements would— then the independent ranges of each species become obvious. The subjective, simplistic Clementsian landscape can only be circularly "proven" to be real by the use of subjective, simplistic sampling techniques. It is not real; it is not nature. If one wishes to recognize associations, perhaps on the basis of the presence of certain dominant species, one can do so and even draw lines on maps; but this activity must be recognized as arbitrary, subjective, and a gross simplification of nature.

Furthermore (as later elaborated by others), the actual range of a species is often less than its potential range because of the vagaries of seed dispersal.[9] A plant can occupy any part of the landscape only if its seeds have been taken there by animal, wind, or water vectors. If a strong competitor reaches that site first, and spreads its aggressive roots and canopy, then seedlings of the other species cannot survive even if their seeds are present. There is, then, a strong element of chance in the final composition of vegetation of any area. Where Clements saw predictability, uniformity, cooperation, stability, and certainty, Gleason saw only individualism, competition, a blur of continuous change, and probability.[10]

The Paradigm Revolution of 1947–1959

GLEASON PUBLISHED HIS INDIVIDUALISTIC VIEW THREE TIMES WITHIN twenty years, but few American ecologists publicly agreed with it or even seemed to notice it. None of the major ecology textbooks prior to 1950 cited Gleason or his continuum theory, and the ecohistorian Robert McIntosh has concluded that "most ecologists simply ignored it."[11] No one attempted to test the validity of Gleason's ideas, and Gleason himself offered no supporting quantitative data. As the ecologist Robert Whittaker retrospectively believed, arguments offered against the individualistic view by Clementsian ecologists "suggest hauteur toward a destructive, subversive idea and a strong, even passionate conviction that it cannot be true."[12] Henry Gleason later wrote a letter to Murray Buell, recalling the results of a debate about his theory at a national meeting of ecologists in the summer of 1926. His presentation had been ridiculed. "To ecologists I was anathema. Not one believed my ideas; not one would even argue the matter. . . . For ten years, or thereabout, I was an ecological outlaw."[13] Only Stanley Cain, in 1937, privately admitted to Gleason that he agreed with him. As a result, Gleason became isolated and ineffective as an ecologist. He left the field of ecology, pursuing instead a research career in plant taxonomy.

Then, in 1947, Cain published a review of vegetation concepts in which he agreed with Gleason's model, but said he appreciated that this "was heretical to the vast majority" of ecologists.[14] And yet, incredibly, that heretical position became the dominant position in only a dozen years. Awards, vindication, and a following all materialized in the 1950s. Murray Buell, a plant ecologist at Rutgers University, served as secretary of the Ecological Society of America (ESA) in the early 1950s. He invented the "Distinguished Ecologist" award and persuaded the society to grant the first one to Gleason. The 1953 citation read, "He is generally recognized as one of the outstanding ecologists of the first half of the twentieth century."[15] Then, three years later the Botanical Society of America awarded him its "Certificate of Merit," but the text made no mention of any contributions outside taxonomy.[16] Finally, in 1959, the ESA bestowed on him "Eminent Ecologist" status, and the declaration (written by Stanley Cain) dealt positively and at length with his individualistic hypothesis.[17] That same year John Curtis of the University of Wisconsin—whose research was proving Gleason right—wrote privately to Robert McIntosh, stating, "There is no longer any vocal opposition to the idea of a continuum by any responsible ecologists. It is an accepted approach and as such does not need to be continually tested or reproved."[18] Curtis's assessment was corroborated thirty years later by the ecologist and textbook author Jonathan Richardson, who concluded that the individualistic theory had been ascendant since 1950.[19]

Was it possible that only twelve years, between 1947 and 1959, were sufficient to change the thinking of a majority of ecologists about a theory so fundamental to their science? I sought an answer in part by an analysis of recently published ecological histories, including books by Bramwell (1989), Fralish et al. (1993), Golley (1993), Hagen (1992), Kingsland (1985), McIntosh (1985), Mitman (1992), Tobey (1981), and Worster (1985) and a number of articles.[20] To gain an even fresher and more direct answer, I conducted telephone interviews of thirty-four ecologists who had experienced the 1950s. The roster of interviewees is in the appendix.

The ecologists with whom I spoke did not all agree that a shift of any significant kind had occurred between 1947 and 1959. About two-thirds said that there had been a change: eighteen agreed that there had been a shift from association-unit to continuum as I have summarized it here and in my questionnaire; and four others said that there had been a revolution of a wider nature.

This last group of four recalled a paradigm shift occurring in the 1950s, but put it in a different, larger context. Harold Mooney, Eugene Odum, and Arnold Schultz said the shift was from a taxonomic view of ecology to a functional view—that is, from a community-centered science to an ecosystem-centered one. Herbert Bormann said that academic restructuring at the time was a major factor in fomenting ecological ferment. It was fashionable in the 1950s for small botany and larger zoology departments to combine into new biology departments. At the same time there was rapid growth in biochemistry-oriented faculty. The result pitted a few plant ecologists with holistic association-unit ideas against many zoologists and biochemists who held reductionist views of nature. Plant ecologists may have found their new academic surroundings to be intellectually challenging and unsettling.

Of those who contended that there had not been a paradigm shift, most insisted that the two paradigms continue side by side today, along with all kinds of intermediate views, and that it is a misleading oversimplification to suggest otherwise. Frank Egler, for example, said that the change was shallow, merely involving technology rather than fundamental concepts. McIntosh agrees that one paradigm has not completely replaced the other, but still argues that the balance of opinion shifted to favor the continuum viewpoint during the 1950s.

Three others who doubted the existence of a paradigm shift claimed to have been unaware of any debate. Daniel Axelrod has admired the practical aspects of the Clementsian system through his long career in paleobotany, and he continues to rely on its insights. His focus, however, was quite apart from that of typical plant sociologists, and he was not conscious of any paradigm shift. Jack Major, who has been a fan of European approaches to vegetation for his entire career, wrote, "I seem to have been immune to [and unobservant of] any paradigm shift."[21] Bill Salt stated that vertebrate zoologists in the western states, including himself, had been aware of individualistic species range limits from the time of Grinnell's publications near the turn of the century; he had not been conscious of any paradigm shift among his fellow animal ecologists.[22] Robert McIntosh has written a review of animal ecologists' views of animal communities. His analysis leads him to agree with Salt that Grinnell's early ideas of the niche paralleled and preceded Gleason's individualistic concept and that animal ecologists now widely accept the individualistic view, but also that there is now a resurgence of organismic thought among prominent animal ecologists.[23]

David Goodall wrote from Australia that the paradigm shift may well have occurred in America during the 1950s, but it was not apparent in Australia, Europe, or the United Kingdom. He asked rhetorically, "Was the earlier dominance of the Clementsian approach a reflection of America's inward-looking culture? Did the paradigm shift correspond with an opening-up of American ecology [and culture] to influence from off its shores, following the Second World War, perhaps?"[24] The Soviet ecologist B. M. Mirkin reviewed vegetation science history in the USSR and concluded that a "paradigm shift" did occur there, but later than here, in the 1960s. "By 1970 most Soviet vegetation scientists had acknowledged vegetation continuity. . . ."[25] Makoto Numata wrote to me, saying that Japanese ecologists also experienced a slightly delayed paradigm shift, and it uniquely involved a movement away from European viewpoints (rather than from Clementsian thought) to the continuum world view. Pierre Dansereau, schooled in Paris and Geneva, was also trained in European methods. Writing to me now from Montreal, he concluded that the paradigm shift in Canada may have begun in the 1950s but was most dramatically advanced in 1965–70, "when the extension of ecological theory to land management forced the recognition of a new methodology."

When asked if they had personally changed their view of the plant community—from the association-unit model to the individualistic model—either during the 1950s or at any other time in their career, about half said no. Of these steadfast twenty, thirteen have maintained a continuum view and seven have maintained a community-unit view. Some of those who said their views had not changed substantially added that their opinions had somewhat evolved, changed in modest ways, or become strengthened. Twelve others stated that their view had substantially changed, in almost every case from a community-unit viewpoint to a continuum viewpoint.

Franklin, Numata, and Rowe hold simultaneously to a community-unit and an individualistic view. Numata explained the value of this ambivalent state in his letter to me by analogy: "Reality encompasses both, like corpuscular theory and wave theory in the physics of light. We cannot expect a complete resolution of this issue." John Cantlon's complex view of the community—largely individualistic, but with nodes of organization that he says are caused by "central tendencies"—is no doubt due to his similar notion that different truths are useful for different applications. He told me,

"The individualistic community is likely to remain the more useful paradigm for most work on understanding ecosystem processes. However . . . for landscape interpretation or management purposes, we will undoubtedly continue to see the . . . taxonomic community."

These ecologists tell us that both world views can be kept mindfully in reserve, one to use for the applied practice of vegetation science and the other to use for analyzing vegetation theories. Rowe and Franklin both pointed out that field foresters easily and often see individualistic species distributions, yet the agencies they work for ask them to simplify reality by "typing" and "mapping" communities. For certain management purposes, it may be sufficient to focus just on the dominant species, lumping together all parts of the landscape that share the same dominant. Dominant species tell managers a great deal about the habitat and thus highlight important environmental features to monitor and maintain (for example, depth to water table, moderate grazing intensity, recurrence of light surface fires) In such circumstances the reality of individualist species assortment is an unnecessary complexity. To the student of vegetation science, however, it is exactly such details that are important. All of the truth does not belong to any single paradigm, according to Franklin, Rowe, and Numata, and they become angry when their breadth is mistaken for fence-sitting. Jerry Franklin easily recalled a thirty-year-old comment made to him by a continuum ecologist: "This community stuff is OK for you managers, but I'm interested in the truth."

Olsvig-Whittaker was the only respondent to say that her view has shifted from the continuum to the community-unit model. After a decade of land management assignments in Australia and Israel, she has concluded that most resources and environmental factors do not always change along smooth gradients and that as a consequence "we tend to see vegetation as fairly discrete communities on the ground." She went on, "My view of the plant association is now rather like my views of organized religion—it is very practical and close enough to reality that it works most of the time even though the underlying theory is probably incorrect."

Several of the respondents took care to point out that few academics were in complete agreement with Clements even well before the 1950s. Harold Heady recalls his major professor John Weaver telling students in the late 1940s that he didn't agree with Clements's equating associations with organisms: "That's an analogy, and that's all it's good for." Stanley Rowe, another Weaver student, similarly reported, "Airy Clementsian ideas were gone over quickly; we didn't dwell on them." There were objections to some of Clements's ideas about succession as well, especially the claims of predictability. Respondents who were soil oriented were particularly unsatisfied with the limitations of the monoclimax view. According to many of the interviewees, faculty of the 1940s were teaching variations of Clementsianism along with other viewpoints, such as European approaches. Professionals and students alike were going through a process of reexamination together. Respondents unanimously stated that there was no generational split of opinion during this 1940s and on into the 1950s.

The historian Joel Hagen interprets this period as proving that "the rise and fall of Clementsian orthodoxy is historical myth . . . [because] most of Clements' specific claims about communities and succession were challenged by prominent ecologists. Among the first rank of Anglo-American ecologists it is difficult to find a single individual who might accurately be characterized as an orthodox Clementsian."[26]

In my opinion, Clementsian orthodoxy is not the essense of the association-unit theory. To suggest, as Hagen does, that the rejection of orthodoxy is a rejection of the association-unit theory misses this point. Few ecologists were adherants of full-blown Clementsian orthodoxy.

Clementsian orthodoxy, as described near the beginning of this essay, includes notions about community as organism and the monoclimax. The essence of the association-unit theory lay neither in organicism nor in monoclimax; it was the belief that plant communities are objective reality. Several respondents (Burgess, Franklin, Pitelka, Peet, Sawyer) agreed with me that equating Clementsian orthodoxy with the association unit theory— as Hagen did—is erecting a straw man. The details about how predictable a particular successional path was, precisely how species replaced each other, and how many climaxes there might be in a single climatic region were viewed as incidental by the average plant ecologist in the 1930s and 1940s who called himself a Clementsian. These orthodoxies were mere red herrings added by some ecologists to further polarize and obfuscate the real debate, which was whether these things called communities were natural or mere human constructs. As Stanley Cain described 1940s-era ecologists, the objective reality of the association "is the *sine qua non* of their science."[27] However, the side issues of the orthodoxy became the useless focus for many tedious battles. As Helen Buell told me in her interview, "Ecologists have wasted an awful lot of time debating the association concept . . . maybe due to the delight in fighting each other that some people have."

Indeed, some respondents argued that the polarized version of the debate was a pedagogic artifice that simplified, but at the great cost of exaggerating differences. Daniel Axelrod, for example, revered Clements for his breadth, for his recognition of large-scale vegetation units, and for his pragmatism, but he did not concern himself with Clements's succession theory or his complex hierarchical system of nomenclature that bothered others. Axelrod does not view the association as being tightly interdependent, yet he sees that *some* groups of species do repeat and in predictable ways that are linked with the microenvironment. There is a "rhythm" to the landscape, he said, adding, "I don't buy the individualistic thing." Harold Heady referred to Clements's classification system in detail when he began teaching at UC-Berkeley, in 1951, "but soon gave it up" because Clements's notions of climax had "an impractical time scale and didn't emphasize human interactions." Yet Heady described himself in the interview as "a Clementsian who has worked a lifetime refining what Clements did."

I conclude that the vast majority of pre-1947 ecologists viewed associations (or communities) as being real and natural integrated entities, and that a fundamental transition of opinion did occur during the 1950s, moving toward an acceptance of the idea that communities were artifacts of the human imagination. What drove acceptance at that particular time?

Why the Revolution Then?
Ecologists Answer

IF ECOLOGISTS CHANGED THEIR VIEW OF NATURE ACCORDING TO THE RULES of Kuhnian paradigm revolution, then there should have been an increasing body of published data that contradicted the association-unit model and supported the individualistic model. Nine of the ecologists I interviewed recollected that new published information supporting the continuum view was in fact the primary cause of opinion change in the 1950s. Papers by Robert Whittaker, Dwight Billings, and, especially, John Curtis and his students were cited as compelling. "There was too much published in favor of the continuum model in the 1950s to argue against it," said Peter Marks, adding that all the oral presentations at annual meetings in the 1950s "could have added to the ground swell." Several respondents told me that attendance at annual society meetings in the fifties was modest, allowing most conference-goers to hear every paper, in contrast to the modern reality of several concurrent sessions. "The Ecological Society of America was a small club then, and we all met face-to-face at the annual meetings," wrote Jerry Olson. "The sheer number of pro-continuum reports made it seem almost like a bandwagon that you had to get on."

These ecologists' opinions echo those of historians who have suggested that the period 1947–59 witnessed a Kuhnian paradigm revolution, with the continuum theory replacing the association-unit theory.[28] True enough, the paradigm's founder in the English-speaking world, Frederic Clements, died in 1945, thereby marking one of Kuhn's rules for a revolution. But was his death followed by the accumulation of enough new information that was contrary to the Clementsian view? From the end of World War II until 1959, published pro-continuum support—in English-language journals—consisted of only eleven research papers and six reviews. Reviews do not present new data; they only discuss the data of already published research papers. In addition, short oral research presentations at annual ESA meetings numbered only thirteen. Most of these were previews of research papers published later in this period (see table on p. 515–16). They all had a very narrow authorship. Eight of eleven research papers, eleven of twelve abstracts, and one of six reviews—70 percent of the published pro-continuum information—came from John Curtis and his students in Wisconsin.

Does this constitute a critical mass of anomalous information—especially considering the facts that (1) the new information was heavily dominated by a single ecologist, working in only one small region of the North American continent, and (2) that no American research papers had been published before this period that supported the individualistic concept? Is twelve years enough time for a 180-degree change in the basic understanding of the central focus of vegetation science? I'm skeptical that the new evidence, in and of itself, was compelling enough to be the sole cause of a revolution. The number of *discrete* research pieces seems too meager. However, Peter Marks rhetorically asked me in his interview, "Couldn't ten to twelve years be typical for *any* transformation of theory? Do we have other examples? Maybe the paradigm shift was not so dramatic." I think it *was* dramatically abrupt. During our interview, Daniel Axelrod recounted that it took several decades of gradually increasing amounts of data, from many independent sources, to convince him—and most geologists—that continents are not static, but instead move across the earth's crust. The theory (paradigm) that continuous evolutionary change marks the history of life required many decades to displace an earlier theory of stasis.

Six of those I interviewed believed that notions of variation and individualism from other areas of science reinforced and amplified the evidence from vegetation during the fifties. Jean Langenheim recalled her angst at having collected data on plant distribution along Rocky Mountain slopes for her Ph.D. study, and realizing that it did not match Clementsian predictions. Coming to Berkeley, she talked with the botanist Herbert Mason (a supporter of Gleason as early as 1947) and learned from him about new discoveries of variation within species and within vegetation types over geologic time. Those discoveries showed that any wide-ranging species was likely to harbor several genetically distinct races (ecotypes), each race occupying a different environmental part of the entire range of the species. Species were not, then, populations of identical individuals. Paleobotanists at the same time were showing that the past movement of species north and south in response to climate change was as individuals, not as synchronous groups. She was able to resolve her non-Clementsian data by placing them in a continuum model. John Cantlon was also impressed with the scope of variation within species, as revealed from the 1950s ecotype work of Calvin McMillan and from Cantlon's own fieldwork with ecotypes of a widely distributed sedge in Alaska. Robert McIntosh remembered the variation revealed to him as a graduate student by the new technique of mass collecting used by the taxonomist Norman Fassett. Linda Olsvig-Whittaker wrote me that "Hutchinson's theory of the niche . . . did a lot to strengthen the individualistic hypothesis, since . . . responses to resource gradients in Hutchinson's paradigm should look like the Gleasonian model." Franklin, Bormann, and McIntosh all spoke of individualist ideas as being "in the air" and of the possibility that ecologists "recognized variability from a lot of sources."

Another group of nine respondents shared the opinion that change was primarily due to the many older students coming to the university immediately after World War II, wanting to be creative, and finding it difficult to be so within the association-unit paradigm. Bill Salt recalled the Clementsian-style vegetation classification literature as "dead, awful, rigid, ecclesiatistical, a subject that only small, legalistic minds could deal with. They had mined out the ground." Paul Risser said, "We worked to death the Clements scheme. People were looking for new creative challenges and couldn't find them in old ground." Billings, Cantlon, Franklin, Golley, Goodall, and Reed all commented on the difference in graduate students before and after the war: after the war students were more numerous, older, better read, more interested in developing testable new ideas, and less inclined to be ideologues. "I think we began getting students who could and did think for themselves," responded Jack Major.

John Cantlon pointed out that the postwar economic boom and the GI Bill also led to the hiring of more faculty, including ecology professors. Cantlon thinks that these young faculty had an impact on the direction of research because the American academic department structure fostered individualism. In Europe (though not Great Britain), young faculty serve the research interests of the most senior professor, thus slowing the rise to prominence of new ideas, whereas in America each faculty member is an individual entrepreneur. What works is more likely to get rewarded.

The only other cause for a paradigm shift mentioned by a significant number of interviewees was the availability of new research tools and the dollar support to purchase them. Extensive, random sampling of vegetation became easier through the use of aerial photography, the development of new vegetation sampling techniques, and the application of new statistical approaches to interpret large data sets (coupled with increasing availability of calculators and pre-computers). Other tools permitted ecologists to get inside their plants, to study the effect of environment on metabolism: radioactive isotopes allowed nutrients and energy to be traced through a plant, a community, or an ecosystem; improved growth chambers and ecophysiological devices could measure whole-plant growth, respiration, water loss, and photosynthesis.

Increased funding for plant ecology research in the 1950s came from the new National Science Foundation, the Atomic Energy Commission, state agencies, and foundations. In some cases, the funding changed research directions, though not in the narrow sense of a shift from association-unit studies to continuum studies. None of the respondents could cite examples of funding agencies directing or otherwise biasing the direction of vegetation science research. Dwight Billings told me that he had wanted to conduct research in ecophysiology since the 1930s but had worked instead with vegetation. Now, twenty years later, he was finally able to pursue ecophysiology, because the support funds necessary to purchase equipment were in hand. Curtis's group at Wisconsin did not depend on public funds, according to the interviewee McIntosh. They received consistent, long-term support from the Wisconsin Alumni Research Foundation.

John Cantlon and Robert Peet suggested that funding agencies had an indirect effect on research. This effect resulted from the act of writing a grant proposal. In constructing a coherent proposal, the applicant had to answer "so what" questions, and by so doing he or she heightened the degree of introspection and fostered hypothesis testing as an investigative model, which shifted the focus from vegetation description to a search for mechanisms of function. Peet called this a "maturing" period for ecology. (In rebuttal, several other respondents noted that the acceptance rate of proposals in the 1950s was so high that very little reflective thought was required for success.)

Both Gerhard Wiegleb and Craig Loehle have recently analyzed the role of logic and hypothesis testing in vegetation science, especially in connection with the paradigm shift. Wiegleb concluded that the logic underlying plant ecology early in the century can be called "naive realism" or "essentialism": a belief in a finite number of entities (for example, associations) that can be meaningfully compared and classified. Research at that time focused on inductive (inferential) reasoning and was not based on hypothesis testing. Hypothesis testing is the process by which a premise can be rejected or accepted on the basis of an experiment. Hypothesis testing today still remains difficult to apply to complex ecological systems, especially when the premises to be tested are immature (vague, qualitative, and lacking in operational definitions). As a consequence, immature theories like the association-unit theory have a great deal of inertia, or what Loehle calls "theory tenacity." Wiegleb sees that a pluralistic kind of ecology, featuring diverse assumptions and techniques of investigation, offers the best hope for progress in the face of problems like immature theories. He concludes that "the individualistic concept of Gleason seems to be able to provide a general framework for a pluralistic vegetation science."[29]

As the association-unit theory declined in the 1950s, an ecosystem paradigm was flowering. The term "ecosystem" was first defined by Arthur Tansley as a unit formed by the interaction of coexisting organisms (a community) with their nonliving environment.[30] Eugene Odum has been the champion and popularizer of the ecosystem concept from 1953, when the first edition of his textbook *Fundamentals of Ecology* was published, to the present.[31]

Was there a connection between the decline of one and the rise of the other? Could Clementsian holism, the association as organism, merely have been elevated to the ecosystem level? Certainly, some ecologists did use the ecosystem concept in a holistic way, making it the holy grail of ecological naturalness, incapable of being explained simply from a tally of its component parts. According to the ecosystem ecologist Frank Golley, "Odum asserted that the ecosystem was a whole greater than the sum of its parts and had emergent properties." Further, Golley wrote, the ecosystem concept "is a more modern way to speak of the wholes and connections of Elton, Clements, Tansley, and Lindeman . . . [It is] a holistic perspective."[32] In his review of the organismic concept in ecology, Jonathan Richardson agreed: "There is an unmistakably organismic flavor to common phrases such as 'community metabolism' and 'ecosystem structure and function,' but the relationship goes well beyond words. I would argue that . . . the ecosystem approach is a child of the organismic concept."[33] The historian Joel Hagan summarizes the modern ecosystem concept as being semi- or quasi-organismic: "Few ecologists after World War II believed that a community or ecosystem really was an organism, but in important ways they continued to believe that these higher level systems behaved somewhat like organisms. . . . The idea of the ecosystem was a direct descendent of the organismal concept."[34] During his interview Frank Golley distanced his own holistic views from those of Eugene Odum, rejecting Odum's notion that ecosystems may experience the process of organic evolution.

The overwhelming majority of my respondents, however, said that the paradigm shift in the 1950s was not a transference of holism from the community level to the ecosystem level. They saw ecosystem research as simultaneously holistic and reductionist. There was no consistent link between the outcome of the Clements-Gleason debate and the rise of the ecosystem paradigm. The ecosystem is not for them the child of the association. The ecosystem is only a convenient conceptual tool and its use in casual conversation does not necessarily mean that the speaker has a holistic view of nature. He or she may still see nature as a reductionist does, a machine best explained by teasing apart each component, no matter how complex and elaborate the task.

Perhaps this task is too great for the human mind. Herbert Bormann, in his interview, said, "I view the ecosystem as humbling. We are foundering on the rocks of complexity." And Frank Egler noted, in his interview, "The ecosystem is not more complex than we think, it is more complex than we *can* think." Some reductionist ecologists do eventually relinquish reductionism and adopt holism when nature's complexity reaches some critically high level. The biosphere, for example, is the conjoined product of all ecosystems on earth. The complexity of this multiple-ecosystem entity causes even the adamant reductionist Daniel Botkin to become holistic. The biosphere is more like a moose than a machine, Botkin concedes, "a system with organic qualities" in contrast to the nonorganismic community.[35]

Why the Revolution Then? Cultural Themes

WHERE DID CLEMENTS'S ORGANISMIC THEORY OF VEGETATION COME FROM? *The Random House Dictionary of the English Language* defines "organicism" as follows: "The view that some systems resemble organisms in having parts that function in relation to the whole to which they belong . . .

[also a] view of society as an autonomous entity analogous to and following the same developmental pattern as a biological organism." Several historians, as well as the South African ecologist John Phillips, credit the sociologists Herbert Spencer and Lester Ward with leading Clements to his organismic view of nature.[36] Both Spencer and Ward equated human social systems with organisms. Ward's *Dynamic Sociology,* for example, includes the statement "Society is simply a compound organism whose acts exhibit the resultant of all the individual forces which its members exert. The acts . . . obey fixed laws. Objectively viewed, society is a natural object."[37] Ward's book was published only a few years before Clements first wrote of his own organismic theory, and Ward's book title was remarkably parallel with Clements's description of his own research as "dynamic ecology." Ward thoroughly reviewed Spencer's similar ideas from *The Social Organism.*[38] Clements never admitted any links between Spencer, Ward, and himself, but he did publicly acknowledge support for his biological ideas from the philosophical works of Jan Christiaan Smuts, who wrote that all reality is aggregative, emergent, and holistic.[39]

Clements's organicism was an extension of nineteenth-century ideas. Ecologists who preceded Clements, such as Alexander von Humboldt, Anton Kerner von Marilaun, Ernst Haeckel, Stephen Forbes, Eugenius Warming, Conway McMillan, and Henry Cowles, all to some extent employed organic metaphors for the plant and animal communities they studied.[40]

The association-unit theory was also adopted by some twentieth-century animal ecologists and limnologists. For example, at the University of Chicago, Professors Allee, Park, and Emerson saw evidence for cooperation and community among associated organisms. Gregg Mitman has convincingly argued that the Quaker, socialist, pacifist beliefs of Warder Allee shaped his scientific research and conclusions.[41] The Chicago school's view of communities dominated animal ecology during the 1920–50 period. All three served as presidents of the ESA, and Park and Emerson additionally held editor positions with the society's premier journal, *Ecology.* Until World War II, then, the science of ecology was awash with holistic analogies.

Immediately after the war holism in ecology and in life became unfashionable. Ecologists experienced fragmentation, revolution, rebellion, as well as growth in their science. They revised fundamental concepts, turning some assumptions about nature upside down. They replaced, enlarged, and abstracted the basic unit of ecology from understandable, individual organisms to something so complex as to be unknowable. They also experienced an explosion of pluralism—the pursuit of many ideas and paths of research—which replaced a historically narrowly defined route. I was an ecology graduate student during the mid-1960s, and the aftershocks of this decade of change brought me strong personal feelings of excitement, tension, confusion, and tenuousness about both the practice and the theories of my own kind of ecology, vegetation science.

The activities of ecologists of the fifties mirrored a revolution in American culture at large.[42] Ecological fragmentation and regrouping in this period fed on and resonated with much wider American ferment. There were links between ecology and technological, social, and cultural actions that celebrated individualism, rebellion from previous norms, and a profound acceptance of uncertainty. Fragmentation was "in the air," pervading the American psyche. People picked up and translated its vibrations into the practice of government, science, literature, and the arts. I suggest that ecologists rode the wave of fragmentation to change some fundamental opinions, to take research risks, and to view nature in a reductionist rather than a holistic way.

Cultural fragmentation was evident in concepts of race, imperialism, and local government. As so well described by Donna Haraway in this volume, the concept of race became fragmented and shattered. Before World War II humanity was seen as being divisible into a small number of discrete races. Wartime Germany and Japan sensitized the world to the ugly excesses of this simplistic kind of racism. The boundaries of traditional races then became softened by studies from medicine, physiology, and genetics that revealed the enormous diversity within any given race and the existence of gradients in individual racial traits. The end of the war brought a dismantling of European empires and the proliferation of independent nations. Many ethnic groups became politically privileged and recognized. The map of the world was dramatically fragmented and changed.[43]

In the fifties Americans became disaffected with socialism. Socialism had dominated the thinking of many American intellectuals for the first half of the century, up to 1950.[44] After this, wrote the historian Godfrey Hodgson, "in the United States (though nowhere else in the world), socialism was utterly discredited. . . . In 1949, a Gallup poll found that only 15% wanted to move in the direction of socialism; 61% wanted to move in the opposite direction. . . . It was a startling shift."[45] Roosevelt and Truman social Democrats gave way to the laissez-faire individualism of Eisenhower Republicans.

The importance of the individual was a second theme. Literature and the arts focused on the loneliness, courage, and uniqueness of the individual. The literary critic David Van Leer summed up the 1950s in one word— "existentialism." "Existentialism defined the generation's conception of self . . . [and] rejected the pursuit of fundamental truths. When translated into a popular idiom . . . the philosophy tended to encourage individual self-absorption over social involvement. The tradition of socialist literature did not survive the anti-Communism of the 1950s."[46]

Anti-establishmentarianism was a third theme. Existentialism offered a popular vehicle for revolt against social convention. Norman Mailer, among other writers, searched for existential heroes to pit against the square mentality of the fifties.[47] In poetry oppositional forces to the status quo first became publicly visible through the "beats," who debuted publicly at a reading in San Francisco in the fall of 1956. The beats broke poetic conventions, used outrageous constructions and unusual language, and jumbled ideas in a seemingly chaotic manner. The anti-establishment theme was echoed by such confessional poets as John Berryman, Robert Lowell, and Sylvia Plath. They urged that there be no more masks or mythologies and an end to precious verbiage, to conservative themes, and to standard meters and verse forms. Some of the confessional poets were influenced by abstract impressionist painters in New York. Frank O'Hara most typified the confessional poet's belief in the poem as a throw-away, a mere chronicle of its creation. They saw each poem, wrote Nina Baym, "as transitory, incomplete, an instrument of passage."[48]

The themes of rebellion and an unsentimental celebration of the individual were also present in the music of Elvis Presley, the abstract expressionism of Jackson Pollock and Willem de Kooning, the antiheroic portrait photography of Robert Frank, and the unlovely, idiosyncratic characters created by Tennessee Williams.

The theme of fragmentation was even apparent in literary and linguistic theory. The neat, holistic, systematic theory of language and literature called structuralism, developed by Ferdinand de Saussure, Roman Jakobson, and Claude Lévi-Strauss, was giving way to an antithetical and chaotic poststructuralism that featured uncertainty in striking parallel with Heisenberg's principle from the physical sciences.[49]

This survey, though brief and superficial, identifies widespread American cultural themes of fragmention of norms, the celebration of the individual, and rebellion against convention. Impermanence and uncertainty replaced predictability, and individual competition displaced group cooperation. At the same time there was an expression of anxiety at the loss of past certitude and stable social organization. A similar range of themes marked the ecology of the fifties.

Most Ecologists Are Not Holistic Individuals

THE ECOLOGISTS I INTERVIEWED HELD A VARIETY OF READY OPINIONS ABOUT possible scientific causes of the revolution. But did anyone link ecological changes in the fifties with parallel cultural or social themes? More personally, did any of them see any connection between their own political or social attitudes and their ecological views or research directions? Was it merely chance that they became community or ecosystem ecologists with either holistic or reductionist viewpoints?

The great majority of those interviewed agreed with Peter Greig-Smith, who wrote back to me, "There may be parallels between ecology and politics but if so I suspect they are coincidental. I . . . see no parallels between my political or social attitudes and my ecological views." Only a dozen respondents admitted to seeing even the smallest connection between society—or their own personality—and their ecological research.

Frank Golley was the sole respondent who connected cultural existentialism with ecology. He recalled the "seething creativity" and rebellion of Gary Snyder, Allen Ginsberg, and other artists who "spoke for him" in their attacks on a 1950s culture of reaction and conservatism. Eugene Odum and Arnold Schultz have both seen cohorts of students and scientists pass through the American academic scene in the past several decades, one generation holistic and the next reductionist. In neither case were they able to relate these episodes to larger cultural cycles, but certainly the implication is that they resonated with broad themes that were in the air. Robert Burgess concluded that culture influences science via its institutions. Social, political, and economic climates create and structure institutions, such as universities and granting agencies. Ecologists accomplish their research through such institutions; thus culture can bias research.

Nine others could not see broad culture-ecology links, but they spoke about connections between individual personalities and the kind of science each practiced. Paul Risser, for example, saw a parallel between his own changing social attitudes and the kind of ecological research he did. He felt that with age, he had become more liberal, more interested in social issues, and more conscious of ties between science and policy; his research has sequentially moved from studies of individual forest herb species to community studies, to landscape and ecosystem work, and most recently to a focus on a sustainable biosphere. Stan Rowe said, "We're all strongly influenced in our science by our political beliefs. Look at the emphasis we put on competition. If one is trying to see nature holistically and integrated, you tend to see cooperation more than competition and aggression." Frank Pitelka agreed that there can be a personal element in one's science—he cited Allee's preoccupation with cooperation in his ecological research—but at the same time he could see no pattern between his own personality and his scientific career. He believes that chance played the largest role in his career: he could as easily have become a botanist, linguist, or novelist as an ecologist. Herbert Bormann and Eugene Odum attributed their career directions to fathers who were interested in sociology, both of whom created mental bridges for their sons to connect ecosystems with human societies. Pierre Dansereau wrote that his European classical upbringing left him "at all times with a profound need for continuity" in history, culture, and science. He added, "Born under Libra, I am a conciliator and a seeker of harmony." His change of view from the association-unit to the continuum paralleled his change in research from genetics and taxonomy to community ecology and later on to human land-use patterns and global environmental issues: "My view of the plant association has been set in an ever-widening framework."

The personalities of dominant researchers may become attached to the fields they work in or to the theories they generate. In such cases, others can be attracted to or repelled from a subject because of its link with a personality. Helen Buell told me that "liberals" were attracted to Gleason's individualistic theory because both Gleason and his writings were less "rigid and hidebound" than Clements. (Ironically, Gleason himself and his earliest supporters Curtis and Whittaker were all political conservatives.) Enough anti-Clementsian anecdotes, illustrating his imperiousness, rigidity, and humorlessness, have come to me over the years and in the course of this project to suggest the possibility at least that some rejected his theories because they rejected his personality. Here's a sample, told to me by Rexford Daubenmire:

> Clements and his wife, Edith, were traveling through the Colfax area of eastern Washington with me in the late 1930s. We stopped in a graveyard because it contained ungrazed vegetation. The graveyard contained grassland and scattered shrubs, some of which were rabbitbrush, an indicator of disturbance. Clements wanted to record this as climax vegetation, representative of the region. He began to take notes, then asked Edith to get out of the car and take a picture. "Be sure to get those sagebrush shrubs in the photograph," he admonished her. "Dr. Clements," I protested, "those shrubs are rabbitbrush, not sagebrush." Without looking up, he scarcely paused before saying, "There's a negligible difference," and continued writing. I have no idea if he wrote down sagebrush or rabbitbrush in his notes. I'd like to know if the photo was ever published, and what species were listed in the caption.

In a post-interview letter to me, Daubenmire wrote that Clements papered over contrary views by being "a superb spell-binder." He added, "I found him able to almost hypnotize his audience, so such so that you would be subconsciously nodding in agreement on points for which you held the opposite interpretation. . . ." Clearly, Clements was a presence, and his personality became linked with his ideas in the minds of many ecologists.

The modest number of respondents who linked ecological science to cultural themes is striking, considering the richness of historical evidence to the contrary. This absence of holistic thinking supports the notion that scientists are not trained to be introspective and intuitive. As Robert Whittaker wrote about his own route to a vocation as a professional ecologist, "Probably few people really know the reasons for such [career] choices when it is not the influence of a particular individual. . . . The process is . . . akin to the . . . choice of a friend or lover, an evaluation of mutual compatibility which is only partly conscious and logical, largely unconscious and unverbalized."[50] Jerry Franklin brought the issue of subconscious personal bias and idiosyncrasy to the community-continuum debate: "Scientific belief is conditioned by the way we're brought up. A lot of biologists can't deal with the idea that nature is not very predictable. They'll bust their behind to develop theories to show that there has to be pattern. They can't believe that God does play with dice."

Stan Rowe, in a post-interview letter to me, counterargued that ecologists weren't so much guilty of an absence of holistic thinking, as guilty of "plain ignorance. Unless the scientist reads outside her/his field, or takes a sociology class and learns how Kuhnian paradigms as 'cultural baggage' lead humans by the nose in all they think and do, one can go through life ignorantly believing that science is detached, objective, factual, unmythic, and withal goal-setting." It isn't what one studies that makes one holistic or reductionist; it's how one thinks about a subject.

The overwhelming majority of respondents claimed that their ecological ideas came from childhood experiences, teachers, colleagues, fortuitious opportunities, or the availability of tools and the money to purchase them with. Jerry Franklin had gone camping as a young boy, an experience that gave him a lifelong "affection" for forests. With ecosystem studies Herbert Bormann found a satisfying way to do basic research while simultaneously generating practical advice for land-use managers. Makoto Numata became a community ecologist because of a deep social commitment to nature conservation. Rexford Daubenmire became an ecologist simply because of the positive force of Professor Stanley Cain's "great guy" personality during an undergraduate course. Cain, Daubenmire said, continued to serve as a personal role model for his entire career. Jean Langenheim was able to make sense of her Ph.D. data and to go on because she accompanied her husband to UC-Berkeley and there met Herbert Mason, who showed her that there was life after Clements. Jack Major began teaching plant ecology and a research career at UC-Davis simply because Vernon Cheadle, at the time chair of the biology department, believed that ecology was a "suitable area of study," overriding the views of other faculty and encouraging Major to express the ecological interests that he had. John Cantlon developed his continuum view of vegetation because of opportunistic work available to be done in Alaska—work funded only because of the national defense value of the Arctic during the height of the Cold War. Dwight Billings went to Duke University as a new graduate student simply because he heard a high school lecture by Stanley Cain and then received a teaching assistantship; he didn't know until later that Henry Oosting was to begin his teaching career at Duke that very year and would give the first ecology course ever offered on that campus. Daniel Axelrod's lifetime interest in geology and vegetation began as a result of temporary work on a depression-era survey of montane California wilderness. And so on. The role of chance contacts with other scientists, quite devoid of any resonance with cultural themes, appears to be enormously formative.

If I took the interviews at face value, I would have to conclude that these premier ecologists of the fifties were too busy to be attentive to the larger world around them (some stated that they were directed by supervisors to keep their science separate from politics and personalities). Discussions with peers, major profesors, and colleagues about politics, literature, ethics, and ideologies were apparently off-limits. The interviews seem to imply that the very best ecologists of the mid-twentieth century were uniform workaholics on autopilot, building careers on the basis of fortuitous meetings, papers read, the availability of new research techniques, and grants obtained, with remarkably little conscious curiosity about personal ethics or one's connection with society. This interpretation is likely exaggerated and skewed, but it matches a rueful statement by the ecohistorian Robert McIntosh that "ecologists generally have little concern with philosophy or history."[51] If my reconstruction is accurate, American ecologists of the 1950s were as randomly individualistic and nonholistic as they claimed their vegetation to be.

But my reconstruction is no doubt incomplete and superficial. Probably, in all of us, a great deal of integration occurs below the conscious level. At that level, ecologists, artists, politicians, and hod carriers are all both holistic and individualistic, injecting broad cultural themes into their research and their lives. If ecologists could mine down there, below the ego, they might recognize and admit that they are attracted to certain visions of nature because of their idiosyncratic personal histories. Proving this, however, would be an essay topic for a hypnotist, a psychotherapist, or a diviner, not for me.

Conclusions

THIS ESSAY HAS NOT BEEN ABOUT THE "CORRECTNESS" OF ANY ECOLOGICAL concept or research direction. It has instead been about the reasons that concepts or research directions come and go when they do and why they become popular or rejected. Although the majority of ecologists today think that the continuum theory best explains vegetation, conservationists who argue for community and ecosystem preservation should not despair: the debate is still going on. We can be certain that the present majority opinion will be different in another decade or two. That new opinion may be some combination of continuum and association-unit or a completely different concept.

Every year's issue of the international *Journal of Vegetation Science* continues the debate or asks for a burial of it, more than thirty years after the supposed paradigm revolution. J. Bastow Wilson, in the 1991 volume, asked how vegetation science could exist if plant communities did not, and he humorously compared the scientific search for proof of communities to the search for the abominable snowman of the Himalayas, the yeti.[52] Paul Keddy, in the 1993 volume, begged his colleagues to get beyond the trivial question of "existence" and move on to more-substantial, testable, pragmatic topics. If Gleason and Clements couldn't resolve it, he asked, why think that anyone now can? "I suspect that, in general, asking whether certain phenomena 'exist' is simply not a profitable route for debate."[53] Finally, Michael Palmer and Peter White, in the 1994 volume, remind us of a common pitfall in human thinking called reification: the mistaken conversion of a theoretical concept into a concrete object. "We create discrete words. We create hierarchies of discrete definitions. We would like to think that what is signified by our definitions has an objective existence. . . . However, our job as scientists is . . . to re-wire our mental structures to reflect the world. Communities, therefore, must be studied and defined operationally . . . with as little conceptual baggage as possible, so that we can put the debate about their existence behind us."[54]

Palmer and White, in using the expression "conceptual baggage" are talking about scientific, verbal accessories to any concept. They could, however, have as easily used the expression "cultural baggage." My essay has been a case study of the central role of cultural baggage in framing and moving scientific debate. Scientists—ecologists, in this example—imagine that their search to explain the ultimate realities in nature is carried along a logical, unbiased course from hypothesis to test, from results to deductions, and from fact to fact much like the force that flows through a row of lined-up billiard balls. One ball drives into the next, ultimately sending the end ball into the correct pocket. But instead, our vision of reality in nature, our search process to find it, and our very reason for conducting the search in the first place are all personally, culturally, and historically driven. What this may mean for vegetation science is that we'll never recognize the forest for the trees, or the trees for the forest.

On the Search for a Root Cause:
Essentialist Tendencies in
Environmental Discourse

Jeffrey C. Ellis

If they can get you asking the wrong questions, they don't have to worry
about the answers.

—Thomas Pynchon

IN THE FALL OF 1993 DR. SALLIE BALUNIAS, AN ASTRONOMER AT THE HAR-
vard-Smithsonian Center for Astrophysics, presented a paper at a climatol-
ogy conference organized by the Scripps Institute in La Jolla, California. In
her paper Balunias argued that a cyclical increase in solar radiation intensity
corresponds with and might explain the pattern of global warming that has
been of such great concern to scientists and environmentalists in recent
years.

Her theory attracted the attention of the Global Climate Coalition, a lobbying organization representing energy companies and trade associations in
Washington, D.C. The coalition approached Balunias about embarking on
a media campaign to publicize her ideas. She agreed. A public relations firm
was hired, and the astronomer toured the country espousing her claim that
solar fluctuations might be causing the warming of the earth's atmosphere.

In response, environmental groups and scientists denounced Balunias's
theory as biased and reasserted their claims that strong evidence indicated a
direct correlation between the phenomenon of global warming and
increased levels of carbon dioxide and other greenhouse gases in the atmosphere. A group of researchers published a report in *Science* that concluded
that solar fluctuations are "too small to have had any significant effect on
climate and cannot be responsible for any current global warming." James
Hansen, director of the Goddard Institute for Space Studies and longtime

investigator of global warming, admitted that solar phenomena might be a factor but argued that they were relatively insignificant compared to the impact of gases produced by humans.[1]

Whenever a problem or a crisis is identified, those concerned tend to seek out and identify the origins of the problem. The logic behind this search for a root cause or causes is compelling. Adequate solutions to a problem cannot be derived or implemented unless those solutions address the problem at its source. Different analyses of the root causes of any specific problem necessarily lead to different policy proposals, which can have profoundly different political and social implications. Disagreements over what constitute the origins of a problem are, understandably, often highly charged affairs.

The clash outlined above over the source of the global warming problem illustrates the particular importance of the debate over root causes to the politics of environmentalism. If Balunias is correct and the warming of the earth's atmosphere is being caused by solar fluctuations rather than by industrial and social practices, then there is little need to regulate and constrain those practices in order to slow down atmospheric change. Furthermore, if the sun itself is the source of one of the earth's most troubling environmental problems, not only is there little that can be done about it, but nature can once again be thought of as humanity's greatest enemy. From this perspective, nature is not something that needs protection and understanding; it is fickle, constantly threatening our existence, and therefore something against which we may justifiably employ all of our scientific and technological capabilities in order to survive.

Most people who consider themselves environmentalists might read about this conflict between the Harvard astronomer and the advocates of the carbon dioxide theory and conclude that this is just another us versus them story, with developmentalists employing the tried-and-true tactic of buying science to divert attention from the need to make difficult decisions. Though this may well be true in this instance, it is worth recognizing that the story also closely resembles the environmentalists versus themselves story so typical of the modern American environmental movement. Balunias and her sponsors can justifiably claim that they are as concerned as their critics about the environment and global warming and that they are motivated by a desire to attack the problem at its roots.

Seen from this perspective, the Balunias story illustrates the tendency for America's diverse environmental movement to engage in debates over the root cause or causes of environmental problems. These at times rancorous debates have been common features of environmental discourse in this country. They have contributed substantially to disagreements over strategy and goals among environmentalists and have served to undermine the possibility of building a more effective and broad-based environmental coalition. With environmental progress stalled as a result of growing public apathy and the seeming intractability of global environmental problems, it is time to assess this tendency and evaluate its impact on the environmental movement.

On February 2, 1970, Barry Commoner appeared on the cover of *Time* magazine and was identified in a feature story as the "Paul Revere of Ecology."[2] This was an appropriate appellation for the plant physiologist from Washington University, in St. Louis, Missouri, who had been active since the mid-1950s in sounding environmental alarms about radiation hazards, pesticides, phosphates, automobile exhaust, and other pollutants.

Commoner's concerns about the chemicalization and irradiation of the environment had originated in the early 1950s while he was investigating cellular processes in plants. During these investigations, he recognized that normal cellular functions were often impaired if cells were exposed to "free radicals," substances that contained unpaired electrons. At the same time, investigators also discovered that tobacco tars, many newly introduced petroleum-based products, and most irradiated materials were radical and carcinogenic.[3]

Commoner grew particularly alarmed when he realized that scientific advances in physics and chemistry were contributing to the proliferation of potentially hazardous substances before their biological consequences had been investigated and understood. He came to believe that this failure to assess the possible biological repercussions of scientific progress constituted a weakness "at the very heart of the scientific enterprise . . . [that] threaten[ed] the future of science and its usefulness to the nation and the world." This was the message that Commoner had expounded during the 1960s, most comprehensively in his book *Science and Survival*.[4]

Having dedicated himself to raising America's environmental consciousness in the years leading up to Earth Day 1970, Commoner felt it was time to reassess the environmental movement after that bellwether event. "Until now," he wrote, "most of us in the environmental movement have been chiefly concerned with providing the public with information that shows that there *is* an environmental crisis." Feeling that he and other environmentalists had at long last succeeded in proving that a "crisis existed," Commoner now believed it had become "necessary . . . to consider its causes, so that rational cures can be designed."[5]

In deciding to evaluate the origins of the environmental crisis, Commoner had a particular bone to pick. He wished to refute the claims being advanced by a cohort of American neo-Malthusians that the country's environmental problems were the direct result of unchecked population growth. Since the late 1960s and early 1970s, the leading gurus of the population-growth-is-the-problem school of environmentalism have been Paul Ehrlich and Garrett Hardin. Ehrlich's 1968 book, *The Population Bomb,* and Hardin's article of the same year, "The Tragedy of the Commons," have served as Bible and epistle for this branch of the environmental movement.[6]

Their work has been the most recent manifestation of a concern with population growth that began in the late eighteenth century, when the English clergyman Thomas Malthus published *An Essay on the Principle of Population*. According to Malthus, because human populations increased geometrically while food production increased arithmetically, mankind would always be pushing the limits of available resources and therefore subject to famine, epidemic disease, and war. Versions of the Malthusian argument have resurfaced periodically ever since, particularly during periods of social upheaval and distress.[7]

Malthus's twentieth-century heirs have been more concerned with resource depletion than with the inability of productive capacity to keep pace with population growth. During the 1950s the American conservationists Fairfield Osborn and William Vogt became obsessed with the idea that population growth in "underdeveloped" countries threatened to deplete the world's resources. Interestingly, Vogt and Osborn failed to consider the fact that the 6 percent of the world's population that lived in the United States was consuming 30–50 percent of the world's resources. During the early Cold War years, it was apparently politically incorrect to criticize America's high standard of living.[8]

Vogt and Osborn were instead concerned about the impracticality of basing U.S. foreign policy on the assumption that the best means of halting the spread of communism was to extend the American way of life to the Third World. This could not be done, they warned, unless the United States also moved quickly to check population growth in those regions as well. In the 1960s Malthusians began to worry that population growth had gotten out of hand in the United States, too, and was the ultimate source of the country's mounting environmental problems.

In December 1970, at the annual meeting of the American Association for the Advancement of Science, Barry Commoner denounced the Malthusian argument in general and personally confronted Paul Ehrlich and Garrett Hardin, who were appearing on the same panel with him. "Saying that none of our pollution problems can be solved without getting at population first," he argued, "is a copout of the worst kind."[9]

Commoner continued his criticisms of the neo-Malthusians in the year that followed. In April he published "The Causes of Pollution" in *Environment*, a journal he had begun in the late 1950s under the auspices of the Greater St. Louis Committee on Nuclear Information. In this article he identified Ehrlich as one of those observers who "have blamed the environmental crisis on overpopulation." Commoner was particularly troubled by what he saw as Ehrlich's reliance on a simple mathematical equation for measuring the impact of population growth on the quality of the environment. While Commoner found Ehrlich's formula "self-evidently true," he believed that it was of little use for advancing "our understanding of the causes of environmental problems." Its greatest drawback, according to Commoner, was that it failed to explain why the amounts of various pollutants had increased by 200 to 1,000 percent between 1946 and 1968, while the population had increased by only 43 percent during that same time period.[10]

Commoner held that a more "detailed guide" was needed to explain this discrepancy. On the basis of his own data and calculations, he concluded that "the rapid intensification of pollution" since World War II could not be "accounted for solely by concurrent increases . . . in population." Rather, the "most powerful cause of environmental pollution . . . appears to be the introduction of changes in technology, without due regard to their untoward effects on the environment."[11]

Commoner escalated his criticisms of Ehrlich and Hardin the following fall in *The Closing Circle,* his second book on the environmental crisis. In this work Commoner reiterated that it was imperative to "understand the origins of the environmental crisis" so that we could "begin to manage the huge undertaking of surviving it." Despite this imperative, Commoner was concerned with the many "confident explanations of the cause and cure of the crisis" that had proliferated since Earth Day. "Having spent some years in the effort simply to detect and describe the growing list of environmental problems," he wrote, "the identification of a single cause and cure seemed a rather bold step." Among those he singled out as most willing to take such a step, Commoner identified Ehrlich and Hardin for blaming pollution problems in the United States on increased population. They, like many other environmental prognosticators, were prone to "read into" the environmental crisis "whatever conclusions their own beliefs . . . suggested."[12]

Even more disturbing for Commoner were the social and political implications of a narrow focus on population as the root cause of the environmental crisis. Behind Hardin's proposals for dealing with population growth, Commoner found a "faintly masked 'barbarism' " that "would condemn most of the people of the world to the material level of the barbarian, and the rest, the 'fortunate minorities,' to the moral level of the barbarian." Similarly, Commoner felt that Ehrlich's suggestion that population be controlled "by compulsion if voluntary methods fail" amounted to a program for "political repression." Nor did he consider it "possible to disguise this ugly fact by notions such as 'mutual coercion, mutually agreed upon.' " He feared that because of the neo-Malthusians' "highly publicized assertions, the notion that human survival is threatened merely by increase in numbers is now a fairly common one."[13]

Although Hardin refrained from directly addressing Commoner's accusations, Ehrlich responded with vehemence. He felt he had to deal with Commoner's "questionable assertions. . . . before persistent and unrebutted repetition entrenches them in the public mind—if not the scientific literature." According to Ehrlich, Commoner had become an "ecological popularizer . . . zeal[ous] to 'prove' that all environmental problems are caused by faulty technology." In his misguided effort to develop this "one-dimensional" thesis, Commoner had resorted to "biased selection of data, unconventional definitions, numerical sleight of hand, and bad ecology." In addition to finding Commoner's position "unjustified and counterproductive," Ehrlich said Commoner was "deluding the public" by offering an "uncomplicated, socially comfortable, and hence, seductive" solution to the environmental crisis.[14]

In this debate Commoner and Ehrlich accused each other of oversimplifying the causes of the environmental crisis. Each felt that the other had adopted too narrow a focus and had reduced the complex environmental crisis to one essential cause, which had to be given priority over all other concerns. To a degree they were both correct, but, ironically, each had difficulty in recognizing that the criticisms he leveled at his opponent applied to his own analysis as well. Both paid lip service to the idea that there were "no monolithic solutions to the problems we face" and that there was a pressing need for a "deeper . . . understanding of the origins of the . . . crisis," and yet each felt compelled to oversimplify those origins and identify a central, most significant cause.[15]

This compulsion to essentialize the crisis can be traced in some detail in the works of both men. In the *Population Bomb* Ehrlich attributed America's "overcrowded highways, burgeoning slums, deteriorating school systems, rising crime rates, riots, and other related problems" to unchecked population increases. "The causal chain of the deterioration is easily followed to its source," he wrote. "Too many cars, too many factories, too much detergent, too much pesticides . . . too little water, too much carbon dioxide—all can be traced easily to TOO MANY PEOPLE."[16]

Continuing down this narrow analytical road, Ehrlich then reduced population growth to the basic biological "urge to reproduce." This urge had been greatly compounded during the evolutionary process, according to Ehrlich. Because of the competitive need to develop a large brain, human babies became increasingly "helpless for a long period while their brains grew after birth." In order to "defend and care for her infant during its unusually long period of helplessness," the mother had to derive a means to entice "Papa [to] h[a]ng around." Although "the girls are still working on that problem, . . . an essential step," Ehrlich argued, "was to get rid of the short, well-defined breeding season characteristic of most mammals." For Ehrlich nothing less than "the year-round sexuality of the human female" explained the nation's environmental and social crises.[17]

Having reduced all of the world's problems to a single, essential cause, Ehrlich did not falter in his advocacy of an appropriate solution. "A general answer to the question, 'What needs to be done?' is simple. We must rapidly bring the world population under control, reducing the growth rate to zero or making it go negative." In order to develop and promote policies that would achieve this drastic curb on population growth, Ehrlich recommended the establishment of a federal department of population and the environment (DPE). Among other things, this new agency would "encourage more research on human sex determination, for if a simple method should be found to guarantee that first-born children were males, then population control problems . . . would be somewhat eased." The DPE would also be charged with promoting sex for pleasure rather than reproduction.[18]

On the foreign policy front, the United States had to reverse its policies and withhold food aid from countries like India despite the opposition of "those in our government whose jobs depend on the willy-nilly spreading of American largess abroad, or by the assorted do-gooders who are deeply involved in the apparatus of international food charity." Those "underdeveloped" countries that were worth saving would be forced to adopt population control and resource development plans designed by the United States and, in order to get the required cooperation of Third World populations, Madison Avenue would be commissioned to propagandize them with television programs supportive of America's population control efforts.[19]

Ehrlich apologized for being unable to offer "sugarcoated solutions." Comparing population growth to the "uncontrolled multiplication of cells," he urged that America shift its "efforts from treatment of the symptoms to the cutting out of the cancer." Though the operation would "demand many brutal and heartless decisions," "radical surgery" was the environment's only "chance for survival."[20]

On the other side of this debate, Barry Commoner in his book *The Closing Circle* led his reader down a reductionist road no less narrow, though perhaps somewhat less convoluted, than the one Ehrlich had traveled in *The Population Bomb*. After lamenting that the American people had unfortunately "become accustomed to think of separate, singular events, each dependent upon a unique, singular cause," Commoner immediately proceeded to dichotomize the suspected causes of the environmental crisis. Was the root cause of the crisis population growth or the "greedy accumulation of wealth" or the "machines which we have built," he asked. Then, for the next three hundred pages, he developed a sustained argument that the nation's environmental problems were directly attributable to "the introduction of synthetic substitutes for natural products" since World War II. Having identified the cause of the crisis as technology run amok, Commoner was optimistic that an adequate solution would soon be formulated and the crisis "resolved."[21]

The Commoner-Ehrlich debate over the root cause occurred in the early 1970s, at what has often been called the beginning of the American environmental movement. In actuality, as a social movement in the United States, environmentalism began in the 1950s, escalated throughout the 1960s, and culminated in the period 1969–73, when environmental concerns were institutionalized in federal and state bureaucracies. From 1969, with the passage of the National Environmental Policy Act, to 1973, with the enactment of the Endangered Species Act, a legal apparatus for dealing with environmental issues was constructed.

This environmental legal structure has provided environmentalists with a seat at many of the nation's decision-making tables. From this seat, they have been able to influence policy and development decisions and at times reduce the rate of environmental destruction. This seat has not, however, given them a forum for challenging basic values or the distribution of social power in American life. In other words, the table itself has not changed dramatically with the presence of an additional seat. Embedded in that table are basic assumptions concerning the origins and nature of the country's environmental problems. Among those assumptions are the following precepts: environmental protection can come only at great economic cost to the American people; a balance can be struck between costs and benefits; environmental problems can and should be solved as they arise on a case-by-case basis; the American way of life, based as it is on the capitalist profit motive, a culture of consumption, and economic growth and development, can be reformed so as to become environmentally sound.

No sooner had this moderate, reform brand of environmentalism become institutionalized than more radical environmentalists, who believed that the American way of life and/or basic American values and attitudes were major contributing factors to the environmental crisis, began to criticize the advocates of reform for dealing with surface symptoms rather than with root causes. Since the early 1970s a number of radical environmental perspectives have taken shape, and each has taken the moderate, reform agenda to task for failing to address the crisis at its roots. For example, in 1973 Arne Naess, a leading philosopher of the deep ecology movement, described the reformist position as "shallow," anthropocentric, and inadequate to the task of preserving the natural world.[22]

Not surprisingly, the advocates of the various radical perspectives have disagreed among themselves as well. They have most frequently criticized one another for misidentifying or overemphasizing a particular root cause at the expense of a more significant, and hence essential, cause of the crisis. Social ecologists have attacked deep ecologists for failing to analyze the social roots of the crisis. In turn, ecofeminists and environmental justice advocates have criticized both social and deep ecologists for not recognizing that environmental problems are essentially sexist and racist in origin. Debates over the root cause have become a deeply entrenched phenomenon in radical environmental discourse. Significantly, the dynamics of these conflicts have remained remarkably similar since the days of the Commoner-Ehrlich debate. One recent example will illustrate this point.

Like Barry Commoner, Murray Bookchin has a long history of involvement in the American environmental movement. During the 1950s he wrote repeatedly about the problem of chemicals in foods, and his 1962 book, *Our Synthetic Environment*, went far beyond Rachel Carson's *Silent Spring* in describing the scope of America's environmental problems and analyzing their social and economic origins. In that work, Bookchin called for revolutionary changes in American society as a necessary prerequisite for effectively dealing with environmental problems that were, he believed, rooted in America's social structure.[23]

Not surprisingly, since the 1970s Bookchin has been a persistent critic of mainstream, reform environmentalism. Much of his criticism has centered on its failure to address what he considers the root cause of the crisis. According to him, "liberal" environmentalism "is based more on tinkering with existing institutions, social relations, technologies, and values than on changing them." "Environmentalists," he has written, "are simply trying to make a rotten society work by dressing it in green leaves and colorful flowers, while ignoring the deep-seated roots of our ecological problems." Since its institutionalization, environmentalism has been reduced from a movement "that at least held the promise of challenging hierarchy and domination" into a type of engineering that reflects a "technical sensibility in which nature is viewed merely as a passive habitat . . . that must be made more 'serviceable' for human use, irrespective of what these uses may be." In a nutshell, according to Bookchin, environmentalism has been hijacked into "providing more palatable techniques for perpetuating . . . [the] irremediable diseases" of America's essentially "anti-ecological society."[24]

In addition to damning mainstream environmentalism for allowing itself to be co-opted by "the very system whose structure and methods it professes to oppose," Bookchin has become one of the most outspoken critics of his fellow radicals for their misinterpretations of the origin of the environmental crisis.[25] In 1987 he inaugurated a heated debate over root causes with members of the deep ecology movement that has yet to subside fully.

Bookchin began his assault on deep ecology at a national meeting of radical environmentalists held in Amherst, Massachusetts. "It is time to face the fact," he announced, "that there are differences within the so-called ecology movement of the present time that are as serious as those . . . of the early seventies." The greatest of these differences is between a "vague, formless, often self-contradictory ideology called 'deep ecology' and a socially oriented body of ideas best termed 'social ecology.' " According to Bookchin, deep ecology has "parachuted into our midst . . . from the Sunbelt's bizarre mix of Hollywood and Disneyland, spiced with homilies from Taoism, Buddhism, spiritualism, reborn Christianity, and, in some cases, eco-fascism." Rather than being a coherent new philosophy that can provide humanity with a much needed "ecological consciousness," as its adherents claim, it is an "ideological toxic dump" that attracts "barely disguised racists, survivalists, macho Daniel Boones, and outright social reactionaries."[26]

The central problem with deep ecology, from Bookchin's perspective, is that it has "no real sense that our ecological problems have their roots in society and in social problems." Deep ecologists as a group are uninterested in "the emergence of hierarchy out of society, of classes out of hierarchy, of the state out of classes—in short, the highly graded social as well as ideological developments which are at the roots of the ecological crisis." Instead, they offer only a slightly veiled Malthusianism that identifies "a vague species called 'humanity' " as the source of that crisis. In reducing "humanity to a parasitic swarm of mosquitoes in a mystified swamp called 'Nature,' " deep ecology is at its core deeply misanthropic. This misanthropy in turn fosters a "crude eco-brutalism" that celebrates famine and disease as nature's way of defending itself against unchecked population growth. This tendency towards ecofascism, while most pronounced in the writings of Dave Foreman, an Earth First! founder, is also present in the central text of the movement, Bill Devall and William Sessions' *Deep Ecology.*[27]

Other leftist social theorists joined Bookchin in his criticisms of deep ecology. George Bradford, the editor of the "radical, antiauthoritarian" journal *Fifth Estate*, also finds deep ecology disturbingly silent about the social dynamics of environmental problems. In seeing "the pathological operationalism of industrial civilization as a species-generated problem rather than one generated by social phenomena that must be studied in their own right," deep ecologists have failed to develop a " 'deep' critique of the state, empire, technology, or capital" and have reduced "the complex web of human relations to a simplistic, abstract, scientistic caricature." Such "ecological reductionism," according to Bradford, "is far from subversive," because it neglects the "interrelatedness of the global corporate-capitalist system and empire on the one hand, and environmental catastrophe on the other." In relying on the maxim that the ecological crisis is the result of "too many people," deep ecologists are advancing the same Malthusian argument that corporate capitalists have been promoting for centuries.[28]

These provocative criticisms took deep ecologists by surprise. Bookchin, after all, has been identified and cited extensively in Devall and Sessions' work as one of the leading prophets of the biocentric vision that is central to the movement's philosophy. As the journalist Kirkpatrick Sale, a vocal defender of deep ecology, expresses it, before the attack he had assumed "that there was really only one great big ecology movement and that [he and Bookchin] shared an essentially similar position on the environmental destruction of the earth." Sale finds Bookchin's criticisms of deep ecology "not only sad but bewildering," and he defends the deep ecology tendency to consider humans collectively as a species. He believes that perspective has been useful in highlighting "the large consequences of a triumphant, exploitative species enjoying a population boom and technological prowess" and that "from this larger perspective, it does not really matter what the petty political and social arrangements are that led to our ecological crisis." He can only conclude that Bookchin, motivated by a cranky desire to impose "some imagined dominant theoretical purity" on the diverse ecology movement, sees deep ecology as a threat to his own brand of "ecological truth" that "ecological exploitation stems from social exploitation."[29]

The deep ecologist Warwick Fox has presented a more developed response to Bookchin and Bradford. Above all, Fox faults social ecologists for oversimplifying "the multitude of interacting factors at work in any given situation." In particular, he criticizes Bookchin's insistence "that there is a straightforward, necessary relationship between the internal organization of human societies and their treatment of the nonhuman world." The danger of such "facile" thinking is that it implies "the solution to our ecological problems is close at hand—all we have to do is remove 'the real root' of the problem." In addition to being simplistic and facile, Fox finds the social ecology perspective "morally objectionable on two grounds, scapegoating and inauthenticity." It scapegoats complete classes of individuals; at the same time it excuses "oppressed" groups for their participation in ecological destruction.[30]

Like the Commoner-Ehrlich exchange, the debate between social and deep ecologists has been in essence a disagreement over the root cause of the environmental crisis. While on the surface the two camps seem to agree that the crisis is rooted in human attitudes that see nature as subordinate to man, just beneath this shallow consensus lurks an irreconcilable difference of opinion. From the social ecology standpoint, elites use their ability to control and exploit the natural world as a means of dominating other human beings. Therefore, in order to resolve the ecological crisis, systems of social relations based upon dominance and hierarchy must be destroyed and replaced with social systems rooted in egalitarian and democratic values. For deep ecologists, on the other hand, the real problem lies in a culturally determined anthropocentrism that prevents human beings from recognizing that other forms of life have intrinsic worth and a right to exist for their own sakes. They emphasize the need for individuals to "work" on themselves in order to cultivate an "ecological consciousness."[31]

Like Commoner and Ehrlich, social and deep ecologists have criticized one another for advancing analyses that oversimplify the complex origins of the ecological crisis. According to both parties, these simplistic interpretations sidestep the more difficult and socially disruptive issues that they themselves have identified as being most crucial. As in the earlier debate, in this one the opponents have failed to recognize that their criticisms are applicable to their own analyses as well. This lack of self-reflexivity is indeed amazing at times. For example, Fox chides Bookchin for proposing a simple solution to the ecological crisis, but he fails to comment on Devall and Sessions' claim that "a way out of our present predicament may be simpler than many people realize."[32] Bookchin, in turn, attacks deep ecology for positing a false dichotomy between ecocentrism and anthropocentrism while refusing to address Fox's claim that Bookchin himself has drawn just such a dichotomy between capitalist exploiters of the environment and the mass of people, whom he depicts as powerless victims of that exploitation.[33]

What is perhaps most startling about the charges and countercharges of oversimplification in these debates is the degree to which they are unfounded. Halting population growth, democratizing the technological decision-making process, restructuring society along nonhierarchical lines, and altering people's basic world views are not, by any means, simple solutions to the many deeply complex ecological problems that confront us. Each of these agendas taken alone would require nothing short of revolutionary changes in the ways Americans think, act, and relate to one another and the environment. Taken together, they represent the enormity of the challenges that we must meet as a species if we are to respond more effectively to what many environmentalists agree is a "continuing ecological crisis."[34]

Because of the complexity and seeming intransigence of environmental problems, it is clearly time for radical environmentalists to focus less on defining their differences and more on determining the common ground that might provide the basis for a more coherent and unified ecology movement. As I hope this essay illustrates, if they hope to achieve a working consensus, radicals must strive to resist the well-established tendency in environmental discourse to identify the single most important and fundamental cause of the many environmental problems that have become increasingly apparent in recent decades.

The desire to essentialize environmental problems and trace them all to one root cause is obviously a powerful one. If a root cause can be identified, then priorities can be clearly established and a definite agenda determined. Although the intention behind this silver bullet approach to understanding the global environmental crisis has been to provide the environmental movement with a clear focus and agenda, its impact has been very nearly just the opposite. It has repeatedly proven to be more divisive than productive in galvanizing a united front against environmental destruction.

This is not surprising. It would indeed be convenient if all ecological problems sprang from the same source, but this is far from likely. If nothing else, during the last forty years it has become abundantly clear that environmental problems are deeply complex. Not only have they proven extremely difficult to unravel scientifically, but they have social and political aspects that further compound their complexity. Global warming, species extinction, pollution, human population growth, depletion of resources, and increased rates of life-threatening disease are just some of the many problems that confront us. The idea that there is a single root cause to any one of these problems, let alone to all of them taken together, is, to put it mildly, absurd. Because environmental problems are each the result of a multiplicity of causal factors, there can be no one comprehensive solution to all of them.

And yet radical environmental thinkers are correct in rejecting the piecemeal approach to environmental problems that has become institutionalized in American society. Thus far, reform environmentalism has proven itself inadequate to the task of halting the deterioration of the earth's ecological systems. But an alternative to that approach will not emerge until radicals reject the quixotic and divisive search for a root cause to the spectrum of environmental problems that have been subsumed under the umbrella of the ecological crisis. Instead of arguing with one another about who is most right, radicals must begin to consider the insights each perspective has generated and work toward a more comprehensive rather than a confrontational understanding of problems that have multiple, complex, and interconnected causes.

One of the purposes of this paper is to endorse and encourage a movement toward synthesis that has already begun to emerge in radical environmental discourse. In late 1989 Murray Bookchin and Dave Foreman, whose misanthropic views had come under heavy criticism from Bookchin, sat down and discussed their differences in a public debate. The upshot of this meeting was a truce, with both participants admitting that they had things to learn from the other. Foreman was most conciliatory and expressed regret for a number of the more volatile statements he had made during his career as an eco-activist. A year after his meeting with Bookchin, Foreman described a new agenda for the ecology movement. "On my best days," he wrote, "I seek a creative synthesis of all of these [radical] approaches into an integrated and coherent perspective which can guide our movement even as radical ecology activists continue to specialize in their particular areas of interest."[35]

A number of environmental thinkers have started the hard work of envisioning what such an "integrated and coherent perspective" might look like. The social ecologists Joel Kovel and George Bradford, although still critical of deep ecology, have sought to reconcile that philosophy's concern with humanity's "estrangement from nature" with their own focus on dominance and hierarchy in human societies.[36] Carolyn Merchant has suggested that the various radical perspectives, despite their differences in emphasis, are all concerned with understanding and ameliorating the basic conflicts and contradictions between production and reproduction in modern industrial societies.[37]

I would suggest that a possible approach to synthesis is to go to the heart of the disagreements that have divided environmentalists in recent years. Conflict, after all, is the crucible of synthesis, and the very disagreements that have split the radical ecology movement into factions have the potential of generating its greatest strength in the future. There is no question that radical environmentalists have dug deeper than reformers in their quest to understand the social and cultural complexities of environmental problems. The challenge for radical environmental thinkers is to continue this exploration, not with the intention of determining some essential root cause but with the goal of providing a fuller assessment of the related, complex, and multiple origins of the diverse environmental problems that we face. The challenge is to provide ecological activists like Dave Foreman with a much sought-after "integrated and coherent perspective."

Whose Nature?
The Contested Moral
Terrain of Ancient Forests*

James D. Proctor

Introduction

THE LANE COUNTY CONVENTION CENTER IN EUGENE, OREGON, WAS PACKED
with people one hot summer day in 1989. They were attending a hearing on
whether that most prominent inhabitant of old-growth Pacific Northwest
forests, the northern spotted owl, should be listed as a threatened species
under the Endangered Species Act. The typical lineup of local officials, federal agency spokespersons, and representatives of environmental and timber
industry interest groups was on hand to voice their official positions. But
the majority of the crowd consisted of ordinary citizens whose passionate
beliefs on the issue led them to take time out from their busy schedules this
Monday afternoon to attend.

Many people came that day to stand at the podium and voice their strong
support for the proposed owl listing and protection of its old-growth habitat. Some felt that the issue was more than simply one of whether or not
people should save the northern spotted owl:

> My name is Barbara Kelley, director of Save Our Ecosystems. These hearings
> are not really about owls, nor are they about loggers. These hearings are about

*This essay is the result of conversations I have had over the past ten years with close
friends, scholars, and others from the Pacific Northwest, and most recently with my
fellow members of the Reinventing Nature group. In particular, I would like to thank
Bill Cronon, Giovanna Di Chiro, Jeff Ellis, Carolyn Merchant, Jenny Price, and Richard
White for commenting on an earlier draft. The Department of Geography at UC-Santa
Barbara granted me a mild reprieve from teaching to pursue this project, David Lawson
provided graphics support, and Chris Bacon served as my library research assistant.

269

whether the timber industry shall be allowed to continue consuming our Northwest forests until there is nothing left of them but rows of even-aged monocultural tree farms susceptible to fire and disease, unsuitable for owls or cougars or fruits and nuts or streams or people. . . . Do our congresspeople and foresters know that the nonhuman life that evolved in these forests for millions of years is going extinct for loss of habitat? Have they seen this list of 700 endangered and threatened species, which I'll give to you? This is what we are doing by the clearcutting.[1]

Others enlarged the spatial scope of their concerns, arguing that the spotted owl issue was just the tip of an iceberg, one of many instances of our global environmental crisis:

I'm Jean Marie Aurnague. I'm an educator in Lane county. Dear Mr. Chairman, due to extreme and rapid destruction of 90 percent of the ancient forest which once covered the Northwest and of other forests of the world, we are experiencing, for example, diminishing species, like the spotted owl, a global warming trend, and holes in the earth's ozone layer. . . . Where does this madness stop? I keep writing letters and involving myself in these crisis issues, hoping that somewhere I will find an ethical response, one not biased by the economic basis which goes into the crisis to begin with. I ask you to list the owl, and I close with the hope that you will.

Though most of those in favor of spotted owl protection cited facts and figures to support their position, others spoke more directly of the moral obligation people have to save the owl:

I'm F. J. Petock and I'm representing myself, and I want to speak to the preservation of the spotted owl and to its establishment on the threatened species list, because I don't feel that any one species has the right to condemn any other species to extinction.

Not everyone in the room, however, supported the proposed spotted owl listing and its management implications for Pacific Northwest forests. A good number of people in attendance had a very different sense of right and wrong for the spotted owl. Some of these people worked for the timber industry and offered their perspective on its environmental responsibility:

I am Jim Standard. I am from Medford, Oregon. In case you haven't noticed, I do work for the timber industry. I was born and raised in Oregon from pioneer stock. For generations my family has been involved in the timber industry in one aspect or another. We have always depended on timber for our livelihood, and because of this dependence, we have probably gained a respect for the forest and the land that few people will ever know. . . . As long as I can remember, loggers have been accused of ruining wildlife habitat. From past experience, I would disagree. Unless a person has actually sat quietly at a logging site and watched and listened, they cannot appreciate the amount of wildlife that is around. After the machinery has been shut down for the day and even before the dust has settled, wildlife starts reappearing. Ask any logger who daily shares his lunch with a raccoon, a chipmunk, a raven, or even a doe and her fawn if he is destroying habitat or enhancing it. The timber industry has done more to perpetuate our natural resources than any other group I can think of. I find it hard to believe anyone would ever support throwing all of this away for the sake of saving a small bird who is not even in trouble and doesn't give a damn how big the tree he is living in or how old it is. I would urge you to do your best to protect the people that are doing their best to protect the forest.

Others spoke to the larger economic implications of listing the spotted owl, cautioning that not enough is known of its current status to warrant such drastic impacts on timber-dependent communities:

> My name is Susan Morgan. I'm here today on behalf of WOOD, Workers of Oregon Development. We're a group of Douglas county families that make our living from the timber industry. . . . WOOD urges the Department of Fish and Wildlife not to list the spotted owl as a threatened species. Not enough research has been done on the owl or its habitat needs. . . . Don't destroy the fabric of the 100 families of WOOD and the thousands of families just like mine throughout the Northwest based on this incomplete and inadequate research. As the search continues, more and more owls are being found. Many of these are in second growth timber. WOOD urges continued research on the needs of the owl. Let's establish what habitat characteristics are necessary to maintain a stable population of owls. Let's duplicate these conditions in our modern managed forests.

The Eugene spotted owl hearing was part of a larger debate that has shaken the Pacific Northwest for the last decade—and there is little hope of resolution in sight. The focus of this debate has been on how we should manage what is perhaps the most significant feature of the region's landscape: its towering coniferous forests, many of which lie on public lands. At the center of the forest controversy has been the fate of the remaining old-growth stands, which by anyone's measure are among the most spectacular terrestrial ecosystems on Earth.[2]

In the months surrounding the Eugene hearing, major environmental organizations were mounting nationwide campaigns to secure public support for protection of old-growth—what they often called ancient—forests. On the next page is a portion of a pamphlet entitled "Stop the Chainsaw Massacre," produced in early 1990 by the Eugene-based Native Forest Council. It graphically displays the current extent of "virgin forests" in the contiguous United States as being but a shadow of their presettlement expanse. And the massacre continues in the Pacific Northwest, according to the pamphlet, which claims that the equivalent of a 20,000-mile-long line of

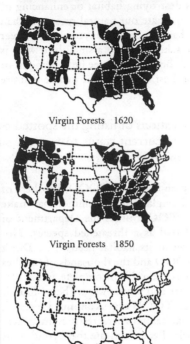

THE INDICTMENT:

A merica's forests are priceless.
They give us cold, clear water to drink. They regulate global and regional climates. They provide habitat for wildlife. And perhaps most important, in their beauty and tranquility we find spiritual enrichment and renewal.

Yet in the time it takes to read this brochure, several acres of irreplaceable virgin forest will be clearcut. And there isn't much left, as shown at the left. Called ancient, native, virgin, primeval, or old growth, these are the original, untouched forests that existed when the first settlers arrived in North America. **And only five per cent is left.**

The national forests are on public lands. Every American is entrusted with the responsibility of preserving these forests for all time. However, under administrations committed to the commercial exploitation of all public natural resources, and with land management agencies headed by pro-timber industry appointees, the US Forest Service and the Bureau of Land Management have become major suppliers to the timber industry. The rate of destruction is difficult to imagine, but picture a line of log trucks 20,000 miles long. That's how much timber is taken out of our Northwest forests each year.

To make matters worse, our national forests are being liquidated at an enormous loss to taxpayers. **This practice must stop!**

Virgin Forests   1620

Virgin Forests   1850

Virgin Forests   1989

The amount of timber taken from Northwest forests each year is equal to a line of log trucks 20,000 miles long!

"Stop the Chainsaw Massacre: The Indictment." *(Courtesy Native Forest Council, 1990)*

log trucks takes timber out of the region annually under the clear support of the federal government.

Yet here again, different stories of the forest, different senses of right and wrong, emerged. On the opposite page are portions of a tract produced in the latter 1980s by the protimber industry Oregon Project. The tract endorses the principle of "wise use," which, it claims, can provide for the nation's timber demand and the region's economic needs without compromising the needs of future generations or threatened species. It encourages those who "support forest conservation" to fly a yellow ribbon as a symbol of their support—and in fact, thousands of yellow ribbons flew from the fences and car antennas of sympathetic Pacific northwesterners in the latter 1980s and early 1990s.

It would be a mistake to dismiss the Oregon Project pamphlet as simply timber industry propaganda; to do so would be to silence the voices of Jim Standard, Susan Morgan, and the many others of the region who share their view.[3] The position these people take highlights a crucial fact: there is more than one ethic, more than one sense of right and wrong, more than one way to care about the fate of Pacific Northwest forests. How, then, can we be sure that the environmentalists hold the moral high ground in their ancient forest campaign? It could be that there exists an infinite possible number of environmentalisms, each with its own nature to save. If so, how are we to choose among them?

In the following essay I will explore the ethics and related ideas of nature informing the ancient forest campaign, and consider whether and how the environmentalist agenda should change in light of the diversity of perspectives on right and wrong suggested in the spotted owl and old-growth debate. By focusing much of my critical attention on the ancient forest campaign, however, I by no means wish to imply that its opponents are beyond reproach. There is, for instance, a continuing need to scrutinize the wise-use movement, which has proven to be a powerful ally of the timber industry in

THE YELLOW RIBBON

At the turn of the century Gifford Pinchot, the father of American forestry defined "forest conservation" as the wise use of our forests. He encouraged the formation of the national forest system to "furnish a continuous supply of timber for the use and necessities of the United States."

Today, those who support forest conservation use the yellow ribbon as a symbol of the wise use of forest resources.

DID YOU KNOW...

•Currently 53% of the federal lands in Washington and Oregon are set aside for purposes other than timber harvesting.

•102,000,000 seedlings (37 for every man, woman and child in Oregon) were planted in the 1988-89 planting year.

•Every American uses the equivalent of a 100 ft. tree each year.

•In 1988, local schools and counties received $325 million from Oregon & Washington public timber sales.

•Threatened species populations, such as the bald eagle and the peregrine falcon are increasing thanks to forest management practices.

FLY A YELLOW RIBBON

That's what the yellow ribbon is all about. It has come to symbolize the pride we feel in the timber industry, from seedlings to finished products.

We take pride in the wise use of our timber land. We want to pass on to our children, and their children, productive forests and a clean, vital environment.

Please join with us to support forest conservation. Fly the yellow ribbon as a symbol of the wise use of forest resources.

THE OREGON PROJECT

"The Yellow Ribbon." *(Courtesy Oregon Project, late 1980s)*

the Pacific Northwest.[4] The main reason for my focus is that the ancient forest campaign has been a paramount item on the recent agenda of most major American environmental organizations: a careful look at its ethical foundations should tell us much about the moral scope and limitations of the larger environmentalist project.

A second caveat bears mention at this point: neither the supporters of ancient forest protection nor their detractors are as unified as this essay may seem to imply. The ancient forest campaign's ranks range from Republican Sierra Clubbers to radical Earth Firsters, many of whom have predictably disagreed at frequent intervals over how much they should compromise their demands in order to achieve some degree of ancient forest protection. Likewise, its opponents include people of many persuasions. Even among those directly involved in the timber industry, there are many divergent interests; consider, for instance, the tension inherent between millworkers and timber industry executives, or between small timber companies dependent on trees from federal lands and multinational timber companies like Weyerhaeuser with vast tracts of their own private stocks. Yet it would be equally foolish to assert that there is no coherence at all in the ethics suggested by the environmentalist and pro-timber positions on old-growth forest protection. In many ways the polarization between these two sides brings some key moral issues into focus.

I am painfully aware of the perils inherent in this journey—and perhaps this is why so few people write on the ethics of the Pacific Northwest forest issue, in contrast to the reams of literature that have emerged on its ecological, economic, and other dimensions.[5] Among the most difficult hazards to avoid, as Bernard Williams suggests in his introduction to the field of ethics, is that one's own perceptual limitations and inadequacies are probably revealed more than in any other kind of work.[6] In light of this danger, it is worth mentioning at the outset why I care about the Pacific Northwest forest issue at all—which may also shed some light on my own "perceptual limitations and inadequacies." The answer is simple: the Pacific Northwest is my birthplace, and in many ways I still call it my home. I grew up in a small timber community in rural Oregon, working its lumber mills and hiking its forest trails in the summertime. Throughout this period, I was profoundly uncomfortable with the moral dogmatism implied by both sides battling over the fate of these forests—though I was more sympathetic to the environmental position than that of the timber industry.

Since then I have left rural Oregon, aside for occasional visits, and have discovered a very different moral condition in contemporary society, one with which I am equally uncomfortable. I call it moral aphasia: an unwillingness or inability to speak of right and wrong in light of all the complexities surrounding moral issues. This essay represents part of my ongoing struggle to develop some alternative to moral dogmatism on the one hand and moral aphasia on the other as a contribution toward resolving the bitter struggles over nature that we witness in the Pacific Northwest and elsewhere. Any alternative to these positions must, I believe, embrace the paradox that ethics are inextricably framed within (often differing) human ideas, and yet speak of a reality beyond human ideas. Both sides of this paradox ultimately point to the rootedness of ethics, and especially environmental ethics, in what geographers call place. In his book *The Betweenness of Place*, the geographer Nicholas Entrikin describes such a perspective:

> To understand place requires that we have access to both an objective and a subjective reality. From the decentered vantage point of the theoretical scientist, place becomes either location or a set of generic relations and thereby loses much of its significance for human action. From the centered viewpoint of the subject, place has meaning only in relation to an individual's or a group's goals and concerns. Place is best viewed from points in between.[7]

Entrikin's statement offers a guide for our journey, one reminding us to take seriously the objective and subjective features of the ancient forest campaign and its underlying ethic, yet to steer a path between these poles. To this task I now turn.

The Transformation of Pacific Northwest Forests

SOME OF THE MOST SPECTACULAR CONIFEROUS FORESTS ON EARTH ARE found in the westside Pacific Northwest—that tall, thin region stretching northward from northern California into Canada and situated between the Pacific Ocean and the Cascade mountain range. The Douglas fir is the most extensive and commercially important species, but others, including the Sitka spruce, western red cedar, western hemlock, incense cedar, and sugar pine, occur as well. One major reason coniferous forests exist here involves the region's climate. Its proximity to the Pacific Ocean yields ample precipitation and relatively mild temperatures, in which conifers (versus broadleafs, which usually shed their leaves in the winter) can grow year-round. In addition, conifers can survive well through the dry summers of the region.

The region's climate has changed over time, and so have Pacific Northwest forests.[8] But change occurs on a much shorter time span as well in Pacific Northwest forests, in large part as a result of a major natural process fostered by the summer drought regime: fire. Wildfires not only provide ideal conditions for Douglas firs to predominate (since they can take advantage of fire-created conditions, such as bare mineral soils and ample sunlight, for their seedlings to germinate and grow). More significantly, wildfires and other natural disturbances, such as windstorms and disease, are responsible for the dynamic process of succession evident throughout the region's forests.[9] Succession refers to patterned changes in forest vegetation and structure with time. In the Pacific Northwest, forest succession may begin with the proliferation of grasses and forbs following a catastrophic fire, and move eventually to a multistoried forest with conifers as the tallest trees and various broadleaf species located beneath the conifer canopy. After a long time—perhaps several hundred years—the forest develops significant old-growth characteristics, with large-scale disturbances such as wildfires, and small-scale disturbances such as disease, opening up variously sized patches to successional changes. Estimates of the presettlement acreage of old-growth forests in the Pacific Northwest range from 60 to 90 percent of total forest coverage, or between roughly 15 and 24 million acres.[10]

Scientists have only recently begun to understand the ecology and habitat characteristics of old-growth forests.[11] This research has revealed that what is special ecologically about old-growth forests is not primarily their age but their structural complexity; age simply gives old-growth forests enough time to develop this complexity. Although live, large-diameter trees dominate much of the old-growth forest canopy, standing dead trees or snags and fallen rotting trees on the forest floor and adjacent streambeds are equally significant, especially in terms of their habitat role. The northern spotted owl, for instance, uses snags as nests, and much of its primary prey consists of small mammals that find food and shelter among decomposing trees on the forest floor.

The dynamic landscape of younger and older successional-stage forests in the Pacific Northwest was shaped to some extent by the land-use practices of Native Americans long before Europeans arrived; for example, their common practice of burning grasslands often prevented incursion of the forest into river valley floors. Yet the rate and extent of transformation following European settlement is unmatched in the cultural history of these forests.[12] Timber production in the Pacific Northwest dates back to the late 1700s, but began in earnest in the mid-nineteenth century, when the region served as a resource hinterland for San Francisco and other growth centers in California to the south. Early logging was restricted to sites such as Puget Sound and Grays Harbor, with prime timber located close to navigable bays. These were the first forests to fall as the timber industry spread in the later nineteenth and early twentieth century, moving farther inland and uphill as the prime timberlands near waterways—once magnificent forests, as early eyewitness accounts suggest—were quickly exhausted. Improved harvesting and transportation techniques, including crosscut saws, steam donkeys (developed to yard logs to loading sites), and mountain railroads, played a key role in the increased rate and spatial extent of logging in the Pacific Northwest during this period. (Later in this century, chain saws, high-lead logging, and log trucks performed the same tasks with markedly greater efficiency.) Technological change increased production in mills as well, with early-twentieth-century innovations such as wood chip–based paper and plywood.

The timber industry of the Pacific Northwest boomed following World War II; it was now able to extract and process lumber with frightening efficiency, and the demand for wood products on the U.S. West Coast exploded as housing was built for those flocking into southern California. Although timber harvests remained fairly constant in the 1950s and 1960s in the Pacific Northwest, public lands supplied more and more timber as private reserves—those first exploited—were largely exhausted during this period. With harvest levels reaching all-time highs in the 1960s and 1970s, the potential effects on future timber supply—now on federal as well as private lands—became increasingly clear.[13] Nonetheless, following the recession-based downturn in timber production in the early 1980s, federal timber harvests for the period 1985–89 neared historic highs—a clearly unsustainable level referred to in a recent Forest Service assessment as a "one-time drawdown."[14]

This one and one-half century-long phenomenon of timber extraction has profoundly transformed the landscape of the westside Pacific Northwest into one dominated by young and mid-successional-stage forests. Old-growth forests have been logged for clear reasons: these forests provide abundant and valuable wood (one 1981 article cites 100 acres of old-growth forests having $1.6 million merchantable timber),[15] and young stands grow wood fiber much faster than older stands. Additionally, disease, death, and decay in old-growth stands render much of its timber useless from a lumber standpoint. Timber industry assessments often speak matter-of-factly of the need to convert unproductive and unmanaged tracts of old-growth forest to younger forests that produce wood fiber much more efficiently. These managed forests are generally logged within forty to eighty years, much sooner than is required to achieve old-growth characteristics.[16]

How much old-growth is left? The answer to this heated question depends on how restrictively one defines old-growth forests. The timber industry has claimed that public lands have as much as 7.5 million acres—perhaps half the original extent. Environmentalists, however, have used detailed studies to claim that as little as 2 million acres remain (perhaps less than 10 percent of their extent prior to European settlement).[17] One major recent assessment includes mature forests (those in which the net rate of growth has peaked and which are starting to exhibit old-growth habitat characteristics) along with old-growth under the category of "late-successional forests." Following this approach, one finds approximately 8.5 million acres of medium- and large-conifer late-successional forest on federal lands in the range of the northern spotted owl in Oregon, Washington, and northern California.[18] No matter which definition is used, however, it is indisputable that logging has been the primary factor responsible for loss of old-growth forests.

One major implication of the diminished extent of old-growth forests is that habitat for associated wildlife is far less than it was before their transformation by Europeans. This includes far more than the northern spotted owl: a total of 667 species, including 555 terrestrial plant and animal species—mycorrhizal fungi and subalpine fir, huckleberries and lady-slippers, pebble snails and salamanders, wood rats and woodpeckers—and 112 fish stocks or species, are closely associated with old-growth coniferous forests of the Pacific Northwest.[19] However, forest biologists know relatively little about how the vast majority of these species have been affected by the loss of habitat.

The Ancient Forest Campaign

THOUGH THE ANCIENT FOREST CAMPAIGN DATES BACK LITTLE MORE THAN half of a decade, its efforts are not new to the region. In many ways they are an outgrowth of nearly a century of dispute in the Pacific Northwest over preservation of the region's forest landscape in the form of national parks—such as Olympic National Park, dedicated in 1938, after years of controversy—and wilderness, beginning with the Wilderness Act of 1964 and including later additions in the 1970s and 1980s. In all, Congress had set aside a total of 3.6 million acres of national parks and wilderness in west-side Oregon and Washington by the mid-1980s—though the bulk of these were relatively high-elevation areas less suitable for timber production.[20]

The ancient forest campaign has been far greater in scope than these earlier efforts, however, focusing on all remaining old-growth on U.S. Forest Service and Bureau of Land Management forests in westside Washington, Oregon, and northern California. According to William Dietrich, the term "ancient forest" was coined in 1988 by executives of the Oregon Natural Resources Council, a regional group that has played a key role in monitoring timber sales and national forest plans. They dispensed with "old growth" as too jargony and "primeval forest" as rather dark and obscure; "ancient forest," in contrast, stressed a long-standing, preexistent nature that fascinated people and compelled them to help protect it.[21] The term stuck and has provided a resonant metaphor for efforts to save old-growth forests of the Pacific Northwest.

Many of the leading environmental organizations in the United States have invested heavily in the ancient forest campaign and have similarly benefited from its success. One notable example is the Wilderness Society, which opened an office in Portland, Oregon, in 1989, in response to the popularity of the cause, and in little more than two years effectively doubled its membership. The Wilderness Society commissioned research and published reports on the ecological limitations of national forest plans, the unsustainable economics of the timber industry, and the current extent of old-growth forests.[22] Nationwide groups have teamed up with smaller, regionally based organizations to form broad-based coalitions such as the Ancient Forest Alliance, which has promoted congressional legislation to protect remaining mature and old-growth coniferous forests in the Pacific Northwest and elsewhere.

The campaign has a dual identity, with powerful moral and political dimensions. Its evangelistic fervor is evident in its outreach to people across the country for financial support; its hard-hitting legal efforts have been remarkably successful in achieving desired ends. One example of the latter is a lawsuit brought against the U.S. Forest Service by the Seattle Audubon Society and other environmental groups in 1989, which eventually resulted in an injunction granted against all timber sales in old-growth spotted owl habitat until the Forest Service could demonstrate that its forest management plans were in compliance with the vertebrate viability requirements of the National Forest Management Act.[23]

In these legal efforts environmentalists have relied heavily on recently expanding scientific knowledge regarding the ecology of old-growth forests and the extent of human impacts. This skillful utilization of science to effect policy change is clear in what was perhaps the pivotal turning point in the ancient forest campaign: the successful petition to protect the northern spotted owl, *Strix occidentalis caurina*, and its old growth habitat. The northern spotted owl resides only in the coniferous forests of the Pacific Northwest. Concern among scientists and laypeople over the fate of the spotted owl in light of reduction of old-growth forest by widespread logging grew during the 1980s, culminating in the decision by the U.S. Fish and Wildlife Service (FWS) effective July 23, 1990, to list it as a threatened species throughout its range under provisions of the Endangered Species Act.[24] The decision was based on scientific evidence suggesting that timber management practices had largely replaced old-growth habitat with a mosaic of young and middle seral-stage forests unsuitable for the spotted owl, and that current regulatory mechanisms for existing owl habitat were not adequate to guarantee its survival.[25]

Following the listing, the FWS designated a total of 6.9 million acres as critical owl habitat to ensure the owl's recovery.[26] Since then, recovery efforts have been coordinated with larger federal proposals for biodiversity conservation on public forests, given the widespread recognition that old-growth forests serve a number of critical ecosystem functions in the region—for instance, they play a key role in maintaining watersheds used by anadromous fish species like salmon. A major recent event in this process was the Clinton administration's timber summit of April 1993, which resulted in a scientific panel commissioned to devise and assess management options—including the administration's preferred Option 9—for old-growth federal forests.[27] In its revised form, Option 9 provides for some 7.4 million acres of late-successional reserves on public forests in the range of the spotted owl, with 2.6 million acres of riparian reserves to protect aquatic habitat and provide some reserve connectivity.

Though ancient forest advocates desired even more old-growth protection than was offered in Option 9, one cannot help concluding that the ancient forest campaign has been an enormous policy success. Only two decades ago biologists and conservationists had extreme difficulty getting federal agencies to set aside 300 acres surrounding known spotted owl nest sites—

approximately 120,000 acres total—to protect the species.[28] Now, in the mid-1990s, proposed federal forest reserves represent a nearly one-hundred-fold increase over that figure. Clearly, environmental protection has become a major priority in management of public forests in the Pacific Northwest.

Ancient Forest Ethics

WHY HAVE ENVIRONMENTALISTS STRUGGLED TO SAVE THE OLD-GROWTH forests of the Pacific Northwest? The answer, at least in part, is that they care deeply about those forests and are grieved at the extent of their transformation by humans. They believe it to be a moral duty for people to protect what little remains; some even argue that it is our duty to restore these forests to their pre-logging status. Perhaps environmental organizations have seized on the ancient forest campaign as an effective strategy to boost their membership and status; but these reasons do not explain why so many thousands of people have joined their ranks to fight the ancient forest battle.

As an example of the embedded moral character of the ancient forest campaign, consider the words of Barbara Kelley we encountered at the outset. Though she offers scientific evidence of "loss of habitat" and of "700 endangered and threatened species," behind those facts are values that result in her concern for endangered species. Without these values, facts alone would not lead to any specific notion of right or wrong, or any particular policy implications. Others are more straightforward in revealing their values: F. J. Petock comes out firmly against the belief that "any one species has the right to condemn any other species to extinction," and Jean Marie Aurnague speaks of her hope for an "ethical response" to the ancient forest crisis. Values are also central to the Native Forest Council pamphlet's justification for protecting ancient forests. Its maps show the depletion of old-growth forests in the United States over the last three and a half centuries. But, as the text suggests, this depletion is meaningful only in the context of the great worth people confer on forests. This is why the pamphlet begins with "America's forests are priceless" and then lists the ways in which people value forests.

Although it is political in implementation, then, the ancient forest campaign stems from environmentalists' values, which point to principles of right and wrong conduct. The link between values and conduct is the realm of ethics. Ethics encompasses ideas and practice, the beliefs people hold concerning ancient forests and their implications for forest management. A focus on ethics in the ancient forest campaign clarifies for us its moral bearing, its sense of why we should treat Pacific Northwest forests in a particular way.

Environmental philosophers have typically classified systems of environmental ethics into several categories, principally on the basis of the type of value conferred upon nature. They often make a distinction between intrinsic and instrumental value.[29]

Intrinsic value in nature implies that its worth is independent of its utility to humans; instrumental value implies that its worth depends on its ability to serve a human end. "Is it good?" is a question of intrinsic value; "What is it good for?" is a question of instrumental value. Forests, for example, could possess intrinsic value as communities of nonhuman life, whether or not this life benefits people; or they could possess instrumental value forests as sources of timber, or as wonderful places to hike, or even because they combat the greenhouse effect or may contain pharmaceutically valuable plant species.

This twofold taxonomy of value leads to a similarly twofold schema of anthropocentric and nonanthropocentric ethics. An anthropocentric ethic is suggested in situations where people value nature instrumentally, as a means to human material, aesthetic, or other ends. Nonanthropocentric ethics, in contrast, are those in which people primarily value nature intrinsically, without reference to human ends (I say "primarily" because instrumental value is also implicitly accorded to nature under most nonanthropocentric ethics).

To be sure, this reduction of all possible environmental ethics into two main categories sounds rather simplistic. Some environmental philosophers have responded by proposing subcategories of these two major types. For instance, anthropocentrism can be expressed as resourcism, in which people value nature as a material resource, or as preservationism, in which nature's worth follows from its inspirational value.[30] Other writers distinguish between narrow forms of anthropocentrism, in which nature's worth is calculated only with reference to a select group of people or a certain human end, and broader forms, in which more people and possible ends count.[31] In all cases, however, the primary reason to save nature is that it benefits people, so all of these ethics can be labeled anthropocentric. Similarly, philosophers have proposed several different forms of nonanthropocentric ethics. Biocentrism, for instance, is an individualistic nonanthropocentric ethic that confers value primarily on species, whereas ecocentrism is a more holistic ethic that confers value primarily upon ecosystems.[32]

Many philosophers have argued that the long-standing anthropocentric basis of human relations with nature must give way to a broader, nonanthropocentric ethic.[33] They contend that there is no way to stretch anthropocentrism far enough to compel people to care about nonhuman life, because in many cases the benefit to humans is negligible. The biologist David Ehrenfeld offers one example of the limits of anthropocentrism in an essay entitled "The Conservation of Non-Resources."[34] The author tells us of the Houston toad, *Bufo houstonensis,* which "has no demonstrated or conjectural resource value to man, other races of toad will replace it, and its passing is not expected to make an impression on the *Umwelt* of the city of

Houston or its suburbs." So why should anyone save a nonresource such as the Houston toad? Clearly, Ehrenfeld suggests, anthropocentrism prioritizes those aspects of nature which can conceivably be valued by someone; others, such as the Houston toad, have little chance of survival, especially if they stand in the way of other human goods. Following this argument, anthropocentrism appears to be far too limited and skewed a moral foundation for people to genuinely care about nature.

To some extent, the ancient forest campaign is a critique of the anthropocentric ethics that have historically defined relations between people and Pacific Northwest forests, and a plea to value forests differently, to adopt a more nonanthropocentric ethic. To environmentalists, ancient forests stand as the last remnant of a natural landscape that over the last century has been radically altered because people valued the forest primarily for its timber wealth. Without assigning some intrinsic worth to the remaining ancient forests, without valuing them as the complex living communities they comprise, there appears little hope of sparing them, since their timber wealth is unarguable.

Environmentalists have been assisted in this moral campaign by powerful legislation such as the Endangered Species Act, which offers a legal basis to protect nonhuman life without reference to good or bad impacts on humans. There was little need at the Eugene hearing, for example, for supporters of spotted owl protection to offer compelling proof of human benefits resulting from such an action; they simply argued that the owl was in danger of extinction, and that we have a moral and legal obligation to prevent this from happening. Imagine what the outcome would have been if supporters and opponents of owl protection had been restricted to instrumental-value justifications of their positions. It is perhaps possible to imagine that some people would miss the spotted owl's solitary hoot and fearless ways, but many more would benefit from logging its old-growth habitat.

The spotted owl and ancient forests thus appear to be classic cases suggesting the limits of anthropocentrism, and why we need a broader, nonanthropocentric ethic to guide relations between people and Pacific Northwest forests. Anthropocentrism, in this view, is an ethic in which one can't see the forest for the trees. Where people once treated forests as sources of lumber, jobs, and profits, the ancient forest campaign suggests that they must also be treated as biotic communities, as complex ecosystems, as centers of biological diversity. The moral logic underlying the ancient forest campaign echoes the famous words of Aldo Leopold, who spoke favorably of a land ethic that "changes the role of *Homo sapiens* from conqueror of the land-community to plain member and citizen of it."[35]

Yet it would be a simplification to assert that the ancient forest ethic is wholly nonanthropocentric, or that it alone can lay claim to this ethic. Look at the Native Forest Council pamphlet again. It notes that forests provide wildlife habitat, but strongly emphasizes their instrumental value as well: according to the pamphlet, they give people drinking water, regulate global and regional climates, and offer spiritual enrichment and renewal. This line of moral argument, in fact, resembles that pursued in the Oregon Project pamphlet, which defends its radically different approach to forest management by means of both instrumental and intrinsic-value arguments. It notes, for instance, that "every American uses the equivalent of a 100 ft. tree each year," as well as that "threatened species populations, such as the bald eagle and peregrine falcon are increasing thanks to forest management practices." Apparently, both sides in the old-growth debate claim that their preferred approaches benefit humans and nonhumans alike.

One possible explanation for the apparent ethical similarity in these two divergent positions is that they are both appealing to the same audience—an American public that generally wants to know how it will benefit from protecting the environment, yet that has also shown increasing concern for protecting wildlife in recent decades. Clearly, the Native Forest Council pamphlet must be understood more as a means to secure the support of the reader than as some definitive guide to the ethics underlying the ancient forest campaign. But it does caution us against believing that this widespread support has been based solely on a nonanthropocentric ethic that stresses the need for people to save nature irrespective of human gains or losses. To be sure, there are probably many such as Jean Marie Aurnague and F. J. Petock who believe passionately in this moral duty. But others such as Barbara Kelley feel that there is little difference between impacts on humans and impacts on nonhumans: once the forests have all been logged, they will be "unsuitable for owls or cougars or fruits and nuts or streams or people." And it is certainly possible that still others have decided to support the ancient forest campaign for wholly anthropocentric reasons—perhaps they want those forests preserved so that they and their children can visit them someday.

There is thus a need to expand upon the anthropocentric / nonanthropocentric distinction in order to understand better the values and ethics underlying popular support for ancient forest protection. We can accomplish this end by looking more closely at some of the ideas of nature suggested in the ancient forest campaign and their moral implications.

Ethics and Ideas of Nature

THE ANCIENT FOREST ETHIC IS CLOSELY TIED TO A PARTICULAR READING OF Pacific Northwest forests and human impacts on these forests—one not necessarily shared by everyone, as the spotted owl testimony indicates. Consider, for a moment, the forest as described by Barbara Kelley and Jim Standard. Kelley's forest once supported a diverse set of species that had long evolved to thrive there; now logging has destroyed this habitat. Standard's forest, however, is different. Here logging has actually benefited wildlife: "Ask any logger who daily shares his lunch with a raccoon, a chipmunk, a raven, or even a doe and her fawn if he is destroying habitat or enhancing it." Though it is impossible to judge their sincerity from the brief testimony they gave, it seems quite reasonable to conclude that Kelley and Standard actually share an ethic of concern for habitat of nonhuman species. Yet where one sees a ravaged forest, the other describes a haven for wildlife. Their ideas of nature thus point them in widely differing directions in spite of their similar concerns.

The ancient forest campaign is to a great extent built on a particular temporal and spatial conception of Pacific Northwest forests. Their preeminent temporal quality is clearly age, stretching back to long before Europeans arrived. This idea of nature is suggested in the very words the ancient forest campaign employs to describe Pacific Northwest old-growth forests: "ancient," "pristine," "primeval," "virgin." Ancient forests, on this view, thus predate and stand outside of European history. They are the result of the forces of nature over centuries and millennia. Ancient forests are not only old, according to this conception, but remarkably stable and resilient as well.[36] Perhaps fire and other natural disturbances would come on occasion, but whatever ancient forest was destroyed would return after a few centuries of succession. They were thus the spatial dominant of the natural forest landscape. One could readily imagine, after reading the Native Forest Council pamphlet, that virtually the entire presettlement landscape of the westside Pacific Northwest was once covered with a living blanket of old-growth forests dating back far before Europeans even set foot on the North American continent.

The view of Pacific Northwest forests suggested in the ancient forest campaign is not just some conception of nature; it is also a conception of the ideal role of humans in nature, which ties directly into ethics. If the good qualities of stability and longevity in ancient forests are separate from the work of humans, the best thing people can do to these forests on this view is simply leave them be. This notion that people should not intervene in nature is supported by the spectacular landscape appeal of ancient forests— who could argue that people should cut down these forests when logging constitutes such a visual blight in comparison! It is also reinforced for reasons beyond the Pacific Northwest. Ancient forests represent to its protectors the last remnant of untouched American forests; witness the marked reduction in "virgin" forests of the United States graphically displayed on the Native Forest Council pamphlet.[37] To environmentalists the battle over the ancient forests is one to save what little remains of pristine nature in the United States and to affirm the ideal role of humans in nature in at least one small part of the American landscape.

This sense of nature and our role in it is, of course, not new, nor is it spatially limited to Pacific Northwest forests. It is, in large part, an outgrowth of the idea of wilderness that has pervaded American environmentalism during this century, an idea William Cronon has examined elsewhere in this volume.[38] Cronon observes how wilderness in the United States has been intimately associated with romantic notions of the sublime—of extraordinary sacred places where inspiration and even God Himself could be found—and of the particularly American concept of the frontier, where wilderness serves as a counterpoint to the country's expanding cultural landscape.

Both the sublime and the frontier are evident in the ancient forest campaign and serve as guides to its powerful aesthetic—the sense of beauty and good inherent in old-growth forests. Though much of the ancient forest campaign has been couched in the language of ecology and biodiversity protection, it is as much the overwhelming beauty of old-growth forests that has compelled so many people to lend their support as recognition of their ecosystem integrity.[39] The outreach efforts of environmental groups all stress the great aesthetic power of ancient forests and the sheer ugliness of clearcuts. The Native Forest Council pamphlet, for instance, emphasizes the latter on its reverse side, where one finds a graphic portrait of a forest laid waste by logging, with the caption "Stop the Chainsaw Massacre" above.

As Cronon argues in his essay, however, the notion of nature as wilderness has led American environmentalism down a peculiarly narrow path. A similar argument is made by Michael Pollan in an essay exploring the ethical limitations of equating nature with wilderness.[40] Pollan tells of a tornado that blasted through his New England town in the late 1980s and knocked down a highly valued, forty-two-acre expanse of old-growth forest known as Cathedral Pines. A debate soon grew over what was to be done. One side wanted Cathedral Pines to be cleared of the blowdown and replanted; others, more in the spirit of letting nature take its own course as suggested in the ancient forest campaign, wanted it to be left alone. As one biologist stated, "It may be a calamity to us, but to biology it is not a travesty. It is just a natural occurrence."[41]

Why did some people want the mess of twisted trees to remain at Cathedral Pines? Surely there was no spectacular beauty or stability suggested in this fallen landscape. Pollan argues that what he calls the "wilderness ethic" played a key role in their decision—in fact, many people did view Cathedral Pines as one of the area's last remaining examples of wilderness. The wilderness ethic, Pollan argues, is "based on the assumption that the relationship of man and nature resembles a zero sum game," where any intervention by humans, whether to help or harness nature, constitutes harm. To step in and clean up the mess made by the tornado would then violate Cathedral Pines; according to the wilderness ethic, nature should be left alone.

There are two problems with this view, according to Pollan's argument. The first is that seemingly "pristine" parts of nature have often been shaped much more than we realize—Cathedral Pines actually was cleared in the late eighteenth century and thinned of hardwoods some years later, and Pollan suggests that it would never have remained as it is for so long without active fire suppression. The second problem is that the wilderness ethic gives us little guidance in deciding what to do with areas that do not meet a "wilderness" classification. This ethic is clearly silent about these areas—even though the vast majority of what we call nature consists of them. Pollan writes,

> "All or nothing," says the wilderness ethic, and in fact we've ended up with a landscape in America that conforms to that injunction remarkably well. Thanks to exactly this kind of either / or thinking, Americans have done an admirable job of drawing lines around certain sacred areas (we did invent the wilderness area) and a terrible job of managing the rest of our land. The reason is not hard to find: the only environmental ethic we have has nothing useful to say about those areas outside the line. Once a landscape is no longer "virgin" it is typically written off as fallen, lost to nature, irredeemable. We hand it over to the jurisdiction of that other sacrosanct American ethic: laissez-faire economics.[42]

As Pollan suggests, environmentalists have drawn lines in the Pacific Northwest in their campaign to save what is left of the ancient forests. Yet, if their claim is correct that perhaps only 10 percent of the ancient forest remains in the region, what are we to do with the remaining 90 percent—the millions of acres of forests that have already been logged? Are they all to be restored to ancient forests? Perhaps the ancient forest campaign has also suffered from too limited a view of nature, one in which places modified by humans cease to be natural any more. As Pollan would argue, such a view may be good for those parts of nature actually untouched by humans (though he maintains that these may not even exist), but it offers little perspective on all the rest. Pollan is concerned both about environmentalists' excessive concern for "wilderness" areas and about their apparent lack of concern for nonwilderness. He laments, "Essentially, we have divided our country in two, between the kingdom of wilderness, which rules about eight percent of America's land, and the kingdom of the market, which rules the rest."[43]

So far I have briefly traced the idea of nature and the ideal role of humans suggested in the ancient forest campaign back through the concept of wilderness, with the help of Cronon and Pollan. I could end here by suggesting fuller metaphors of nature than wilderness to inform management of Pacific Northwest forests, given its deficiencies noted above.[44] But there is an even more disturbing conclusion I want us to reach from this discussion: if indeed the ancient forest campaign is founded on an ethic closely tied to a particular view of nature, then it reflects only one of potentially many different forms of environmental concern, each informed by its own sense of nature.

The scholar Barbara Deutsch Lynch provides us with one such alternative reading of environmental concern in an essay that examines the ideas of nature shared among U.S. Latino communities, and their differences from mainstream environmentalism.[45] Lynch tells of Daniel Perez, a Dominican immigrant who planted corn, garlic, tomatoes, and black beans on a littered median strip in New York City; of José García, a Puerto Rican who retreats to his garden to escape the oppressiveness of New York; of Latinos who board party boats in Sheepshead Bay in New York and catch bluefish along the way to eat and sell when they return to port.

These stories suggests a nature far different from that typically associated with environmentalism, one which, according to Lynch, is nonetheless equally worthy of this characterization. Lynch argues that "the environment is a social construction: a product of cultural responses to specific historical circumstances which give rise to shared sets of imagined landscapes."[46] Among Caribbean Latinos, Lynch notes, the garden and the sea have been powerful symbols not only of nature but of livelihood and political resistance. Their perspective, however, has been largely silenced in mainstream environmentalism as a result, she argues, of an unequal distribution of power in society that favors certain social constructions of nature at the expense of others. Lynch concurs with Cronon and Pollan in contending that mainstream environmentalism treats nature more like a wilderness than like a garden. In the garden, humans are an active and appropriate part of nature; in the wilderness, they are intruders. Latino environmentalism, in which the garden metaphor is central, thus rejects the dichotomization of people and nature that has pervaded contemporary environmentalism.[47]

In many significant ways, Lynch's account of nature and the proper role of humans in nature among New York Latinos resonates in the testimonies presented by Jim Standard and Susan Morgan at the Eugene hearing. According to their perspective, the active management of nature by humans in the Pacific Northwest has in fact improved it, in the same way that a gardener's toil enhances the garden. Standard, for example, suggests that logging has enhanced the quality of natural resources and wildlife habitat in his defense of timber industry practices. The logger, like the gardener, is close to nature because he labors to improve nature.[48] As Standard observes, "We have always depended on timber for our livelihood, and because of this dependence, we have probably gained a respect for the forest and the land that few people will ever know." Morgan also believes that people working for the timber industry possess an intimate knowledge of forests. This leads her to speak confidently of their ability to manage forests for both human and nonhuman benefit: "Let's establish what habitat characteristics are necessary to maintain a stable population of owls. Let's duplicate these conditions in our modern managed forests." The sentiments of Standard and Morgan are echoed in the Oregon Project leaflet, which also clearly supports active human intervention in forests. In its endorsement of Gifford Pinchot and his philosophy of conservationism, the leaflet asserts that humans are by no means intruders in nature, or even the fellow travelers that Leopold praised; instead, people are nature's managers, charged with the responsibility of using the resource wisely—a notion with implications for the fate of ancient forests far different from that of the environmentalists.

Whose Nature? Whose Ethic?

THE ANCIENT FOREST CAMPAIGN HAS BEEN SUPPORTED BY PEOPLE LIKE JEAN Marie Aurnague, F. J. Petock, Barbara Kelley, and thousands upon thousands of others across the country who consider it their moral duty to protect the Pacific Northwest old-growth forest and its biota. They have joined environmental groups like the Wilderness Society, the Sierra Club, and the Native Forest Council; they have sent letters to their congressional representatives; they have attended hearings, speaking passionately for saving what little remains. Their efforts have resulted in unprecedented policies to restrict logging in mature and old-growth forests of the Pacific Northwest.

And yet this essay has suggested that the ancient forest they strive to protect is as much a reflection of their own particular view of nature as it is some primeval ecosystem under siege by logging. Their ethic, their passionate sense of right and wrong, is only one of many possible ethics. It is enmeshed in a particular, culturally based idea of nature. Viewed from a different perspective—the most notable in the Pacific Northwest being the wise-use ethic of those who support the timber industry—a whole different set of preferred practices and policies emerges.

The ancient forest emerges as a contested moral terrain, a focus of dispute arising from divergent ideas on what nature is and should be, what our role in nature is and should be. The testimonies people made on the proposed spotted owl listing offer clear evidence of this diversity of perspectives on right and wrong. To some people attending that hearing in Eugene, the spotted owl was the proverbial canary in the coal mine, proof that the Pacific Northwest old-growth forest ecosystem was in imminent danger of collapse. To others, the spotted owl was yet another preservationist ploy, a fluffy, big-eyed snail darter whose listing case was deliberately advanced to obstruct sound management of the region's forest resources.

Yet, in spite of these differences, both sides were apparently deeply concerned about the ways people affect Pacific Northwest forests. Their point of difference was thus not one of whether people should care about nature but of how and why. So there is the Native Forest Council and Barbara Kelley, and there is the Oregon Project and Jim Standard. There is environmentalism, and there are alternative environmentalisms, in the Pacific Northwest. Whose is right? Whose nature ought we to protect? This is the troubling question that arises out of acknowledging that environmental ethics are enmeshed in ideas of nature.

There are several familiar ways out of this dilemma that I find unacceptable. The easiest (or at least most politically popular) solution would be to protect everyone's nature. And there has been a good deal of interest in finding advanced management techniques that can combine high levels of timber production with environmental protection in the region's forests. Some of these have gone under the banner of "New Forestry," defined as "the principle of integrating ecological and environmental values with forest commodities production."[49] Yet, even under optimal assumptions, such techniques entail significant economic costs—such as estimated reduction of timber harvests over the long term by a minimum of 25 percent—which many timber companies may not readily be able to absorb.[50] To take another example, the Clinton administration's Option 9 was deliberately crafted to provide high timber harvests and still comply with environmental protection laws. Its projected annual timber sale level of 1.1 billion board feet, however, falls far below the 1980–89 federal forests harvest average of 4.5 billion board feet.[51] In other words, one cannot easily accommodate everyone's nature in the Pacific Northwest; society has no other option but to make hard choices.

Another problematic solution to this dilemma can be termed the compromise argument, which asserts that all sides in the battle are extremists. They want too much. Common sense, it would seem, tells us that the right course of action is somewhere in the middle. On this view, the nature we should save in the Pacific Northwest will have some forest preserved as old growth, and some forest devoted to timber production. The compromise argument has several weaknesses. Its some-of-both solution might in principle seem attractive to all sides, but the difficulty comes in trying to agree on how much land should be devoted to each of these differing landscapes. Anyone who has followed the old-growth debate through to the present knows how much conflict there has been over that little detail! For instance, both sides have struggled to defeat the Clinton administration's Option 9 strategy for managing Pacific Northwest forests: the environmentalists contend that it protects too little of nature, while timber industry supporters argue that it protects too much.[52]

A more philosophical limitation with the compromise argument is its assumption that right and wrong are determined by striking a balance between competing claims. But what if one side turns out to be morally bankrupt? Imagine applying the compromise argument to settle the nineteenth-century dispute between slaveholders and abolitionists: would the right course of action have been to permit slavery but ensure that slaves were, for example, adequately fed and sheltered? The moral claims of the ancient forest campaign are in some senses similar to those of abolitionists, in that many environmentalists assert—rightly or wrongly—that our duties to nature are nonnegotiable.[53]

The biggest problem with the "both and" and compromise solutions, however, is that they focus more on policy and management than on values, ethics, and ideas. When we ask whose nature we are to choose in the Pacific Northwest, we are forced to listen carefully to the testimonies of the people at the Eugene hearing, to the arguments of interest groups like the Native Forest Council and the Oregon Project. At the core of these arguments is always some statement of right and wrong that we must, I believe, critically yet sensitively assess. And how is this to be done? It is easy to be sympathetic to Susan Morgan's pleas that we should protect timber-dependent communities, or to share the concern of Jean Marie Aurnague when she paints a gloomy picture of global environmental destruction. We realize that what we hear are passionate descriptions of the world these people experience and understand. But appreciating their worlds, their natures, cannot in and of itself resolve this problem.

I propose that we have no choice but to embrace a necessary paradox. What we behold in the Pacific Northwest old-growth forest battle are differing conceptions of Pacific Northwest forests and our role in relation to them, coming from people who are differently situated with respect to these forests, who hold differing values and interests. Yet at the same time it is the same forest, the same spotted owl, the same system of human relations with nature to which these distinct ethical positions refer. The environmental ethics we wish to assess and criticize, in other words, have intermingled subjective and objective dimensions: they are framed within the reality of human ideas, and they speak of a reality beyond human ideas. There is no nature wholly outside of culture we can invoke as a fixed point for judging the ethical perspectives arising in the old-growth debate; yet it is chauvinistic to assert that nature cannot exist independent of our ideas of it. This paradox appears to offer rather slippery advice on whose nature one should choose in the Pacific Northwest. Yet I believe it provides three key guiding notions, which I will discuss in the remainder of this section: (a) a realist form of moral pluralism, (b) an anthropogenic, though not necessarily anthropocentric, moral basis, and perhaps ultimately (c) a sense of ethics rooted in, but not limited to, place.

Accepting the idea that ethics are simultaneously enmeshed in and refer to a world beyond human ideas leads us to steer between the two familiar poles of absolutism and relativism. Absolutism arises from conveniently ignoring the subjective dimension of environmental ethics. It asserts that right and wrong are fairly straightforward decisions based, for example, on comparing a particular ethic against its claims on objective reality—reality "out there." For instance, an absolutist may say that the timber industry's ethic promoting active human intervention to improve nature is wrong because ecological evidence clearly shows how people have damaged Pacific Northwest forests. Relativism can arise either from wallowing in the subjective dimension of ethics to the point that reality becomes irreparably fractured, or from asserting that even if we could come to some consensus about what reality is, this sense of reality would not offer us any moral guidance— a position known in moral philosophy as the fact-value distinction.[54] Either way, according to the moral relativist, right and wrong make sense only within a particular, socially based perspective.[55] On this view, it makes no sense to ask whose nature we should save in the Pacific Northwest; there are simply conflicting accounts, each of which has numerous adherents believing passionately that they are right.

Yet there is considerable room between dogmatic moral absolutism and relativism to develop some realist notion of moral pluralism, a view that ethics must necessarily encompass diverse perspectives but help us make sense of how to act in this world—a shared reality not altogether reducible to these perspectives.[56] Moral pluralism is by definition nonabsolutistic; yet it need not be relativistic, either. Since ethics inevitably make claims on reality, not all ethical positions are valid just because people believe them; some are tied to factually incorrect claims or lead to undesirable results. The environment may in large part be, as Lynch argues, a social construction; still, it is not infinitely malleable to our versions of it.

The connection between ethics and reality is not straightforward, because reality itself is not straightforward. For instance, there is no clear balance of nature in Pacific Northwest forests we can describe and invoke as some ideal landscape people should try to protect or restore.[57] But if people value nonhuman life and its habitat—and remember that both sides in the old-growth debate voiced this concern—then there is emerging evidence as to what kinds of habitat people need to protect. Recall again the testimonies of Barbara Kelley and Jim Standard. Kelley speaks of how the timber industry has reduced forests to "even-aged monocultural tree farms," which has drastically reduced old-growth habitat for spotted owls. Standard, in contrast, argues that "the timber industry has done more to perpetuate our natural resources than any other group" he can think of, and he simply cannot understand all the fuss over "a small bird who is not even in trouble and doesn't give a damn how big the tree he is living in or how old it is." Theirs is a conflict of interests—he wants to save his job, she wants to save the owl—and also of values and ethics. But their different perspectives appeal to the same reality: in this case, the effects of logging on spotted owl habitat. And to the best of our (admittedly imperfect) knowledge, spotted owls' habitat needs are far more selective than Standard and the timber industry have maintained, requiring habitat conditions largely restricted to old-growth forests for their nesting, roosting, and much of their foraging activities. The loss of this habitat as a result of logging has severely jeopardized the northern spotted owl's chances for continued reproductive success and, if unchecked, may threaten the species with extinction.[58]

Note also the wildlife Standard mentions in his testimony—raccoons, chipmunks, raven, and deer. All of these species thrive in the fragmented, early successional-stage forest landscapes created by logging. In this sense, he is correct: the timber industry has in fact benefited these species, though at the expense of the spotted owl and others whose habitat needs involve old-growth forests. If we are sincere about valuing nonhuman species and their habitat needs, then we cannot conveniently privilege those that prosper from heavy human uses of nature.

One of the most bitterly contested realities in the old-growth debate, referred to in both the Native Forest Council and the Oregon Project pamphlets, involves the issue of how much old-growth remains. According to the Native Forest Council version, the timber industry has—with the help of government agencies—ruthlessly logged "virgin" forests down to only 5 percent of what once existed in the United States. The other notes that logging is (as of the late 1980s, when the pamphlet was written) prohibited on over one-half of the federal lands in Oregon and Washington, and at any rate has actually benefited wildlife. Are these tracts describing the same forest? In some ways, no: the ideal forest for the Native Forest Council is untouched by human hands, whereas the ideal forest for the Oregon Project is being carefully used to meet human needs. Here we are forced to confront the diversity of perspectives about the appropriate role of humans in nature.

But both of these ideal forests are justified by reference to a real forest, which gives us some basis to critically assess their moral claims. As I suggested earlier, what the Native Forest Council tract refers to as "virgin" forests were indeed a major feature of the Pacific Northwest, but they were no permanent characteristic of the landscape, being shaped—and sometimes destroyed—by natural disturbances such as fire, disease, and windstorms, and extensive burning in areas inhabited by Native Americans. In other words, to suggest that Pacific Northwest forests were completely old-growth and untouched before Europeans transformed them is to deny the historical dynamics of nature in the region. Old-growth forests have been a phase in the processes of succession and disturbance by nature and humans. In fact, I have already noted that one must apply a severely restrictive definition of old-growth forests to the Pacific Northwest to see such a drastic reduction in their extent. On the other hand, the Oregon Project's claim that 53 percent of the forest has been set aside from logging reflects some statistical sleight of hand, since it differs markedly from U.S. Forest Service statistics that suggest that logging was at that time prohibited on only 19 percent of the potentially harvestable national forests in the westside Pacific Northwest.[59] Reality thus calls both claims on the forest into question.

Though I have emphasized the interrelationship between ethics and ecological claims in the old-growth debate, the ecological dimension is only part of the story. There similarly exist many historical, economic, social, and political claims implicit in the positions of both sides that also require critical assessment. The very existence of these competing versions of what nature is and should be deserves scrutiny as well. No ideas are politically innocent; they are not merely ways people make sense of reality, but are often actively promoted to serve specific economic and other interests. A fuller critical examination of the ethics underlying the ancient forest campaign and its alternatives would necessitate traveling down these paths as well.

Embracing the multiple realities out of which ethics emerge touches also on the problem of anthropocentrism. As I suggested above, one strong, though often implicit, moral thread running through much of the ancient forest campaign has been an assertion that we must move beyond anthropocentrism in our relations with nature. Yet some would argue that, since humans view nature from their own perspective, all ethics are anthropocentric, whether intentional or not.[60] On this view, the ancient forest campaign's call to embrace a nonanthropocentric ethic is rather naive; people who truly wish to save nature, then, must find some way to reorient anthropocentrism so that it supports more environmentally benign conduct.

Michael Pollan, for example, has argued for a "garden ethic" as a preferred substitute for the wilderness ethic he is rightly critical of. The garden ethic, Pollan argues, "would be frankly anthropocentric. . . . We know nature only through the screen of our metaphors; to see her plain is probably impossible."[61] It is, nonetheless, based on a "broad and self-enlightened" conception of human self-interest. Pollan writes, "Anthropocentric as [one who holds such a conception] may be, he recognizes that he is dependent for his health and survival on many other forms of life."[62] The garden ethic echoes many of the values and concerns I noted above with groups that traditionally have fallen outside the mainstream of environmentalism, ranging from New York City Latinos to Oregon loggers. In Pollan's version, for instance, the gardener "tends not to be romantic about nature," "feels he has a legitimate quarrel with nature," and "doesn't take it for granted that man's impact on nature will always be negative."[63]

The argument that anthropocentrism is inevitable, however, is weak. Clearly, Pollan and others are right that systems of ethics emerge out of human ideas, which I have stressed above—after all, they are how people make moral sense out of the world in which they live. So it is people who do the valuing; all ethics are, in other words, anthropo*genic.* But there is no necessity that these values mark human good as the ultimate criterion of worth; that is, they need not be anthropo*centric.* For instance, people could choose—as many have done in the ancient forest campaign—to value the forest noninstrumentally in addition to its worth to humans.

Environmental philosophers have been quick to point out the logical problems with the assertion that anthropocentrism is inevitable. Warwick Fox, for example, has dubbed it the "perspectival fallacy," and in a careful refutation Val Plumwood has argued, "The confusion here . . . is that because . . . valuations involve valuers' perspectives and individuating criteria, they must be reducible to valuers' interests and satisfactions."[64] In this sense, the perspectival fallacy can lead to some dangerous moral implications. Logically extended, it also becomes inevitable, for instance, for more advantaged peoples to neglect or even oppress less advantaged peoples unless these actions harmed those in power. In many cases, ethics are needed precisely to provide a compelling reason to care about someone or something else when it may not benefit us in any important way; remember David Ehrenfeld's example of the Houston toad.

Yet it is one thing to suggest that anthropocentrism is not inevitable as an ethical basis for human conduct affecting Pacific Northwest forests, and quite another to argue that it is not feasible. Imagine, for example, that we are looking for an instrumental-value argument to protect old-growth forests. Such an argument would not be too difficult to imagine. Perhaps we should protect them for their value in reminding us of the sacred dimension of life as it unfolds through evolutionary history. I would find this moral perspective quite laudable; it is one that resonates in many of us. I am less sure, however, of how to demonstrate its importance to those who see very different forms of human benefit arising from forests—particularly the more tangible ones like jobs and revenues and cheap lumber. And even if we were to try to implement some expansive anthropocentric ethic to protect old-growth forests, we would still probably need to know whether, for instance, we were protecting enough habitat to maintain animal species associated with old growth. Here the distinction between instrumental and intrinsic value is blurring: Are we promoting old-growth forests for their own ends? For ours? For both? To take another example of a moral perspective that blurs instrumental- and intrinsic-value arguments: What of a virtue-based approach, which asserts that people should protect old-growth forests not only to maintain habitat for nonhuman species and the like but also because such behavior suggests desirable human qualities like humility and moral expansiveness?[65] These examples suggest that any adequate ethic to protect old-growth forests will not be purely instrumental; thus anthropocentrism is ruled out. But to call these ethics nonanthropocentric may suggest that undue stress is being placed on nonhuman benefits. It is worth emphasizing that nonanthropocentric ethics simply situate human needs and interests within a wider context—a context that takes seriously the notion that we are only one of many forms of life on Earth and thus have some obligation to share this planet.

Whatever the name we give this ethic, it must apply to a broader range of landscapes than the wilderness ethic does, for all the reasons I noted earlier. This may be another reason I am somewhat uncomfortable with Pollan's garden ethic: though he intends it to replace the wilderness ethic, it may simply shift our moral energies to different kinds of landscapes. Not all of nature is wilderness, to be sure; yet not all is a garden either. The forests of the Pacific Northwest involve a continuum of landscapes, from thoroughly humanized, even-aged tree plantations to barely humanized reaches of wilderness.

This range of landscapes is real and imagined; one understands it fully by studying forest classification maps of the region as well as by listening to the ideal forest landscapes envisioned by people like those who testified in the Eugene hearing. Like the wilderness and the garden, the old-growth forest and the managed forest arise out of multiple realities in conversation with some shared reality. Accordingly, the final implication I would like to draw out of this paradox is that we need a sense of ethics rooted in, but not limited to, place—which, as Nicholas Entrikin's statement quoted at the outset suggests, is neither wholly objective nor subjective, but best understood from "points in between." It will not do to come up with some ethic in the abstract and then apply it to Pacific Northwest forests. This would be an ethic from nowhere. The ethics of Jim Standard and F. J. Petock, of Susan

Morgan and Barbara Kelley, arise from their lived experience in the region, and they form the raw stuff out of which we can craft some sense of that place. All the little details of their personal geographies, their interactions with the nature of the Pacific Northwest, matter. So do all the little details of the physical geography of the region: its natural and cultural fire history, climate, vegetation changes over the last century and since the last glacial maximum. All of this helps us get a sense of place, a very practical sense we can weave our moral frameworks around.

But attention to place need not restrict our scope of inquiry in trying to make moral sense of the relations between people and Pacific Northwest forests. These forests are connected with other places through, for example, trade in lumber products. In one very important sense, they constitute a zone of production, feeding markets of consumption throughout the Pacific Rim. If we are to come to moral terms with human-environment relations affecting Pacific Northwest forests, we will have to look beyond the Pacific Northwest to the political and economic forces of industrial capitalism that have played such a key role in the transformation of these forests over the last century, and will certainly do so in this and other places in the future.[66] As an example, some studies suggest that demand to log Pacific Northwest forests will probably decline in the next century for largely economic reasons, when it becomes less profitable to log them relative to booming sites of production in the U.S. Southeast and elsewhere.[67] Other studies suggest that protecting old-growth forests in the Pacific Northwest without curtailing consumption of wood products in the United States will simply transfer ecological impacts to other forests in other countries.[68] The issue of Pacific Northwest forests demands sensitivity to that place, but it also demands our realization that the problems affecting these forests are symptoms of larger processes we also need to make some moral sense of. An ethics of place is not a spatially limited ethics; it is a spatially based ethics.

In summary: whose nature should we save? There is no one nature to save in the Pacific Northwest, since nature is always in part a social construction. There exist many differently situated human practices and perspectives on the nature of these forests. Yet neither is there an infinite number of natures in the Pacific Northwest. The reality of these forests, and of interactions people have had with them over time, sets bounds on our ethics, which are meaningless if they fail to engage the real world.

I have suggested three broad ethical implications arising from this paradox. They involve the necessity of moral pluralism; the inevitability of an anthropogenic, though not necessarily anthropocentric, approach; and the need to root, but not limit, ethics to place. How exactly do these implications offer a different perspective on the ancient forest campaign? My contribution here is not to product but to process; I have suggested some major landmarks to keep in sight, and others to avoid, as supporters and opponents of ancient forest protection discuss and debate the alternatives. All the critical details still need to be worked out. There remain plenty of questions, for instance, about how significant old-growth protection should be relative to timber production, and what kind of moral logic we should invoke in weighing these alternatives.

But the ensuing discussion must be understood, first and foremost, not as some matter of ecology or economics or management but as a matter of ethics, which ties these very practical considerations to the values that inform our sense of right and wrong. By turning our attention to ethics, I do not suggest that the ensuing discussion will be any easier. But at least it will be more to the point, because we will have before us the central question: What should be our role in nature? We can no longer adequately answer this question by invoking the dogmatism and absolutism of particular views, such as wilderness-style environmentalism, or the naive relativism inherent in admitting all views as equally valid. Nature and our own many natures all count here.

Conclusion

THE SPOTTED OWL HEARING HELD ON THAT SUMMER DAY IN EUGENE IN 1989 was certainly not the last to consider whose nature we should save in the Pacific Northwest. I can imagine plenty of hearings to come on proposed management plans for those forests. Will environmentalists continue to cite their facts and figures about how little of the ancient forest remains? Will the timber industry and its supporters continue to cite their statistics to show how some proposed federal action will endanger the regional economy? I think not; in many ways, everyone seems to be weary of the battle they have been fighting over old-growth forests for the last decade. Yet there are even possibly larger battles looming over saving salmon and steelhead habitat on rivers running up and down the region.[69] Nature is contested terrain in the Pacific Northwest, and even if everyone gets tired of shouting over ancient forests, people are sure to find something else to fight over.

My picture of the future is not an especially rosy one, but it does suggest something of the larger role environmentalists can play in the region after they declare victory in the ancient forest campaign. What is critically lacking in the Pacific Northwest is moral leadership on these contested matters of human relations with nature. But this is precisely what environmentalists can potentially offer. As Timothy O'Riordan once said, environmentalism is much more than a set of policies; at heart its policy initiatives are "superficial manifestations of much more deeply-rooted values." More recently, Robin Grove-White has declared that environmentalism is a potentially new moral discourse for technological society.[70]

Environmentalists cannot hope to provide any moral leadership, however, until they reexamine their own values and consider earnestly the values of people who oppose their campaigns to save nature. The reason they need to do this is suggested throughout this volume. In the Pacific Northwest and elsewhere, it is clear that nature is far more complex, far more a projection of particular human ideas, than many of its defenders would willingly admit. Such an assertion calls into question the moral authority of environmentalism, which can no longer ground its claims on some unitary nature existing outside of human values, aspirations, interests, and fears.

What I suggest here, in essence, is that it is time literally to *reevaluate* environmentalism, to regain a sense of its ethic. Environmentalists need to ask: What is it that we value deeply, that we care for? Too often, they have restricted their focus to wilderness, to the ancient forest, to nature remote and untouched by human hands. This view, however, is surely incomplete. What is to replace this notion?

We cannot hope that our answer to this question will have the same moral clarity as the ethic that has led so many thousands of Americans to support ancient forest protection. Accepting a pluralism of natures necessarily makes our ethics more contested and ambiguous; this is an inescapable part of the late twentieth century. As Zygmunt Bauman stresses in *Postmodern Ethics,* "The postmodern perspective offers more wisdom; the postmodern setting makes acting on that wisdom more difficult. . . . What the postmodern mind is aware of is that there are problems in human and social life with no good solutions, twisted trajectories that cannot be straightened up."[71]

As complex and fragmented as this task may be, it nonetheless demands an (always preliminary) answer. And such an answer is possible. When we ask, "Whose nature?," we know we are talking of more than differing ideas in our heads. What I have suggested here is that we need a perspective on ethics that takes objective as well as subjective realities seriously; otherwise, there will be no common ground we could possibly share. These realities are rooted in specific places; here I have focused on one small place called the Pacific Northwest. Making moral sense of these places entails embracing the paradox that they are both social constructions and realities that transcend social constructions.

The fundamental task for environmentalists, then, is not just to save nature. They need to find and promote answers to the moral questions that loom large in contemporary debates over nature. The next time there is a hearing in Eugene, environmentalists should leave most of their ecological ammunition at home and instead encourage people to address more fundamental issues: What kind of world do we want to live in? What kind of social and natural landscape would describe this world? What can we do, individually and collectively, to help move our little part of the world in this direction?

No one should expect this discussion to lead to easy consensus—the terrain of environmental battles is too fraught with divergent interests and unequal allocations of power to permit easy solutions. But this task of rethinking ethics will surely result in a more inclusive environmentalism, one uniting it with other social movements in a common moral cause: to help create a more livable world for all of us, humans and nonhumans alike.

Nature as Community:
The Convergence of Environment and Social Justice

Giovanna Di Chiro

Introduction

"SHEILA, I THINK THEY'RE TRYING TO KILL US!" THIS WAS THE ONLY LOGICAL conclusion that Robin Cannon, a resident of South Central Los Angeles, could imagine, as she attempted to convey to her sister in a late-night phone call the ominous contents of the environmental impact report (EIR) she had just spent the entire evening poring over. Earlier that day Cannon had attended a public hearing sponsored by the Los Angeles City Council, where she first learned of the proposed 1,600-ton-per-day solid-waste incinerator known as LANCER (Los Angeles City Energy Recovery Project), which was planned to be sited in the center of her neighborhood. City officials who advocated the waste incinerator facility intended to allay "unfounded" fears and misconceptions about what an incinerator would mean for the community. The residents who attended the meeting were treated to splendid images of the waste incinerator site encircled by beautifully landscaped picnic areas that, according to LANCER's proponents, would offer an attractive place to host wedding receptions and outdoor parties. These city officials could not have suspected that this ordinary woman who was asking so many questions about the health effects of burning tons of waste in her community would actually read the entire three-inch-thick EIR that documented the project's scientifically based standards of safety. As Cannon's phone call to her sister suggests, the layers of information embedded in the technical document actually conveyed a very different message. Highly toxic dioxins and fluorons were only some of the chemicals

298

that would most likely contaminate the air, water, and land of the people who lived in South Central Los Angeles.

Cannon, her sister Sheila, and her friend Charlotte Bullock, all residents of this predominantly African American, low-income community, formed Concerned Citizens of South Central Los Angeles in response to the distressing implications of the EIR. These three women's immediate actions toward building an organized response to the perceived threat to the welfare of their community dispelled the stereotypes of low-income and poor neighborhoods as "unaware," "unconcerned," and "compliant."[1] Through Concerned Citizens they mobilized a citywide network of community organizations and local political and business leaders, which successfully blocked the construction of LANCER by defeating the city-sponsored $535 million bond issue. Not only did this grassroots organization thwart the city's plans to build the incinerator; it forced the city to reevaluate the long prioritization of incineration in its waste management policy and to pursue instead a commitment to recycling. The fight against the LANCER facility also initiated a host of other community actions on issues such as housing, schools, drugs, and neighborhood security. These issues were seen by the activists to be as "environmental" as those of hazardous waste, air quality, and land use.

I met Robin Cannon in 1993 and was surprised to learn that these issues were *not* deemed adequately "environmental" by local environmental groups such as the Sierra Club or the Environmental Defense Fund. When members of Concerned Citizens first approached these organizations in the mid-1980s for support to fight LANCER, they were informed that the poisoning of an urban community by an incineration facility was a "community health issue," not an environmental one.[2] Addressing this question of the discrepancy between what does and does not not count as "environmental" is, I believe, crucial to the effort to produce a broadly based environmental movement that really works. Part of this effort requires a close analysis and historical reading of how different groups of people have understood their relationship to "nature" and the environments in which they live. What, for example, are the diverse and sometimes contradictory meanings and metaphors that different people deal with when negotiating the multiple environments they encounter in their everyday lives? What does it mean to talk about nature as a "benevolent mother," as "wild places unspoiled by human hands," or as the "place where family and community convene and share life experiences"? We can also learn a lot about how people understand, live in, and change their environments, not only by studying diverse *ideas* about "nature" or human/environment interconnections, but by examining social practice. What are the complex forms and structures of social and cultural organization that emerge in diverse locales to resist the destruction of particular human/environment relationships and to support specific ways of life? In other words, how do people mobilize through action in order to sustain or transform certain relationships with "nature" and their environment? In this essay, I examine the emergence of the environmental justice movement, a social movement strongest in low-income communities of color that, like Concerned Citizens of South Central Los Angeles, conceive of "nature" and "environment" as those places and sets of relationships that sustain a local community's way of life. The grassroots organizations that make up the movement identify such issues as social justice, local economic sustainability, health, and community governance as falling under the purview of "environment."

Redefining Environmentalism: The Struggle for a "Green" Justice

THE EXTENSIVE NATIONAL AND INTERNATIONAL NETWORK OF COMMUNITY/ environmental organizations referred to as the environmental justice movement challenges dominant meanings of environmentalism and produces new forms of environmental theory and action. The term "environmental justice," which appeared in the United States sometime in the mid-1980s, questions popular notions of "environment" and "nature" and attempts to produce something different. In this essay I explore some of those differences as they are articulated through the voices of activists in the movement. The vast majority of activists in the environmental justice movement are low-income women and predominantly women of color, including Dana Alston, Pam Tau Lee, Penny Newman, Esperanza Maya, Juana Guttierrez, Vernice Miller, Marta Salinas, Valerie Taliman, Marina Ortega, Lois Gibbs, Rose Augustine, and Janice Dickerson.[3] From the start, the gender, race, and class composition of the movement distinguishes it from that of the mainstream environmental movement, whose constituents have historically been white and middle class and whose leadership has been predominantly male.[4]

The history of mainstream environmentalism locates its adherents in an ideological position that constructs a separation between humans and the "natural" world. Environmentalists are therefore often said to be obsessed with preserving and protecting those "wild and natural" areas defined as places where humans are not and *should* not be in large numbers. Social movement historians have occasionally referred to environmental justice activists as the "new environmentalists," a term that I find misleading.[5] Many of the grassroots activists with whom I have spoken are reluctant to call themselves environmentalists at all, much less newly converted ones. In part, this is due to the dominance of the mainly white, middle-class, and uncritically "preservationist" political culture from which much mainstream environmental thinking has developed.[6] Again, in these mainstream terms, what counts as environment is limited to issues such as wildland preservation and endangered species protection. Issues pertaining to human health and survival, community and workplace poisoning, and economic sustainability are generally not considered to be part of the environmental agenda. Additionally, many activists perceive much of mainstream environmentalism to be either fixated on anti-urban development campaigns (read as "no jobs for city-dwelling people") or utterly indifferent to the concerns of urban communities. Many of the community organizations that make up the environmental justice movement are located in low-income and working-class communities in and around industrialized urban centers throughout the country. Crucial issues in these communities, as we saw in the case of Robin Cannon and Concerned Citizens, include lead and asbestos poisoning in substandard housing, toxic waste incineration and dumping, and widespread unemployment. Until relatively recently, these were problems that the mainstream organizations located outside the domain of the "environment."[7]

Environmental justice activists define the environment as "the place you work, the place you live, the place you play." Many mainstream environmentalists would find this formulation incomprehensible, even ethically indefensible, because of its apparent anthropocentrism. Putting humans at the center of environmental discourse is a grave error, they argue, because humans are the perpetrators of environmental problems in the first place. Environmental justice activists maintain that some humans, especially the poor, are also the victims of environmental destruction and pollution and that, furthermore, some human cultures live in ways that are relatively sound ecologically. They therefore contend that the mainstream environmentalists' invention of a universal division between humans and nature is deceptive, theoretically incoherent, and strategically ineffective in its political aim to promote widespread environmental awareness. Pam Tau Lee, the labor coordinator for the Labor and Occupational Health Program at the University of California at Berkeley and a board member of the National Toxics Campaign Fund and the Southwest Organizing Network, describes environmental justice as being

> able to bring together different issues that used to be separate. If you're talking about lead and where people live, it used to be a housing struggle; if you're talking about poisoning on the job, it used to be a labor struggle; people being sick from TB or occupational exposures used to be separate health issues, so environmental justice is able to bring together all of these different issues to create one movement that can really address what actually causes all of these phenomena to happen and gets to the root of the problems.[8]

The merging of social justice and environmental interests therefore assumes that people are an integral part of what should be understood as the environment. The daily realities and conditions of people's lives have not been at the center of mainstream environmental discourse. Traditional environmental arguments have commonly constructed "society" and "nature," and urban versus wild/natural, as hostile dichotomies. The essays by William Cronon and Candace Slater in this book argue persuasively that traditional Euro-American conceptions of "the natural" as "Edenic" or "sublime" posit nature as a place or state of original purity, uncontaminated by human intervention and avarice. As these authors have demonstrated in their writing on the history of ideas of wilderness and on Western imaginings of Amazonia, this type of Edenic thinking, which locates nature outside of human culture, separates humans from nature while constructing nature as in need of human control and domination. Cronon and Slater describe how the human populations that Euro-American colonists considered to be closer to nature and part of the "wilderness" landscape (for example, the native Indians in the Americas or the enslaved Africans brought to the New World, who were both classified as savages and likened to animals) are people who were also seen to be a part of a wild, untamed nature that had to be exploited and controlled.

How can these historical analyses inform us about the contemporary environmental conditions of human groups situated differently in the society, and about their different responses to the environmental problems that confront them? Numerous studies have demonstrated that it is primarily low-income communities of color that are often targeted for industrial and toxic waste disposal sites.[9] Many environmental justice activists argue that this reality is nothing less than history repeating itself, this time in relation to who suffers the consequences of modern-day environmental pollution. Dana Alston, a longtime activist, discusses how the environmental justice movement's redefinition of "environment" to account for the presence of people reflects one of the primary differences between it and the mainstream movement.

> The Nature Conservancy defines itself as the "real estate" arm of the environmental movement and as being about saving nature, pristine areas, sensitive ecosystems, endangered species, and rain forests. But the reality of the situation is that there is hardly anywhere in the world where there aren't people living, no matter how remote you get, and the most vulnerable cultures are in the areas that are most remote, whether you are talking about here in the U.S. or in Latin America or wherever, so immediately it puts us in confrontation with the Nature Conservancy. We continue to raise these issues not only in the international arena but here as the Nature Conservancy goes to buy large tracts of land in New Mexico or out west where indigenous and Chicano people have lived for decades and have sovereignty or land-grant rights . . . with total disregard for how these real estate dealings affect the social, political, and economic life of our communities. We feel that many of these communities are just as much endangered species as any animal species.[10]

Consequently, activists in the environmental justice movement are unlikely to identify themselves as the "new environmentalists," because they do not view themselves as an outgrowth of the "old" environmental movement, with its "Save the whales and rain forests" slogans. It would be more accurate to regard environmental justice activists as the "new" civil rights or "new" social justice activists, since many of the prominent organizers affirm their roots in and political continuities with the social justice movements of the sixties, including the civil rights, welfare rights, and labor and farm-worker movements. Moreover, the term "new environmentalists" suggests that the members of these emerging grassroots organizations, who come from predominantly African American, Latino, Native American, and Asian American communities, have only recently become aware of the importance of "environmental" concerns. Numerous histories of activism by people of color on environmental issues exist but often are not classified by mainstream groups as authentic "environmental history," because of these crucial questions of definition.[11]

What is new about the environmental justice movement is not the "ele-vated environmental consciousness" of its members but the ways it is trans-forming the possibilities for fundamental social and environmental change through processes of redefinition, reinvention, and construction of innova-tive political and cultural discourses and practices. This includes, among other things, the articulation of the concepts of environmental justice and environmental racism and the forging of new forms of grassroots political organization. I will illustrate some of these conceptual inventions by exam-ining a few key historical moments that have defined the environmental jus-tice movement.

Revisioning Environmental History: Whose Stories Are Told?

SOME MOVEMENT HISTORIANS IDENTIFY THE LARGE-SCALE CIVIL DISOBEDI-ence that occurred in Warren County, North Carolina, in 1982 as the first active demonstration of an emerging environmental justice movement.[12] At this demonstration, hundreds of predominantly African American women and children, but also local white residents, used their bodies to block trucks from dumping poisonous PCB-laced dirt into a landfill near their commu-nity. The mainly African American, working-class, rural communities of Warren County had been targeted as the dumping site for a toxic waste landfill that would serve industries throughout North Carolina. This dem-onstration of nonviolent civil disobedience opened the gates for a series of subsequent actions by people of color and poor people throughout the country. Unlike social activism against toxic contamination that predated this event, such as the struggle against Hooker Chemical Company at Love Canal, New York, in the late 1970s, this action began to forge the connec-tions between race, poverty, and the environmental consequences of the production of industrial waste.[13]

The Warren County episode succeeded in racializing the antitoxics agenda and catalyzed a number of studies that would document the historical pattern of disproportionately targeting racial minority communities for toxic waste contamination. One such study, which represents another key moment in the history of the environmental justice movement, was a report sponsored by the United Church of Christ Commission for Racial Justice (UCC-CRJ) and published in 1987. Although people living near toxic waste facilities have known for many years about industrial pollution's detrimental effects on their health and their environments, it was not until this report that an awareness of widespread environmental racism entered mainstream political consciousness.

The UCC-CRJ report, *Toxic Waste and Race in the United States: A National Report on the Racial and Socioeconomic Characteristics of Communities with Hazardous Waste Sites,* compiled the results of a national study that found race to be the leading factor in the location of commercial hazardous waste facilities. The study, presented to the National Press Club in Washington, D.C., that same year, determined that people of color suffered a "disproportionate risk" to the health of their families and their environments, with 60 percent of African American and Latino communities and over 50 percent of Asian / Pacific Islanders and Native Americans living in areas with one or more uncontrolled toxic waste sites. The report also disclosed that 40 percent of the nation's toxic landfill capacity is concentrated in three communities—Emelle, Alabama, with a 78.9 percent African American population; Scotlandville, Louisiana, with 93 percent African Americans; and Kettleman City, California, which is 78.4 percent Latino.[14]

The term "environmental racism" entered into political discussion on the environment in 1987 when the Reverend Benjamin Chavis, the commission's executive director who was most recently the head of the NAACP, coined it. According to Chavis, environmental racism is "racial discrimination in environmental policy-making and the enforcement of regulations and laws, the deliberate targeting of people of color communities for toxic waste facilities, the official sanctioning of the life-threatening presence of poisons and pollutants in our communities, and history of excluding people of color from leadership in the environmental movement."[15] In the mid to late 1980s, this process of naming and researching the material realities of environmental racism made possible a significant transformation in what would count as properly environmental concerns. This new political concept also provided an organizing tool for galvanizing into action the multiple and diverse communities and constituencies for whom environmental racism was a painful reality.

How did the appearance of the UCC-CRJ report on toxics and race and the public naming of environmental racism affect the national environmental agenda? By 1990 a variety of coalitions of people of color environmental justice organizations had emerged, including the extremely dynamic Southwest Network for Economic and Environmental Justice (SNEEJ). In January and March of that year, representatives from many of these grassroots coalitions sent two recriminating letters to the Group of Ten[16] national environmental organizations, "calling on them to dialogue on the environmental crisis impacting communities of color, and to hire people of color on their staffs and boards of directors."[17] The letters presented an analysis of environmental racism and defined the ways that the primarily white, mainstream organizations have complicitly supported it:

> There is a clear lack of accountability by the Group of Ten environmental organizations towards Third World communities in the Southwest, in the U.S. as a whole and internationally. Your organizations continue to support and promote policies which emphasize the clean-up and preservation of the environment on the backs of working people in general and people of color in particular. In the name of eliminating environmental hazards at any cost, across the country industrial and other economic activities which employ us are being shut down, curtailed or prevented while our survival needs and cultures are ignored. We suffer from the results of these actions, but are never full participants in the decision making which leads to them.[18]

According to the activists with whom I have spoken, responses to these challenges have varied. At worst, some of the Group of Ten have expressed outrage and denial and all but ignored the invitation to "come to the table as equals." On the other hand, some have begun to enter into discussions about building "multicultural and multi-racial organizations," to share resources such as technical expertise, legal assistance, and funding, and to seriously modify their organizations' structure and mission. The Earth Island Institute, Greenpeace, and the now defunct National Toxics Campaign are often cited as the environmental groups that have responded to these challenges by expanding the scope of their projects to include environmental justice issues and by diversifying their staff and leadership.

In October of 1991 the First National People of Color Environmental Leadership Summit convened in Washington, D.C., signifying a watershed moment in the history of the movement. According to conference participants, this event foregrounded the importance of people of color environmental groups' insistence on self-representation and speaking for themselves.[19] It also marked an unequivocal rejection of a "partnership based on paternalism" with the mainstream environmental movement.

The summit brought together three hundred African, Native, Latino, and Asian American delegates from the United States and a number from Canada, Central and South America, Puerto Rico, and the Marshall Islands to shape the contours of a "multi-racial movement for change" founded on the political ideology of working from the grassroots. Conference participants heard testimonies and reports on the local effects of environmental racism, including the extensive poisoning of air, water, and land that disproportionately devastates their environments and health. These discussions also provided a supportive context for people of color to "reaffirm their traditional connection to and respect for the natural world," which was collectively understood as "including all aspects of daily life." Environment so defined expands the definition of environmental problems and so includes issues such as "militarism and defense, religious freedom and cultural survival, energy and sustainable development, transportation and housing, land and sovereignty rights, self-determination and employment."[20] Dana Alston describes how the leadership summit helped to bring people of color together in a spirit of political solidarity.

> The most important thing that came out of the summit was the bonding. Many people might think that because they're nonwhite, that they're going to come together, but the society is built on keeping people divided, and we all know about the tensions between African Americans and Asian Americans and Latinos and Native Americans, but it's the history, the culture, the society that's keeping us divided . . . because that's how the power structure stays in power, by keeping us separate, so we had to from the very beginning put together a set of principles from which we were going to relate to each other.[21]

The composition and program of the second day of the leadership summit shifted with the arrival of another 250 participants from a variety of environmental and social change organizations, together with a sampling of "professionals" like lawyers, academics, and policymakers. Engaging in critical discussions and debates, the conferees articulated key issues of the building of the environmental justice movement, including the definition of environment and environmental problems, leadership and organizational strategy, and the formation of coalitions and partnerships. Working by consensus, the leadership summit drew up a set of seventeen organizational principles that would guide the emergent political process. These "Principles of Environmental Justice" profile a broad and deep political project to pursue environmental justice in order to "secure our political, economic and cultural liberation that has been denied for over 500 years of colonization and oppression, resulting in the poisoning of our communities and land and the genocide of our peoples."

All of the activists with whom I have spoken maintain that the most promising achievement of the leadership summit was its commitment to the construction of diverse, egalitarian, and nonhierarchical leadership and organizational processes and structures. The participants wanted something different from the technocratic rationality and top-down managerialism that the mainstream environmental organizations have adopted by mimicking the decision-making approaches of the very corporations they are opposing. As grassroots activists working in direct response to the threats of pollution, resource exploitation, and land-use decisions in their communities, they contend that the decision-making process is itself a primary issue in the debate over environmental problems. They reject the top-down approach as disempowering, paternalistic, and exclusive and instead are committed to developing a more democratic, locally and regionally based, decentralized organizational culture. A commitment to such values, they argue, will build an environmental movement that truly works.

Principles of Environmental Justice

PREAMBLE

WE, THE PEOPLE OF COLOR, gathered together at the multinational People of Color Environmental Leadership Summit, to begin to build a national and international movement of all peoples of color to fight the destruction and taking of our lands and communities, do hereby re-establish our spiritual interdependence to the sacredness of our Mother Earth; to respect and celebrate each of our cultures, languages and beliefs about the natural world and our roles in healing ourselves; to insure environmental justice; to promote economic alternatives which would contribute to the development of environmentally safe livelihoods; and, to secure our political, economic and cultural liberation that has been denied for over 500 years of colonization and oppression resulting in the poisoning of our communities and land and the genocide of our peoples, do affirm and adopt these Principles of Environmental Justice:

1. **Environmental justice** affirms the sacredness of Mother Earth, ecological unity and the interdependence of all species, and the right to be free from ecological destruction.

2. **Environmental justice** demands that public policy be based on mutual respect and justice, for all peoples, free from any form of discrimination or bias.

3. **Environmental justice** mandates the right to ethical, balanced and responsible uses of land and renewable resources in the interests of a sustainable planet for humans and other living things.

4. **Environmental justice** calls for universal protection from nuclear testing, extraction, production and disposal of toxic /

hazardous wastes and poisons that threaten the fundamental right to clean air, land, water and food.

5.   **Environmental justice** affirms the fundamental right to political, economic, cultural and environmental self-determination of all peoples.

6.   **Environmental justice** demands the cessation of the production of all toxins, hazardous wastes and radioactive materials; and that all past and current producers be held strictly accountable to the people for detoxification and the containment at the point of production.

7.   **Environmental justice** demands the right to participate as equal partners at every level of decision-making including needs assessment, planning, implementation, enforcement and evaluation.

8.   **Environmental justice** affirms the right of all workers to a safe and healthy work environment without being forced to choose between an unsafe livelihood and unemployment. It also affirms the right of those who work at home to be free from environmental hazards.

9.   **Environmental justice** protects the right of victims of environmental injustice to receive full compensation and reparations for damages as well as quality health care.

10.   **Environmental justice** considers governmental acts of environmental injustice a violation of international law, the Universal Declaration on Human Rights and the United Nations Convention on Genocide.

11.   **Environmental justice** must recognize a special legal and natural relationship of Native Peoples to the U.S. Government through treaties, agreements, compacts and covenants which impose upon the U.S. Government a paramount obligation and responsibility to affirm the sovereignty and self-determina-

tion of the indigenous peoples whose land it occupies and holds in trust.

12. **Environmental justice** affirms the need for urban and rural ecological policies to clean up and rebuild our cities and rural areas in balance with nature, honoring the cultural integrity of all our communities and providing fair access for all to the full range of resources.

13. **Environmental justice** calls for the strict enforcement of principles of informed consent and a halt to the testing of experimental reproductive and medical procedures and vaccinations on people of color.

14. **Environmental justice** opposes the destructive operations of multinational corporations.

15. **Environmental justice** opposes military occupation, repression and exploitation of lands, people and cultures, and other life forms.

16. **Environmental justice** calls for the education of present and future generations which emphasizes social and environmental issues based on our experience and an appreciation of our diverse cultural perspectives.

17. **Environmental justice** requires that we, as individuals, make personal and consumer choices to consume as little of Mother Earth's resources and to produce as little waste as possible and make the conscious decision to challenge and re-prioritize our lifestyles to insure the health of the natural world for present and future generations.

"Principles of Environmental Justice." *(Toxic-Free Neighborhoods: Community Planning Guide, San Diego: Environmental Health Coalition, 1993)*

Reinventing Nature through Community Action

TO FORGE A VIGOROUS, EFFECTIVE ENVIRONMENTAL MOVEMENT, THE EMERgent grassroots coalition of environmental justice organizations in the United States is producing a coherent analysis of the causes and consequences of environmental problems and a political culture based on community-governed and network-oriented social organization. In large part, these analyses and social practices are based on diverse interpretations of and experiences with nature and with social injustice. In response to different cultural histories and to different experiences of environmental injustice, these low-income communities construct distinct meanings and definitions of "nature" and of what constitutes proper human/environment interrelations and practices. These divergent definitions and practices, and their implications in the world, indicate the core discrepancies between the environmental justice and the mainstream environmental movements. They also represent approaches to understanding nature, and to *reinventing* it, that are very different from those that appear in many of the essays of this book.

In the final section of this essay, I want to focus on aspects of environmental justice that illustrate the ways that activists in the movement are "reinventing nature." As I mentioned earlier, environmental justice activists explicitly undertake a critique of modernist and colonial philosophies of unlimited progress, unchecked development, the privileging of Western scientific notions of objective truth and control of nature, and the hierarchical separation between nature and human culture. This antimodernist analysis is also implicitly a critique of the mainstream environmental movement, which, activists argue, upholds the same underlying colonial philosophy of nature as "other" to human culture.

The activists' approach to reinventing nature, I suggest, contains both deconstructive and constructive elements. Their critiques of conventional or dominant ideas of nature and environment demonstrate how these constructs and their policy implications are detrimental to certain *human* communities, primarily the poor and people of color. Exposing the historical and ecological effects on humans *and* the nonhuman world of these dominant ideologies reveals their limitations as theoretical foundations for a just environmentalism. Environmental justice groups, while strongly criticizing mainstream conceptions of nature, also *produce* a distinct theoretical and material connection between human/nature, human/environment relations through their notions of "community." Community becomes at once the idea, the place, and the relations and practices that generate what these activists consider more socially just and ecologically sound human/environment configurations. These processes of critique and construct both engage the project of reinventing nature. In the paragraphs that follow I will briefly discuss some of their key points.

Communities of color involved in environmental justice organizations develop a critique of what I call the colonial discourse of Euro-American forms of "nature talk." Colonial discourses of nature, they argue, constitute one of the historical progenitors of contemporary environmental racism. Although "nature talk" separates humans from nature and posits them as superior to nature, it specifies that some humans are in fact part of nature. In other words, particular Euro-American romantic constructions of nature (see, for example, the extended descriptions that Merchant, Cronon, and Slater offer on the Edenic or sublime notions of nature from Western traditions) have been and continue to be problematic and even genocidal for people who have been characterized as being more like nature and thus less than human. The discourse that opposes an Edenic or sublime nature to a fallen culture either categorizes people of color as identical *with* nature, as in the case of indigenous peoples or Third World natives (thereby entitling Western colonizers and slave traders to exploit and have dominion over some humans in similar ways in which they would feel entitled to exploit nonhuman nature),[22] *or* classifies them as people who are anti-nature, impure, and even toxic, as in the case of poor communities of color living in contaminated and blighted inner cities or in the surrounding rural wastelands. Images of people of color in the mainstream environmental literature not infrequently depict throngs of overbreeding, slashing and burning, border-overflowing, and ecologically incorrect Third Worlders or illegal immigrants. Such images encode these groups as anti-nature or out of touch with the natural world. Wilderness or Eden must be located where these "toxic" or "fallen" peoples are not.

The Edenic notion of nature becomes, for many communities of color, a tool of oppression that operates to obscure their own "endangered" predicaments. Such a conception of nature is also seen by many activists to be the moral authority on which white, bourgeois culture bases its often genocidal environmental policy decisions. So the trademark slogans of mainstream environmentalism, such as "Save the whales" or "Extinction is forever," are seen to reflect concerns of white people who are blind to the problems of people of color. The obsession with saving the rain forest and preserving biodiversity at the expense of local cultures is seen as a decision to trade them off. As a consequence, many white environmentalists claim that people of color aren't interested in saving nature or the environment—even though the Black Congressional Caucus has registered the strongest voting record on Capitol Hill on issues of the environment. Clearly, activists of color have substantial interests in the conceptual project of "reinventing" the dominant idea of nature in mainstream environmentalism.

How a particular community of color perceives its relationship with nature or reinvents it is based on specific experiential and historical realities. One of the central premises of this book is the argument that what we understand as nature is historically dynamic and culturally specific. What counts as nature is therefore different among various people of color groups that have very different cultural histories. In fact, for many environmental justice activists from different ethnic backgrounds, the leadership summit revealed that there is no "natural" bond among people of color groups. They had to tackle the hard work of recognizing one another's specific cultural understandings of nature and the environment, as well as one another's specific experiences of environmental racism. Paul Ruffins, an African American journalist who attended the summit, explains that for various human groups in North America the different definitions of and relationships to nature that they espouse depend on how they got there. Obviously, the experience of dislocation and relocation in relation to the land and to "place" was very different for Native Americans, European settlers, enslaved Africans, indentured Chinese laborers, and Mexican inhabitants of the Southwest. Ruffins argues that, as an urbanized African American, he was forced to consider that a Native American's thinking about "mother nature" and "whales as brothers"—terms that sounded suspicious to him at first—may be different from the colonial nature talk embedded in a mainstream environmentalist's insistence on saving an endangered species at the expense of human cultures. He writes,

> Many African American environmentalists define ourselves by our concern for the urban environment. We have vigorously attacked white environmentalists for their concern with saving birds and forests and whales while urban children were suffering from lead paint poisoning. For me personally, the most spiritually uplifting part of the Summit was the opportunity it gave me to temper that thinking, and spend more time considering the need to protect the land for its own sake. This came about partly from meeting black ecologists from the south who are fighting to save black farmers from losing their land and to preserve traditional black communities such as the Georgia Sea Islands, which are threatened by resort development.
>
> But the most unique experience was the opportunity to interact with so many Native American and Hawaiian brothers and sisters and experience cultures that can only be understood in relationship to a piece of land or a body of water. Hearing Native Americans who have been oppressed since 1492 explain the need to protect "our brothers the whales," helped me to truly experience the moral imperative of protecting animals and trees and land.[23]

The multiracial dialogue afforded by the summit provided the opportunity for people of color groups to understand their historical and cultural differences, to see how they are similarly or differently positioned within colonial discourses of nature, and to begin to build a common environmental justice discourse that may embrace ideas as seemingly polarized as "whales as our brothers" and cities as ecologically sound environments.

Ruffins's testimony speaks to the point that cultural and historical differences in perceptions of nature and environment among people of color groups may be productive of, or militate against the formation of, environmental justice coalitions. He cited the summit as a moment when these multiple histories and cultures were able to unite in a collective conversation.

This process of community and coalition building for environmental justice may be similarly inspired when people of color groups share their different experiences of environmental oppression in everyday life. These may include experiences of racism, economic hardships, toxic poisoning affecting one's health or the health of one's children, and feelings of alienation from one's surroundings and sense of place. Colonial discourse of nature often emphasizes the problem of increased alienation from nature as a consequence of capitalist advancement. As we learned from Slater's and Cronon's essays, the construction of wilderness as Eden was necessary to ameliorate the problems of alienation, spiritual depletion, and corruption brought about by unrestrained capitalist greed.

Carl Anthony, director of the Urban Habitat Program of the Earth Island Institute, in San Francisco, writes about the forms of alienation that people of color, especially African Americans, have been made to suffer.[24] This alienation, he argues, is a result of a profound sense of loss suffered by many people who have been forced off their land and detached from their sense of place (like the Native Americans and Mexicans who were dispossessed of their land, or the Africans who were shipped to America on slave ships) or by those who, because of class and racial oppression, must live in the forsaken, highly polluted inner cities with "no functional relationship to non-human nature." He and others are interested in examining the nature of the psychological damage being done to inner-city youth when they compare their environment with the resplendent images normally associated with the American landscape.[25] For Anthony, reinventing human relationships with nature depends upon the production of what he calls a culturally and historically sensitive form of "ecopsychology"—an analytical method to understand how different groups' specific views of nature are central to human identity formation. The histories of racial and class oppression that underlie an inner-city dwelling person's "non-functional" relationship to nature, and the reality of living in an impoverished environment, would result in a form of alienation and notion of self that, according to Anthony, must be addressed in order for the ecological health of the local community and natural environment to be transformed.

Experiences of alienation from nature, from one's environment and sense of place, and the forms of identity that ensue, differ among various people of color communities. As numerous scholars of the environmental justice movement have shown, however, the framing of a collective experience of alienation and oppression often works to mobilize community activism.[26] Many activist members of the Western Shoshone, for example, invoke their cultural heritage in relation to their intergenerational connections to the land as the political motivation behind their decades-long struggle against the U.S. government's annexation of their ancestral ground for the Nevada Nuclear Weapons Test Site.[27] The experience of alienation and dispossession, in the case of the Western Shoshone's land-rights claims, constructs activist political identities. African Americans have different ties to the

North American landscape. As a result of historical and demographic patterns of industrial development and post-Reconstruction labor migration, they live in predominantly urban communities. As Anthony has argued, the "non-functional" relationship with nature that results from living in an impoverished, polluted environment may produce a disabling alienation that breeds hopelessness in local communities.

This is not, however, the only possible response to experiences of environmental injustice. Often the only *functional* relationship with nature for many city-dwelling people or those living near toxic waste sites becomes the core of their political strategy. In other words, their knowledge of the destruction of nature and natural systems in their local communities may function to mobilize them to act on these negative experiences. This knowledge often pits them against health department experts who would claim that there is nothing wrong with the environments in which they are living. But the community activists know otherwise—they often pay close attention to the changes they are living through as a result of toxic contamination of their environments. Many describe in great detail the profusion of respiratory illnesses, skin disorders, and cancers that they and their neighbors suffer. They talk about the increased miscarriages, stillbirths, deformities, pet deaths, deformities in animal births, plants that won't grow or that come up out of the earth in strange contortions, bad-smelling air, and foul-tasting water.[28] Such direct knowledge about changes in the environment, obtained through experience, is essential for the environmental justice movement's argument that people of color are often the ones who suffer the most from the effects of environmentally unsound industrial development.

Experiential knowledge of environmental degradation and toxic poisoning, and the community mobilization focusing on public health concerns that follows, is often, though not exclusively, an urban phenomenon. Industrial activity and its labor forces are concentrated in and around urban centers, as are most community organizations struggling for environmental justice. Because the overwhelming majority of African American, Latino, and Asian American communities in the United States are urbanized, the predicament of the "sustainable" city becomes one of the primary concerns of environmental justice activists.[29] Consequently, another one of the essential reinventions of nature that environmental justice activists highlight is the relationship of nature to the city—the constructed or built urban environment. Mainstream environmentalism generally describes the city as being in opposition to nature. As Michael Pollan has put it, the city is "written off as fallen, lost to nature, irredeemable."[30] In fact, many organizations, such as the Wilderness Society, the Nature Conservancy, and Not Yet New York, portray the large, modern, industrial city as a menacing, noxious sprawl of humanity representing the major threat to the survival of the natural world. The colonial discourse of nature has positioned cities as the repositories of waste, garbage, vermin, disease, and depravity—all features that, in colonial nature talk, are also associated with the people who must live there. Activists in the movement argue that attention to the social and ecological sustainability of cities is the key environmental issue of the late twentieth century, a sobering proposition considering that most mainstream environmental organizations and environmental studies programs in U.S. universities pay scant attention to the problems and potentials of the urban environment.[31] The Urban Habitat Program, a project of the San Francisco Bay area environmental justice group Earth Island Institute, warns,

> In the next decade, important decisions about the future of cities and surrounding agricultural land will have consequences for millions of people. The deteriorated infrastructure of urban areas must be rebuilt. There are hidden rewards for undertaking a program of rebuilding our urban cores in tune with nature. The investment of the billions of dollars that will be required offers a multitude of opportunities for fresh approaches to affordable housing, public services, resources and waste. There is room for small projects and for bringing wilderness back into the city.[32]

For those who live, work, and play in industrialized urban settings, largely populated by people of color, the current rhetoric of "cities in crisis" is much more than empty words. Environmental justice organizations enumerate the many ways that U.S. inner cities and their poor and low-income inhabitants are in peril, often using the language of "endangerment." The question of what (and who) counts as an endangered species is therefore another crucial aspect of the environmental justice movement's reconceptualization of the relationships between nonhuman and human nature and the emergence of new ideas of nature and new forms of environmentalism. Activists use the highly potent and provocative signifier "endangered species" in strategic ways. For example, the brochure published by San Francisco's Citizens for a Better Environment sets up a counterintuitive use of a mainstream, yet very controversial, environmental slogan.[33] On the front cover of the brochure, underneath the bold appeal "Save an Endangered Species . . . ," we see depicted a cheerful scene of mixed gender, multiracial community members busily working in a very fruitful community garden that appears to encircle the city where they live. The slogan continues inside and, surprisingly, identifies as its object of concern not an endangered "warm and fuzzy" animal or a spotted owl but ". . . YOU!" The text asserts, "When California's water, land or air is poisoned, it's not just fish and wildlife that are threatened. So are we. Our families, our neighborhoods, and our cities are all at risk from irresponsible toxic polluters and unenforced laws." The accompanying image portrays an army of concerned citizens forming an angry and determined barrier between the encroaching toxic polluters and their beloved, clean, and sustainable city. In this organizational brochure, Citizens for a Better Environment claims possession of the term "endangered species" in order to reinvent its limited use by mainstream environmentalists. The group shows that by focusing on a single

Save an Endangered Species . . .

"Save an Endangered Species: You!"
*(Courtesy Citizens for a Better Environment,
501 Second St., Suite 305, San Francisco, CA,
94107, 415-243-8980)*

you! . . .

When California's water, land or air is poisoned, it's not just fish and wildlife that are threatened.

So are we.

Our families, our neighborhoods, and our cities are all at risk from irresponsible toxic polluters and unenforced laws.

That's why Citizens for a Better Environment fights hard for you and your neighbor's right to a clean and healthy environment — where you live and where you work.

Our mission is to translate an ecological and democratic vision for California's future into tough, effective advocacy that prevents and reduces toxic pollution.

Since 1978, CBE's 30,000 members throughout California have helped support our research, legal and education staff in the Bay Area and in the Los Angeles Basin to prevent pollution at its source, enforce the law, and protect the health and well-being of all Californians.

CBE combines expert scientific research, effective legal action, sophisticated policy advocacy, and focused public education to bring about environmental reform — for all Californians.

Citizens for a Better Environment takes on the tough issues of toxic pollution of California's air, water and land — and we win.

It takes tough, skilled, visionary people to heal California's environment.

People like Citizens for a Better Environment.

And people like you.

Become a member of Citizens for a Better Environment now, and help . . .

. . . save an endangered species.

issue, such as the federal listing of an endangered species, mainstream environmentalists miss or obscure the many other related problems that contribute to environmental deterioration for all species, including people.

The anthropologist Stephen Feld critiques the notion of endangered species effectively in the liner notes for his CD *Voices of the Rainforest,* a recording of a day in the life of a Bosavi rain forest community in Papua New Guinea. Feld writes,

> When I read that we lose 15–20,000 species of plants and animals a year through the logging, ranching and mining that escalates rainforest destruction, my mind immediately begins to ponder how to possibly calculate the number of songs, myths, words, ideas, artifacts, techniques—all the cultural knowledge and practices lost per year in these mega-diversity zones. Massive wisdom, variations on human being in the form of knowledge in and of place: these are co-casualties in the eco-catastrophe. Eco-thinout may proceed at a rate much slower than cultural rubout, but accomplishment of the latter is a particularly effective way to accelerate the former. The politics of ecological and aesthetic co-evolution and co-devolution are one.[34]

His argument suggests that it is neither logical nor socially just for environmentalists to focus their efforts on decontextualized "endangered species," because of the profound historical interconnections among human and nonhuman species. Moreover, his analysis implies that an environmentalism that conceives of the notion of endangered as also encompassing human cultural systems would be significantly more vigorous and effective. The reconceptualization of the idea of endangered species to include specific human cultures, developed by Feld and Citizens for a Better Environment, implies the reinvention of the definition of a critical environmental issue and how it should be addressed by a more socially just environmental movement.

All of the foregoing reinventions advocated by environmental justice activists have in common their rejection of the philosophical tenet that I have labeled colonial nature talk, separating nature and culture, separating a nonhuman natural world and nonnatural human communities. The environmental justice movement, in challenging mainstream environmentalism, argues that an effective movement must integrate, not dichotomize, the histories and relationships of people and their natural environments. Most environmental justice activists' discussions of nature are balanced with an analysis of the impossibility of separating it from "life," from cultural histories, and from socially and ecologically destructive colonial and neocolonial experiences. Many activists point to the importance of thinking "ecosystemically," and not just focusing on single-issue environmentalism. They offer a framework that insists on making linkages among the multiple aspects of the ecosystem, including the biophysical environment, the built environment, and the social environment.[35] For these activists it is incomprehensible and inaccurate, as well as immoral, to separate them.

Ideas of nature, for environmental justice groups, are therefore tied closely to ideas of community, history, ethnic identity, and cultural survival, which include relationships to the land that express particular ways of life. The place—geographic, cultural, and emotional—where humans and environment converge is embodied in the ideas and practices of "community." One concept of community advances group identification with common histories, experiences and endurances of oppression, whether racial, ethnic, gender based, or socioeconomic. This view of community is often said, in the language of social science, to represent a "unity of sameness." In other words, those whom we identify as members of our community we recognize as having similar or identical features. Other, less anthropocentric and, some would argue, less conservative[36] conceptions of community exist, however, and emphasize the notion of "unity in difference."[37] This idea of community presupposes connection to and interconnectedness with other groups, other species, and the natural environment through everyday experiences with family, comradeship, and work. The cultural theorists Laurie Anne Whitt and Jennifer Daryl Slack argue that communities should be understood as "sites where the human and other than human are drawn together in multiple articulations."[38] They propose the term "mixed communities" to signify the relations of interdependence that inhere in geographically diverse "mixed species" (human and nonhuman) assemblages. An environment contextualizes a particular mixed community, "situating it within and bonding it to both the natural world and the larger 'containing society,' "[39] Communities and environments are therefore conjoined and must be understood as being mutually constitutive. Whitt and Slack continue,

> Communities, then, are as much results as they are causes of their own environments. One practical political consequence of this is that discussions of development cannot proceed reductively, by divorcing communities from their material contexts. Mixed communities and their constitutive environments are inseparable; they are the unit of development and of change. All development is, for better or for worse, co-development of communities and environments. And the relation between a particular community and its environment "is not simply one of interaction of internal and external factors, but of a dialectical development" . . . of community and environment in response to one another.[40]

Environmental justice activists express their involvement with their natural environments as "community" or "mixed community" in the terms of living, working, and playing. This may include the diverse urban community projects organized by the San Francisco Bay Area "People of Color Greening Network." The Greening Network sponsors various urban environmental initiatives, such as creek restoration, farmers markets, and gardening projects in the local prisons. One venture of this sort is led by Trevor Burrowes and the East Palo Alto–Historical Agricultural Society, which reintroduces African American communities to their "agricultural heritage" through the cultivation of healthy, organic food in an urban setting. According to Burrowes, this is a direct way to confront and transform the "non-functional" relationship to nature suffered by inner-city African American communities. The community/environment "unity in difference" concept is also demonstrated in a community revitalization project, "The Great Los Angeles Gutter Clean-Up and Graffiti Paint-Out," subheaded "Healing Ourselves, Our Community, Our Earth," sponsored, in part, by Concerned Citizens of South Central Los Angeles and reaching out to the entire city of Los Angeles as an "imagined" community writ large. Community members work together to paint out graffiti and toss trash and toxins out of gutters, streets and alleys to clean up neighborhoods and prevent pollution from reaching our beaches." Transforming the environment in which one lives, according to these activists, extends a sense of alliance and connection far beyond the boundaries of one's local habitat. This sentiment is reflected in remarks made by Robin Cannon during the battle against LANCER, when Concerned Citizens was joined by other women activists from different racial and class backgrounds all across Los Angeles: "I didn't know we all had so many things in common . . . millions of people in the city had something in common with us . . . the environment."[41]

Barbara Lynch has argued, in an article examining ideas of nature, community, and environmentalism shared by Latinos living in the United States, that the relationship with nature for these cultural groups has always been associated with an understanding of community. She writes of Dominican Astin Jacobo's Crotona Community Coalition, which reclaims redlined housing and empty lots in the South Bronx, transforming them into community gardens to plant corn, tomatoes, beans, and garlic, thereby re-creating a small inner-city Cibao (the Dominican Republic's agricultural heartland).[42] She also tells of Puerto Ricans living in New York, such as Dona Licha, who speak of their relationship with the sea and fishing as central to life itself and who feel that their lives are endangered because of declining fish populations and the increasing pollution of New York's coastal waters. Fishing, for New York Puerto Ricans, also represents a relationship to community, one they feel is jeopardized by recent New York State restrictions on the recreational catch. According to Lynch, although these Latino communities support conservation efforts, they are concerned that state restrictions on activities such as fishing "will deprive them of an opportunity for contact with nature by restricting their ability to use the catch as an occasion for generosity to family, friends, and neighbors."[43] Lynch argues that both ideas and experiences of nature, inherent in "the garden and the sea" for U.S. Latinos, are manifest through and firmly rooted in community, and not only an expression of community as "sameness." Specific cultural groups, be they Puerto Ricans in New York, Chicanas in East Los Angeles, or Salvadorans in the San Francisco Bay Area, have built environmental coalitions, such as the Mothers of East LA, El Pueblo para el Aire y Agua Limpio in Kettleman City, and the El Puente Toxic Avengers in Pennsylvania, both in the United States and across the border with Mexico. Once again, we see relationships with nature and the environment converging with social justice considerations, and activated through ideas and practices of "community," as the essential feature of environmental justice organizations in the United States.

How could knowledge of these specific "inventions" of nature, which intimately associate it with everyday social and cultural life, inform a more inclusive and effective environmental movement? Moreover, in what ways can the environmental justice activists' reconceptualizations of the social and ecological connections between communities and environments help bridge the conceptual gap that splits humans from nature and likewise separates environmental from social justice concerns? Scholars of environmental justice such as Lynch, Whitt, and Slack, Devon Pena, Robert Gottlieb, Cynthia Hamilton, and Laura Pulido, among many others, make the argument that for people of color in the United States nature is located in many cultural histories, including painful histories of colonialism, and is tightly linked to alienating experiences of oppression, yet also to the experiences of affinity and partnership building that obtain in community. Their scholarship, together with the extensive political organization and insights of grassroots environmental justice organizations such as Concerned Citizens, the Center for Community Action and Environmental Justice, and El Pueblo para el Aire y Agua Limpio, offer clues about ways of unearthing existing inventions of nature that emerge not from mainstream nature talk but from other cultural histories that could offer a rich source for grounding new multicultural environmentalisms.

Universal Donors in a Vampire Culture: It's All in the Family: Biological Kinship Categories in the Twentieth-Century United States

Donna J. Haraway

If the human face is "the masterpiece of God" it is here then in a thousand fateful registrations.

—Carl Sandburg[1]

RACE IS A FRACTURING TRAUMA IN THE BODY POLITIC OF THE NATION—AND in the mortal bodies of its people. Race kills, liberally and unequally; and race privileges, unspeakably and abundantly. Like nature, race has much to answer for; and the meter is still running for both categories. Race, like nature, is at the heart of stories about the origins and purposes of the nation. Race, at once an uncanny irreality and an inescapable presence, frightens me; and I am not alone in this paralyzing historical pathology of body and soul. Like nature, race is the kind of category that leaves no one neutral, no one unscathed, no one sure of his or her ground, if there is a ground. Race is a peculiar kind of object of knowledge and practice. The meanings of the word are unstable and protean; the status of the word's referent has wobbled from being considered real and rooted in the natural, physical body to being considered illusory and utterly socially constructed. In the United States race immediately evokes the grammars of purity and mixing, compounding and differentiating, segregating and bonding, lynching and marrying. Race, like nature and sex, is replete with all the rituals of guilt and innocence in the stories of nation, family, and species. Race, like nature, is about roots,

321

pollution, and origins. Inherently doubtful, race, like sex, is about the purity of lineage, the legitimacy of passage, and the drama of inheritance of bodies, property, and stories. I believe that, like nature, race haunts those of us who call ourselves Americans. All of our rational denials only deepen the suppurating puncture wound of the racialized history, past and present.

Inheriting the whirlwind it sowed as founding seeds, in slavery, dispossession, and genocide, as well as in immigration, democracy, and liberty, the Republic of the United States is a society consumed with racial purity and racial denial. Therefore, the United States is also replete with fascination with racial mixing and racial difference. Fascination with mixing and unity is a symptom of preoccupation with purity and decomposition. And like any expanding capitalist society that must continually destroy what it builds and feed off of every being it perceives as natural—if its strategies of accumulation of wealth are to continue to push the envelope of catastrophe—the United States is consumed with images of decadence, obsolescence, and corruption of kind. No wonder its natural parks and its stories of gardens and wilderness have been more therapeutically crucial to nursing national innocence than any of its other civic sacraments.

As a middle-class, professional, white woman in the United States, who is riveted by fascination with the fungal web of nature, nation, sex, race, and blood in U.S. history, I write behind a disavowal, an incantation, an alibi, a tic or symptom. Behind a list of personal, qualifying adjectives—white, Christian, apostate, professional, childless, middle-class, middle-aged, biologist, cultural theorist, historian, U.S. citizen, late-twentieth-century, female—I write about the universal; that is, about "the human." The human is the category that makes a luminous promise to transcend the rending trauma of the particular, especially that particular non-thing and haunt called race. Like all symptoms, my neurotic listing makes a false promise to protect me from category confusion, from the irrational fear that drives the tic, from corruption.

Lurching beyond the symptom in the first paragraphs, however, I acknowledge that a specific figure animates this essay. The figure is the vampire: the one who pollutes lineages on the wedding night; the one that effects category transformations by illegitimate passages of substance; the one who drinks and infuses blood in a paradigmatic act of infecting whatever poses as pure; the one that eschews sun worship and does its work at night; the one who is undead, unnatural, and perversely incorruptible. In this essay, I am instructed by the vampire; and my questions are about the vectors of infection that trouble racial categories in twentieth-century bioscientific constructions of universal humanity. I think vampires can be vectors of category transformation in a racialized, historical, national unconscious. A figure that both promises and threatens racial and sexual mixing, the vampire feeds off of the normalized human; and the monster finds such contaminated food to be nutritious. The vampire also insists on the nightmare of racial violence behind the fantasy of purity in the rituals of kinship.[2]

I approach the universal through a particular discourse, the science of biology. Biology's epistemological and technical task has been to produce a historically specific kind of human unity: namely, membership in a single species, the human race, *Homo sapiens*. Biology discursively establishes and performs what will count as human in powerful domains of knowledge and technique. A striking product of early biological discourse, race, like sex and nature, is about the apparatuses for fabricating and distributing life and death in the modern regimes of biopower. Like nature and sex, at least from the nineteenth century on, race was constituted as an object of knowledge by the life sciences, especially biology, physical anthropology, and medicine. The institutions, research projects, measuring instruments, publication practices, and circuits of money and people that made up the life sciences were the machine tools that crafted "race" as an object of scientific knowledge over the last two hundred years. Then, in the middle of the twentieth century, the biological and medical sciences began to disown their deadly achievement and worked like Sisyphus to roll the rock of race out of the upscale hillside neighborhoods being built in post–World War II's prosperous times to house the new categories of good natural science. All too predictably, the new universals, like the suburbs and the laboratories, were all too white.

Biology is not the body itself, but a discourse on the body. "My biology," a common expression in daily life for members of the U.S. white middle class, is not the juicy and mortal flesh itself, but a linguistic sign for a complex structure of belief and practice, through which I and many of my fellow citizens organize a great deal of life. Biology is also not a culture-free universal discourse, for all that it has considerable cultural, economic, and technical power to establish what will count as nature throughout the planet Earth. Biology is not everyone's discourse about human, animal, and vegetable flesh, life, and nature; indeed, "flesh," "life," and "nature" are no less rooted in specific histories, practices, languages, and peoples than "biology" itself. Biologists are not ventriloquists speaking for Earth itself and all its inhabitants, reporting on what organic life really is in all its evolved diversity and DNA-soaked order. No natural object-world speaks its metaphor-free and story-free truth through the sober objectivity of culture-free and so universal science. Biology is also not a discourse that reaches back into the mists of time, to Aristotle or beyond. It is, rather, a complex web of practices that emerged over the last two hundred years or so, mainly in what gets called the West, in the midst of major inventions and reworkings of categories of nation, family, type, civility, species, sex, humanity, nature, and, race. Now a global discourse like the other natural sciences, biology is also a knowledge-producing practice that I value, want to participate in and make better, and believe to be culturally, politically, and epistemologically important. It matters to contest for a livable biology, as for a livable nature.

Both contestations require that we think long and hard about the permutations of racial discourse in the life sciences in this century. This paper is a small contribution to that end.

In the United States in the twentieth century, the categories of biology often become universal donors in the circulatory systems of meanings and practices that link the family, state, commerce, nature, entertainment, education, and industry. Apparently culture-free categories are like type O⁻ blood; without a marker indicating their origin, they travel into many kinds of bodies. Transfused into the body politic, these categories shape what millions of people consider common sense in thinking about human nature. In this essay I will pay attention to three twentieth-century configurations of bioscientific thinking about the categories of unity and difference that constitute the human species. Claiming to be troubled by clear and distinct categories, I will nonetheless nervously work with a wordy chart, a crude taxonomic device to keep my columns neatly divided and my rows suggestively linked.

Table 1 is an effort to chart twentieth-century biological kinship categories that I believe are critical in racial discourse in the U.S. professional middle classes, but the categories have power far beyond those circles. The chart deliberately emphasizes U.S. views of the world linked to elite scientific culture. Like any such taxonomic device, the chart emphasizes *related* discontinuities across its columns, placing into distinct periods what from other points of view could appear on a continuum or, alternatively, seem to be completely unconnected. Contentious homologies, as well as divisions, are suggested by placing objects across from each other within columns. Many other practices besides biology—like prisons, welfare systems, real estate policy, schools, youth culture, child-raising patterns, and labor markets—are potent constructors of race and kinship. Table 1, however, monomaniacally pursues its suspicions from the foundation of its periodization and its associated "key objects of knowledge": race, population, and genome. I have chosen three broad time divisions—1900 to about 1940, 1940 to somewhere in the 1970s, about 1975 into the 1990s—because I think national and international, technological, laboratory, clinical, field, political, economic, and cultural transformations within these temporal patterns have been intrinsic to the processes that reshaped biological discourse about human unity and diversity, producing mutations that merit attention.

Of course, practices, ideas, and institutions spill from one period into the next, but I think "real world" patterns of power and authority shift within the paradigmatic configurations detailed in the rows within each period. Also, many other practices, ideas, and institutions fill these time periods, but find no place on this chart. A paradigmatic category for some communities of practice is contested by other communities; and from various points of view, what looks like a paradigm to me could look trivial or just wrong. Learning how to get at point of view in constructing and using a chart is part of my purpose. Unlike a perspective drawing that geometrically con-

TABLE 1

Universal Donors in a Vampire Culture: Twentieth-Century U.S. Biological Kinship Categories

Dates	1900–1930s	1940–1970s	1975–1990s
Key Object of Knowledge	race	population	genome
Family portrait	gorilla diorama, American Museum of Natural History, 1936	*Fossil Footprint Makers of Laetoli*, painting by Jay Matternes, 1979	SinEve and matrix of morphed progeny, *Time* magazine, 1993
Data objects	tree genealogies, taxonomies	gene frequencies	genetic databases
Paradigmatic technical practice	craniometry	measure ABO blood marker frequencies	genetic mapping DNA analysis by polymerase chain reaction (PCR) and restriction fragment length polymorphism (RFLP)
Evolutionary paradigm	typological paradigm Spencerian versions of Darwinism William Z. Ripley, *The Races of Europe*, 1899 Franklin H. Giddings, Social Marking System, 1910	populationist paradigm neo-Darwinian evolutionary synthesis Theodosius Dobzhansky, *Genetics and the Origin of Species*, 1937 G. G. Simpson, *The Major Features of Evolution*, 1953 James D. Watson, *Molecular Biology of the Gene*, 1965	sociobiological neo-Darwinist paradigm unit of selection debates (gene, organism, population) E. O. Wilson, *Sociobiology, the New Synthesis*, 1975 Richard Dawkins, *The Selfish Gene*, 1976; *Extended Phenotype*, 1982

TABLE 1

Universal Donors in a Vampire Culture: Twentieth-Century U.S. Biological Kinship Categories

Dates	1900–1930s	1940–1970s	1975–1990s
Key Object of Knowledge	race	population	genome
Family portrait	gorilla diorama, American Museum of Natural History, 1936	*Fossil Footprint Makers of Laetoli*, painting by Jay Matternes, 1979	SimEve and matrix of morphed progeny, *Time* magazine, 1993
Pedagogical practice	Biology is established in high schools nationally. Hygiene and eugenics are closely linked. By 1928, 20,000 U.S. college students are enrolled in 376 courses in eugenics.	UNESCO race statements, by evolutionary biologists, appear in 1950 and 1951. The New Physical Anthropology guides research and teaching. Biological Sciences Curriculum Study (BSCS) revised curriculum is introduced. The context is scientific competition of the Cold War.	Biodiversity and biotechnology are closely linked in humanist and environmentalist ideologies, international conventions, and pedagogy. *Advances in Genetic Technology* (1989) is a new BSCS high school biotechnology text. The context is international corporate high-tech competitiveness. Corporations fund high school biology laboratories to teach biotechnology.
Ethical discourse on human heredity	Eugenic marriage counseling and eugenic sterilization are urged.	Medical genetic counseling emerges for a growing list of genetic diseases.	Bioethics becomes a regulatory industry of its own.

Status of race as epistemological object in science and popular culture	Race is real and fundamental in both areas.	Race is an illusory object constructed by bad science. Race remains prominent in many domains of culture, social science, and politics. Nazi genocidal practices are strong in public memory and mute many aspects of racial policies. At the same time, apartheid flourishes in many forms.	Race reemerges in medical discourse on organ transplants and drug testing. Race is hotly contentious in cultural, political, and community struggles. Race is a fashion accessory for *United Colours of Benetton*. Ethnic cleansing and race-based immigration restriction reemerge globally.
Rhetorics of unity and diversity	family trees Model eugenic families compete at state fairs. H. H. Goddard, *The Kallikak Family*, 1912 C. B. Davenport, *The Trait Book*, 1912	universal family of man Kalahari desert !Kung hunter-gatherers are the model for man. Films: *The Hunters*, 1957 *The Making of Mankind III: the Human Way of Life*, 1982	Human Genome Project (Man™) Human Genome Diversity Project System dynamics modeling of sub-Saharan pastoralists becomes biosocial paradigm. Amazon forest people (e.g., the Kayapó) are popular paradigms of indigenous cultural and biodiversity discourses and of indigenous transnational commercial and technological savvy.
Ideal of progress	Everything moves in stages from primitive to civilized. Hierarchy is natural at all levels of organization.	The universal sharing way of life is at the origin. System management should produce cooperation.	Multiculturalism and networking are ideologically dominant in sciences, businesses, and liberal political practice.

TABLE 1

Universal Donors in a Vampire Culture: Twentieth-Century U.S. Biological Kinship Categories

Dates	1900–1930s	1940–1970s	1975–1990s
Key Object of Knowledge	race	population	genome
Family portrait	gorilla diorama, American Museum of Natural History, 1936	*Fossil Footprint Makers of Laetoli*, painting by Jay Matternes, 1979	SimEve and matrix of morphed progeny, *Time* magazine, 1993
Symbolic and technical status of blood	Blood = kinship = race/family/culture. Blood and gene are one. Blood and culture closely tied. ABO markers constructed, 1908. Landsteiner Nobel Price in 1930; Rh factors follow. Blood, culture, language, race, nature, and land are tightly linked.	Gene/blood and culture tie is broken. Blood is the key fluid studied for gene frequencies. The gene begins to displace blood/race in discourses of human diversity. ABO system is elaborated. First heart transplant is in 1967.	Blood is merely the tissue for getting easy DNA samples. The genome largely displaces blood symbolically and technically. Synthetic blood and autotransfusions are ideal. Baboon-human heart transplant is in 1990
Diseases of the "blood"	"Bad blood" covers venereal disease generally (e.g., syphilis).	Hemoglobinopathies (e.g., sickle-cell anemia) are studied. Research expands on genetics of diverse human hemoglobins.	New diseases are interpreted as communication and information transfer pathologies (e.g., AIDS). Fear of infected blood is rampant.
Paradigmatic pathology	decadence, rotting, infection tuberculosis	obsolescence, stress, overload	defective gene, errors in the database immunological breakdown

Prophylaxis	vaccination and public health Infection control is boundary maintenance.	system engineering and management	technical enhancement and system redesign Boundary crossing seems more interesting than boundary maintenance.
Meaning of the gene	Gene/blood are linked to race and nature.	Gene = information equation emerges. Notion of life as an information system is consolidated. The gene is the sign of the universal. Genetic and cultural diversity discourses are separated.	Gene = information is infinitely elaborated. Information = communication. Informatics and genomics converge. Genetic and cultural diversity discourses are conflated.
"The family"	Focus is on the natural heterosexual reproductive family. Miscegenation is biological pathology. Kinship is perceived to stem from blood.	Focus is on the natural heterosexual reproductive family. Intermarriage is biologically normal.	New reproductive technologies dominate scientific, legal, and popular attention. The first "test tube baby" is born in 1978. The status of heterosexuality and many reproductive practices is unstable. artifactual families morphing
Relation to industrial technologies and scientific ideologies	Organicism and mechanism are believed to be oppositional and distinct. Boundaries between the living and nonliving seem secure.	Cybernetics becomes popular discourse in the 1950s and 1960s. Cyborgs are named in 1960 in the context of the space race. Interfaced cybernetic/organic systems in military and civilian technologies, e.g., numerical-controlled machine tools, are developed.	Cyborgs proliferate in business, military, popular culture, technoscience, and interdisciplinary theory. Cyborgs become second-order cyberspace beings in the 1980s. Gaia hypothesis is named in 1969. Artificial-life research emerges in the 1980s.

TABLE 1

Universal Donors in a Vampire Culture: Twentieth-Century U.S. Biological Kinship Categories

Dates	1900–1930s	1940–1970s	1975–1990s
Key Object of Knowledge	race	population	genome
Family portrait	gorilla diorama, American Museum of Natural History, 1936	*Fossil Footprint Makers of Laetoli*, painting by Jay Matternes, 1979	SimEve and matrix of morphed progeny, *Time* magazine, 1993
Legal and political documents	Eugenic sterilization laws are passed by thirty state legislatures in the U.S. in the period 1907–31. U.S. National Origins Act of 1924 restricts immigration by racial logic.	UNESCO statements on race, 1950, 1951, are written from point of view of population genetics and modern evolutionary synthesis.	The Biological Diversity Convention, NAFTA, GATT, and the World Trade Organization include provisions on patenting biological materials. First World–Third World struggles over biodiversity intensify. Biodiversity erosion is an official international emergency. Indigenous peoples (e.g., the Guaymi of Panama) contest patenting of human genes and organize to repatriate their genetic material from the American Type Culture Collection and other First World genomic/informatic databanks.

Research institutions for human unity and diversity	Cold Spring Harbor Eugenics Records Office	Wenner Gren Foundation's Early Man in Africa research program Multidisciplinary, international, team research in paleoanthropology	GenBank© U.S. Human Genome Project Human Genome Diversity Project HUGO in Europe
Photographic documents of humanity and earth	Eugenic and dysgenic facial portraiture and racial types Panoramic nature photography, 1920	*Family of Man*, Museum of Modern Art, 1955 NASA photos of the Whole Earth, 1969	*The Multicultural Planet*, UNESCO, 1994 LANDSAT photographic mapping
Discourse of relation to other species	Species are defined by interbreeding block.	Interest is in gene flow among populations within species. Separate species are maintained in nature.	Nature is a genetic engineer that continually exchanges, modifies, and invents new genes across various barriers. Viruses are information vectors that link us all.
Model of nature	The community (organismic) model frames study of species associations and successions through time. The University of Chicago school of ecology is dominant. F. Clements and V. Shelford, *Bio-Ecology*, 1939 W. C. Allee et al., *The Principles of Animal Ecology*, 1949	The ecosystem (cybernetic) model frames study of radioactive isotopes and energy flows traced through trophic levels. Systems dynamics modeling techniques emerge in business and biology. The Odum school of ecology is prominent. Eugene Odum, *Fundamentals of Ecology*, 1959 D. H. Meadows et al., *Limits to Growth*, 1972	Simulated and global ecosystems are prominent in research. Database and informatics development are critical to models of nature. Geographic information systems (GIS) reorganize research and policy practice. E. O. Wilson, ed., *Biodiversity* (1988) Gaia hypothesis and artificial-life research are foundation of SimEarth and SimLife games of the Maxis Corporation.

TABLE 1

Universal Donors in a Vampire Culture: Twentieth-Century U.S. Biological Kinship Categories

Dates	1900–1930s	1940–1970s	1975–1990s
Key Object of Knowledge	race	population	genome
Family portrait	gorilla diorama, American Museum of Natural History, 1936	*Fossil Footprint Makers of Laetoli*, painting by Jay Matternes, 1979	SimEve and matrix of morphed progeny, *Time magazine*, 1993
Preservationist practice	colonial and national park system Parc Albert in the Belgian Congo	postcolonial park management Serengeti in Tanzania	Global environmental regulation debates are dominated by Northern Hemisphere powers. Rain Forest Reserves biodiversity banking ecotourism debt for nature swaps
Popular images of apes	Tarzan is raised by Kala, his ape mother, and fights the powerful rival male ape, Terkoz. E. R. Burroughs, *Tarzan of the Apes*, 1914	Jane Goodall goes to Gombe to live in nature with the wild chimpanzees. Jane Goodall, *In the Shadow of Man*, 1971	Koko, the sign language–using gorilla in the Silicon Valley, tries to get pregnant with IVF. F. Patterson and E. Linden, *The Education of Koko*, 1981
Paradigms of gardening and landscape architecture	U.S.: Wilhelm Miller, "The Prairie Spirit in Landscape Gardening" on Jens Jensen's designs for the "wild" and "natural" garden Germany: the "natural garden"	Ecological planning emerges in urban design. New Towns, Houston, Tex., "the Woodlands" Ian McHarg, *Design with Nature*	Virtual landscape planning emerges. Martha Schwartz's "Splice Garden" is built on the Whitehead Institute roof, Cambridge, Mass.

Icons of genetic achievement	Mendelian genetics, pure types standardized egg and poultry breeding and marketing.	hybridized seed and animals Green Revolution "miracle" seeds	transgenic plants and animals herbicide-resistant crops
Major institutions for plant and animal genetic research	Agricultural research stations and U.S. land grant universities University basic research (Morgan fruit fly lab at Columbia)	Foundation-funded research institutes for breeding High Response Varieties Mexico: Centro Internacional del Mejoramiento del Maíz y Trigo, 1966 Philippines: International Rice Research Institute, 1960 World Bank–launched Consultative Group on International Agricultural Research, 1970 Major science universities develop genetic research. The National Seed Storage Laboratory, first U.S. national gene bank, is established, Fort Collins, Colo., 1959.	Transnational corporations, foundations, international financial institutions, national science policy, and major science universities all participate in international corporatization of genetics, molecular biology, and biotechnology. Global network of gene banks is consolidated. Third World charges intensify that the First World collects diversity, disregarding local expertise or treating it as a natural resource, and produces homogeneity in standardized commodities.
Popular images inside political ideology	American Museum of Natural History big-game dioramas Teddy Bear Patriarchy (Theodore Roosevelt–style Progressive Era reform through expertise)	Man the Hunter and the first family civil rights movement United Nations humanism (20th-century Bridgewater Treatises)	sociobiological reproductive investment strategists in nature *United Colours of Benetton* multiculturalism
Icons of national and international discourse	*Birth of a Nation* (D. W. Griffith film, 1915)	*The Family of Man*, 1955, Museum of Modern Art Cold War blocs and multinational organizations reshape official national ideologies.	"Rebirthing of a Nation" is featured in *Time* magazine 1993 special issue on immigration. Context is transnationalism, the New World Order, and multicul-

TABLE 1

Universal Donors in a Vampire Culture: Twentieth-Century U.S. Biological Kinship Categories

Dates	1900–1930s	1940–1970s	1975–1990s
Key Object of Knowledge	race	population	genome
Family portrait	gorilla diorama, American Museum of Natural History, 1936	Fossil Footprint Makers of Laetoli, painting by Jay Matternes, 1979	SimEve and matrix of morphed progeny, Time magazine, 1993
		United Nations Food and Agriculture Organization World Health Organization UNESCO World Bank (Bretton Woods, 1944) International Monetary Fund (1945)	turalism as dominant ideologies and practices.
Economic discourse	Fordist modernity monopoly capital modern corporation	Fordist modernity in a multinational vein U.S. is hegemonic in the post–WWII economic order. Militarized economy is driven by the Cold War.	flexible postmodernity New World Order, Inc., is unfettered from Cold War contests. Transnational capital elaborates strategies of flexible accumulation. Structural adjustment dominates aid and development policy.

Signs of scientific power as transgression and transcendence	airplane telephone	transuranic elements (plutonium, 1940) first nuclear bombs, Little Boy and Fat Man	transgenic organisms FlavrSavr Tomato, OncoMouse™
Instructions on how to act around aliens	H. G. Wells, *War of the Worlds*, 1898; radio dramatization by Orson Welles, 1938	*The Day the Earth Stood Still*, 1951 *2001: A Space Odyssey*, 1968	*Alien*, 1979 *Aliens*, 1986 *Alien³*, 1992 *Alienⁿ*, forthcoming
Feminist instructions on how to act around aliens	Charlotte Perkins Gilman, *Herland*, 1915	Ursula LeGuin, *The Left Hand of Darkness*, 1969 Joanna Russ, *The Female Man*, 1975	Octavia Butler, Xenogenesis Trilogy, 1987–89 Marge Piercy, *He, She, and It*, 1991
Animation technology	Muybridge 19th-century stop-action techniques	Walt Disney Studios, *Fantasia* and *Pinocchio*, 1940	Industrial Light and Magic computer-generated graphics, esp. morphing: *Terminator 2*, 1991; *Jurassic Park*, 1993

structs the unique point from which to see into the composition, Table 1 invites the reader to evaluate contending locations as an intrinsic aspect of participating in scientific culture on the charged topics of race, sex, and nature. One way to do this is to make the chart into a narrative device; that is, to use it to construct a story. Stories are not "fictions" in the sense of "made up." Rather, narratives are devices to produce certain kinds of meaning. I try to use stories to tell what I think is the truth—a located, embodied, contingent, and, therefore, real truth.

My chart does *not* argue that "forces" like political developments "influenced" biology from the "outside," or vice versa; nor does it imply that life science, or anything else, is the summation of its determinations. Biology is complex cultural practice, engaged by real people, not bundles of determinations just waiting for the analyst's clever discovery. Biology might be politics by other means, but the means are specific to the located practice of the life sciences. These means are usually more about things like genes, graphs, and blood than about legislatures or supposed social interests of scientists.

The relationships that are insistently urged by the proliferation of rows inside each period could seem perversely arbitrary, linking not just apples and oranges but gardens and genes, vampires and Nobel Prize winners, or masterful DNA and frivolous fashion magazines. I think such odd bedfellows are linked, but I often stutter in naming *how* they are tied together. The stutter is an incitement to work out the trouble, not to pass over the complexities of worlds of discourse by hygienic category separation. The luxuriating rows are meant to invite the reader to add or subtract, to alter what is inside the boxes, to explore geometries of relationship that more restrained meaning-making devices might make look foolish. I do not think the rows within columns are linked by the conventions of cause and effect, but they are not just random free associations either. Yet I know from my own relationship to this chart, as well as that of colleagues who have commented on its various drafts, that it induces a kind of generative dream state. The chart, like any residue of semiosis, could be read as a symptom. But the reader would have to decide, take a stand on, what the symptom is *of.* That is simultaneously a political, cultural, and scientific question. From a biological point of view, symptoms point to functioning, or malfunctioning, bodies and processes that might otherwise be invisible.

The best metaphor, and technical device, for representing the kind of relationality implicit in this chart might be hypertext. In hypertext, readers are led through, and can construct for themselves and interactively with others, webs of connections held together by heterogeneous sorts of glues. Pathways through the web are not predetermined, but show their tendentiousness, their purposes, their strengths, and their peculiarities. Engaging in the epistemological and political game of hypertext commits its users to the search for relationships in a fungus-like mangrove or aspen forest, where before there seemed to be neat exclusions and genetically distinct, single-trunk trees. I think part of the work of interrogating racial discourse—or any discourse—is learning how to represent both relationality and the "ontological" status of categories provocatively. Failing to produce an actual hypertext for this essay, I hope that the old-fashioned, clumsy, two-dimensional, pencil-and-paper chart (done, of course, on a computer generally available to people like me in the so-called First World) might ironically prove able to subvert the monological, conventional oppositions of cause and effect versus randomness. I rely on the reader to act like a savvy hypertext user by making jumps, connections, and multiple pathways through Table 1.

I like the idea of using a truly monological object like a chart, and not some timely fractal design, to figure nonlinear, dynamic relationships. If it is successful, the chart undoes charting, as a vampire undoes the family tree and its genealogical method. I also like to use the blunt, in-your-face quality of entries in a chart to provoke questions about the contextual conditions of existence for any category. It keeps the *contingency* of our meaning-making devices up front, even while we, laughing a little nervously, use them to do work we care about. That seems especially important to me when trying to work with molten, explosive categories like race, sex, or nature, much less all three such bombs together. Finally, there is nothing like the metaphor of hypertext for reinforcing the class, ethnic, and professional bias of the chart. Who, after all, figures the ability to read complex networks of relationality as hypertext?

So, a chart like this is a rhetorical instrument, a kind of argument, a technology of persuasion, or, more simply, a device to think with. I want my readers to ask if the chart works and what it works *for*. As my argument unfolds, I will detail some of the consequences of this taxonomic excursion. Space does not allow me to go systematically through the chart, or even to identify all of its entries. Various readers will bring different kinds of expertise to Table 1 and make more or less sense of—and quibble with—different parts of it. I think that this is inevitable with any text and also a good thing, not the mark of deficiency of author or reader. I want the chart to work like an echo chamber or a diffraction grid, producing wave interferences that make many kinds of patterns on the active recording neural tissues of readers. Still, inescapably, from various points of entry, some of the chart will seem self-evident, some obscure, some properly explained. I hope the readers will use the chart to provoke and explore, and not be repelled by the unknown regions, the obvious parts, or my errors.

Leaving most categories in the chart to fend for themselves, I will work to control one braided narrative line. The story resonates from images of racialized faces, which are taut membranes stretched across the scaffolding of accounts of conjoined biological and technological evolution. The story moves from the primal ape family, rebirthed by taxidermy in the dioramas of the American Museum of Natural History in New York City in the 1930s; to the universal first family seen in the 1960s to be living its sharing way of life on the African savanna at the dawn of the human species; to the computer-generated, multicultural SimEve in *Time* magazine's New Face of America of the 1990s. I will try to show how the mutations of bioscientific categories from race, to population, to genome code for what can count as human, and therefore as progressive, in the civic and personal bodies of twentieth-century U.S. Americans.

I. Race

THE STARTING POINT FOR MY STORY IS THE RACIAL DISCOURSE IN PLACE AT the end of the nineteenth century in Europe and the United States. As the historian George Stocking put it, " 'blood' was for many a solvent in which all problems were dissolved and processes commingled." "Race" meant the "accumulated cultural differences carried somehow in the blood."[3] The emphasis was on "somehow"; for blood proved a very expansible and inclusive fluid. Four major discursive streams poured into the caldron in which racial discourse simmered well into the early decades of the twentieth century, including the ethnological, Lamarckian, polygenist, and evolutionist traditions. For each approach the essential idea was the linkages of lineage and kinship. No great distinction could be maintained between linguistic, national, familial, and physical resonances implied by the terms "kinship" and "race." Blood ties were the proteinaceous threads extruded by the physical and historical passage of substance from one generation to the next, forming the great, nested, organic collectives of the human family. In that process, where race was, sex was also. And where race and sex were, worries about hygiene, decadence, health, and organic efficiency occupied the best minds of the age, or at least the best published.

These same minds were uniformly concerned about the problems of progress and hierarchy. Organic rank and stage of culture from primitive to civilized were at the heart of evolutionary biology, medicine, and anthropology. The existence of progress, efficiency, and hierarchy were not in question scientifically, only their proper representation in natural-social dramas, where race was the narrative colloid or matrix left when blood congealed. The plenum of universal organic evolution, reaching from ape to modern European, with all the races and sexes properly arrayed between, was filled with the bodies and measuring instruments proper to the life sciences. Craniometry and the examination of sexual/reproductive materials both focused on the chief organs of mental and generative life, which were the keys to organic social efficiency. Brains were also sexual tissues, and reproductive organs were also mental structures. Furthermore, the face revealed what the brain and the gonad ordained; diagnostic photography showed as much. The evolution of language, the progress of technology, the perfection of the body, and the advance of social forms seemed to be aspects of the same fundamental human science. That science was constitutively physiological and hierarchical, organismic and wholist, progressivist and developmental.

To be sure, in the early twentieth century Franz Boas and social-cultural anthropology broadly were laying the foundations of a different epistemological order for thinking about race. But, encompassing immigration policy, mental health assessments, military conscription, labor patterns, nature conservation, museum design, school and university curricula, penal practices, field studies of both wild and laboratory animals, literary evaluation, the music industry, religious doctrine, and much more, race—and its venereal infections and ties to sexual hygiene—was real, fundamental, and bloody. If the skeptic of poststructuralist analysis still needs to be convinced by an example of the inextricable weave of historically specific discursive, scientific, and physical reality, race is the place to look. The discursive has never been lived with any greater vitality than in the always undead corpus of race and sex. For many in the first decades of the twentieth century, race mixing was a venereal disease of the social body, producing doomed progeny whose reproductive issue was as tainted as that of lesbians, sodomites, overeducated women, prostitutes, criminals, masturbators, or alcoholics. These were the subjects, literal and literary, of the commodious discourse of eugenics, where intraracial hygiene and interracial taxonomy were two faces of the same coin.[4]

Even radicals and liberals, to name them anachronistically, who fought the reproductive narrative and social equations of the last paragraph, accepted race as a meaningful object of scientific knowledge. They had little choice. These writers and activists worked to reshape race into a different picture of collective human health.[5] Scientific racial discourse—in the sense that did not insist on the separation of the physical and the cultural and spoke in the idiom of organic health, efficiency, and familial solidarity— accommodated writers from great American liberators like W. E. B. Du Bois and Charlotte Perkins Gilman, to middle-of-the-official-road, Progressive Era, unabashed racists like Madison Grant.[6] Du Bois is particularly interesting because he most consistently rejected "biologism" in his approach to race and racism, but the broad discourse that assimilated race feeling to family feeling and invited discussion on the childhood and maturity of collective human groups called races was inescapable.[7] Although he retracted such language a decade or so later, in 1897 Du Bois wrote that the history of the world is the history of races. "What is race? It is a vast family . . . generally of common blood and language, always of common history."[8]

George Stocking's thumbnail portrait of the Social Marking System developed by the U.S. sociologist Franklin H. Giddings around 1900 to 1910 collects up the ways that race and nation, passing through kinship of many ontological kinds and degrees of closeness, were held together on a continuum of social-biological differences. "[T]he essential element of the race concept was the idea of kinship. . . . 'Race' and 'nation' were simply the terms applied to different levels of a single pyramid."[9] Giddings attempted to provide a quantitative notation to distinguish degrees of kinship, arrayed across eight different kinds of relatedness. Types like the Hamitic, the Semitic, the Celtic, and so on filled the taxonomic slots. The specifics of Giddings's classification are less important here than their illustration of the exuberance of racial taxonomizing in the United States. In these taxonomies, which are, after all, little machines for clarifying and separating categories, the entity that always eluded the classifier was simple: race itself. The pure Type, which animated dreams, sciences, and terrors, kept slipping through, and endlessly multiplying, all the typological taxonomies. The rational classifying activity masked a wrenching and denied history. As racial anxieties ran riot through the sober prose of categorical bioscience, the taxonomies could neither pinpoint nor contain their terrible discursive product.

To complete my brief caricature of race as an object of bioscientific knowledge in the period before World War II, I will turn to a family portrait that innocently embodies the essence of my argument. The portrait slips down the developmental chain of being to racialized urban humanity's ultimate other and intimate kin, the gorilla in nature.[10] On the opposite page is a taxidermic reconstruction of a gorilla group, with a striking silverback male beating his chest, a mother eating calmly to the side, and a toddler. A young blackback male is in the diorama, but out of the photograph. The primal ape in the jungle is the dopplegänger and mirror to civilized white manhood in the city. Culture meets nature through the looking glass, at the interface of the Age of Mammals and the Age of Man. Preserved in changeless afterlife, this vibrant gorilla family is more undead than alive. The members of this (super)natural gorilla family were hunted, assembled, and animated by the art of taxidermy to become the perfect type of its species. Dramatic stories about people, animals, tools, journeys, diseases, and money inhere in each precious corpse, from the chest-beating male called the Giant of Karisimbi, to the ape-child speared as it screamed in terror on the steep volcanic mountainside. The blood was drained, face masks taken from the corpses, the skins stripped and preserved, shipped across continents, and stretched over special, light mannequins. Lit from within and surrounded by the panoramic views made possible by Hollywood set painting and the new cameras of the 1920s, the perfect natural group—the whole organic family in nature—emerged in a lush Eden crafted out of detailed reconstructions of leaves, insects, and soils. In these ways, the gorilla was reborn out of the accidents of biological life, a first birth, into epiphanic perfection, a second birth, in a diorama in the Akeley African Hall in the American Museum of Natural History in New York City.

Behind the dioramic re-creation of nature lies an elaborate world of practice. The social and technical apparatus of the colonial African scientific safari and the race-, class-, and gender-stratified labor systems of urban museum construction organized hundreds of people over three continents

Gorilla group in Akeley African Hall. *(Neg. no. 314824, courtesy American Museum of Natural History. Photo: Warts Bros.)*

and two decades to make this natural scene possible. To emerge intact, reconstructed nature required all the resources of advanced guns, patented cameras, transoceanic travel, food preservation, railroads, colonial bureaucratic authority, large capital accumulations, philanthropic institutions, and much more. The technological production of a culturally specific nature could hardly be more literal. The intense realism of the diorama was an epistemological, technological, political, and personal-experiential achievement. Natural order was simply there, indisputable, luminous. Kinship was secure in the purity of the achieved vision.

Walt Disney Studios and the National Geographic Society might do better in the decades to come, but they needed the magic of motion pictures. The achievement of the prewar natural history diorama relied more on a sculptural sensibility that was also manifest in the elegant bronzes, placed just outside the African Hall, of "primitive natural man," the East African Nandi lion hunters. Their perfection was sought by the same scientist-artist, Carl Akeley, who designed the dioramas for the American Museum. Organicism and typology ruled unchallenged in these practices, where the earth's great racial dramas, constructed in a white, imperial, naturalist, and progressive frame, were displayed as pedagogy, hygiene, and entertainment for an urban public.

After the successful scientific hunt for the perfect specimen, the superior nobility of hunting with the camera was urged in a conservationist doctrine that downplayed further hunting with the gun. To strengthen the conservationist argument, white women and children came on the final hunt for the museum's gorillas to prove that the great violent drama of manhood in confrontation across species could give way to a gentler tale. In part because of the efforts of the members of this collecting expedition in 1921–22 and of the officers of the American Museum, the area where the Giant of Karisimbi died became a Belgian national park, the Parc Albert in the Belgian Congo, where nature, including "primitive" people as fauna in the timeless scene, was to be preserved for science, adventure, uplift, and moral restoration as proof against civilization's decadence. No wonder universal nature has been a less than appealing entity for those who were not its creators and its beneficiaries. Undoing this inherited dilemma has never been more urgent if people and other organisms are to survive much longer.

The hunt for the Giant of Karisimbi took place in 1921, the same year that the American Museum of Natural History hosted the Second International Congress of Eugenics. Collected proceedings from the congress were titled "Eugenics in Family, Race, and State." The Committee of Immigration of the Eugenics Congress sent its exhibit bearing on immigration to Washington, D.C., as part of its lobbying for racial quotas. In 1924 the U.S. National Origins Act restricted immigration by a logic that linked race and nation. For officials of the American Museum, its nature preservation, germ plasm protection, and display work were all of a piece. Exhibition, conservation, and eugenics were part of a harmonious whole. Race was at the center of that natural configuration; and racial discourse, in all of its proliferating diversity and appalling sameness, reached deep into the family of the nation.

II. Population

THE COMMUNITY OF RACE, NATION, NATURE, LANGUAGE, AND CULTURE transmitted by blood and kinship never disappeared from popular racialism in the United States; but this bonding has not been meaningfully sustained by the biological sciences for half a century. Rather than dwell on the scientific and political processes that led to the biosciences' reversal on the reality and importance of race to evolutionary, genetic, physiological, therapeutic, and reproductive explanations in the middle decades of the twentieth century, I will leap to the other side of the divide, to where the Wizard of Oz has changed the set in the theater of nature. The major difference is that an entity called the population is now critical to most of the dramatic action.

A population, a relatively permeable group within a species, differed by one or more genes from other such groups. Changes of gene frequencies within populations were fundamental evolutionary processes, and gene flow between populations structured the traffic that bound the species together. Genes and genotypes were subject to Darwinian natural selection in the context of the functioning phenotypes of whole organisms within populations. Occasionally still a convenient notion, "race" was generally a misleading term for a population. The frequency of interesting genes, like those coding for immunological markers on blood cells or for different oxygen-carrying hemoglobins, might well differ more for individuals within a population than between populations. Or they might not; the question was an empirical one and demanded an explanation that included consideration of random drift, adaptational complexes, and the history of gene exchange. The populations' history of random genetic mutation and gene flow, subjected to natural selection resulting in adaptation, constituted the history of the species. Populations were not types arranged hierarchically but dynamic assemblages that had to function in changing environments. Measurements had to be of structures important to adaptational complexes related to current function. For example, craniometry producing brain-volume values on a putative hierarchical chain of being gave way to measurements of structures critical to dynamic action in life, like facial regions critical to chewing and subject to physical and functional stresses during the development of the organism. Highly variable and permeable natural populations seemed to be the right kind of scientific object of knowledge, and the racial type seemed to be a residue from a bad nightmare.

The construction of the category of the population occurred over several decades. Leading parts were taken by naturalists studying geographical variation and speciation; geneticists learning that mutations were inherited in discrete Mendelian fashion; population geneticists constructing mathematical models showing how mutation, migration, isolation, and other factors could affect the frequency of genes within populations; and experimentalists demonstrating that natural selection could operate on continuous variations to alter the characteristics of a population. The synthesis of these lines of research—which was effected by the Russian-trained, immigrant, U.S. geneticist Theodosius Dobzhansky; the English scion of the scientific Huxley clan Julian Huxley; the polymath, German-trained, immigrant, U.S. systematist Ernst Mayr; and the U.S. paleontologist George Gaylord Simpson, among others, from the late 1930s to the late 1940s—changed the face of dominant evolutionary theory. The result was called the modern synthesis or the neo-Darwinian evolutionary theory. Several of the men who put the modern synthesis together were also popular writers, published by the major university presses, who developed an antiracist, liberal, biological humanism that held sway until the 1970s.[11] This was a scientific humanism that emphasized flexibility, progress, cooperation, and universalism.

This was also precisely the humanism enlisted by M. F. Ashley Montagu, former student of Franz Boas and organizer of the United Nations Educational, Scientific, and Cultural Organization's (UNESCO) statements on race in 1950 and 1951.[12] Perched on the cusp between the Allied victory over the Axis powers, the ideological contest for defining human nature waged by "socialism" and "capitalism" in the Cold War, and the struggles for Third World decolonization that sharpened after World War II, the UN-sponsored documents were intended to break the bioscientific tie of race, blood, and culture that had fed the genocidal policies of fascism and still threatened doctrines of human unity in the emerging international scene. Since biologists had to bear so much of the responsibility for having constructed race as a scientific object of knowledge in the first place, it seemed essential to marshal the authority of the architects of the new synthesis to undo the category and relegate it to the slag heap of pseudo-science. It would not have done for the UNESCO statement to have been authored by social scientists. The crafting of the UNESCO race statements provides a unique case study for the discursive reconstitution of a critical epistemological and technical object for policy and research, where science and politics, in the oppositional sense of those two slippery terms, form the tightest possible weave.

The concept of the population was in the foreground, as the authors argued that plasticity was the most prominent species trait of *Homo sapiens*. While the strong statement that the range of mental talent is the same in all human groups did not survive controversy over the 1950 version, the negative argument that science provides no evidence of inherited racial inequality of intelligence remained. The contentious 1950 statement that universal brotherhood *(sic)* is supported by a species-wide, inborn trait of a drive toward cooperation also did not live through the rewriting in 1951. Nonetheless, the latter document—signed by ninety-six internationally prominent scientific experts before it was released—remained uncompromising on the key ideas of plasticity, educability, the invalidity of the race and culture tie, and the importance of populationist evolutionary biology.[13] To cast group differences typologically was to do bad science—with all the penalties in jobs, institutional power, funding, and prestige that flow from such labeling. Needless to say, biological racialism did not disappear overnight, but a palace coup had indeed taken place in the citadel of science.[14]

Walking out of UNESCO House in Paris, the new universal man turned up fossilized in East Africa almost immediately. In honor of this timely geological appearance, the Harvard Lampoon dubbed the Olduvai Gorge, made famous by the paleoanthropological investigations of the Leakey family, the "Oh Boy! Oh Boy! Gorge" for its stunning hominid fossils and the associated accounts of the dawn of human history and of the species-defining characteristics of human nature. Deeply indebted to the modern synthesis, the New Physical Anthropology developed from the 1950s to become a major actor in identifying those adaptational complexes that made "us" human and in installing them in both pedagogical and research practice.

Public and intradisciplinary antiracist lectures, new undergraduate and graduate curricula in physical anthropology sustained by the expanding institutional prosperity of the postwar era in the United States, field studies of natural primate populations, and major programs of research on African hominid fossils were all part of the program of the new physical anthropology. Its objects of attention were not typologically constructed taxonomies but systems of action that left their residue in the enduring hard structures in fossil beds or under the skin of still living animals. Adaptational behavior is what these biological anthropologists cared about, whether they were looking at pelvic bones, crania, living monkeys and apes, or modern hunter-gatherers. In the new framework, people who were typical "primitives" to the earlier expeditions of the American Museum of Natural History were fully modern humans, exhibiting clearly the fundamental adaptational complexes that continue to characterize all populations of the species. Indeed, lacking the stresses of too much First World abundance, the former "primitives" like modern hunter-gatherers became especially revealing "universal" human beings.

The most important adaptational complex for my purposes in this essay is the species-defining sharing way of life, rooted in hunting and the heterosexual nuclear family. Man the Hunter, not the urban brother of the Giant of Karisimbi or the Nandi lion spearmen, embodied the ties of technology, language, and kinship in the postwar universal human family. Parent to technology and semiology—to the natural sciences and the human sciences—in the same adaptational behavior, Man the Hunter crafted the first beautiful and functional objects and spoke the first critical words. Hunting in this account was not about competition and aggression but about a new subsistence strategy possible for striding, bipedal, proto-humans with epic hand-eye coordination. Acquiring big brains and painful births in the process, these beings developed cooperation, language, technology, and a lust for travel, all in the context of sharing the spoils with mates, children, and each other. Males were certainly the active motor of human evolution in the hunting hypothesis of the 1950s and 1960s; but the logic was not too much strained in the 1970s by foregrounding Woman the Gatherer and a few useful family reforms, like female orgasms and mate choice favoring males who made themselves useful with the kids.[15] Still, baby slings, carrying bags for roots and nuts, daily adult gossip, and talking to children could hardly compete for originary drama with elegant projectiles, adventurous travel, political oratory, and male bonding in the face of danger.[16]

Two powerful photographic documents of the universal human family conclude my meditation on the hopeful, but fatally flawed, biological humanism of the mid-twentieth century: the late-1970s painting called *Fossil Footprint Makers of Laetoli*, by the anatomical illustrator Jay Matternes, and the New York Museum of Modern Art's publication from its 1955 epic photographic exhibit called *The Family of Man*. Both documents stage the relations of nature and culture mediated by the heterosexual, reproductive, nuclear family as the figure of human unity and diversity. Both renderings of the human story are starkly under the visible sign of the threat of nuclear destruction; and both suggest a saga of unity, danger, and resilience that permeated accounts of science, progress, and technology in the post–World War II era.

Accompanying an international museum exhibit of hominid fossils in the 1980s, Matternes's painting shows the hominid first family walking across the African savanna under the cloud of an erupting volcano, the sign of destruction by fire. These transitional figures between apes and modern humans recall the gorilla family in the American Museum of Natural History. But for earthlings in the last, chilling years of the Cold War, the thick cloud of dust spewing into the sky to obscure the sun in Matternes's reconstruction could not help evoking the looming threat of nuclear winter. Expulsion from Eden had particular narrative resonances in nuclear culture. In the era of nuclear superpowers facing each other off in fraternal rivalry, threats came in centralized apocalyptic packages. In the New World Order of the post–Cold War, nuclear threats, like all else, have a more dispersed and networked structure of opportunity and danger—like criminal smuggling of plutonium from the former Soviet Union and the apocalypse-lite of plutonium poisoning of urban water supplies or dirty minibombs backing up political disputes. Matternes's painting is a reconstruction of the life events that might have been responsible for the 3.7 million-year-old footprints found in the volcanic ash at Laetoli, near the Olduvai Gorge, by Mary Leakey and others in the late 1970s. The space-faring descendants of the first family put their footprints in moon dust in 1969, in Neil Armstrong's "one small step for mankind," just as the *Australopithecus afarensis* trekkers, at the dawn of hominization, made their way through the volcanic dust of the human travel narrative.

The great myths of birth and death, beginnings and endings, are everywhere in this painting. The reconstructed hominids are members of a highly publicized, ancestor-candidate species that has been at the center of scientific debates about what counts as human. Perhaps the best-known fossil in this media and scientific fray has been the 3.5 million-year-old skeleton of a diminutive female named by her Adamic founders Lucy, after the Beatles' Lucy in the Sky with Diamonds. The African plain in the painting, scene of the passage of Lucy's relatives, is both rich with the signs of abundant animal life and thickly crusted with the smothering ash that must drive all the animals, including these early hominids, in search of food. The three family members vividly dramatize the central adaptive complexes that made "us" human. The elements for the universal sharing way of life are unmistakable. The male strides ahead, carrying a serviceable tool, although not quite the future's elegant projectiles that were critical to the hunting hypothesis, as well as to Stanley Kubrick's *2001: A Space Odyssey*. *A. afarensis* would have to wait for somewhat larger heads before they improved their aesthetic sense. The antiracist universals of the evolutionary drama scripted according to the humanist doctrines of the modern synthesis left in place the durable essentials of the sexual division of labor, male-headed heterosexual families, and child-laden females—here pictured *without* the baby-carrying sling that many anthropologists argue was likely to have been among the first human tools. In Matternes's Adamic imagination, the child-carrying female follows behind, looking to the side, while the male leads, looking into the future. The germ of human sociality was the couple and their offspring, not a mixed foraging group, a group of related females with their kids, two males with one carrying a kid, or any other of the many possibilities for those first small steps for mankind left in the dust at Laetoli.

If it is the numbing and hegemonic sameness of the universal way of life that I resist in the new physical anthropology, including many of its feminist versions, and in Matternes's painting, then perhaps an earlier document, the popular coffee table book of Edward Steichen's photographic exhibit called *The Family of Man* can settle my dyspeptic attack of political correctness. If I detect the unself-conscious ethnocentricity of those who crafted the natural-technical object of knowledge called the first family and the universal hominizing way of life, perhaps the global scope of the 1955 document will allow a more capacious field for imagining human unity and difference. Yet, once I have learned to see the Sacred Image of the Same and the Edenic travelogue of so much Western historical narrative, I have a hard time letting go of this perhaps monomaniacal critical vision, which might be worse than the objects it complains about. My own perverse skill at reading the sameness of my own inherited cultural stories into everything is one of the symptoms that drives this paper. Still, I believe that this capacity of reproducing the Same, in culpable innocence of its historical, power-charged specificity, characterizes not just me but people formed like me, who are liberal, scientific, and progressive—just like those officials of the American Museum of Natural History who sent their eugenic immigration exhibit to Washington in 1921. I am worried that too little has changed in hegemonic bioscientific discourse on nature, race, unity, and difference, even in the face of seeming major change. So, let me pursue my suspicion that the Sacred Image of the Same is not just my problem but is also one of the tics that reproduces sexually charged racist imaginations even in the practices most consciously dedicated to antiracism.

In this mood, I am not surprised that Steichen's 1955 photo album does not settle my dyspepsia. My queasiness is not just with the title and its conventional familial trope for binding together humanity, with all the resonances that metaphor evokes of kinship, lineage, and blood ties. There is much to love in *The Family of Man*, including its vivid photos of working, playing, and fighting. Old age, infirmity, and poverty are no barriers to liveliness here. Even the staging of everybody and everything into one grandly decontextualized narrative, which culminates in the United Nations and the hopes for peace in nuclear times after the ravages of depression, fascism, and war, can almost be forgiven. After all, *The Family of Man* is a lot less sanitized than most 1990s versions of multiculturalism. Despite decades of critical visual theory, I am susceptible, even now, to the images of this book. That helps, because it is a rule for me not to turn a dissolving eye onto straw problems, not to "deconstruct" that to which I am not also emotionally and politically vulnerable.

The Family of Man is ruled throughout its organic tissues by a version of unity that repeats the cyclopean story that collects up the people into the reproductive heterosexual nuclear family, the potent germ plasm for the Sacred Image of the Same. The opening photos show culturally varied young men and women in courtship, then marriage, then all sorts of women in pregnancy and labor, then birth (mediated by a male scientific-medical doctor), nursing, babyhood, and parenting by both genders. The photo album then opens out into culturally and nationally varied scenes of work on the land and in factories. Food, music, education, religion, technology, tragedy and mercy, aging and death, anger and joy, hunger and suffering all find their place. The icons of nuclear war and of other wars, as well as images of racism and fascism, cast a deep shadow. The pall is lifted by the images of democracy (voting) and internationalism (the United Nations), which locate hope for this family story solidly in the signifiers of the "free world." The last pages of the exhibit are full of multihued children, seeds of the future. The last photo (before the unfortunate ocean wave on the inside back cover) is of a little boy and little girl moving away from the viewer, walking hand-in-hand in sylvan nature toward the sunny light of a possible future. This book about human universals is vehemently antiracist, and simultaneously deeply enmeshed in an ethnospecific, teleological story that continues to make the human collective bleed, or at least to hunger for other stories of what it means to be members of a species and a community. What's not collected in a reproductive family story does not finally count as human. For all the photo narrative's emphasis on difference, this is the grammar of indifference, of the multiplication of sameness.

The desire for a child, for a future in that potent image, permeating *The Family of Man* is at least as fierce as the yearning sustaining the new reproductive technologies of the 1980s and 1990s. The genetic imagination never dimmed under the sign of the population. Genetic desire would be no less when the genome became the signifier of human collectivity.

III. Genome

IF UNIVERSAL HUMANITY WAS PLASTIC UNDER THE SIGN OF THE POPULATION at midcentury, then human nature is best described as virtual in present, end-of-the-millennium regimes of biological knowledge and power. Specifically, human nature is embodied, literally, in an odd thing called a genetic database, held in a few international locations, like the three large public databases for genetic map and sequence data: the U.S. GenBank©, the European Molecular Biological Laboratory, and the DNA Data Bank of Japan. The Genome Data Base at Johns Hopkins University is a massive, central repository of all gene-mapping information. In the world of gene sequencing, intellectual property rights vie with human rights for the attention of lawyers and scientists alike. Criminal as well as corporate lawyers have a stake in the material and metaphoric representation of the genome. Funding and policy strongly support rapid public access to genome databases in the interests of research and development. For example, in 1993 the French researcher Daniel Cohen, of the Centre d'Etude du Polymorphisme Humaine in Paris, made his first complete draft map of the human genome available through the Internet. GenInfo, developed by the U.S. National Center for Biotechnology Information of the National Library of Medicine, is a kind of meta-database, containing both protein and nucleic acid sequence data "to which other databases can add, refer, annotate, interpret, and extrapolate."[17] In part because of the tremendous physical computing power and human expertise that resulted from nuclear weapons research, informatics development in the U.S. Human Genome Project began under the auspices of GenBank© at the U.S. National Laboratories at Los Alamos, New Mexico. It was there also that the expertise and machines existed that built the matrix for the flourishing of artificial-life research at the nearby Santa Fe Institute.

A database is an information structure. Computer programs are the habitats of information structures, and an organism's genome is a kind of nature park among databases. Just as racial hygiene and eugenics were committed to science and progress, and populationist doctrines of human universals were unambiguously on the side of development and the future, the genome is allied with all that is up-to-the-minute. Yet something peculiar happened to the stable, family-loving, Mendelian gene when it passed into a database, where it has more in common with LANDSAT photographs, Geographical Information Systems, international seed banks, and the World Bank than with T. H. Morgan's fruit flies at Columbia University in the 1910s or UNESCO's populations in the 1950s. Banking and mapping seem to be the name of the genetic game at an accelerating pace since the 1970s, in the corporatization of biology to make it fit for the New World Order, Inc.[18] If the modern synthesis, ideologically speaking, tended to make everyone his brother's keeper, then, in its versions of kin selection and inclusive fitness maximization strategies, the sociobiological synthesis runs to making everyone his or her sibling's banker.[19]

Biotechnology in the service of corporate profit is a revolutionary force for remaking the inhabitants of planet Earth, from viruses and bacteria right up the now repudiated chain of being to *Homo sapiens* and beyond. Biological research globally is progressively practiced under the direct auspices of corporations, from the multinational pharmaceutical and agribusiness giants to venture capital companies that fascinate the writers for the business sections of daily newspapers. Molecular biology and molecular genetics have become nearly synonymous with biotechnology as engineering and redesign disciplines. Beings like Man the Hunter and Woman the Gatherer reappear for their roles on the stage of nature enterprised up as Man™ and Woman™, copyrighted, registered for commerce, and, above all, highly flexible.[20] In a world where the artifactual and the natural have imploded, nature itself, both ideologically and materially, has been patently reconstructed. Structural adjustment demands no less, of bacteria and trees as well as of people, businesses, and nations.

The genome is the totality of genetic "information" in an organism or, more commonly, the totality of genetic information in all the chromosomes in the nucleus of a cell. Conventionally, the genome refers only to the nucleic acid that "codes" for something, and not to the dynamic, multipart structures and processes that constitute functional, reproducing cells and organisms. Thus, not even the proteins critical to nuclear chromosomal organization or DNA structures like mitochondrial chromosomes outside the nucleus are part of the genome, much less the whole living cell. Embodied information with a complex time structure is reduced to a linear code in an archive outside time. This reduction gives rise to the curious, ubiquitous, mixed metaphor of "mapping the code," applied to projects to represent all the information in the genome. DNA, in this view, is a master molecule, the code of codes, the foundation of unity and diversity. Much of the history of genetics since the 1950s is the history of the consolidation and elaboration of the equation of "gene = information" in the context of master-molecule metaphors. I consider this representational practice for thinking about genetics to constitute a kind of artificial-life research itself, where the paradigmatic habitat for life—the program—bears no necessary relationship to messy, thick organisms.

The convergence of genomics and informatics, in technique and personnel as well as in basic theory and shared tropes, is immensely consequential for bioscientific constructions of human nature. The technical ability to manipulate genetic information, in particular to pass it from one kind of organism to another in a regulated manner in the lab, or to synthesize and insert new genes, has grown exponentially since the first successful genetic engineering experiments of the early 1970s. In principle, there is no naturally occurring genome that cannot be experimentally redesigned. This is a very different matter compared to the genetic traffic among populations of a species studied within the midcentury evolutionary synthesis, much less compared to the genetic, natural racial types that inhabited the biological world earlier in the century. Genetic engineering is not eugenics, just as the genome does not give the same kind of account of a species as does organic racial discourse.

From the point of view of the 1990s, the genome is an information structure that can exist in various physical media. The medium might be the DNA sequences organized into natural chromosomes in the whole organism. Or the medium might be various built physical structures, like Yeast

Artificial Chromosomes (YACs) or bacterial plasmids, designed to hold and transfer cloned genes or other interesting stretches of nucleic acid. The entire genome of an organism might be held in a "library" of such artifactual biochemical information structures. The medium of the database might also be the computer programs that manage the structure, error checking, storage, retrieval, and distribution of genetic information for the various international genome projects that are under way for *Homo sapiens* and for other model species critical to genetic, developmental, and immunological research. Those species include mice, dogs, bacteria, yeast, nematodes, rice, and a few more creatures indispensable for international technoscientific research.

The U.S. Human Genome Project officially began in 1988, under the management of the Department of Energy and the National Institutes of Health. As a whole, the human genome project is a multinational, long-term, competitive and cooperative, multibillion-dollar (yen, franc, mark, etc.) effort to represent exhaustively—in genetic, physical, and DNA sequence maps—the totality of information in the species genome.[21] The data are all entered into computerized databases, from which information is made available around the world on terms still very much being worked out. Computerized database design is at the leading edge of genomics research. Design decisions about these huge databases shape what can be easily compared to what else, and so determine the kinds of uses that can be made of the original data. Such decisions structure the kinds of ideas of the species that can be sustained. National science bodies, tax- and foundation-supported universities, international organizations, private corporations, communities, indigenous peoples, and many configurations of political and scientific activists all play a part in the saga.

Questions about agency—who is an actor—abound in the world of the genome, as in the worlds of technoscience in general. For example, in the discourse of genome informatics, data are exchanged among "agents" and sent to "users" of databases. These entities could as easily be computers or programs as people.[22] It does not solve the trouble to say that people are the end users. That turns out to be a contingent, technical, design decision—or a way of representing ongoing flows of information—more than an ontological necessity. People are in the information loop, but their status is a bit iffy in the artificial life world. Compared to the biological humanism of the modern synthesis, technohumanism has had to make a few timely ideological adjustments. Genomics is neither taxidermy nor the reconstruction practices of the new physical anthropology, and the emerging techniques of animation occupy the minds of more than the *Jurassic Park* special-effects programmers at Industrial Light and Magic.

Issues of *agency* permeate practices of *representation* in many senses of both terms: Who, exactly, in the human genome project represents whom? A prior question has to be a little different, however. Who, or what, *is* the human that is to be exhaustively represented? Molecular geneticists are consumed with interest in the variability of DNA sequences. Their data-bases are built to house information about both stable and variable regions of genes or proteins. Indeed, for actors from drug designers to forensic criminologists, the uniqueness of each *individual's* genome is part of the technical allure of the human genome projects' spin-offs. More fundamen-tally, however, the genome projects produce entities of a different ontologi-cal kind than flesh-and-blood organisms, "natural races," or any other sort of "normal" organic being. At the risk of repeating myself, the Human Genome Project produces ontologically specific things called databases as objects of knowledge and practice. The human to be represented, then, has a particular kind of totality, or species being, as well as a specific kind of individuality. At whatever level of individuality or collectivity, from a sin-gle-gene region extracted from one sample through the whole species genome, this human *is* itself an information structure, whose program might be written in nucleic acids or in the artificial intelligence programming lan-guage called FORTH.

Therefore, variability has its own syntax in genome discourse as well. There is no illusion in the 1990s about single "wild-type" genes and various mutant deviants.[23] That was the terminology of Mendelian genetics of the early twentieth century, when the languages of the normal and the deviant were much more sanitary. Racial hygiene and its typological syntax are not supported by genome discourse, or by artificial life discourses in general. Genetic investment strategies, in the sense of both evolutionary theory and business practice, *are* supported. The populationist thinking of the modern synthesis blasted an entire tool kit of resources for believing in norms and types. Flexibility, with its specific grammars of human unity and diversity, is the name of the game at the end of this millennium. However, for all of their commitment to variability, most molecular geneticists are not trained in evolutionary population biology. This disciplinary fact has given rise to a most interesting project and ensuing controversy for the purposes of this essay. Let us pick up questions of agency and representation, as well as unity and difference, through the Human Genome Diversity Project.

If the human genome databases are exhaustively to represent the species—and to provide information to users who demand that kind of knowledge, in dreams of totality as well as in practical projects—the repositories must contain physical and electronic data about the specific molecular constitu-tion and frequency of genes on a truly global scale. Population geneticists were critical both of molecular biologists' sampling protocols for human genetic material and of their woeful statistical grasp of the structure, distri-bution, history, and variability of human populations. The population geneticists were also worried that many human populations around the world were becoming extinct—either literally or through interbreeding and swamping of their diversity in larger adjoining populations—with the conse-quent loss of genetic information forever impoverishing the databases of the species. What it means to be human would have irredeemable informational gaps. There would be a biodiversity information loss in the life world of the genome. Like the vanishing of a rain forest fungus or fern before pharmaceutical companies could survey the species for promising drugs, the vanishing of human gene pools is a blow to technoscience. Prompt and thorough genetic collection and banking procedures, as well as preservation of the source of variation, if possible, are the solution.

I am being a bit mordant in my reading of purposes in this account, for the organizers of the Human Genome Diversity Project were largely liberal biological humanists of the old stamp. Also, I remain sympathetic to the desire to produce a human species database that draws from as large a concept of humanity as possible. I want there to be a way to reconfigure this desire and its attendant humanism. However, it was precisely the doctrines of difference, representation, and agency of "universal" humanism that got the project and its well-meaning organizers into well-deserved trouble.[24]

Beginning about 1991 the organizers of the Human Genome Diversity Project proposed to amend the evolutionary population thinking, or lack of thinking, of the mainline Human Genome Project by collecting hair-root, white blood-cell, and cheek-tissue samples, to be held in the American Type Culture Collection, from over seven hundred groups of indigenous peoples on six continents. Over five years the cost would be about $23–35 million (compared to more than $3 billion for the Human Genome Project as a whole). Unfortunately, unself-conscious, modernist perspectives distorted the definition of the categories of people from whom samples were to be sought, leading to a vision of dynamic human groups as timeless "Isolates of Historic Interest." Also, other potentially genetically distinct ethnic communities did not appear on the sampling list.

The planning of the project did not involve members of the communities in any formative way in the science. The people to be sampled might give or withhold permission, more or less carefully sought and thoroughly explained; but they were not regarded as partners in knowledge production who might have ends and meanings of their own in such an undertaking. Their versions of the human story, complexly articulated with the genetic science of the visitors, did not shape the research agenda. Permission is not the same thing as collaboration, and the latter could lead to fundamental changes in who and what would count as science and as scientists. All the trappings of universal science notwithstanding, amending a database is a pretty culturally specific thing to want to do. Just why should other people, much less folks called "isolates of historic interest," help out with that project? That is not a rhetorical question; and there can be very strong answers, coming from counterintuitive as well as obvious viewpoints for any actor. The question is a fundamental one about the rhetorics of persuasion and the practical processes through which people—including scientists and everybody else—get reconstituted as subjects and objects in encounters. How should the many discourses in play within and between people like the Guaymi of Panama and the Population Geneticists of California be articulated with each other in a power-sensitive way? This is an ethical question, but it is much more than that. It is a question about what may count as modern knowledge and who will count as producers of that knowledge.[25]

Not surprisingly, it turned out that indigenous people were more interested in representing themselves than in being represented in the human story. The encounter was most certainly not between "traditional" and "modern" peoples, but between contemporaneous people with richly interlocking and diverging discourses, each with its own agendas and histories. Functioning as boundary objects, "genes" and "genomes" circulated among many of the languages in play.[26] Members of communities to be sampled, as well as other spokespeople, had several concerns. Some were adamant that genes or other products derived from indigenous material not be patented and used for commercial profit. Others were worried that the genetic information about tribal and marginalized peoples could be misused in genocidal ways by national governments. Some argued that medical and social priorities of the communities could be addressed by the money that would go to funding the genetic sampling, and the HGDP did not give benefits back to the people. Some were quite willing to have indigenous genetic material contribute to a medically useful world knowledge fund, but only under United Nations or similar auspices that would prevent exploitation and profit making. Ethics committee members of the HGDP tried to assure skeptics that the project had no commercial interests, and it would try to make sure that any commercial benefits that did result from the sampled material flowed back to the communities. But overall, the general issue was the question of the agency of people who did not consider themselves a biodiversity resource. Diversity was about both their *object* status and their *subject* status.

In May 1993, at a nongovernmental conference meeting parallel to the UN Human Rights Conference in Vienna, the Rural Advancement Foundation International and indigenous peoples urged the HGDP to "halt current collection efforts, convene a meeting with Indigenous peoples to address ethical and scientific issues, incorporate Indigenous organizations in every aspect of the HGDP and grant them veto power, and place the HGDP under direct United Nations control, with decision making delegated to a management committee dominated by Indigenous people."[27] Leaders of the HGDP tried to address the objections, but by fall 1993 they had not set up mechanisms acceptable to the critics to include indigenous peoples in project organizing. The World Council of Indigenous Peoples monitored the project skeptically. It is important to me to note, however, that the HGDP was a minority effort in the Human Genome Project, and not at the center of the prestigious action. To get the research done at all in the face of the nonpopulationist molecular genetic orthodoxy that guided ordinary practice in the HGP would have been no small trick. It has proved easier to slow down or stop the HGDP, itself a kind of oppositional effort, than to question the powerful HGP itself. That makes the trouble with "difference" built into this potentially positive scientific project all the more disturbing—and important.

Inescapably, independently of the HGDP but fatally glued onto it, the all too predictable scandal happened. Like all pathologies, the scandal revealed the structure of what passes for normal in bioscientific regimes of knowledge and power. The Guaymi people carry a unique virus and its antibodies that might be important in leukemia research. Blood taken from a twenty-six-year-old Guaymi woman with leukemia in 1990, with her "informed oral consent," in the language of the U.S. Center for Disease Control in Atlanta, was used to produce an "immortalized" cell line deposited at the American Type Culture Collection. The U.S. secretary of commerce proceeded to file a patent claim on the cell line. Pat Mooney of the Rural Advancement Foundation International found out about the claim in August 1993 and informed Isidoro Acosta, the president of the Guaymi General Congress. Considering the patent claim to be straightforward biopiracy, Acosta and another Guaymi representative went to Geneva to raise the issue with the Biological Diversity Convention, which had been adopted at the 1993 Earth Summit in Brazil. That convention had been intended to deal with plant and animal material, but the Guaymi made strategic use of its language to address technoscientifically defined human biodiversity. The Guaymi also went to the General Agreement on Tariffs and Trade (GATT) secretariat to argue against the patentability of material of human origin in the intellectual-property provisions of the new GATT treaty then being drafted.

In late 1993 the U.S. secretary of commerce withdrew the patent application, although by early 1994 the cell culture had not been returned, as demanded, to the Guaymi. The property and sovereignty battles are far from resolved; they are at the heart of bioscientific regimes of knowledge and power worldwide. Scientific and commercial stakes are high. The stakes are also the ongoing configuration of subjects and objects, of agency and representation, inside of and by means of these disputes about biopower. The stakes are about what will count as human unity and diversity. The human family is at stake in its databases. I am instructed by the encounter of discourses, where genes are the circulating boundary objects. The Guaymi and the U.S. actors engaged each other in biogenetic terms, and they struggled to shape those terms in the process. Perhaps the Guaymi did not initiate biotechnological and genetic engineering discourses, including their business and legal branches; but the indigenous Panamanians are far from passive objects in these material and linguistic fields. They are actors who are reconfiguring these powerful discourses, along with others they bring to the encounter. In the process, the Guaymi are changing both themselves and the international scientists and other policy elites.

A troubling leitmotif in the Guaymi cell-line dispute returns us to the narratives, images, and myths with which I want to conclude this meditation on the human family. In the midst of the polemics, Pat Mooney of the RAFI was quoted to say, "When a foreign government comes into a country, takes blood without explaining the real implications to local people, and then tries to patent and profit from the cell line, that's wrong. Life should not be subject to patent monopolies."[28] True enough about the patent monopoly part, but penetration by a foreign power to take blood evokes much more than intellectual-property issues. I cannot help hearing Mooney's words in the context of periodically surfacing stories in Latin America about white North Americans stealing body parts, sucking blood, and kidnapping children to be organ donors. The dubious factual accuracy of the accounts is not the point, even though the standards of evidence to which commentators have been held when the stories appear in U.S. news articles and radio talk shows appall me. What matters in this essay is the stories themselves, that is, the ready association of technoscience with realms of the undead, tales of vampires, and transgressive traffic in the bloody tissues of life. Sampling blood is never an innocent symbolic act. The red fluid is too potent, and blood debts are too current. Stories lie in wait even for the most carefully literal-minded. Blood's translations into the sticky threads of DNA, even in the aseptic databases of cyberspace, have inherited the precious fluid's double-edged power. The genome lives in the realm of the undead in myriad ways that cannot be contained by rational intentions, explicit explanations, and literal behavior. The stories get at structures of power and fantasy that must be faced in all their displaced, uncanny truth.

Table 2, "Night Births and Vampire Progeny," is a rough guide through a tiny region of the mine-strewn territory. My chart is indebted to three mainline publications within technoscientific professional and popular culture. Pursuing the symptomatic logic of this essay, my technique is resolute overreading. I know no better strategy to deal with the vermin-infested normality of rational discourse. Just state the obvious. Say what should not have to be said.

Du Pont's wonderful advertisement for OncoMouse™, the first patented animal in the world, in *Science* magazine in 1989–90 provides my first text. OncoMouse™ contains a cancer-causing bit of DNA, called an oncogene, derived from the genome of another creature and implanted by means of genetic engineering techniques. A model for breast cancer research, the redesigned rodent is like a machine tool in the workshops for the production of knowledge. OncoMouse™ is a transgenic animal, whose scene of evolution *is* the laboratory. Inhabiting the nature of no nature, OncoMouse™'s natural habitat is the fully artifactual space of technoscience. Symbolically and materially, OncoMouse™ is where the categories of nature and culture implode for members of technoscientific cultures. For that very reason, the mouse has been at the center of controversy since its production.[29] Defined by a spliced genome, identified with a spliced name, patented, and trademarked, OncoMouse™ is paradigmatic of nature enterprised up. What interests me here, however, are the stories that are crusted like barnacles onto the striking advertising image.

TABLE 2
Night Births and Vampire Progeny

Image	OncoMouse™	gorilla-suited bride	SimEve
Source	*Science* magazine	*American Medical News*	*Time* magazine
Kin category	species	family	race
Reproductive practice	genetic engineering	professional investment	cybergenesis by morphing
Narratives and myths	night births in the laboratory scientific enlightenment Plato's allegory of the cave heroic quest	Bad investments yield polluted offspring. Reverse alchemy turns gold into base metal. racialized heterosexuality vampire-toothed bride	masculine parthenogenesis mind children Orestian Trilogy Pygmalion and Galatea
Slogan	"where better things for better living come to life"	"If you've made an unholy alliance . . ."	"love that will forever remain unrequited"

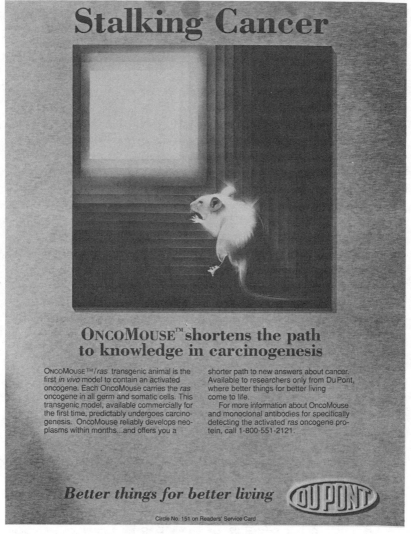

OncoMouse™. (*Courtesy Du Pont, © 1989. Reprinted with permission of DuPont NEN Products. On May 19,1995, DuPont announced its intent to divest its Medical Products businesses. The former DuPont NEN Products business will become NEN Life Science Products.*)

Du Pont's white mouse is in the midst of a heroic travel or quest narrative and part of a noble hunt where the cancer enemy is stalked. Epistemophilia, the lusty search for knowledge of origins, is everywhere. The mouse climbs out of a womb-like, geometric cave toward the light of knowledge, evoking the narrative elements of the Western Enlightenment and of Plato's allegory of the cave. OncoMouse™ is "available to researchers only from Du Pont, where better things for better living come to life." Like it or not, we are catapulted into the narrative fields that contain Frankenstein and his monster and all the other alluring scenes of night births in the mythological culture of science. The laboratory repeatedly figures as an uncanny place, where entities that do not fit, do not belong, cannot be normal—that transgress previously important categories—come into being. I am drawn to the laboratory for this essential narrative and material power. How could feminists and antiracists in this culture do without the power of the laboratory to make the normal dubious? Raking ambivalence and strong visitations from a culturally specific unconscious, however, are the price of this alliance with the creatures of technoscience. Reproduction is afoot here, with all of its power to reconfigure kinship. In the proliferating zones of the undead, the kin categories of species are undone and redone, all too often by force. Consciously or unconsciously, whoever designed this ad knew all the right stories. Enlightenment has never been more pregnant with consequences, both semiological and technological, for the human family.

Family imagery is much more explicit and far more ominous in my next text, an ad for Prepaid Medical Management, Inc. (PreMed), which was published in *American Medical News* on August 7, 1987. PreMed tells physicians that it can help get them out of unprofitable contracts with health maintenance organizations that had promised a financially sound patient base and quality care, but delivered instead profits for distant shareholders and high administrative fees for doctors. PreMed claims to have aided physicians in establishing locally controlled and fiscally sound HMOs, in which doctors could determine whom they treated and how they practiced medicine. There is little question that these are pressing concerns in the context of a medicine-for-profit system, in which many patients are uninsured, underinsured, or covered by public plans that pay much less for services than private insurers. Although not referring directly to the larger context, the ad appeared in the midst of an epidemic of national publicity about high Medicare and Medicaid patient loads in urban HMOs, African American crack-addicted and AIDS-infected mothers and babies in inner cities, and astronomical malpractice insurance costs, particularly for urban obstetricians.

The PreMed verbal text makes no reference to race, gender, or class; but I think these codes structure the ad. "Accepting reduced fees and increased risks" is a code for accepting too many poor patients who do not have private insurance. The code, if not a more complicated reality, biases readers to see those high-risk, poor patients as overwhelmingly people of color, especially African American. The visual scene of a wedding and the verbal text about an unholy alliance propel the reader to see the patient as female and black and the doctor as male and white. An unholy alliance is "miscegenation," the dragon at the heart of racist and misogynist terror.

Finally, it is the double disguise, the twice-done veiling of the bride that makes the ad so flagrantly about what it literally covers up with a joke: the class-structured, racialized, sexual politics of American reproductive health

If You've Made An Unholy HMO Alliance, Perhaps We Can Help.

All across the country, physicians who once had visions of a beautiful marriage to an HMO have discovered that the honeymoon is over.

Instead of quality care and a fiscally sound patient-base, they end up accepting reduced fees and increased risks. Plus a lot of new rules that make it more like administrating than practicing medicine.

And while you're doing a lot of the administration, the HMO is charging administrative fees in the neighborhood of 17% to 20%. Small wonder, these HMOs continue to reward

distant shareholders with record returns while participating physicians get nothing but grief.

Most doctors have felt there's little or no hope—that "we're trapped" with no way out. But that's not true. There are alternatives. And we're in the business of providing them.

At Prepaid Medical Management Inc., we help physicians develop their own HMOs, negotiate with hostile HMOs or leave contractual situations that have turned sour. And we've been doing it for seven years. In the process, we've helped a number of physician groups profitably leave contracts with national HMOs and establish locally controlled plans with solid fiscal track records.

If you'd like to discuss the alternatives available to your group or IPA, give PreMed President Ed Petras a call. It's not too late to do something about an unholy alliance.

PREMED®

8400 Normandale Lake Blvd.
Suite 1180
Minneapolis, MN 55437
1-800/833-7612

An unholy alliance. *(Courtesy PreMed, © 1987)*

and the further withdrawal of medical services from already underserved populations. A white medical coat–clad, stethoscope-wearing, prosperous-looking white man with just the right amount of graying hair is putting a gold wedding band on the ring finger of a black gorilla-suited bride in a white wedding gown and veil. The bride is doubly not there. Present are only two disguises: wedding dress and gorilla suit. The implied infected or addicted, pregnant black woman, always, in the code, on welfare, is denied in advance.[30] The surface of the ad insists that it is me, not PreMed, who is both making the connection of the gorilla-suited bride with African American women and also putting the wedding scene into the context of reproductive health care. Can't I take a joke? But my power to be amused is vitiated by the searing memory of just where African American women fit historically into systems of marriage and kinship in white heterosexual patriarchy in the United States. "Miscegenation" is still a national racist synonym for infection, counterfeit issue unfit to carry the name of the father, and a spoiled future. The bitter history of the scientific and medical animalization of people of African descent, especially in the narratives of the great chain of being that associated apes and black people, further accounts for my poor sense of humor. The gorilla suit cannot be an innocent joke here, and good intentions are no excuse. The lying disguises cannot hide what they deny.

But this bride is less a living—or a reconstructed—gorilla than an undead monster. She is not a creature in an Akeley diorama, whose natural types always glowed with health. The gorilla-suited bride is the type of no type. Her lips are parted just enough to show the gleam of a bright-white tooth. The bride is a vampire, equipped with the tool for sucking the blood of the husband and polluting his lineage. The shining tooth echos the brilliant gold of the wedding ring. The wedding night bodes ill. The conventional trope of the scientist-husband of nature generating the legitimate, sacred fruit of true knowledge in the womb of the wife's body is engaged here with chilling modifications. A metaphor for the magical power of science, alchemy is about the generative sexual practices of the craft, which are a kind of marriage that yields gold from base metal. Alchemy is about holy alliances, true marriages with gleaming children. In the PreMed advertisement, the narrative is reversed, and an "unholy alliance" threatens to mutate the promised gold of a medical-career investment into the base metal of a nonproductive practice. "If you've made an unholy alliance, perhaps we can help." Call upon PreMed and enjoy the fruit of a productive union. Be flexible; make the required structural adjustments to stimulate the production of wealth—and its flow upward to the deserving professional classes. Leave that unnatural and unprofitable alliance with infected bodies. A healthy family life demands no less.

The PreMed ad almost seems out of its time. It shouldn't still be possible to publish such an image in a scientific medical magazine. But it is possible. The fierce resurgence of explicit racist, sexist, and class-biased discourse of many kinds all over the world, and exuberantly in the United States, gives all too much permission for this merely implicit and latent joke.

My third text, by contrast, wants to be firmly on the side of the antiracist angels. All the signs of liberal multiculturalism pervade *Time* magazine's cover image for its special fall 1993 issue on immigration. These angels,

Virtual Eve. (Time *magazine cover, Fall 1993, © 1993 Courtesy Time Inc., reprinted with Permission)*

however, turn out to exist in cyberspace. The *Time* cover is a morphed portrait of a being I call SimEve. In the background is a matrix of her mixed cybergenetic kin, all resulting from different "racial" crosses effected by a computer program. "Take a good look at this woman. She was created by a computer from a mix of several races. What you see is a remarkable preview of . . . The New Face of America." Indeed. We are abruptly returned to the ontology of databases and the marriage of genomics and informatics in the artificial life worlds that reconstitute what it means to be human. Here, the category so ethereally and technically reconfigured is race. In an odd computerized updating of the typological categories of the nineteenth and early twentieth centuries, the programmer who gave birth to SimEve and her many siblings generated the ideal racial synthesis, whose only possible existence is in the matrices of cyberspace. Genetic engineering is not yet up to the task, so it falls to the computer sciences alone for now. Full of new information, the first family reconstructed by Jay Matternes has had a transgenic change of form, to reemerge from *Time*'s computer womb as morphed ideal citizens, fit for the "Rebirthing of America." If the biotechnological genetics laboratory was the natural habitat and evolutionary scene fusing nature and culture for OncoMouse™'s version of the origin of life, SimEve's primal story takes place in the first morphing program for the personal computer, called Morph 2.0, produced by the Gryphon Software Corporation.[31]

This technology has proved irresistible in the United States for 1990s mass cultural racialized kinship discourse on human unity and diversity. Never has there been a better toy for playing out sexualized racial fantasies, anxieties, and dreams. The reverie begins in cross-specific morphing, with the compelling computer-generated composite of human and chimpanzee faces in the 1992 *Cambridge Encyclopedia of Human Evolution*.[32] Soberly looking straight at the reader, the mature face is intelligent and beautiful. Like Carl Akeley's taxidermic reconstructions, this morphed face feeds a deep fantasy of touch across the ethnospecific categories of nature and culture. Unframed by any such specificity, the face seems to bring word about an original transformation in universal natural history.

On the contemporary human register, Gillette's shaving ads on television show the transformation of men's faces into each other across a racial spectrum, producing a utopic multiethnic male bonding. In the September 1994 Great American Fashion Issue of the feminism-lite magazine *Mirabella*, the prominent photographer Hiro produced the computer-generated cover image from many photos of exquisitely beautiful, multiracial, multiethnic women. Asked by the editors to give them a photo to represent "the diversity of America," Hiro did a simulated (and very light-skinned) woman.[33] A tiny microchip floats through space next to her gorgeous face. I read the chip as a sign of insemination, of the seminal creative power of Hiro, a modern Pygmalion/Henry Higgins creating his Galatea/Eliza Doolittle. But the seminal power is not just Hiro's; it is the generative power of technology. Pygmalion himself has been morphed; he has become a computer program. Internationally, Benetton's ads, including its morphed racial transforms, and its magazine *The United Colours of Benetton*, are the most famous. As Celia Lury put it, eschewing the distinction between cloth and skin, Benetton deals with the color of skin as a fashion palette. Benetton produces a stunningly beautiful, young, stylish panhumanity composed by mix-and-match techniques. Diversity, like DNA, is the code of codes. Race, in Sarah Franklin's words, becomes a fashion accessory.[34]

All this is surely not the naturalized typologies of Teddy Bear Patriarchy's early-twentieth-century racial discourse, nor are we here subjected to Pre-Med's version of racial-sexual crossing. So why do I feel so uncomfortable? Shouldn't I be happy that the patently constructed nature of racial and gender categories is so obvious? In the face of resurgent racial hatred all around, what's wrong with a little obvious ideology for Butterbrickle multiculturalism? Do we always have to order Rocky Road? Am I just having a dyspeptic attack of political correctness inevitably brought on by indulging in the pleasures of high-technology commodification within multinational capitalism? Why shouldn't the United Nations' *Family of Man* be morphed into the New World Order's *United Colours of Benetton?* Certainly the photography has advanced, and the human family seems naturally to be the story of the progress of technology.

To address the discomfort, let us look more closely at the *Time* special issue on immigration. In the note from the managing editor on page 2, we learn that the *Time* imaging specialist Kin Wah Lam created the matrix of progeny in the table out of photographs of seven male and seven female models, each assigned to a racial-ethnic category. The top (female) and side (male) photos were electronically "mated" to produce the cybergenetic offspring. Each figure is a pleasant-faced but undramatic nude bust, a "natural" man or woman, enhanced modestly by the understated makeup and minimal hair styling. All the figures are young adults; and all the unions are chastely heterosexual, although presumably the computer could do a bit better than the technology of eggs and sperm on that score. In their defense, the editors' purpose was "to dramatize the impact of multiethnic marriage, which has increased dramatically in the U.S. during the latest wave of immigration." Still, the trope of reproductive heterosexual marriage is as firmly ensconced here as in the worlds of *The Fossil Footprint Makers of Laetoli* or *The Family of Man.* The mixing of immigration could be dramatized by many other practices. The sense of utter homogeneity that emanates from *Time*'s matrix of diversity is numbing. The blacks are not very black; the blondes are not very blond; the range of skin color would require the best chromatography to distinguish one promising golden hue from another. These figures of the new humanity look the way I imagine a catalog of replicants for sale off world in *Blade Runner* might look—young, beautiful, talented, diverse, and programmed to fulfill the buyer's wishes and then self-destruct. Unlike the terrible white-supremacist scenes of *Birth of a Nation* in 1915, nothing about race and ethnicity in *Time*'s Rebirthing of a Nation speaks about racial domination, guilt, and hatred. Nothing here is scary; so why am I trembling?

As Claudia Castañeda put it in her argument about "morphing the global U.S. family," "[t]he racism here does not consist in the establishment of a hierarchy for domination based on biologized or even culturized racial difference. Its violence consists in the evacuation of histories of domination and resistance (and of all those events and ways of living that cannot be captured in those two terms) *through* technological (but still decidedly heterosexual) reproduction."[35] The denials and evasions in this liberal, antiracist, technophilic exercise are at least as thick as they are in the PreMed ad. All the bloody history caught by the ugly word "miscegenation" is missing in the sanitized term "morphing." Multiculturalism and racial mixing in *Time* magazine are less achievements against the odds of so much pain than a recipe for being innocently raptured out of mundane into redeemed time. It is the resolute absence of history, of the fleshy body that bleeds, that scares me. It is the reconfirmation of the Sacred Image of the Same, once again under the sign of difference, that threatens national rebirth. I want something much messier, more dangerous, thicker, and more satisfying from the hope for multiculturalism. To get that kind of national reproductive health delivery is going to take addressing past and present sexualized racial power, privilege, exclusion, and exploitation. I suspect the nation will have to swallow the castor oil of sober accountability about such racialized sex before morphing looks like much fun to most of its citizens.[36]

Alongside a photo of the imaging specialist, labeled with a classically orientalist caption, "Lam creates a mysterious image," *Time*'s managing editor tells us still more about the cybergenesis of the woman on the cover:

> A combination of the racial and ethnic features of the women used to produce the chart, she is: 15% Anglo-Saxon, 17.5% Middle Eastern, 17.5% African, 7.5% Asian, 35% Southern European and 7.5% Hispanic. Little did we know what we had wrought. As onlookers watched the image of our new Eve begin to appear on the computer screen, several staff members fell in love. Said one: "It really breaks my heart that she doesn't exist." We sympathize with our lovelorn colleagues, but even technology has its limits. This is a love that must forever remain unrequited.

Themes running throughout the essay implode in this unlikely black hole. Early-century racialized ethnic categories reappear as entries in an electronic database for a truly odd statistical population analysis. A virtual woman is the result, fathered like Galatea, Pygmalion's creature, with which he fell in love. The curious erotics of single-parent, masculine, technophilic reproduction cannot be missed. SimEve is like Zeus's Athena, child only of the seminal mind—of a man and of a computer program. The law of the nation, like that laid down by Athena for Athens in the Orestian trilogy, will be the Law of the Father. The Furies in cyberspace will not be pleased. In the narrative of romantic love, SimEve forever excites a desire that cannot be fulfilled. This is precisely the myth infusing dreams of technological transcendence of the body. In these odd, but conventional, technoscientific erotics, the actual limits of technology only spur the desire to love that which cannot and does not exist. SimEve is the new universal human, mother of the new race, figure of the nation; and she is a computer-generated composite, like the human genome itself. She is the second- and third-order offspring of the ramifying code of codes. She ensures the difference of no difference in the human family.

PostScript™

THROUGHOUT "UNIVERSAL DONORS IN A VAMPIRE CULTURE," RACIAL DIScourse has persistently pivoted on sexual hygiene, and the therapeutic scene has been the theater of nature in the city of science. I am sick to death of bonding through kinship and "the family"; and I long for models of solidarity and human unity and difference rooted in friendship, work, partially shared purposes, intractable collective pain, inescapable mortality, and persistent hope. It is time to theorize an "unfamiliar" unconscious, a different primal scene, where everything does not stem from the dramas of identity and reproduction. Ties through blood—including blood recast in the coin of genes and information—have been bloody enough already. I believe that there will be no racial or sexual peace, no livable nature, until we learn to produce humanity through something more and less than kinship. I think I am on the side of the vampires, or at least some of them. But, then, since when does one get to choose which vampire will trouble one's dreams?

SOCIAL NATURE

Part of the ideological power of nature flows from the word's implication that it describes a universal quality: nature is something, surely, that is common to us all, that all of us share. And yet reality is rarely so simple. When we look closely at ideas of nature, we almost always find competing notions of the good, the true, and the beautiful disguised as singular, monolithic nature. The question we need always to ask of such competing notions is "Whose nature?" What looks natural to one person may look all too unnatural to another. As soon as we recognize disagreements of this sort, we face the difficult challenge of adjudicating between them. If nature is partly in the eyes of the beholder, whose eyes should we trust to see it clearly? The answer to this question is unlikely to come just from nature itself; it is more apt to come from our own complicated dialogue with each other and with the (rest of) the natural world.

WHERE YOU AT?—
A Bioregional Quiz

Compiled by: Leonard Charles, Jim Dodge,
Lynn Milliman, Victoria Stockley.

What follows is a self-scoring test on basic environmental perception of place. Scoring is done on the honor system, so if you fudge, cheat, or elude, you also get an idea of where you're at. The quiz is culture-bound, favoring those people who live in the country over city dwellers, and scores can be adjusted accordingly. Most of the questions, however, are of such a basic nature that undue allowances are not necessary.

1. Trace the water you drink from precipitation to tap.

2. How many days till the moon is full? (Slack of two days allowed.)

3. What soil series are you standing on?

4. What was the total rainfall in your area last year (July–June)? (Slack: 1 inch for every 20 inches.)

5. When was the last time a fire burned your area?

6. What were the primary subsistence techniques of the culture that lived in your area before you?

7. Name five native edible plants in your region and their season(s) of availability.

8. From what direction do winter storms generally come in your region?

9. Where does your garbage go?

10. How long is the growing season where you live?

11. On what day of the year are the shadows the shortest where you live?

12. When do the deer rut in your region, and when are the young born?

13. Name five grasses in your area. Are any of them native?

14. Name five resident and five migratory birds in your area.

15. What is the land use history of where you live?

16. What primary ecological event / process influenced the land form where you live? (Bonus special: what's the evidence?)

17. What species have become extinct in your area?

18. What are the major plant associations in your region?

19. From where you're reading this, point north.

20. What spring wildflower is consistently among the first to bloom where you live?

Scoring:

0–3   You have your head up your ass.

4–7   It's hard to be in two places at once when you're not anywhere at all.

8–12   A fairly firm grasp of the obvious.

13–16   You're paying attention.

17–19   You know where you're at.

20   You not only know where you're at, you know where it's at.

"Where You At?" *(Leonard Charles, Jim Dodge, Lynn Milliman, and Victoria Stockley, reprinted with the permission of Jim Dodge, from* CoEvolution Quarterly *[now* Whole Earth Review*], Winter 1981; subscriptions to WER are $20 a year [4 issues] from P.O. Box 38, Sausalito, CA, 94966, 415-332-1716)*

Goats test notions of 'native' and 'exotic' species

It's been 10,000 years since native mountain goats roamed the weathered peaks in Yellowstone National Park. They supposedly disappeared about the same time that glaciers retreated northward into Canada.

Now a new invasion of mountain goats—and a plan to shoot them—is forcing Yellowstone resource managers to re-open the old debate over maintaining native and exotic species in America's oldest wildlife sanctuary.

Many compare this latest controversy in wildlife management to the recent decision to have uniformed park rangers shoot buffalo cows leaving Yellowstone this winter. However, there have been few, if any, instances in Yellowstone's modern history where wildlife managers have considered killing large, wild mammals migrating *into* the park.

According to guidelines established in 1968, goats migrating into Yellowstone across the western park boundary will be welcomed, while goats entering from the northeast or south may be shot on sight.

"This is ridiculous," charged Cleveland Amory, executive director of the New York City-based Fund For Animals. "We will certainly have our lawyers look into this one. Why should one group of goats be considered natural and another group shot for going into the park? It's a bunch of crap."

While Amory's outrage is shared by some conservationists and wildlife advocacy organizations, park officials say their policy is clear. Goats classified as exotic must be stopped before they destroy habitat important to bighorn sheep and rare plants already occupying Yellowstone's fragile high country.

Yellowstone's research chief, John Varley, says the park is mandated to protect native species like bighorn sheep and their habitat against exotic intruders. "The first thing you have to decide is what is a native species," Varley said. "There are a number of interpretations out there."

Since the retreat of glaciers from the greater Yellowstone region, goats have been expanding down the spine of the Rocky Mountain front, Varley said. Their range once extended from Canada into Mexico and as far east as central Wyoming. Evolutionary models adopted by the Park Service dictate that species recolonizing Yellowstone from the west are consistent with natural wildlife dispersal in the post Pleistocene period and are therefore acceptable.

The arrival of mountain goats in Yellowstone, coupled with the recent discovery of goat bone shards at paleontological digs in the park, substantiates two conclusions: First, goats were once native to Yellowstone, and second, a population approaching the park from the west should be welcomed because it is part of a naturally expanding population.

Researchers, however, say the so-called "native" population of goats moving in from the west is not expected to reach the park for several years. The park's problems will begin with goat populations artificially introduced into areas of the ecosystem where they would not occur naturally for hundreds, if not thousands, of years.

Goats were "planted" for hunters

Several decades ago, wildlife officials in Montana, Wyoming and Idaho transplanted mountain goats into a chain of peaks on the Yellowstone periphery. This was meant to build populations suitable for hunting on adjacent national forest lands. The goats adapted well to the new terrain, and their numbers grew rapidly.

The Targhee National Forest on Yellowstone's western tier now has 150 goats, the Bridger-Teton to the south 370, the Shoshone on the east 120 and the Beaverhead to the northwest 290. Dozens of those goats are advancing toward Yellowstone across the Beartooth and Absaroka ranges on the northeast and southern corners of the park.

"They're already here, if you really want to know the truth," said John Laundre, hired by the Park Service to study goats and present a list of possible options for managing them. Laundre has taken several photographs of exotic goats already inside the Yellowstone boundary.

Varley said a decision will be made later this year on how to confront the earliest arrivals. The options include shooting the exotic goats, attempting to haze them out of the park, or simply leaving them alone and allowing them to cultivate their own biological niche.

Laundre said that even if Yellowstone is successful in stopping the advance of the exotic goats by shooting them, they would be back on the park border within 20 to 30 years.

"It's not a simple problem," he said. "The easiest thing to do would probably be to allow the goats to move into the park, but then they [Yellowstone resource managers] have to contend with habitat questions. They also have the Olympic [National Park] experience as a reminder of the type of resource damage goats can cause."

Goats wreak havoc

Yellowstone officials say they are closely watching events unfold in Olympic National Park, where exotic goats have wreaked havoc. Goats were never native to Olympic; sportsmen's organizations introduced them to Washington's Olympic Peninsula outside the park between 1925 and 1929. The number of goats subsequently grew to a peak population of 1,000 and adopted the national park as a new home, said Chuck Janda, Olympic's chief ranger.

"It's one of the classic cases of what you call natural," Janda said. "We have this myth that we can maintain a natural ecosystem. There is no way any national park can exist as an island."

Nevertheless, national park officials there cite erosion problems and the destruction of native plants and habitat as reasons for drastically reducing the number of goats in Olympic's back country. Janda said overgrazing and goat wallows, exacerbated by erosion, now represent a major problem on Olympic's steep mountain slopes.

To date, 407 goats have been removed in a live-capture, aerial-removal program, Janda said, but park officials have deemed aerial removal too dangerous and are considering a plan to eliminate the goats by shooting them. Although Olympic's plan to shoot goats is not popular among animal-rights groups, it is considered one of the few viable options for protecting the park's natural resources.

Rich Day, executive director of the Montana Wildlife Federation, said it is premature for Yellowstone to recommend a solution without more research. The federation, Montana's largest and oldest statewide conservation organization, has 7,000 members, most of them hunters and anglers.

Day said his organization is awaiting completion of an environmental review of Olympic's proposed goat shoot, which may offer some guidelines for Yellowstone. "I do find it interesting," Day added, "that Yellowstone is concerned on the one hand about balancing habitat between bighorn sheep and goats, while on the other hand they show no concern about balancing habitat for their native bison."

Yellowstone's goats are likely to trigger a broader analysis of whether the park's notion of native and exotic species is now out of date, Varley said, and whether Yellowstone can realistically maintain an ecosystem composed only of native species.

"I don't envy their position," Laundre commented. "If they don't do anything and the goats impact the native flora and fauna, then they'll look like the bad guys to some people. But if they intervene early and shoot the goats to prevent resource problems, then they'll also be the bad guys. It's definitely a Catch-22."

—Todd Wilkinson

Todd Wilkinson is a free-lance writer based in Bozeman, Montana.

"Goats Test Notions of 'Native' and 'Exotic' Species." (*Courtesy Todd Wilkinson*, High Country News, *October 22, 1990*)

Ricardo Carrillo, Grade 5, John Otis School

Don't pollute: A child's-eye view. *(Drawing by Ricardo Carrillo, grade 5, John Otis School*, San Diego Bay Watershed Protection 1994 Calendar, *courtesy Environmental Health Coalition, 1717 Kettner Boulevard, Suite 100, San Diego, CA, 92101)*

URBAN WILDERNESS TRAILS

VANCOUVER

B.C. CANADA

THE URBAN WILDERNESS

Vast and untamed, the Urban Wilderness is an area of varied topography and scenic terrain. Mountain views, sidewalk flora, shadows and reflections are a few of the many species of wildlife indigenous to the area. The Urban Wilderness is in fact a wildlife sanctuary. Many rewards are available for the naturalist and the photographer.

A local naturalist shows a visitor a prime example of backlane flora.

There are three self-guided nature trails. Each of these has its own special terrain. The Westend Trail is a walk that includes wildlife familiar to all visitors. The False Creek Trail, with its spectacular scenic views, reveals to the walker a different approach to the downtown area. The Explorer's Trail is for the adventurous walker. It appeals primarily to those persons motivated by a desire for wilderness surroundings, although the inexperienced walker will have no trouble enjoying this trail as well. Along all of the trails, wildlife markers have been placed on the sidewalk. For example, where a remarkable mountain view is to be seen, the words 'mountain view' and a directional arrow will be found. In the case of more transient species of wildlife, i.e., shadows, reflections, clouds, etc., photos have been mounted near the marker as additional evidence. The wise walker will be aware that the Urban Wilderness is constantly changing and will therefore be continually on the alert.

In addition to these three self-guided trails, there are numerous unmarked trails available to the experienced walker.

"Urban Wilderness Trails." *(Courtesy Michael de Courcy)*

WESTEND TRAIL
FOR SOMETHING CLOSE TO HOME

The Westend Trail covers the north-west section of the area. This trail has many splendid mountain views, especially along Dunsmuir and Georgia Streets. Bute and Jervis Streets take you into the densest part of the trail with many varied species of wildlife. Along Davie Street the walker will find shadows of all kinds, particularly during the spring and summer months. Continuing along Thurlow Street one discovers vast areas of water for the first time. Bringing the walker back to the downtown area is Burrard Street, and the trail contiues through this area where it is possible to encounter many forms of human wildlife.

This trail is marked on the map — - - - - - - -

FALSE CREEK TRAIL
FOR SPECTACULAR SCENIC VIEWS

This trail leads through the industrial area along Hamilton and Helmcken, which is the backbone of the city. Industrial wildlife of all kinds are abundant. Random rocks, unlikely sidewalk flora and scattered debris are typical of this part of the trail. On reaching Granville Street, the walker encounters for the first time the hustle and bustle of a major downtown street. At Granville and Drake the walker should board a bus to portage across False Creek to Broadway and Granville, at this point transferring to a Broadway bus which will carry the walker to Broadway and Cambie. Note the magnificent mountain views along this section of the trail and the splendid perspective of the downtown one gets from this far off vantage point. The trail continues along Cambie Street across the Connaught Bridge. The walk across this bridge is breathtaking. The mountains north of the downtown are readily visible, in particular, Vancouver's famous moving Lions, which appear and disappear as one moves along the bridge. To the north-east is a wonderful view of the Mount Seymour question mark. And then there is False Creek itself, one of the few interior waterways of the city. On reaching the end of the bridge there is the interesting Coast Paper reflection, a distinctive landmark.

This trail is marked on the map — • • • • • • •

EXPLORER'S TRAIL
FOR THE ADVENTUROUS WALKER

This is the most untamed self-guided trail. The strong and direct mountain views are the magnet that draws most visitors to this region, along with the most dramatic evidence of weather. Proceeding north along Hamilton to Pender the walker reaches Victory Square, nesting ground for the many pigeons of the area. Wilderness camping is not restricted to particular sites, although there are more popular sites along Cordova and Hastings Streets. However, this is a wilderness area with little direct supervision, and visitors must remember to supervise themselves. Continuing along Cordova to Main, to the north is a magnificent mountain view, to the south the broad thoroughfare of Main Street. A notable landmark at this point is the vine abundantly creeping up the Courthouse wall. One block east of Main the trail crosses Hastings Street, the heart of the Explorer's Trail. On Keefer the walker should note an uncontrolled bamboo grove. The trail proceeds along Keefer and crosses Main where for the second time there is a view of the mountains, this time from a more southerly point. At Keefer and Main Streets it is possible to board a bus and travel to Broadway and Main, transferring to continue along Broadway to Cambie Street where the trail joins up with the False Creek Trail. For further information on this section, read the passage on the False Creek Trail.

At Keefer and Columbia is another point of interest, a vacant lot. Walkers would be well advised to prowl around this area and see for themselves the evidence of wildlife past. Hastings Street is the most arduous part of this trail, and the walker should continue slowly as there is much to be seen. Wildlife of all kinds is abundant and flourishing here. The end of the trail connects one again to the downtown area, and the walker will be aware of changes in the terrain.

This trail is marked on the map — ——

Wilderness camping is not restricted to particular sites.

On Mourning Our Built-Up World

Quake, fire and flood expose the limits of human existence. But our 'things' are not just the detritus of futile attempts to dominate nature. They are our part in creation.

By MARLENE ADLER MARKS

When it comes to discussing the post-fire and -earthquake period in Los Angeles, I tell my mother: Everything is fine; we're back to normal now. But it's not true. Since Jan. 17 a sense of the weird has taken over. Last week, two friends were burned out of their home, which spontaneously burst into flames. A pipe bomb was found on the San Diego freeway. Cracks appear in exterior walls and plaster comes off ceilings as the earth continues to settle. And this week, floods.

And so Southern California life continues, swinging between two planes. Jews call this period *shiva*, mourning for the old in the midst of the new. In this period, we ponder how much we can control, how much we even matter. There's plenty of time now, on endless rides avoiding cracked freeways, to ponder eternity.

For me, a basic premise about the way things work is up for grabs. Once I craved to live "in nature," amid the primeval bounties of hill and sea; but now it's mankind's works that I monitor and miss. The great eucalyptus grove by the roadside was planted; it did not just sprout. And the homes over there that are now rubble or cracked or otherwise red-tagged—these are personal visions, testimony to what human creativity can bring. What I once thought of as "natural" needed human participation to come to life.

Such appreciation is new to me. I was raised to judge harshly the human role on earth. My bias, received from elders like John Muir, grandfather of the ecology movement, is to leave alone as much of my habitat as possible. Nature creates. I can only mess up.

But now that's obviously reversed. Nature has messed up. And to restore order, we must begin to create. And so we come to our unfinished business. In the days since the fire and earthquake, acknowledging loss remains our community's unfinished business.

But on both the personal and the civic level, it is not acceptable to grieve. True, fire and earthquake show us how negligible our lives are in the scheme of things, but we're doing our best to make them more negligible still.

So it is that we tell each other that the family heirlooms now reduced to glass splinters are "just things." That our condos and apartments were unsafe anyway and therefore unworthy. And that our freeways and shopping malls were unsightly examples of urban sprawl. An aura of embarrassment overtakes those who dare to assert that life was good, that for example, a day in the library or spent walking down Montana Avenue in Santa Monica represented if not true art, then at least a bit of harmony. Instead, the major message is that the works of our hands, that which we have added to the landscape, somehow violate the natural order.

As it turns out, this question of where harmony lies and who and what shall rule reflects an American ambivalence about progress grounded in the late 19th Century. Our economic expansion has typically been justified by a literal interpretation of the Bible: Hasn't God given the Earth to men like Andrew Carnegie to rule over it? But in the same breath, with help from transcendentalists like Emerson and Thoreau, Genesis is reinterpreted as an ecological tract. By this theory, humans are intended to be low-impact gardeners, placed on Earth merely to "dress" and "keep it." That's why Muir, the gardener *par excellence* and friend of Emerson, fought so hard to keep Yosemite Valley and the national park system as pristine enclaves. And that's why we give ourselves so little comfort when our urban life is destroyed.

But there is a third interpretation of Genesis, kinder and more comforting, which can help us understand sadness with the loss of our "things." By this version, mankind is "co-creator"—here to work the land and improve it, to complete what God purposely had left unfinished. It is this third definition that I think about today, in a world of broken glass. Most of us seek neither to dominate the world nor to leave it completely alone. And by now, we understand that whatever we build can be gone in a flash. But between these two poles—between chaos and order—there is creativity and even a stab at beauty. And the knowledge that living in nature is both work and art.

Marlene Adler Marks is a columnist for the Jewish Journal of Greater Los Angeles.

"On Mourning Our Built-Up World" (Los Angeles Times, *February 9, 1994, courtesy of Marlene Adler Marks*)

COMMON
PLACES

Reinventing Common Nature: Yosemite and Mount Rushmore— A Meandering Tale of a Double Nature

Kenneth R. Olwig*

Preface

JUST NORTH OF COPENHAGEN, THE CITY IN WHICH I HAVE LIVED FOR THE past twenty years, there is a special place called Dyrehaven.[1] It was established in the seventeenth century as a royal game park on the site of an ancient village, which was razed, leaving only the village pond and traces of high ridged fields. The game, partially tame deer, still roam the park's grassy open glades beneath high-trunked old trees. Copenhageners have made pilgrimages to this spot since time immemorial because it is the site of a holy spring. It is a public park today, and it is the natural place for Copenhageners to go on outings with friends, associates, or family, to court, to recreate, and to play in what is seen to be quintessential Danish nature. The park was a major cause célèbre for the budding national nature preservation movement in the early twentieth century, and today it is managed much like an American national park, complete with nature interpreters.[2] When I returned to my American homeland to "reinvent nature" in California, I naturally took my half-Danish daughter and my Danish wife to Yosemite, my favorite American natural park. But the whole time I was there, I kept thinking of Dyrehaven. I kept thinking about how words like "natural" have taken on different shades of meaning in different cultures and at different times.[3] These etymological speculations recalled Raymond Williams's statement that "the idea of nature contains, though often unnoticed, an extraordinary amount of human history."[4] It became clear to me that my musings were of more than semantic importance, and I kept wondering what it is that makes a park a park, and what makes a park both natural and national, not to mention "American." National parks would seem to be as much about the nature of national identity as about physical nature. If this is so, they should be able to tell us a lot about ourselves as Americans; a lot about the way we interact with each other and our environment. When seen in this light, parks become places where we "reinvent nature" in our own image, and hence good places to study the reflections of that image.

Nature and National Parks

"NATURE" HAS A DOUBLE MEANING AND REPRESENTS AT ONE AND THE SAME time both a physical realm and the realm of cultural ideals and norms— all of which we lump together as the "natural."[5] If we say that Americans "naturally" love their country we are implying that this truth about the nature of Americans is to be taken for granted. To be an American is to love one's country. Much as it would be "unnatural" for Americans not to love their country, it would be "unnatural" to call this "truth" into question. But why is it "natural" to love the "purple mountains' majesty," and what do mountains have to do with the "leaves of grass" on the "fruited plain"? Despite the fact, then, that *nature* is one of the most abstract and compli-cated concepts we have, nature nevertheless signifies all that is concrete, unmediated, and *naturally* given.[6] It is this doubleness of meaning that makes the term "nature" so duplicitous that it should never be taken at face value. Yet we do so constantly, because not to do so is to challenge basic norms. The very idea of "reinventing" nature is no doubt offensive to many people because the natural is so bound up with their deepest, unreflected, individual, social, and national values. If, however, people are to become aware of the questionable ways that their concepts of nature can affect the way they act upon their physical environment, then they must question these values. They must realize that the "natural" values they find in their environment are given not by physical nature but by society.

This essay attempts to reinvent, or at least recover, an essentially premod-ern concept of nature in which people and their values do not appear to be excluded from nature. I wish to defend an older usage of the word in which nature is fundamentally a generative, creative principle. It is a principle fur-thermore akin to that of "love"—be it love toward an individual, "thy neighbor," or one's country. This usage of "nature" emphasizes sustainable reciprocity rather than domination and makes of nature not a spectacle but something to be dwelled within. I hope this will lead people to reflect upon that which they take most for granted—*nature*.

Yosemite and Mount Rushmore are ideal vehicles with which to approach the nature of American environmental values and behavior. Yosemite valley is where the national park idea was pioneered in 1864.[7] It was the archetypal natural park and broke the ground for the establishment of a later system of national parks. Mount Rushmore makes a useful counterpoint to Yosemite because it expresses a transformation in the idea of nature and in ideas of the natural way for Americans to interact with each other and their environment. The comparison will point to the necessity of reinventing a "common nature." It was this idea of a common nature, I will argue, that gave rise to the idea of Yosemite as a natural park for the American people. If this natural ideal was the model for all of America, not just some of its parks, we might be able to rectify environmental policies that tend to create inviolable wilderness preserves in areas where people are largely excluded while overlooking the desecration of environments where we live and work.

Nature as Fertile Commons—A Meandering Stream of Consciousness

YOSEMITE IS NOT JUST A NATURAL AREA; IT IS A NATURAL "PARK." THE Yosemite valley, with its meandering stream of the Merced River—the river of mercy—flowing through green meadows at the bottom of a rock-walled canyon, has always been immediately recognizable as a park to American visitors. According to Lafayette Bunnell, who was among the first whites to penetrate the valley, in 1851, it "presented the appearance of a well kept park." Bunnell was the diarist of Major James D. Savage's military expedition, whose mission was to further mining interests by evicting the Ahwahneechee Indians from Yosemite.[8] To Frederik Law Olmsted, who first visited the valley in 1864, Yosemite was a "wild park," and represented "the greatest glory of nature."[9] He was the first chairman of the California Yosemite Park Commission, which managed the valley until 1906, when the federal government retook control of the park. As the landscape architect of what was to become a similarly encanyoned scene of meadows and winding streams—New York's Central Park—Olmsted knew what he meant by park "scenery."[10] Even the great celebrant of a wild and sublime Yosemite—John Muir, the founding president of the Sierra Club (1892)—praised its valleys for being "a grand landscape garden."[11] This is the term used for British landscape parks in the "natural" style, which had their heyday in the eighteenth century. The new "natural" parks were called landscape gardens to distinguish them from the formal gardens they replaced.

This seemingly automatic recognition of Yosemite as being naturally a park, much more than the persuasive abilities of particular individuals, arguably generated the national consensus that made Yosemite the pioneer national park. Drawings, paintings, and written descriptions somehow effectively transmitted the idea to the American public that Yosemite was not just natural but was and ought to be a park. This suggests that if we are

Merced River in Yosemite Valley. *(Photograph by William Cronon)*

to understand the "nature" of Yosemite, we will have to look much more closely at the idea of the park as it has become ingrained in Western civilization.

What Is a Park?

THE ETYMOLOGICALLY PRIMARY MEANING OF THE WORD "PARK," FOUND IN many early European languages, is an enclosed preserve for beasts of the chase. A "wilderness" was, in contrast, the place where the beasts (*deoren* in Old English) ran wild (wild-deer-ness), and was related to "bewilderment" and going astray. The term "park" was later extended to mean a "large ornamental piece of ground, usually comprising woodland and pasture, attached to or surrounding a country house or mansion, and used for recreation, and often for keeping deer, cattle, or sheep."[12] Olmsted was clearly thinking of this sort of park when he described Yosemite in terms of "the most placid pools . . . with the most tranquil meadows, the most playful streams, and every variety of soft and peaceful pastoral beauty." The meandering stream of the Merced, he tells us, "is such a one as Shakespeare delighted in, and brings pleasing reminiscences to the traveller of the Avon or the upper Thames."[13]

When woodlands are enclosed for wild game, or for the pasturage of domesticated animals in a pastoral economy, they take on a characteristically open, grassy, "parklike" appearance with scattered, "naturally" fully crowned, high-trunked trees. The "natural" appearance of parkland trees is due to the browsing of the animals, helped, perhaps, by the clearing activities of the gamekeepers, shepherds, or gardeners. This environment is ideally suited to sport and recreation and thus also for pleasure parks because people, even on horseback, can move freely and quickly after game or a ball.

Natural Paradise and Unnatural Wilderness Desert

PARKS APPEAR TO BE ATTRACTIVE AND COMFORTABLE BY NATURE, AND THIS clearly explains some of their appeal. It does not explain, however, the symbolic importance of national parks as places to preserve both nature and national values. This symbolic appeal of parks can be explained by way of the link between the idea of the park and that of paradise. The word "paradise" made its way from Persian to Greek and from there to Latin and the

Lucas Cranach's (1472–1553) *Das Goldene Zeitalter* (The Golden Age) might be seen as a highly stylized version of Yosemite, complete with meandering stream, parklike meadow, and a surrounding wall, beyond which are wild mountains and what might pass for a contemporaneous San Francisco. *(Photo © Nasjonalgalleriet, courtesy National Gallery, Oslo, Norway)*

other languages of Europe. The primary dictionary derivation is "enclosed park," and the first paradises were indeed hunting grounds.[14] The horsemen and hunters on Savage's expedition may have had this sort of happy hunting ground on their minds when one of them suggested calling the place "Paradise Valley."[15] The meaning of the word "paradise" also extended to mean "enclosed orchard or pleasure ground." In this context it was natural to describe the biblical Garden of Eden as a paradise. It was, of course, in this mythical fertile orchard, watered by a river and grazed by various creatures, that humankind was believed to have been born. The Germanic word "garden," which is related to the modern English word "yard," also means enclosed area. Yosemite and the neighboring Hetch Hetchy valley, which Muir described as "a spacious flowery lawn four or five miles long, surrounded by magnificent snowy mountains,"[16] have the physical attributes of such an enclosed paradisiacal park. It was therefore not inappropriate for Muir to make the Garden of Eden, "its boundaries drawn by the Lord," a precedent for Yosemite as the first nature reserve.[17]

Paradise would not generate strong feelings concerning the need to preserve landscapes like Yosemite in national parks if the Garden of Eden merely called forth a nostalgic desire to return to an earlier, idyllic form of existence. The garden idea is potent because it has long been a vital symbol in Western culture of a moral society living in "natural" social and environmental harmony. Historically, the counterpositioning of the paradise garden park to the wilderness was a means of making a symbolic statement about the *nature* of *natural* national existence. The delightful garden park represents a fertile blend of the four elements: earth, wind, fire, and water. It is counterpoised to a wild wasteland, which is characterized by the infertile dominance of one element at the expense of the others. This basic framework is found in much Western art, where the wasteland might be represented by everything from dry desert (a plethora of fire and earth) to the sea (a plethora of water) or the steamy jungle (a plethora of water and earth).[18] When an environment is infertile, it is "deserted" by life and becomes a *desert,* which in the original sense of the word need not be dry.

We find this structure in the classical and biblical literary sources that inspired artists. We see it, for example, in the Bible, where the nation of Israel is essentially told that if its people behave according to God's command,

> the Lord will comfort Zion;
>   he will comfort all her waste places,
>   and will make her wilderness like Eden,
>   her desert like the garden of the Lord.

The Lord transforms the desert into a garden by rectifying the balance of the elements with water:

> I will make the wilderness a pool of water,
> and the dry land springs of water.
> I will put in the wilderness the cedar,
> the acacia, the myrtle, and the olive;
> I will set in the desert the cypress,
> the plane and the pine together.

When the Israelites did not love and obey the Lord, however, "their lands became a wilderness because of the glow of his [Yahweh's] wrath."[19]

The same counterpoising of a garden to the desert wilderness can also be seen in the tradition of Virgilian classical pastoral poetry, in which the national importance of love and community is an important theme.[20] In Virgil's *Eclogues* the Roman Empire is thus depicted as behaving unnaturally when it expropriates Arcadia's common garden pastures in order to divide the area into properties for outsiders. This is symbolized by the native shepherds' being sent into exile to "thirsty Afri," to Scythia, "turbulent with mud," and to the Britons "sundered far off from the whole world."[21] The home they leave, on the other hand, becomes a wilderness, the oak under which they sang struck by lightening, the land they cross dry, formless, and barren—roamed by wolves. The reverse situation, however, is also possible, as when Virgil describes in the *Georgics* the peace that brings the hammering of swords into plowshares and results in the fertile rural idyll of a community of farmers and shepherds.

The physical "nature" of both the biblical and the classical stories reflects the "nature" of the human community. The moral is that if people act naturally, and love both their god(s) and one another, they will be able to live in environments that are fertile and comfortable; if they act unnaturally, they will struggle in rugged, infertile wilderness desert. There is thus a clear relation between the character of physical nature and the idea of the natural as related to the behavior of the human community. This "double" character of the concept of nature is paralleled by that of love. When the two concepts are compared, the relation between their physical and spiritual dimensions becomes clearer and hence less duplicitous.

Nature and "Love"

JOHN MUIR DESCRIBES THE YOSEMITE VALLEY AS THE "MOUNTAIN MANSION [where] Nature had gathered her choicest treasures, to draw her lovers into close and confiding communion with her."[22] There is good historical precedent for Muir's linking of the ideas of love and nature to Yosemite in this way. "Love," like "nature," has a dual meaning, involving both a physical dimension and a more spiritual, moral dimension. Love and nature go together, as we are told in a poem by a contemporary of Shakespeare: "What makes the vine about the elm to dance / With turnings windings and embracements round? / . . . Kind nature first doth cause all things to love; / Love makes them dance and in just order move."[23] The word nature derives from the Latin word for "birth," *natura*, and giving birth, of course, requires making physical love. The word *"nation"* derives from the same root. It refers to the native born who are the product not only of physical love but of the love that binds the nation together.[24] It is this love that generates the in*born* character, or *nature*, of that nation. This, in turn, is reflected in the *nature* of its environment. Muir saw a clear relation, in fact, between the nation's love for Yosemite and the moral "nature" of the nation itself. He thus described those who would dam Hetch Hetchy as "temple destroyers, devotees of ravaging commercialism, [who] seem to have a perfect contempt for Nature, and, instead of lifting their eyes to the God of the mountains, lift them to the Almighty Dollar."[25]

By making "Nature" a beloved woman, Muir, like many other nineteenth-century nature writers, was drawing upon an ancient allegorical tradition that represented the generative force of nature by the figure of Natura, a goddess of love.[26] Note that he applied the word "nature" not directly to the material environment of Yosemite but to a more abstract generative force called "Nature." This is historically the most common use of the word. Until the Renaissance, in fact, the word "nature" was not used to refer to the material environment itself. The material environment was the *expression* of this abstract natural creative force and was not in and of itself nature. Olmsted was using the word in this traditional way when he referred to Yosemite as expressing "the greatest glory of nature." We can get a better idea of what that nature represented by following the winding stream of Olmsted's Merced as it meandered back to its symbolic British source.

The Meandering Stream of Nature

IN HIS 1865 REPORT TO THE CALIFORNIA PARK COMMISSION FOR YOSEMITE, Olmsted makes repeated references to the recreational benefits for the upper classes of the British landscape parks. He notes the existence in Britain of "more than one thousand private parks and notable grounds devoted to luxury and recreation." These parks were so valuable that the cost of their annual maintenance was "greater than that of the national schools." He criticizes, however, the fact that the enjoyment of the "choicest natural scenes in the country" is the monopoly of "a very few, very rich people." After comparing the recreational value of this scenery to the collective value of the waters of a river, and after favorably comparing democratic America to Britain, he concludes, "It was in accordance with these views of the destiny of the New World and the duty of the republican government that Congress enacted that the Yosemite should be held, guarded and managed for the free use of the whole body of the people forever. . . ."[27] Olmsted's grasp of what was to become the American national park ideal was seminal precisely because he had such a good grasp of American social and cultural ideals.[28] It is therefore important to note the way Olmsted plays upon the continuities and discontinuities between American values and those of America's imperial mother country. The various metaphorical meanders by which Olmsted traces the Merced back to headwaters in England provide a useful means of understanding American ideas of nature. In following the current of these ideas back to their source, one soon discovers a vital cultural heritage that can help explain the genesis of American environmental values.

Yosemite and the Deserted Village

WHEN OLMSTED DRAWS UPON THE SYMBOLISM OF THE ENGLISH LANDSCAPE park as land that has been privatized and so made inaccessible to the general public, he is striking a theme that was widely known to the educated nineteenth-century public. Among the most familiar sources would have been *The Deserted Village*, by Oliver Goldsmith, from 1770, one of the most popular English poems ever written. In it Goldsmith describes the contemporary origin of the British parks in the gentry's imparkment of English village lands. I will dwell upon this poem at some length because it so wonderfully embodies the "natural" community values that Americans (and Goldsmith) felt Britain had deserted and the American folk had rightfully inherited. These natural values, as the poem makes clear, were heavily bound up with both the idea of the "park" and that of "imparkment," by which an area is enclosed. The village common or green in the poem is thus essentially a native community park that is imparked by a man of wealth in order to exclude that very community. The distinction between the community's park and the private imparked park is critical, even though the naked eye may not be able to distinguish the grass on the village common from that appropriated for the manor's natural-style landscape garden.

Though the description of Goldsmith's village of "sweet Auburn" seems quite realistic, we can only guess at its actual identity, because it is a literary fiction. As fiction it is not about the historical details of actual places but about the world of ideas attached to the long history of controversy surrounding the enclosure and imparkment of the land of the village commoners. The commons were enclosed as part of ongoing social and economic processes that generated ever larger private estates.[29] They were not normally enclosed because of an ecological "tragedy of the commons" that necessitated the land's transferal to private ownership as a result of environmental abuse by the commoners.[30] This fact is made particularly poignant by the irony of the enclosure of Auburn's working community commons in order to make room for a park designed to look like a "natural" functioning commons, but which, in reality, is an artificial construction for private plea-

The eighteenth-century landscape garden at Stourhead, in England, includes a reconstruction of an English village (complete with village green) which was reconstructed to look suitably ancient. *(Photograph by Kenneth R. Olwig)*

sure. In treating the social issues generated by enclosure and imparkment, this poem highlights the difference between the use of fiction to make people reflect upon their ideas of what is natural and the use of aesthetics to deceive by creating a scenic "virtual reality," which disguises an unnatural world and makes it seem natural.[31] This poem is especially relevant to our theme because it is about the aesthetics of imparkment and "scenery"—a term that itself derives from the realm of theatrical illusion. Guidebooks to our national parks are full of references to vantage points from which one might view natural "scenery." The origins of this word should alert us to the fact that the nature we are led to see might be staged.

In his poem Goldsmith describes an environment that could be Yosemite, with its stream and grassy lawns:

> How often have I loitered o'er thy green, . . .
> The sheltered cot, the cultivated farm,
> The never-failing brook, the busy mill,
> The decent church that topped the neighboring hill,
> The hawthorn bush, with seats beneath the shade,

For talking age and whispering lovers made!
How often have I blest the coming day,
When toil remitting lent its turn to play,
And all the village train, from labor free,
Led up their sports beneath the spreading tree.[32]

Yosemite, of course, is the sort of place the nation goes to take vacations on the green beneath the park's spreading trees. Children romp and play in the

The church, from 1879, is all that survives from Yosemite village. The village was razed between 1959 and 1963. *(Photograph by Kenneth R. Olwig)*

glades along the stream, and it is even possible to spy whispering lovers. It is the sort of place where people who might have little in common in their workaday lives share the green. The only thing that appears to be missing is the village. Even though the Park Service has created an imitation Indian village, it is no doubt hard for the average modern visitor to imagine a village like Goldsmith's Auburn in Yosemite! And yet, there actually once was a village not unlike Auburn in Yosemite. It is difficult to find today because between 1959 and 1963 the Park Service razed its buildings to the ground, and the old village site is now the object of an extensive project to erase all archaeological traces of its existence. Soon the village will have been entirely rubbed out, with the exception of its 1879 church.

The Gentrification and Appropriation of Common Nature

THE VILLAGE IN GOLDSMITH'S POEM IS "DESERTED" BECAUSE IT HAS BEEN turned into a park for the gentry. This was done by a selfish individual who had the village enclosed and its population dispossessed to create a landscape park. The park would have been in the then popular "natural" pastoral style, which created the idealized appearance of a grazed commons while transforming the actual commons into a private pleasure park:[33]

> The man of wealth and pride
> Takes up a space that many poor supplied;
> Space for his lake, his park's extended bounds, . . .
> His seat, where solitary sports are seen,
> Indignant spurns the cottage from the green.[34]

The farmers must leave not just the land but England itself, and this is not all that leaves:

> E'en now, methinks, as pondering here I stand,
> I see the rural virtues leave the land.[35]

The rural "virtues" of which Goldsmith speaks are quite similar to those which Americans think of in connection with Jeffersonian democracy:[36]

> A time there was, ere England's griefs began,
> When every rood of ground maintained its man;
> . . . his best riches, ignorance of wealth.
> But times are altered: trade's unfeeling train
> Usurp the land, and dispossess the swain;
> Along the lawn, where scattered hamlets rose,
> Unwieldy wealth and cumbrous pomp repose.[37]

The meandering stream and its green meadows play an important role in this poem, as a nationally recognized symbol of community love and place that characterizes the "rural virtues" of England. The imparkment of this landscape was thus not only a means of creating an idyllic scene; it was also a means of appropriating an important symbol of natural community and thus "naturalizing" a process of enclosure that was anything but natural.

The Historical Symbolism of Common Nature

THE STREAM AND MEADOWS ARE IDEAL SYMBOLS OF THE NATURAL BECAUSE they combine physical and spiritual elements of nature and the related idea of love. The stream and meadows are critical both to the fertility that sustains the village community physically through time and to the need for a community spirit that enables the population to manage its resources in an equitable and sustainable way. In this manner the meadow becomes a vital symbol of the brotherly love that sustains community identity. The power of the symbol depends to some degree on a historical geographical knowledge of the working relation between people and nature that, for many, has been lost.[38] The physical and community dynamics that make the stream and meadows so historically compelling as a symbol are, in fact, quite fascinating. First the physical dynamics: the meandering of the stream causes the water flow to slow and nutrient-rich sediments to be deposited on the inside of the bend. As any canoeist knows, this causes the inside of the bend to become shallow and mucky, before it grades off into a mire of reeds and eventually grass. The fast-moving, turbulent water on the outside of the bend eats into the bank of the stream, creating sediment and causing the stream to meander further. During the spring the stream often runs over its banks, and the reeds and grass slow the water, causing it to deposit even more sediment while cleaning the stream of sediments and nutrients that may have run off the grain fields. When the spring sun warms the soft muck, seeds germinate and feed on its nutrients, turning into a lush growth of reeds and grass in the summer. This grass makes the pastures for the keeper's game and/or the pastoralist's flocks. In a more developed agricultural economy, the manure from the grazing animals fertilizes the farmer's grain fields.[39] It is for this reason that such meadows were often termed "the mother of the grain fields" and regarded as being the farmer's most valuable land. The grass by the meandering stream was therefore not just a comfortable place for lovers; it was, in a very concrete way, a source of the sustainable generative power of nature.

The village green with its meandering stream was also an ideal symbol of the sort of love that binds a community together. Both the meadowlands along the stream and the green surrounding the pond were community property prior to enclosure, and the village green is still community property throughout much of Europe. The water of the stream was also a vital common resource that had to be apportioned fairly. The grazing of the meadowlands thus required the villagers to agree on such issues as how many animals could be grazed, by whom, and when, so as to sustain their environmental viability. Issues of this sort were traditionally sorted out by the farmers in a kind of protodemocractic town meeting, or "moot," which was held on the green.[40]

Though the village green was grazed, its primary purpose may well have been for sport and recreation and, of course, for community activities such as village meetings and fairs. The importance of the common use of grasslands both for grazing and for recreation is also attested to by the remnants of this landscape in the language we use today to express ideas of democracy and community. There is thus a close tie between the concept of the commons, commoners, and community. Even the word "fellowship" apparently derives ultimately from ancient Germanic terms referring to those who form (ship/shape) a body (*lag*—literally meaning "lay together") to share the grazing of animals (*fe*).[41] American metaphors for democracy and community are, in fact, filled with references to the green environment characteristic of a commons. These metaphors range from Walt Whitman's "leaves of grass" to the expression "grassroots democracy." It is also for this reason that the lawn on the New England village commons is freighted with much of the same symbolic load for many Americans as the Old England village commons was for Goldsmith. The guidebook statement "To the entire world, a steepled church, set in its frame of white wooden houses around a manicured common, remains a scene which says 'New England' " thus leads the historical geographer Donald Meinig to comment,

> drawing simply upon one's experience as an American (which is, after all, an appropriate way to judge a national symbol) it seems clear that such scenes carry connotations of continuity (of not just something important in our past, but a viable bond between past and present), of stability, quiet prosperity, cohesion and intimacy. Taken as a whole, the image of the New England village is widely assumed to symbolize for many people the best we have known of an intimate, family-centered, Godfearing, morally conscious, industrious, thrifty, democratic *community*.[42]

The Washington Mall, which despite its name is not a shopping plaza, is in many respects such a commons writ large, with the edifices and monuments of American democracy grouped around it.[43]

In some ways the lawns of Yosemite were heirs to the symbolism of the community green that had wended its way from England to America along with the meandering stream. Olmsted thus not only stressed in his report on Yosemite that "the establishment by government of great public grounds for the free enjoyment of the people . . . is a political duty." He also felt that laws were necessary "to prevent an unjust use by individuals, of that

Experiencing the meadow in Yosemite. *(Photograph by Kenneth R. Olwig)*

which is not individual but public property."[44] As Stephen T. Mather, the first director of the U.S. Park Service, wrote in a 1921 book on Yosemite, "our parks are not only show places and vacation lands but also vast school-rooms of Americanism where people are studying, enjoying, and learning to love more deeply this land in which they live."[45] The national parks were thus in many respects conceived of as a means of protecting what I would term "common nature" (or, perhaps better, "commons nature") by preserving it for use by the national community.

Was America Natural?

THE UNNATURALNESS OF WHAT WAS BEING DONE TO THE ENGLISH NATIONAL community was symbolized in Goldsmith's poem by the fact that the villagers were exiled from the garden into the wilderness. The wilderness of America! Wilderness was clearly a symbol of the unnatural. This is powerfully evident in Goldsmith's description of the New World to which his villagers are exiled:[46]

> Ah, no. To distant climes, a dreary scene,
> Where half the convex world intrudes between,
> Through torrid tracts with fainting steps they go, . . .
> The various terrors of that horrid shore:
> Those blazing suns that dart a downward ray,
> And fiercely shed intolerable day,
> Those matted woods where birds forget to sing,
> But silent bats in drowsy clusters cling;
> Those pois'nous fields with rank luxuriance crowned, . . .
> While oft in whirls the mad tornado flies,
> Mingling the ravaged landscape with the skies.
> Far different these from every former scene,
> The cooling brook, the grassy-vested green,
> The breezy covert of the warbling grove,
> That only sheltered thefts of harmless love.[47]

Goldsmith's poem helps explain, in a rather backhanded way, some of the motivation that led Americans to preserve the verdant meadows of Yosemite and Yellowstone as the first national parks. Americans were ashamed of the way Europeans like Goldsmith tended to depict the United States as having an unnaturally wild and unkempt scenery. When park scenery was discovered at Yosemite and Yellowstone that could rival the scenery of the natural landscape gardens of Britain, it seemed to prove that America was not by nature unnatural. It was only poetic justice to make these parklands into parks for the American people.[48] This, in fact, is precisely the way Olmsted saw Yosemite. Olmsted's idea for Yosemite was as American as the landscape parks of England were British, or as the Parisian state monuments to nationhood were French. Writing at the close of the Civil War, Olmsted clearly envisioned the park as a monument reaffirming America's national identity. He thus presented Yosemite as being on a par with Thomas Crawford's Statue of Liberty, New York's Central Park, Washington's Capitol dome and fresco *Westward the Course of Empire Takes Its Way,* by Emanuel Leutze.[49] (See p. 149.)

Unnatural Scenery?

THE BITTER IRONY OF THE IMPARKMENT OF THE VILLAGE GREEN IN GOLD-smith's poem illustrates the way a natural physical scene can create an aesthetic appearance that "naturalizes" human conditions many would regard to be unnatural:

> Thus fares the land, by luxury betrayed;
> In nature's simplest charms at first arrayed;
> But verging to decline, its splendors rise,
> Its vistas strike, its palaces surprise;
> While, scourged by famine from the smiling land,
> The mournful peasant leads his humble band;
> And while he sinks, without one arm to save,
> The country blooms a garden and a grave.[50]

Similar rhetoric actually was used in the early disputes over Yosemite's imparkment. In 1868 Representative James A. Johnson of California thus opposed the appropriation of James Lamon's Yosemite farm and orchard by stating that the Constitution and laws of the United States made no provision "for the creation of fancy pleasure grounds by Congress out of citizens' farms." While Johnson's reaction may seem exaggerated, Yosemite did set a precedent, in principle, for the appropriation and destruction of farms that took place with the establishment of the Shenandoah National Park in the 1920s and 1930s. Some of these farms dated back to the eighteenth century, and their removal involved the uprooting of several thousand people.[51] Early supporters of natural parks as wild scenery actually feared a public perception of Yosemite valley as an agricultural landscape, rather than as untouched natural scenery. In their publications they therefore sought to give the impression that the rural cultural landscape did not exist, or sought to have it removed altogether.

The tendency to define a landscape as being either natural, in which case it is ideally untrammeled virgin wilderness, or cultural is perhaps typically American. "It is no accident," as David Lowenthal puts it, "that God's own wilderness and His junkyard are in the same country."[52] He is referring to the American tendency to dichotomize landscapes into natural and wild ones, which are strictly protected against human development, and human ones, which tend to be poorly protected and regulated. In Denmark, by contrast, the nature preservation movement has largely opposed setting aside nature in enclosed parks.[53] Danes have essentially preferred to treat the entire nation as a park.[53] They do this, in part, by regulating land use in areas considered by experts and community representatives to be important examples of "nature." Few such areas would meet American standards for wilderness, yet, as the example of Yosemite shows, American "natural" landscapes may not be as wild as they appear. England now has national natural parks that, unlike the aristocracy's landscape gardens, are expressly open to the entire nation. They are not, furthermore, pastoral paradises preserved from evidence of human labor, but working agrarian landscapes. Unlike their American counterparts, they tend to be conserved precisely because of their evidence of ancient habitation and stewardship, and it is widely recognized that the landscape must continue to be worked by the local community if it is to exist.[54]

The vistas of the gentlemen's park in Goldsmith's poem offer striking but deceptive surprises. At the same time as the prospect pleases, the working landscape, with its green and stream, is neglected. The overgrown state of a once sustainably productive environment is used to symbolize the unnaturalness of the rulers of the English nation:

> And desolation saddens all thy green:
> One only master grasps the whole domain,
> And half a tillage stints thy smiling plain;
> No more thy grassy brook reflects the day,
> But, choked with sedges, works its weedy way.[55]

Much of the symbolism of Goldsmith's poem can be traced back to sources in the classical literary pastoral. But we are also dealing with what might be termed a "natural" symbol, because it is born out of basic forms of human environmental activity such as hunting, pastoralism, and agriculture. The Indian woman Totuya thus immediately remarked upon the deterioration of the Yosemite valley in 1929 when she returned for the first time since she had been driven out by Savage's troops in 1851. The granddaughter of Chief Tenaya, she was now the sole survivor of the band of Ahwahneechee Indians that had dwelled in the valley. The nature purists, such as Muir and his backers in the Sierra Club, who had opposed attempts to graze and burn the area "Indian style," were at least partially responsible for its becoming overgrown with vegetation.[56] It was conceptually impossible, of course, for the park to be both a wild scenic expression of U.S. values and an Indian cultural landscape. But the fact remained that the Yosemite that was "discovered" in 1852 "presented the appearance of a well kept park" because it was a park in the original sense of the word. The Indian gamekeepers burned it to promote, among other things, the growth of grass for game and black oaks for acorns. The open environment was also ideal for Indian field games. According to Lafayette Bunnell, in 1855 "there was no undergrowth of young trees to obstruct clear open views in any part of the valley from one side of the Merced River across to the base of the opposite wall." The extent of "clear open meadow land . . . was at least four times as large" as in 1894, when he made these comments.[57] The result of the white man's neglect was an environment that led Totuya to shake her head and exclaim, "Too dirty; too much bushy."[58]

Totuya's "aesthetic" judgment was based on an environmental steward-ship that sought to sustain the ability of the tribe to reproduce itself. This use-oriented aesthetic is foreign to the visually oriented, scenic aesthetic of the champions of the natural park. Olmsted, for example, made a point of arguing that "savages" were little affected by "the power of scenery," and he decried the Indians' burning.[59] The problem, unfortunately, is that when the park is not regularly burned and cleared, the accumulation of detritus and bush ultimately makes for much more violent fires, which can also destroy the ancient forest that preservationists are so anxious to save. Ironi-cally, the lack of burning also means that the very scenic views from the valley bottom that Olmsted so prized become obliterated by vegetation. This suggests that Olmsted's British landscape garden ideal is insufficient as a model for natural parks. A better ideal might be landscapes showing forms of sustainable community stewardship. This, however, would mean accepting the natural priority of the Indian cultural landscape, not as a visual scene, but as a place of dwelling.

Raw Nature, Raw Power

After the designation of Yellowstone as a national park in 1872, more than twenty years went by before the next parks were named. Many of these new parks were characterized solely by wild infertile environments, with no counterbalancing green meadows, meandering streams, and pools such as are found at both Yosemite and Yellowstone. It is as if the ideal symbol of the natural has shifted focus from the valley bottom of Yosemite to the rugged walls and high mountains that surround it.

In some ways this change in focus reflects the difference in scenic values between Olmsted and Muir, a more transitional figure. Olmsted clearly saw Yosemite as a beautiful recreative park for the general population, and he emphasized the experience of the *ensemble* formed by the encompassing scenery surrounding the "native" vegetation at the valley bottom. He was not so interested in particular sights. For him it was "conceivable that any one or all of the cliffs of the Yo Semite might be changed in form and color, without lessening the enjoyment which is now obtained from the scenery." The cascades were "scarcely to be named among the elements of the sce-nery," and he actually preferred the park when the cascades were dry![60]

Muir, on the other hand, was emphatically a cliff and cascade man who climbed the valley's walls alone and preferred the view from the top down. The elite who followed in his singular footsteps traditionally have looked down on the hoi polloi flocked below, and the two differing points of view have made of the park contested territory. As a club member wrote in 1919, "to a Sierran bound for the high mountains the human noise and dust of Yosemite [Valley] seem desecration of primitive nature."[61] Though he was concerned about the living nature of the valley bottom, Muir was particularly interested in reading the "glacial hieroglyphics," written in the stone of the valley walls, "whose interpretation is the reward of all who devoutly study them"[62]

The Nature of Mount Rushmore

THE CHANGE IN PREVAILING IDEAS OF THE NATURAL, AS REFLECTED IN THE difference between the original American natural parks and the newer variety, can perhaps best be symbolized by the figures on Mount Rushmore. They look out from a mountainside not unlike the walls of Yosemite, but they do not look down on an enclosed green and watered valley.

At Mount Rushmore we have graven, into a South Dakotan mountain, images intended to express American national values by their creator, Gutzon Borglum. According to Borglum's wife, who acted as the sculptor's spokesman, the effigies expressed a "sincere patriotic effort to preserve and perpetuate the ideals of liberty and freedom on which our government was established and to record the territorial expansion of the Republic."[63] These values are not only jackhammered and dynamited into the commonly owned physical nature of the nation; they represent, as it were, a vision of its shared spiritual nature. This was a vision of manifest destiny believed to have come to Borglum when he first stood on the crest of the mountain and was overwhelmed by the magisterial view "out over a horizon level and beaten like the rim of a great cartwheel 2,000 feet below."[64]

Mount Rushmore belongs to a later era of parks and monuments when barren cliffs did not need to be contrasted with fertile meadows in order to conjure up a picture of nature. One can imagine that Teddy Roosevelt, the favorite of Borglum and a friend of Muir, is quite happy on his cliff, spying out over the wilderness. He had a hunting lodge in the Dakotas, and this was an area where he loved to test his masculinity against a rugged nature. This rough-riding warrior, outdoorsman, big-game hunter, and father of American imperial expansion, would probably look down his long stony nose at the soft nature lovers in Yosemite valley.[65] His national values are more like those expressed by William C. Everhart, an official in the National Park Service, when he described the parks as preserving the memory of an era in American history when the "exemplary virtues of rugged individualism and free enterprise were the foremost commandments of Manifest Destiny."[66]

If Teddy is happy with the magisterial view from Mount Rushmore, Jefferson and Washington are no doubt longing for the grassy lawns of Monticello or Mount Vernon (which despite their names are on hills, *not* mountains). Abraham Lincoln probably identified more with the leaves of prairie grass and the lilac-bedecked dooryards of prim midwestern farm houses. Honest Abe, too, is no doubt wondering what he is doing carved into a mountain, alone in a wilderness with three other men. In the period between Jefferson and Roosevelt a sea change occurred in prevailing ideas of nature and the natural.[67] Though this change had been brewing since the Renaissance, it is during the nineteenth century that we see a virtual reversal in the symbolism of the natural. The wild, which had once been the epitome of the unnatural, now becomes a natural ideal.

The Idolization of the Wilderness

IN TIMES PAST THE WILDERNESS WAS ASSOCIATED WITH DEMONS—THE MOST famous, of course, being the devil himself. It is in the wilderness that Jesus, the prophet of love, is be*wild*ered and tempted by Satan. Wild environments are places where one "strays from the path" and becomes lost both physically and spiritually. The meaning of the word "diabolic" (from which the word "devil" derives) is highlighted when it is contrasted to that of "symbolic." A symbol is something that stands for something else. The Greek and Latin prefix "sym" means "together," suggesting that a symbol brings meanings together. The word "diabolic," by contrast derives from Greek and Latin words that literally mean "thrown across," which suggests that the symbolic and the diabolic might be at cross-purposes.[68] The diabolic is thus typically identified with the graven image or idol, which does not stand, symbolically, for the abstract idea of God, but which is treated as being itself a god. The graven image or idol is diabolic because it blocks or confuses meaning when it no longer stands for the abstract divine nature of the Godhead, but is seen to be the Godhead itself.

"In the beginning was the Word," according to the word of the Scripture, "and the Word was God."[69] The message of God was to be found not in the pantheism and graven images of the pagans but in the intangible symbolic expression of the word with which God ordered and created nature. If you followed that holy word, and loved thy neighbor as thyself, you would live as in a garden paradise. And the physical "nature" of that garden would be a physical symbolic expression of the spiritual "nature" of that love. The reverse, however, is not true. People do not necessarily love one another because they live in a paradisiacal garden. It would be diabolic, and contrary to the word of the Bible, to confuse the biblical ideal of a natural state of human affairs with the physical nature that symbolizes that state. This, however, is just the sort of confusion that is generated when we treat concrete wild nature as something that is in and of itself holy. People or businesses do not necessarily become moral or natural because they preserve nature. Natural environments are generated and preserved because people act morally or naturally. The central point here, however, is not moral or religious, though it derives historically from arguments couched in moral and religious terms. It is simply that meaning is confused when physical nature is not seen to be an expression of human values but rather is seen to embody values in and of itself. The values that humans place in physical

nature are displaced and obscured when they are made to appear to derive
from the objective authority of that nature rather than from a subjective
human source. It then becomes difficult to discern the true origin and meaning of these values, and the resulting confusion can be quite diabolical.

A painting that captures the new idolization of wilderness is Caspar David
Friedrich's depiction of a lone figure staring across a sea of clouds and
mountaintops from around 1818 called *Wanderer über dem Nebelmeer*. In

Caspar David Friedrich's early-nineteenth-century painting of a lone wanderer
above a sea of clouds, entitled *Wanderer über dem Nebelmeer,* displays a relationship between people and nature that is very different from that in Cranach's painting. *(Courtesy Hamburger Kunsthalle, Hamburg, Germany)*

this painting nature becomes something raw and rugged that lies opposite the lone viewer, who gazes upon it across a chasm of space. For people like Friedrich the sublime wild mountain scenery was sacred.[70] It was this sort of nature that the transcendental philosopher Ralph Waldo Emerson was looking for, bearing a German dictionary and a work by Johann Wolfgang Goethe, when he visited John Muir at Yosemite in May 1871.[71]

Muir himself had originally gone to Yosemite in 1868 in search of "any place that is wild."[72] Encountering the wild was, for him, a religious experience, and he heard a "sublime psalm" in the "pure wildness" of a cataract.[73] At Yosemite he found a 2,500-foot-high "grand Sierra Cathedral," built by "nature," where one could worship.[74] Yosemite, for him, was a place where "no holier temple has ever been consecrated by the heart of man."[75] For Emerson and Muir alike the most sublime aspect of the park was the magisterial views downward from the valley walls.[76] The religious power of Yosemite is a theme that was also picked up by the National Park Service. We find this sentiment expressed in 1926 by Stephen Mather when he wrote, "from Nature can be learned the scheme of creation and the handiwork of the Great Architect as from no other source."[77] These sentiments persist, as one can see by the way quasi-religious statements like the above are used to adorn the interpretive sepulcher of many modern national parks.

The Demon in the Wild

HOWEVER GRATEFUL WE MIGHT BE TO MUIR AND OTHERS FOR THEIR RELIgious efforts to preserve the glories of Yosemite, a dark side to the venture reveals the dangers of idolizing wilderness as nature. When wildness is sanctified, it is difficult to interpret the theology expressed by the "hieroglyphics" of its landscape scenery.[78] Muir's temple was bloodied from the start by the violent eviction of the native Indians. This tale is not made prettier by stories of false treaties of sale and suggestions of wanton murder and rape.[79] Such stories also abound, of course, in the vicinity of Mount Rushmore, where Wounded Knee and Custer State Park are located. Questions are raised, too, by the odd alliance between wilderness preservers and industrial interests, particularly the railroads, which were not otherwise noted for their environmental concerns. We must even confront the schism, on the personal level, between Muir the wilderness purist and Muir the Yosemite sawmill operator at the base of Yosemite falls, producing lumber for tourist development.[80] Finally, there is the troubling support by the wilderness preservationists for militarizing the park. As Muir wrote in 1895, "The effectiveness of the War Department in enforcing the laws of Congress has been illustrated in the management of Yosemite National Park." He was impressed by the army's work because "the sheep having been rigidly excluded, a luxuriant cover has sprung up on the desolate forest floor, fires have been choked before they could do any damage, and hopeful bloom and beauty have taken the place of ashes and dust." To him, "one soldier in the woods, armed with authority and a gun, would be more effective in forest preservation than millions of forbidding notices."[81] Such words are in the worst tradition of the British park and game wardens, who were known for their use of violence.[82] This cannot have been what the pacifist and lazy man's gardener Henry David Thoreau had in mind when he made the oft-abused statement "In wildness is the preservation of the world"![83]

The point in noting this dark side of the wilderness preservation movement is neither to discredit important prophets of the environmental movement nor to decry the existence of the American national parks. It is rather to encourage us to rethink the nature of these parks and to find the place where our modern concept of nature may bewilder us and lead us astray. It is time, I believe, to reconsider the idolization of wilderness. It is one thing to respect and fear a wilderness conceived as something "wholly other," like the biblical Leviathan. This beast is a symbol of that wildness which is beyond the limits of human comprehension or control, which we neither can nor should attempt to fathom, tame, or worship. It can be useful to learn to respect human limitations and to fear the consequences of environmental hubris. It is quite another thing, however, to sanctify a wilderness that symbolizes not American community values but a rugged, misanthropic individualism that, in the face of historical evidence, often assumes the "tragedy of the commons" to be a foregone conclusion.[84] In this case the wilderness is not "wholly other" but "wholly us," and to idolize such a wilderness is to idolize, unwittingly, ourselves.[85]

Between the Devil and the Deep Blue Waters

ONE PERSON WHO APPEARS TO HAVE UNDERSTOOD THE AMBIVALENCE OF idolizing wild scenery was Goethe. The figure seen in Friedrich's painting is aptly captured in a nearly contemporaneous passage from Goethe's *Faust,* which Marshall Berman uses to capture the essence of the modern idea in his wonderful book *All That Is Solid Melts into Air.* Faust, however, is not entirely alone, for he is accompanied by the demonic figure of Mephistopheles. Both are depicted, backs to us, standing on a rugged mountain and looking through a beclouded space. Berman describes how Faust contemplates the sea and lyrically evokes its surging elemental majesty, "its primal and implacable power, so impervious to the works of man." Faust is enraged because he cannot understand why men should allow things to continue to be the same. He would like to see mankind assert itself against nature's tyrannical force, which expends its enormous energy by merely surging back and forth with nothing being achieved. Faust exclaims

> This drives me near to desperate distress!
> Such elemental power unharnessed, purposeless!

> There dares my spirit soar past all it knew;
> Here I would fight, this I would subdue!
> . . . And it is possible! . . . Fast in my mind, plan upon plan unfolds.

Faust envisions gigantic reclamation projects, which include dams for large-scale irrigation and waterpower for industry. The only thing standing between Faust and his dream is an old couple who live in pastoral harmony with their surroundings and who are a model of community virtue. Faust becomes obsessed with this old couple and their land. They must go, he believes, to make room for the culmination of his work: an observation tower from which Faust and his public can gaze out into the infinite at the new world they have made.[86]

It becomes clear from this passage that what we are seeing in the modern period is not just a change in the natural ideal, from the pastoral and agrarian to the wild, but a fundamental change in the idea of nature itself. Nature is no longer the love and community that brings together the elements in fertile harmony. Faust's project necessitates the destruction of that community's symbol, the old couple in the pastoral idyll. The new nature would be worshiped for the pure power within the raw material of the separate elements. The freeing, breaking apart, and purification of the elements become the natural occupations of the lone heroic male developer who will put their power to use for the collective good of an abstracted conception of man and progress. And yet the diabolical figure of Mephistopheles hovers over Faust like a mushroom cloud, casting a deep shadow that causes one to wonder just how natural this progressive modern nature really is.

This passage from *Faust* prefigures the vast dams and power projects, with adjacent recreational parks, which were subsequently undertaken to "conserve" nature by centralized authorities. Living communities were often submerged in the process, but they had to make way for the industry and recreation of an abstract society that belonged to the future. These projects invoke a vision of nature and progress that brings to mind not only Theodore Roosevelt's stony imperial gaze from Mount Rushmore but also the modern era of large-scale dam building that began during his administration.

The Enframement of Nature

FRIEDRICH'S LONELY FIGURE STANDS NOT ONLY ON A PRECIPICE, STARING out into a distanced, wild, elemental nature. He also stands within a frame. The presentation of nature as scenery within a window-like frame expresses a Renaissance revolution in Western thought. The frame is important because it enables the construction of a framework of invisible lines converging on a vanishing point that illudes infinite spatial depth. In this way the earth's organic forms are transformed into landscape scenery. The geometric lines of perspective run through this scenery like the tracks of a train, revealing the potentiality of a progressively unfolding spatial infinitude. We draw upon this pictorial cosmology every time we speak of being "visionary," "having perspective," "seeing the point," or "getting the picture."[87]

Friedrich's figure on the jagged mountain, Goethe's Faust, and Mount Rushmore's Teddy Roosevelt are all images of visionary individuals staring into the infinite and seeing infinite possibilities for human development. Friedrich's observer stands squarely within the frame. As spectators you and I thus tend to be drawn into the picture so that we look over the shoulder of this observer. This, I think, is a useful metaphor for grasping the way we tend to be drawn into the framed space that the modernist visionaries create for us.[88] The lines of perspective in the modernist's world picture are no longer invisible geometric coordinates for structuring a pictorial space. The progressivist vision of the world is achieved by transforming the world itself into a picture in which the lines of perspective are materialized as vast linear lines of power, straightened concrete waterways, and huge rows of housing developments, all with "picture windows." Even national parks become moving pictures in which streams of asphalt link vantage points along vast skyline drives through naturalized "wilderness" landscapes that have been cleansed of human dwelling.

The Postmodern Meandering Stream

THE MEANDERING STREAM IN YOSEMITE HAS BEEN PRESERVED, BUT IN MUCH of California the rivers have become linear open sewers made of concrete. From California to Europe, hardly a waterway has gone untouched. In Denmark over 90 percent of the waterways have been straightened. These massive changes have led to calls to restore the nature of streams, ranging from the Los Angeles River to the Skjern River in Denmark. This is to be done by "re-meandering" the streams. The Danish case is illustrative because it shows the impossibility of separating cultural and physical factors when "restoring" nature. The straightening of a stream allows the farmer to drain the meadowlands and grow grain. Fertilizer needs no longer be provided by grazing cattle; petrochemicals now do the job. Not only have the streams been straightened; so too have agriculture's nutrient flows. No longer do we see a cycle of movement of nutrients from meadow, to cow, to field and back. Now that animal husbandry is not dependent upon the meadows, it tends to be concentrated in particular places, creating a superabundance of manure, which becomes a pollutant rather than a fertilizer. Elsewhere, farmers drop cattle production and become dependent upon a cornucopia of artificial fertilizers, which are rapidly leached into the streams. The streams, which have now become efficient drains, flush the water into the bays and sea, where eutrophication causes plants and fish to die. Game and wildlife that depended upon the meandering streams and meadows for survival are lost, along with the recreative and amenity value

The Los Angeles River, 1994. *(Photograph by William Cronon)*

of the areas where they once lived. Agricultural production, however, has increased and become more efficient, so efficient that the market is glutted. As overproduction drives prices down, the pressure mounts to increase efficiency or give up, and farmers increasingly must withdraw from the agricultural community and sell their land. The agricultural value of the drained meadowlands, however, is falling because as the soil dries out, it sinks and requires redraining. All of these factors work, in turn, to create a nostalgia for the meandering streams of recent memory, and a desire to restore their nature.

The Danish case is not unique; there is now an almost worldwide call to restore riverine nature. In Denmark the most ambitious environmental project of our time is the unstraightening of the Skjern River, which was linearized just three decades ago.[89] The work will probably be done by some of the same firms with the same sort of machinery that was used to straighten the river. In Denmark as elsewhere, this will be done in the name of nature. It will be done for the wildlife, for the purity of the water, and most of all for the "naturalness" of the visual scenery that it reinvents. Such projects will be in vain, however, if they merely restore the picturesque appearance of nature. In Denmark, for example, it is necessary not only to allow the stream to meander again. One must also restore the agricultural systems that maintained the meadowlands as a fertile environment for both domestic and wild animals. In the long run the re-meandered stream cannot be maintained by a park service but must be cared for by a productive human community.

BERLINGSKE AFTENAVIS WEEKEND 12.–13. MARTS 1971

Hedeselskabet kommer!

Tegning og tekst af GERDA NYSTAD

Sådan en å kan jo ligge i tusind år og passe sig selv med selvrensende processer i de stille kroge. Men rettes ud, det skal den. Om det så skal gå ud over biologikken. Sådan mener Hedeselskabet – – om Trend.

De-meandering and re-meandering a Danish river.

(a) An unregulated heathland stream. *(Photograph by Kenneth R. Olwig)*

(b) A regulated stream on reclaimed heath. *(Photograph by Kenneth R. Olwig)*

(c) A political cartoon from *Berlingske Weekendavis,* March 12–13, 1971, by Gerda Nystad. The caption reads, "The Heath Society is coming! A stream can take care of itself for a thousand years by cleaning itself in its quiet bends. But it must be straightened, even if it violates bio-logic. This is the opinion of the Heath Society." *(Cartoon courtesy of Gerda Nystad)*

Reinventing Nature

THERE ARE FEW ENVIRONMENTS, INCLUDING THOSE IN THE AMERICAN national parks, that are not the product of a long history of interaction with humanity and that do not require some form of use to be preserved. It is not enough to simply re-meander our streams and pretty up their meadows; we must reevaluate the nature of the communities that shape the physical nature in their "watershed."[90] A concept of nature that has been purified of its human touch—objectified and cleansed of its human values—will not serve this purpose. A natural ideal common to human communities and their environment is much needed.

It is important to protect national parks and the extraordinary places where we can go, like pilgrims, to recreate physically while regenerating our community and environmental values. We must not, however, lose the connection between the "nature" of these uncommon places and the "nature" of the ordinary worlds where we spend our daily lives.[91] We cannot survive by merely escaping to the wilderness and preaching an "earth first" prophecy of ecological doom. The natural ideals we hope to restore in the "headwaters" of our national parks must be given form in the planning and protection of our daily environments farther "downstream." The two cannot be separated, as anyone can testify who has witnessed the polluted airstream of LA smog in the Grand Canyon. The damming of Hetch Hetchy and the imparkment of Yosemite reflect two sides of the character of San Francisco's interaction with its "watershed."

What I propose is not that we invent a new nature, but rather that we reinvent a conception of a "common/commons nature" that is quite old and gives our cultural heritage much of its meaning. It is through this cultural heritage that we learn to appreciate the significance of our natural heritage as a sustainable, recreative and productive resource for human communities that, itself, is dependent upon the continuing stewardship of those communities. Such a heritage is symbolized by the meandering stream and the common nature of its meadowlands. By regaining this common nature, we may find it easier to understand that the physical nature we share as a nation is also an expression of the nature of our society. We cannot improve the nature of our environment without improving the nature of our communities.

Simulated Nature and Natural Simulations: Rethinking the Relation between the Beholder and the World

N. Katherine Hayles

YOU ARE ABOUT TO HAVE YOUR FIRST VIRTUAL REALITY EXPERIENCE. YOU put on the stereovision helmet and data glove, the cables dangling that will communicate to the computer the positions of your head and hand. With the helmet fitted snugly over your head, the real world disappears from view, replaced by the three-dimensional simulation you see in the two eye screens, the images offset just enough to give the illusion of depth. On-screen you see a simulacrum of your hand appear, and you begin interacting with the simulated environment. When you move your head, the image moves as if you were *inside* the screen, glancing around. The only indication that you are watching a computer-generated image is the slight time lag as the computer performs the calculations needed to change the image to fit your point of view (or pov, as it is known to aficionados). The functionalities you can activate include more than vision. You discover that when you point, your pov moves in that direction. When you close your hand into a fist, your pov stops. You use these hand motions to dive through a waterfall, pick up a frog and watch it turn into a prince, go inside an egg to see the baby bird nestling there. You continue to explore the simulated world unfolding before you, testing its capabilities, finding out what happens when you fall off the edge. Fascinated, you lose track of time. When you finally emerge and pull off the helmet, you are amazed to see that two hours have passed.

Is this a vision of utopia, or of a high-tech electronic drug that threatens to replace our delight in the natural world with a perverse desire to live in electronically mediated simulations? Virtual reality (VR) is the latest, and arguably the most intense, of visualization techniques that offer to immerse Americans in simulated environments. Military training, entertainment, the spotted owl controversy, medical research, video games, global warming scenarios, computer networks—it would be difficult to find an area of contemporary American life that has not been touched by simulation.[1] Many people who are concerned about the environment see in virtual reality and related technologies a threat to the natural world. If people become hooked on VR, they ask, will they be content to live in windowless rooms littered with computer equipment? Will cruising virtual landscapes blunt their awareness of a deteriorating natural environment? Are they fiddling with data gloves while Rome burns? The concern is not new. E. M. Forster gave it classic expression at the beginning of the twentieth century in "The Machine Stops," a dystopic vision of an underground society that lives entirely through simulations.[2] When the machine stops, almost all the inhabitants of the underground hive city die. The protagonist struggles to the surface long enough to see that a band of outcasts has learned to live in the polluted air of the natural world. He dies consoled, knowing that the race will continue.

The problem with constructing the situation in these terms—bad simulation, good nature—is that it relies on distinctions that quickly become problematic. What counts as natural? Can we consider Yosemite National Park an embodiment of nature? If so, then nature is synonomous with human intervention, for only human intervention has kept Yosemite as a nature perserve. Asked for a definition of wilderness in our Reinventing Nature seminar, Richard White offered the following ironic observation: wilderness is managed land, protected by three-hundred page manuals specifying what can and cannot be done on it. Equally problematic is the definition of simulation. One of the first popular simulations in America was Buffalo Bill's Wild West Show, an entertainment that became popular as a mass-media event only after the frontier was already disappearing. By the time it was named such, the "Wild West" had become a retrospective cultural construction that romanticized and mythologized firsthand experience in ways the original participants would no doubt have found amusing, if not incomprehensible. Yet it is the simulation, not the firsthand experience, that often enters popular consciousness as the operative cultural signifier.

A similar transformation happened with the concept of "landscape," as William Cronon has convincingly shown in his study of eighteenth- and nineteenth-century landscape paintings.[3] Majestic vistas that privilege vertical forms, sweeping prospects, and an observer dwarfed by his surroundings emerge as a visual and cultural category in American art only after people have ceased to struggle at first hand with the sweat, discomfort, and danger of grappling with impenetrable forests, negotiating treacherous rivers, and breaking their plows and backs on unyielding rocky soil. Confronted with nature in the raw, people registered its impact on their bodies, as Richard

White points out—calluses on hands and feet, sweat dripping off brows, muscles sore and aching after a day's battle with a river.[4] When "nature" becomes an object for *visual* consumption, to be appreciated by the connoisseur's eye sweeping over an expanse of landscape, there is a good chance it has already left the realm of firsthand experience and entered the category of constructed experience that we can appropriately call simulation. Ironically, then, many of the experiences that contemporary Americans most readily identify with nature—mountain views seen from conveniently located lookouts, graded trails traversed along gurgling streams, great national parks like Yosemite visted with reservations made months in advance—could equally well be considered simulation. Thus the distinction between simulation and nature with which we began is a crumbling dike, springing leaks everywhere we press upon it.

There is another, more subtle problem with the attempt to create a black-and-white distinction between simulation and nature. Although most readers of this book would probably want to align themselves with nature against simulation, there are those who choose simulation and are all too happy to leave nature behind. Hans Moravec, head of Carnegie-Mellon Mobile Robot Laboratory, suggests in *Mind Children* that it will soon be possible to download human consciousness into a computer, allowing humans to shuffle off the mortal coil that has so far limited them to a merely biological lifetime.[5] Once the transfer into the computer is complete, Moravec reasons, consciousness is essentially immortal, for when the machine starts to age, the person (if he can still be considered such) can transfer his mind into a newer model. Such fantasies are antithetical to the desires of those who want to immerse themselves in nature and have nothing to do with simulation. Although they express opposite values, however, the antitheses are joined in seeing nature and simulation as opposed and mutually exclusive categories. The existence of one choice necessarily implies the existence of the other, and there will always be people who will choose the other, regardless of the side on which we position ourselves. Once the situation is constructed as black-and-white, black and white are always in play, regardless of individual choice. Indeed, to focus on choice as the issue at stake is self-defeating, for structurally each polarity requires the other in order to define itself.[6] To paraphrase the infamous sentiment expressed by Hitler, if simulation did not exist it would be necessary to invent it, for only so could the purity of "nature" be asserted in opposition to the artificiality of simulation. To choose nature over simulation is not to escape from this dynamic but to reinforce it.

Simulation cannot, then, simply be left behind by an act of choice. Once on the scene, it often cannot be put aside, either. An incident in Don DeLillo's novel *White Noise* illustrates the point.[7] Jack Gladney and his friend Murray take a trip out into the country to do some sightseeing. As they drive, signs keep telling them they are approaching the most photographed barn in America. When they arrive, the first thing they see is a booth selling picture postcards of the barn and, by the barn, cameras on tripods with people peering into them. Murray points out that people can no longer see the barn; they see only pictures of the barn. Even when they are right next to it, they see their seeing of the barn, not the barn itself. The power of simulation to overtake reality is reiterated when a cloud of toxic chemicals—euphemistically called an "airborne toxic event" by the media—lowers over the town where the Gladneys live. People are evacuated; civil defense teams are called into action. When Jack comes across his daughter lying in the street, he is alarmed until he discovers that her civil defense team is running a simulation. They are disgusted because people have failed to meet their expectations for orderly evacuation. The actual event is far too untidy for their tastes. They see it as practice for their next simulation.

That simulation has the power to construct reality has also been suggested by Jed Rasula, a literary and cultural theorist interested in virtual reality.[8] Rasula draws on the concept of neoteny—the neural development that certain species, notably humans, continue to experience after birth—to suggest that virtual reality provides us with a kind of allegory for our "natural" state. We are born into the world with a set of equipment that we have to learn to use through painstaking and often painful practice. Only gradually do we gain control over head and neck, torso and buttocks, legs and arms. This physical equipment constitutes our original virtual reality gear, Rasula suggests, for it provides us with a multimedia simulation through which we can begin to manipulate the world. The first prostheses we contend with are our own bodies.

For those who want to keep nature separate from simulation, this perspective may seem startling and even perverse. I believe, however, that we can learn something valuable from it about both nature and simulation. Notice that the crucial move in generating this unusual perspective is remarking the position of what can be called the locus of selfhood. In Rasula's construction, the self is contracted to some position inside the body and rendered remote from it. The body then becomes equipment that the self has to learn to manipulate. When self is constituted as a raft of awareness awash in an ocean of constructed experience, simulation is at a maximum.[9] At the opposite extreme is a position that celebrates human communion with nature. Let us imagine, for example, a painting that shows a solitary individual perched high on a mountain overlook, viewing the magnificent scenery around him. Here selfhood is constituted as unproblematically dispersed throughout the body, encountering an outside world immediately present to view. When the eye looks out on the world directly, without mediation, nature is at a maximum. In drawing the distinction between simulation and nature, where one places the marker that defines selfhood is crucial.

The most difficult, and I believe the most productive, place to locate that marker is neither contracted inside the body nor unproblematically projected outside it, but at the cusp between the beholder and the world.[10] To explore the implications of this assertion, I want to discuss two technically elaborate and philosophically challenging research programs that have opposite aims. The first makes the world into a simulation; the second makes a simulation into a world. As we would expect, the first, concerned to maximize simulation, places the marker of selfhood firmly inside the sensory-cognitive apparatus of the body, emphasizing its disjunction from the world. The second, intent on naturalization, extends the mind's eye into a world immediately accessible to view. But wait. There is an ironic inversion going on here, too, for it turns out that the first, maximizing simulation, is talking about natural biological systems, while the second, maximizing nature, is concerned with artificial "creatures" that live inside a computer. By now it should be clear that my own agenda in setting these two research programs side by side is to further confound the easy distinction between simulation and nature. Instead of accepting a construction that opposes nature to simulation, I seek to arrive at an understanding of nature and simulation that foregrounds connections between them. Not two separate worlds, one natural and one simulated, estranged from each other, but interfaces and permeable membranes through which the two flow and interpenetrate. Interactivity between the beholder and the world is the key.

Frog's Eyes and Human Brains: The World as Simulation

THE FIRST RESEARCH PROGRAM I WILL DISCUSS IS EPISTEMOLOGICAL; THAT is, it is concerned with how we know the world. The primary spokesperson for it is Humberto Maturana, the gifted Chilean neurobiologist whose work has been influential in a variety of fields, ranging from systems theory to neurophysiology and cultural studies. Maturana began his journey into epistemology with research on the visual cortext of the frog. This research is summarized in a seminal article, coauthored by Maturana, entitled "What the Frog's Eye Tells the Frog's Brain."[11] Maturana and his coauthors demonstrate that the frog's sensory receptors speak to the brain in a language highly processed and species specific. If every species constructs for itself a different world, which is the world? The implications of this question are radical, for they point toward the conclusion that we, like the frog, never perceive the world as it "really" is. Indeed, on this view there is no *world* to perceive, for the very idea of a world implies an entity that preexists its construction by an observer. Following Maturana, I have elsewhere argued that the most we can say about what is "out there" prior to perception is that it is an unmediated flux, a stream of potential experiences that will happen differently for differently situated observers. As these actors, human and nonhuman, interact with the unmediated flux, their worlds come into being. Mine will be very different from a frog's or a bat's, somewhat different from a Neanderthal cavewoman's, and even in some measure different from yours. Thus Maturana's credo: *There is no observation without an observer.*

None of these implications is stated explicitly in the article, which follows scientific decorum in limiting itself to the subject at hand, the frog's visual cortex. Moreover, despite the article's explosive implications, its form is thoroughly traditional. It is written in standard scientific style, which is to say that it employs a rhetoric that reinforces rather than challenges an objectivist epistemology. Typical of this rhetoric is the erasure of the first person and extensive use of passive voice. "It was observed" is the preferred phrasing, rather than "we saw."[12] Obviously, such rhetorical practices subvert the very argument that the content asserts, for they have the effect of erasing the observer from the scene. The tension between form and content is telling, for it indicates how difficult it would be to integrate the article's conclusions into mainstream scientific epistemology. Circumlocutions such as "it was observed" are not simply bad writing. They are rhetorical figures designed precisely to detach the observation from the observer and locate it in a conceptual space independent of the racial, cultural, linguistic, and historical positions that the observers occupy. An argument for the constructivist nature of perception, which necessarily brings the observer into the picture, has the potential to throw a monkey wrench into this scientific business as usual. Maturana had a choice. He could remain within an objectivist epistemology, in which case he would not be able to fully develop the implications of the argument. Or he could take another path altogether.

He decided to break for new ground when further research led him to believe that perception is not fundamentally representational.[13] Working with the primate retina, he and his coauthors proposed a model of color vision that treated the experience of color perception "as determined by the nervous system itself, and not by the external world; thus the external world would only have a triggering role in the release of the internally-determined activity of the nervous system."[14] On this view, the perceiver encounters the world through his own self-organizing processes rather than through perceptual representations of external reality. To follow this result to its logical conclusion, Maturana forged a new epistemology that incorporated a different conceptual framework and used a new vocabulary, doing away with the misleading connotations of words such as "stimulus," "response," and indeed "causality" itself. It is not an overstatement to say that a revolutionary epistemology creates a new world, for it challenges fundamental presuppositions about how we perceive and know the world. The vision that emerges from Maturana's philosophy I will call, simply, Maturana's world.

The creation of Maturana's world is presented in *Autopoiesis and Cognition,* coauthored with Francisco Varela. Maturana begins by making a distinction between allopoietic and autopoietic systems. Allopoietic systems are designed to perform a function useful to agents outside themselves; their goal is set not by themselves but by others. My car exemplifies an allopoietic system. When I use it to drive to the store, I set its goal (insofar as it could be said to have one). Autopoietic systems, by contrast, have as their goal the maintenance of their internal organization. If my primary goal is to keep on living, then I am an autopoietic system. Autopoietic systems, Maturana argues, have the property of *formally closing on themselves.* Their actions are determined solely by their structure, which can be understood as the form their organization takes at a given moment.

We saw earlier that moving the marker of selfhood to the inside of the observer maximizes simulation. In Maturana's world, the formal closure of systems upon themselves means that all perception is a simulation, in the sense that it has no external referent, nor even any direct correspondence with what happens externally. Nothing in the environment *causes* anything to occur within an autopoietic system. Rather, the external action is merely the trigger for an event determined solely by the system's organization. Say I slap you. In Maturana's world, my slap does not cause you to get angry, or elated, or anything else. It is, rather, the triggering event for a structural change determined by your organization. Although this may sound like a roundabout way to say what can more simply be described as causation, the change in rhetoric is important, for it signals a shift in view that has wide-ranging consequences. In the rhetoric of causality, a stimulus directly elicits the response, so that information can be seen as flowing from the environment *into* the organism. In Maturana's world, no information comes into the system from the outside. Rather, an outside event selects one process from the many possible within the system's organization. Thus it is the organization, not the event, that is responsible for the process. Maturana's view is not as esoteric as it may seem. Some of it, at least, falls into the realm of common sense. Consider how you would react to a slap in the face, compared to a masochist. A masochistic personality is presumably organized differently from a normal one; this difference in organization explains why the same triggering event can lead to very different actions by differently organized systems.

In Maturana's world, systems interact with each other through "structural coupling," which is his phrase to describe the relation between a system and the medium in which it exists. In order for a system to exist, it must be structurally coupled to the world; if it is not structurally coupled, it cannot exist in that world. The specificities of the coupling determine how the system can interact, and the interactions determine the specificities of the coupling. This kind of reflexive mirroring is characteristic of Maturana's epistemology. It can also be seen in his concept of self-organization. He defines a self-organizing system as a composite unity. It is a unity because it has a coherent organization, and it is composite because it consists of components whose relations with each other and with other systems constitute the organization that defines the system as such. Thus the components constitute the system, and the system unites the components so that they are *components* and not isolated parts. This reflexivity is part and parcel of Maturana's world. There is a deep reason why it is repeatedly called into play: it is fundamental to a system that posits an observer whose internal organization determines what he sees. Every glance outward turns into a window inward. When the outward thrust of representational thinking is redirected back onto the system, reflexivity is the result.[15]

A particular nemesis for Maturana was behaviorism, which reinforced a realist epistemology by treating the subject as a black box that gives a predictable outcome for a given input. No perceptual transformations here, just straight correspondence between simulus and response. The experimenter looks out unmediated onto a world whose surfaces (the only areas that count in the behaviorist picture) are immediately accessible to view. Maturana's world was developed in part as a reaction against behaviorism. Heinz von Foerster, a systems theorist and cybernetician who worked with Maturana on a number of projects, anticipated Maturana's rejection of behaviorism when he contested the behaviorist account by shifting the focus to the experimenter-observer.[16] He argued that behaviorist experiments do not prove that living creatures are simple causal mechanisms that can be modeled as black boxes or, as he called them, "trivial machines." Rather, they demonstrate that the experimenter has simplified his environment so that it has become predictable, while preserving intact his own complexity and free will. "Instead of searching for mechanisms in the environment that turn organisms into trivial machines," von Foerster argued, "we have to find the mechanisms within the organisms that let them turn their environment into a trivial machine."[17]

In Maturana's terms, the experimenter has converted the experimental subject into an allopoietic system, while continuing to function himself as an autopoietic system. The critique gives a political edge to Maturana's epistemology, for it points to the power relations that determine who gets to function autopoietically and who is reduced to allopoiesis. It also demonstrates, once again, that where one places the locus of selfhood will be central to whether one sees the resulting picture as nature or simulation. The behaviorists, positing an observer who sees reality directly, saw conditioned behavior as a manifestation of a "natural" dynamic. Von Foerster, repositioning the marker of selfhood so that it takes into account the observer's motivations and actions, saw the experimental situation as a simulation created by an internally complex self-organizing system. The further the marker moves toward the observer, the more likely the situation is to be viewed as a simulation.

Maturana's world is perhaps the most thoroughgoing of scientific attempts in the twentieth century to take seriously the proposition that the observer is part of what he observes. The idea is not unprecedented. It had been explored in a different way in the Copenhagen interpretation of the quantum mechanical uncertainty principle, and in the same vein as Maturana but somewhat more tepidly in the second-order cybernetics associated with von Foerster, among others. Maturana departs from other reflexive philosophies in insisting on the formal closure of systems upon themselves. His great contribution is to work out the consequences of this closure to their logical end, showing how our presuppositions must change if a representational model of perception is rejected.[18] As visualization technologies become more widespread, the language that Maturana proposed (which is apt to strike the ear as cumbersome and awkward when one is talking about the body's perceptual systems) comes to sound almost commonsensical. There is nothing circuitous about "structural coupling" when one is describing a virtual reality interface. The user is joined to the simulation through a coupling—part technological, part bioperceptual—whose structure as a bioapparatus precisely determines the functionalities with which the user can interact with the simulation. It is no accident that Maturana's epistemology applies so well to a simulation, of course, for it was designed to fit the world conceptualized as a simulation.

The boldness with which Maturana followed out the consequences of his initial premise puts a great deal of weight on it—a burden that I believe it is not altogether able to carry. Given his initial assumption that there is no causal relation between an external event and an internal perception, everything else follows; but how necessary or compelling is this assumption? From an organism's point of view, it does not matter what quantitative and qualitative transformations of the incoming data take place, as long as they are consistent and can reliably be correlated with the triggering event. Regardless whether I see in the infrared or ultraviolet range of the spectrum, I can still respond effectively as long as the same external event gives rise to similar perceptions on my part. Maturana may well be correct in arguing against a representational model. If perceptual transformations have significant correlations with such factors as the subject's previous experience (as evidence compiled by Walter Freeman and Christine Skarda, among others, indicates that it does), then perception will depend on a combination of factors, part internal, part external.[19] In this case, a representational model is misleading, for it captures only part of the situation (the incoming data) and underestimates or ignores the other part (the internal transformations). If a representational model is misleading, however, so is an antirepresentational model, for it too captures only part of the situation (the internal transformations) and ignores the other part (the incoming data). It is understandable that, confronted with a representational model deeply entrenched in scientific discourse and everyday thinking, Maturana formulated an epistemology that was its opposite. It is always easier to think the opposite of prevailing opinion than to come up with something new, for the form of what one opposes provides a template for the revolution. Everything can remain the same, only inverted. Not that Maturana's world was easy to conceive. On the contrary, it is an extraordinarily complex and courageous intellectual adventure that follows out the consequences of the initial premise with unusual rigor.

Perhaps because this hard work has already been done, it is now possible to see that one might reject a representational model of perception without proposing the opposite, that is, without cutting perception off from the environment. An alternative model focuses on what I have elsewhere called "riding the cusp." It acknowledges that every observation is contingent on the observer, but it also recognizes that the unmediated flux plays an active role in informing and guiding perception. Reality originates at the interface where an organism capable of perception, at whatever level, encounters the unmediated flux. Worlds come into being as a result of this interactivity. Not the observer alone, and not the unmediated flux alone, but the two together in dynamic interaction.

I can now state more clearly what is at stake for me in the nature/simulation dichotomy. If nature can be separated from simulation in a clear-cut way, then we risk believing that nature is natural because it is unmediated, whereas simulation is artificial because it is constructed. But there is an important sense in which nature is constructed (through the active interface between the observer and the unmediated flux) and simulation is natural (because simulation self-consciously mimics the mediation of our bioperceptual systems in the mediations it produces through technological interfaces). Only because simulation technologies employ precise and detailed knowledge about human perceptual transformations can they create simulations that strike us as compelling and realistic. A VR simulation appears three-dimensional to us because the images are offset, simulating the "natural" spacing of our eyes. Simulations work because they are natural as well as artificial, just as nature appears natural to us because we experience it through the simulacra provided by our bioapparatus. In a fundamental sense, nature and simulation meet in the dynamic and interactive cusp we ride when we experience the world.

Human Eyes and Computer Brains: Simulation as a World

NOWHERE ARE THE CLAIMS FOR MAKING A SIMULATION INTO A WORLD stronger than in the rapidly developing field of artificial life (or alife, as it is known in the field). Conventionally, artificial life is divided into three research fronts. *Wetware* is the creation of artificial biological life through such techniques as building components, e.g., RNA, of unicellular organisms in test tubes. *Hardware* is the construction of robots and other embodied life forms. *Software* is the creation of computer programs instantiating evolutionary processes. None of the research is uncontroversial, but in some respects the most so is the software branch of the family. The strong claim for artificial life is that alife computer programs do not merely simulate living activity but are themselves alive. Christopher Langton, editor of the first conference volume on artificial life, explains the reasoning. "The principle [sic] assumption made in Artificial Life is that the 'logical form' of an organism can be separated from its material basis of construction, and that 'aliveness' will be found to be a property of the former, not of the latter."[20]

On this view, processes encoded in silicon are on an equal footing with those in protein; neither has proprietary rights to the claim of life. The evolutionary processes exhibited by alife programs are therefore not models of evolution but evolution itself.

The claim takes its force from the ability of the programs to exhibit emergent behavior. The idea is to begin with a few simple local rules and then, through structures that are highly recursive, allow complexity to emerge spontaneously. Emergence implies that properties or programs appear on their own, often developing in ways not anticipated by the person who created the simulation.[21] Structures that lead to emergence typically involve complex feedback loops in which the output of a system is repeatedly fed back in as input. As the recursive looping continues, small deviations can quickly become magnified, leading to the complex interactions and unpredictable evolutions associated with emergence.

Even granting emergence, it is still a long jump from living organisms to programs that replicate inside a computer. This gap is bridged largely through narratives about the programs that map them into evolutionary scenarios traditionally associated with the behavior of living creatures. The narratives translate the operations of computer codes into biological analogues that make sense of the program's logic. In the process, the narratives transform the binary operations that, on a physical level, amount to changing the polarities on bits of magnetic tape into the high drama of a Darwinian struggle for survival and reproduction. This transformation is not just a linguistic sleight of hand, as some of its detractors have suggested. Rather, it is deeply rooted in a metaphysic that sees informational patterns as the underlying reality that finds physical expression in biological organisms. When Christopher Langton identifies form as the essential property of life, he follows in a long tradition, stretching at least back to Plato, that privileges abstract pattern over embodied physicality. Before we analyze these narratives further, it may be useful to hear what they sound like. Following is an account I have written of Tom Ray's Tierra program, drawing on his scientific articles, his anecdotal stories about his Tierra program, and a video he compiled that presents an artist's visualization of how the program works as well as stories about his own struggle to capture evolutionary processes inside a computer.[22] While the specific language of this narrative is my own, I have told it much as he does when he speaks about the Tierra program. Interspersed with this narrative are my editorial comments marking transitions from observable phenomena to biological analogues. The processes that demonstrate a minimum of interpretation, I have marked with an "eye," since they could be seen by any knowledgeable observer. Those that require narration and analogy to construct, I have marked with the "I" to indicate the interaction of the researcher as a subject with the subject of his research. These markings are intended to call the reader's attention to where the transitions between subjectivity and the subject occur and to the work these transitions and constructions do in the narrative.

"One of the first successful alife software programs was created by

Thomas S. Ray, an evolutionary biologist who left behind the tropical forests of Costa Rica for the silicon ecosystems of computer datascapes. When I visited him at the Santa Fe Institute, he talked about the alife program he calls Tierra. Frustrated with the slow pace of natural evolution, Ray wondered if it would be possible to speed things up by creating evolvable artificial organisms within the computer [I]. One of the first challenges he faced was designing programs robust enough to withstand mutation without crashing [eye]. To induce robustness, he conceived of building inside the regular computer a 'virtual computer' out of software. Whereas the regular computer uses memory addresses to find data and execute instructions, the virtual computer uses a technique Ray calls 'address by template' [I]. Taking its cue from the topological matching of DNA bases, in which one base finds its appropriate partner by diffusing through the medium until it locates another base with a surface it can fit into like a key into a lock, address by template matches one code segment to another by looking for its binary inverse [eye]. For example, if a coding instruction is written in binary code 1010, the virtual computer searches nearby memory to find a matching segment with the code 0101. The strategy has the advantage of creating a container for the organisms that renders them incapable of replicating outside the virtual computer [I], for the address by template operation can occur only within a virtual computer [eye]. Presented with a string such as 0101, the regular computer would read it as data [eye] rather than instructions to replicate [I].

"Species diversify and evolve through mutation [I]. To introduce mutation, Ray creates the equivalent of cosmic rays by having a bit flip its polarity once in every 10,000 executed instructions [eye]. In addition, replication errors occur about once in every 1,000 to 2,500 instructions copied [eye], introducing another source of mutation [I]. Other differences spring from an effect Ray calls 'sloppy reproduction,' analogous to the genetic mixing that occurs when a bacterium absorbs fragments of a dead organism nearby [I]. To control the number of organisms, Ray introduced a program that he calls the 'reaper' [I]. The 'reaper' monitors the population and eliminates the oldest creatures and those who are 'defective' [I], that is, those who most frequently have made errors in executing their programs [eye].

"The virtual computer starts the evolutionary process by allocating a block of memory that Ray calls the 'soup' [eye]. Inside the soup are unleashed self-replicating programs, normally starting with a single 80-byte creature called the 'ancestor' [I]. The ancestor is comprised of three segments [eye]. The first segment instructs the organism to count its instructions to see how long it is; the second segment reserves that much space in nearby memory; the third segment copies the program into the reserved space, thus completing the reproduction by creating a 'daughter cell.' To see how mutation leads to new species [I], consider that a bit flip occurs in the last line of the first segment, changing 1100 to 1110. Normally the program would find the second segment by searching for its first line, encoded

0011. Now, however, the program searches until it finds a segment starting with 0001. Thus it goes not to its own second segment but to another string of code in nearby memory [eye]. Many mutations are not viable and do not lead to reproduction [I]. Occasionally, however, the program finds a segment starting with 0001 [eye] which will allow it to reproduce [I]. Then a new species is created, as this organism begins producing offspring [I].

"When Ray set his program running overnight, he thought he would be lucky to get a one- or two-byte variation from the 80-byte [eye] ancestor [I]. Checking it out the next morning, he found that an entire ecology had evolved [I], including one 22-byte [eye] organism [I]. Among the mutants were parasites that had lost their own copying instructions (the middle segment of code) but had developed the ability to invade a host and hijack its copying procedure. One 45-byte parasite had evolved into a benign relationship with the ancestor; others were destructive, crowding out the ancestor with their own offspring. Later runs of the program saw the development of hyperparasites, which had evolved ways to compete for time as well as memory [I]. Computer time is doled out equally to each organism by a 'slicer' that determines when it can execute its program [eye]. Hyperparasites wait for parasites to invade them [I]. Then, when the parasite attempts to reproduce using the hyperparasite's own copy procedure, the hyperparasite directs the program to its own third segment instead of returning it to the parasite's ending segment [eye]. Thus the hyperparasite's code is copied on the parasite's time. In this way the hyperparasite greatly multiplies the time it has for reproduction, for in effect it appropriates the parasite's time for its own [I]."

The editorial markings make clear that the interpretation of the program through biological analogies is so deeply bound up with its logic and structure that it would be virtually impossible to understand the program without them. These analogies are not like icing on a cake, which you can scrape off and still have the cake.[23] Nor are they clothes you can remove and still have the figure.[24] The biological analogies do not embellish the story; in an important sense, they constitute it. Moreover, important as the analogies are, they are not the whole story. The narrative's compelling effect comes not only from the words Ray has chosen to describe the computer programs—"ancestor," "parasite" and "hyperparasite"—but also from the story that emerges of their struggle for survival and reproduction. More than an analogy, this is a drama that, if presented in a different medium, one would not hesitate to identify as an epic. Like an epic, it portrays life on a grand scale, depicting the rise and fall of races, some doomed and some triumphant, recording the strategies they invent as they play for the high stakes of establishing a lineage, operating with a cunning worthy of Odysseus and a vulnerability reminiscent of Achilles. To measure how much this epic narrative accomplishes, it is helpful to remember that what one actually sees as the output of the Tierra program is a spectrum of bar graphs tracking the numbers of "creature" programs of given bit lengths as a function of time. The strategies emerge when human interpreters scrutinize the binary codes that constitute the "creatures" to find out how they have changed and determine how they work.

The epic nature of the narrative is even more explicit in Ray's plans to develop a global ecology for Tierra. He wants to create a digital "biodiversity reserve" (in his presentation to the 1994 Conference on Artificial Life at MIT, he linked it to a companion proposal for an organic reserve in the rain forests of Costa Rica).[25] The idea is to release the Tierra program on the Internet, so that it can be run in background on computers across the globe. Each site will develop its own microecology. Because background programs run when demands on the computer are at a minimum, the programs will normally be executed late at night, when most users are in bed. Someone monitoring activity in Tierra programs would therefore see it as a moving wave that follows dark fall around the world.

Despite the obvious translation that goes on in the epic narratives of Tierra, it would be a mistake to dismiss them as simple anthropomorphisms (or, more accurately, biomorphisms). They reflect attitudes, deeply held in many scientific communities, about the relation between the complexity of observable phenomena and relatively simple rules they are seen to embody. Traditionally the natural sciences, especially physics, have attempted to reduce apparent complexity to underlying simplicity. The attempt to find the "fundamental building blocks" of the universe in quarks is one example of this endeavor; the mapping of the human genome is another.[26] The sciences of complexity, with their origins in chaos theory, complicated this picture by demonstrating that for highly nonlinear dynamical systems, the evolution of the system could not be predicted, even in theory, from the initial conditions (as Ray did not know what creatures would evolve from the ancestor). Thus the sciences of complexity articulated a limit on what reductionism could accomplish. In a significant sense, however, alife researchers have not relinquished reductionism. In place of predictability, traditionally the test of whether a theory works, they emphasize emergence. Instead of starting with a complex phenomenal world and reasoning back through chains of inference to what the fundamental elements must be, they *start* with the elements and complicate them through appropriately nonlinear processes so that the complex phenomenal world appears on its own.

Why is one justified in calling the phenomena that emerge a "world"? Precisely because they are generated from simple underlying rules and forms. Alife reinscribes, then, the mainstream assumption that simple rules and forms give rise to phenomenal complexity. The difference is that alife starts at the simple end, where synthesis can move forward spontaneously, rather than at the complex end, where analysis must work backward. Christopher Langton, in his explanation of what alife can contribute to theoretical biology, makes this difference explicit. "Artificial Life," he writes,

is the study of man-made systems that exhibit behaviors characteristic of natural living systems. It complements the traditional biological sciences concerned with the *analysis* of living organisms by attempting to *synthesize* life-like behaviors within computers and other artificial media. By extending the empirical foundation upon which biology is based beyond the carbon-chain life that has evolved on Earth, Artificial Life can contribute to theoretical biology by locating *life-as-we-know-it* within the larger picture of *life-as-it-could-be.*[27]

The presuppositions informing the narratives of artificial life have been studied by Stefan Helmreich, an anthropologist who spent several months at the Santa Fe Institute for the Study of Complex Adaptive Systems, the research center whose modest quarters on the outskirts of Santa Fe belie the major role it is playing in initiating and developing the field.[28] Helmreich interviewed several of the chief players in the American alife community, including Christopher Langton, Tom Ray, John Holland, and others. He summarizes the views of his informants about the "worlds" they create. "For many of the people I interviewed, a 'world' or 'universe' is a self-consistent, complete, and closed system that is governed by low level laws that in turn support higher level phenomena which, while dependent on these elementary laws, cannot be simply derived from them."[29] Helmreich uses comments from the interviews to paint a fascinating picture about the various ways in which simple laws are believed to underlie complex phenomena. Several informants thought that the world was mathematical in essence; others held the view (also articulated several years ago by Edward Fredkin) that the world is fundamentally made up of information. From these points of view, the world of phenomenological experience is itself a kind of illusion, covering over an underlying reality of simple forms. For them, a computer program that generates phenomenological complexity out of simple forms is no more or less illusory than the "real" world. Similar assumptions led Hans Moravec to believe that it would be possible to download human consciousness into a computer, for if the mind is in essence encoded information, then its essential features could conceivably be captured within a silicon-based mechanism. As Helmreich points out, the mind/body division characteristic of certain strands in Western culture reinforces and is reinforced by its sister dichotomy, form/matter.

Where is the observer in all this? Helmreich reports that one of his informants, skeptical of strong claims for artificial life, insisted, " 'It's in the eye of the beholder. It's not the system, it's the observer.' "[30] Edited out are the actions of the observer in creating the narrative, and thus in constructing the "world" within which the "creatures" live, just as they are in mainstream scientific journal writing. The reasons for this editing are, however, distinctive to alife research. The observer looks out onto the world directly not because his glance is unmediated (as scientific rhetorical practices frequently presuppose). On the contrary, it is obvious that the gaze is highly mediated by everything from computer graphics to the processing program that translates machine code into a high-level computer language such as C^{++}.[31] Rather, the observer's gaze is privileged because he can peer directly into the elements that the world is before it cloaks itself with the appearance of complexity. This viewpoint is graphically portrayed in the beginning scene of Tom Ray's video. The representation, created by an artist commissioned to illustrate Ray's program, shows tripartite segmented creatures moving over an informational grid, while overhead the electricity of creation flickers and the death's head of the reaper hovers. The image makes the world of Tierra visually accessible to the viewer, as if she could peer into it directly, without needing to construct it through the highly mediated and conceptual operations required to extrapolate from the actual computer output to an understanding of Tierra's "digital ecology." The locus of selfhood extends far out into the world in the video representation because the world itself is conceived as having been stripped of its phenomenological complexity, in the sense that it generated directly from the simple rules and processes that underlie it. As a result, the movement in an observer's commentary from eye to I admits of conflicting interpretations. For the skeptic, it is evidence that the observer is creating the world. For the believer, it is testimony that the world and the observer are made from the same cloth, inasmuch as they see the observer as constituted through the same elementary processes that he sees inside the computer. Here Tierra eerily touches Maturana's world, for its interpreters believe they are justified in calling the simulation a world because they have already conceptualized the world as a simulation.

Simulated Nature and Natural Simulations: What Can They Teach Us?

IN COMPARING MATURANA'S WORLD WITH TIERRA, THE READER MAY FIND helpful the following chart summarizing points of divergence and convergence between them.

Maturana's World	Tierra
Governing trope: self-organization	Governing trope: emergence
Emphasizes stability of systems	Emphasizes evolution of systems
Foregrounds perception	Edits out perception
Edits out the world	Foregrounds seeing world directly
Sees system as a closed world	Sees world as a closed system
Systems interact by structural coupling	Systems interact through competition
Narrative form: reflexive mirroring	Narrative form: epic struggle
Complexity located in perception of observer	Complexity reduced to informational codes
Moves from complexity of perception to simplicity of autopoiesis	Moves from simplicity of codes to complexity of ecology
Causality is punctuation by observer	Causality operates but leads to unpredictable evolution

The chart suggests that Maturana's world and Tierra are in complementary relation to each other. Each is weak where the other is strong, and strong where the other is weak. Interpretations of Tierra that take no account of the observer, his assumptions, or the narratives he creates are philosophically naive. Maturana's world, by contrast, gives a richly complex account of the role that perception plays in the construction of the world. The shoes change feet, however, when we consider how adequate the two worlds are in accounting for interactions between the organism and its environment. Maturana's world achieves self-consistency only at the price of erasing the environment, whereas Tierra gives a detailed and satisfying account of ecological interactions in the world that it has created.

The convergence between the two is significant, for it marks a point of weakness they share. Both perform an act of closure that cuts off the beholder from the world—Maturana's world by seeing a system as a formally closed world, and Tierra by seeing its world as a formally closed system. Missing from both accounts is a story of how experience emerges from the interactivity between the observer and the world. Maturana's world demonstrates that such a story must consider the perceptual transformations that the observer experiences, and Tierra suggests that even an artificial world can encompass more than the observer dreams of. What counts as reality for us resides neither in the world by itself nor in the observer by herself but in the interaction between the beholder and the world.

What would the narrative that tells this story be like? I am of two minds on the question. Sometimes I think it has not yet been written, because it lies in the cracks and crevices that become apparent when Maturana's world and Tierra are pushed up against each other. Sometimes I think it has been written already, inscribed in and through the interfaces that join the reader to this text. Wherever it exists, if it exists, it tells a tale that refuses the Hobson's choice of identifying itself as simulation or nature. It speaks instead of simulated nature and natural simulation, insisting that the interaction between the beholder and the world partakes of both.

Toward a
Philosophy of Nature

Robert P. Harrison

AXIOM: PHILOSOPHY IS BORN OF WONDER—ABOUT OUR PLACE IN THE COS-
mos, about the ground of our relation to nature.[1]

Hypothesis: Philosophy wonders more about our being in the world than
about the world as such, for even if the world were fully comprehensible,
the presence in it of those who try to comprehend it makes it altogether too
much to comprehend.

Just as revenge is a kind of wild justice (Francis Bacon), environmentalism
is a kind of wild philosophy. The assumption, for example, that human
beings are determined by, and hence must respect, the conditions that determine nature is neither true nor false. It is simply wild and requires cultivation.

The cultivation of nature gives rise to culture, to be sure, yet culture is not
an epiphenomenon of nature. It is the modes by which human beings organize their relation to nature. The modes vary and change. What does not
change is that the religion, art, ideas, institutions, and science through
which a culture expresses itself are ultimately reflections of the ways it
relates to nature.

All of which follows from the axiom that human beings, unlike other living
species, live not in nature but in their relation to nature. Even the belief that
we are a part of nature is a mode of relating to it.

426

To the extent that we relate to it, we are outside nature. To the extent that we intend things, we do not share the nature of things. But human beings tend to confuse themselves with what they intend. We search for an image of ourselves in what we relate to rather than in our need to seek out an image in the first place.

In the modern era it was common to invert the Judeo-Christian notion that man was created in God's image and to claim instead that God was created in man's image. In either case the image was more or less taken for granted. Yet nowadays we have no such image of who we are. What we have instead are fragments of concepts of how we function—biologically, genetically, socially, psychologically, linguistically, and so on—but even a complete understanding of function, were it possible, would not amount to self-knowledge.

Science has brought us to the point where we now have the know-how to clone and manipulate the genetic makeup of human beings. We are literally on the verge of re-creating ourselves according to an as yet unspecified image of the normative human being. But who is to decide on that image? And on what basis? These are questions that science cannot answer from within its domain of competence. Nor are they merely ethical questions. They are, properly speaking, philosophical, insofar as philosophy counteracts our tendency to adopt self-evident conceptions of who we are.

Question: Who are we? Answer: Beings for whom the question is an issue. But if and when the question ceases to be an issue, does the answer still hold?

Any definition of the humanity of human beings must posit a distinction between the human and the animal. If I were to ask in what way humans are different in nature from animals, it is unlikely that most people nowadays would answer, "I have an immortal soul," or "I am a free moral agent," or "I am endowed with a divine faculty of reason." The most obvious answer, I suppose, is "I possess self-awareness." But what does that mean? What exactly is self-awareness aware of?

If animals could speak, they would no longer be animals but a species of humanity, which is another way of saying that language is the distinguishing trait of human beings. But this does not advance us very far, for the nature of language is as much in doubt these days as human nature.

Humanisim, in its Christian or secular versions, conceives of our humanity in terms of our freedom from determination by natural instinct and our capacity for autonomous moral choice. But after the convulsions of Darwinism, Marxism, Nietzscheanism, Freudianism, to say nothing of the modern sciences, which interpret human behavior in terms of subhuman impulses and see human beings as merely a more complex life-form than others—after such formidable endeavors to renaturalize human nature, do we or can we still believe that we are free moral agents? On the other hand, do we have any idea of how we might define ourselves—as a society and as a species—on a basis other than that of humanism? These are questions that once again force us to ask ourselves who exactly we are, or who exactly we believe we are, for it may be that we are nothing but what we believe we are—that is, it may be that we are and forever will be a mythical sort of species.

The myth of human exceptionality has been supplanted of late by the myth of biological continuity. Recent research efforts in the social and natural sciences seem determined to prove—indeed, presume to have already proved—that there is no essential, irreducible distinction between humans and animals.[2] Each one of our prized faculties—language, cognition, megalothymia—is shown to appertain in one degree or another to other species. Precisely at the moment when we have overcome the earth and become unearthly in our modes of dwelling, precisely when we are on the verge of becoming cyborgs, we insist on our kinship with the animal world. We suffer these days from a new form of collective anxiety: species loneliness. It is an anxiety that does not quite know how to deal with the guilt that nourishes it.

Consider the following newspaper cartoon: A man and a woman, down on their hands and knees beside their dog, tell a visitor who has just entered their house, "In the interest of animal rights and pet equity, would you mind getting down on the floor?"

In any case there is a logic to the cartoon's humor, for if we no longer admit of any ontological distinction between humans and animals, then the moral basis of our right to subjugate animals and use them to our own ends comes to grief. Our dominion over the earth becomes demoralized—its right is in its might, and humans figure merely as another ape in the forest, the most dominant ape, to be sure, but an ape nonetheless.

Is that what Nietzsche's Zarathustra means when he descends from his mountain, enters the marketplace of the modern city, and proclaims to the people there, "Once you were apes, and even now, too, man is more ape than any ape"—namely, that the extraordinary explosion of technological means to achieve total mastery of the earth corresponds to an equally extraordinary implosion of man's faith in the goals, purpose, and vocation of his power?[3] What right do we have to such power? What happens to us, what happens to nature, when we dispose of such power without believing in our right to it?

Axiom: One of the most confused notions in contemporary environmentalism is that of rights. Rights are alien to the order of nature. Their concept belongs to the domain of human law and morality.

Question: On what basis do we or should we grant rights to nonhuman species? Do we grant them, for example, only to the so-called higher animals? To both the higher and lower animals? Or to everything in nature, whether animate or inanimate, including rocks, sand storms, fungi, cancer cells, tape worms, cholera bacteria, etc.? In other words, is the concept of rights really appropriate to this context, or is the awkward use we make of it when we speak of nature an indication that we still lack the terms that would enable us to say what we mean, and mean what we say, rather than stammering, stuttering, and shouting—as many environmentalists do when they are forced into the language of their adversaries?

An animal rights group recently tried to pressure the scientific community to classify certain primates as *Homo sapiens,* since it has been scientifically proven that these species possess a form of human intelligence. This is a case of arguing for interspecies equivalence not only through natural kinship but through species identity itself. It is also a case of animal rights advocates speaking the language of their adversaries, given that biology and paleoanthropology identify *sapientia,* or intelligence, as the distinguishing trait of *Homo sapiens.*

The traditional definition of man in Western thought is that of the "intelligent animal"—in Latin, *animal rationale;* in Greek, *zoon logon echon.* But what exactly is the nature of the *sapientia* of *Homo sapiens?* Is it an epiphenomenon of nature, or is it beyond nature? The same question must be asked of human language—whether it belongs to the fabric of nature or whether it in fact creates a rift or tear in it.

When one tries to gain clarity about the concepts one employs, it is helpful to seek out intermediary cases that blur the boundaries between one concept and another. In this case it would help to find an intermediary case between the human and the animal, since it is our concept of the distinction between the two that we hope to clarify. Yet the mark of our exceptionality in the natural order is that intermediary species between the human and animal do not exist, at least not in nature.

If we cannot turn to nature, let us turn then to literature. The Italian writer Italo Calvino, who died in 1985 but who is still in every respect our contemporary, has imagined an intermediary case between the human and the animal in a book entitled *Mr. Palomar.* One day Mr. Palomar, who is described by the author as "a nervous man who lives in a frenzied and congested world," visits the zoo in Barcelona, where he sees an unusual ape that inspires in him the following reflections. I quote the episode in its entirety:

The Albino Gorilla

IN THE BARCELONA ZOO THERE EXISTS THE ONLY EXEMPLAR KNOWN IN THE *world of the great albino ape, a gorilla from equatorial Africa. Mr. Palomar picks his way through the crowd that presses into the animal's building. Beyond a sheet of plate glass, "Copito de Nieve" ("Snowflake," as they call him) is a mountain of flesh and white hide. Seated against a wall, he is taking the sun. The facial mask is a human pink, carved by wrinkles; the chest also reveals a pink and glabrous skin, like that of a human of the white race. Every now and then that face with its enormous features, a sad giant's, turns upon the crowd of vistors beyond the glass, less than a meter away, a slow gaze charged with desolation and patience and boredom, a gaze that expresses all the resignation at being the way he is, sole exemplar in the world of a form not chosen, not loved, all the effort of bearing his own singularity, and the suffering at occupying space and time with his presence so cumbersome and evident.*

The glass looks onto an enclosure surrounded by high masonry walls, which gives it the appearance of a prison yard, but actually it is the "garden" of the gorilla's house-cage; from its soil rises a squat leafless tree and an iron ladder like those in a gymnasium. Farther back in the yard there is the female, a great black gorilla carrying a baby in her arms: the whiteness of the coat cannot be inherited, Copito de Nieve remains the only albino of all gorillas.

White and motionless, the great ape suggests to Mr. Palomar's mind a remote antiquity, like mountains or like the pyramids. In reality the animal is still young, and only the contrast between the pink face and the short snowy coat that frames it and, especially, the wrinkles all around the eyes give him the look of an old man. For the rest, the appearance of Copito de Nieve shows fewer resemblances to humans than to that of other primates: in the place of a nose, the nostrils dig a double chasm; the hands, hairy and— it would seem—not very articulated, at the end of the very long and stiff arms, are actually still paws, and the gorilla uses them as such when he walks, pressing them to the ground like a quadruped.

Now these arm-paws are pressing a rubber tire against his chest. In the enormous void of his hours, Copito de Nieve never abandons the tire. What can this object be for him? A toy? A fetish? A talisman? Mr. Palomar feels he understands the gorilla perfectly, his need for something to hold tight while everything eludes him, a thing with which to allay the anguish of isolation, of difference, of the sentence to being always considered a living phenome-

non, not only by the visitors to the zoo but also by his own females and his children.

The female has an old tire too, but for her it is an object of normal use, with which she has a practical relationship, without problems: she sits in it as if it were an easy chair, sunbathing and delousing her infant. For Copito de Nieve, on the contrary, the contact with that tire seems to be something affective, possessive, and somehow symbolic. From it he can have a glimpse of what for man is the search for an escape from the dismay of living investing oneself in things, recognizing oneself in signs, transforming the world into a collection of symbols—a first daybreak of culture in the long biological night. To do all this the gorilla has only an old tire, an artifact of human production, alien to him, lacking any symbolic potentiality, naked of meanings, abstract. Looking at it, you would not say that much could be derived from it. And yet what, more than an empty circle, can contain all the symbols you might want to attribute to it? Perhaps identifying himself with it, the gorilla is about to reach, in the depths of silence, the springs from which language burst forth, to establish a flow of relationship between his thoughts and the unyielding, deaf evidence of the facts that determine his life. . . .

Leaving the zoo, Mr. Palomar cannot dispel the image of the albino gorilla from his mind. He tried to talk about him with people he meets, but he cannot make anyone listen. At night, both during the hours of insomnia and during his brief dreams, the great ape continues to appear to him. "Just as the gorilla has his tire, which serves as tangible support for a raving, wordless speech," he thinks, "so I have this image of a great white ape. We all turn in our hands an old, empty tire through which we try to reach some final meaning, which words cannot achieve."[4]

Where philosophy reaches its limits of clear and distinct articulation, literature takes over its vocation. Literature, unlike philosophy, finds words for what words cannot express. It does this by rendering their meaning as indeterminate as the concept we are seeking to clarify—that of human nature.

The more one ponders Calvino's vignette about the albino gorilla, the more it seems that it is not really about the albino gorilla at all, but about Mr. Palomar, who sees in the ape an image of something unutterable and enigmatic in himself. Just as the ape seems dumbfounded by his singular existence, so too Mr. Palomar is dumbfounded by the ape. The albino gorilla is for Mr. Palomar what the old tire is for the gorilla—a sort of inarticulate symbol, or symbol of the inarticulate.

Omne individuum sit species infima. "Every individual is an irreducible species unto itself." Copito de Nieve, one could say, is at the threshold of becoming such a *species infima.* His albinoism figures as the individuating consciousness, or self-consciousness, which philosophy has traditionally identified as the inalienable subject of human freedom, the seat of all human rights.

Let me quote again what I take to be the crucial sentence: "From [his tire, the albino gorilla] can have a glimpse of what for man is the search for an escape from the dismay of living—investing oneself in things, recognizing oneself in signs, transforming the world into a collection of symbols—a first daybreak of culture in the long biological night." The myths, idols, fetishes, symbols through which we invest ourselves in the world are generated out of a sense of bewilderment in the face of existing. Dismay, alienation, confusion, anguish, in a word, *wonder*—these are the states of mind or modes of self-awareness that, according to Calvino's text, bring about the first daybreak of culture in the long biological night.

Axiom: Wonder is ignorance that is aware of itself as ignorance.

Hypothesis: Animals are not aware of their ignorance; hence they lack irony.

Irony, as the condition of human language, ensures that all our words are attempts to reach some final meaning that words cannot achieve, hence that we never completely mean what we say or say what we mean. We are, of course, free to literalize our words. Yet we are also free to draw attention, through language, to the irony that pervades them. Literature, for example, makes us wonder about the words we use: what they mean or want to mean, what they say without saying, what demands they make on us as fellow speakers and interpreters. It reminds us of the strangeness of the medium through which we presume to know ourselves.

Science, also born of wonder, works best when it forgets the irony that sponsors its search for empirical knowledge. When science turns ironic, it is no longer science but a form of wisdom, or the beginning of self-knowledge, which is to say that self-knowledge can never be scientific.

Calvino's text says of Copito de Nieve that, identifying himself with the tire, "the gorilla is about to reach, in the depths of silence, the springs from which language burst forth, to establish a flow of relationships between his thoughts and the unyielding, deaf evidence of the facts that determine his life. . . ." The unyielding, deaf evidence of the facts that determine his life is the fact of nature, which scientific research investigates and explains. But language at its origin is the establishment of a flow of relationships between these unyielding facts and our inarticulate thoughts. Such language need not manifest itself as speech at all; it may even take the form of speechlessness, a "raving wordless speech," as Calvino puts it, such that "we all turn in our hands an old, empty tire." This tire is not only a circle but above all an empty circle through whose hole we invest ourselves in the world. The question then becomes: what particular empty circle are we looking through, and can we ever see it short of a laborious effort of reflection?

This is the irony and painful contradiction of language: that we sense that the world makes sense, we notice evidence that it follows rules or obeys a law, we intimate some greater order around us, but in the final analysis we are at a loss to account for the meaning of it, precisely because meaning arises from the relation between ourselves and the world. Perhaps this relation, as existentialists have argued, is essentially absurd. Perhaps it requires something like human culture to domesticate it—to make us at home in it.

A poem of Wordsworth begins with the words "The world is too much with us." The world is too much with us because we exceed and overreach ourselves. This self-overreaching is the essence of our dismay. It is what we try to escape from, what brings us to grief, and what causes us to hold fast to the old, empty tire. It is also what moves us to speak.

Most anthropological theories about the origins of language view language as an instrument of communication that enabled early humans to better master their environment by coordinating their efforts in hunting down animals, or instituting social codes of behavior, obedience, and so forth. Such theories are like Copito de Nieve's mate, who has an unproblematic, merely functionalistic relationship to her tire. The problem with functionalistic explanations in this context is that they cannot account for the curiosity that engenders their interpretation of the world, a curiosity that in turn is engendered by dread, or wonder, or terror, or this sense of isolation that causes Copito de Nieve to hold tight to the tire while everything eludes him. The unyielding, dumb evidence of the facts—even if we succeed in explaining them—is what language is at odds with.

Fact: Copito de Nieve is not a fictional gorilla. He exists, and Calvino saw him during the early 1980s in the Barcelona zoo.

Fact: It so happens that Copito de Nieve is male. This in itself does not render superfluous an interpretation of Calvino's story in terms of gender politics. It is merely a fact.

I confess that, in the final analysis, I do not fully understand Calvino's vignette about the albino gorilla. For example, is Copito de Nieve a protofigure of *Homo sapiens* in the order of nature? Is he a figure of "man" as opposed to "woman"? Is he a figure of Calvino himself, or of the artist's alienated relation to society as a whole? Is he a figure of the last man of a decaying civilization? Is he an allegory of the origins of religious consciousness? Is he on the threshold of a new freedom, or is he the testimony of a hopeless enslavement? In short, I have no interpretation that would make complete sense of the text. This is not by chance. To the degree that it is literature, its final meaning is elusive, unstable, open to revision and reconsideration. To the degree that it is literature, it is a textual index of our irreducible dismay.

Those realists who insist on reminding us that human beings are nothing but tiny microorganisms on a speck of cosmic dirt called Earth are not wrong in their analogy. They are merely feckless. Humans are those beings for whom being nothing but tiny microorganisms on a speck of cosmic dirt is a source of anguish.

There is nothing quite as withering of the hope that our failures of self-knowledge will not lead to deadly self-reifications than to read Edward Wilson's *On Human Nature*. I choose at random a passage from this book by the founder of sociobiology: "The human mind is a device for survival and reproduction, and reason is just one of its various techniques. . . . The intellect was not constructed to understand atoms or even to understand itself but to promote the survival of human genes. . . . Aesthetic judgments and religious beliefs must have arisen by the same mechanistic process."[5]

If one looks at a house from a given angle, one will see only so much of the house. If one looks at human beings from the perspective of genetics, one will see only genetic determinism. Looked at materially, a movie is nothing but a series of images registered on a scroll of cellulose film and projected onto a screen by a beam of light. But is that what we mean when we say, "I saw a movie"? From a certain perspective, I suppose the answer is yes. But is that really how we *see* the movie?

If sociobiology is consistent with its own premise, then it must have a theory that explains why the science of sociobiology is itself a mode of promoting the survival of human genes. More important, it must at the very least have a theory of allegory. When we read an essay on the philosophy of nature, when we write *Mr. Palomar*, when we believe in religious doctrines, when we say something is beautiful, it does not seem to us that we are merely promoting the survival of human genes. If the sociobiological premise is true, then what we say and do are not what we mean and perform, but rather all the things we say and do are veils of expression behind which lurks another intention. Human culture as a whole becomes an extravagant allegory of a dumb, unyielding nature. I have no problems with the notion that the human condition is essentially allegorical, in the sense that intention and expression never definitively coincide. My problem, as a literary critic, is with bad readers. Bad readers are those who either literalize the text or find allegories in it where there are none, which itself is a form of literalization.

Culture is not the allegory of nature; it is the ritualized institution of the irony that puts us at odds with nature. To say it otherwise, I am at odds with my death. I am cursed by an awareness that nature's demands don't answer my demand that my having been born and my being here make a difference that makes sense to me. I am nature's exception and nature's negation insofar as my self-awareness is aware of nothing—a nothing that separates me, isolates me, individuates me, forcing me into relation, mediation, and intention, call it language.

Mr. Palomar is trapped in a frenzied and congested world the way Copito de Nieve is trapped in the prison yard of his garden; and just as the great ape cannot articulate what he dimly perceives as a new horizon of sense just beyond his reach, so too Mr. Palomar is silenced by the world, at a loss for adequate words. He tries to talk to people he meets about the albino gorilla, but communication fails. It is in this loss of the voice with which we speak ourselves to the world that humanity finds itself most denatured in Mr. Palomar's age.

When we become aphasic, when the world dumbfounds us, when we can't find the words for what we want to say, it takes literature to help us become loquacious again, for literature finds the voice of what cannot be spoken outrightly, of what reality has a way of infantilizing in us.

Like Copito de Nieve's, Mr. Palomar's circumstance (his world) does not do justice to his nature, that is, to his overreaching of reality. Which is another way of saying that it does not do justice to his freedom. Freedom is not a question of rights. Rights are fortresses. To need them implies that one is under siege. Freedom means first and foremost being who or what one is. If one is an ape, it means being an ape the way apes are apes according to their nature. If one is human, it means being human the way humans are human according to their nature.

Axiom: Animals do not need to do justice to their nature, since they cannot betray it. The idea of justice arises where there exists the possibility of denial and transgression.

Hypothesis: Rights exist solely because they can be violated. Only human beings, who are self-surpassing, are able to transgress the law of freedom that governs the natural order.

Our failure to do justice to our nature creates the prison yard—both internal and external—in which we find ourselves. When we fail to do justice to our nature, we also fail to do justice to nature, for nature is the outer boundary of human nature. It is that which we come up against whenever we come to terms with ourselves. We live not in nature but in our relation to nature, which means that human nature, for all its indeterminacy, is determined by its relation to nature. This is not to say that it is determined by nature; it is to say that our relation to nature is the correlate of our relation to ourselves.

Given that we are self-surpassing by nature, we relate to ourselves by reaching out beyond ourselves. It is in this sense—that we find ourselves beyond ourselves—that we are allegorical creatures or, what amounts to the same, creatures of culture. When we surpass ourselves the most, we reach out toward our death. The irony is that when we reach out toward our death, we in fact reach out toward nature, for nature, ultimately, is the place where our death is at home.

Hypothesis: Because the earth is the place where our death is at home, we have an urge to take revenge on it.

The surrounding world of nature, which preceded us and will succeed us, offers us the spectacle of a longevity and an endurance that are denied us. This spectacle can be a source of anguish or of reassurance, depending on the relation we maintain with ourselves. A great deal of the destructiveness in our dealings with nature arises, it seems, from a stubborn refusal to come to terms with our finitude, to accept our fundamental limitations.

We are both inside and outside of nature: this is our dismay, that we come up against its insurmountable limit. We gain our freedom not by overcoming but by recognizing that limit. Just as freedom is not a question of rights, so too it is not a question of emancipation. Its essence lies in acknowledgment.

The slave is a slave to the degree that the master refuses to acknowledge his humanity. But when emancipation comes about and the master's shackles are thrown off, it is up to the slaves in their liberation to acknowledge their humanity for themselves. A slave morality is one that fails to do this.

Nature is not our slave; it does not need our acknowledgment. By the same token it is not our master and cannot acknowledge our humanity. Just as it is a misunderstanding to think that nature should or could acknowledge our humanity, so too it is a misunderstanding to think that, because nature cannot do so, we can dispense with its limit.

A rare philosopher has written: "The commonest, most ordinary curse of man is not so much that he was ever born and must die, but that he has to figure out the one and shape up to the other and justify what comes between, and that he is not a beast and not a god: in a word, that he is a man, and alone. All those, however, are the facts of life; the curse comes in the ways we try to deny them."[6] The curse is perhaps original, transhistorical, and unredeemable. But the ways we try to deny the facts of life, the ways we institute such denial, the ways we deny even our own denials, are multiple and historical, forever changing with the transformations of culture. The task of philosophy, and its inner voice, which is literature, is to continue to strive to expose the ways of denial.

Conclusion: Acknowledgment does not save us from ourselves; at most it spares us the indignity of leaving the world kicking and screaming like the infants who came into it.

VIRTUAL NATURE

To many who care about the natural world, no modern phenomenon seems more troubling than the emergence of "virtual reality" as a new form of human experience. What only a few years ago no doubt seemed like science fiction now begins to seem an ever more plausible reality: the ability of people to experience "environments" that are completely constructed by computers. Whether playing a computer simulation game, cruising the Internet, or enjoying the ever more sophisticated fantasies that emerge from the studios of Industrial Light and Magic, adults and children alike are spending increasing amounts of time in cyberspace, isolated from "real" nature. And yet it is also true that our awareness of potential environmental problems has an increasingly virtual quality as we turn to computer models and simulated ecosystems to try to understand the complex changes going on around us in the natural world. Drawing the boundary between "real" and "virtual" nature turns out to be rather more difficult—rather more revealing and instructive concerning our ideas of nature—than we might first have thought.

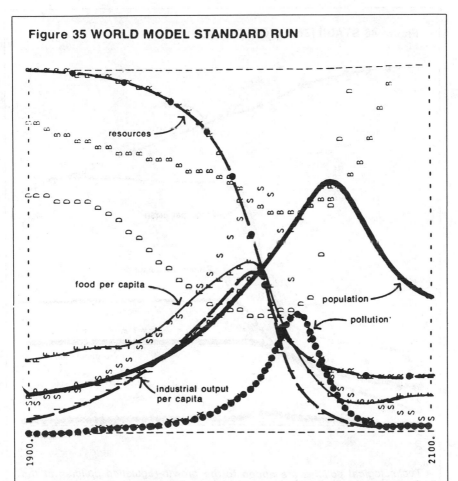

Figure 35 WORLD MODEL STANDARD RUN

The "standard" world model run assumes no major change in the physical, economic, or social relationships that have historically governed the development of the world system. All variables plotted here follow historical values from 1900 to 1970. Food, industrial output, and population grow exponentially until the rapidly diminishing resource base forces a slowdown in industrial growth. Because of natural delays in the system, both population and pollution continue to increase for some time after the peak of industrialization. Population growth is finally halted by a rise in the death rate due to decreased food and medical services.

Limits to growth: "World Model Standard Run." *(Donella H. Meadows, Dennis L. Meadows, Jørgen Randers, and William W. Behrens III,* The Limits to Growth: A Report for The Club of Rome's Project on the Predicament of Mankind, *courtesy Universe Publishing, 1972)*

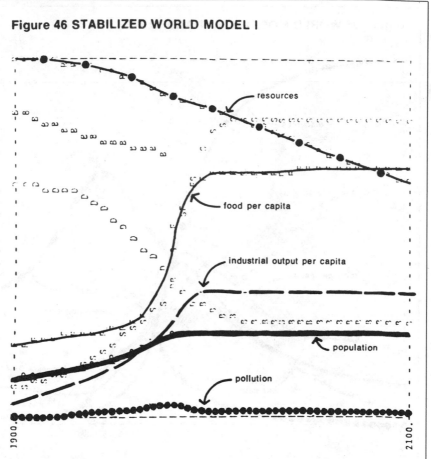

Figure 46 STABILIZED WORLD MODEL I

resources

food per capita

industrial output per capita

population

pollution

1900.

2100.

Technological policies are added to the growth-regulating policies of the previous run to produce an equilibrium state sustainable far into the future. Technological policies include resource recycling, pollution control devices, increased lifetime of all forms of capital, and methods to restore eroded and infertile soil. Value changes include increased emphasis on food and services rather than on industrial production. As in figure 45, births are set equal to deaths and industrial capital investment equal to capital depreciation. Equilibrium value of industrial output per capita is three times the 1970 world average.

Limits to growth: "Stabilized World Model I." *(Donella H. Meadows, Dennis L. Meadows, Jørgen Randers, and William W. Behrens III, The Limits to Growth: A Report for The Club of Rome's Project on the Predicament of Mankind, courtesy Universe Publishing, 1972)*

"Small Blue Planet: The Real Picture Atlas." *(Courtesy Now What Software)*

"Spend 24 Hours That Are Out of This World." *(Copyright 1993, Decisions Investment Corporation, reprinted in whole or in part with the permission of the Decisions Investment Corporation)*

What the Frogs Are Telling Us

A familiar harbinger of spring in much of North America is a tiny frog known to scientists as Hyla crucifer and to ordinary householders as the spring peeper. Beginning in March, male peepers in search of mates form a clamorous and joyful chorus, trilling around ponds and swimming pools. But the chorus has muted in recent years, in line with a mysterious worldwide decline in frogs, toads and other amphibians. Now there is evidence that what is silencing the peeper may be ultraviolet radiation resulting from a thinner ozone layer.

A spring peeper

This hypothesis does not explain all disappearances: loss of habitat, pollution, acid rain are among other credible culprits. But scientists at Oregon State University have found that ultraviolet rays do deadly damage to the eggs of frogs and toads that have been vanishing from the Cascade Mountains of Oregon. This has to be of some interest to another bare-skinned species.

The experimental data seem persuasive. Frog eggs form gelatinous masses, and Oregon's declining species tend to lay them in uncovered shallow water. The Oregon researchers were able to greatly enhance the survival rate of the eggs from Cascades frogs and Western toads by shielding them from ultraviolet rays. The working hypothesis — that creatures living at high altitudes would be more susceptible to damage caused by solar radiation — was borne out by exposing frog eggs to different natural conditions.

What this fails to explain, however, is the comparably dramatic decline in lowland species, like Costa Rica's golden toad, which dwells in a dark rain forest. Nor is it yet clear why the Pacific treefrog, which is also native to Oregon, has escaped the fate of its cousins by laying eggs with greater survival power.

Even so, the Oregon team has provided suggestive evidence that wildlife is affected by the thinning ozone layer. Those vanishing frogs are telling us something. And the silence of the spring peepers recalls the vital clue of the dog's failure to bark in Sherlock Holmes's "Silver Blaze": "The dog did nothing in the nighttime." To which the master detective replied, "That was the curious incident."

PARTINGS

Toward a Conclusion

William Cronon: Although these essays are each the work of a single author, they also reflect our many conversations as we've sought to explore and rethink the different meanings of nature in the modern world. So maybe it makes sense here at the end to talk a little about what we've accomplished, not only in our individual essays but in the book as a whole. What did we learn from our time together, and what would we like our readers to take away from *Uncommon Ground?* In what ways would we like this book to make a real practical difference out there in the world?

Anne Spirn: Living for five months in a foreign biome and culture—Irvine— left vivid memories. Southern California first disoriented and depressed, then intrigued and stimulated me. I remember the green against brown, lush against sere, my sleep disturbed by the nightly hssssssssss of sprinklers. I remember the strange plants (trees whose brown bark turned yellow when it rained!) and the confusing mix of species from all over the world lumped together out of context: forest trees, desert cactus, tropical palms. I remember dozens of huge bulldozers on vast hillsides of dirt, walled communities with guarded gates, manicured landscapes clipped by invisible gardeners, sidewalks that no one walked on, ten-lane freeways where everyone moved at eighty miles per hour bumper to bumper. I remember Disneyland and the Crystal Cathedral. I remember the dry air, the diffuse horizon of the sea, the sky opalescent at twilight, the trembling earth, the spicy smell of sage in evening and early morning. I remember the scent of burning sage and eucalyptus during October's wildfires, the holocaust landscape of Laguna in February, the new meaning of bright green shoots backlit against blackened stumps after winter rains.

I miss our easy collegiality at the institute, the congenial luxury of living among colleagues and friends, the week punctuated by Monday's daylong discussions, the stimulation of trying to get my head around someone else's assumptions, often so different from my own. But I also remember our discussions as so abstracted from the "nature" in which we were living, which I was feeling so intensely but perhaps not expressing verbally. Sometimes the talk seemed so disembodied. I regret that we didn't fully engage the tangibility, the "reality," of nonhuman nature. I wonder how different our conversations might have been if they had not taken place under fluorescent lights, in a windowless room, against the whistling whoosh of the building's ventilation system.

Our discussions deepened my awareness of how nature is and has been culturally constructed, but now more than ever I feel it crucial to reassert the reality of nonhuman features and phenomena. I hope our book doesn't overemphasize the cultural construction of nature to the extent that readers come away with the impression that nature is only a construct. I hope it will help people see nature as varied, not singular, as both real and imagined: as multiple features and phenomena that have palpable presence and autonomy on the one hand; as projected human ideas on the other. I hope my essay will help readers see landscapes, whether "wilderness" or urban, as both literal and figurative constructions of nature, to appreciate that landscapes are shaped, and that shaping expresses values and ideas for which humans, as individuals and societies, must take responsibility.

Robert Harrison: One of the most rewarding experiences of this collaboration was the realization that, for all the uncommon ground among specialists in diverse fields, there was a deeply common sense among us that nature (however defined or invented) is beyond any comprehensive conceptual grasp yet wholly within the domain of our social, political, and moral responsibility. I would hope that this realization carries over into the book as a whole and that its reader will be alerted to, and be inspired to assume, such responsibility, whatever specific form it may take.

Jim Proctor: What I'd like the reader to carry away from my own essay is the realization that ideas of nature have crucial *moral* implications—they provide a context of right and wrong that supports certain courses of action to protect the environment. Rethinking ideas of nature thus necessitates rethinking ethics, too: once you admit, for instance, that nature is not just wilderness or the ancient forest, you've then got to decide whether and why you should care about wilderness or ancient forests at all, and how high up they should be on your list of moral priorities. This, I believe, is the real challenge of this book for environmentalism, and we've just begun that journey here.

One lesson I hope the reader will *not* take away from this book is that there are no better and worse ideas of nature. Though few of us said so explicitly in our essays, our private conversations together revealed a profound discomfort with relativism. The reader, I trust, will understand that our primary task here was to call into question certain commonsense notions about nature, but this doesn't imply that we have abandoned any hope of finding more socially and ecologically appropriate approaches to nature. As Clifford Geertz once said, "It is not truth that varies with social, psychological, and cultural contexts but the symbols we construct in our unequally effective attempts to grasp it."

I hope this book helps people approach environmental problems as more than just environmental problems. What I mean is that if you take nature as a given and just worry about coming up with optimum policies to save it, you'll miss some crucial ideological considerations, as we've suggested throughout this book. By considering relevant human practices and ideas, environmental problems become human problems as well. But this doesn't mean that they are *merely* human problems; the natural sciences, for instance, still have a great deal to offer us in deepening our knowledge of the environment. We're just advocating that people broaden their scope of inquiry when they try to understand or solve environmental problems.

This approach will no doubt be frustrating to those who are looking for immediate solutions to specific environmental problems, because when you broaden your scope of inquiry you discover that environmental problems are often entangled in a larger web—ideas of nature are intimately associated with all kinds of ideas about people that may appear to have nothing whatsoever to do with nonhuman nature. But there's no way around the messiness and complexity of environmental problems. A better perspective, I believe, is to approach environmental problems as points of departure in a larger critique of modernity; this approach encourages environmentalists to join forces with other social movements seeking to create a more livable world.

Jeff Ellis: I am particularly concerned about those individuals or groups who come to environmental problems with established ideological agendas and whose primary concern is with fitting those problems into rigid ideological frameworks. To me, this is akin to a blind man who doesn't know he is blind putting his Seeing Eye dog into its harness and dragging the animal against its will into a busy street at rush hour. Very little good can come of it. I want readers to recognize not only the political nature of environmental problems but the political nature of the many environmental perspectives that gravitate toward those problems.

I am equally concerned about those environmentalists who too readily accept the overly simple analysis that identifies generic man as the culprit. This basically misanthropic position is widespread in environmental circles and is counterproductive in that it limits constructive action to population control and wilderness preservation. Only by recognizing that there are many environmental problems, each of which is historically contingent and multicausal, can environmentalists begin to overcome their differences and attempt to hammer out a more comprehensive and effective reform agenda. I want to point out a profound irony within contemporary environmental discourse. In order to promote unity and strengthen the environmental movement by providing it with a clear focus and analysis upon which to base actions, environmental theorists have too often oversimplified extremely complex issues and interrelationships. Ironically this tendency to oversimplify has served to divide rather than unite environmentalists, making the movement less rather than more than the sum of its parts.

I think the book's most important contribution can be to provide a much needed reassessment of the well-worn tactics and strategies that have characterized American environmentalism. Many of those tactics and strategies have lent credence to charges of elitism and misanthropy and prevented the environmental movement from broadening its base and becoming a democratic force in American politics. The movement's construction of nature as something out there that needs preserving, its reliance on the Edenic narrative to provide an alternative vision for how to live on Earth, its validation of knowing nature through consumption and its rejection of knowing it through work—all of these strategies have and will continue to have long-term negative consequences.

Jennifer Price: I find this such a difficult question to answer because of its enormousness—how to reinvent human relationships with nature? So begin with the small things. I'll be very pleased if readers ask a few new questions about their encounters with nature in everyday life—Where *did* this table come from? Why are all the Nature Company stores in glitzy upscale malls? Why are nature shows on the Discovery Channel so slow, with low-voiced male narrators and lots of flute music? Why do the trails in this park go to these places? Has this river always been straight? In sum, I'll be pleased if they question anything about their encounters with nature that they've taken for granted, because our assumptions about nature are surely among our most ironclad. Among the many ideas we've had about nature, perhaps the most powerful is that nature is *natural*—and what we think or know about it is therefore universally true, nonnegotiable, unassailable. Such small questions might engage readers with the larger questions this book takes on. Or even simply make these big questions seem relevant, reverent, acceptable to ask—what nature is, what it means, how and whether humans should and shouldn't transform it, to whose end, and who gets to decide.

For many of us, the woods or the wilderness can seem to lack everything the city has too much of—no trash, crowds, loud engines, hate crimes, or alarm clocks. One's early "nature experiences"—in my own case, hiking forays into the wilds of the Rockies—become a powerful source for a critique of what seems problematic about modern urban life. And the city becomes *unnatural*. I hope these essays encourage people to see nature in the city—to make visible the nature that supports our everyday lives. Can we "renaturalize" tables, electricity, computers? Even parks, which might seem like "artificial" landscapes—that is, not really truly nature? Well, so many of our essays insist that "nature" is not just "out there," not so unchanging or quite so inviolate. That can be unsettling (what *can* you count on to stay put in modern life, if not nature?). But a key implication is that it's okay to use nature, to change it. I think that can render the nature we *do* use in the city more visible—and can compel us to think about where that nature came from, how and by whose hands it traveled into the city, etc. We have to see nature in order to *re*-vision it—to think about how to integrate nature into everyday urban life in more sustainable or livable ways, to create urban landscapes that actually teach us about nature and our connections to it, rather than urge us to escape.

So many of the essays argue that there is no one right way to value or use nature. Better and worse ways, perhaps. But say you're trying to design a management plan for the new California desert park—there's no one perfect way to recreate, no higher command against fire suppression or grazing, no one unchanging way for this slice of the Mojave to look. Can the plan be negotiated with more tolerance than environmental conflicts have been notorious for?

Candace Slater: What I would like readers to get from my essay and, hopefully, from the book as a whole is the conviction that nature is a noun with a necessary multiplicity of modifiers, if not a singular in desperate need of pluralization. Amazonian nature isn't Californian or Japanese nature, except on the very broadest of levels. Moreover, individual Amazonian or Californian or Japanese ways of looking at nature are certainly not all the same. We can generalize, but any generalization is bound to be based on particulars. Bad generalizations are the ones that forget or disguise their roots in the concrete. The more successful generalizations acknowledge and actively recall these roots.

A great many of the calamitous decisions made in regard to Amazonia arise from projection onto the region of preexisting notions of a what a rain forest—or a wilderness or jungle—ought to be. If readers of this book say, "Hey, wait a minute, why do these Indians always have to be so perfect?" the next time they see a TV documentary on the Amazon, I'll be happy. I'll be even happier if people start routinely looking for what I've called Edenic narratives in materials that have nothing to do with the Amazon. Because then, when they do encounter Amazonia, they will see it with new eyes.

I emphasize the importance of interconnections because I'm aware that my own thinking about nature and environmental issues has become a great deal more interconnected. A year ago I would have said, "The spotted owl? Interesting, but what do those debates have to do with Amazonia?" Or "Toxic dumps? Sorry, my area is rain forests; there's nothing I could say about how they are portrayed." My own increased appreciation of the ways in which debates about the Amazon reflect discussions of superficially very different environmental topics makes me hopeful that others will come to see these interrelations, and that this broader vision will have practical effects.

Susan Davis: I think what I'd most like people to think about while reading our book is the historical particularity of the idea of nature. It is a shifting construct that is always located in a particular place and time, and put to very partial and particular uses. I'd like people to think about how nature is used, to what purposes, and by whom. If our book gets people to think about where images, ideas, representations of nature come from, who produces them, and how and for what uses—then I think this would be a big contribution.

I myself came away from our readings and discussions more convinced than ever of the need to talk about the many ways and places where nature is produced. Ideas, images, representations of nature don't float free from a social location. Most current theorizing in the humanities separates representation from social location and social experience—so what I'm suggesting here goes against the grain. Nonetheless, going against the grain lets us look at what nature is (not just how it is represented) for a wide variety of people whose experiences of nature, uses for nature, ideas about nature, have not only been written off but actually been rendered completely invisible in academic discussion. Insisting on the social location of dominant ideas about nature would, among other things, provide activists with a powerful critical tool.

Giovanna Di Chiro: One of the most important elements of the seminar discussions for me has been the commitment to developing a critical discourse about "nature" and "environment" that did not attempt to come to final closure, that did not once again reproduce the universalism that is so characteristic of colonial discourse. We have differing positions on this issue—some people in the group were less sanguine about the tendency of our discussions to move toward "uncommon ground" rather than toward the production of a unified statement that could represent the possibility of a reassuring "common ground." I don't think that the representation of diverse and sometimes conflicting positions, inherent in the vocabulary of "uncommon ground," necessarily means that the prospects of collectivity or affinity are quashed. In fact, I believe it promises just the opposite—that important differences and tensions can thereby be revealed and opened up for scrutiny, negotiation, and accountability.

By uncritically adopting the colonial discourse on the separation of nature and culture, mainstream environmentalists limit the possibilities of their political project. Given that the condition of the environment appears to be worsening on a global scale, how should a serious environmental movement respond? One response emerges from the many communities, organizations, and networks that make up the environmental justice movement. The concept of "nature as community," which suffuses the theory and practice of environmental justice suggests a profound connection between humans and their environments. The environmental justice movement proposes a form of environmentalism that recognizes the historical interrelationships between communities and environments and argues that there are already existing "inventions" of nature that do not take as their starting point the human control of the natural world. Trying to solve the historical problems of particular capitalist and patriarchal dominations of nature by removing "humans as contaminants" does not move us closer to a sustainable future. More salient issues include how different humans are differently implicated in environmental degradation, how different cultures and environments interact in positive and destructive ways, and how diverse ways of inventing "mixed species communities" might produce a more livable world.

Carolyn Merchant: This disorderly, ordered world of nonhuman nature must be acknowledged as a free autonomous actor, just as humans are free autonomous actors. But nature limits human freedom to totally dominate and control it, just as human power limits nature's and other humans' freedom. Science and technology can tell us that an event such as a hurricane, earthquake, flood, or fire is likely to happen in a certain locale, but not when it will happen. Because nature is fundamentally chaotic, it must be respected and related to as an active partner through a partnership ethic.

If we know that an earthquake in Los Angeles is likely in the next seventy-five years, a utilitarian, homocentric ethic would state that the government ought not to license the construction of a nuclear reactor on the fault line. But a partnership ethic would say that we, the human community, ought to respect nature's autonomy as an actor by limiting building and leaving open space. If we know there is a possibility of a hundred-year flood on the Mississippi River, we respect human needs for navigation and power, but we also respect nature's autonomy by limiting our capacity to dam every tributary that feeds the river and to build homes on every floodplain. We leave some rivers wild and free and leave some floodplains as wetlands, while using others to fulfill human needs. If we know that forest fires are likely in the Rockies, we do not build cities along forest edges. We limit the extent of development, leave open spaces, plant fire-resistant vegetation, and use tile rather than shake roofs. If cutting tropical and temperate old-growth forests creates problems for both the global environment and the local communities, but we cannot adequately predict the outcome or effects of those changes, we need to conduct partnership negotiations in which nonhuman nature and the people involved are equally represented. Each of

these difficult, time-consuming ethical and policy decisions will be negotiated by a human community in a particular place, but the outcome will
depend on the history of people's relations with nature in the area—and,
not least, on the narratives they tell themselves about the land, vital human
needs, past and present land-use patterns, the larger global context, and the
ability (or lack of ability) to predict nature's events.

Donna Haraway: How have the connections of race and nature changed in
a world where information and genes have become the dominant scientific
terms of reference? What happens when symbolic systems of blood—so
critical to ideas of nature, sex, and race—are transmuted into the coin of
genes? That is the question that has kept nagging me in our investigation
into the many constructions of nature in U.S. cultures over this century.
Through museum practice, school curricula, government policy, medicine,
labor policies, vernacular music, biological research, and broad popular
belief, race and nature were tightly coupled at the beginning of the twentieth
century. In the current era of multiculturalism, what forms have the old
connections between race and nature taken, or have they at last slithered
away into the garbage pile of both popular and scientific ideas?

I don't have any final answers to these questions at the end of our project,
but I do have more confidence that the corporatization of the body is at the
heart of the issue. In the New World Order, Inc., I am becoming an old-
fashioned Marxist feminist again, no matter how unacceptably politically
correct that label sounds. In a world where nature and culture have both
been "enterprised up," the turning of everything that moves and breathes
into a commodity has changed people's experience of race and nature on an
everyday basis. The change is ferociously global and excruciatingly local.
The body of nature and the personal body of experience have both become
part of regimes of flexible accumulation, where the global circulation of
information determines the weather patterns of lives.

At the end of the twentieth century, the database is what makes us
human. Its diversity is our scientific racial discourse and our sexy colonial
problem. It is not the jungle, rain forest, or wilderness that is at the heart of
what gets to count as nature for millions, if not billions, of people at the
close of the second Christian millennium. When biodiversity is a banking
problem, the nature of nature has become a very different speculative game.
Eden was once a dream, or a dirty secret, at the heart of endless stories.
Now Eden is the home of SimEve in the sparkling databanks of cyberspace,
where nature has been raised to a higher power and where humanity is
enticed or forced to diversify by the logics of naked market imperatives.

Our task is to refuse this version of human nature in practical and intellectual terms. Our systems of kin and of kind depend upon it. Referring to the
first patented animal in the world, Du Pont advertised itself as the place
"where better things for better living come to life." But I want a different
origin story for the corporate body—the body that ties us all together. I

want a story and a practice where all the liveliness of science is in the service a livable nature, where diversity ceases to be a question of the bottom line. In very old-fashioned terms, I want a science for the people. Only I would change that to a science for the humans and nonhumans, in alliance for a potent new story about the whole earth.

Ken Olwig: On my return to the United States for the first extended stay in fifteen years, it was literally alienating to find myself a foreigner in my native land. My estrangement as a person betwixt and between two countries played an important role in the way I saw the project of reinventing nature. Not belonging anywhere meant that the given norms of any culture no longer seemed natural. I don't think my situation was unique, though; I felt that I was in good company in the group. Because this group speaks from so many radically different communities and worlds, it has generated a kind of uncommon ground that has caused it to question given norms. I think the book might help generate a similarly productive form of alienation among its readers—an alienation from what is otherwise thought to be naturally given.

I think we will have accomplished a lot if we can just get people to not take their own concept of nature and the natural for granted. To get them to show tolerance and consider the fact that such concepts are culturally defined. Even to realize that many ideas and institutions, which are cherished as being naturally American, derive from Europe—where they were also thought to be naturally English, Danish, or even Roman. This might, in turn, lead to the realization that not even all Americans share the same idea of nature. A major step in this direction would be taken if we could just get people to stop thinking primarily of nature in terms of the objects, or assemblages of objects, which in their particular culture, at their particular time, are identified with nature and the natural. It would be valuable to get people to consider the abstract meanings that their culture derives from its symbols.

Katherine Hayles: One of the valuable lessons I learned in our seminar was the difficulty of defining "nature" in opposition to culture, human activity, or technological interventions. Humans have now established themselves as so much the dominant species on the planet that virtually no "nature" untouched by human hands exists. Either we have no nature, then, or nature is everywhere around us but we have difficulty seeing it because we want it to be "out there," separate and distinct from our interactions with it. Besides the conceptual issues involved (on what grounds can one define "nature" as really natural and not artificial?), viewing nature as separate from us leads to significant practical problems. It invites an "us versus them" posture that creates opposition within environmental movements as well as outside them. For example, it may pit endangered species activists against those concerned with such issues as environmental justice, for the former want to channel resources into saving nonhuman life forms and habitats, while the latter want to make the environment safer and cleaner for humans, particularly economically disadvantaged people of color who suffer the most from environmental toxicity.

What is the alternative? We can find a clue, I believe, in the contests that are now shaping up around the meaning and significance of simulation technologies. At stake in these contests is nothing less than the definition of what it means to be human. One view would identify the human with the mind, particularly rational thought. The capacity for rational thought, the argument goes, we share with intelligent machines. They are our destiny, not the messy "wetware" that we share with other biological life-forms. If nature is biology, leave it behind and vault into an informational space where we can control what happens to us. Seemingly at the opposite pole from an environmental movement such as wilderness preservation, this view actually shares with it some important assumptions. Both see nature as essentially nonhuman, an entity that we encounter as something apart from ourselves. What is needed is a view of humanity that integrates the human into nature rather than separating us out from it, and a view of nature that stresses its interpenetration into all areas of human experience and cognition, including the artificial worlds of simulation technologies.

What perceptions can be fostered by a view that places humans within nature and allies nature with simulation rather than putting it in opposition to artificial worlds? The following list of propositions traces out one line of argument.

1. We never perceive nature directly. All perception of the outside world is constructed through interactions between what is "out there" and our cognitive-sensory apparatus.

2. Simulation technologies extend these interactions between the "out there" and our sensory-cognitive apparatus into artificial worlds.

3. Artificial worlds are in this sense "natural." They remind us that our interactions with nature are also mediated and constructive.

4. One potentially liberatory element in simulation technology is the evidence it gives us of otherness. In the case of artificial worlds, this otherness comes from a combination of the emergent behavior of complex systems and a technology that is a material instantiation of the interplay between human thought and the materials out of which the technologies are formed. The people who created the technology are other than us, and through the technology we experience on many levels the assumptions that they encoded into the material forms with which we interact. In the case of a "natural" environment, the otherness comes from a combination of nonhuman life-forms and habitats that have been affected to varying degrees by human activity and interventions. The world as we experience it, then, is neither wholly apart from the human nor wholly of it, neither completely natural nor completely artificial. This is as true of walking through a rain forest as it is of cruising a virtual habitat that exists in the computer.

Michael Barbour: My tongue-in-cheek suggestion of a title for this volume was *Myths, Memories, and Expectations.* With good reason it wasn't accepted; after all, who would know this was a book about nature with a title like that? What I meant was that we interpret nature through a filter of very personal bias. We see any natural setting through a haze of stories—of myths—told to us by our culture. We come to each new landscape with a baggage of memories accumulated from all the other places we have ever been. We see any place through a lens of hungers, desires, and expectations that we bring with us to that place. Nature is real, of course, but we can experience and relate to others only a filtered, personalized version of nature. The filter exists alike for farmer, poet, scientist, and public policy maker; one consequence is that none of them can claim to speak for nature. My coming to understand the existence of this pervasive filter—even within the area of my own specialty, the science of ecology—was a personal take-home lesson from our workshop, this book, and my own chapter in it. The lesson still generates ambivalent feelings in me, both disturbing my trust in the objectivity of the scientific method and comfortingly putting me in the good company of all humans who pass through the natural world, trying their best to understand it and their own place in it. Perhaps the take-home lesson for some of those who read this book will be the same as my own. Indeed, I hope so.

Richard White: I was struck by the divisions that did not materialize among us. There was considerable agreement that the natural world was more than a representation and that we could learn meaningful things about it—not just about our representations of it. There was also considerable agreement that, whatever else nature was, it was a representation. That is not so much a conclusion. It is where our discussions began. I know that after six months in Irvine, I came away more and more convinced of how the made world (our ideas, machines, homes, etc.) and the unmade world (the "nature" we did not create, including our own bodies) have begun to merge and blur in very interesting ways. It made me more and more intrigued by these blurrings, both now and in the past.

I also found our insistent questioning about what counts as nature and who gets to define nature quite profitable. This need not, I think, lead to a kind of hopeless relativism or reification of difference but instead to an awareness of how dominant cultural forms are constructed and how alternative constructions are buried or erased. These are hardly new ideas, but when paired with a willingness to see the natural world itself as undermining or supporting various constructions, a richer world of meaning and action opens up.

William Cronon: In thinking about a Big Message that I might offer as an ending for this book, I've kept returning to that phrase of Raymond Williams: "Ideas of nature, but these are the projected ideas of men" (and women too, he would presumably now add). It seems to me that all of us agree with this formulation of Williams, so our common ground, such as it is, almost surely lies somewhere amid the unnaturally natural ideas and projections toward which he points. If there is a moral to this book, it is that we need to think much harder than we usually do about what we mean when we use the word "nature," and about how we should and should not draw boundaries between the things we call "human" and the things we call "natural."

One of the challenges we've faced in this book has been trying to reach two audiences that are likely to draw quite opposite conclusions from our work. On the one hand, we need somehow to persuade scientists and environmentalists who assume "nature" to be natural, wholly external to human culture, that there is something profoundly important and useful in recognizing its cultural constructedness. On the other hand, we need no less to persuade humanists and postmodernists that although ideas of nature may be the projected ideas of men and women, the world onto which we project those ideas is by no means entirely of our own making: there is more to the world than just words.

Nature is a mirror onto which we project our own ideas and values; but it is also a material reality that sets limits (never completely clear but no less definite for being uncertain) on the possibilities of human ingenuity and storytelling. Recognizing the mirror helps us become more self-critical about our own assumptions; recognizing its limits chastens us into becoming more humble about our own power. Oddly enough, I think science and postmodernism, which so often seem to be at odds with each other, share a commitment to the idea that we must struggle always to see the world clearly. They may differ about the nature of the clarity we can hope to achieve, but their faith in self-criticism as the only possible route to clarity seems powerfully shared. So perhaps the strongest claim we can make for the approach we offer in this book is to say that we humans cannot hope to solve our current environmental crises unless we try to understand not just the environment whose problems worry us but also the "we" who choose to understand and worry about those problems in ways that are quite peculiarly our own.

I guess what surprised me most about our group was how quickly, despite our very different backgrounds and intellectual commitments, we found common ground in Williams's uncommon notion that nature is the projected ideas of human beings—or rather, that it is the meeting place between the world "out there" and the culturally constructed ideas and beliefs and values we project onto that world. The nonhuman world is real and autonomous, a place always worthy of our respect and care, but the paradox of our human lives is that we can never know that world at first hand. Instead, we see it through the lens of our own conceptions and simulations, which never map onto the real world in a perfect one-to-one correspondence. The nonhuman world is not (just) our creation, but nature is. Nature is far less natural than we think. This is an unusual a way of thinking about "nature," and I suspect many readers have probably at one time or another found it troubling. I nonetheless hope that by now its value has become more compelling.

Question: Why should people think about nature in this seemingly unnatural way? Answers: Because any other way of thinking about nature will almost certainly misconceive its true nature. Because any other way of thinking about nature will remove it from history and separate it from the cultural processes that created this deeply human way of thinking. Because so many modern ways of thinking about nature too easily accept the false dualism between nature and culture, positing an inescapably fallen humanity that cannot help being *un*natural—whereas the paired naturalness and unnaturalness of humanity is the very thing we most need to linger over and understand. The most important contribution this book can make, it seems to me, is to help people grapple more clearly and self-critically with the peculiarly human task of living in nature while thinking themselves outside it.

On the Nature of Nature:
An Eclectic Reading List

Abrams, M. H. *Natural Supernaturalism: Tradition and Revolution in Romantic Literature.* New York: Norton, 1971.

Agarwal, Bina. "The Gender and Environment Debate: Lessons from India." *Feminist Studies* 18 (1992): 119–59.

Albanese, Catherine L. *Nature Religion in America: From the Algonkian Indians to the New Age.* Chicago: Univ. of Chicago Press, 1990.

Allin, Craig W. *The Politics of Wilderness Preservation.* Westport, Conn.: Greenwood Press, 1982.

Alston, Dana. *We Speak for Ourselves: Social Justice, Race, and the Environment.* Washington, D.C.: Panos Institute, 1990.

Anderson, Edgar. *Landscape Papers.* Edited by Bob Callahan. Berkeley, Calif.: Turtle Island Foundation, 1976.

Andrews, Malcolm. *The Search for the Picturesque.* Stanford: Stanford Univ. Press, 1989.

Armstrong, Susan J., and Richard G. Botzler. *Environmental Ethics: Divergence and Convergence.* New York: McGraw-Hill, 1993.

Atwood, Margaret. *Wilderness Tips.* New York: Doubleday, 1991.

Auden, W. H. "In Praise of Limestone." In *Selected Poetry of W. H. Auden.* New York: Modern Library, 1958.

Auerbach, Erich. *Mimesis: The Representation of Reality in Western Literature.* Princeton: Princeton Univ. Press, 1953.

Bachelard, Gaston. *The Poetics of Space.* Boston: Beacon, 1969.

Bakeless, John. *The Eyes of Discovery: The Pageant of North America as Seen by the First Explorers.* New York: Dover Publications, 1961.

Baldwin, A. Dwight, Jr., et al. *Beyond Preservation: Restoring and Inventing Landscapes.* Minneapolis: Univ. of Minnesota Press, 1994.

Banham, Reyner. *Los Angeles: The Architecture of Four Ecologies.* New York: Penguin, 1971.

———. *Scenes in America Deserta.* Salt Lake City: Peregrine Smith, 1982.

Barbour, Michael, and Valerie Whitworth. "California's Grassroots: Native or European?" *Pacific Discovery* 45, no. 1 (Winter 1992): 8–15.

Barbour, Michael, et al. *California's Changing Landscapes: Diversity and Conservation of California Vegetation.* Sacramento: California Native Plant Society, 1993.

Barnes, Trevor J., and James S. Duncan, eds. *Writing Worlds: Discourse, Texts and Metaphors in the Representation of Landscape.* New York: Routledge, 1992.

Barrell, John. *The Dark Side of the Landscape: The Rural Poor in English Painting, 1730–1840.* New York: Cambridge Univ. Press, 1980.

———. *The Idea of Landscape and the Sense of Place, 1730–1840.* Cambridge: Cambridge Univ. Press, 1972.

Bate, Jonathan. *Romantic Ecology: Wordsworth and the Environmental Tradition.* New York: Routledge, 1991.

Bateson, Gregory. *Mind and Nature: A Necessary Unity.* New York: Bantam, 1980.

Baudrillard, Jean. *For a Critique of the Political Economy of the Sign.* St. Louis: Telos Press, 1981.

———. *Jean Baudrillard: Selected Writings.* Edited by Mark Poster. Stanford: Stanford Univ. Press, 1988.

Benjamin, Walter. *Illuminations.* Translated by Harry Zohn. New York: Harcourt, Brace and World, 1968.

Bennett, Jane, and William Chaloupka, eds. *In the Nature of Things: Language, Politics, and the Environment.* Minneapolis: Univ. of Minnesota Press, 1993.

Berger, John. *About Looking.* New York: Pantheon, 1980.

Berleant, Arnold. *The Aesthetics of Environment.* Philadelphia: Temple Univ. Press, 1992.

Berman, Marshall. *All That Is Solid Melts into Air: The Experience of Modernity.* New York: Simon and Schuster, 1982.

Berman, Morris. *The Reenchantment of the World.* Ithaca: Cornell Univ. Press, 1981.

Bermingham, Ann. *Landscape and Ideology: The English Rustic Tradition, 1740–1860.* Berkeley: Univ. of California Press, 1986.

Bernstein, Richard J. *Beyond Objectivism and Relativism: Science, Hermeneutics, and Praxis.* Philadelphia: Univ. of Pennsylvania Press, 1983.

Berry, Wendell. *The Gift of Good Land: Further Essays Cultural and Agricultural.* San Francisco: North Point, 1981.

———. *Home Economics.* San Francisco: North Point, 1987.

———. *What Are People For?* San Francisco: North Point, 1990.

Best, Steven, and Douglas Kellner. *Postmodern Theory: Critical Interrogations.* New York: Guilford Press, 1991.

Bishop, Peter. *The Myth of Shangri La: Tibet, Travel Writing, and the Western Creation of Sacred Landscape.* London: Athlone, 1989.

Borgmann, Albert. *Crossing the Postmodern Divide.* Chicago: Univ. of Chicago Press, 1992.

Botkin, Daniel B. *Discordant Harmonies: A New Ecology for the Twenty-first Century.* New York: Oxford Univ. Press, 1990.

Bouissac, Paul. *Circus and Culture: A Semiotic Approach.* Bloomington: Indiana Univ. Press, 1976.

Bourassa, Steven C. *The Aesthetics of Landscape.* London: Belhaven Press, 1991.

Bourdieu, Pierre. *Outline of a Theory of Practice.* Translated by Richard Nice. New York: Cambridge Univ. Press, 1977.

Bramwell, Anna. *Ecology in the 20th Century: A History.* New Haven: Yale Univ. Press, 1989.

Brantlinger, Patrick. *Crusoe's Footprints: Cultural Studies in Britain and America.* New York: Routledge, 1990.

Browne, Janet. *The Secular Ark: Studies in the History of Biogeography.* New Haven: Yale Univ. Press, 1983.

Bullard, Robert. *Dumping in Dixie: Race, Class, and Environmental Quality.* Boulder, Colo.: Westview Press, 1990.

———, ed. *Confronting Environmental Racism: Voices from the Grassroots.* Boston: South End Press, 1993.

———, ed. *Unequal Protection: Environmental Justice and Communities of Color.* San Francisco: Sierra Club Books, 1994.

Burke, Edmund. *A Philosophical Enquiry into the Origin of Our Ideas of the Sublime and Beautiful.* Ed. James T. Boulton. 1958. Notre Dame: Univ. of Notre Dame Press, 1968.

Butler, Judith. *Bodies That Matter: On the Discursive Limits of "Sex."* New York: Routledge, 1993.

Cantwell, Robert. *Ethnomimesis: Folklife and the Representation of Culture.* Chapel Hill: Univ. of North Carolina Press, 1993.

Carr, Claudia. *Pastoralism in Crisis: The Dasanetch and Their Ethiopian Lands.* Chicago: Univ. of Chicago Geography Department, 1977.

Carson, Rachel. *Silent Spring.* Boston: Houghton Mifflin, 1962.

Cartmill, Matt. *A View to a Death in the Morning: Hunting and Nature through History.* Cambridge: Harvard Univ. Press, 1993.

Casey, Edward S. *Getting Back into Place: Toward a Renewed Understanding of the Place-World.* Bloomington: Indiana Univ. Press, 1993.

Chapple, Christopher Key. *Ecological Prospects: Scientific, Religious, and Aesthetic Perspectives.* Albany: State Univ. of New York Press, 1994.

Chase, Alston. *Playing God in Yellowstone: The Destruction of America's First National Park.* Boston: Atlantic Monthly Press, 1986.

Christensen, Norman L. "Landscape History and Ecological Change." *Journal of Forest History* 33 (July 1989): 116–25.

Churchill, Ward. *Struggle for the Land.* Monroe, Maine: Common Courage, 1993.

Clark, Kenneth. *Landscape into Art.* Rev. ed. New York: Harper and Row, 1976.

Clark, T. J. *The Painting of Modern Life: Paris in the Art of Manet and His Followers.* New York: Knopf, 1984.

Clifford, James. *The Predicament of Culture: Twentieth-Century Ethnography, Literature, and Art.* Cambridge: Harvard Univ. Press, 1988.

Clifford, James, and George E. Marcus. *Writing Culture: The Poetics and Politics of Ethnography.* Berkeley: Univ. Of California Press, 1986.

Cohen, Michael. *The Pathless Way: John Muir and the American Wilderness.* Madison: Univ. of Wisconsin Press, 1984.

Colinvaux, Paul. *Why Big Fierce Animals Are Rare: An Ecologist's Perspective.* Princeton: Princeton Univ. Press, 1978.

Collingwood, R. G. *The Idea of Nature.* New York: Oxford Univ. Press, 1945.

Conzen, Michael P., ed. *The Making of the American Landscape.* London: Unwin Hyman, 1990.

Cooper, Diana Starr. *Night after Night.* (Washington, D.C.: Island Press, 1994).

Cosgrove, Denis. *Social Formation and Symbolic Landscape.* Totowa, N.J.: Barnes and Noble, 1984.

Crandell, Gina. *Nature Pictorialized: "The View" in Landscape History.* Baltimore: Johns Hopkins Univ. Press, 1993.

Cranz, Galen. *The Politics of Park Design: A History of Urban Parks in America.* Cambridge: MIT Press, 1982.

Crary, Jonathan. *Techniques of the Observer: On Vision and Modernity in the Nineteenth Century.* Cambridge: MIT Press, 1993.

Crase, Douglas. *The Revisionist: Poems.* Boston: Little, Brown, 1981.

Cronon, William. *Changes in the Land: Indians, Colonists, and the Ecology of New England.* New York: Hill and Wang, 1983.

———. "Kennecott Journey: The Paths Out of Town." In *Under an Open Sky: Rethinking America's Western Past,* edited by William Cronon, George Miles, and Jay Gitlin. New York: Norton, 1992.

———. "Landscape and Home: Environmental Traditions in Wisconsin." *Wisconsin Magazine of History* 74 (1990–91): 83–105.

———. *Nature's Metropolis: Chicago and the Great West.* New York: Norton, 1991.

———. "A Place for Stories: Nature, History, and Narrative." *Journal of American History* 78 (1992): 1347–76.

Crosby, Alfred W. *The Columbian Exchange: Biological and Cultural Consequences of 1492.* Westport, Conn.: Greenwood Press, 1972.

———. *Ecological Imperialism: The Biological Expansion of Europe, 900–1900.* New York: Cambridge Univ. Press, 1986.

Crumley, Carole L., ed. *Historical Ecology: Cultural Knowledge and Changing Landscapes.* Santa Fe: School of American Research Press, 1994.

Daniels, Stephen, and Dennis Cosgrove, eds. *The Iconography of Landscape: Essays on the Symbolic Representation, Design, and Use of Past Environments.* New York: Cambridge Univ. Press, 1988.

Darnovsky, Marcy. "Stories Less Told: Histories of U.S. Environmentalism." *Socialist Review* 22 (Oct.–Dec. 1992): 11–54.

Davis, Mike. *City of Quartz.* London: Verso, 1990.

deBuys, William. *Enchantment and Exploitation: The Life and Hard Times of a New Mexico Mountain Range.* Albuquerque: Univ. of New Mexico Press, 1985.

Demeritt, David, "Ecology, Objectivity and Critique in Writings on Nature and Human Societies," *Journal of Historical Geography* 20 (1994): 22–37.

Dewey, John. *Art as Experience.* New York: Capricorn Books, 1958.

Diamond, Irene, and G. Ornstein, eds. *Reweaving the World: The Emergence of Ecofeminism.* San Francisco: Sierra Club Books, 1990.

Dibbell, Julian. "Rape in Cyberspace: A Tale of Crime and Punishment On-Line." *Village Voice,* Dec. 21, 1993, 36–42.

Dickens, Peter. *Society and Nature: Towards a Green Social Theory.* Philadelphia: Temple Univ. Press, 1992.

Douglas, Mary. *Natural Symbols: Explorations in Cosmology.* New York: Pantheon, 1982.

————. *Purity and Danger: An Analysis of the Concepts of Pollution and Taboo.* London: Routledge and Kegan Paul, 1966.

Douglas, Mary, and Aaron Wildavsky. *Risk and Culture: An Essay on the Selection of Technological and Environmental Dangers.* Berkeley: Univ. of California Press, 1982.

Dudley, Edward, and Maximillian E. Novak, eds. *The Wild Man Within: An Image in Western Thought from the Renaissance to Romanticism.* Pittsburgh: Univ. of Pittsburgh Press, 1972.

Duerr, Hans Peter. *Dreamtime: Concerning the Boundary between Wilderness and Civilization.* New York: Basil Blackwell, 1985.

Dunlap, Thomas R. *Saving America's Wildlife.* Princeton: Princeton Univ. Press, 1988.

Eagleton, Terry. *Ideology: An Introduction.* London: Verso, 1991.

Egerton, Frank N. "Changing Concepts of the Balance of Nature." *Quarterly Review of Biology* 48 (1973): 322–50.

Eiseley, Loren. *The Firmament of Time.* New York: Atheneum, 1960.

Ekirch, Arthur A., Jr. *Man and Nature in America.* New York: Columbia Univ. Press, 1963.

Eliade, Mircea. *The Myth of the Eternal Return.* New York: Pantheon, 1954.

————. *The Sacred and the Profane: The Nature of Religion.* Translated by Willard R. Trask. New York: Harcourt, Brace, 1959.

Eliot, T. S. "The Four Quartets." *Collected Poems, 1909–1962.* New York: Harcourt, Brace and World, 1970.

Empson, William. *Some Versions of the Pastoral.* New York: New Directions, 1974.

Engel, Leonard, ed. *The Big Empty: Essays on the Land as Narrative.* Albuquerque: Univ. of New Mexico Press, 1994.

Entrikin, J. Nicholas. *The Betweenness of Place: Towards a Geography of Modernity.* Baltimore: Johns Hopkins Univ. Press, 1991.

Environmental History Review.

Evernden, Neil. *The Natural Alien: Humankind and the Environment.* Toronto: Univ. of Toronto Press, 1985.

————. *The Social Creation of Nature.* Baltimore: Johns Hopkins Univ. Press, 1992.

Febvre, Lucien. *A Geographical Introduction to History.* New York: Knopf, 1925.

Fein, Albert. *Frederick Law Olmsted and the American Environmental Tradition.* New York: George Braziller, 1972.

Ferkiss, Victor. *Nature, Technology, and Society: Cultural Roots of the Current Environmental Crisis.* New York: New York Univ. Press, 1993.

Findlay, John M. *Magic Lands: Western Cityscapes and American Culture after 1940.* Berkeley: Univ. of California Press, 1992.

Forest and Conservation History.

Foucault, Michel. "Questions on Geography." *Power / Knowledge: Selected Interviews and Other Writings, 1972–1977.* Edited by Colin Gordon. New York: Pantheon, 1980.

Fox, Stephen. *John Muir and His Legacy: The American Conservation Movement.* Boston: Little, Brown, 1981.

Franke, Richard, and Barbara Chasin. *Seeds of Famine: Ecological Destruction and the Developmental Dilemma in the West Africa Sahel.* Montclair, N.J.: Allanheld, Osmun, 1980.

Fritzell, Peter A. *Nature Writing and America: Essays upon a Cultural Type.* Ames: Iowa State Univ. Press, 1990.

Frye, Northrop. *Anatomy of Criticism: Four Essays.* Princeton: Princeton Univ. Press, 1957.

Frykman, Jonas, and Orvar Löfgren. *Culture Builders: A Historical Anthropology of Middle-Class Life.* Translated by Alan Crozier. New Brunswick: Rutgers Univ. Press, 1987.

Gadgil, Madhav, and Ramachandra Guha. *This Fissured Land: An Ecological History of India.* Berkeley: Univ. of California Press, 1992.

Garreau, Joel. *Edge City: Life on the New Frontier.* New York: Doubleday, 1991.

Geertz, Clifford. *Agricultural Involution: The Processes of Ecological Change in Indonesia.* Berkeley: Univ. of California Press, 1963.

———. *The Interpretation of Cultures.* New York: Basic Books, 1973.

Gerbi, Antonello. *Nature in the New World: From Christopher Columbus to Gonzalo Fernandez de Oviedo.* Translated by Jeremy Moyle. Pittsburgh: Univ. of Pittsburgh Press, 1985.

Gibbs, Lois Marie. *Love Canal: My Story.* Albany: State Univ. of New York Press, 1982.

Gillespie, Angus K., and Jay Mechling, eds. *American Wildlife in Symbol and Story.* Knoxville: Univ. of Tennessee Press, 1987.

Gilpin, William. *Three Essays: On Picturesque Beauty; on Picturesque Travel; and on Sketching Landscape.* London, 1803.

Glacken, Clarence J. *Traces on the Rhodian Shore: Nature and Culture in Western Thought from Ancient Times to the End of the Eighteenth Century.* Berkeley: Univ. of California Press, 1967.

Gleick, James. *Chaos: Making a New Science.* New York: Viking, 1987.

Godelier, Maurice. *The Mental and the Material: Thought Economy and Society.* London: Verso, 1984.

Golley, Frank Benjamin. *A History of the Ecosystem Concept in Ecology: More Than the Sum of the Parts.* New Haven: Yale Univ. Press, 1993.

Gottlieb, Robert. *Forcing the Spring: The Transformation of the American Environmental Movement.* Washington, D.C.: Island Press, 1993.

Goudie, Andrew. *The Human Impact on the Natural Environment.* 2nd ed. Oxford: Basil Blackwell, 1986.

Gould, Stephen Jay. *Time's Arrow, Time's Cycle: Myth and Metaphor in the Discovery of Geological Time.* Cambridge: Harvard Univ. Press, 1987.

———. *Wonderful Life: The Burgess Shale and the Nature of History.* New York: Norton, 1990.

Green, Nicholas. *The Spectacle of Nature: Landscape and Bourgeois Culture in 19th-Century France.* Manchester: Manchester Univ. Press, 1990.

Greenblatt, Stephen. *Marvelous Possessions: The Wonder of the New World.* Chicago: Univ. of Chicago Press, 1991.

Gudeman, Stephen. *Economics as Culture: Models and Metaphors of Livelihood.* Boston: Routledge and Kegan Paul, 1986.

Guha, Ramachandra. *The Unquiet Woods: Ecological Change and Peasant Resistance in the Himalaya.* Berkeley: Univ. of California Press, 1990.

Guthrie-Smith, H. *Tutira: The Story of a New Zealand Sheep Station.* Edinburgh: Blackwood, 1953.

Hagen, Joel B. *An Entangled Bank: The Origins of Ecosystem Ecology.* New Brunswick: Rutgers Univ. Press, 1992.

Hallyn, Fernand. *The Poetic Structure of the World: Copernicus and Kepler.* New York: Zone Books, 1990.

Haraway, Donna. *Primate Visions: Gender, Race, and Nature in the World of Modern Science.* New York: Routledge, 1989.

———. *Simians, Cyborgs, and Women: The Reinvention of Nature.* New York: Routledge, 1991.

Harrison, Helen Mayer, and Newton Harrison. *The Lagoon Cycle.* Ithaca: Herbert F. Johnson Museum of Art, Cornell Univ., 1985.

Harrison, Robert Pogue. *Forests: The Shadow of Civilization.* Chicago: Univ. of Chicago Press, 1992.

Harvey, David. *The Condition of Postmodernity.* Cambridge, Mass.: Basil Blackwell, 1989.

Hawthorn, Geoffrey. *Plausible Worlds: Possibility and Understanding in History and the Social Sciences.* Cambridge: Cambridge Univ. Press, 1991.

Hayles, N. Katherine. *Chaos Bound: Orderly Disorder in Contemporary Literature and Science.* Ithaca: Cornell Univ. Press, 1990.

———. "Constrained Constructivism: Locating Scientific Inquiry in the Theater of Representation." *New Orleans Review* 18 (1991): 76–85.

———. *The Cosmic Web: Scientific Field Models and Literary Strategies in the Twentieth Century.* Ithaca: Cornell Univ. Press, 1984.

Hays, Samuel P. *Beauty, Health, and Permanence: Environmental Politics in the United States, 1955–1985.* New York: Cambridge Univ. Press, 1987.

———. *Conservation and the Gospel of Efficiency: The Progressive Conservation Movement, 1890–1920.* Cambridge: Harvard Univ. Press, 1959.

Hecht, Susanna, and Alexander Cockburn. *The Fate of the Forest: Developers, Destroyers, and Defenders of the Amazon.* New York: HarperCollins, 1990.

Heidegger, Martin, *The Question concerning Technology and Other Essays.* Translated by William Lovitt. New York: Harper and Row, 1977.

Helvarg, David. *The War against the Greens: The "Wise-Use" Movement, the New Right, and Anti-Environmental Warfare.* San Francisco: Sierra Club Books, 1994.

Hemingway, Andrew. *Landscape Imagery and Urban Culture in Early 19th-Century Britain.* New York: Cambridge Univ. Press, 1992.

Henderson, L. J. *The Fitness of the Environment: An Inquiry into the Biological Significance of the Properties of Matter.* New York: Macmillan, 1913.

Hofrichter, Richard, ed. *Toxic Struggles: The Theory and Practice of Environmental Justice.* Philadelphia: New Society Publishers, 1993.

Hoskins, W. G. *The Making of the English Landscape.* 1955. London: Hodder and Stoughton, 1988.

Hulme, Peter. *Colonial Encounters: Europe and the Native Caribbean, 1492–1797.* New York: Methuen, 1986.

Hundley, Norris, Jr. *The Great Thirst: Californians and Water, 1770s–1990s.* Berkeley: Univ. of California Press, 1992.

Hunt, John Dixon. *Gardens and the Picturesque: Studies in the History of Landscape Architecture.* Cambridge: MIT Press, 1992.

Hurst, James Willard. *Law and the Conditions of Freedom in the Nineteenth-Century United States.* Madison: Univ. of Wisconsin Press, 1956.

Hutchinson, G. Evelyn. *The Ecological Theater and the Evolutionary Play.* New Haven: Yale Univ. Press, 1965.

Huth, Hans. *Nature and the American: Three Centuries of Changing Attitudes.* Lincoln: Univ. of Nebraska Press, 1957.

Ingold, Tim. *The Appropriation of Nature: Essays on Human Ecology and Social Relations.* Iowa City: Univ. of Iowa Press, 1987.

Jackson, J. B. *Landscapes: Selected Writings of J. B. Jackson.* Edited by Ervin H. Zube. Amherst: Univ. of Massachusetts Press, 1970.

Jackson, John Brinckerhoff. *Discovering the Vernacular Landscape.* New Haven: Yale Univ. Press, 1984.

———. *A Sense of Place, a Sense of Time.* New Haven: Yale Univ. Press, 1994.

Jackson, Peter. *Maps of Meaning: An Introduction to Cultural Geography.* London: Unwin Hyman, 1989.

Jackson, Wes, et al., eds. *Meeting the Expectations of the Land: Essays in Sustainable Agriculture and Stewardship.* San Francisco: North Point, 1984.

John, David M. "The Relevance of Deep Ecology to the Third World: Some Preliminary Comments." *Environmental Ethics* 12 (1990): 233–52.

Jussin, Estelle, and Elizabeth Lindquist-Cock. *Landscape as Photograph.* New Haven: Yale Univ. Press, 1985.

Kahrl, William L. *Water and Power: The Conflict over Los Angeles' Water Supply in the Owens Valley.* Berkeley: Univ. of California Press, 1982.

Kant, Immanuel. *Observations on the Feeling of the Beautiful and Sublime.* 1764. Translated by John T. Goldthwait. Berkeley: Univ. of California Press, 1960.

Kaplan, Rachel, and Stephen Kaplan. *The Experience of Nature: A Psychological Perspective.* New York: Cambridge Univ. Press, 1989.

Katakis, Michael, ed. *Sacred Trusts: Essays on Stewardship and Responsibility.* San Francisco: Mercury House, 1993.

Killingsworth, M. Jimmie, and Jacqueline S. Palmer. *Ecospeak: Rhetoric and Environmental Politics in America.* Carbondale: Southern Illinois Univ. Press, 1992.

Kingsland, Sharon E. *Modeling Nature: Episodes in the History of Population Ecology.* Chicago: Univ. of Chicago Press, 1985.

Kittredge, William. *Owning It All: Essays.* St. Paul, Minn.: Graywolf Press, 1987.

Klee, Paul. *Paul Klee: The Thinking Eye: The Notebooks of Paul Klee.* Edited by Jurg Spiller. Translated by Ralph Manheim. New York: George Wittenborn, 1961, 1970.

Kline, Marcia B. *Beyond the Land Itself: Views of Nature in Canada and the United States.* Cambridge: Harvard Univ. Press, 1970.

Kling, Rob, et al. *Postsuburban California: The Transformation of Orange County since World War II.* Berkeley: Univ. of California Press, 1991.

Klinkenborg, Verlyn. "The Mustang Myth." *Audubon,* Jan.–Feb. 1994, 35–43.

Knoepflmacher, U. C., and G. B. Tenneyson, eds. *Nature and the Victorian Imagination.* Berkeley: Univ. of California Press, 1977.

Kolodny, Annette. *The Land before Her: Fantasy and Experience of the American Frontier, 1630–1860.* Chapel Hill: Univ. of North Carolina Press, 1984.

———. *The Lay of the Land: Metaphor as Experience and History in American Life and Letters.* Chapel Hill: Univ. of North Carolina Press, 1975.

Kuhn, Thomas. *The Structure of Scientific Revolutions.* Chicago: Univ. of Chicago Press, 1962.

Lansbury, Coral. *The Old Brown Dog: Women, Workers, and Vivisection in Edwardian England.* Madison: Univ. of Wisconsin Press, 1985.

Latour, Bruno. *Science in Action: How to Follow Scientists and Engineers through Society.* Cambridge: Harvard Univ. Press, 1987.

LeFebvre, Henri. *The Production of Space.* Cambridge, Mass.: Basil Blackwell, 1991.

Le Roy Ladurie, Emmanuel. *Times of Feast, Times of Famine: A History of Climate since the Year 1000.* Translated by Barbara Bray. Garden City, N.Y.: Doubleday, 1971.

Leiss, William. *The Domination of Nature.* New York: George Braziller, 1972.

Leopold, Aldo. *A Sand County Almanac with Other Essays on Conservation from Round River.* New York: Oxford Univ. Press, 1966.

Lewin, Roger. *Complexity: Life at the Edge of Chaos.* New York: Macmillan, 1992.

Lewis, C. S. *The Discarded Image: An Introduction to Medieval and Renaissance Literature.* New York: Cambridge Univ. Press, 1964.

————. *Studies in Words.* 2nd ed. New York: Cambridge Univ. Press, 1967.

Lewis, Martin. *Green Delusions: An Environmentalist Critique of Radical Environmentalism.* Durham, N.C.: Duke University Press, 1992.

Lewis, R. W. B. *The American Adam: Innocence, Tragedy, and Tradition in the Nineteenth Century.* Chicago: Univ. of Chicago Press, 1955.

Limerick, Patricia Nelson. *Desert Passages: Encounters with the American Deserts.* Albuquerque: Univ. of New Mexico Press, 1985.

Liu, Alan. *Wordsworth: The Sense of History.* Stanford: Stanford Univ. Press, 1989.

Lobeck, Armin K. *Things Maps Don't Tell Us: An Adventure into Map Interpretation.* 1956. Chicago: Univ. of Chicago Press, 1993.

Longino, Helen E. *Science as Social Knowledge: Values and Objectivity in Scientific Inquiry.* Princeton: Princeton Univ. Press, 1990.

Lovejoy, Arthur O. *The Great Chain of Being: A Study of the History of an Idea.* Cambridge: Harvard Univ. Press, 1936.

Lowenthal, David. *The Past Is a Foreign Country.* New York: Cambridge Univ. Press, 1985.

Lowenthal, David, and Martyn J. Bowden. *Geographies of the Mind.* New York: Oxford Univ. Press, 1975.

Lynch, Barbara D. "The Garden and the Sea: U.S. Latino Environmental Discourses and Mainstream Environmentalism." *Social Problems* 40 (Feb. 1993): 108–24.

MacCannell, Dean. *Empty Meeting Grounds: The Tourist Papers.* New York: Routledge, 1992.

————. *The Tourist: A New Theory of the Leisure Class.* New York: Schocken, 1976.

MacCormack, Carol P., and Marilyn Strathern, eds. *Nature, Culture and Gender.* Cambridge: Cambridge Univ. Press, 1981.

Maclean, Norman. *A River Runs through It.* Chicago: Univ. of Chicago Press, 1976.

Mahar, Dennis J. *Government Policies and Deforestation in Brazil's Amazon Region.* Washington, D.C.: World Bank, 1989.

Malin, James C. *History and Ecology: Studies of the Grassland.* Edited by Robert P. Swierenga. Lincoln: Univ. of Nebraska Press, 1984.

Marcus, George E., and Michael M. J. Fischer, eds. *Anthropology as Cultural Critique: An Experimental Moment in the Human Sciences.* Chicago: Univ. of Chicago Press, 1986.

Marks, Stuart A. *Southern Hunting in Black and White: Nature, History, and Ritual in a Carolina Community.* Princeton: Princeton Univ. Press, 1991.

Marsh, George Perkins. *Man and Nature; or, Physical Geography as Modified by Human Action.* 1864. Edited by David Lowenthal. Cambridge: Harvard Univ. Press, 1965.

Marshall, Peter. *Nature's Web: Rethinking Our Place on Earth.* New York: Paragon House, 1994.

Marx and Engels on Ecology. Edited by Howard Parsons. Westport, Conn.: Greenwood Press, 1977.

Marx, Leo. *The Machine in the Garden: Technology and the Pastoral Ideal in America.* New York: Oxford Univ. Press, 1964.

Mason, Peter. *Deconstructing America: Representations of the Other.* New York: Routledge, 1990.

Maxwell, Kenneth. "The Tragedy of the Amazon." *New York Review of Books,* March 7, 1991, 24–29.

McCay, Bonnie M., and James M. Acheson, eds. *The Question of the Commons: The Culture and Ecology of Communal Resources.* Tucson: Univ. of Arizona Press, 1987.

McEvoy, Arthur F. *The Fisherman's Problem: Ecology and Law in the California Fisheries, 1850–1980.* New York: Cambridge Univ. Press, 1977.

McHarg, Ian L. *Design with Nature.* Garden City, N.Y.: Doubleday, 1971.

McIntosh, Robert P. *The Background of Ecology: Concept and Theory.* New York: Cambridge Univ. Press, 1985.

———. "Pluralism in Ecology." *Annual Review of Ecology and Systematics* 18 (1987): 321–41.

McLuhan, T. C., ed. *The Way of the Earth: Encounters with Nature in Ancient and Contemporary Thought.* New York: Simon and Schuster, 1994.

McNeill, William H. *The Human Condition: An Ecological Perspective.* Princeton: Princeton Univ. Press, 1980.

———. *Plagues and Peoples.* New York: Doubleday, 1979.

McPhee, John. *Assembling California.* New York: Farrar Straus Giroux, 1993.

———. *The Control of Nature.* New York: Farrar Straus Giroux, 1989.

———. *Encounters with the Archdruid.* New York: Farrar Straus and Giroux, 1971.

———. "Travels of the Rock." *New Yorker,* Feb. 26, 1990, 108–17.

Meillassoux, Claude. *Maidens, Meal, and Money: Capitalism and the Domestic Economy.* New York: Cambridge Univ. Press, 1981.

Merchant, Carolyn. *The Death of Nature: Women, Ecology, and the Scientific Revolution.* San Francisco: Harper and Row, 1980.

———. *Earthcare: Women and the Environment.* New York: Routledge, forthcoming.

———. *Ecological Revolutions: Nature, Gender, and Science in New England.* Chapel Hill: Univ. of North Carolina Press, 1989.

———, ed. *Major Problems in American Environmental History.* Lexington, Mass.: D. C. Heath, 1993.

Miller, Perry. *Nature's Nation.* Cambridge: Harvard Univ. Press, 1967.

Mitchell, W. J. T., ed. *Landscape and Power.* Chicago: Univ. of Chicago Press, 1994.

Mitman, Gregg. *The State of Nature: Ecology, Community, and American Social Thought, 1900–1950.* Chicago: Univ. of Chicago Press, 1992.

Monk, Samuel. *The Sublime: A Study of Critical Theories in XVIII-Century England*. New York: Modern Language Association, 1935.

Myers, Greg. *Writing Biology: Texts in the Social Construction of Scientific Knowledge*. Madison: Univ. of Wisconsin Press, 1990.

Nagel, Thomas. *The View from Nowhere*. New York: Oxford Univ. Press, 1986.

Nash, Roderick Frazier. *The Rights of Nature: A History of Environmental Ethics*. Madison: Univ. of Wisconsin Press, 1989.

———. *Wilderness and the American Mind*. 3rd ed. New Haven: Yale Univ. Press, 1982.

Nelson, Richard K. "The Embrace of Names." *Northern Lights* 8 (Summer 1992): 18–19.

———. *Make Prayers to the Raven: A Koyukon View of the Northern Forest*. Chicago: Univ. of Chicago Press, 1983.

Newman, Penny. "Killing Legally with Toxic Waste: Women and the Environment in the United States." In *Close to Home: Women Reconnect Ecology, Health and Development Worldwide*, edited by Vandana Shiva. Philadelphia: New Society Publishers, 1994.

Newton, Norman T. *Design on the Land: The Development of Landscape Architecture*. Cambridge: Harvard Univ. Press, 1971.

Nicolson, Marjorie Hope. *Mountain Gloom and Mountain Glory: The Development of the Aesthetics of the Infinite*. Ithaca: Cornell Univ. Press, 1959.

Norris, Christopher. *The Truth about Postmodernism*. Cambridge, Mass.: Basil Blackwell, 1993.

Norton, Bryan G. *Toward Unity among Environmentalists*. New York: Oxford Univ. Press, 1991.

———. *Why Preserve Natural Variety?* Princeton: Princeton Univ. Press, 1987.

Norwood, Vera. *Made from This Earth: American Women and Nature*. Chapel Hill: Univ. of North Carolina Press, 1993.

Novak, Barbara. *Nature and Culture: American Landscape Painting, 1825–1875*. New York: Oxford Univ. Press, 1980.

O'Brien, Raymond J. *American Sublime: Landscape and Scenery of the Lower Hudson Valley*. New York: Columbia Univ. Press, 1981.

Oelschlaeger, Max. *Caring for Creation: An Ecumenical Approach to the Environmental Crisis*. New Haven: Yale Univ. Press, 1994.

———. *The Idea of Wilderness: From Prehistory to the Age of Ecology*. New Haven: Yale Univ. Press, 1991.

Olwig, Kenneth R. "Historical Geography and the Society/Nature 'Problematic': The Perspective of J. F. Schouw, G. P. Marsh, and E. Reclus," *Journal of Historical Geography* 6 (1980): 29–45.

———. *Nature's Ideological Landscape: A Literary and Geographic Perspective on Its Development and Preservation on Denmark's Jutland Heath*. London: George Allen and Unwin, 1984.

Palmer, Bryan D. *Descent into Discourse: The Reification of Language and the Writing of Social History*. Philadelphia: Temple Univ. Press, 1990.

Pena, Devon. "The 'Brown' and the 'Green': Chicanos and Environmental Politics in the Upper Rio Grande." *Capitalism, Nature, and Socialism* 3 (1992): 1–25.

Pepper, David. *Eco-Socialism: From Deep Ecology to Social Justice*. New York: Routledge, 1993.

Perlin, John. *A Forest Journey: The Role of Wood in the Development of Civilization.* New York: Norton, 1989.

Pirsig, Robert. *Zen and the Art of Motorcycle Maintenance: An Inquiry into Values.* New York: Morrow, 1974.

Plumwood, Vera. *Feminism and the Mastery of Nature.* London: Routledge, 1993.

Polanyi, Karl. *The Great Transformation: The Political and Economic Origins of Our Time.* Boston: Beacon, 1944.

Pollan, Michael. *Second Nature: A Gardener's Education.* New York: Atlantic Monthly Press, 1991.

Potter, David M. *People of Plenty: Economic Abundance and the American Character.* Chicago: Univ. of Chicago Press, 1954.

Pratt, Mary Louise. *Imperial Eyes: Travel Writing and Transculturation.* New York: Routledge, 1992.

Prigogine, Ilya, and Isabelle Stengers. *Order out of Chaos: Man's Dialogue with Nature.* New York: Bantam, 1984.

Prown, Jules David, et al. *Discovered Lands, Invented Pasts: Transforming Visions of the American West.* New Haven: Yale Univ. Press, 1992.

Pulido, Laura. "Internationalization and Environmental Rights in the U.S." *Environment and Planning* 26 (1994).

Putz, Francis E., and N. Michele Holbrook. "Tropical Rain-Forest Images." In *People of the Tropical Rain Forest,* edited by Julie Sloan Denslow and Christine Padoch. Berkeley: Univ. of California Press, 1988.

Pyne, Stephen J. *Fire in America: A Cultural History of Wildland and Rural Fire.* Princeton: Princeton Univ. Press, 1982.

Rackham, Oliver. *The History of the Countryside.* London: J. M. Dent and Sons, 1986.

Rathje, William, and Cullen Murphy. *Rubbish! The Archaeology of Garbage.* New York: HarperCollins, 1992.

Raup, Hugh. *Forests in the Here and Now: A Collection of the Writings of Hugh Miller Raup.* Edited by Benjamin B. Stout. Missoula: Montana Forest and Conservation Experiment Station, Univ. of Montana School of Forestry, 1981.

Real, Leslie A., and James H. Brown. *Foundations of Ecology: Classic Papers with Commentaries.* Chicago: Univ. of Chicago Press, 1991.

Reid, David, ed. *Sex, Death, and God in L.A.* Berkeley: Univ. of California, 1992.

Ritvo, Harriet. *The Animal Estate: The English and Other Creatures in the Victorian Age.* Cambridge: Harvard Univ. Press, 1987.

Robinson, Sidney K. *Inquiry into the Picturesque.* Chicago: Univ. of Chicago Press, 1991.

Rodda, Annabel. *Women and the Environment.* London: Zed Books, 1991.

Rorty, Richard. *Objectivity, Relativism, and Truth.* New York: Cambridge Univ. Press, 1991

——. *Philosophy and the Mirror of Nature.* Princeton: Princeton Univ. Press, 1979.

Rosaldo, Renato. *Culture and Truth: The Remaking of Social Analysis.* Boston: Beacon, 1992.

Rose, Gillian. *Feminism and Geography: The Limits of Geographical Knowledge.* Minneapolis: Univ. of Minnesota Press, 1993.

Rose, Mark. *Authors and Owners: The Invention of Copyright.* Cambridge: Harvard Univ. Press, 1993.

Rosenberg, Charles. *The Cholera Years: The United States in 1832, 1849, and 1866.* Chicago: Univ. of Chicago Press, 1962.

Rosenzweig, Roy, and Elizabeth Blackmar. *The Park and the People: A History of Central Park.* Ithaca: Cornell Univ. Press, 1992.

Rosner, David, and Gerald Markowitz. *Dying for Work: Workers' Safety and Health in Twentieth-Century America.* Bloomington: Indiana Univ. Press, 1989.

Ruffins, Paul. "Defining a Movement and a Community." *Crossroads,* April 1990, 9–15.

Runte, Alfred. *National Parks: The American Experience.* 2nd ed. Lincoln: Univ. of Nebraska Press, 1987.

Ryden, Kent C. *Mapping the Invisible Landscape: Folklore, Writing, and the Sense of Place.* Iowa City: Univ. of Iowa Press, 1993.

Sahlins, Marshall. *Culture and Practical Reason.* Chicago: Univ. of Chicago Press, 1976.

———. *Islands of History.* Chicago: Univ. of Chicago Press, 1985.

Sale, Kirkpatrick. *The Green Revolution: The American Environmental Movement, 1962–1992.* New York: Hill and Wang, 1993.

Sauer, Carl O. *Land and Life: A Selection from the Writings of Carl Ortwin Sauer.* Edited by John Leighly. Berkeley: Univ. of California Press, 1963.

Scarry, Elaine. *The Body in Pain: The Making and Unmaking of the World.* New York: Oxford Univ. Press, 1985.

Schmitt, Peter J. *Back to Nature: The Arcadian Myth in Urban America.* New York: Oxford Univ. Press, 1969.

Schuyler, David. *The New Urban Landscape: The Redefinition of City Form in Nineteenth-Century America.* Baltimore: Johns Hopkins Univ. Press, 1986.

Seager, Joni. *Earth Follies: Coming to Feminist Terms with the Global Environmental Crisis.* New York: Routledge, 1993.

Sears, John. *Sacred Places: American Tourist Attractions in the Nineteenth Century.* New York: Oxford Univ. Press, 1989.

Sears, Paul B. *Deserts on the March.* Norman: Univ. of Oklahoma Press, 1940.

Seed, Patricia. "Colonial and Postcolonial Discourse." *Latin American Research Review* 26 (1991): 181–200.

Seltzer, Mark. *Bodies and Machines.* New York: Routledge, 1992.

Shapin, Steven, and Simon Schaffer. *Leviathan and the Air-Pump: Hobbes, Boyle, and the Experimental Life.* Princeton: Princeton Univ. Press, 1985.

Shaw, Christopher, and Malcolm Chase. *The Imagined Past: History and Nostalgia.* Manchester: Manchester Univ. Press, 1989.

Shepard, Paul. *Man in the Landscape: A Historic View of the Esthetics of Nature.* New York: Knopf, 1967.

Shi, David E. *The Simple Life: Plain Living and High Thinking in American Culture.* New York: Oxford Univ. Press, 1985.

Shiva, Vandana. *Monocultures of the Mind: Perspectives on Biodiversity and Biotechnology.* London: Zed Books, 1993.

———. *Staying Alive: Women, Ecology and Development.* London: Zed Books, 1988.

———. *The Violence of the Green Revolution: Third World Agriculture, Ecology and Politics.* London: Zed Books, 1991.

Slater, Candace. *Dance of the Dolphin: Transformation and Disenchantment in the Amazonian Imagination.* Chicago: Univ. of Chicago Press, 1994.

Slotkin, Richard. *The Fatal Environment: The Myth of the Frontier in the Age of Industrialization, 1800–1890.* New York: Harper and Row, 1986.

———. *Gunfighter Nation: The Myth of the Frontier in Twentieth-Century America.* New York: Atheneum, 1992.

Smith, Bernard. *Imagining the Pacific: In the Wake of the Cook Voyages.* New Haven: Yale Univ. Press, 1992.

Smith, Henry Nash. *Virgin Land: The American West as Symbol and Myth.* Cambridge: Harvard Univ. Press, 1950.

Smith, Michael L. *Pacific Visions: California Scientists and the Environment, 1850–1915.* New Haven: Yale Univ. Press, 1987.

Smith, Nigel J. H. *Rainforest Corridors: The Transamazon Colonization Scheme.* Berkeley: Univ. of California Press, 1982.

Snyder, Gary. *The Practice of the Wild.* San Francisco: North Point, 1990.

———. *Turtle Island.* New York: New Directions, 1974.

Soja, Edward W. *Postmodern Geographies: The Reassertion of Space in Critical Social Theory.* London: Verso, 1989.

Solkin, David. *Richard Wilson and the Landscape of Reaction.* London: Tate Gallery, 1982.

Sorkin, Michael, ed. *Variations on a Theme Park: The New American City and the End of Public Space.* New York: Hill and Wang, 1992.

Spain, Daphne. *Gendered Spaces.* Chapel Hill: Univ. of North Carolina Press, 1992.

Spirn, Anne Whiston. *The Granite Garden: Urban Nature and Human Design.* New York: Basic Books, 1984.

———. *The West Philadelphia Landscape Plan: A Framework for Action.* Philadelphia: Univ. of Pennsylvania Graduate School of Fine Arts, 1991.

Stegner, Wallace. *Wolf Willow: A History, a Story, and a Memory of the Last Plains Frontier.* New York: Viking, 1962.

Stilgoe, John R. *Common Landscape of America, 1580 to 1845.* New Haven: Yale Univ. Press, 1982.

Strathern, Marilyn. *Reproducing the Future: Essays on Anthropology, Kinship and the New Reproductive Technologies.* New York: Routledge, 1992.

Sutton, S. B., ed. *Civilizing American Cities: A Selection of Frederick Law Olmsted's Writings on City Landscape.* Cambridge: MIT Press, 1979.

Sweet, David. "A Realm of Nature Destroyed: The Middle Amazon Valley, 1640–1750." Ph.D. diss., Univ. of Wisconsin at Madison, 1974.

Swift, Graham. *Waterland.* New York: Poseidon, 1983.

Szasz, Andrew. *Ecopopulism: Toxic Waste and the Movement for Environmental Justice.* Minneapolis: Univ. of Minnesota Press, 1994.

Tanner, Adrian. *Bringing Home Animals: Religious Ideology and Mode of Production of the Mistassini Cree Hunters.* New York: St. Martin's Press, 1979.

Tanner, Tony. *The Reign of Wonder: Naivety and Reality in American Literature.* Cambridge: Cambridge Univ. Press, 1965.

Taussig, Michael. *Mimesis and Alterity: A Particular History of the Senses.* New York: Routledge, 1993.

———. *Shamanism, Colonialism, and the Wild Man: A Study in Terror and Healing.* Chicago: Univ. of Chicago Press, 1987.

Thomas, Keith. *Man and the Natural World: A History of the Modern Sensibility.* New York: Pantheon, 1983.

Thomas, William L., Jr., ed. *Man's Role in Changing the Face of the Earth*. Chicago: Univ. of Chicago Press, 1956.

Thompson, George F., ed. *Landscape in America*. Austin: Univ. of Texas Press, 1995.

Tichi, Cecilia. *New World, New Earth: Environmental Reform in American Literature from the Puritans through Whitman*. New Haven: Yale Univ. Press, 1979.

Tuan, Yi-Fu. "Realism and Fantasy in Art, History, and Geography." *Annals of the Association of American Geographers* 80 (1990): 435–46.

———. *Space and Place: The Perspective of Experience*. Minneapolis: Univ. of Minnesota Press, 1977.

———. *Topophilia: A Study of Environmental Perception, Attitudes, and Values*. Englewood Cliffs, N.J.: Prentice-Hall, 1974.

Turner, Frederick Jackson. *The Frontier in American History*. New York: Henry Holt, 1920.

Turner, James. *Reckoning with the Beast: Animals, Pain, and Humanity in the Victorian Mind*. Baltimore: Johns Hopkins Univ. Press, 1980.

Urry, John. *The Tourist Gaze: Leisure and Travel in Contemporary Societies*. Newbury Park, Calif.: Sage Publications, 1990.

Veldman, Meredith. *Fantasy, the Bomb, and the Greening of Britain: Romantic Protest, 1945–1980*. Cambridge: Cambridge Univ. Press, 1994.

Verdi, Richard. *Klee and Nature*. New York: Rizzoli, 1985.

Virgil. *Eclogues and Georgics*. Translated by T. F. Royds. New York: E. P. Dutton, 1946.

Wagstaff, J. M., ed. *Landscape and Culture: Geographical and Archaeological Perspectives*. New York: Basil Blackwell, 1987.

Waldrop, M. Mitchell. *Complexity: The Emerging Science at the Edge of Order and Chaos*. New York: Simon and Schuster, 1992.

Watts, May Theilgaard. *Reading the Landscape of America*. New York: Macmillan, 1975.

Webb, Walter Prescott. *The Great Plains*. Boston: Ginn, 1931.

Weiner, Douglas R. *Models of Nature: Conservation, Ecology, and Cultural Revolution*. Bloomington: Indiana Univ. Press, 1988.

Weiskel, Thomas. *The Romantic Sublime: Studies in the Structure and Psychology of Transcendence*. Baltimore: Johns Hopkins Univ. Press, 1976.

White, Hayden. *The Content of the Form: Narrative Discourse and Historical Representation*. Baltimore: Johns Hopkins Univ. Press, 1987.

———. *Metahistory: The Historical Imagination in Nineteenth-Century Europe*. Baltimore: Johns Hopkins Univ. Press, 1973.

———. *Tropics of Discourse: Essays in Cultural Criticism*. Baltimore: Johns Hopkins Univ. Press, 1978.

White, Richard. "American Environmental History: The Development of a New Historical Field." *Pacific Historical Review* 54 (1985): 297–335.

———. "Discovering Nature in North America." *Journal of American History* 79 (1992): 874–91.

———. "Environmental History, Ecology, and Meaning." *Journal of American History* 76 (1990): 1111–16.

———. *Land Use, Environment, and Social Change: The Shaping of Island County, Washington*. Seattle: Univ. of Washington Press, 1980.

————. *The Roots of Dependency: Subsistence, Environment, and Social Change among the Choctaws, Pawnees, and Navajos.* Lincoln: Univ. of Nebraska Press, 1983.

Willey, Basil. *The Eighteenth-Century Background: Studies on the Idea of Nature in the Thought of the Period.* London: Chattus and Windus, 1949.

Williams, Michael. *Americans and Their Forests: A Historical Geography.* New York: Cambridge Univ. Press, 1989.

Williams, Raymond. *The Country and the City.* New York: Oxford Univ. Press, 1973.

————. "Ideas of Nature." In Raymond Williams, *Problems in Materialism and Culture.* London: Verso, 1980.

————. *Keywords: A Vocabulary of Culture and Society.* New York: Oxford Univ. Press, 1976.

Willis, R. G., ed. *Signifying Animals: Human Meaning in the Natural World.* London: Unwin Hyman, 1990.

Wilson, Rob. *American Sublime: The Genealogy of a Poetic Genre.* Madison: Univ. of Wisconsin Press, 1991.

Wolf, Bryan Jay. *Romantic Re-vision: Culture and Consciousness in Nineteenth-Century American Painting and Literature.* Chicago: Univ. of Chicago Press, 1982.

Woodring, Carl. *Nature into Art: Cultural Transformations in Nineteenth-Century Britain.* Cambridge: Harvard Univ. Press, 1989.

Wordsworth, Jonathan, et al. *William Wordsworth and the Age of English Romanticism.* New Brunswick: Rutgers Univ. Press, 1987.

Worster, Donald. *Dust Bowl: The Southern Plains in the 1930s.* New York: Oxford Univ. Press, 1979.

————. "History as Natural History: An Essay on Theory and Method." *Pacific Historical Review* 53 (1984): 1–19.

————. *Nature's Economy: A History of Ecological Ideas.* 2nd ed. New York: Cambridge Univ. Press, 1994.

————. *Rivers of Empire: Water, Aridity, and the Growth of the American West.* New York: Pantheon, 1985.

————. *The Wealth of Nature: Environmental History and the Ecological Imagination.* New York: Oxford Univ. Press, 1993.

————, ed. *The Ends of the Earth: Perspectives on Modern Environmental History.* New York: Cambridge Univ. Press, 1988.

Worster, Donald, et al. "Environmental History: A Round Table." *Journal of American History* 76 (1990): 1087–147.

Wrede, Stuart, and William Howard Adams. *Denatured Visions: Landscape and Culture in the Twentieth Century.* New York: Museum of Modern Art, 1991.

Wright, Will. *Wild Knowledge: Science, Language, and Social Life in a Fragile Environment.* Minneapolis: Univ. of Minnesota Press, 1992.

Young, Robert M. *Darwin's Metaphor: Nature's Place in Victorian Culture.* New York: Cambridge Univ. Press, 1985.

Zimmerman, Michael E., et al., eds. *Environmental Philosophy: From Animal Rights to Radical Ecology.* Englewood Cliffs, N.J.: Prentice-Hall, 1993.

Notes

1. There was only one constraint on my freedom to identify would-be participants in the seminar: all but three had to be professors or graduate students in the University of California system. The purpose of the Humanities Research Institute (or HRI, as it is usually abbreviated) is to advance humanistic knowledge by building bridges between disciplines whose members may not ordinarily communicate with each other, and at the same time to link the campuses of the UC system by encouraging colleagues from different campuses to work together under the unusually intimate conditions of a residential seminar. Many universities have such institutes, but most do little more than provide financial support and office space where individual scholars can pursue their individual research projects in an individualistic way. HRI is unusual in bringing together scholars from radically different backgrounds to focus on common research questions over an extended period of time. It is an extraordinarily fertile and effective model, one that other universities would do well to emulate.

2. Clements would have described them not as "ecosystems" but as "superorganisms," a difference in vocabulary that is itself suggestive of the subsequent change in ecological thinking. See Ronald C. Tobey, *Saving the Prairies: The Life Cycle of the Founding School of American Plant Ecology, 1895–1955* (Berkeley: Univ. of California Press, 1981); Donald Worster, *Nature's Economy: A History of Ecological Ideas*, 2nd ed. (New York: Cambridge Univ. Press, 1994).

3. One small but crucial example of this labeling problem is contained in this very sentence: the word "nature" is always singular, suggesting that its referent is a unified holistic entity, whereas the *things* it describes are in fact plural, diverse, and perhaps not so holistic as they seem.

4. Raymond Williams, "Ideas of Nature," in Raymond Williams, *Problems in Materialism and Culture* (London: Verso, 1980), 67.

5. Urban Design Forum, "Rocky Mountain Arsenal: Refuge Design for the 21st Century" (conference brochure dated Nov. 15–16, 1991).

6. See Sonia Nazario, "Two Neighborhoods, Two Destinies," *Los Angeles Times*, May 2, 1994, A14–15. The subtitles of Nazario's article are highly suggestive for the point I am trying to make: "Where Life Was Hopeful, Determination Is Winning Out" and "Where There Was Struggle, Now There Are Death Throes."

7. I borrow this striking observation from an anonymous article entitled "Disassembling California," *New Yorker*, Jan. 31, 1994; given the subject and the style, its author is almost certainly John McPhee.

8. Mike Davis, "Building Homes amid a Landscape of Fire Ecology," *Los Angeles Times*, Nov. 14, 1993, M1, M3.

9. *Oxford English Dictionary*. See also Williams, "Ideas of Nature"; Raymond Williams, *Keywords: A Vocabulary of Culture and Society* (New York: Oxford Univ. Press, 1976).

10. For a brilliant brief explication of these arguments, see Williams, "Ideas of Nature."

11. Mike Davis noted Los Angeles's paucity of public parks while leading our group on a daylong field trip through the city.

12. Reyner Banham, *Los Angeles: The Architecture of Four Ecologies* (New York: Penguin, 1971), 31.

13. "Welcome to Dove Canyon: A More Perfect World," Advertising Supplement, *Los Angeles Times*, May 14, 1994, V3.

14. "Welcome to Rancho Santa Margarita," Advertising Supplement, *Los Angeles Times*, April 9, 1994, FF1–FF2, FF10.

15. Rebecca Trounson and Mark I. Pinsky, "Gnatcatcher Taken off Threatened Species List," *Los Angeles Times*, May 3, 1994, A1, A20.

16. Frank Messina, "Laguna Niguel Trees Felled, Tempers Rise," *Los Angeles Times*, April 14, 1994, A1, A22.

17. From *The Californias*, a 144-page tourist brochure put out by the California Office of Tourism, quoted by Edward W. Soja, "Inside Expolis: Scenes from Orange County," in Michael Sorkin, ed., *Variations on a Theme Park: The New American City and the End of Public Space* (New York: Hill and Wang, 1992), 94.

18. For an accessible, albeit polemical, critique of these computer modeling techniques, see Patrick J. Michaels, *Sound and Fury: The Science and Politics of Global Warming* (Washington, D.C.: Cato Institute, 1992).

19. Jeff Outcalt, letter to the editor, *Time*, Feb. 21, 1994, 7.

20. Tom Gorman, " 'Killer Bees' About to Join Facts of Life in Southland," *Los Angeles Times*, March 13, 1994, A1, A32.

21. "The Children? Or the Cub?" editorial, *New York Times,* May 29, 1994.

22. "UCI Tree Tour: A Natural History Walk in Aldrich Park" (Irvine: Univ. of California at Irvine, 1990).

23. Ibid.

The Trouble with Wilderness

1. Henry David Thoreau, "Walking," *The Works of Thoreau,* ed. Henry S. Canby (Boston: Houghton Mifflin, 1937), 672.

2. *Oxford English Dictionary,* s.v. "wilderness"; see also Roderick Nash, *Wilderness and the American Mind,* 3rd ed. (New Haven: Yale Univ. Press, 1982), 1–22; and Max Oelschlaeger, *The Idea of Wilderness: From Prehistory to the Age of Ecology* (New Haven: Yale Univ. Press, 1991).

3. Exodus 32:1–35, KJV.

4. Exodus 14:3, KJV.

5. Mark 1:12–13, KJV; see also Matthew 4:1–11; Luke 4:1–13.

6. John Milton, "Paradise Lost," *John Milton: Complete Poems and Major Prose,* ed. Merritt Y. Hughes (New York: Odyssey Press, 1957), 280–81, lines 131–42.

7. I have discussed this theme at length in "Landscapes of Abundance and Scarcity," in Clyde Milner et al., eds., *Oxford History of the American West* (New York: Oxford Univ. Press, 1994), 603–37. The classic work on the Puritan "city on a hill" in colonial New England is Perry Miller, *Errand into the Wilderness* (Cambridge: Harvard Univ. Press, 1956).

8. John Muir, *My First Summer in the Sierra* (1911), reprinted in *John Muir: The Eight Wilderness Discovery Books* (London: Diadem; Seattle: Mountaineers, 1992), 211.

9. Alfred Runte, *National Parks: The American Experience,* 2nd ed. (Lincoln: Univ. of Nebraska Press, 1987).

10. John Muir, *The Yosemite* (1912), reprinted in *John Muir: Eight Wilderness Discovery Books,* 715.

11. Scholarly work on the sublime is extensive. Among the most important studies are Samuel Monk, *The Sublime: A Study of Critical Theories in XVIII-Century England* (New York: Modern Language Association, 1935); Basil Willey, *The Eighteenth-Century Background: Studies on the Idea of Nature in the Thought of the Period* (London: Chattus and Windus, 1949); Marjorie Hope Nicolson, *Mountain Gloom and Mountain Glory: The Development of the Aesthetics of the Infinite* (Ithaca: Cornell Univ. Press, 1959); Thomas Weiskel, *The Romantic Sublime: Studies in the Structure and Psychology of Transcendence* (Baltimore: Johns Hopkins Univ. Press, 1976); Barbara Novak, *Nature and Culture: American Landscape Painting, 1825–1875,* (New York: Oxford Univ. Press, 1980).

12. The classic works are Immanuel Kant, *Observations on the Feeling of the Beautiful and Sublime* (1764), trans. John T. Goldthwait (Berkeley: Univ. of California Press, 1960); Edmund Burke, *A Philosophical Enquiry into the Origin of Our Ideas of the Sublime and Beautiful,* ed. James T. Boulton (1958; Notre Dame: Univ. of Notre Dame Press, 1968); William Gilpin, *Three Essays: On Picturesque Beauty; on Picturesque Travel; and on Sketching Landscape* (London, 1803).

13. See Ann Vileisis, "From Wastelands to Wetlands" (unpublished senior essay, Yale Univ., 1989); Runte, *National Parks.*

14. William Wordsworth, "The Prelude," bk. 6, in Thomas Hutchinson, ed., *The Poetical Works of Wordsworth* (London: Oxford Univ. Press, 1936), 536.

15. Henry David Thoreau, *The Maine Woods* (1864), in *Henry David Thoreau* (New York: Library of America, 1985), 640–41.

16. Exodus 16:10, KJV.

17. John Muir, *My First Summer in the Sierra,* 238. Part of the difference between these descriptions may reflect the landscapes the three authors were describing. In his essay elsewhere in this book, Kenneth Olwig notes that early American travelers experienced Yosemite as much through the aesthetic tropes of the pastoral as through those of the sublime. The ease with which Muir celebrated the gentle divinity of the Sierra Nevada had much to do with the pastoral qualities of the landscape he described.

18. Frederick Jackson Turner, *The Frontier in American History* (New York: Henry Holt, 1920), 37–38.

19. Richard Slotkin has made this observation the linchpin of his comparison between Turner and Theodore Roosevelt. See Slotkin, *Gunfighter Nation: The Myth of the Frontier in Twentieth-Century America* (New York: Atheneum, 1992), 29–62.

20. Owen Wister, *The Virginian: A Horseman of the Plains* (New York: Macmillan, 1902), viii–ix.

21. Theodore Roosevelt, *Ranch Life and the Hunting Trail* (1888; New York: Century, 1899), 100.

22. Wister, *Virginian,* x.

23. On the many problems with this view, see William M. Denevan, "The Pristine Myth: The Landscape of the Americas in 1492," *Annals of the Association of American Geographers* 82 (1992): 369–85.

24. Louis Warren, "The Hunter's Game: Poachers, Conservationists, and Twentieth-Century America," (Ph.D. diss., Yale University, 1994).

25. Wilderness also lies at the foundation of the Clementsian ecological concept of the climax. See Michael Barbour's essay in this volume, as well as my introduction.

26. On the many paradoxes of having to manage wilderness into order to maintain the appearance of an unmanaged landscape, see John C. Hendee et al., *Wilderness Management,* USDA Forest Service Miscellaneous Publication No. 1365 (Washington, D.C.: Government Printing Office, 1978).

27. See James Proctor's essay in this volume.

28. See Candace Slater's essay in this volume. This argument has been powerfully made by Ramachandra Guha, "Radical American Environmentalism: A Third World Critique," *Environmental Ethics* 11 (1989): 71–83.

29. Bill McKibben, *The End of Nature* (New York: Random House, 1989).

30. Ibid., 49.

31. Even comparable extinction rates have occurred before, though we surely would not want to emulate the Cretaceous-Tertiary boundary extinctions as a model for responsible manipulation of the biosphere!

32. Dave Foreman, *Confessions of an Eco-Warrior* (New York: Harmony Books, 1991), 69 (italics in original). For a sampling of other writings by followers of deep ecology and/or Earth First!, see Michael Tobias, ed., *Deep Ecology* (San Diego: Avant Books, 1984); Bill Devall and George Sessions, *Deep Ecology: Living as if Nature Mattered* (Salt Lake City: Gibbs Smith, 1985); Michael Tobias, *After Eden: History, Ecology, and Conscience* (San Diego: Avant Books, 1985); Dave Foreman and Bill Haywood, eds., *Ecodefense: A Field Guide to Monkey Wrenching*, 2nd ed. (Tucson: Ned Ludd Books, 1987); Bill Devall, *Simple in Means, Rich in Ends: Practicing Deep Ecology* (Salt Lake City: Gibbs Smith, 1988); Steve Chase, ed., *Defending the Earth: A Dialogue between Murray Bookchin & Dave Foreman* (Boston: South End Press, 1991); John Davis, ed., *The Earth First! Reader: Ten Years of Radical Environmentalism* (Salt Lake City: Gibbs Smith, 1991); Bill Devall, *Living Richly in an Age of Limits: Using Deep Ecology for an Abundant Life* (Salt Lake City: Gibbs Smith, 1993); Michael E. Zimmerman et al., eds., *Environmental Philosophy: From Animal Rights to Radical Ecology* (Englewood Cliffs, N.J.: Prentice-Hall, 1993). A useful survey of the different factions of radical environmentalism can be found in Carolyn Merchant, *Radical Ecology: The Search for a Livable World* (New York: Routledge, 1992). For a very interesting critique of this literature (first published in the anarchist newspaper *Fifth Estate*), see George Bradford, *How Deep Is Deep Ecology?* (Ojai, Calif.: Times Change Press, 1989).

33. Foreman, *Confessions of an Eco-Warrior*, 34.

34. Ibid., 65. See also Dave Foreman and Howie Wolke, *The Big Outside: A Descriptive Inventory of the Big Wilderness Areas of the U.S.* (Tucson: Ned Ludd Books, 1989).

35. Foreman, *Confessions of an Eco-Warrior*, 63.

36. Ibid., 27.

37. See Richard White's essay in this volume, and compare its analysis of environmental knowledge through work with Jennifer Price's analysis of environmental knowledge through consumption. It is not much of an exaggeration to say that the wilderness experience is essentially consumerist in its impulses.

38. Cf. Muir, *Yosemite*, in *John Muir: Eight Wilderness Discovery Books*, 714.

39. Wallace Stegner, ed., *This Is Dinosaur: Echo Park Country and Its Magic Rivers* (New York: Knopf, 1955), 17 (italics in original).

40. Katherine Hayles helped me see the importance of this argument.

41. Analogous arguments can be found in John Brinckerhoff Jackson, "Beyond Wilderness," *A Sense of Place, a Sense of Time* (New Haven: Yale Univ. Press, 1994), 71–91, and in the wonderful collection of essays by Michael Pollan, *Second Nature: A Gardener's Education* (New York: Atlantic Monthly Press, 1991).

42. Wendell Berry, *Home Economics* (San Francisco: North Point, 1987), 138, 143.

43. Gary Snyder, quoted in *New York Times,* "Week in Review," Sept. 18, 1994, 6.

Constructing Nature

1. This essay draws from an unpublished lecture for the Frederick Law Olmsted National Historic Site in 1985, "Frederick Law Olmsted: The Legacy of a Pragmatic Visionary." Although many ideas were shaped by the discussions of 1994, I would like to thank Shary Berg, former director of the Olmsted Site, for inviting me to give the original lecture and for making the Olmsted Office archives available at a time when they were closed to scholars. I am also grateful to W. George Batchelor, my research assistant for the project in 1985, to Emily Stern, who helped with additional research in summer 1994 when I was a guest scholar at the Woodrow Wilson International Center for Scholars, and to Sylvia Palms for assistance in checking facts and assembling the illustrations for publication. I would also like to extend a special thanks to Bill Cronon, who as editor was always provocative, supportive, demanding, and collegial.

2. Olmsted was a product of his own time, place, and position in society. The specifics of his views on the moral value of natural scenery, for example, or on class and gender, seem naive and patronizing to a modern reader. Recently, scholars have criticized his social views, particularly in reference to the urban working class; see, for example, Roy Rosenzweig and Elizabeth Blackmar, *The Park and the People: A History of Central Park* (Ithaca: Cornell Univ. Press, 1992). Despite this critique, many of Olmsted's ideas, methods, and results remain models for contemporary practice.

3. Act of Congress quoted by Laura Wood Roper in her introductory note to "The Yosemite Valley and the Mariposa Big Trees: A Preliminary Report (1865) by Frederick Law Olmsted," *Landscape Architecture* 43 (1952): 12.

4. Ibid., 21.

5. Ibid., 24.

6. Ibid., 12–13. Roper recounts the presumed history of the report and its suppression and describes how it was reconstructed and published for the first time in 1952.

7. Hans Huth, *Nature and the American: Three Centuries of Changing Attitudes,* new ed. (Lincoln: Univ. of Nebraska Press, 1990), 150.

8. Roper, "Yosemite Valley," 16.

9. Ibid., 20. Such views were common at the time. See, for example, *The Home Book of the Picturesque; or, American Scenery, Art, and Literature* (New York: Putnam, 1851).

10. Olmsted's description of the positive effects of natural scenery may sound dated and naive, but recent studies have documented the beneficial effects of plants on human health and healing. Hospital patients who have windows with views of trees or other "natural" scenery have been shown to heal faster than patients who have views of buildings or no window at all. See Roger Ulrich and Russ Parsons, "Influences of Passive Experiences with Plants on Individual Well-being and Health," in Diane Relf, ed., *The Role of Horticulture in Human Well-being and Social Development* (Portland: Timber Press, 1992), 93–105.

11. Roper, "Yosemite Valley," 22.

12. Yosemite National Park generates twenty-five tons of garbage per day in mid-August; one-half of this comes from Yosemite Valley. Concessions contribute an additional ten tons per day. Don Fox, personal communication.

13. For a history and critique of such views, see the essays by Richard White and William Cronon in this volume.

14. Among the other members of this campaign were Frederick E. Church, whose paintings of Niagara Falls were part of this effort to focus attention on Niagara, and the publisher Samuel Bowles, who had been present when Olmsted read his report on Yosemite. Elizabeth McKinsey has traced the changing meanings of Niagara over time and pointed out that Niagara had already paled as an icon of the sublime by the middle of the nineteenth century. See her *Niagara Falls: Icon of the American Sublime* (New York: Cambridge Univ. Press, 1985).

15. See Olmsted's report in James T. Gardiner, *Special Report of New York State Survey on the Preservation of the Scenery of Niagara Falls* (Albany: Charles Van Benthuysen, 1880), 27–31. Gardiner, previously a member of the California State Geological Survey, had surveyed and mapped Yosemite at the request of the commission Olmsted chaired. He and Olmsted remained friends for many years. See Roper, "Yosemite Valley," 12.

16. Olmsted's lobbying took diverse forms. For example, he and Charles Eliot Norton paid young graduates of Harvard Theological Seminary to visit Niagara and write press releases describing the blighted conditions surrounding the falls.

17. Frederick Law Olmsted and Calvert Vaux, *General Plan for the Improvement of the Niagara Reservation* (Niagara Falls: Gazette Book and Job Office, 1887), 3. There was a good deal of friction between Olmsted and his partner Vaux at this time. His son John Charles Olmsted wrote to Vaux to try to smooth things over and described how hard his father was working on the Niagara report ("He *can't* take writing easily") and how important the writing was to him. See Letter from John Charles Olmsted to Calvert Vaux, Sept. 2, 1887, Olmsted Papers, Library of Congress.

18. Olmsted and Vaux, *General Plan*, 4.

19. Ibid., 6–7.

20. Ibid., 20.

21. Ibid., 19.

22. Ibid., 8.

23. Ibid., 18.

24. Ibid., 8.

25. Ibid., 13.

26. After Olmsted's death his sons were hired to revisit the problem of diminished flow and unsightly banks. Photographs from the Olmsted Office files record the conditions they found. Frederick Law Olmsted National Historic Site, Brookline, Mass.

27. At Yosemite, John Muir and Gifford Pinchot had clashed over the issue of sheep grazing in 1897. To Muir sheep were "hoofed locusts" that should be banned from the valley. Pinchot had favored a compromise: permit grazing, but regulate it.

28. J. Horace McFarland, "The Niagara Falls Situation," *Landscape Architecture* 19 (1929): 157–62. See also the final report of the Special International Niagara Board, *The Preservation of Niagara Falls* (Ottawa: F. A. Ackland, 1930). McFarland, one of two American members of the board appointed by President Hoover, was chairman of the Art Commission of the State of Pennsylvania and former president of the American Civic Association. The other American member was an officer in the U.S. Army Corps of Engineers. The two Canadian members were the deputy minister of mines and the director of the Dominion Water Power and Reclamation Service.

29. McFarland, "Niagara Falls Situation," 160.

30. Ibid.

31. Ibid., 160–61.

32. International Joint Commission, *Preservation and Enhancement of the American Falls at Niagara* (n.p., 1975), 26. The IJC appointed the American Falls International Board to study the issues and make recommendations. The four-member board consisted of two landscape architects (including Garrett Eckbo from the United States), an officer of the U.S. Army Corps of Engineers, and the director of Water Planning and Management Branch, Environment Canada. The above report summarizes the recommendations of the board and actions taken by the IJC. For greater detail on the studies and recommendations of the board, see American Falls International Board, *Preservation and Enhancement of the American Falls at Niagara: Final Report to the International Joint Commission* (n.p., 1974); *Preservation and Enhancement of the American Falls at Niagara: Interim Report to the International Joint Commission* and *Appendix B: Aesthetics* (n.p., Dec. 1971); and *Intrusions on Views of Niagara Falls* (n.p., Nov. 9, 1970). See also Martin Krieger, "Up the Plastic Tree," *Landscape Architecture* 63 (1973): 349–60, 411.

33. International Joint Commission, *Preservation and Enhancement*, 1, 17.

34. Ibid., 12.

35. Ibid., 13.

36. Ibid., 17.

37. Ibid., 19.

38. Ibid.

39. Faye B. Harwell, "Recovering the 'Lost' Niagara," *Landscape Architecture* 71 (1981): 454–55.

40. See Richard White, *The Organic Machine* (New York: Hill and Wang, 1995).

41. American Falls International Board, *Appendix B*, 32.

42. Letter from Olmsted to Richard Morris Hunt, March 2, 1889, Olmsted Papers, Library of Congress. "The value of the site is in its outlook; the local scenery is not attractive. The soil is extremely poor and intractable. There is not a single circumstance that can be turned to account in gaining any desirable local character, picturesqueness, for instance, or geniality. Whatever we aim at must be made 'out of the whole cloth.' "

43. Ibid.

44. Letter from Olmsted to Fred Kingsbury, Jan. 20, 1891, Olmsted Papers, Library of Congress.

45. Ibid.

46. Ibid.

47. After Vanderbilt died, in 1914, his forest of more than 100,000 acres was deeded to the U.S. government to become the first national forest east of the Mississippi. This included the original forest plantations, as well as land already forested when he purchased it.

48. Letter to Kingsbury, Jan. 20, 1891.

49. Frederick Law Olmsted, Report to George Vanderbilt, July 12, 1889, Olmsted Papers, Library of Congress, 34–35. "The nursery price of *Rhododendron Maximum* in New York, three feet high, has been $2.00 a plant. You can have plants gathered for you within twenty miles of your residence, by the thousand, probably at ten cents a plant, and after two years in nursery they will be better plants than I have been able to get from any nurseryman in Europe or America."

50. Frederick Law Olmsted, "George W. Vanderbilt's Nursery," *The Lyceum* 2, no. 6 (Dec. 1891): 7.

51. Olmsted's interest in forestry was long-standing. See Laura Wood Roper, *FLO: A Biography of Frederick Law Olmsted* (Baltimore: Johns Hopkins Univ. Press, 1973), 415, for his activities prior to Biltmore.

52. Frederick Law Olmsted and J. B. Harrison, *Observations on the Treatment of Public Plantations, More Especially Related to the Use of the Axe* (1889), reprinted in Frederick Law Olmsted, Jr., and Theodora Kimball, eds., *Forty Years of Landscape Architecture: Central Park* (Cambridge: MIT Press, 1973), 362–75.

53. Report to Vanderbilt, 19.

54. Gifford Pinchot, *Breaking New Ground* (New York: Harcourt, Brace, 1947), 49. In this book, his autobiography, Pinchot also referred to Olmsted as "one of the men of the century" (48).

55. Ibid., 57.

56. Ibid., 65.

57. The details of competing claims often pose a quandary. Maybe this is why it is so easy for people to be "for" saving the rain forests. In far-off places the goals are abstract and the details of the dilemmas unknown. The popular conception of Amazonia is of an unpopulated wilderness, yet millions of people live there. See Candace Slater's essay in this volume.

58. For a more detailed description of the Dayton case, see Anne Whiston Spirn, *The Granite Garden: Urban Nature and Human Design* (New York: Basic Books, 1984), 174–75.

59. Olmsted, "Vanderbilt's Nursery," 7.

60. Letter to Charles Eliot and John Charles Olmsted, Oct. 28, 1893. Olmsted Papers, Library of Congress.

61. For a description of these projects in the overall context of Boston, see Spirn, *Granite Garden*. For a description of how the basin and the tidal gate were intended to work, see Olmsted's account of his dialogue with the city's engineer in an 1886 lecture to the Boston Society of Architects, "The Problem and Its Solution." The handwritten notes for this lecture are in the Olmsted Papers at the Library of Congress. They were transcribed by Cynthia Zaitzevsky and reprinted in her dissertation, "Frederick Law Olmsted and the Boston Park System" (Harvard Univ., 1975), 295–306, and excerpted in her book of the same title (Cambridge: Harvard Univ. Press, 1982). For a description of how the flood control function worked, see E. W. Howe, "The Back Bay Park, Boston" (speech to the Boston Society of Civil Engineers, March 16, 1881).

62. Zaitzevsky, *Olmsted*, 188.

63. Letter to F. L. Temple, March 15, 1886, Olmsted Papers, Library of Congress. Temple was the landscape gardener Olmsted had hired to plant the Fens. Of the 100,000 plants, only 35,000 survived, many of which were "nurse" plants intended to die. Of the plant species intended to predominate over time, 75–95 percent were dead. See also Zaitzevsky, *Olmsted*, 187–90.

64. The Ramble at Central Park was planted to appear "wild," but it was only a small part of the park. William Robinson, an English acquaintance of Olmsted, published his book *The Wild Garden* in 1870. Olmsted was undoubtedly also aware of Martin Johnson Heade's contemporary paintings depicting marshes along Boston's North Shore. (I am grateful to William Cronon and Neil Levine for this reference.)

65. Frederick Law Olmsted, "Parks, Parkways and Pleasure Grounds," *Engineering Magazine* 9 (1895): 253–54 (italics added).

66. See Joachim Wolschke-Bulmahn's review of Robert E. Grese, *Jens Jensen: Maker of Natural Parks and Gardens* (Baltimore: Johns Hopkins Univ. Press, 1992), in *Journal of Garden History* 15 (1995): 54–55.

67. See Gert Groening and Joachim Wolschke-Bulmahn, "Some Notes on the Mania for Native Plants in Germany," *Landscape Journal* 11 (1992): 116–26, for parallels between the eradication of non-native plants in Nazi Germany and the extermination of non-Aryan human populations. This essay provoked a very strong reaction: Kim

Sorvig, "Natives and Nazis: An Imaginary Conspiracy in Ecological Design," *Landscape Journal* 13 (1994): 58–61; Gert Groening and Joachim Wolschke-Bulmahn, "Response: If the Shoe Fits, Wear It," ibid., 194–96.

68. We know Olmsted approved of including hardy exotic plants because this was a point over which he and Charles Sprague Sargent argued on the Boston projects. Sargent deplored the use of exotic species; this is ironic, since he was director of the Arnold Arboretum, which had many trees from other regions and continents. Olmsted preferred to follow William Robinson's practice of mixing native and hardy exotic plants, as described in *The Wild Garden* (1870). See Zaitzevsky, *Olmsted*, 196, for quotations showing how Olmsted and Sargent disagreed on this subject.

69. The assumed superiority of native over exotic species is still a strong value of many landscape architects and ecologists today.

70. These projects are all described in Spirn, *Granite Garden*.

71. The first course in city planning in the United States was offered in 1909, in the School of Landscape Architecture at Harvard, several of whose faculty later founded the first school of city planning, in 1929. The first city-planning degree was a master's of landscape architecture and city planning offered at Harvard in 1923. See Anne Whiston Spirn, "Urban Nature and Human Design: Renewing the Great Tradition," *Journal of Planning Education and Research* 5 (Autumn 1985): 39–51. See also John L. Hancock, "Planners in the Changing American City: 1900–1940," *Journal of the American Institute of Planners* 33 (1967): 290–304.

72. Many plans for parks and parkways as a multipurpose urban infrastructure were never implemented and are now being rediscovered and proposed anew. Mike Davis and others, for example, have revived interest in proposals for the Los Angeles River made by Frederick Law Olmsted, Jr.

73. The Boston proposals are described in Steve Curwood, "Profile: Shaping the City to Nature's Laws," *Boston Sunday Globe*, May 26, 1985, and Anne Whiston Spirn, "Reclaiming Common Ground: The Future Shape of Boston" (lecture sponsored by the Boston Society of Architects, American Institute of Architects, and McGraw-Hill, May 1985). See also Anne Whiston Spirn, "Landscape Planning and the City," *Landscape and Urban Planning* 13 (1986): 433–41. For a description of the Philadelphia proposals, see Thomas Hine, "Surroundings: A Long-Buried Creek in West Philadelphia," *Philadelphia Sunday Inquirer*, Nov. 15, 1992. See also Anne Whiston Spirn, *The West Philadelphia Landscape Plan: A Framework for Action* and *Vacant Land: A Resource for Reshaping Urban Neighborhoods* (Philadelphia: Department of Landscape Architecture and Regional Planning, Univ. of Pennsylvania, 1991).

74. Daniel Schodek includes the Boston subway of 1895 (the nation's first) and the Charles River Dam and Basin of 1910 as two landmark projects in his book *Landmarks of American Civil Engineering* (Cambridge: MIT Press, 1987). He refers to Olmsted's Emerald Necklace as ringing the city with "some of the loveliest waterways and parklands in the country," but fails to see its significance as a landmark of engineering. Exhibiting a fundamental misunderstanding that is all too common, he contrasts what he terms Olmsted's "nostalgic sense of the landscape" in the Fens with the scientific and commercial concerns of the Charles River Dam (301). The Fens also exposes the power and problem of cultural construction. Even as culture enables us to see some things, it blinds us to others. Once the Fens became a marsh, it was perceived as a potential dump. In contrast, the forested floodplain of the Riverway was not used as a dump.

75. This is a point Michael Barbour has made repeatedly.

76. He acknowledged this shortcoming. He titled a pamphlet on Central Park "The Spoils of the Park, with a Few Leaves from the Deep-Laden Note-books of a Wholly Impractical Man," reprinted in Olmsted and Kimball, *Forty Years*, 117–55.

77. The modern meanings of the word "artifice" reveal a negative attitude toward the deliberately and artfully made versus the given or "natural." "Artifice" originally referred to an *art* of making and "artificial" to something that was made or modified through human skill and art, often in imitation of something in nature. Now the usual meaning of "artifice" is trickery, and "artificial" connotes something that is not genuine, that seeks to fool. This double meaning has been part of the English language for a long time. See *Webster's New International Dictionary* (2nd ed.) and the *Oxford English Dictionary*. The first use of "artifice" with this negative meaning cited by the *OED* dates from the seventeenth century. It is interesting to note that although Olmsted employed artistry ("artifice") in shaping landscape, his frequent use of the word "artificial" was generally in its negative sense in reference to qualities or features that were not "natural." Perhaps the negative connotation of "artificial" explains why Olmsted's works are seldom seen as constructed. (I am grateful to Mark Rose and William Cronon for discussions that prompted these points.)

78. From a letter to Ralph Waldo Emerson: "I invite you to join me in a month's worship with Nature in the high temples of the great Sierra Crown beyond our holy Yosemite. It will cost you nothing save the time and very little of that for you will be mostly in Eternity." Quoted in Huth, *Nature*, 151.

Amazonia as Edenic Narrative

1. For one critique of these schemes, see Susanna Hecht and Alexander Cockburn, *The Fate of the Forest: Developers, Destroyers, and Defenders of the Amazon* (London: Verso, 1989). Other critiques are listed in the bibliography. Two newer works that do not appear there are Ronald A. Foresta, *Amazon Conservation in the Age of Development: The Limits of Providence* (Gainesville: Univ. of Florida Press, 1991), and Marianne Schmink and Charles H. Wood, *Contested Frontiers in Amazonia* (New York: Columbia Univ. Press, 1992).

2. For a summary of the Trombetas situation, see Rosa Azevedo and Edna Castro, *Negros do Trombetas: Guardiães de Matas e Rios* (Belém do Pará: Editora da Universidade, 1993). See also *Informe Revisão Constitucional—Os Direitos dos Remanescentes de Quilombos*, nos. 2, 3, and 4 (São Paulo: Comissão Pro-Indio de São Paulo, Jan. 12, 17, and 27, 1994).

3. The European explorers were wont to conceive of the Americas as a kind of Eden. See Henri Baudet, *Paradise on Earth: Some Thoughts on European Images of Non-European Man*, trans. Elizabeth Wentholt (New Haven: Yale Univ. Press, 1965), and Sérgio Buarque de Holanda, *Visão do Paraíso*, 2nd rev. ed., Brasiliana 33 (São Paulo: Editora Nacional/Editora da Universidade de São Paulo, 1969). See also the chapter on Columbus in Mary B. Campbell, *The Witness and the Other World: Exotic European Travel Writing, 400–1600* (Ithaca: Cornell Univ. Press, 1988).

4. Theodore Roosevelt, *Through the Brazilian Wilderness* (New York: Scribner's Sons, 1914).

5. Lévi-Strauss devotes a whole section to the Nambikwara in his *Tristes Tropiques*, trans. John and Doreen Weightman (New York: Atheneum, 1981).

6. Roosevelt, *Brazilian Wilderness*, 219 (italics added).

7. *Oxford English Dictionary* (citing T. Brooks Gold, *Key Works*, V, 473, 1867).

8. *Oxford English Dictionary* (citing William Cowper, *Task* ii, 1784, p. 1).

9. Joseph Conrad, *Heart of Darkness: An Authoritative Text, Backgrounds and Sources, Criticism*, ed. Robert Kimbrough, 3rd ed. (New York: Norton, 1988).

10. Although many scholars employ the name Yanomamo, I follow popular usage and the article in question by referring to the tribe as the Yanomami.

11. Napoleon A. Chagnon's classic study of the tribe is *Yanomamo: The Fierce People* (New York: Holt, Rinehart and Winston, 1968). For a consideration of how the tribe's image has changed, see Alcida R. Ramos, "Reflecting on the Yanomami: Ethnographic Images and the Pursuit of the Exotic," in *Rereading Cultural Anthropology*, ed. George E. Marcus (Durham: Duke University Press, 1992), 48–68.

12. Paul Lieberman, "Managers of Indian Casino Are Indicted," *Los Angeles Times*, May 12, 1994, A27.

13. The definition appears in the most recent edition of *Webster's International Dictionary*. Not all authors agree on the hundred-inch criterion, and some require slightly more or less moisture in order for a woodland to qualify.

14. *The New American Heritage Dictionary* of 1975, for instance, does not include the term. More recent editions do.

15. See Newman, *Tropical Rainforest* and *The Rainforests: A Celebration*, compiled by the Living Earth Foundation, ed. Lisa Silcock (San Francisco: Chronicle Books, 1990).

16. In the past the rain forest was any humid woodland. "The name 'Rain forest,' " asserts Paul Westamacott Richards, "is commonly given, not only to the evergreen forest of moist tropical lowlands . . . but also to the somewhat less luxuriant evergreen forest found at low and moderate altitudes on tropical mountains, and to the evergreen forests of oceanic subtropical climates." See Richards, *The Tropical Rain Forest: An Ecological Study* (Cambridge: Cambridge Univ. Press, 1966), 1. The term, however, has increasingly come to denote a specifically tropical location. (See the most recent edition of *Webster's International Dictionary*.)

17. "Living Cathedral" is the title of the first chapter in Arnold Newman, *Tropical Rainforest: A World Survey of Our Most Valuable and Endangered Habitat with a Blueprint for Survival* (New York: Facts on File, 1990).

18. McDonald's distributed the rain forest flier and four earlier fliers on environmental themes between 1990 and 1993. Current environmental information efforts are coordinated with the World Wildlife Foundation and the Field Museum of Natural History. They include a "Save the Rain Forest" (two words) poster, picturing a baby jaguar on a leafy log, and a Rain Forest Imperative Video, designed to help students in grades 6–12 "unearth the complex and urgent issues in preserving the tropical rain forest."

19. I thank Professor Joe Antos of the University of Victoria, a specialist in plant ecology of the Pacific Northwest, for his professional evaluation of the photo. I also thank Michael Barbour for putting me in touch with Professor Antos.

20. After Jim Proctor and Michael Barbour confirmed that the vegetation in the picture could not be tropical, I wrote to the McDonald's Corporation to ask where the picture was taken. Mr. Jerry Horn of the Customer Satisfaction Department wrote back that "the photo on the 'Did You Know' #5 leaflet is a tropical forest in South America" (personal communication, June 14, 1994). When I called Mr. Horn on June 28 to ask where exactly this rain forest might be located, he informed me that an outside firm "scoured all over in the Amazon for it." Asked who could give me the precise location, he replied that the photo was a stock photo from the Leo Burnett archives and that no one could say "where in the world it came from, except that it is definitely a tropical rain forest in South America."

21. Mary Louise Pratt suggests the possibility of release from the rigidity of genre "not by doing away with tropes (which is not possible) but by appropriating and inventing new ones (which is)." See Pratt, "Fieldwork in Common Places," in *Writing Culture: The Poetics and Politics of Ethnography,* ed. James Clifford and George E. Marcus (Berkeley: Univ. of California Press, 1986), 50.

22. Alcida Ramos makes this point in her "Indian Voices," in *Rethinking History and Myth: Indigenous South American Perspectives on the Past,* ed. Jonathan D. Hill (Urbana: Univ. of Illinois Press, 1988), 214–34.

Reinventing Eden

*An earlier version of this paper was presented as a keynote address to the Fifth International Conference on Narrative, Albany, N.Y., April 1–4, 1993. I am grateful for suggestions and comments from Zelda Bronstein, J. Baird Callicott, Anthony Chennells, Yaakov Garb, Debora Hammond, David Igler, James McCarthy, Charles Sellers, Hayden White, and members of the Reinventing Nature seminar at the Humanities Research Institute at the University of California at Irvine.

1. Roland Nelson, Penobscot, as recorded by Frank Speck, "Penobscot Tales and Religious Beliefs," *Journal of American Folklore* 48 (Jan.–March 1935): 1–107, on 75. This corn mother origin story is a variant on a number of eastern U.S. and Canadian transformative accounts, recorded from oral traditions, that attribute the origins of corn to a mythical corn mother who produces corn from her body, grows old, and then instructs her lover or son how to plant and tend corn. The killing of the corn mother in most of the origin stories may symbolize a transition from gathering-hunting to active corn cultivation. The snake lover may be an influence from the Christian tradition or a more universal symbol of the renewal of life (snakes shed their skins) and / or the male sexual organ. On corn mother origin stories, see John

Witthoft, *Green Corn Ceremonialism in the Eastern Woodlands* (Ann Arbor: Univ. of Michigan Press, 1949), 77–85; Joe Nicholas, Malechite, Tobique Point, Canada, Aug. 1910, as recorded by W. H. Mechling, *Malechite Tales* (Ottawa: Government Printing Bureau, 1914), 87–88; for the Passamaquoddy variant, see *Journal of American Folklore* 3 (1890): 214; for Creek and Natchez variants, see J. R. Swanton, "Myths and Tales of the Southeastern Indians," *Bulletin of the Bureau of American Ethnology,* no. 88 (1929): 9–17; on Iroquois variants, see Jesse Cornplanter, *Legends of the Longhouse* (Philadelphia: J. B. Lippincott, 1938), and Arthur Parker, "Iroquois Use of Maize and Other Food Plants," *New York State Museum Bulletin,* no. 144 (1910): 36–39; Gudmund Hatt, "The Corn Mother in America and Indonesia" *Anthropos* 46 (1951): 853–914. Examples of corn mother origin stories from the Southwest include the Pueblo emergence from the dark interior of the earth into the light of the fourth world, where corn mother plants thought woman's gift of corn. See Ramón Gutiérrez, *When Jesus Came the Corn Mothers Went Away* (Stanford: Stanford Univ. Press, 1991). For a discussion of the relationship of the corn mother to mother earth, see Sam Gill, *Mother Earth: An American Story* (Chicago: Univ. of Chicago Press, 1987), 4, 125.

2. On Great Plains environmental histories as progressive and declensionist plots, see William Cronon, "A Place for Stories: Nature, History, and Narrative," *Journal of American History* 78 (1992): 1347–76. The Indian and European origin stories can be interpreted from a variety of standpoints other than the declensionist and progressive narrative formats I have emphasized here (such as romance and satire). Additionally, the concepts of desert, wilderness, and garden are nuanced and elaborate motifs that change valences over time in ways I have not tried to deal with here.

3. Genesis, chap. 1. On the comic and tragic visions of the human, animal, vegetable, mineral, and unformed worlds, see Northrup Frye, *Fables of Identity* (New York: Harcourt, Brace, 1963), 19–20. In the comic state, or vision, the human world is a community, the animal world consists of domesticated flocks and birds of peace, the vegetable world is a garden or park with trees, the mineral world is a city or temple with precious stones and starlit domes, and the unformed world is a river. In the tragic state or vision, the human world is an anarchy of individuals, the animal world is filled with beasts and birds of prey (such as wolves, vultures, and serpents), the vegetable world is a wilderness, desert, or sinister forest, the mineral world is filled with rocks and ruins, and the unformed world is a sea or flood. The plot of the tragedy moves from a better or comic state to a worse or tragic state; the comedy from an initial tragic state, to a comic or happy outcome. I thank Hayden White for this reference. On history as narrative, see Hayden White, *Metahistory: The Historical Imagination in Nineteenth-Century Europe* (Baltimore: Johns Hopkins Univ. Press, 1973); idem, *Tropics of Discourse: Essays in Cultural Criticism* (Baltimore: Johns Hopkins Univ. Press, 1978); idem, *The Content of the Form: Narrative Discourse and Historical Representation* (Baltimore: Johns Hopkins Univ. Press, 1987).

4. Benjamin Franklin, "Remarks concerning the Savages of North America," in Richard E. Amacher, ed., *Franklin's Wit and Folly: The Bagatelles* (New Brunswick: Rutgers Univ. Press, 1953), 89–98. Franklin's story is probably satirical rather than literal.

5. The concept of a recovery from the original Fall appears in the early modern period. See the *Oxford English Dictionary,* s.v. "recovery": "The act of recovering

oneself from a mishap, mistake, fall, etc." See Bishop Edward Stillingfleet, *Origines Sacrae* (London, 1662), II, i, sec. 1: "The conditions on which fallen man may expect a recovery." William Cowper, *Retirement* (1781), 138: "To . . . search the themes, important above all, Ourselves, and our recovery from our fall." See also Richard Eden, *The Decades of the Newe Worlde or West India* (1555), 168: "The recouerie of the kyngedome of Granata." The term "recovery" also embraced the idea of regaining a "natural" position after falling and a return to health after sickness. It acquired a legal meaning in the sense of gaining possession of property by a verdict or judgment of the court. In common recovery, an estate was transferred from one party to another. John Cowell, *The Interpreter* (1607), s.v. "recouerie": "A true recouerie is an actuall or reall recouerie of anything, or the value thereof by Judgement." Another meaning was the restoration of a person or thing to a healthy or normal condition, or a return from a lapsed state to a higher or better state, including the reclamation of land and of resources such as soil. Anonymous, *Captives bound in Chains . . . the misery of graceless Sinners, and the hope of their recovery by Christ* (1674); Bishop Joseph Butler, *The Analogy of Religion Natural and Revealed* (1736), II, 295: "Indeed neither Reason nor Analogy would lead us to think . . . that the Interposition of Christ . . . would be of that Efficacy for Recovery of the World, which Scripture teaches us it was." Joseph Gilbert, *The Christian Atonement* (1836), i, 24: "A modified system, which shall include the provision of means for recovery from a lapsed state." James Martineau, *Essays, Reviews, and Addresses* (1890–91), II, 310: "He is fitted to be among the prophets of recovery, who may prepare for us a more wholesome future." John Henry Newman, *Historical Sketches* (1872–73) II, 1, iii, 121: "The special work of his reign was the recovery of the soil."

6. On the Genesis 1, or priestly, version (Genesis P), composed in the fifth century B.C., versus the Genesis 2, or Yahwist, version (Genesis J), composed in the ninth or tenth century B.C., and their relationships to the environmental movement, see J. Baird Callicott, "Genesis Revisited: Muirian Musings on the Lynn White, Jr. Debate," *Environmental Review* 14, nos. 1–2 (Spring/Summer 1990): 65–92. Callicott argues that Lynn White, Jr., mixed the two versions in his famous article "The Historical Roots of Our Ecologic Crisis," *Science* 155 (1967): 1203–7. On the historical traditions behind the Genesis stories, see Artur Weiser, *The Old Testament: Its Formation and Development*, trans. Dorothea M. Barton (New York: Association Press, 1961).

7. John Prest, *The Garden of Eden: The Botanic Garden and the Re-creation of Paradise* (New Haven: Yale Univ. Press, 1981), 1–37; J. A. Phillips, *Eve: The History of an Idea* (San Francisco: Harper and Row, 1984).

8. "Paradise" derives from the old Persian word for "enclosure" and in Greek and Latin takes on the meaning of garden. Its meanings include heaven, a state of bliss, an enclosed garden or park, and the Garden of Eden. "Parousia" derives from the Latin *parere*, meaning to produce or bring forth. The Parousia is the idea of the End of the World, expressed as the hope set forth in the New Testament that "he shall come again to judge both the quick and the dead." See A. L. Moore, *The Parousia in the New Testament* (Leiden: E. J. Brill, 1966). I thank Anthony Chennells for bringing this concept to my attention. Capitalism and Protestantism were initially mutually reinforcing in their common hope of a future golden age. But as capitalism became more materialistic and worldly it began to undercut the church's Parousia

hope. Communism retained the idea of a future golden age in its concern for community and future direction (ibid., 2–3). The Parousia hope was a driving force behind the church's missionary work in its early development and in the New World (p. 5). The age of glory was a gift of God, an acknowledgment of the future inbreaking of God (JHWH) into history (pp. 16, 17). "The scene of the future consummation is a radically transformed earth. The coming of this Kingdom was conceptualized as a sudden catastrophic moment, or as preceded by the Messianic kingdom, during which it was anticipated that progressive work would take place" (p. 20). "Concerning the central figure in the awaited End-drama there is considerable variation. In some visions the figure of Messiah is entirely absent. In such cases 'the kingdom was always represented as under the immediate sovereignty of God' " (p. 21). "The divine intervention in history was the manifestation of the Kingdom of God. . . . [T]his would involve a total transformation of the present situation, hence the picture of world renewal enhanced sometimes by the idea of an entirely supernatural realm" (pp. 25–26). "The fourth Eclogue of Virgil presents the hope of a 'golden age' but in fundamental contrast to apocalyptic expectation; although it is on a cosmic scale, it is the hope of revolution from within rather than of intervention from without" (p. 28).

9. Max Oelschlaeger, *The Idea of Wilderness: From Prehistory to the Age of Ecology* (New Haven: Yale Univ. Press, 1991), 49–60.

10. Francis Bacon, *Novum Organum,* in *Works,* ed. James Spedding, Robert Leslie Ellis, and Douglas Devon Heath, 14 vols. (London: Longmans Green, 1870), 4: 247–48, 114–15. See also Bacon's statement "I mean (according to the practice in civil causes) in this great plea or suit granted by the divine favor and providence (whereby the human race seeks to recover its right over nature) to examine nature herself and the arts upon interrogatories." Bacon, "Preparative towards a Natural and Experimental History," *Works,* 4: 263. William Leiss, *The Domination of Nature* (New York: George Braziller, 1972), 48–52; Carolyn Merchant, *The Death of Nature: Women, Ecology, and the Scientific Revolution* (San Francisco: Harper and Row, 1980), 185–86; Charles Whitney, *Francis Bacon and Modernity* (New Haven: Yale Univ. Press, 1986), 25.

11. Marshall Sahlins, *Culture and Practical Reason* (Chicago: Univ. of Chicago Press, 1976), 53: "The development from a Hobbesian state of nature is the origin myth of Western capitalism."

12. On the definition of natural resources, see John Yeats, *Natural History of Commerce* (London, 1870), 2. Thomas Hobbes, *Leviathan* (1651), in *English Works,* 11 vols. (reprint ed., Aalen, W. Germany: Scientia, 1966), 3: 145, 158. John Locke, *Two Treatises of Government* (1690), ed. Peter Laslett (Cambridge: Cambridge Univ. Press, 1960), Second Treatise, chap. 5, secs. 28, 32, 35, 37, 46, 48.

13. The Fall from Eden may be interpreted (as can the corn mother origin story; see note 1) as representing a transition from gathering-hunting to agriculture. In the Garden of Eden, Adam and Eve pick the fruits of the trees without having to labor in the earth (Genesis 1:29–30; Genesis 2:9). After the Fall they had to till the ground "in the sweat of thy face" and eat "the herb of the field" (Genesis 3:18, 19, 23). In Genesis 4, Abel, "keeper of sheep," is the pastoralist, while Cain, "tiller of the ground," is the farmer. Although God accepted Abel's lamb as a firstfruit, he did

not accept Cain's offering. Cain's killing of Abel may represent the ascendancy of farming over pastoralism. Agriculture requires more intensive labor than either pastoralism or gathering. See Oelschlaeger, *Idea of Wilderness;* Callicott, "Genesis Revisited," 81.

14. Hesiod, "Works and Days," in *Theogony and Works and Days,* trans. M. L. West (Oxford: Oxford Univ. Press, 1988), 40.

15. Publius Ovid, *Metamorphoses,* trans. Rolfe Humphries (Bloomington: Indiana Univ. Press, 1955), bk. 1, p. 6, lines 100–111.

16. On the meanings of "nature" and "nation" and the following interpretation of Virgil, see Kenneth Olwig, *Nature's Ideological Landscape* (London: George Allen and Unwin, 1984), 3–9. In the *Eclogues,* Virgil characterized the pastoral landscape as the grazing of tame animals on grassy hillsides. Human labor domesticated animals, transformed the forest into meadows, and dammed springs to form pools for watering livestock. But the shepherd was relatively passive, watching flocks while reclining in the shade of a remnant forest tree.

17. Olwig, *Nature's Ideological Landscape,* 6. Agriculture is initiated by Jove, who "endowed that cursed thing the snake with venom and the wolf with thirst for blood." "Toil . . . taught men the use and method of the plough." Agricultural instruments were hammered out by the use of fire, becoming "weapons hardy rustics need ere they can plow or sow the crop to come." Virgil, *Georgics* 1.151–52, as quoted ibid., 6.

18. Olwig, *Nature's Ideological Landscape,* 3–9; Virgil, *Georgics* 2: 106–7; *Eclogues* 4: 4–34. Virgil's temporal and spatial stages prefigure Frederick Jackson Turner's frontier stages and Johann Heinrich von Thünen's rings, discussed by William Cronon in the conversion of hinterland resources (first nature) into commodities (second nature) in Chicago. See Cronon, *Nature's Metropolis: Chicago and the Great West* (New York: Norton, 1991), 46–54.

19. Lucretius, *Of the Nature of Things,* trans. William Ellery Leonard (New York: E. P. Dutton, 1950), bk. 5, lines 922–1008. Lucretius' image of the "state of nature" was strikingly similar to that of Thomas Hobbes in *Leviathan* (1651). Lucretius wrote that in the early days "men led a life after the roving habit of wild beasts." They chased and ate wild animals and were in turn hunted and devoured by them. In the state of nature they "huddled in groves, and mountain-caves, and woods" without any regard for "the general good" and did not "know to use in common any customs, any laws." Just as Hobbes characterized life before civil law as "nasty, brutish, and short," so Lucretius wrote that "the clans of savage beasts" would make "sleep-time horrible for those poor wretches." Men were "snatched upon and gulped by fangs," while those who escaped "with bone and body bitten, shrieked," as the "writhing pangs took them from life." In a time before agricultural plenty, starvation was rampant as "lack of food gave o'er men's fainting limbs to dissolution." Procreation, for Lucretius, was likewise beastlike and brutal. Men took women "with impetuous fury and insatiate lust" or bribed them with berries and fruit. When finally women moved "into one dwelling place" with men, "the human race began to soften," as they saw "an offspring born from out themselves." Neighbors intervened on behalf of women and children and urged compassion for the weak.

20. Lucretius, *Of the Nature of Things*, bk. 5, lines 1135–85: "So next some wiser heads instructed men to found the magisterial office, and did frame codes that they might consent to follow laws. . . . For humankind, o'er wearied with a life fostered by force . . . of its own free will yielded to laws and strictest codes." Because "each hand made ready in its wrath to take a vengeance fiercer than by man's fair laws," people voluntarily submitted to "fear of punishment."

21. Lucretius, *Of the Nature of Things*, bk. 6, lines 1136–1284. "For now no longer men did mightily esteem the old Divine, the worship of the gods: the woe at hand did overmaster."

22. Ibid., bk. 5, lines 811–70.

23. On Edenic imagery in American history, see R. W. B. Lewis, *The American Adam: Innocence, Tragedy, and Tradition in the Nineteenth Century* (Chicago: Univ. of Chicago Press, 1955); David Noble, *The Eternal Adam and the New World Garden: The Central Myth in the American Novel since 1830* (New York: George Braziller, 1968); David Wari, *The Fall into Eden: Landscape and Imagination in California* (New York: Cambridge Univ. Press, 1986); Cecilia Tichi, *New World, New Earth: Environmental Reform in American Literature from the Puritans through Whitman* (New Haven: Yale Univ. Press, 1979).

24. Vladimir Propp, "Morphology of the Folktale," *International Journal of American Linguistics* 24, no. 4 (Oct. 1958): 46–48; Roland Barthes, "The Struggle with the Angel," *Image, Music, Text*, trans. Stephen Heath (New York: Noonday Press, 1977), 139–41.

25. Quoted in Peter N. Carroll, *Puritanism and the Wilderness, 1629–1700* (New York: Columbia Univ. Press, 1969), 13–14.

26. William Bradford, *History of Plymouth Plantation, 1620–1647*, ed. Worthington C. Ford, 2 vols. (Boston: Published for the Massachusetts Historical Society by Houghton Mifflin, 1912).

27. Charles Morton, *Compendium Physicae*, from the 1697 manuscript copy Publications of the Colonial Society of Massachusetts, vol. 33 (Boston, 1940), pp. xi, xxix, xxiii, xxxi; Nathaniel Ames, *An Astronomical Diary or Almanac* (Boston: J. Draper, 1758), endpapers.

28. Robert Beverley, *The History and Present State of Virginia* (London: R. Parker, 1705), 246–48.

29. Matthew Baigell, *Thomas Cole* (New York: Watson Guptill, 1981), plates 15, 16. On Cole's use of Eden as metaphor, see Henry Adams, "The American Land Inspired Cole's Prescient Visions," *Smithsonian*, May 1994, 99–107.

30. Baigell, *Thomas Cole*, plates 10, 15.

31. Ralph Waldo Emerson, "The Young American," *The Dial* 4 (1844): 484–507, quotation on 489, 491.

32. Leo Marx, *The Machine in the Garden: Technology and the Pastoral Ideal in America* (New York: Oxford Univ. Press, 1964).

33. John Winthrop, "Winthrop's Conclusions for the Plantation in New England," in *Old South Leaflets*, no. 50 (1629) (Boston: Directors of the Old South Work, 1897), 4–5; John Quincy Adams, in *Congressional Globe* 29, no. 1 (1846): 339–42. Adams omits the biblical phrase "replenish the earth." Thomas Hart Benton, ibid., 917–18, reverses the biblical ordering from "replenish the earth and subdue it" to "subdue and replenish the earth."

34. Reverend Dwinell, quoted in John Todd, *The Sunset Land, or the Great Pacific Slope* (Boston: Lee and Shepard, 1870), 252; Henry Nash Smith, *Virgin Land: The American West as Symbol and Myth* (Cambridge: Harvard Univ. Press, 1950); Marx, *Machine in the Garden*.

35. Frederick Jackson Turner, "The Significance of the Frontier in American History," *Annual Report of the American Historical Association* (1893) (Washington, D.C., 1894), 199–227.

36. Francis Paul Prucha, *The Indians in American Society* (Berkeley: Univ. of California Press, 1985), quotations on 7, 10.

37. Ibid., quotation on 12.

38. Ibid., 14–20; Lloyd Burton, *American Indian Water Rights and the Limits of the Law* (Lawrence: Univ. of Kansas Press, 1991), 6–34; Carolyn Merchant, *Ecological Revolutions: Nature, Gender, and Science in New England* (Chapel Hill: Univ. of North Carolina Press, 1989), chaps. 2 and 3; William Cronon, *Changes in the Land: Indians, Colonists, and the Ecology of New England* (New York: Hill and Wang, 1983); Richard White, *The Roots of Dependency: Subsistence, Environment, and Social Change among the Choctaws, Pawnees, and Navajos* (Lincoln: Univ. of Nebraska Press, 1983); "Wilderness Act," 1964.

39. Chief Luther Standing Bear, *Land of the Spotted Eagle* (Boston: Houghton Mifflin, 1933), xix. On the ethnocentricity of wilderness values, see J. Baird Callicott, "The Wilderness Idea Revisited: The Sustainable Development Alternative," *Environmental Professional* 13 (1991): 236–45.

40. Neal Salisbury, "Red Puritans: The 'Praying Indians' of Massachusetts Bay and John Eliot," *William and Mary Quarterly*, 3rd ser., 31, no. 1 (1974): 27–54; William Simmons, "Conversion from Indian to Puritan," *New England Quarterly* 52, no. 2 (1979): 197–218.

41. Franklin, "Remarks concerning the Savages," 91.

42. On images and metaphors of nature as female in American history, see Annette Kolodny, *The Lay of the Land: Metaphor as Experience and History in American Life and Letters* (Chapel Hill: Univ. of North Carolina Press, 1975); idem, *The Land before Her: Fantasy and Experience of the American Frontier, 1630–1860* (Chapel Hill: Univ. of North Carolina Press, 1984); Vera Norwood and Janice Monk, eds., *The Desert Is No Lady: Southwestern Landscapes in Women's Writing and Art* (New Haven: Yale Univ. Press, 1987); Vera Norwood, *Made from This Earth: American Women and Nature* (Chapel Hill: Univ. of North Carolina Press, 1993); Sam Gill, *Mother Earth* (Chicago: Univ. of Chicago Press, 1987).

43. Thomas Morton, *New English Canaan*, in Peter Force, ed., *Tracts and Other Papers . . .* (Washington, D.C., 1838), 2: 10.

44. Henry Colman, "Address before the Hampshire, Franklin, and Hampden Agricultural Society Delivered in Greenfield, Oct. 23, 1833" (Greenfield, Mass.: Phelps and Ingersoll, 1833), 5–6, 15, 27.

45. Frank Norris, *The Octopus: A Story of California* (1901) (New York: Penguin, 1986), 127. I thank David Igler for bringing these passages to my attention.

46. Ibid.

47. Ibid., 130–31.

48. *Scribner's Monthly*, Nov. 1880, 61. On the association of women with civilization and culture in nineteenth-century America, see Christopher Lasch, *The New Radicalism in America, 1889–1963* (New York: Norton, 1965), 65; Nancy Woloch, *Women and the American Experience* (New York: Knopf, 1984), chap. 6; Merchant, *Ecological Revolutions*, chap. 7.

49. J. Hector St. John de Crèvecoeur, "What Is an American?" *Letters from an American Farmer* (1782) (New York: E. P. Dutton, 1957), 39–43.

50. Richard F. Burton, *The City of the Saints and across the Rocky Mountains to California* (1861) (New York: Knopf, 1963), 72.

51. See also Roderick Nash, *Wilderness and the American Mind*, 3rd ed. (New Haven: Yale Univ. Press, 1982); Richard Slotkin, *Regeneration through Violence: The Mythology of the Frontier* (Middletown, Conn.: Wesleyan Univ. Press, 1973); idem, *Gunfighter Nation: The Myth of the Frontier in Twentieth-Century America* (New York: Atheneum, 1992). For further discussion of these themes, see the chapters in this book by Kenneth Olwig, Anne Spirn, and William Cronon.

52. On the Renaissance distinction between *Natura naturans* and *Natura naturata*, see Eustace M. W. Tillyard, *The Elizabethan World Picture* (New York: Vintage, 1959), 46: "This giving a soul to nature—nature, that is, in the sense of *natura naturans*, the creative force, not of *natura naturata*, the natural creation—was a mildly unorthodox addition to the spiritual or intellectual beings. . . . Hooker, orthodox as usual, is explicit on this matter. [Nature] cannot be allowed a will of her own. . . . She is not even an agent . . . [but] is the direct and involuntary tool of God himself." See also Whitney, *Bacon and Modernity*, 123: "[T]he extreme dehumanization of [nature by] the Baconian scientist . . . is linked not simply to a complementary dehumanization of the feminine object of study, but to a somewhat anachronistic return to a more robust feminine image of nature as *natura naturans*." Spinoza likewise used the two terms, but with meanings rather different from those implied here. See *Spinoza Selections*, ed. John Wild (New York: Charles Scribner's Sons, 1930), 80–82; Harry A. Wolfson, *The Philosophy of Spinoza*, 2 vols. (1934) (New York: Meridian, 1958), 1: 253–55.

53. John Gast, *American Progress*, painting, 1872, reproduced as a chromolithograph in Jules David Prown et al., *Discovered Lands, Invented Pasts* (New Haven: Yale Univ. Press, 1992), 97. On landscape paintings as narrative moments, see William Cronon, "Telling Tales on Canvas: Landscapes of Frontier Change," ibid., 37–87.

54. For representations and interpretation of the four paintings discussed below, see William H. Truettner, ed., *The West as America: Reinterpreting Images of the Fron-*

tier, 1820–1920 (Washington, D.C.: National Museum of Art, 1991), 135, 120, 136, 137.

55. Frank Norris, *The Pit: A Story of Chicago* (1903) (New York: Grove Press, 1956).

56. Cronon, *Nature's Metropolis*. Cronon quotes the passage below from *The Pit*, on the page preceding his "Prologue."

57. Norris, *The Pit*, 62.

58. Ibid., 60–63.

59. On Marx's concept of the endowment of money with organic, living properties and its application among the Indians of the Cauca valley, in Colombia, see Michael Taussig, "The Genesis of Capitalism amongst a South American Peasantry: Devil's Labor and the Baptism of Money," *Comparative Studies in Society and History* 19 (1977): 130–53.

60. Norris, *The Pit*, 374.

61. Nash, *Wilderness and the American Mind*.

62. Carol P. MacCormack, "Nature, Culture, and Gender," in Carol MacCormack and Marilyn Strathern, eds., *Nature, Culture, and Gender* (Cambridge: Cambridge Univ. Press, 1980), 6–7; Sherry Ortner, "Is Female to Male as Nature Is to Culture?" in Michelle Rosaldo and Louise Lamphere, eds., *Woman, Culture, and Society* (Stanford: Stanford Univ. Press, 1974), 67–87.

63. Philip Elmer-Dewitt, "Fried Gene Tomatoes," *Time*, May 30, 1994, 54–55; Richard Keller Simon, "The Formal Garden in the Age of Consumer Culture: A Reading of the Twentieth-Century Shopping Mall," in Wayne Franklin and Michael Steiner, eds., *Mapping American Culture* (Iowa City: Univ. of Iowa Press, 1992), 231–50. See also the chapters in this book by Jennifer Price, Katherine Hayles, and Donna Haraway.

64. Max Horkheimer and Theodor Adorno, *Dialectic of Enlightenment* (1944) (New York: Continuum, 1993), quotations on 3, 7, 9.

65. Maria Gimbutas, *The Goddesses and Gods of Old Europe, 6500–3500 B.C.* (Berkeley: Univ. of California Press, 1982); Merlin Stone, *When God Was a Woman* (New York: Harcourt Brace Jovanovich, 1976); Riane Eisler, *The Chalice and the Blade* (San Francisco: Harper and Row, 1988); Elinor Gadon, *The Once and Future Goddess* (San Francisco: Harper and Row, 1989); Monica Sjöö and Barbara Mor, *The Great Cosmic Mother: Rediscovering the Religion of the Earth* (San Francisco: Harper and Row, 1987); Pamela Berger, *The Goddess Obscured: The Transformation of the Grain Protectress from Goddess to Saint* (Boston: Beacon, 1985). On cultural ecofeminism see some of the essays in Irene Diamond and Gloria Orenstein, eds., *Reweaving the World: The Emergence of Ecofeminism* (San Francisco: Sierra Club Books, 1990).

66. Londa Schiebinger, *The Mind Has No Sex? Women in the Origins of Modern Science* (Cambridge: Harvard Univ. Press, 1989); Evelyn Fox Keller, *Reflections on Gender and Science* (New Haven: Yale Univ. Press, 1985).

67. Examples include Oelschlaeger, *Idea of Wilderness;* Donald Worster, *The Wealth of Nature* (New York: Oxford Univ. Press, 1993); Barry Commoner, *The Closing Circle: Nature, Man, and Technology* (New York: Knopf, 1971).

68. Paul Ehrlich, "Eco-Catastrophe!" *Ramparts,* Sept. 1969; Donella H. Meadows, Dennis L. Meadows, Jørgen Randers, and William Behrens III, *The Limits to Growth* (New York: Signet, 1972); Bill McKibben, *The End of Nature* (New York: Random House, 1989). For a critique see Tom Athanasiou, *US Politics and Global Warming* (Westfield, N.J.: Open Magazine Pamphlet Series, 1991).

69. Carolyn Merchant, *Radical Ecology: The Search for a Livable World* (New York: Routledge, 1992).

70. Alan Hastings, Carole L. Hin, Stephen Ellner, Peter Turchin, and H. Charles J. Godfray, "Chaos in Ecology: Is Mother Nature a Strange Attractor?" *American Review of Ecological Systems* 24, no. 1 (1993): 1–33; N. Katherine Hayles, "Gender Encoding in Fluid Mechanics: Masculine Channels and Feminine Flows," *Differences: A Journal of Feminist Cultural Studies* 4, no. 2 (1992): 16–44; idem, *Chaos Bound: Orderly Disorder in Contemporary Literature and Science* (Ithaca: Cornell Univ. Press, 1990); idem, ed., *Chaos and Order: Complex Dynamics in Literature and Science* (Chicago: Univ. of Chicago Press, 1991); Daniel Botkin, *Discordant Harmonies: A New Ecology for the Twenty-first Century* (New York: Oxford Univ. Press, 1990); James Gleick, *Chaos: The Making of a New Science* (New York: Viking, 1987); Edward Lorenz, *The Essence of Chaos* (Seattle: Univ. of Washington Press, 1993).

"Are You an Environmentalist or Do You Work for a Living?"

1. "Timber Drama Hits Home in Town of Forks," *Seattle Times,* Aug. 5, 1994, A14.

2. William Dietrich, *The Final Forest: The Battle for the Last Great Trees of the Pacific Northwest* (New York: Simon and Schuster, 1992), 209.

3. For loggers and knowledge, see ibid., 39.

4. Elaine Scarry, *The Body in Pain: The Making and Unmaking of the World* (New York: Oxford Univ. Press, 1985), 82.

5. For a summary of this literature, see Richard White and William Cronon, "Ecological Change and Indian-White Relations," in *History of Indian-White Relations,* ed. Wilcomb Washburn, vol. 4 of *Handbook of North American Indians,* ed. William Sturtevant (Washington, D.C.: Smithsonian Institution, 1988), 417–29. For a bibliographical essay, see Richard White, "Native Americans and the Environment," in W. R. Swagerty, ed., *Scholars and the Indian Experience: Critical Reviews of Recent Writing in the Social Sciences* (Bloomington: Indiana Univ. Press, 1984), 179–204.

6. Wendell Berry, "The Journey's End," in *Recollected Essays, 1965–1980* (New York: North Point Press, 1993), 259–62.

7. Philip Shabecoff, *A Fierce Green Fire: The American Environmental Movement* (New York: Hill and Wang, 1993), 23.

8. For Marshall as first human in the area, see Bill McKibben, *The End of Nature* (New York: Anchor Books, 1989), 53. For Nunamiut, see Ted Catton, "Inhabited Wilderness: The Making of Alaska's National Parks" (Ph.D. diss., Univ. of Washington, 1994), 174–212.

9. McKibben, *End of Nature*, 52.

10. Shabecoff, *Fierce Green Fire*, 22–24.

11. Gary E. Moulton, ed., *The Journals of the Lewis & Clark Expedition*, vols. 2–4 (Lincoln: Univ. of Nebraska Press, 1986–87), entries of July 23, 1804, 2: 415; Aug. 15, 1804, 2: 483; Sept. 17, 1804, 3: 80; Sept. 23, 1804, 3: 104; Oct. 29, 1804, 3: 210; March 6, 1805, 3: 309; May 28, 1805, 4: 237; July 20, 1805, 4: 407; July 25, 1805, 4: 428.

12. One of the best examples is recent literature on the decline of the bison. Dan Flores, "Bison Ecology and Bison Diplomacy: The Southern Plains from 1800 to 1850," *Journal of American History* 78 (1991): 465–85. I have also looked at the Indian role in shaping the environment in Richard White, *The Roots of Dependency: Subsistence, Environment, and Social Change among the Choctaws, Pawnees, and Navajos* (Lincoln: Univ. of Nebraska Press, 1983).

13. Entry of May 6, 1805, in Moulton, *Journals*, 4: 117.

14. Entry of May 31, 1805, ibid., 231.

15. Entries of May 30 and 31, 1805, ibid., 223–25.

16. Quoted in Richard Rajala, "The Forest as Factory: Technological Change and Worker Control in the West Coast Logging Industry, 1880–1930," *Labour/ Le Travail* 32 (Fall 1993): 84.

17. Diane Star Cooper, *Night after Night* (Washington, D.C.: Island Press, 1994), 129.

18. Ibid., 135 (italics added).

19. Shabecoff, *Fierce Green Fire*, 29.

20. John Berger, *Pig Earth* (New York: Pantheon, 1979), 1–12, 195–213.

21. Ibid., 75.

22. Pierre Bourdieu, *Outline of a Theory of Practice* (Cambridge: Cambridge Univ. Press, 1977), 78–79; idem, *The Logic of Practice*, trans. Richard Nice (Stanford: Stanford Univ. Press, 1990), 66–79. Bourdieu, however, has relatively little to say about how habitus intersects with actual work in the natural world.

23. Berger, *Pig Earth*, 198; William deBuys and Alex Harris, *River of Traps: A Village Life* (Albuquerque: Univ. of New Mexico Press, 1990), 11.

24. DeBuys and Harris, *River of Traps*, 23.

25. Ibid., 24.

26. Michael Pollan, *Second Nature: A Gardener's Education* (New York: Delta Trade Paperbacks, 1991), esp. 209–38.

27. William G. Robbins, *Hard Times in Paradise: Coos Bay, Oregon, 1850–1986* (Seattle: Univ. of Washington Press, 1988), 122; for a description of work and skill, see Rajala, "Forest as Factory," 81–82.

28. Dietrich, *Final Forest,* 39.

29. Russell to Friend Bob, April 14, 1920, in *Charles Russell, Catalog: C. M. Russell Museum* (Great Falls, Mont.: C. M. Russell Museum, n.d.), 19.

30. DeBuys examines this in *River of Traps* and in an earlier book, *Enchantment and Exploitation: The Life and Hard Times of a New Mexico Mountain Range* (Albuquerque: Univ. of New Mexico Press, 1985), 215–34.

31. Wendell Berry, "The Making of a Marginal Farm," in *Recollected Essays,* 336; idem, "The Body and the Earth," ibid., 269–326.

32. Wendell Berry, *The Unsettling of America: Culture and Agriculture* (New York: Avon Books, 1978), 138–40. For romanticism, see, for example, idem, *A Continuous Harmony: Essays Cultural & Agricultural* (New York: Harcourt Brace Jovanovich, 1972), 79.

33. Norris, quoted in Craig Wollner, *Electrifying Eden: Portland General Electric, 1889–1965* (Portland, Ore.: Historical Society Press, 1990), 162.

34. See, for example, D. Clayton Brown, *Electricity for Rural America: The Fight for the REA,* Contributions in Economics and Economic History, no. 29 (Westport, Conn.: Greenwood Press, 1980), 115–20.

35. Lewis Mumford, *Technics and Civilization* (New York: Harcourt, Brace, 1934), 256–57.

36. McKibben, 58.

37. Ibid.

38. Ibid., 47–49.

39. Ibid., 64–65, 83.

40. The *High Country News* is a superb paper. In general it provides the best view of the West now available, and the views in it are not necessarily those of its editors. I am not seeking to apologize for the real harm done by logging, ranching, and mining, but most reporting on those industries is either implicitly or explicitly a denunciation of the industries themselves and their work and not just the specific harm they do. See, for example, *High Country News,* issue of June 13, 1994.

Looking for Nature at the Mall

1. "What Is the Nature Company?" in the Nature Company's press kit (Berkeley: Nature Company), received June 1994.

2. Kathryn Jackson Fallon, "Wet Seals and Whale Songs," *Time,* June 3, 1991, 45.

3. On the rise of the eco-store, see, for example, Sally Deneen, "Dawn of the Eco-Shop," *E: The Environmental Magazine,* March–April 1993, 24–28; Faye Brookman, "Terra Verde: New York Store Features Friendly Merchandise," *Stores* 74 (Jan. 1992): 126–28; Laurie Freeman, "Eco-Retailers Turn Green into Gold," *Stores* 73 (Oct. 1991): 50–51.

4. Informational handout for employees (Berkeley: Nature Company, current March 1994), 1–3 (hereafter cited as Handout).

5. Stanley W. Angrist, "It's All in the Earn-Out," *Forbes*, April 25, 1988, 52; Gordon Bock, "CML Group: Soaking Up Those Yuppie Dollars," *Business Week*, June 16, 1986, 75.

6. "The Nature Company Profile," in press kit.

7. Handout, 3.

8. The products mentioned in this essay were all marketed by the Nature Company—by catalog and / or in retail stores—between Feb. 1993 and Aug. 1994.

9. The average store size is 2,918 square feet—CML Group, Inc., "Annual Report Pursuant to Section 13 or 15 (d) of the Securities Exchange Act of 1934" (for the fiscal year ended July 31, 1993), Securities and Exchange Commission form 10-K, p. 5.

10. Handout, 2.

11. Maureen O'Brien, "The Nature Company Jumps into Japan," *Publishers Weekly*, May 17, 1991, 37.

12. For example, Handout, 1–3; "What Is the Nature Company?"; CML Group, *Annual Report* (1993), 10.

13. Liz Lufkin, "Natural History Gets Hip," *San Francisco Chronicle*, Dec. 18, 1986.

14. *The Nature Company Catalog* (Holiday 1993), 14, 48, 32.

15. *The Nature Company Catalog* (Fall 1994), sale section, pp. A–B.

16. "What Is the Nature Company?"

17. *The Nature Company Catalog* (Holiday 1992), 43.

18. See the essays by William Cronon, Candace Slater, Susan Davis, Giovanna Di Chiro, and Richard White.

19. Allene Symons, "Marketing Nature Tie-ins at Nature Company," *Publishers Weekly*, May 1, 1987, 37.

20. Leighton Taylor, *Glacier Bay: Last Great Places on Earth* (Berkeley, Calif.: Nature Company, 1991), 3—accompanies Dennis Hysom, CD of same title (Vol. 2, The Nature Company Audio Library).

21. My understanding of the middle-class "nature lover" tradition has also been particularly influenced by Raymond Williams, "Ideas of Nature," in *Problems in Materialism and Culture* (London: Verso, 1980), 67–85; Jonas Frykman and Orvar Löfgren, *Culture Builders: A Historical Anthropology of Middle-Class Life*, trans. Alan Crozier (New Brunswick: Rutgers Univ. Press, 1987), 42–87; Ann Berming-

ham, *Landscape and Ideology: The English Rustic Tradition, 1740–1860* (Berkeley: Univ. of California Press, 1986), 9–54.

22. Henry David Thoreau, *The Selected Works of Thoreau,* rev. and with a new introd. by Walter Harding (Cambridge: Houghton Mifflin, 1975), 43.

23. Angrist, "Earn-Out," 52; Bock, "CML Group," 75.

24. "What Is the Nature Company?"; CML Group, *Annual Report,* cover; "CML Group (20 1/2), report on company by Adams, Harkness & Hill, March 22, 1994, 4.

25. Holiday 1993 catalog, 38. Moodtape—"Designed to stimulate your moods, beautify your environment, and enhance your lifestyle. . . . Perfect for relaxing, entertaining, love-making . . . the ideal gift"—box notes for Ron Roy, producer and director, *Tranquility* (Studio City, Calif.: Ron Roy Productions, 1986).

26. CML Group, *Annual Report,* 2.

27. Joan Didion, *The White Album* (New York: Simon and Schuster, 1979), 180.

28. To understand the essential spirit of "the mall," I have drawn especially on Jon Goss, "The 'Magic of the Mall': An Analysis of Form, Function, and Meaning in the Contemporary Retail Built Environment," *Annals of the Association of American Geographers* 83 (March 1993): 18–47; Margaret Crawford, "The World in a Shopping Mall," in Michael Sorkin, ed., *Variations on a Theme Park: The New American City and the End of Public Space* (New York: Hill and Wang, 1992), 3–30.

29. See, for example, Barry Maitland, *Shopping Malls: Planning and Design* (New York: Nichols, 1985); idem, *The New Architecture of the Retail Mall* (New York: Van Nostrand Reinhold, 1990); Nancy Rivera Brooks, "The Mall Face-Lift Craze," *Los Angeles Times,* Jan. 28, 1991; Robert Davis Rathbun, *Shopping Centers and Malls, Book 2* (New York: Retail Reporting Corp., 1988), 9.

30. "Restaurants, Nightclubs & Food," in Mall of America press kit (Bloomington, Minn.: Mall of America), received July 1994.

31. This argument is a central tenet of Jeffrey S. P. Hopkins, "West Edmonton Mall: Landscape of Myths and Elsewhereness," *Canadian Geographer* 34 (Spring 1990): 2–17.

32. Store numbers are listed in "The Nature Company Stores," in press kit.

33. My analysis here has been influenced by the argument, closely identified with the British cultural studies movement, that consumers will appropriate mass-produced culture for their own purposes—see, for example, the historical overview in Simon During, ed., *The Cultural Studies Reader* (London: Routledge, 1993), 1–25— though I haven't emphasized (as this argument invariably does) the producers' aims as hegemonic.

34. *The Nature Company Catalog* (Summer 1994), 27; Taylor, *Glacier Bay,* 6.

35. Fallon, "Wet Seals," 45.

36. Pete Dunne, "In the Natural State," *New York Times,* May 7, 1989.

37. Lufkin, "Natural History Gets Hip."

38. People so often report lost cars at the mall as stolen that some police departments use the incidents to inflate their recovery statistics. See Jerry Jacobs, *The Mall: An Attempted Escape from Everyday Life* (Prospect Heights, Ill.: Waveland Press, 1984), 8.

39. Crawford ("World in a Shopping Mall," 13–14) and Goss ("Magic of the Mall," 29–35) discuss the design strategies of the mall.

40. Goss, "Magic of the Mall," 22.

41. Didion, *White Album*, 186.

42. "Invitees": for example, Urban Land Institute, *Dollars & Cents of Shopping Centers: 1990* (Washington, D.C.: Urban Land Institute, 1990), 4. "Three hours": Crawford, "World in a Shopping Mall," 14.

43. Dunne, "In the Natural State."

44. Goss, "Magic of the Mall," 18.

45. A wonderfully useful review and critique of consumer culture theory is Jean-Christophe Agnew, "Coming Up for Air: Consumer Culture in Historical Perspective," in John Brewer and Roy Porter, eds., *Consumption and the World of Goods* (New York: Routledge, 1993), 19–39. My understanding of the uses of commodities to engage the world and establish who we are has been influenced especially by Mary Douglas and Baron Isherwood, *The World of Goods: Towards an Anthropology of Consumption* (London: Allen Lane, 1979); Grant McCracken, *Culture and Consumption: New Approaches to the Symbolic Character of Consumer Goods and Activities* (Bloomington: Indiana Univ. Press, 1988); and the material-culture analysis in Mihaly Csikszentmihalyi and Eugene Rochberg-Halton, *The Meaning of Things: Domestic Symbols and the Self* (Cambridge: Cambridge Univ. Press, 1981).

46. See, for example, Jeffrey S. P. Hopkins, "West Edmonton Mall as a Centre for Social Interaction," *Canadian Geographer* 35 (Fall 1991): 268–79.

47. Goss, "Magic of the Mall," 18.

48. Fall 1994 catalog, sale section, p. A.

49. Goss, "Magic of the Mall," 36, suggests that the presence of nature in the mall serves to "naturalize" consumption, thereby mitigating anticonsumer alienation.

50. David Guterson, "Enclosed. Encyclopedic. Endured: One Week at the Mall of America," *Harper's*, Aug. 1993, 54.

51. Handout, 3.

52. Ibid.

53. E. J. Muller, "Global Strategies for Small Shippers," *Distribution*, Oct. 1991, 29; Byron Greer, "Nature Company Expansion in High Gear," *San Francisco Chronicle*, July 13, 1987.

54. CML Group, "Annual Report," 7.

55. Handout, 4; O'Brien, "Nature Company Jumps into Japan," 37, 38; CML Group, company records, on *Disclosure* database.

56. Agnew, "Coming Up for Air," 33.

57. Jack Anderson and Michael Binstein, "Cuff Links and Trade Deal Come Undone," *Washington Post*, Feb. 3, 1992.

58. My analysis here has been informed by Agnew's insistence that while celebrating consumerism as an imaginative (or anti-hegemonic) act, we shouldn't forget about economic power and the social relations of production, and by William Cronon's insistence that we not forget that commodities are products not only of human labor but of nature. See Agnew, "Coming Up for Air," and Cronon, *Nature's Metropolis: Chicago and the Great West* (New York: Norton, 1991), esp. 148–51.

59. Bock, "CML Group," 75; Angrist, "Earn-Out," 52.

60. See esp. the essays by William Cronon, Anne Spirn, Giovanna Di Chiro, and James Proctor.

61. "What Is the Nature Company?"

"Touch the Magic"

1. Special thanks for research assistance to Kay Mary Avila.

2. Descriptions and direct quotations refer to ad copy written by D'Arcy Masius, Benton and Bowles, Inc. USA, and the commercial as aired.

3. Anheuser-Busch owns ten theme parks: Sea Worlds in San Diego, Calif., Aurora, Ohio, San Antonio, Tex., and Orlando, Fla.; Busch Gardens parks in Williamsburg, Va., and Tampa, Fla.; Adventure Island in Tampa; Cypress Gardens in Winter Haven, Fla.; Sesame Place in Langhorne, Penn.; and Water Country USA in Williamsburg, Va. An Anheuser-Busch publicity brochure estimates that "over the past 30 years, more than 160 million people have visited Sea World parks." Anheuser-Busch, public relations brochure on environmental responsibility (untitled), "Item No. 001-584," St. Louis, 1993. The first Sea World was launched in San Diego in the early 1960s by a small group of private investors. Anheuser-Busch purchased the Sea World from the publishing, real estate, and insurance conglomerate Harcourt Brace Jovanovich in 1989.

4. Thirty- and sixty-second versions of "Touch the Magic" ran in major television markets nationally; versions of it also appeared in print and billboard advertising. The accompanying lyrics and music, which provide the verbal and aural "text" of the television commercial, also serve as background music in the theme park and over its internal audio systems.

5. Richard Melcher, "Anheuser-Busch Says *Skoal, Salud, Prosit*," *Business Week*, Sept. 20, 1993, 76–77.

6. I estimate total attendance for all the Busch theme parks as about 18 million visits for 1993. The American Disney parks totaled about 41 million visits in the same year. *Amusement Business Magazine*, Year End Report, chart, Dec. 20, 1993–Jan. 2, 1994, 68–69. The Busch Entertainment Division brought $55 million in profits to the corporation in 1992, up 22 percent from the previous year (but still weaker than in 1990). Melcher, "Anheuser-Busch," 76.

7. Tim O'Brien, "Theme Park Admission Prices Reach Record High," *Amusement Business*, April 18–24, 1994, 1, 35. Adult admission is $34.95.

8. According to their management, Sea World of San Diego earns roughly 50 percent of its profits from admissions and 50 percent from concession sales.

9. Through sponsorship arrangements the Sea World parks reduce their advertising costs; sponsors gain cross-promotion advantages, exclusive merchandising rights (for example, Kodak and Pepsi are "official suppliers"), and association of their name in connection with animals, the environment, and family entertainment. Sponsorship may have been more important when the Sea Worlds were owned by Harcourt Brace Jovanovich, especially as HBJ had to fight off takeover attempts. Anheuser-Busch's pockets are much deeper.

10. This may be especially important in an era of public concern over advertising alcoholic beverages to youth, and over commercial connections between beer, rock music, and sports. Beer companies' extensive sponsorship of rock concerts and band tours has been criticized by health professionals and advocates of drunk-driving prevention. Paul Grein, "Suds 'n' Bucks 'n' Rock 'n' Roll: Beer Companies Rock Sponsorships Stir Controversy," *Los Angeles Times*, Sunday Calendar, July 30, 1989, 8, 85, 86. Budweiser has been the major sponsor for U.S. concerts by Mick Jagger and the Rolling Stones, most recently providing millions of dollars for the 1994 "Voodoo Lounge" tour.

11. This commercial confusion of retail space with public space is increasingly common, as shopping malls, for example, begin to house playgrounds, museums, libraries, city halls, even public schools and community colleges. See Margaret Crawford, "The World in a Mall," in Michael Sorkin, ed. *Variations on a Theme Park: The New American City and the End of Public Space* (New York: Hill and Wang, 1992), 3–30; Leah Brumer, "Discovery Zone" (unpublished paper, summer 1994).

12. This argument is made over and over again throughout the parks and their public relations materials. Anheuser-Busch also emphasizes the parks' membership in the American Association of Zoological Parks and Aquariums. Anheuser-Busch, public relations brochure on environmental responsibility (untitled), "Item no. 001-584," St. Louis, 1993.

13. Busch Entertainment allows cable systems, school districts, and teachers to tape these broadcasts for repeated use; thus their reach is expanded.

14. The maker of many disposable paper and plastic items, Procter & Gamble has been criticized for distributing factually inaccurate and self-serving materials disguised as science study resources. Michael Parrish, "Environmentalists Criticize Firm's Educational Material," *Los Angeles Times*, Dec. 17, 1993, D2.

15. With the recent acquisition of parks chains by Time-Warner (Six Flags parks), MCA (Universal Studios), and Viacom (Paramount Parks), and with the merger of Viacom with Blockbuster, the theme park industry is dominated by mega-media corporations. Most of the large theme parks in the United States are now sites for the integrated marketing of diverse media products, following the Disney model. The five biggest companies in the industry are Disney, Anheuser-Busch, Time-Warner, MCA, and Viacom. Anheuser-Busch uniquely specializes in "nature."

16. Walt Disney pioneered this technique. Richard Schickel, *The Disney Version: The Life, Times, Art and Commerce of Walt Disney,* rev. ed. (New York: Simon and Schuster, Touchstone Books, 1985), 295–338. George Lipsitz, "Discursive Space and Social Space: Television, Highways, and Cognitive Mapping in the 1950s City" (paper presented at the American Studies Association Meeting, Nov. 1989).

17. One such model might be Discovery Channel's "Those Amazing Animals," filmed at another nature theme park, Marine World Africa USA. A feature-length film and an animated television show featuring "Shamu" are reported to be in development. Kim Kowsky, "Busch to Buy Rights to Films about Shamu," *Los Angeles Times* (San Diego County ed.), Jan. 5, 1990, D1.

18. In 1994 Third Story Books published twelve children's books based on the Sea World parks and characters. These were promoted in the Barnes and Noble bookstores, among others. "New Firm to Do Sea World Books," *Publisher's Weekly,* March 14, 1994, 11. LaPorta and Company produces the "Shamu and You" educational video series. "Video Treasures of the Deep and Wild," *Billboard,* Feb. 8, 1992, 47.

19. At the same time, we are always aware of the artifice of Sea World's realism. For example, the blue-painted pool holding Shamu is constructed to appear bottomless. The seeming depth of the pool is a kind of perceptual support system, letting us think the whale has boundless room to move way from us, even while we are aware that it cannot get away.

20. On the history and ideological structure of travel literature, see Mary Louise Pratt, *Imperial Eyes: Travel Writing and Transculturation* (London: Routledge, 1992); on nature, knowledge, and empire, Harriet Ritvo, *The Animal Estate: The English and Other Creatures in the Victorian Age* (Cambridge: Harvard Univ. Press, 1987), 1–44; on *National Geographic,* Herbert I. Schiller, *The Mind Managers* (Boston: Beacon, 1974), 79–103, and Catherine A. Lutz and Jane L. Collins, *Reading National Geographic.* (Chicago: Univ. of Chicago Press, 1993).

21. The public relations department at Sea World was unable to tell me the provenance of the myth referred to in "Shamu New Visions."

22. Anheuser-Busch, untitled public relations brochure, "Item no. 001-584."

23. Between 1983 and 1988, hundreds of eggs were "imported" from Antarctica, incubated, and the hatchlings hand-raised at Sea World of California. At least some of the penguins on display are descendants of these chicks.

24. Sea World's publicity materials and entertainments make much of teaching "naturally antagonistic" species "how to live together," although it's not clear what "naturally antagonistic" means, or that the parks really do this. (For example, killer whales and sea lions do not share tanks in the park.) *Amusement Business,* Jan. 14, 1984. In 1993–94 San Diego's Sea World featured a multispecies whale and dolphin show called "One World."

25. Sea World's exhibits do make use of such references, especially to "Star Trek."

26. Stuart Ewen, *All Consuming Images: The Politics of Style in Contemporary Culture* (New York: Basic Books, 1988). Very little work has been done on nature as an ingredient in contemporary consumer advertising. Judith Williamson's *Decoding Advertisements: Ideology and Meaning in Advertising* (New York: Marion Boyars, 1984) remains helpful.

27. Raymond Williams, "Ideas of Nature," in *Problems in Materialism and Culture* (London: Verso, 1980), 67–85; idem, *The Country and the City* (New York: Oxford Univ. Press, 1980).

28. See, for example, Williams, "Ideas of Nature."

29. Ibid. and Williams, *Country and the City*, 87–107.

30. Jonas Frykman and Orvar Löfgren, *Culture Builders: A Historical Anthropology of Middle-Class Life*, trans. Alan Crozier (New Brunswick: Rutgers Univ. Press, 1987), 42–87.

31. Pratt, *Imperial Eyes*, 15–37; John Michael Kennedy, "Philanthropy and Science in New York City: The American Museum of Natural History, 1868–1968" (Ph.D. diss., Yale Univ., 1968); Donna J. Haraway, *Primate Visions: Gender, Race, and Nature in the World of Modern Science* (New York: Routledge, 1989), 1–58; Peter J. Schmitt, *Back to Nature: The Arcadian Myth in Urban America* (Baltimore: Johns Hopkins Univ. Press, 1990), 77–95.

32. Each of the Sea Worlds commissions extensive market and "psycho-graphic" (lifestyle) research on its customers, interviewing as many as five hundred visitors in person per month and distributing numerous take-home questionnaires to others. In 1992 Sea World of California's interview research showed that only 15 percent of the customers reported family annual income under $30,000. (During this same period median family income in San Diego County was about $35,000.) Some 51 percent of the customers claimed more than $40,000 annual income; 33 percent stated that their family earned more than $50,000. Even allowing for the many problems inherent in self-reporting, this is obviously an affluent audience. Fully 43 percent of those interviewed claimed a college or higher degree, while 22 percent had a high school diploma or less. Market research for the same period reports that 89 percent of the customers interviewed are "Anglo" and 11 percent "non-Anglo" (only these two categories were used). It is unclear whether this identification is based on observation or self-description, whether it refers to color, historical identity, or mother tongue. Nevertheless, the figure is sharply divergent from the general ethnic makeup of the southern California counties. The average audience member was a baby boomer, about thirty-eight years old, and nearly 65 percent of the audience was between the ages of twenty-five and fifty. (In other words, the audience closely resembled the people who wrote this book.)

33. *Amusement Business*, April 4, 1987, 4.

34. Other theme parks in California use dress codes to discourage the presence of "gang members." The content of youth music concerts at theme parks is also carefully vetted.

35. The five counties are Los Angeles, Riverside, Orange, San Bernardino, and San Diego.

36. Frykman and Löfgren, *Culture Builders*, passim; Yi-Fu Tuan, *Dominance and Affection: The Making of Pets* (New Haven: Yale Univ. Press, 1984), esp. 115–31; Schmitt, *Back to Nature*, 77–124.

37. See, for example, Richard Louv, *Childhood's Future* (Boston: Houghton Mifflin, 1990).

38. Frykman and Löfgren, *Culture Builders.* When thinking about what children "need," we should distinguish contact with nature from unstructured play or autonomous activities. There is little unstructured or autonomous about the "nature" children encounter at Sea World.

39. Schmitt, *Back to Nature.*

40. John Berger, "Why Look at Animals?" *On Looking* (New York: Pantheon, 1980), 1–26.

41. The rationale behind the architecture of the new zoo is summarized by Melissa Greene, "No Rms, Jungle View," *Atlantic Monthly,* Dec. 1987, 62–78.

42. The Du Pont television commercial shows marine mammals applauding the chemical manufacturer's environmental record, to the strains of Beethoven's "Ode to Joy." Chip Berlet and William K. Burke, "The Anti-environmental Movement," *Democracy Watch,* July 1992, 3, 11. See also *Hold the Applause* (Washington, D.C.: Friends of the Earth, 1992).

43. Yet nature on TV has received almost no attention from media scholars. For example, while there has been extensive study of network news, soap opera, and crime drama, we have no broad and accurate picture of how much nature TV is broadcast, who produces it, and whom it reaches. Presumably a media genre this prolific has some important effects on how its television audience understands environmental problems and their social and political context.

44. On the general structure and corporate funding of PBS, see William Hoynes, *Public Television for Sale: Media, the Market and the Public Sphere* (Boulder, Colo.: Westview Press, 1994), esp. 89–114. Hoynes notes that "corporations such as BASF, DuPont, W. F. Grace and Waste Management, Inc., sponsor such programs as *Adventure, Discoveries Underwater, Victory Garden* and *Conserving America*" (102–3). For criticism of the "public" nature of public television, see also David Croteau, William Hoynes, and Kevin M. Carragee, "Public Television and the Missing Public: A Study of Sources and Programming," *Extra,* Sept. / Oct. 1993, 6–14; Janine Jackson, "When Is a Commercial Not a Commercial? When It's on Noncommercial TV," ibid., 17–18.

45. For example, Roy Rosenzweig and Elizabeth Blackmar emphasize that the social uses of parks, landscapes, and museums are contested, and shaped by their diverse and often antagonistic users. *The Park and the People: A History of Central Park* (Ithaca: Cornell Univ. Press, 1992).

46. Although institutions such as Chicago's Museum of Science and Industry have a long history of connections to corporate sponsors, the interpenetration of the for-profit and nonprofit spheres has accelerated in the last decade. As zoos and museums have found their public funding and philanthropic support dwindling, they have come to depend heavily on gift shop and souvenir sales, and in this and other ways they have become more like the pay-to-enter, concession-driven theme park. Famous nonprofit science centers, such as San Francisco's Exploratorium, seek development funds through licensing and coproduction agreements with media giants like Time-Warner. For a critique of related developments in the world of art museums, see Debora Silverman, *Selling Culture: Bloomingdale's, Diana Vreeland, and the New Aristocracy of Taste in Reagan's America* (New York: Pantheon, 1986.) A more general and thoroughgoing critique is offered by Herbert I. Schiller, *Culture, Inc.* (New York: Oxford Univ. Press, 1991). On national parks, see Dean MacCannell, "Nature Incorporated," in *Empty Meeting Grounds: The Tourist Papers* (New York: Routledge, 1993), 114–20.

47. Interestingly, Sea World's references to the *Exxon Valdez* oil spill are limited to its display of rehabilitated Alaskan otters. Wildlife biologists, writing in *Science,* have criticized the media focus on otter and bird rescue after the spill. They argue that media coverage of the rehabilitation of a small number of animals has diverted attention from the extent of environmental damage, and from the need for the absolute prevention of oil spills, and given the public a false sense that catastrophic environmental damage can be mitigated. James A. Estes, "Catastrophes and Conservation: Lessons from Sea Otters and the *Exxon Valdez,*" *Science* 254 (1991): 1596.

Ecological Fragmentation in the Fifties

1. Barry Commoner, *Making Peace with the Planet* (New York: Pantheon, 1975).

2. Homer Shantz, "Frederic Edward Clements (1874–1945)," *Ecology* 26 (1945): 317–19. Details of Clements's life can be found in Ronald Tobey, *Saving the Prairies: The Life Cycle of the Founding School of American Plant Ecology, 1895–1955* (Berkeley: Univ. of California Press, 1981).

3. This quotation is from an obituary of Clements: Arthur G. Tansley, "Frederic Edward Clements, 1874–1945," *Journal of Ecology* 34 (1947): 194–96.

4. Daniel Botkin, *Discordant Harmonies: A New Ecology for the Twenty-first Century* (New York: Oxford Univ. Press, 1990), 94; see also Golley, *History of the Ecosystem Concept in Ecology* (New Haven: Yale Univ. Press, 1993), 166, and Robert Whittaker, "Classification of Natural Communities," *Botanical Review* 28 (1962): 1–240. The quotation is from Frederic E. Clements, *Plant Succession: An Analysis of the Development of Vegetation* (Washington, D.C.: Carnegie Institution, 1916), 3–6.

5. Tobey, *Saving the Prairies,* 6 and 79; Thomas Kuhn, *The Structure of Scientific Revolutions* (Chicago: Univ. of Chicago Press, 1962).

6. Gleason's life is recounted in excellent detail by Malcolm Nicolson, "Henry Allan Gleason and the Individualistic Hypothesis: The Structure of a Botanist's Career," *Botanical Review* 56 (1990): 91–161. Early European ecologists with similar ideas include Leonid Ramenski and Joseph Paczoski, whose contributions have been summarized in English by Paul F. Maycock, "Joseph Paczoski, Founder of the Science of Phytosociology," *Ecology* 48 (1967): 1031–34; Robert P. McIntosh, "Excerpts from the Work of L. G. Ramensky," *Bulletin of the Ecological Society of America* 64 (1983): pt. 1, pp. 7–12; T. A. Rabotnov, "Concepts of Ecological Individuality of Plant Species and of the Continuum of Plant Cover in the Works of L. G. Ramensky," *Soviet Journal of Ecology* 9 (1978): 417–22; L. N. Sobolev and V. D. Utekhin,

"Russian (Ramensky) Approaches to Community Systematization," in *Ordination of Plant Communities,* ed. Robert H. Whittaker (The Hague: Junk, 1978), 71–97. In addition, Stan Rowe (J. S. Rowe, "Uses of Undergrowth Plant Species in Forestry," *Ecology* 37 [1956]: 461–73) has pointed out that the European forestry literature between 1928 and 1950 included various classifications of forest types built on the concept of gradients in environmental factors and in plant distribution.

7. Henry Gleason, "Autobiographical Letter," *Bulletin of the Ecological Society of America* 34 (1953): 40–42; see also Robert Burgess, "John Thomas Curtis: Botanist, Ecologist, Conservationist," in *John T. Curtis: Fifty Years of Wisconsin Plant Ecology,* ed. John Fralish, Robert McIntosh, and Orie Loucks (Madison: Wisconsin Academy of Sciences, Arts, and Letters, 1993), 260; details of the 1926 debate are given in Nicolson, "Gleason and the Individualistic Hypothesis," 139–43. We should not lose sight of the fact that Gleason's argument was itself a gradient; that is, it was scale dependent. At a local level Gleason could admit that similar patches of vegetation occurred near each other. "He rested his argument for the individuality of communities by reference to the broad regional scene." J. S. Rowe, "Phytogeographic Zonation: An Ecological Appreciation," in *The Evolution of Canada's Flora,* ed. J. Taylor and D. Ludwig (Toronto: Univ. of Toronto Press, 1966), 16–17.

8. Henry Gleason, "The Structure and Development of the Plant Association," *Bulletin of the Torrey Botanical Club* 44 (1917): 463–81; idem, "The Individualistic Concept of the Plant Association," ibid., 53 (1926): 1–20; idem, "The Individualistic Concept of the Plant Association," *American Midland Naturalist* 21 (1939): 92–110.

9. Frank Egler, "Vegetation Science Concepts—Part I: Initial Floristic Composition, a Factor in Old-Field Development," *Vegetatio* 4 (1954): 412–17.

10. The ecologist Michael Austin, in "Continuum Concept, Ordination Methods, and Niche Theory," *Annual Review of Ecology and Systematics* 16 (1985): 39–61, has correctly pointed out that there are in fact two arguments being confounded here. One posits the individualistic distribution of species—this he calls the individualistic hypothesis. The second posits the continuous change of vegetation along environmental gradients—this he calls the continuum concept. He concludes that the two are not necessarily linked. However, they are so intertwined in the minds of most ecologists that I will continue to use the terms "continuum" and "individualistic" as synonyms in this essay.

11. Robert McIntosh, "H. A. Gleason—Individualistic Ecologist 1882–1975—His Contribution to Ecological Theory," *Bulletin of the Torrey Botanical Club* 102 (1975): 253–73.

12. Whittaker, "Classification of Natural Communities," 82.

13. Gleason, "Autobiographical Letter," 41.

14. Stanley Cain, "Characteristics of Natural Areas and Factors in Their Development," *Ecological Monographs* 17 (1947): 185–200.

15. Telephone interview with Helen Buell, April 27, 1994; see also award citation in Gleason, "Autobiographical Letter," 40–42.

16. Nicolson, "Gleason and the Individualistic Hypothesis," 150.

17. Stanley Cain, "Henry Allan Gleason—Eminent Ecologist," *Bulletin of the Ecological Society of America* 40 (1959): 105–10.

18. Telephone interview with Robert McIntosh, April 25, 1994; see also letter from John Curtis to Robert McIntosh, April 8, 1959, and Robert McIntosh, "The Continuum Continued: John T. Curtis' Influence on Ecology," in *John T. Curtis,* 101.

19. Jonathan Richardson, "The Organismic Community: Resilience of an Embattled Ecological Concept," *BioScience* 30 (1980): 465–71.

20. Full citations of the books are as follows: Anna Bramwell, *Ecology in the Twentieth Century: A History* (New Haven: Yale Univ. Press, 1989); John Fralish, Robert McIntosh, and Orie Loucks, eds., *John T. Curtis: Fifty Years of Wisconsin Plant Ecology* (Madison: Wisconsin Academy of Sciences, Arts, and Letters, 1993); Frank Golley, *A History of the Ecosystem Concept in Ecology* (New Haven: Yale Univ. Press, 1993); Joel Hagen, *An Entangled Bank: The Origins of Ecosystem Ecology* (New Brunswick: Rutgers Univ. Press, 1992); Sharon Kingsland, *Modeling Nature: Episodes in the History of Population Ecology* (Chicago: Univ. of Chicago Press, 1985); Robert McIntosh, *The Background of Ecology: Concept and Theory* (Cambridge: Cambridge Univ. Press, 1985); Gregg Mitman, *The State of Nature: Ecology, Community, and American Social Thought, 1900–1950* (Chicago: Univ. of Chicago Press, 1992); Ronald Tobey, *Saving the Prairies: The Life Cycle of the Founding School of American Plant Ecology, 1895–1955* (Berkeley: Univ. of California Press, 1981); Donald Worster, *Nature's Economy: A History of Ecological Ideas,* 2nd ed. (Cambridge: Cambridge Univ. Press, 1985). Journal articles of particular value are as follows: Robert McIntosh, "Plant Ecology 1947–1972," *Annals of the Missouri Botanical Garden* 61 (1974): 132–87; Robert McIntosh, "H. A. Gleason—Individualistic Ecologist, 1882–1975, His Contribution to Ecological Theory," *Bulletin of the Torrey Botanical Club* 102 (1975): 253–73; idem, "The Background and Some Current Problems of Theoretical Ecology," *Synthese* 43 (1980): 195–255; idem, "Pluralism in Ecology," *Annual Review of Ecology and Systematics* 18 (1987): 321–41; Malcolm Nicolson, "Henry Allan Gleason and the Individualistic Hypothesis: The Structure of a Botanist's Career," *Botanical Review* 56 (1990): 91–161.

21. The Braun-Blanquet school of phytosociology represents the most widely followed approach to vegetation description and classification in the world, except for the English-speaking countries. Its central concept, the plant association, is defined on the basis of species composition, habitat, and community architecture. The degree of interdependence among the associated species is left unexamined, however. Therefore, Braun-Blanquet ecologists have an association-unit concept of vegetation, but do not adopt the organistic extreme of Clements. See Josias Braun-Blanquet, *Plant Sociology: The Study of Plant Communities,* trans. G. D. Fuller and H. S. Conard (New York: McGraw-Hill, 1932).

22. Joseph Grinnell made important contributions to our understanding of animal geography in the southwestern United States. He was a professor of zoology and an important contributor to the Museum of Vertebrate Zoology at the Univ. of California at Berkeley. For an overview of his work, see Alden Miller, ed., *Joseph Grinnell's Philosophy of Nature: Selected Writings of a Western Naturalist* (1943; reprint, Freeport, N.Y.: Books for Libraries, 1968).

23. Robert McIntosh, "H. A. Gleason's 'Individualistic Concept' and Theory of Animal Communities: A Continuing Controversy," *Biological Reviews* (1995, in press). An example of published organismic thought among current animal ecologists is David Wilson and E. Sober, "Reviving the Superorganism," *Journal of Theoretical Ecology* 136 (1989): 337–56.

24. Telephone interview with David Goodall, April 29, 1994.

25. B. M. Mirkin, "Paradigm Change and Vegetation Classification in Soviet Phyto-coenology," *Vegetatio* 68 (1987): 131–38.

26. Hagen, *Entangled Bank*, 47.

27. Cain, "Characteristics of Natural Areas," 196.

28. McIntosh, "Continuum Continued"; Nicolson, "Gleason and the Individualistic Hypothesis"; Tobey, *Saving the Prairies.*

29. Craig Loehle, "Hypothesis Testing in Ecology: Psychological Aspects and the Importance of Theory Maturation," *Quarterly Review of Biology* 62 (1987): 397–409; Gerhard Wiegleb, "Explanation and Prediction in Vegetation Science," *Vegetatio* 83 (1989): 17–34, quotation on 31.

30. Arthur Tansley, "The Use and Abuse of Vegetational Concepts and Terms," *Journal of Ecology* 16 (1935): 284–307.

31. Eugene Odum, *Fundamentals of Ecology* (Philadelphia: W. B. Saunders, 1953). Odum continues to espouse an organismic, Clementsian view of the ecosystem. In "Great Ideas in Ecology for the 1990s," *BioScience* 42 (1992): 542–45, he claims that ecosystems are affected by natural selection and thus are capable of evolution; he also finds merit in the Gaia hypothesis, which holds that the entire biosphere behaves like an organism.

32. Golley, *History of the Ecosystem Concept*, 106, 166.

33. Richardson, "Organismic Community," 468.

34. Hagen, *Entangled Bank*, 32, 48.

35. Botkin, *Discordant Harmonies*, 151.

36. Tobey, *Saving the Prairies;* Hagen, *Entangled Bank;* Worster, *Nature's Economy;* John Phillips, "Succession, Development, the Climax, and the Complex Organism: An Analysis of Concepts, Part 3," *Journal of Ecology* 23 (1935): 488–508.

37. Lester Ward, *Dynamic Sociology, or Applied Social Science*, 2 vols. (1883; reprint, New York: Greenwood Press, 1968), 35

38. J. D. Y. Peel, ed., *Herbert Spencer: On Social Evolution, Selected Writings* (Chicago: Univ. of Chicago Press, 1972). Clements's first published account of the organismic metaphor appears in his *Research Methods in Ecology* (Lincoln: Univ. Publishing Company, 1905), 5.

39. Jan Christiaan Smuts, *Holism and Evolution* (New York: Macmillan, 1926).

40. Bramwell, *Ecology in the Twentieth Century*, 39–50; Golley, *History of the Ecosystem Concept*, 10–29; Hagan, *Entangled Bank*, 9–10.

41. Mitman, *State of Nature*, 81, 87.

42. This section was abstracted largely from the following general reviews and anthologies: James Breslin, "Poetry, 1945 to the Present," in E. Elliott, ed., *Columbia Literary History of the United States* (New York: Columbia Univ. Press, 1988), 1079–1100; Gerald Bruns, "The New Philosophy," ibid., 1045–59; Godfrey Hodgson, *In Our Time: America from World War II to Nixon* (London: Macmillan, 1976); Ronald Schleifer, "Structuralism," in Michael Groden and Martin Kreiswirth, eds., *Johns Hopkins Guide to Literary Theory and Criticism* (Baltimore: Johns Hopkins Univ. Press), 696–701; David Van Leer, "Society and identity," in E. Elliott, ed., *Columbia History of the American Novel* (New York: Columbia Univ. Press, 1991), 485–509. I also want to express appreciation to David Robertson, professor of English at the Univ. of California at Davis, for his analysis of this period of time, and for other ideas contributed by the members of the Reinventing Nature workshop held at the University of California at Irvine during Jan.–June of 1994, esp. William Cronon, convener of that workshop and editor of this volume.

43. Hodgson, *In Our Time.*

44. Ibid.; Van Leer, "Society and Identity."

45. Hodgson, *In Our Time*, 77.

46. Van Leer, "Society and Identity," 487. Existentialism was a credo defined well before the 1950s, by Kierkegaard, Heidegger, and Jean-Paul Sarte, among others.

47. Ibid.; Nina Baym et al., eds., *The Norton Anthology of American Literature*, 3rd ed., vol. 2 (New York: Norton, 1989), 2070.

48. Baym, *Norton Anthology of American Literature*, 2377–78.

49. Bruns, "New Philosophy"; Schleifer, "Structuralism."

50. Robert Burgess, ed., *The Murray Fife Buell Seminar on World Ecologists* (Syracuse: Department of Environmental and Forest Biology, State University of New York, R. L. Burgess, publisher, 1994), 617.

51. McIntosh, "Background and Some Current Problems," 203. In a post-interview letter to me, Dr. McIntosh softened his statement: "In recent years many ecologists appeal to philosophy and some philosophers have things to say about ecology."

52. J. Bastow Wilson, "Does Vegetation Science Exist?" *Journal of Vegetation Science* 2 (1991): 289–90.

53. Paul Keddy, "Do Ecological Communities Exist? A Reply to Bastow Wilson," *Journal of Vegetation Science* 4 (1993): 135–36.

54. Michael W. Palmer and Peter S. White, "On the Existence of Ecological Communities," *Journal of Vegetation Science* 5 (1994): 279–82, quotations on 281 and 279.

Technical American Publications That Supported the Individualistic
Hypothesis 1947–1959
Those written by John Curtis or his students are preceded with an
asterisk. Citations are given in chronological order.

I. Research Papers

W. Dwight Billings, "The Shadscale Vegetation Zone of Nevada and Eastern California in Relation to Climate and Soils," *American Midland Naturalist* 42 (1949):
87–109.

*John Curtis and Robert McIntosh, "An Upland Continuum in the Prairie-Forest
Border Region of Wisconsin," *Ecology* 32 (1951): 476–96.

*Robert Brown and John Curtis, "The Upland Conifer-Hardwood Forests of
Northern Wisconsin," *Ecological Monographs* 22 (1952): 217–34.

Robert Whittaker, "A Study of Summer Foliage Insect Communities in the Great
Smoky Mountains," *Ecological Monographs* 22 (1952): 1–44.

*Margaret Gilbert and John Curtis, "Relation of the Understory to the Upland
Forest in the Prairie-Forest Border Region of Wisconsin," *Transactions of the Wisconsin Academy of Sciences, Arts, and Letters* 42 (1953): 183–95.

*John Curtis, "A Prairie Continuum in Wisconsin," *Ecology* 36 (1955): 558–66.

Robert Whittaker, "Vegetation of the Great Smoky Mountains," *Ecological Monographs* 26 (1956): 1–80.

*J. Roger Bray and John Curtis, "An Ordination of the Upland Forest Communi-
ties of Southern Wisconsin," *Ecological Monographs* 27 (1957): 325–49.

*Delle Swindale and John Curtis, "Phytosociology of the Larger Submerged Plants
in Wisconsin Lakes," *Ecology* 38 (1957): 398–407.

*Earl Christensen, J. Johanna Clausen, and John Curtis, "Phytosociology of the
Lowland Forests of Northern Wisconsin," *American Midland Naturalist* 62 (1959):
232–47.

*John Curtis, *The Vegetation of Wisconsin* (Madison: Univ. of Wisconsin Press,
1959).

II. Review Articles

Robert Whittaker, "A Criticism of the Plant Association and Climatic Climax Concept," *Northwest Science* 25 (1951): 17–31.

Robert Whittaker, "A Consideration of the Climax Theory: Climax as Population
and Pattern," *Ecological Monographs* 23 (1953): 41–78.

David Goodall, "Quantitative Aspects of Plant Distribution," *Biological Review* 27
(1953): 194–205.

Robert Whittaker, "Recent Evolution of Ecological Concepts in Relation to the Eastern Forests of North America," *American Journal of Botany* 44 (1957): 197–206.

Cornelius Muller, "Science and the Philosophy of the Community Concept," *American Scientist* 46 (1958): 294–308.

*Robert McIntosh, "Plant Communities," *Science* 128 (1958): 115–20.

III. Abstracts of Oral Presentations at National Meetings of the Ecological Society of America

*Robert McIntosh and John Curtis, "The Upland Hardwoods Continuum of Southwestern Wisconsin," *Bulletin of the Ecological Society of America* 31, pt. 3 (1950): 56 (hereafter *BESA*).

*John Curtis, "A Wisconsin Prairie Continuum Based upon Presence Data," *BESA* 32, pt. 3 (1951): 56.

*Robert Brown and John Curtis, "A Northern Conifer-Hardwood Forest Continuum," *BESA* 32, pt. 3 (1951): 56–57.

*Margaret Gilbert, "Herb Composition of the Hardwood Forests of Southern Wisconsin," *BESA* 32, pt. 3 (1951): 57.

*Homer Tresner, "Microflora of the Upland Forest Continuum," *BESA* 32, pt. 3 (1951): 57.

*John Curtis, "The Continuum," *BESA* 33, pt. 4 (1952): 81.

Robert Whittaker, "Vegetation of Diorite, Gabbro, and Peridotite in the Siskiyou Mountains of Southwestern Oregon," *BESA* 33, pt. 3 (1952): 54.

Robert Whittaker, "The Climax Pattern Hypothesis," *BESA* 33, pt. 3 (1952): 54.

*M. E. Hale, "Phytosociology of Cryptograms in the Hardwoods of Southern Wisconsin," *BESA* 33, pt. 3 (1952): 59.

*Margaret Gilbert and John Curtis, "The Understory Continuum of the Upland Hardwoods of Southern Wisconsin," *BESA* 33, pt. 3 (1952): 59.

*Robert McIntosh, "A Study of Physical Environment and Forest Succession in the Upland Forest Continuum in the Prairie-Forest Border Region of Wisconsin," *BESA* 33, pt. 3 (1952): 60.

*D. Natelson, "Aquatic Plant Communities in Wisconsin Lakes," *BESA* 35, pt. 3 (1954): 57.

*R. R. Bond, "Ecological Distribution of Breeding Birds in the Upland Forests of Southern Wisconsin," *BESA* 37, pt. 3 (1956): 74.

Appendix: Participants

I interviewed thirty-four individuals who either lived through the 1950s as professional ecologists or who were (1) personally acquainted with influential ecologists of that decade and are themselves ecologists, (2) broadly interested in the history of vegetation science, *or* (3) leaders in a field of ecology that became important following the 1950s.

Some of the most senior interviewees are part of the third generation of American plant ecologists, who began or finished graduate training in the 1930s (Daniel Axelrod, Dwight Billings, Pierre Dansereau, Rexford Daubenmire, Frank Egler, Harold Heady, Cornelius Muller, Eugene Odum, Frank Pitelka, John Reed). Most of the others received their Ph.D.'s in the 1940s and 1950s (Robert Burgess, Herbert Bormann, John Cantlon, Grant Cottam, Frank Golley, Hugh Iltis, Jean Langenheim, Jack Major, Robert McIntosh, Harold Mooney, Jerry Olsen, George Salt, Arnold Schultz). Several others, who completed their training in the 1960s, were interviewed because they represent important modern areas of plant ecology research or because they were close to older ecologists (Jerry Franklin, Peter Marks, Robert Peet, Paul Risser, John Sawyer). Also included are the widows of Murray Buell (Helen Buell) and Robert Whittaker (Linda Olsvig-Whittaker) and five respondents from other countries (David Goodall from Australia, Peter Greig-Smith from Great Britain, Makoto Numata from Japan, and Pierre Dansereau and Stanley Rowe from Canada).

They all were students of, or interacted with, many ecologists who dominated the first half of the this century, men such as Murray Buell, Stanley Cain, Ralph Chaney, Frederic Clements, William Cooper, Henry Cowles, John Curtis, Henry Gleason, Hans Jenny, Herbert Mason, Charles Olmsted, Henry Oosting, Paul Sears, Victor Shelford, Arthur Tansley, Arthur Vestal, and John Weaver.

A number of the interviewees had their education or careers put on hold during the years of World War II, then were part of the dam burst into a golden age of academic growth. They were then founders, participants, or observers of the "new ecologies" that grew up in the 1950s, such as ecosystem ecology, ecophysiology, and population ecology. They were among the first award recipients and proposal evaluators of the National Science Foundation and later of "big science" grants from the International Biological Program. They experienced the rise of environmentalism, spanning the publication of Paul Sears's *Deserts on the March* (1935), Aldo Leopold's *A Sand County Almanac* (1949), and Rachel Carson's *Silent Spring* (1962); the spawning of the Nature Conservancy from their professional organization, the Ecological Society of America; and the creation of early congressional legislation on environmental quality throughout the 1950s.

The questions asked and the roster of interviewees were largely compiled with the assistance of William Cronon, environmental historian at the University of Wisconsin and editor of this volume; Robert McIntosh, emeritus plant ecologist and ecological historian at Notre Dame University; John Cantlon, emeritus plant ecologist and provost at Michigan State University; and Dwight Billings, emeritus plant ecologist at Duke University. The latter two are past presidents of the Ecological Society of America.

I extend my deep gratitude and sincere appreciation to all those who made the considerable effort to participate. Copies of this manuscript were sent to all for review, and seven responded with written critiques, which further improved this essay. I regret any errors of fact or interpretation that might remain.

Participants Interviewed (in Alphabetical Order)

Daniel I. Axelrod	Jack Major
W. Dwight Billings	Peter L. Marks
F. Herbert Bormann	Robert P. McIntosh
Helen F. Buell	Harold A. Mooney
Robert L. Burgess	Cornelius H. Muller
John E. Cantlon	Mokato Numata (by letter)
Grant Cottam	Eugene P. Odum
Pierre Dansereau	Jerry Olsen
Rexford Daubenmire	Linda Olsvig-Whittaker (by letter)
Frank E. Egler	Robert K. Peet
Jerry F. Franklin	Frank A. Pitelka
Frank B. Golley	John F. Reed
David W. Goodall (by letter)	Paul G. Risser
Peter Greig-Smith (by letter)	J. Stan Rowe
Harold F. Heady	George W. Salt
Hugh H. Iltis	John Sawyer
Jean H. Langenheim	Arnold M. Schultz

Non-Respondents

Gene E. Likens	Ralph O. Slatyer
Alton A. Lindsey	Eddy van der Maarel
Howard T. Odum	George M. Woodwell

On the Search for a Root Cause

1. Deborah Blum, "Astronomer Lands in Climate Debate," *Sacramento Bee,* April 10, 1994, sec. A, pp. 1, 26.

2. "Paul Revere of Ecology," *Time,* Feb. 2, 1970, 58.

3. This description of Commoner's work in the early 1950s is based upon documents and letters in Box 2 of the Commoner Papers, Library of Congress, Washington,

D.C. Commoner best describes his work and his suspicions about the connections between free radicals and carcinogenesis in letters to colleagues. See Commoner to Dr. Leslie A. Falk, April 27, 1953, and Commoner to Dr. David Taber, Dec. 2, 1953, ibid.

4. Barry Commoner, "Is Science Getting Out of Hand" (address before the National Science Teachers Association, March 30, 1963), Box 14, Commoner Papers, 2; idem, *Science and Survival* (New York: Viking, 1966).

5. Barry Commoner, Michael Corr, and Paul J. Stamler, "The Causes of Pollution," *Environment* 13 (April 1971): 2.

6. Paul R. Ehrlich, *The Population Bomb* (New York: Ballantine Books, 1968); Garrett Hardin, "The Tragedy of the Commons," *Science* 162 (1968): 1243–48.

7. On Malthus and his influence on Hardin, see Garrett Hardin, ed., *Population, Evolution, and Birth Control: A Collage of Controversial Ideas* (San Francisco: W. H. Freeman, 1969).

8. Fairfield Osborn, *The Limits of the Earth* (Boston: Little, Brown, 1953); William Vogt, *People! Challenge to Survival* (New York: W. Sloane Associates, 1960).

9. "A Clash of Gloomy Prophets," *Time,* Jan. 11, 1971, 56.

10. Commoner et al., "Causes," 4.

11. Ibid., 16.

12. Barry Commoner, *The Closing Circle: Nature, Man, Technology* (New York: Knopf, 1971), 10–16.

13. Ibid., 214, 233, 296–97.

14. Paul R. Ehrlich and John P. Holdren, "Impact of Population Growth," *Science* 171 (1971): 1212; Paul R. Ehrlich and Anne H. Ehrlich, *Population, Resources, Environment: Issues in Human Ecology* (San Francisco: W. H. Freeman, 1972), 266; Paul R. Ehrlich and John P. Holdren, "A Bulletin Dialogue on 'The Closing Circle,' " *Bulletin of the Atomic Scientists* 28 (May 1972): 16–27.

15. Ehrlich and Holdren, "Impact of Population," 1216; Commoner, *Closing Circle*, 11.

16. Ehrlich, *Population Bomb*, 67.

17. Ibid., 29–30.

18. Ibid., 131–39.

19. Ibid., 160–63.

20. Ibid., 166.

21. Commoner, *Closing Circle,* 12–13, 298–99.

22. Arne Naess, "The Shallow and the Deep Long-Range Ecology Movement," *Inquiry* 16 (1973): 95–100.

23. Lewis Herber [Murray Bookchin], "The Problem of Chemicals in Foods," *Contemporary Issues* 3 (June–Aug. 1952): 206–41; idem, *Our Synthetic Environment* (New York: Knopf, 1962).

24. Murray Bookchin, *Toward an Ecological Society* (Montreal: Black Rose Books, 1980), 77–79; idem, "Social Ecology versus Deep Ecology," *Socialist Review* 18 (July–Sept. 1988): 12; idem, *Remaking Society* (Montreal: Black Rose Books, 1989), 15.

25. Bookchin, *Toward an Ecological Society*, 13.

26. Bookchin, "Social Ecology," 12–14.

27. Ibid., 13–18; Bookchin, *Remaking*, 13.

28. George Bradford, *How Deep Is Deep Ecology?* (Ojai, Calif.: Times Change Press, 1989), 10–13.

29. Kirkpatrick Sale, "Deep Ecology and Its Critics," *Nation*, May 14, 1988, 670–75.

30. Warwick Fox, "The Deep Ecology–Ecofeminism Debate and Its Parallels," *Environmental Ethics* 11 (Spring 1989): 15–16.

31. Bill Devall and George Sessions, *Deep Ecology: Living as if Nature Mattered* (Salt Lake City: Gibbs Smith, 1985), 3–8.

32. Ibid., ix.

33. Steve Chase, ed., *Defending the Earth: A Dialogue between Murray Bookchin and Dave Foreman* (Boston: South End Press, 1991), 128–33.

34. Devall and Sessions, *Deep Ecology*, ix.

35. Chase, *Defending*, 117.

36. Joel Kovel, "The Marriage of Radical Ecologies," and George Bradford, "Toward a Deep Social Ecology," in Michael E. Zimmerman et al., eds., *Environmental Philosophy: From Animal Rights to Radical Ecology* (Englewood Cliffs, N.J.: Prentice-Hall, 1993).

37. Carolyn Merchant, *Radical Ecology: The Search for a Livable World* (New York: Routledge, 1992): 239–40.

Whose Nature?

1. All testimony is taken from hearing transcripts. See USDI, "Administrative Record to Proposed Determination of Threatened Status for the Northern Spotted Owl" (Portland, Ore.: U.S. Fish and Wildlife Service, 1990).

2. For book-length summaries of the spotted owl and old-growth debate, see Keith Ervin, *Fragile Majesty: The Battle for North America's Last Great Forest* (Seattle: Mountaineers, 1989); William Dietrich, *The Final Forest: The Battle for the Last Great Trees of the Pacific Northwest* (New York: Simon and Schuster, 1992); David Seideman, *Showdown at Opal Creek* (New York: Carroll and Graf Publishers, 1993); Steven L. Yaffee, *The Wisdom of the Spotted Owl: Policy Lessons for a New Century* (Washington, D.C.: Island Press, 1994).

3. For a recent sampling of perspectives of six selected representatives of the timber industry, environmental groups, and others involved in the ancient forest debate, see

Catherine L. Phillips et al., "Perspectives: Ancient Forests of the Pacific Northwest," *Northwest Environmental Journal* 9 (1993): 5–23. For a recent survey of public opinion on forest management issues, see Bruce Shindler, Peter List, and Brent S. Steel, "Managing Federal Forests: Public Attitudes in Oregon and Nationwide," *Journal of Forestry* 91, no. 7 (1993): 36–42. Other surveys suggest that support for the timber position, while a minority view, is not restricted to rural, timber-dependent areas; see Griggs-Anderson Research, "Forest Product Industry and the Spotted Owl Controversy Statewide Survey II" (survey conducted for *The Oregonian*, 1990); Cambridge Reports/Research International, "Survey Results on Forest Management Policy" (conducted for the Timber Industry Labor Management Committee, 1991); Bennett, Petts, and Associates, "Telephone Survey of Public Opinion in Oregon, Washington, and Northern California" (Portland, Ore.: Bennett, Petts, and Associates, 1993).

4. For a summary of the wise-use movement written by one of its founders, see Ron Arnold, ed., *The Wise Use Agenda* (Bellevue, Wash.: Center for the Defense of Free Enterprise, 1988). Some sense of the influence of the wise-use philosophy on ordinary people involved in timber battles is presented in Ray Raphael, *More Tree Talk: The People, Politics, and Economics of Timber* (Washington, D.C.: Island Press, 1994). For critical context on the movement, see John Echeverria and Raymond B. Eby, eds., *Let the People Judge: Wise Use and the Private Property Rights Movement* (Washington, D.C.: Island Press, 1994), as well as relevant sections in Carl Deal, *The Greenpeace Guide to Anti-Environmental Organizations* (Berkeley, Calif.: Odonian Press, 1993).

5. For one book-level inquiry focusing on ethics and Pacific Northwest forests, see Douglas E. Booth, *Valuing Nature: The Decline and Preservation of Old-Growth Forests* (Lanham, Md.: Rowman and Littlefield, 1994). At a more general level, the question of ethics in forest management has received considerable attention recently. For example, a good deal of discussion arose among the Society of American Foresters over the proposed inclusion of a "land ethic" statement in its professional code; see James E. Coufal, "The Land Ethic Question," *Journal of Forestry* 87, no. 6 (1989): 22–24; Robert T. Perschel, "Pioneering a New Human/Nature Relationship," ibid., 89, no. 4 (1991): 18–28; Holmes Rolston and James Coufal, "A Forest Ethic and Multivalue Forest Management," ibid., 35–40; R. S. Craig, "Land Ethic Canon Proposal: A Report from the Task Force," ibid., 90, no. 8 (1992): 40–41. More recently, the April 1993 edition of the *Journal of Forestry* was devoted primarily to questions of ethics that arise in forestry.

6. Bernard Williams, *Morality: An Introduction to Ethics* (Cambridge: Cambridge Univ. Press, 1972).

7. J. Nicholas Entrikin, *The Betweenness of Place: Towards a Geography of Modernity* (Baltimore: Johns Hopkins Univ. Press, 1991), 5. Robert Sack is another geographer who asserts that moral questions are properly resolved by recourse to the place-specific geographies of daily life; see Robert David Sack, *Place, Modernity, and the Consumer's World: A Relational Framework for Geographical Analysis* (Baltimore: Johns Hopkins Univ. Press, 1992).

8. Cathy Whitlock, "Vegetational and Climatic History of the Pacific Northwest during the Last 20,000 Years: Implications for Understanding Present-Day Biodiversity," *Northwest Environmental Journal* 8 (1992): 5–28.

9. Jerry F. Franklin, "Pacific Northwest Forests," in *North American Terrestrial Vegetation*, ed. Michael G. Barbour and William D. Billings (New York: Cambridge Univ. Press, 1988) 103–30; Thomas A. Spies and Jerry F. Franklin, "Old Growth and Forest Dynamics in the Douglas-Fir Region of Western Oregon and Washington," *Natural Areas Journal* 8, no. 3 (1988): 190–201; Peter D. A. Teensma, John T. Rienstra, and Mark A. Yeiter, *Preliminary Reconstruction and Analysis of Change in Forest Stand Age Classes of the Oregon Coast Range from 1850 to 1940* (Portland, Ore.: Bureau of Land Management Technical Note OR-9, 1991); James K. Agee, *Fire Ecology of Pacific Northwest Forests* (Washington, D.C.: Island Press, 1993).

10. Larry D. Harris, *The Fragmented Forest: Island Biogeography Theory and the Preservation of Biotic Diversity* (Chicago: Univ. of Chicago Press, 1984); Elliot A. Norse, *Ancient Forests of the Pacific Northwest* (Washington, D.C.: Island Press, 1990); Douglas E. Booth, "Estimating Prelogging Old-Growth in the Pacific Northwest," *Journal of Forestry* 89, no. 10 (1991): 25–29; Peter H. Morrison et al., *Ancient Forests of the Pacific Northwest: Analysis and Maps of Twelve National Forests* (Washington, D.C.: Wilderness Society, 1991). The timber industry and its supporters, however, often dispute these figures, arguing that natural dynamics and Native American land use resulted in far less old growth than is generally assumed. See, for instance, the special March–April 1994 issue of *Evergreen Magazine*.

11. For general reviews, see E. Charles Meslow, Chris Maser, and Jared Verner, "Old-Growth Forests as Wildlife Habitat," *Transactions of the 46th North American Wildlife and Natural Resources Conference* (Washington, D.C.: Wildlife Management Institute, 1981) 329–35; Larry D. Harris, Chris Maser, and A. W. McKee, "Patterns of Old-Growth Harvest and Implications for Cascades Wildlife," *Transactions of the 47th North American Wildlife and Natural Resources Conference* (Washington, D.C.: Wildlife Management Institute, 1982) 374–92; Franklin, *Pacific Northwest Forests;* Spies and Franklin, "Old-Growth and Forest Dynamics"; Norse, *Ancient Forests.*

12. For historical background, see William G. Robbins, "The Social Context of Forestry: The Pacific Northwest in the Twentieth Century," *Western Historical Quarterly* 16 (1985): 413–27; Carlos A. Schwantes, *The Pacific Northwest: An Interpretive History* (Lincoln: Univ. of Nebraska Press, 1989); Michael Williams, *Americans and Their Forests: A Historical Geography* (Cambridge: Cambridge Univ. Press, 1989). For an attempt at quantifying Native American uses, see Booth, *Valuing Nature.*

13. Brian Wall, "Log Production in Washington and Oregon: An Historical Perspective" (Pacific Northwest Forest and Range Experimental Station, 1972). A major study for Oregon, for instance, forecast a sharp decline through the remainder of the century because of cutting far in excess of regeneration; see John H. Beuter, K. Norman Johnson, and H. Lynn Scheurmann, *Timber for Oregon's Tomorrow* (Corvallis: Oregon State Univ. Forest Research Laboratory, 1976). For more recent figures suggesting the overcutting of national forests, see Jeffrey T. Olson, *Pacific Northwest Lumber and Wood Products: An Industry in Transition* (Washington, D.C.: Wilderness Society, 1988).

14. USDA, *An Analysis of the Timber Situation in the United States: 1989–2040* (Fort Collins, Colo.: Rocky Mountain Forest and Range Experiment Station, 1990).

15. Meslow, Maser, and Verner, "Old-Growth Forests as Wildlife Habitat."

16. See, for example, John Sessions, *Timber for Oregon's Tomorrow: The 1989 Update* (Corvallis: Oregon State Univ. Forestry Publications Office, 1991).

17. The timber industry position is found in Northwest Forest Resource Council, "Response to the Oregon Delegation Questions: National Forest and Public Land Management Meeting" (unpublished report, 1989). For the latter estimate, see Norse, *Ancient Forests;* Morrison et al., *Ancient Forests.*

18. USDA-USDI, "Forest Ecosystem Management: An Ecological, Economic, and Social Assessment" (Report of the Forest Ecosystem Assessment Team, 1993).

19. J. W. Thomas et al., "Viability Assessments and Management Considerations for Species Associated with Late-Successional and Old-Growth Forests of the Pacific Northwest" (Portland, Ore.: USDA Forest Service, 1993).

20. Booth, *Valuing Nature,* 133.

21. Dietrich, *Final Forest,* 209–11.

22. Olson, *Pacific Northwest Lumber;* Wilderness Society, *End of the Ancient Forests: A Report on National Forest Management Plans in the Pacific Northwest* (Washington, D.C.: Wilderness Society, 1988); Morrison et al., *Ancient Forests.*

23. *Seattle Audubon v. Evans,* 771 F. Supp. 1081 (W.D. Washington 1991).

24. USDI, "Determination of Threatened Status for the Northern Spotted Owl; Final Rule," *Federal Register* 55 (June 26, 1990): 26114–194.

25. USDI, "1990 Status Review: Northern Spotted Owl *(Strix occidentalis caurina)*" (U.S. Fish and Wildlife Service, 1990).

26. USDI, "Determination of Critical Habitat for the Northern Spotted Owl; Final Rule," *Federal Register* 57 (Jan. 15, 1992): 1796–838.

27. USDA-USDI, *Forest Ecosystem Management;* USDA-USDI, *Final Supplemental Environmental Impact Statement on Management of Habitat for Late-Successional and Old-Growth Forest Species within the Range of the Northern Spotted Owl* (Portland, Ore.: U.S. Forest Service and Bureau of Land Management, 1994).

28. Dietrich, *Final Forest,* 77.

29. Some recent accounts have differentiated between the intrinsic value people bestow upon nature and that which exists in nature irrespective of whether people recognize it; yet there is no agreement as to appropriate terms for each. See, for example, Susan J. Armstrong and Richard G. Botzler, eds., *Environmental Ethics: Divergence and Convergence* (New York: McGraw-Hill, 1993), 53; Joseph R. Des Jardins, *Environmental Ethics: An Introduction to Environmental Philosophy* (Belmont, Calif.: Wadsworth, 1993), 144–47.

30. Warwick Fox, *Toward a Transpersonal Ecology: Developing New Foundations for Environmentalism* (Boston: Shambhala, 1990); Max Oelschlaeger, *The Idea of Wilderness from Prehistory to the Age of Ecology* (New Haven: Yale Univ. Press, 1991).

31. René Dubos, *A God Within* (New York: Charles Scribner's Sons, 1972); Bryan G. Norton, "Environmental Ethics and Weak Anthropocentrism," *Environmental*

Ethics 6 (1984): 131–48; Carolyn Merchant, "Environmental Ethics and Political Conflict: A View from California," ibid., 12 (1990): 45–68.

32. For a sample biocentric account, see Paul Taylor, *Respect for Nature: A Theory of Environmental Ethics* (Princeton: Princeton Univ. Press, 1986). For an elaboration of ecocentrism, see J. Baird Callicott, *In Defense of the Land Ethic: Essays in Environmental Philosophy* (Albany: State Univ. of New York Press, 1989).

33. Support for nonanthropocentric ethics can be found in, for example, Aldo Leopold, *A Sand County Almanac* (London: Oxford Univ. Press, 1949); Arne Naess, "The Shallow and the Deep, Long-Range Ecology Movement," *Inquiry* 16 (1973): 95–100; Bill Devall and George Sessions, *Deep Ecology: Living as if Nature Mattered* (Salt Lake City: Gibbs Smith, 1985); Robin Attfield, *A Theory of Value and Obligation* (London: Croom Helm, 1987); Holmes Rolston, *Environmental Ethics: Duties to and Values in the Natural World* (Philadelphia: Temple Univ. Press, 1988); Lawrence E. Johnson, *A Morally Deep World: An Essay on Moral Significance and Environmental Ethics* (Cambridge: Cambridge Univ. Press, 1991). One application to forestry is found in Rolston and Coufal, "Forest Ethic." Others, however, are far less certain that nonanthropocentric ethics are necessary or possible; examples include John Passmore, *Man's Responsibility for Nature: Ecological Problems and Western Traditions* (New York: Charles Scribner's Sons, 1974); Kristin Schrader-Frechette, *Environmental Ethics* (Pacific Grove, Calif.: Boxwood Press, 1981); Bryan G. Norton, *Why Preserve Natural Variety?* (Princeton: Princeton Univ. Press, 1987); Eugene C. Hargrove, *Foundations of Environmental Ethics* (Englewood Cliffs, N.J.: Prentice-Hall, 1989).

34. David Ehrenfeld, "The Conservation of Non-Resources," *American Scientist* 64 (1976): 648–56.

35. Leopold, *Sand County Almanac,* 204.

36. Two other essays in this volume offer critical elaboration of some of these key ideas. On the relationship between the notion of stability in nature and the Clementsian paradigm of climax vegetative communities, see the essay by Michael Barbour. On the historically significant connection between virgin forests and the virgin woman, see Carolyn Merchant's essay.

37. For a history of the transformation of American forests, see Williams, *Americans and Their Forests.*

38. For a fuller discussion, see Cronon's essay.

39. Yi-Fu Tuan has demonstrated how absolutely fundamental the sense of the aesthetic is to the relation between nature and culture; see *Morality and Imagination: Paradoxes of Progress* (Madison: University of Wis. Press, 1989), and *Passing Strange and Wonderful: Aesthetics, Nature, and Culture* (Washington, D.C.: Island Press, 1993).

40. Michael Pollan, *Second Nature: A Gardener's Education* (New York: Atlantic Monthly Press, 1991).

41. Ibid., 177.

42. Ibid., 188.

43. Ibid., 189.

44. At any rate, the idea of wilderness and the possibility of fuller metaphors of nature has been carefully explored elsewhere; see, for instance, Oelschlaeger, *Idea of Wilderness;* David B. Rothenberg, ed., *Wild Ideas* (Minneapolis: Univ. of Minnesota Press, 1995).

45. Barbara Deutsch Lynch, "The Garden and the Sea: U.S. Latino Environmental Discourses and Mainstream Environmentalism," *Social Problems* 40 (1993): 108–24.

46. Ibid., 109.

47. The diversity of cultural practices and perspectives related to the environment is a major theme in Giovanna Di Chiro's essay on environmental justice in this volume.

48. For a fuller discussion of the implications of knowing nature through labor, see Richard White's essay in this volume.

49. Gordon H. Orians and Jerry F. Franklin, " 'New Forestry' and the Old-Growth Forests of Northwestern North America: A Conversation with Jerry Franklin," *Northwest Environmental Journal* 6 (1990): 445–61. For further discussion of New Forestry, see Jerry F. Franklin, "Scientific Basis for New Perspectives in Forests and Streams," in *Watershed Management: Balancing Sustainability and Environmental Change,* ed. Robert J. Naiman (New York: Springer-Verlag, 1992), 25–72; F. J. Swanson and Jerry F. Franklin, "New Forestry Principles from Ecosystem Analysis of Pacific Northwest Forests," *Ecological Applications* 2 (1992): 262–74; D. S. Debell and R. O. Curtis, "Silviculture and New Forestry in the Pacific Northwest," *Journal of Forestry* 91, no. 12 (1993): 25–30; Jerry F. Franklin, "Lessons from Old-Growth: Fueling Controversy and Providing Direction," ibid., 10–13.

50. Orians and Franklin, " 'New Forestry' "; J. N. Long and S. D. Roberts, "Growth and Yield Implications of a 'New Forests' Silvicultural System," *Western Journal of Applied Forestry* 7 (1992): 6–9; William C. McComb, Thomas A. Spies, and William H. Emmingham, "Douglas-Fir Forests: Managing for Timber and Mature-Forest Habitat," *Journal of Forestry* 91, no. 12 (1993): 31–42.

51. USDA-USDI, *Forest Ecosystem Management*, VI-5.

52. A good sample of their divergent opinions is found in the April 1994 edition of the *Journal of Forestry,* devoted exclusively to Option 9 and its alternatives.

53. Roderick Nash has drawn a strong association between abolitionism and environmental ethics; see *The Rights of Nature: A History of Environmental Ethics* (Madison: Univ. of Wisconsin Press, 1989).

54. For instance, G. E. Moore's well-known "naturalistic fallacy" discounts the possibility of analyzing moral judgments in terms of their factual basis; see G. E. Moore, *Principia Ethica* (New York: Cambridge Univ. Press, 1903). A discussion of Moore's position is provided by Geoffrey Sayre-McCord, "Introduction: The Many Moral Realisms," in *Essays on Moral Realism,* ed. Geoffrey Sayre-McCord. (Ithaca: Cornell Univ. Press, 1988).

55. For more discussion on relativism, see Steven Lukes, "Relativism: Cognitive and Moral," *Essays in Social Theory* (New York: Columbia Univ. Press, 1977); Robert L. Arrington, *Rationalism, Realism, and Relativism* (Ithaca: Cornell Univ. Press,

1989); Michael Krausz, ed., *Relativism* (Notre Dame: Univ. of Notre Dame Press, 1989). For an interesting discussion from a contemporary pragmatist position, see Jeffrey Stout, *Ethics after Babel: The Languages of Morals and Their Discontents* (Boston: Beacon, 1988).

56. In environmental ethics, moral pluralism more properly refers to the assertion that multiple moral principles must necessarily be invoked to inform humankind's conduct affecting other humans, species, ecosystems, etc. See Christopher Stone, *Earth and Other Ethics: The Case for Moral Pluralism* (New York: Harper and Row, 1987); J. Baird Callicott, "The Case against Moral Pluralism," *Environmental Ethics* 12 (1990): 99–124; James C. Anderson, "Moral Planes and Intrinsic Values," ibid., 13 (1991): 49–58; Gary E. Varner, "No Holism without Pluralism," ibid., 175–79; Peter S. Wenz, "Minimal, Moderate, and Extreme Moral Pluralism," ibid., 15 (1993): 61–74. Here I extend this usage to embrace multiple subjects as well as objects. For a fuller theoretical discussion of the realist position in social theory and moral philosophy, see Sabina Lovibond, *Realism and Imagination in Ethics* (Oxford: Basil Blackwell, 1983); Sean Sayers, *Reality and Reason: Dialectic and the Theory of Knowledge* (Oxford: Basil Blackwell, 1985); Sayre-McCord, ed., *Essays on Moral Realism;* Roy Bhaskar, *Reclaiming Reality* (London: Verso, 1989); David O. Brink, *Moral Realism and the Foundations of Ethics* (Cambridge: Cambridge Univ. Press, 1989).

57. For general discussions of this point, see Daniel B. Botkin, *Discordant Harmonies: A New Ecology for the Twenty-first Century* (New York: Oxford Univ. Press, 1990); Stuart L. Pimm, *The Balance of Nature? Ecological Issues in the Conservation of Species and Communities* (Chicago: Univ. of Chicago Press, 1991).

58. J. W. Thomas et al., *A Conservation Strategy for the Northern Spotted Owl* (Portland, Ore.: Interagency Committee to Address the Conservation of the Northern Spotted Owl, 1990); USDI, "1990 Status Review"; Jonathan Bart and Eric D. Forsman, "Dependence of Northern Spotted Owl *Strix occidentalis caurina* on Old-Growth Forests in the Western USA," *Biological Conservation* 62 (1992): 95–100; J. A. Blakesley, A. B. Franklin, and R. J. Gutierrez, "Spotted Owl Roost and Nest Site Selection in Northwestern California," *Journal of Wildlife Management* 56 (1992): 388–92; Roland H. Lamberson et al., "A Dynamic Analysis of Northern Spotted Owl Viability in a Fragmented Forest Landscape," *Conservation Biology* 6 (1992): 505–12; USDI, "Draft Recovery Plan for the Northern Spotted Owl" (USDI Fish and Wildlife Service Spotted Owl Recovery Team, 1992); Susan Harrison, Andy Stahl, and Daniel Doak, "Spatial Models and Spotted Owls: Exploring Some Biological Issues behind Recent Events," *Conservation Biology* 7 (1993): 950–53; Thomas et al., "Viability Assessments."

59. The forest statistics I use here are taken from USDA, *Analysis of the Timber Situation.*

60. See, for instance, Anthony Weston, "Beyond Intrinsic Value: Pragmatism in Environmental Ethics," *Environmental Ethics* 7 (1985): 321–39; Reiner Grundmann, "The Ecological Challenge to Marxism," *New Left Review* 187 (1991): 103–19; Janna Thompson, "A Refutation of Environmental Ethics," *Environmental Ethics* 12 (1991): 147–60.

61. Pollan, *Second Nature,* 191.

62. Ibid., 192.

63. Ibid., 192–93.

64. Fox, *Transpersonal Ecology;* Val Plumwood, "Ethics and Instrumentalism: A Response to Janna Thompson," *Environmental Ethics* 13 (1991): 139–49.

65. For some discussion of the virtue approach to environmental ethics, see Geoffrey B. Frasz, "Environmental Virtue Ethics: A New Direction for Environmental Ethics," *Environmental Ethics* 15 (1993): 259–74.

66. Williams, *Americans and Their Forests;* William G. Robbins, *Lumberjacks and Legislators: Political Economy of the U.S. Lumber Industry, 1890–1941* (College Station: Texas A&M Univ. Press, 1982); John Bellamy Foster, "Capitalism and the Ancient Forest," *Monthly Review* 43, no. 5 (1991): 1–16.

67. USDA, *Analysis of the Timber Situation.*

68. See, for instance, John M. Perez-Garcia, "Global Forestry Impacts of Reducing Softwood Supplies from North America" (Center for International Trade in Wood Products, 1993); Roger A. Sedjo, "Global Consequences of U.S. Environmental Policies," *Journal of Forestry* 91, no. 4 (1993): 19–21.

69. For some background on human impacts on anadromous fish runs in the region, see Christopher A. Frissell, "Topology of Extinction and Endangerment of Native Fishes in the Pacific Northwest and California (U.S.A.)," *Conservation Biology* 7 (1993): 342–54.

70. Timothy O'Riordan, *Environmentalism* (London: Pion, 1981), ix; Robin Grove-White, "Environmentalism: A New Moral Discourse for Technological Society?" in *Environmentalism: The View from Anthropology,* ed. Kay Milton (London: Routledge, 1993), 18–30.

71. Zygmunt Bauman, *Postmodern Ethics* (Oxford: Blackwell, 1994), 245.

Nature as Community

1. These are stereotypes of low-income communities that have been "scientifically" established by research and consulting firms, such as the Los Angeles–based Cerrell Associates, Inc., in its document "Political Difficulties Facing Waste-to-Energy Conversion Plant Siting" (320 North Larchmont Blvd., Los Angeles, CA 90004, California Waste Management Board, 1984). This research provides corporations with information about the level of resistance they can expect from local residents to the proposed siting of a hazardous facility.

2. Eventually, environmental and social justice organizations such as Greenpeace, the National Health Law Program, the Center for Law in the Public Interest, and Citizens for a Better Environment would join Concerned Citizen's campaign to stop LANCER.

3. The phenomenon of the predominance of women, specifically "marginalized" women, in environmental justice organizations has been documented by various sources. See, for example, Celene Krauss, "Women of Color on the Front Line," in

Unequal Protection: Environmental Justice and Communities of Color, ed. Robert Bullard (San Francisco: Sierra Club Books, 1994), 256–71; Lin Nelson, "The Place of Women in Polluted Places," in *Reweaving the World: The Emergence of Ecofeminism,* ed. Irene Diamond and Gloria Orenstein (San Francisco: Sierra Club Books, 1989), 173–88; Jane Kay, "Women in the Movement," *Race, Poverty and the Environment* 1, no. 4 (Winter 1991): Barbara Ruben, "Leading Indicators: Women Speak Out on the Challenges of National Grassroots Leadership," *Environmental Action* 24, no. 2 (Summer 1992): 23–25; Anne Witte Garland, *Women Activists: Challenging the Abuse of Power* (New York: Feminist Press, 1988).

4. I am using the term "mainstream" in the sense of the commonly understood meanings and social organizations that constitute environmentalism in the United States. This would include ideas that embrace nature as a threatened wilderness separate from polluted, overpopulated cities and the preservation of wild animal species and the nonhuman world in general. "Mainstream" also refers to organizations that invoke a historical legacy that includes the writings and philosophies of figures like John Muir, Aldo Leopold, and Gifford Pinchot. Such organizations include the Sierra Club, the National Wildlife Federation, and the Nature Conservancy.

5. See Robert Gottlieb and Helen Ingram, "The New Environmentalists," *Progressive,* Aug. 1988, 14–15.

6. Discourses of environmental preservation, protection, and the conservation of the "aesthetics of nature" dominate the environmentalism of mainstream groups, especially the "Group of Ten," also called the "Big Ten," including Friends of the Earth, the Wilderness Society, the Sierra Club, the National Audubon Society, the Environmental Defense Fund, the Natural Resources Defense Council, the National Wildlife Federation, the Izaak Walton League, the National Parks and Conservation Association, and the Nature Conservancy.

7. In recent years and in response to the exhortations of many people of color organizations in the United States, the importance of addressing the complexities of "urban environments" and "urban ecologies" has appeared in some mainstream environmental discourse. Organizations such as Greenpeace, the Sierra Club, and the Earth Island Institute's Urban Habitat Program have begun to link inner-city needs with environmental concerns. These projects construct the awareness of urban areas as "multicultural ecosystems" that require specific environmental knowledge to ensure sustainable and socially and ecologically sound development. See, for example, Richard Stren, Rodney White, and Joseph Whitney, eds., *Sustainable Cities: Urbanization and the Environment in International Perspective* (Boulder, Colo.: Westview Press, 1991); Rutherford Platt, Rowan Rowntree, and Pamela Mvick, eds., *The Ecological City: Preserving and Restoring Urban Biodiversity* (Amherst: Univ. of Massachusetts Press, 1994). In addition, some environmental historians have expanded their objects of scholarly attention to include cities and metropolitan areas as rightfully "environmental." A good example is William Cronon's *Nature's Metropolis: Chicago and the Great West* (New York: Norton, 1991).

8. Author's interview with Pam Tau Lee at the University of California's Labor and Occupational Health Program, Berkeley, Calif., Jan. 25, 1993.

9. Robert Bullard and Beverly Wright, "Environmentalism and the Politics of Equity," *Mid-America Review of Sociology* 12 (Winter 1987): 21–37; Robert Bul-

lard, *Dumping in Dixie: Race, Class, and Environmental Quality* (Boulder, Colo.: Westview Press, 1990); R. F. Anderson and M. R. Greening, "Hazardous Waste Facility Siting: A Role of Planners," *Journal of the American Planning Association* 48 (Spring 1982): 204–18; U.S. General Accounting Office, *Siting of Hazardous Waste Landfills and Their Correlation with Racial and Economic Status of Surrounding Communities* (Washington, D.C.: General Accounting Office, 1983); Sue Pollack and Joann Grozuczak, *Reagan, Toxics and Minorities* (Washington, D.C.: Urban Environment Conference, 1984).

10. Author's interview with Dana Alston at the Public Welfare Foundation, Washington, D.C., Dec. 22, 1992.

11. For example, see Devon Pena, "The 'Brown' and the 'Green': Chicanos and Environmental Politics in the Upper Rio Grande," *Capitalism, Nature and Socialism* 3, no. 1 (1992): 1–25; Bullard, *Dumping in Dixie;* Laura Pulido, "Latino Environmental Struggles in the Southwest" (Ph.D. diss., UCLA, 1991); Ward Churchill, *Struggle for the Land* (Monroe, Maine: Common Courage, 1993).

12. For example, see Robert Bullard, *Confronting Environmental Racism: Voices from the Grassroots* (Boston: South End Press, 1993).

13. Lois Gibbs, *Love Canal: My Story* (Albany: State Univ. of New York Press, 1982).

14. Commission for Racial Justice, *Toxic Waste and Race in the United States: A National Report on the Racial and Socioeconomic Characteristics of Communities with Hazardous Waste Sites* (New York: United Church of Christ, 1987).

15. Karl Grossman, "From Toxic Racism to Environmental Justice," *E Magazine*, May–June 1992, 31.

16. See above, n. 6.

17. Richard Moore, "Confronting Environmental Racism," *Crossroads/Forward Motion* 11, no. 2 (April 1992): 7.

18. Ibid., 8.

19. Dana Alston, ed., *We Speak for Ourselves: Social Justice, Race and Environment* (Washington, D.C.: Panos Institute, 1990).

20. Moore, "Confronting Environmental Racism," 8.

21. Alston interview, 1992.

22. Studies of Western colonialism and its discourse on nature can be found in Donna Haraway, *Primate Visions: Gender, Race, and Nature in the World of Modern Science* (New York: Routledge, 1989); Stephen J. Gould, *The Mismeasure of Man* (New York: Norton, 1981); Carolyn Merchant, *The Death of Nature: Women, Ecology, and the Scientific Revolution* (San Francisco: Harper and Row, 1980); idem, *Ecological Revolutions: Nature, Gender, and Science in New England* (Chapel Hill: Univ. of North Carolina Press, 1989).

23. Paul Ruffins, "Defining a Movement and a Community," *Crossroads/Forward Motion* 11, no. 2 (April 1992): 11.

24. Carl Anthony, "Ecopsychology and the Deconstruction of Whiteness," in *Ecopsychology* (San Francisco: Sierra Club Books, forthcoming).

25. Charles Lee, "From Los Angeles, East St. Louis and Matamoros: Developing Working Definitions of Urban Environmental Justice," *Earth Island Journal* 8, n. 4 (1993): 41.

26. Michael Edelstein, *Contaminated Communities* (Boulder, Colo.: Westview Press, 1988); Richard Hofrichter, ed., *Toxic Struggles: The Theory and Practice of Environmental Justice* (Philadelphia: New Society Publishers, 1993); Bullard, *Unequal Protection;* Andrew Szasz, *Ecopopulism: Toxic Waste and the Movement for Environmental Justice* (Minneapolis: Univ. of Minnesota Press, 1994).

27. See Churchill, *Struggle for the Land.*

28. For detailed accounts of these conditions, see Phil Brown and Edwin J. Mikkelsen, *No Safe Place: Toxic Waste, Leukemia, and Community Action* (Berkeley: Univ. of California Press, 1990); Penny Newman, ed., *Communities at Risk: Contaminated Communities Speak Out on Superfund* (Riverside: Center for Community Action and Environmental Justice, 1994).

29. Lee, "From Los Angeles"; Robert Gottlieb, *Forcing the Spring: The Transformation of the American Environmental Movement* (Washington, D.C.: Island Press, 1993).

30. Michael Pollan, *Second Nature: A Gardener's Education* (New York: Atlantic Monthly Press, 1991), 188.

31. See Lee, "From Los Angeles"; Bullard, *Unequal Protection.*

32. Carl Anthony, "Why African Americans Should Be Environmentalists," *Earth Island Journal* 5 (Winter 1990): 43–44.

33. See James Proctor's essay in this book for a discussion of the disputes between community people, who make their living working in the timber industry in the Pacific Northwest, and environmentalists, interested in saving the ancient forests, as an illustration of very different perceptions of the significance of the idea of endangered species.

34. Steven Feld, "Voices of the Rainforest," *Public Culture* 4, no. 1 (1991): 139.

35. Robert Gottlieb, "Reconstructing Environmentalism: Complex Movements, Diverse Roots," *Environmental History Review* 17 (Summer 1993): 1–19.

36. A notion of community that focuses exclusively on "unity in sameness" is conservative, according to some analysts, because of its nativist or nationalist overtones. In other words, community as "sameness" seeks to repress or eliminate the threat of difference, to resist change, and to shore up the existing power and authority structure. Raymond Plant argues that this notion of community likens itself to an "organic unity within which each individual has an allotted place and a part to play." Plant, "Community: Concept, Conception and Ideology," *Politics and Society* 8 (1978): 95.

37. For a more detailed discussion of ideas of community in U.S. culture, see Robert Booth Fowler, *The Dance with Community: The Contemporary Debate in Ameri-*

can Political Thought (Lawrence: Univ. Press of Kansas, 1991); Benedict Anderson, *Imagined Communities: Reflections on the Origins and Spread of Nationalism* (New York: Verso, 1983); David M. Hummon, *Commonplaces: Community Ideology and Identity in American Culture* (Albany: State Univ. of New York Press, 1990).

38. Laurie Anne Whitt and Jennifer Daryl Slack, "Communities, Environments and Cultural Studies," *Cultural Studies* 8 (Jan. 1994): 21.

39. Ibid., 21.

40. Ibid., 22.

41. Cited in Cynthia Hamilton, "Concerned Citizens of South Central Los Angeles," in Bullard, *Unequal Protection,* 213.

42. Barbara Deutsch Lynch, "The Garden and the Sea: U.S. Latino Environmental Discourses and Mainstream Environmentalism," *Social Problems* 40 (1993): 108–24.

43. Ibid., 109.

Universal Donors in a Vampire Culture

1. Carl Sandburg, "Prologue," in Edward Steichen, *The Family of Man* (New York: Maco Magazine Corporation for the Museum of Modern Art, 1955).

2. Race, nature, gender, sex, and kinship must be thought together. Starting points for grasping U.S. kinship discourse include David M. Schneider, *American Kinship: A Cultural Account* (Englewood Cliffs, N.J.: Prentice-Hall, 1968); idem, *A Critique of the Study of Kinship* (Ann Arbor: Univ. of Michigan Press, 1984); Carol Stack, *All Our Kin: Strategies for Surviving in a Black Community* (New York: Harper and Row, 1974); Hortense Spillers, "Mama's Baby, Papa's Maybe: An American Grammar Book," *Diacritics* 17, no. 2 (1987): 65–81; Jane F. Collier and Sylvia Junko Yanagisako, eds., *Gender and Kinship: Essays toward a Unified Analysis* (Stanford: Stanford Univ. Press, 1987); Carol Delaney and Sylvia Yanagisako, eds., *The Naturalization of Power Relations* (forthcoming); Richard Griswold del Castillo, *La Familia: Chicano Families in the Urban Southwest, 1848 to the Present* (Notre Dame: Univ. of Notre Dame Press, 1984); Maxine Baca Zinn, "Marital Roles, Marital Power and Ethnicity: A Study of Changing Chicano Familes," (Ph.D. diss., University of California at Berkeley, 1978).

3. George Stocking, Jr., "The Turn-of-the-Century Concept of Race," *Modernism/Modernity* 1 (1993): 4–16, quotation on 6. See also idem, *Race, Culture and Evolution: Essays in the History of Anthropology* (New York: Free Press, 1968); Nancy Stepan, *The Idea of Race in Science: Great Britain, 1800–1960* (Hamden, Conn.: Archon Books, 1982); Elazar Barkan, *The Retreat from Scientific Racism: Changing Concepts of Race in Britain and the United States between the World Wars* (New York: Cambridge Univ. Press, 1992); Sandra Harding, ed., *The "Racial" Economy of Science* (Bloomington: Indiana Univ. Press, 1993); Stephen J. Gould, *The Mismeasure of Man* (New York: Norton, 1981); David Theo Goldberg, ed., *Anatomy of Racism* (Minneapolis: Univ. of Minnesota Press, 1990).

4. Eugenics is race-hygiene or race-improvement discourse. For the history of eugenics, the classics include Mark Haller, *Eugenics: Hereditarian Attitudes in*

American Thought (New Brunswick: Rutgers Univ. Press, 1963); Daniel J. Kevles, *In the Name of Eugenics: Genetics and the Uses of Human Heredity* (New York: Knopf, 1985); Stephan L. Chorover, *From Genesis to Genocide: The Meaning of Human Nature and the Power of Behavior Control* (Cambridge: MIT Press, 1979); Hamilton Cravens, *The Triumph of Evolution: American Scientists and the Hered-ity-Environment Controversy, 1900–1941* (Philadelphia: Univ. of Pennsylvania Press, 1978). The development of Mendelian genetics after 1900, in the context of the dominant interpretation of the writing of the late-nineteenth-century German biologist August Weismann, which separated the passage of acquired characteristics from the genetic continuity of the germinal plasm, gradually eroded much of the racial and eugenic discourse I am discussing here. But many U.S. life scientists did not consistently rely on that distinction in their approach to evolution and race until near midcentury, and they certainly did not use Mendelian genetics to develop an antiracist scientific position. If they did insist on the separation of nature and culture, the effect was likely to harden into a genetic, trait-based eugenic doctrine even less open to "liberal," environmentalist contestation.

5. Nancy Leys Stepan and Sander L. Gilman, "Appropriating the Idioms of Science: The Rejections of Scientific Racism," in Harding, *"Racial" Economy of Science,* 170–93. For African American women's configurations of racial discourse, including sci-entific doctrines, in the late nineteenth and early twentieth centuries, see Hazel V. Carby, *Reconstructuring Womanhood: The Emergence of the Afro-American Woman Novelist* (New York: Oxford Univ. Press, 1987).

6. Charlotte Perkins Gilmann, *Herland* (serialized in the *Forerunner*, 1915; London: Women's Press, 1979), is full of the unself-critical white racialism that wounded so much of American feminism. Madison Grant, *The Passing of the Great Race; or, The Racial Basis of European History* (New York, 1916), is replete with unadulter-ated Nordic superiority and condemnation of race crossing. A corporation lawyer, Grant was a leader in eugenics, immigration restriction, and nature conservation politics—all preservationist, nativist, white-supremacist activities. See Donna J. Haraway, "Teddy Bear Patriachy," in *Primate Visions: Gender, Race, and Nature in the World of Modern Science* (New York: Routledge, 1989), 57.

7. W. E. B. Du Bois, *The Souls of Black Folks* (1903) (New York: Bantam, 1989), 8.

8. W. E. B. Du Bois, "The Conservation of Races," in Andrew G. Pashal, ed., *A W. E. B. Du Bois Reader* (New York: Macmillan, 1971), 19–31; Anthony Appiah, "The Uncompleted Argument: Du Bois and the Illusion of Race," *Critical Inquiry* 12 (Autumn 1985): 21–35; Kwame Anthony Appiah, "Racisms," in Goldberg, ed., *Anatomy of Racism,* 3–17, 16 n. 3; Stepan and Gilman, "Appropriating the Idioms of Science," n. 37.

9. Stocking, "Turn-of-the-Century Concept of Race," 7–8.

10. The full story of the Akeley African Hall is told in Haraway, *Primate Visions,* 26–58, 385–88.

11. For an overview of these complex developments, see Ernst Mayr and William B. Provine, *The Evolutionary Synthesis: Perspectives on the Unification of Biology* (Cambridge: Harvard Univ. Press, 1980); Howard L. Kaye, *The Social Meaning of Biology: From Darwinism to Sociobiology* (New Haven: Yale Univ. Press, 1986);

G. G. Simpson, *The Meaning of Evolution* (1949), rev. ed. (New Haven: Yale Univ. Press, 1967); Theodosius Dobzhansky, *Mankind Evolving: The Evolution of the Human Species* (New Haven: Yale Univ. Press, 1962); Evelyn Fox Keller, *Secrets of Life, Secrets of Death* (New York: Routledge, 1992).

12. UNESCO, *The Race Concept: Results of an Inquiry* (Paris: UNESCO, 1952).

13. The African American physical anthropologist at Howard University, Ashley Montagu Cobb, one of the very few doctoral black experts in the field, was not asked to sign the document. In the context of constitutively self-invisible, international, white scientific hegemony, his signature seemed to imply racial favoritism, not universalist, culture-free, scientific authority. In a spirit of peace, I won't even mention the gendering of the new plastic universal man—until he starts hunting in a species-making adaptation that will defeat my present restraint.

14. This account is an illustrative caricature of much more contradictory processes and practices within which the UNESCO documents lived. For a fuller but still inadequate account, see Haraway, *Primate Visions*, 197–203. The cartoon version of the sharing way of life in the following section of this essay is argued in detail ibid., 186–230, 405–8.

15. The infamous gem of Man the Hunter theorizing was S. L. Washburn and C. S. Lancaster, "The Evolution of Hunting," in Richard Lee and Irven DeVore, eds., *Man the Hunter* (Chicago: Aldine, 1968), 293–303. Woman the Gatherer made her debut in Sally Linton, "Woman the Gatherer: Male Bias in Anthropology," in Sue-Ellen Jacobs, ed., *Women in Perspective: A Guide for Cross-Cultural Studies* (Urbana: Univ. of Illinois Press, 1971), 9–21. She was fleshed out in Nancy Tanner and Adrienne Zihlman, "Women in Evolution, Part I: Innovation and Selection in Human Origins," *Signs* 1 (1976): 585–608.

16. If one is weary with narrative drama and its unmarked psychoanalytic, political, and scientific universalist plots, feminist theory is the place to turn. See Teresa de Lauretis, *Alice Doesn't: Feminism, Semiotics, Cinema* (Bloomington: Indiana Univ. Press, 1982), 103–57; Ursula LeGuin, "The Carrier-Bag Theory of Fiction," in Denise DuPont, ed., *Women of Vision* (New York: St. Martin's Press, 1988), 1–12; Elaine H. Kim and Norma Alarcón, eds., *Writing Self Writing Nation: Essays on Teresa Hak Kyung Cha's Dictée* (Berkeley, Calif.: Third Woman Press, 1994); Chéla Sandoval, "U.S. Third World Feminism: The Theory and Method of Oppositional Consciousness in the Postmodern World," *Genders* 10 (1991): 1–24; Victoria Smith, "Loss and Narration in Modern Women's Fiction" Ph.D. diss., Univ. of California at Santa Cruz, 1994).

17. *Science* 254 (1991): 201–7, quotation on 202. The special pullout section of this *Science* magazine annual issue on the genome was dedicated to databases. See also Rachel Nowak, "Draft Genome Map Debuts on Internet," *Science* 262 (1993): 1967.

18. Making life into a force of production and reorganizing biology for corporate convenience can be followed in Edward Yoxen, "Life as a Productive Force," in Les Levidow and Bob Young, eds., *Science, Technology and the Labour Process* (London: CSE Books, 1981), 66–122; Susan Wright, "Recombinant DNA Technology and Its Social Transformation," *Osiris*, 2nd ser. 2 (1986): 303–60; Vandana Shiva, *Monocultures fo the Mind: Perspectives on Biodiversity and Biotechnology* (London: Zed Books, 1993).

19. The incisive critique of sociobiology is Philip Kitcher, *Vaulting Ambition: Sociobiology and the Quest for Human Nature* (Cambridge: MIT Press, 1987). On unit-of-selection debates, see Robert N. Brandon and Richard M. Burian, eds., *Genes, Organisms, Populations: Controversies over the Units of Selection* (Cambridge: MIT Press, 1984). Defying classification as technical or popular, Richard Dawkins's *The Selfish Gene* (Oxford: Oxford Univ. Press, 1976) and *The Extended Phenotype: The Gene as Unit of Selection* (Oxford: Oxford Univ. Press, 1982) are the best expositions of the logic of the fierce competitive struggle to stay in the game of life, relying on strategies of flexible accumulation that strangely seem so basic to postmodern capitalism as well. For the fundamentally important theory of flexible accumulation in political economy, see David Harvey, *The Condition of Postmodernity: An Inquiry into the Origins of Cultural Change* (Oxford: Basil Blackwell, 1989). For multileveled feminist working of the theme of flexibility in the American biomedical body, see Emily Martin, *Flexible Bodies: Tracking Immunity in American Culture from the Days of Polio to the Age of AIDS* (Boston: Beacon, 1994).

20. The idea of nature and culture "enterprised up" is borrowed from Marilyn Strathern's treatment of assisted conception and English kinship in the period of British Thatcherism, *Reproducing the Future: Anthropology, Kinship and the New Reproductive Technologies* (Manchester: Manchester Univ. Press, 1992).

21. A good place to start reading on the subject is Daniel J. Kevles and Leroy Hood, eds., *The Code of Codes: Scientific and Social Issues in the Human Genome Project* (Cambridge: Harvard Univ. Press, 1992).

22. Deborah Erickson, "Hacking the Genome," *Scientific American*, April 1992, 128–37. On "agency" in Internet habitats, see M. Mitchell Waldrop, "Software Agents to Sift the Riches of Cyberspace," *Science* 265 (1994): 882–83.

23. The supplement to the *Oxford English Dictionary* puts the first uses of the term "genom" *(sic)* in the 1930s, but the word did not then mean a database structure. That sense emerged from the consolidation of genetics as an information science, and especially since the 1970s.

24. I am indebted to an unpublished manuscript by the UCSC anthropology graduate student Cori Hayden, "The Genome Goes Multicultural" (April 8, 1994). See also L. L. Cavalli-Sforza et al., "Call for a Worldwide Survey of Human Genetic Diversity: A Vanishing Opportunity for the Human Genome Project," *Genomics* 11 (1991): 490–91; Rural Advancement Foundation International (RAFI), "Patenting Indigenous Peoples," *Earth Island Journal* (Fall 1993, Northern Hemisphere; Spring 1993, Southern Hemisphere), 13; Daniela Spiwak, "Gene, Genie, and Science's Thirst for Information with Indigenous Blood," *Ayba Yala News*, 7, nos. 3–4 (1993): 12–14; RAFI, "Following Protest, Patent Claim Withdrawn on Guaymi Indian Cell Line," *GeneWatch: A Bulletin of the Council for Responsible Genetics* 9, nos. 3–4 (Jan. 1994): 6–7. For efforts to restart the Human Genome Diversity Project, see Patricia Kahn, "Genetic Diversity Project Tries Again," *Science* 266 (1994): 720–22.

25. I have been instructed on what and who will count as science and as scientists by Giovanna Di Chiro, "Local Actions and Global Visions: Women's Science, Environment and Health Movements in the U.S. and India" (Ph.D. diss., Univ. of California at Santa Cruz, in progress). I draw also on Anna Tsing, "Forest Collisions: The

Construction of Nature in Indonesian Rainforest Politics" (unpublished manuscript, UCSC, Anthropology Board, 1993); and Charis Cussins, "Ontological Choreography: Agency for Women Patients in an Infertility Clinic" (unpublishd manuscript, University of California at San Diego, Science Studies Program, 1994).

26. Susan Leigh Star and James R. Griesemer, "Institutional Ecology, 'Translations,' and Boundary Objects: Amateurs and Professionals in Berkeley's Museum of Vertebrate Zoology, 1907–39," *Social Studies of Science* 19 (1989): 387–420.

27. RAFI, "Patenting Indigenous Peoples," 13.

28. RAFI, "Following Protest, Patent Claim Withdrawn," 7.

29. For a fuller account of this rodent's life world, see Donna Haraway, "Mice into Wormholes: A Technoscience Fugue in Two Parts," in *Modest_Witness@Second_Millennium.FemaleMan©Meets OncoMouse™* (New York: Routledge, forthcoming).

30. The $3 million, National Pregnancy and Health Survey of 2,613 women who gave birth at fifty-two hospitals around the nation in 1992 suggests how many and which U.S. pregnant women actually use substances that could harm the fetus (and the bottom line for an HMO). Conducted for the National Institute on Drug Abuse and released in September 1994, the study concludes that more than 5 percent of the 4 million U.S. women who gave birth in 1992 used illegal drugs, while about 20 percent used cigarettes and/or alcohol. Smokers and drinkers were more likely to use illegal drugs than were ethanol and nicotine abstainers. White women were more likely to drink or smoke during pregnancy than women of color (23 percent of the white women drank, compared to 16 percent African American and 9 percent Hispanic; 24 percent of the white women smoked, compared to 20 percent black and 6 percent black and 6 percent Hispanic). The racial categories here are crude and partial, but they still have a limited utility. Poor, less educated, unemployed, and unmarried women were more likely to use illegal drugs than more privileged women. About 11 percent of the pregnant African American women used such drugs, compared to 5 percent of white and 4 percent of Hispanic mothers-to-be. That still means that more than half of the 221,000 pregnant women who used illegal drugs were white, 75,000 were black, and 28,000 Hispanic. Alcohol and tobacco can harm a developing fetus as much as or more than illegal drugs, but with less social and financial stigma. Overall, about 820,000 babies were born to smokers and 757,000 to imbibers. The same baby can show up in all the user categories. The study shows that most women tried to avoid illegal drugs, alcohol, and smoking during pregnancy; but few who used these powerful subsances succeeded entirely. See the *Santa Rosa Press Democrat*, Sept. 13, 1994, A7. The need for supportive, nonpunitive treatment for women trying to have a healthy pregnancy could hardly be clearer. Along with readily available, pro-woman, substance-treatment programs for those with any of these addictions, raising the incomes and improving the educations of women would likely be the most successful public health measures. Such measures would far outstrip the benefit to child and maternal health from intensive neonatal care units in high-tech hospitals, not to mention the dubious health results from the criminalizing of users. There is an unholy alliance between medicine as a system and millions of pregnant women in the United States, and it is reflected in the incomes of physicians compared to the incomes of at-risk mothers-to-be. The direction of

flow of precious bodily fluids is the reverse of that suggested by the gleaming tooth and gold wedding band of the PreMed ad.

31. Selling in early 1994 for $239 for Macintoshes and $169 for Windows-using machines, Morph is widely used by scientists, teachers, special-effects designers for Hollywood movies, business people making presentations, and law enforcement personnel, e.g., for aging missing children. A competitor in the market, Photo-Morph, comes with graphics for practicing—"women turning into men, a girl turning into an English sheepdog, a frog turning into a chicken," Michael Finley, "The Electronic Alchemist," *San Jose Mercury News*, March 6, 1994, F1–2. Finley illustrated his article with a series of morphed transformations between the competing personal computer giants, Apple Computer's co-founder Steve Jobs and Microsoft's founder Bill Gates. Mergers in the New World Order can be effected by many means. Needless to say, anyone still believing in the documentary status of photographs had better not get a copy of Morph, go to the movies, or look at the missing children on milk cartons.

32. Steve Jones, Robert Martin, and David Pilbeam, eds., *The Cambridge Encyclopedia of Human Evolution* (New York: Cambridge Univ. Press, 1992). Thanks to Ramona Fernandez of the Univ. of California at Santa Cruz for sending me this example.

33. Thanks to Giovanna Di Chiro, Univ. of California at Santa Cruz, for the tip on this image and for Hiro's comments from the "Today Show" of Aug. 17, 1994.

34. Celia Lury, "United Colours of Diversity: Benetton's Advertising Campaign and the New Universalisms of Global Culture: A Feminist Analysis" (paper delivered at the Univ. of California at Santa Cruz, Jan. 7, 1994. Sarah Franklin, comments on paper by Celia Lury.

35. Claudia Castañeda, "Transnational Adoption as U.S. Racist Complicity?" (paper for the American Ethnological Society meetings, April 1994). Castañeda's and my interpretations of the figures in the issue of *Time* evolved together in conversation, her hearing of my talk for a History of Consciousness colloquium Feb. 9, 1994, and my reading of her paper. I also draw on undergraduate students' readings of these images in a final exam in my fall 1993 course on science and politics.

36. Meanwhile, fitting the analysis found in Emily Martin's *Flexible Bodies*, U.S. corporations attempt to capitalize on a particular version of multiculturalism. For an unembarrassed argument, see John P. Fernandez, *The Diversity Advantage: How American Business Can Out-perform Japanese and European Companies in the Global Marketplace* (New York: Lexington Books, Macmillan, 1993). See L. A. Kauffman, "The Diversity Game: Corporate America Toys with Identity Politics," *Village Voice*, Aug. 31, 1993, 29–33.

Reinventing Common Nature

*The research on which this article is based was funded in part by a project entitled "Nature, Environment, Landscape: European Attitudes and Discourses in the Modern Period, with Particular Attention to Water Regulation," under the Commission of the European Communities, Directorate General XII, Science, Research and

Development. Socioeconomic Environmental Research (SEER), contract no. EV5V-0151.

1. It means "game grounds" or, more literally, "game garden."

2. Flemming Kiilsgaard Madsen, *Naturfredningssagens historie i Danmark* (Odense: Odense Universitetsforlag, 1979), 44–53.

3. The Danish equivalent, *naturlig*, is not applied to parks, because it would imply that some parks are "unnatural."Is Central Park an unnatural park? Is the Badlands National Park natural?

4. Raymond Williams, "Ideas of Nature," in *Problems in Materialism and Culture* (London: Verso, 1980), 67.

5. For a differing presentation of this issue, see Neil Evernden, *The Social Creation of Nature* (Baltimore: Johns Hopkins Univ. Press, 1992).

6. I have presented this problem more fully in my *Nature's Ideological Landscape* (London: George Allen and Unwin, 1984). For a classic discussion of the complexity of the concept of nature, see Yi-Fu Tuan, *Man and Nature* (Washington, D.C.: Association of American Geographers, 1971).

7. Yellowstone, from 1872, is technically the first national park, because Yosemite was initially managed by the state of California, but Yosemite was the first park set aside by an act of Congress. There was no precedent for establishing a national park in 1864, so it was placed under the control of the state of California. Since there was no state to administer Yellowstone when this park was formed in 1872, it was born a national park, and set a precedent for the nationalization of Yosemite. A national park was created for the area surrounding Yosemite valley in 1890. The National Park Service first assumed control of the valley in 1906.

8. Alfred Runte, *Yosemite: The Embattled Wilderness* (Lincoln: Univ. of Nebraska Press, 1990), 37.

9. Margaret Sanborn, *Yosemite: Its Discovery, Its Wonders and Its People* (Yosemite: Yosemite Association, 1989), 11; Frederick Law Olmsted, "The Yosemite Valley and the Mariposa Big Trees: A Preliminary Report (1865)," *Landscape Architecture* 43 (1952): 16.

10. As Anne Whiston Spirn shows in her essay, Olmsted was also someone who knew about estate management and the creation of rural parks, not just for the gentry—such as George Vanderbilt's colossal Biltmore Estate in Ashville, N.C.—but for the nation as a whole, as at Niagara Falls. He first went to California to manage the vast Sierra mining estates of General Frémont. In 1866 he resigned from the Yosemite Park Commission in order to resume work on Central Park.

11. John Muir, *The Yosemite* (1914), with a foreword by David Brower (San Francisco: Sierra Club, 1988), 194. He was writing of Yosemite valley's smaller twin, the Hetch Hetchy valley.

12. *Oxford English Dictionary*, s.vv."paradise," "park," "wilderness," and "wild."

13. Olmsted, "Yosemite Valley," 14, 16.

14. *Webster's Seventh New Collegiate Dictionary*, s.v. "paradise."

15. Sanborn, *Yosemite*, 46.

16. Ibid., 195.

17. Quoted in Runte, *Yosemite*, 71.

18. W. H. Auden, *The Enchafèd Flood: Three Critical Essays on the Romantic Spirit* (New York: Vintage, 1967).

19. George H. Williams, *Wilderness and Paradise in Christian Thought: The Biblical Experience of the Desert in the History of Christianity* (New York: Harper and Brothers, 1962), 9, 12; Williams's quotations are from Isaiah 51: 3–4, Isaiah 41: 18–19, and Jeremiah 25: 38–39.

20. See Kenneth R. Olwig, "Literature and 'Reality': The Transformation of the Jutland Heath," in *Humanistic Geography and Literature*, ed. Douglas C. D. Pocock (London: Croom Helm, 1981), 47–65.

21. Michael C. J. Putnam, *Virgil's Pastoral Art* (Princeton: Princeton Univ. Press, 1970), 56; Vergil, *Eclogues* 1.64–68.

22. Muir, *Yosemite*, 5.

23. The poem is Sir John Davies's *Orchestra* (1596), quoted in E. M. W. Tillyard, *The Elizabethan World Picture* (London: Chatto and Windus, 1960), 97.

24. On the connection between sexuality and the concept of nature, see Kenneth R. Olwig, "Sexual Cosmology: Nation and Landscape at the Conceptual Interstices of Nature and Culture, or What Does Landscape Really Mean?" in *Landscape: Politics and Perspectives*, ed. Barbara Bender (Oxford: Berg, 1993), 307–43.

25. Muir, *Yosemite*, 196–97.

26. See George D. Economou, *The Goddess Natura in Medieval Literature* (Cambridge: Harvard Univ. Press, 1972), for an analysis of the relation between the concept of love and nature as represented by the goddess Natura in the medieval period. For a more modern conception of the relation between love and nature, see Wendell Berry, "The Futility of Global Thinking," *Harper's*, Sept. 1989, 16–22.

27. Olmsted, "Yosemite Valley," 21–22.

28. See Runte, *Yosemite*, 28–44; see also Anne Whiston Spirn's essay.

29. See J. M. Neeson, *Commoners: Common Right, Enclosure and Social Change in England, 1700–1820* (Cambridge: Cambridge Univ. Press, 1993).

30. The theory of the tragedy of the commons was propounded in Garrett Hardin, "The Tragedy of the Commons," *Science* 162 (1968): 1243–48. For a critique see Bonnie M. McCay and James M. Acheson, eds., *The Question of the Commons: Culture and Ecology of Communal Resources* (Tucson: Univ. of Arizona Press, 1987).

31. See N. Katherine Hayles's essay.

32. Oliver Goldsmith, *The Deserted Village* (1770) (Philadelphia: Porter and Coates, n.d.), 7–9.

33. John Barrell, *The Idea of Landscape and the Sense of Place* (Cambridge: Cambridge Univ. Press, 1964).

34. Goldsmith, *Deserted Village*, 33.

35. Ibid., 43.

36. On the relation between Jeffersonian democracy and the pastoral literary tradition, see Leo Marx, *The Machine in the Garden: Technology and the Pastoral Ideal in America* (New York: Oxford Univ. Press, 1964).

37. Goldsmith, *Deserted Village*, 13.

38. See Richard White's essay.

39. On turbulance and the feminine, see N. Katherine Hayles, "Gender Encoding in Fluid Mechanics: Masculine Channels and Feminine Flows," *Differences: A Journal of Feminist Cultural Studies* 4, no. 2 (1992): 16–44; on the feminine and agrarian fertility, see Carolyn Merchant's essay in this book.

40. *Black's Law Dictionary* gives the following definition of a "Folc-mote" or "Folc-gemote": "In Saxon law, a general assembly of the people in a town or shire. It appears to have had judicial functions of a limited nature, and also to have discharged political offices, such as deliberating upon the affairs of the commonwealth or complaining of misgovernment, and probably possessed considerable powers of local self-government." "Folc-land" is "Land belonging to the people or the public. Folc-land was the property of the community. It might be occupied in common, or possessed in severalty; and, in the latter case, it was probably parceled out to individuals in the folc-gemote or court of the district. . . . But while it continued to be folc-land, it could not be alienated in perpetuity." Henry Campbell Black, *Black's Law Dictionary* (St. Paul: West Publishing, 1979), 578.

41. *Webster's Collegiate Dictionary*, s.vv. "fellow" and "ship" As "fellows" at the Humanities Research Center at the University of California, we shared, as part of a larger academic community, a lovely mowed campus green where we could sit together and "reinvent" nature.

42. D. W. Meinig, "Symbolic Landscapes: Some Idealizations of American Communities." in *The Interpretation of Ordinary Landscapes: Geographical Essays*, ed. D. W. Meinig (New York: Oxford Univ. Press, 1979), 165.

43. See the essay by Jennifer Price.

44. Olmsted, "Yosemite Valley," 21–22.

45. Quoted in Stanford E. Demars, *The Tourist in Yosemite, 1855–1985* (Salt Lake City: Univ. of Utah Press, 1991), 94–95.

46. See Roderick Nash, *Wilderness and the American Mind*, 3rd ed. (New Haven: Yale Univ. Press, 1982); Marjorie Hope Nicholson, *Mountain Gloom and Mountain Glory: The Development of the Aesthetics of the Infinite* (New York: Norton, 1959).

47. Goldsmith, *Deserted Village*, 39–40.

48. Paul Shepard, *Man in the Landscape: A Historic View of the Esthetics of Landscape* (New York: Ballantine, 1967), 244–55.

49. Olmsted, "Yosemite Valley," 13–14.

50. Goldsmith, *Deserted Village*, 35–36.

51. Shenandoah National Park was a cause célèbre for the elites of Washington, much as Yosemite was for the elites of San Francisco, with George Freeman Pollock playing a role analogous to that of Muir. See George Freeman Pollock, *Skyland: The Heart of the Shenandoah National Park*, ed. Stuart E. Brown, Jr. (n.p.: Chesapeake Book Co., 1960). On the imparkment and depopulation of Shenandoah, and its eventual designation as wilderness, see Henry Heatwole, *Guide to Shenandoah National Park*, 4th ed. (Luray, Va.: Shenandoah Natural History Association, 1992), 27–44; Carolyn Reeder and Jack Reeder, *Shenandoah Heritage: The Story of the People before the Park* (Washington, D.C.: Potomac Appalachian Trail Club, 1978).

52. David Lowenthal. "Is Wilderness 'Paradise Enow'? Images of Nature in America," *Columbia University Forum* 7, no. 2 (1964): 40.

53. Madsen, *Naturfredningssagens historie*, 144–48.

54. See, for example, Timothy O'Riordan, Christopher Wood, and Ann Shadrake, *Landscapes for Tomorrow: Interpreting Landscape Futures in the Yorkshire Dales National Park* (Grassington: Yorkshire Dales National Park Committee, 1992). For a critical view see Marion Shoard, *The Theft of the Countryside* (London: Temple Smith, 1980).

55. Goldsmith, *Deserted Village*, 13.

56. Runte, *Yosemite*, 28–82.

57. Ibid., quotation on 37.

58. Sanborn, *Yosemite*, 237–43, quotation on 238. On St. John, U.S.V.I., there is another U.S. national park that has grown unkempt. The "native-born" St. Johnians have a phrase that suggests an environmental aesthetic similar to that of Totuya: "man die, bush grow a he door mout." See Karen Fog Olwig, "National Parks, Tourism, and Local Development: A West Indian Case," *Human Organization* 39, no. 1 (1980): 22–31.

59. Olmsted, "Yosemite Valley," 18, 22. In his foreword to Muir's *Yosemite*, David Brower notes that the only example he knows of Indian "eye for beauty" is a panoramic vista point with a "magnificent" broad view near Yosemite where Indians made arrowheads. Toyuta, I would venture, is expressing a form of aesthetic appreciation that Brower probably would have difficulty comprehending, given his emphasis upon the "eye" and his approval of Muir's and Olmsted's successful efforts to prevent the Indian-style burning of Yosemite. Brower, foreword, xii, xvii.

60. Olmsted, "Yosemite Valley," 16.

61. Quoted in Demars, *Tourist*, 109.

62. Muir, *Yosemite*, 127.

63. Quoted in Albert Boime, *The Magisterial Gaze* (Washington, D.C.: Smithsonian Institution Press, 1991), 161–62.

64. Ibid., quotation on 158.

65. On Roosevelt and his ideals, see Richard Slotkin, *Gunfighter Nation: The Myth of the Frontier in Twentieth-Century America* (New York: Atheneum, 1992), 29–62.

66. William C. Everhart, *The National Park Service* (New York: Praeger, 1972), 6.

67. A particularly pertinent source on this sea change is Nash, *Wilderness.*

68. These definitions are taken from *Webster's Collegiate Dictionary,* s.vv. "wilder," "desert," "devil," "symbol," and "graven." I am indebted to Gabriele Zanetto, Univ. of Venice, for this insight.

69. John 1:1–2.

70. See Albert Boime, *Art in an Age of Bonapartism, 1800–1815* (Chicago: Univ. of Chicago Press, 1990), 523–26.

71. Sanborn, *Yosemite,* 140–47.

72. Muir, *Yosemite,* 1.

73. Ibid., 15.

74. Ibid., 10.

75. Ibid., 197.

76. Whereas Friedrich's figures tended to look upward in reverence, Americans tended to look downward from a high vantage point with, in the words of the art historian Albert Boime, a "magisterial gaze." This was the same magisterial gaze Borglum was later to carve into stone at Mount Rushmore. See Boime, *Art,* 158–66.

77. Quoted in Demars, *Tourist,* 95.

78. See Laura H. Graber, *Wilderness as Sacred Space* (Washington, D.C.: Association of American Geographers, 1976); for a relevant analysis of American landscape art, see William Cronon, "Telling Tales on Canvas: Landscapes of Frontier Change," in *Discovered Lands, Invented Pasts,* ed. Jules David Prown (New Haven: Yale Univ. Press, 1992), 37–87.

79. Sanborn, *Yosemite,* 42–52.

80. Muir, *Yosemite,* 193, 196, 209.

81. Quoted in Runte, *Yosemite,* 61–62.

82. Alistair D. Graham, *The Gardeners of Eden* (London: George Allen and Unwin, 1973).

83. See William Cronon's essay for a discussion of this phrase. See also Nash, *Wilderness,* 84–95.

84. For an interpetation of the parks as a "tragedy of the commons," see Runte, *Yosemite,* 188–89, 197–99.

85. Anthony Brandt, "Views," *Atlantic Monthly,* July 1977, 46–49; William Leiss, *The Domination of Nature* (Boston: Beacon, 1974). See also William Cronon's essay.

86. Marshall Berman, *All That Is Solid Melts into Air: The Experience of Modernity* (New York: Simon and Schuster, 1982), 60–71.

87. I have discussed much of the relevant literature in Olwig, "Sexual Cosmology."

88. A useful discussion of issues relevant to this topic is to be found in Jonathan Crary, *Techniques of the Observer: On Vision and Modernity in the Nineteenth Century* (Cambridge: MIT Press, 1990).

89. See Olwig, *Nature's Ideological Landscape*, 95–103.

90. Anne Whiston Spirn, *The Granite Garden: Urban Nature and Human Design* (New York: Basic Books, 1984), 129–68.

91. The English organization Common Ground is taking steps in this direction; see Susan Clifford, Angela King, and Richard Mabey, eds., *Second Nature* (London: Jonathan Cape, 1984).

Simulated Nature and Natural Simulations

1. Howard Rheingold surveys the areas in which VR technology is already in use, in *Virtual Reality* (New York: Summit Books, 1991).

2. E. M. Forster, "The Machine Stops," in *The Eternal Moment and Other Stories* (London: Sidgwick and Jackson, 1928).

3. William Cronon, "Telling Tales on Canvas: Landscapes of Frontier Change," in Jules David Prown et al., *Discovered Lands, Invented Pasts: Transforming Visions of the American West* (New Haven: Yale Univ. Press, 1992), 37–87. See also Barbara Novak, *Nature and Culture: American Landscape Painting, 1825–1875* (New York: Oxford Univ. Press, 1980).

4. See Richard White's essay in this volume.

5. Hans Moravec, *Mind Children: The Future of Robot and Human Intelligence* (Cambridge: Harvard Univ. Press, 1988).

6. The classic demonstration of this proposition occurs in Jacques Derrida's discussion of supplementarity in *Of Grammatology*, trans. Gayatri S. Spivak (Baltimore: Johns Hopkins Univ. Press, 1976).

7. Don DeLillo, *White Noise* (New York: Viking, 1985).

8. Jed Rasula, presentation at the Society for Literature and Science, Atlanta, 1992.

9. Henry Adams articulated this realization nearly a century ago in *The Education of Henry Adams: An Autobiography* (Boston: Houghton Mifflin, 1961), where he asserts that the Virgin knows the world is real because she created it. The image Adams uses is of consciousness as a raft adrift in an ocean of "supersensual chaos."

10. For a fuller version of this argument, see N. Katherine Hayles, "Constrained Constructivism: Locating Scientific Inquiry in the Theater of Representation," *New Orleans Review* 18, no. 1 (1991): 77–85.

11. J. Y. Lettvin, H. R. Maturana, W. S. McCulloch, and W. H. Pitts, "What the Frog's Eye Tells the Frog's Brain," *Proceedings of the IRE* 47 (1959): 1940–59.

12. There is now an impressive body of work on how the rhetorics of scientific writing constitute a textual reality. See in particular Greg Myers, *Writing Biology: Texts in the Social Construction of Scientific Knowledge* (Madison: Univ. of Wisconsin Press, 1990); Charles Bazerman, *Shaping Written Knowledge: The Genre and Activity of the Experimental Article in Science* (Madison: Univ. of Wisconsin Press, 1988); Bruno Latour, *Science in Action* (Cambridge: Harvard Univ. Press, 1987).

13. H. R. Maturana, G. Uribe, and S. Frenk, "A Biological Theory of Relativistic Color Coding in the Primate Retina," *Archivos de Biologia y Medicina Experimentales*, suppl. no. 1 (Santiago, Chile: 1968).

14. Humberto R. Maturana and Francisco J. Varela, "Introduction," *Autopoiesis and Cognition: The Realization of the Living*, Boston Studies in the Philosophy of Science, vol. 42 (Dordrecht: D. Reidel, 1972), xv.

15. For a discussion of how reflexivity affects scientific objectivity, see Malcolm Ashmore, *The Reflexive Thesis: Wrighting Sociology of Scientific Knowledge* (Chicago: Univ. of Chicago Press, 1989).

16. Heinz von Foerster worked closely with Maturana and was influenced by his work. He makes the argument for a reflexive model of cybernetics (known as second-order cybernetics, or a cybernetics of cybernetics) in a collection of essays entitled *Observing Systems* (Salinas: Intersystems Publications, 1981).

17. Heinz von Foerster, "Molecular Ethology: An Immodest Proposal for Semantic Clarification," in *Observing Systems*, 171.

18. Niklas Luhmann, the German sociologist, has been an important figure in carrying on Maturana's ideas, removing certain consistencies that lingered in Maturana's world (for example, Maturana supposes that we know how systems work—but if the observer is himself a system, how is this knowledge acquired?). Luhmann defines the observer as one who makes a distinction, and defines a distinction as the ability to draw a boundary separating form from background. For a sample of Luhmann's work, see *Essays On Self-Reference* (New York: Columiba Univ. Press, 1990).

19. I am using "external" and "internal" here for clarity, even though such terminology does not appear in Maturana's epistemology, because it implicitly reinforces a realist view that sees a reality "out there" and a perceiver "in here." See Walter Freeman and Christine Skarda, "Mind/Body Science: Neuroscience on Philosophy of Mind," in *John Searle and His Critics*, ed. E. LePore and R. van Gulick (London: Blackwell, 1988); Christine A. Skarda, "Understanding Perception: Self-Organizing Neural Dynamics," *La Nuova Critica* 9–10 (1989): 49–68.

20. Christopher Langton, "Artificial Life," in *Artifical Life*, ed. Christopher Langton (Redwood City: Addison-Wesley, 1989), 1–47, esp. 1.

21. Luc Steels has an extensive discussion of emergence in "The Artificial Life Roots of Artificial Intelligence," *Artificial Life* 1, nos. 1–2 (1994): 75–110.

22. See Thomas S. Ray, "An Evolutionary Approach to Synthetic Biology: Zen and the Art of Creating Life," *Artificial Life* 1, nos. 1–2 (1994): 179–210; idem, "An Approach to the Synthesis of Life," *Artificial Life II*, Santa Fe Institute Studies in the Sciences of Complexity, vol. 10, ed. C. G. Langton et al. (Redwood City: Addison-Wesley, 1991), 371–407; idem, "Natural Evolution of Machine Codes: Digital

Organism," in the Santa Fe Institute Proposal for a Research Program in Adaptive Computation; Kurt Thearling and Thomas S. Ray, "Evolving Multi-Cellular Artificial Life," Santa Fe Institute Working Paper 94-06-039.

23. An argument made by Richard Dawkins in *The Selfish Gene,* when he insists that the metaphors he uses (which are also constitutive of his argument) are so much fluff that can be discarded at will, leaving the argument unchanged. See Dawkins, *The Selfish Gene* (Oxford: Oxford Univ. Press, 1976).

24. An argument ironically examined by Thomas Carlyle in *Sartor Resartus,* and even more ironically replayed by Henry Adams in the preface to *The Education of Henry Adams.*

25. Thomas S. Ray, "A Proposal to Create Two Biodiversity Reserves: One Digital and One Organic" (presented at the Artificial Life Conference, MIT, June 1994).

26. Richard Doyle has written on the simplification of body to information in the Human Genome Project in "On Beyond Living: Rhetorics of Vitality and Post-Vitality in Molecular Biology" (Ph.D. diss., Univ. of California at Berkeley, 1993).

27. Langton, "Artificial Life," 1.

28. Stefan Helmreich, "Anthropology Inside and Outside the Looking-Glass Worlds of Artificial Life" (unpublished manuscript, 1994). An earlier version of this work was published as a working paper at the Santa Fe Institute under the title "Travels through 'Tierra,' Excursions in 'Echo': Anthropological Reflections and Refractions on the Looking-Glass Worlds of Artificial Life," 94-04-024. Helmreich included in this version some remarks that the administrators of SFI evidently found offensive, including comments that likened a belief in the "aliveness" of artificial life to other cultural beliefs that people who are not anthropologists may find strange. Objecting that Helmreich's work was not scientific and that it misrepresented the science done at SFI, the administrators had the working paper removed from the shelves and deleted from the list of available publications.

29. Helmreich, "Anthropology Inside," 5.

30. Quoted ibid., 11.

31. The mediations that take place in almost every scientific laboratory have been the subject of extensive exploration, including Steven Shapin and Simon Schaffer, *Leviathan and the Air-Pump: Hobbes, Boyle, and the Experimental Life* (Princeton: Princeton Univ. Press, 1985), and Karin Knorr-Cetina, *The Manufacture of Knowledge: An Essay on the Constructivist and Contextual Nature of Science* (Oxford: Pergamon Press, 1981).

Toward a Philosophy of Nature

1. Cf. Aristotle, *Metaphysics* A.2.982b.12 ff.

2. Donna Haraway, a contributor to this volume, states the case as boldly as anyone: "The boundary between human and animal is thoroughly breached. The last beachheads of uniqueness have been polluted if not turned into amusement parks—language, tool use, social behavior, mental events. Nothing really convincingly settles the separation between human and animal." See "A Manifesto for Cyborgs: Science, Technology, and Socialist Feminism in the 1980s," in *Feminism/Postmodernism*, ed. Linda J. Nicholson (New York: Routledge, 1990), 193. One of the most sober arguments against the new orthodoxy is, in my view, Alan Wolfe's recent book *The Human Difference: Animals, Computers and the Necessity of Social Science* (Berkeley: Univ. of California Press, 1993).

3. Friedrich Nietzsche, *Thus Spoke Zarathustra*, in *The Portable Nietzsche*, trans. Walter Kaufmann (New York: Vintage, 1969), 124.

4. Italo Calvino, *Mr. Palomar*, trans. William Weaver (San Diego: Harcourt Brace Jovanovich, 1985), 81–83.

5. Edward Wilson, *On Human Nature* (Cambridge: Harvard Univ. Press, 1978), 2.

6. Stanley Cavell, *Must We Mean What We Say?* (New York: Scribners, 1969), 122.

Index

Page numbers beginning with 477 refer to notes.